# William McIntosh

# and

# Maria Caldwell McIntosh

Beverly Jean McIntosh Brown

William McIntosh and Maria Caldwell McIntosh:

The Life and Journey of William and Maria Caldwell McIntosh From Lanark, Ontario, Canada to Mount Pleasant, Utah, United States 1841-1899



ISBN 978-0-578-33402-8 (Hardcover)

ISBN 978-0-578-33403-5 (Paperback)

Library of Congress Control Number 9780578334028



Book design by Nan Barnes, StoriesToTellBooks.com

# William McIntosh

and

# Maria Caldwell McIntosh

*Dedicated*

*to the posterity of*

*William McIntosh*

*and*

*Maria Caldwell*

*May this teach future generations to appreciate the strength and fortitude of their honorable ancestors.*

# Contents

# List of Illustrations

# List of Maps

# Preface

William McIntosh felt it his duty to make a record of his life, and so he did. He was my great-great grandfather who came to North America from Scotland in 1821. I did not hear any specific stories about him, but reading his diary made me feel close to him, to read about his struggles to make a good life for himself and his family. His diary was passed down through four generations. In the 1970's, it was transcribed, and a typed copy placed in the Brigham Young University Library in Provo, Utah. In 2002, my sister, Marsha McIntosh, and I wrote an abridgement of William's diary and placed it in the Family History Library of the Church of Jesus Christ of Latter-day Saints in Salt Lake City, Utah. The abridgement was written to shorten William's diary while retaining its basic content. This version of his diary is written in story format and supplements his diary with maps, photographs, illustrations, and text clarifications, so a modern reader can better understand his remarkable story.

My only regret is what William did not say. In several places, he leaves us hanging with such tantalizing statements as "I will say no more about this" and "for reasons I will not mention here."

The original diary now resides in the Special Collection Section of the Family History Library in Salt Lake City, Utah. This makes it available to all William's descendants as well as descendants of friends and neighbors whom William mentions. It is also available to the public.

# Acknowledgments

This book would not have been possible without the help of family and friends. McIntosh family members provided information, comments and background to improve the understanding of William and Maria's story.

My brother Gary McIntosh and his wife Carol Molnia produced most of the maps used in this book. Carol also served as my manuscript editor. My sister Marsha McIntosh also helped edit my work.

I thank my husband, Douglas Brown, for understanding and appreciating my need to tell the stories of these intriguing people who have come before me and are a part of me.

# Introduction

William McIntosh was born in Barony, Lanark, Scotland, on Thursday, September 16, 1819. See Appendix B for a copy of the record of his birth from the National Archives of Scotland, Old Parish Records, Edinburgh, Scotland.

He sailed across the Atlantic Ocean from Scotland to Canada on a crowded immigrant ship when he was only 18 months old. It was a four-month voyage.

He immigrated to Canada in 1821 with his parents, John and Girsey Rankin McIntosh, and his older sister Agnes. They, and others, were given land grants from England to settle this particular area.

They settled in Lanark, Ontario, Canada, a land that was wild and undeveloped. His parents had to chop down trees to get logs to build a house. They had to break the rocky ground to plant crops. They raised their children there. Like many immigrants, they named their new home in Lanark, Canada after their former home in Lanark, Scotland.

William's wife, Maria Caldwell, was born in Lanark, Ontario, Canada in 1824. Her family had emigrated from Scotland to Canada in 1820. The Caldwell's were also given a land grant. The two families settled land near each other and became neighbors and friends.

About twenty years later, missionaries from the Church of Jesus Christ of Latter-day Saints, also called LDS, Mormons, and Saints, brought the two families into the Church. William and Maria wanted to join members of the Church in the United States. Both their families would later follow them.

William McIntosh married Maria Caldwell on Monday, September 27, 1841 in Bathurst, Lanark, Canada. They had both become members of the Church of Jesus Christ of Latter-day Saints. The Saints were gathering in Zion. Zion was initially Nauvoo, Illinois, but later became Utah. Zion would be the place where William and Maria could live with other members of their faith.

In their lifetime together, William and Maria made homes in at least five locations on their way to Zion, and seven locations in Utah. Maria gave birth to 11 children. They experienced joy and heartbreak. They lived a full life with family and friends. I believe they had a good life.

Maria died on Tuesday, July 27, 1897 of epilepsy. She was 73.

William died on Thursday, May 4, 1899 of the flu. He was 79.

He and Maria were guided by their Church in all ways and had been able to live in Zion among the Saints for over 45 years.

This book is William's diary about the journey he and his wife, Maria, took to be with their Church in Utah. It is also about the life they had as they settled and raised their family.

This is not a word-for-word transcription. Although William's handwriting is readable, it can be difficult to decipher in some places. He used his pen until the ink ran dry and the words became faint. He wrote on every page until it was full.

I have tried to faithfully represent William's spellings, grammar, and use [or lack] of punctuation.

His diary entries appear in italics.

I inserted non-italicized words or short phrases in brackets within his entries to add explanation or clarification.

Where I had a longer explanation, my words appear between William's diary entries and are not indented, italicized or in brackets.

Here is a sample of William's handwriting from his diary. It is his first entry.

9

Great Salt Lake Utah Territory March 25th 1857
[illegible] my [illegible]

[illegible] the [illegible] of making
[illegible] of my life in as brief [illegible] as I can and
as near the truth as I can recollect I sit down this
[illegible] with good Spirit to write a small history
of my life as correct as I can . . .

I was born September [illegible] 1840 — Scotland
and I crossed the ocean when about 20 months old with
my Parents John and Jenny McIntosh . . .
to a new country there experienced some of the inconveniences
of a new country there we remained a great many years
previous to the coming of the Gospel to whereever we were
[illegible] Elders of Israel came to our house and told us the glad
tidings of great joy to the world saying the kingdom
of God was at hand and we must repent and be
baptized for the remission of our sins and that the Lord
hath raised up a Prophet even Joseph Smith with the
Book of Mormon and so forth for which I feel thankful
[illegible] that I [illegible] a desire to [illegible] when I [illegible] it is
my desire to have the spirit of this dispensation even
the spirit of God to direct me in all things that I may
[illegible] the truth I lived with my Parents without thinking
much about [illegible] the true God careless about religion but when
the truth [illegible] came [illegible] the Gospel of the new covenant
I was not so careless about that the Spirit bore testimony to
[illegible] and I received it and rejoiced in the truth until now
[illegible] in Canada a number of years after I received the [illegible]
the Gospel soon after I began to have the spirit of gathering
[illegible] my parents [illegible] the [illegible] and my [illegible]

The Diary of William McIntosh

His words in the first paragraph:

*Feeling it my duty, also seeing the necessity of making a record of my life in as brief a manner as I can and as near the truth as I can recollect, I sit down this afternoon with good spirits to write a small history of my life as correct as I can.*

William started his diary with this entry on Saturday, March 28, 1857, more than likely a cold winter day, after finishing his chores. He summarized his life up to that date and then began to write regularly.

On March 23, 1858, almost a year later, he wrote:

*I am sorry that I did not keep a journal from the day that I was baptized or rather from my childhood. I would feel a great deal better, more satisfied with myself. Now I have to labor under a great disadvantage in trying to record just a few circumstances that are the most prominent in my memory. Perhaps I may write about some things more particular further along in this book if I can recollect them.*

His last entry was on Sunday, December 25, 1898. He died on Thursday, May 4, 1899 in Mount Pleasant, Utah. He was 79 years old.

## Chapter 1

# Lanark, Canada to Ohio, United States 1841 – 1845

The journey starts with the wedding of William McIntosh and Maria Caldwell.

The wedding was Monday, September 27, 1841 in Bathurst, Ontario, Canada. William was 22 and Maria was 17. The wedding ceremony was performed by Reverend MacAlister, a Presbyterian minister, and witnessed by David Caldwell, Maria's father, and John Barrowman, a Mormon missionary.

*William and Maria Caldwell McIntosh*
*Picture from personal collection of Beverly McIntosh Brown*

A few days earlier, William's parents, with his brothers and sisters, left their home in Canada to start their journey to the United States. We do not know why they did not wait until after the wedding.

As William wrote in his diary:

> *We stayed behind them for reasons that I will not mention here.*

Maria's family was not ready for the trip to the United States. They would follow three years later.

After the wedding, William wrote in his diary:

> *We then started on foot with our bundles under our arms to gather with the Saints. We then took our journey of many thousand's miles with all the courage we could muster.*

They walked to Toledo, Ohio, arriving on Thursday, October 28, 1841. It was a journey of about 500 miles, completed in 30 days. They would have averaged 17 miles a day.

Here is an illustration of Kingston Road, near Lake Erie in Canada in the 1840's. Perhaps this is the road William and Maria took as they walked to the United States.

*Kingston Road near Lake Erie in Canada, circa 1840*
*Sketch used with permission of the Library of Congress, Washington, D.C.*

They arrived in Toledo, Ohio, which is at the southwest tip of Lake Erie [**Map 1**].

They could have followed the north shore of the lake, taking the Kingston Road. However, Maria had a sister, Ann Caldwell Yates, living in Buffalo, New York. They may have walked between Lake Ontario and Lake Erie, visited her sister, and then walked along the southern shore of Lake Erie to Toledo.

In October 1841, they arrived in Toledo, Ohio, and William wrote in his diary:

*We came to Toledo, Ohio. We had about fifty cents when we landed at Toledo, as sickly a place as I ever saw. We lived there for several years and suffered much sickness.*

He also wrote:

*I found my father's folks.* [He meant his father, mother, brothers, and sisters, not his father's parents].

Toledo was a port city, so William, his father and brothers, may have worked at the port. There were also farms nearby where they could have worked. It was near the area called The Great Black Swamp. Malaria was endemic at that time. The disease was a chronic problem for residents, until the swamp was drained in 1859 and the former mosquito-breeding grounds dried up.

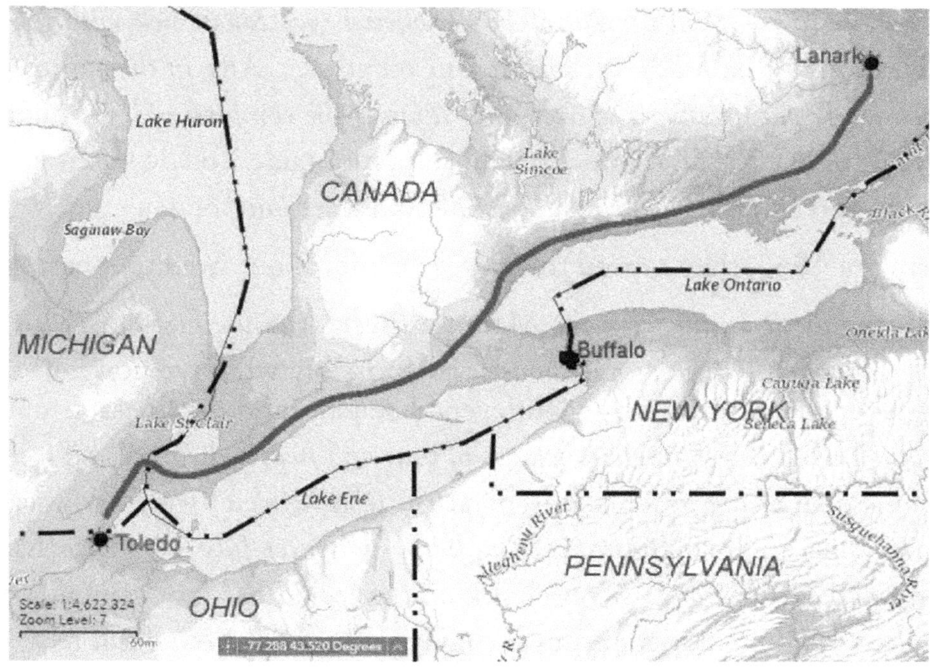


**Map 1**. *Map of area around Lake Ontario and Lake Erie, showing a possible route [red line] taken by William and Maria from Lanark, Canada, to Toledo, Ohio. Map from "The National Map" of the United States Geological Survey.* https://viewer.nationalmap.gov/advanced-viewer/

*The Great Black Swamp near Toledo, Ohio*
*Picture used with permission of the Library of Congress, Washington, D.C.*

William and Maria's first child was born in Toledo, Ohio, on Monday, June 13, 1842, which means Maria was pregnant for the last part of their 500-mile walk. The baby, John Ephraim, was born strong and healthy.

William again recorded in his diary:

*I labored very hard there till the fall of 1842 when I was taken sick with the fever and ague* [malaria] *and it did not leave me for four months.... And in the summer of 1843, I done some work, got us a yoke of oxen and some of the comforts of life. And in 1844, I cut cordwood and boated to Toledo* [they lived just outside Toledo] *on a flat boat and worked in the harvest for a cow. I had the chills and fever but not down sick.*

In the spring of 1845, they moved to Oregon, Ohio, about five miles east of Toledo. :

*I rented a farm about a mile from the Maumee River. And the first day that I harvested in 1845, I was taken with Nervis Tifous fever* [possibly what we now call typhus, an infectious fever characterized by high fever, headache, and dizziness, usually carried by ticks] *and I went through several stages of that and nearly died. We all were sick and was not able, some of the time, to help ourselves to a drink of water. My wife, Maria, was confined under these circumstances and had a daughter July 27, 1845* [Mary Ann]. *John Ephraim, our oldest boy, was very sick and we could not take care of him. He was two years old. Acquaintances of ours by the name of Mr. and Mrs. Treat took him home. We had had a good deal of dealings with them. They took him home and took care of him for six weeks for which we have the warmest gratitude.*

They lived in Toledo and Oregon, Ohio until August 1845, almost four years. William worked hard to earn money for the next part of their journey.

## Chapter 2

# Ohio to Michigan
# 1845 – 1846

In August 1845, William, Maria, John Ephraim and newborn baby, Mary Ann, moved from Oregon, Ohio [just outside of Toledo] to Erie, Michigan [just outside of Monroe, Michigan].

William wrote:

*In the year 1845, we moved to Michigan suffering much and deprived of many of the comforts of life by sickness. My father's folks lived there. It was not quite as sickly a place as Toledo. My brother James took sick in Michigan, and died there about eight miles from Monroe City, towards Toledo. We lived there until the spring of 1846.*

James McIntosh was buried in the LaSalle Pioneer Cemetery.

In the spring of 1846, William wrote:

*Early in the spring I done some work for a man by the name of John Lonston. When cropping time came I hired with a man by the name of John Hall for all summer at ten dollars per month. A very good man. He paid me honorably as did Lonston. All this time my health was very poor yet I labored diligently and the Lord blessed me.*

William's desire was to gather with the Saints in Zion.

Zion has many meanings, but in this case, it refers to a central physical location to which the Latter-day Saints have or will gather. Zion is often used to connote a utopian association of the righteous. In 1839, Joseph Smith, founder of the Church of Jesus Christ of Latter-day Saints, led the Saints to Nauvoo, Illinois as their Zion. The move was to escape conflict with the state government in Missouri. Mormons flocked there. Its peak population was 12,000. But, by the end of 1845, it became clear that no peace was possible between LDS church members and the local people. Violence by the local non-Mormons led the Mormons to make plans to evacuate Nauvoo in early 1846. Most went to the area called Winter Quarters, later named Omaha, Nebraska. They set up a place where they could live through the winter before traveling west to their new Zion in Utah. Winter Quarters, Nebraska was on the west side of the Missouri River, across from Council Bluffs, Iowa.

William and his family never made it to Nauvoo, Illinois, but met the Saints in Winter Quarters, Nebraska in 1851.

On Thursday, January 29, 1847, a tragic accident happened.

William wrote:

*At that time, we lived about a half mile from Abraham Vaughan, my wife Maria's uncle who had married my sister Agnes. She had a child* [Isaac Vaughn] *and was not able to be up yet. Maria went over to help her to do some work. I was dragging up some wood with the oxen. And while I was after a drag of wood, Mary Ann's clothes caught fire. Before I could get to her, her clothes was all on fire. In this condition she came out to me. John Ephraim had called to me that sissy's clothes was on fire and I came as fast as I could. She met me at the corner of the house. By this time the blaze was above her head. I put the fire out very quick. Water and snow being close by. After I had done this, her mother was not there, and I did not know what to do with her. I concluded I would take her to her mother. I had called several times but Maria she did not hear me. Consequently I started. Maria came out to meet me. Reader, you may judge how our feelings was in those circumstances. John Hall, the man I worked for at the moment, heard it and started his boy and a horse at the height of his speed for a doctor and soon had one there. We all did the best we could but all seemed of no use. She died in the eighth day of her illness. I was glad in one way to see her out of pain. This was in the 9th day of February 1847.*

Mary Ann McIntosh was only 18 months old when she died. She was buried in the LaSalle Pioneer Cemetery.

LaSalle was a cemetery, which no longer exists, in Monroe County, Michigan. A researcher in the area found records that indicate an old pioneer cemetery was located there, but no records as to who was buried there. Family records show that James McIntosh was buried there in 1845. Jane Cooper Caldwell Leonard was buried there in 1846. Mary Ann McIntosh was buried there in Feb 1847. David Caldwelll was buried there in Nov 1849.

Agnes McIntosh Vaughn, Williams's sister whom Maria was visiting at the time of Mary Ann's accident, probably died around the same time; sometime after giving birth to their second child, Isaac. There are no records for her after 1847. Her burial place is unknown, but was probably LaSalle Pioneer Cemetery.

In the 1850 U.S. Census, there is no record of Abraham Isaac Vaughn, but his and

Agnes' children, Mary and Isaac, were living with William's parents, John and Girsey McIntosh in Monroe, Michigan. The 1860 U.S. Census shows Isaac living with a Caldwell aunt, Mary Caldwell Stewart, in Frenchtown, Michigan. We cannot find Isaac after that. There were many Isaac Vaughns who served in the Civil War; perhaps he was one of those. There is no further record of Mary. But the 1860 U.S. Census does show Abraham Isaac living in Erie, Monroe, Michigan in a boarding house. In the 1870 U.S. Census, he is living with the family of Mary Caldwell Stewart. He is not found in any census record after that.

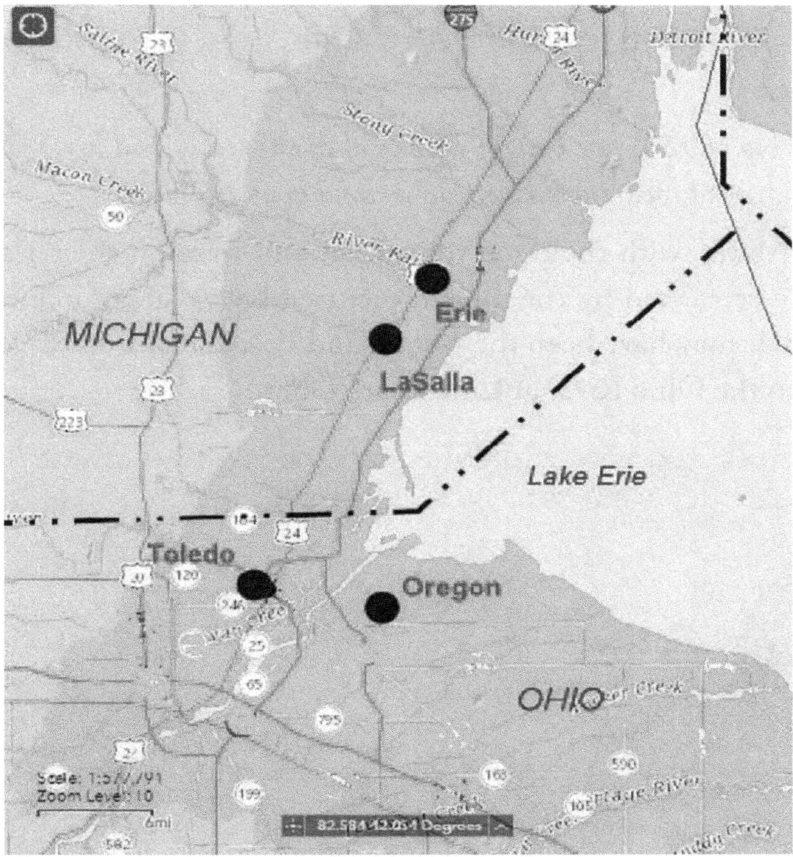


**Map 2.** *William and Maria lived near Toledo, then moved to Oregon, Ohio; then they moved to Erie, Michigan. The cemetery mentioned below was in LaSalla [more commonly spelled LaSalle]. Map from "The National Map" of the United States Geological Survey.* https://viewer.nationalmap.gov/advanced-viewer/

## Chapter 3

# Michigan to Saint Louis, Missouri 1847

William wrote:

*And in the spring of 1847 we bought a yoke of oxen, a cow and a wagon, about all the property we had. And took our passage on a canal boat at Toledo.*

William and Maria, with their son John Ephraim, were on their way to Saint Louis, Missouri. They were carried by canal boat, pictured below, along one of the canals built throughout Ohio. It may have been the Miami and Erie Canal from Toledo to Cincinnati. It brought them to the Ohio River at Cincinnati, Ohio.

*Canal boat on an Ohio canal*
*Picture used with permission of the Library of Congress, Washington, D.C.*

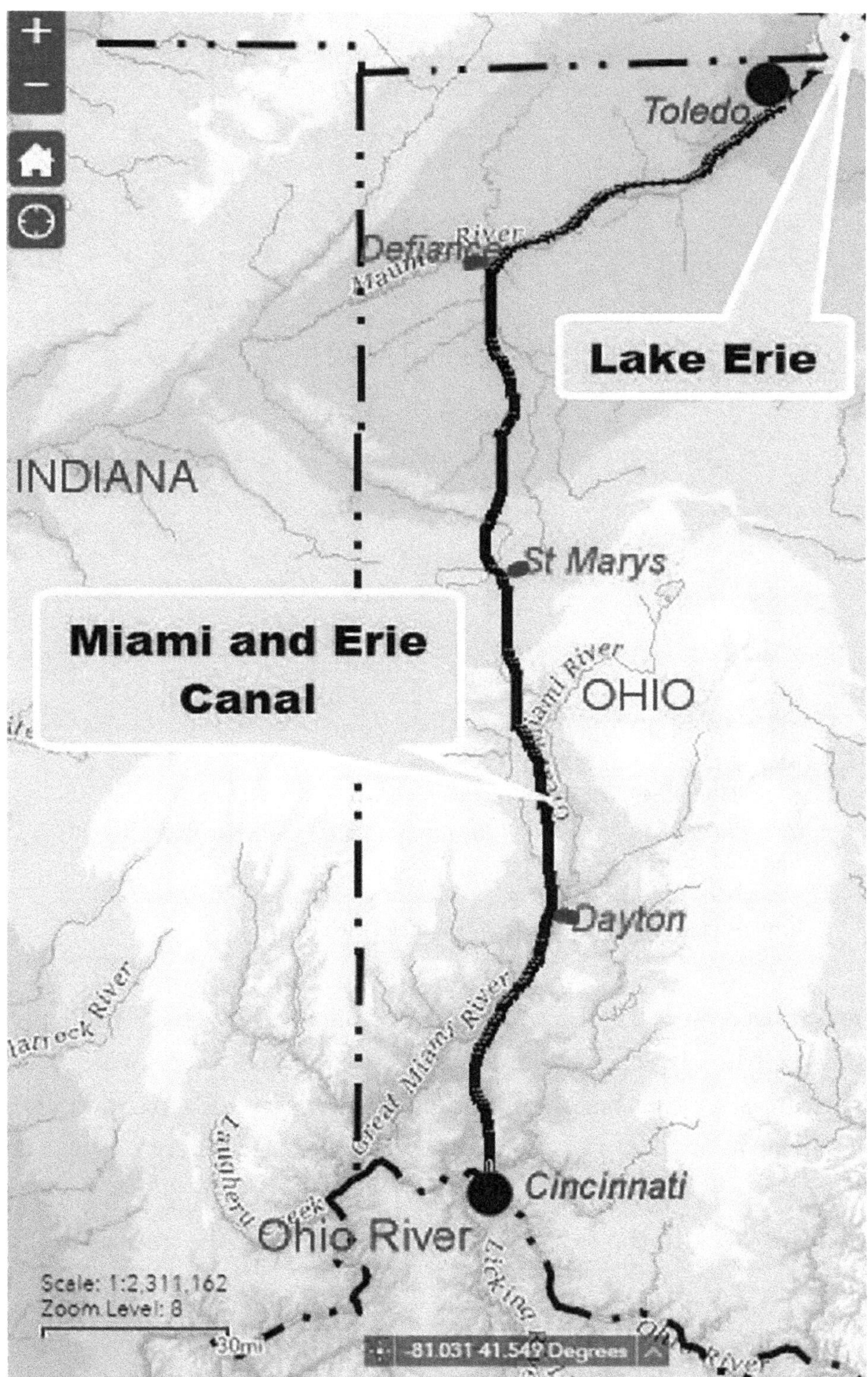


**Map 3**. *Map of the Miami and Erie Canal which connected Lake Erie with the Ohio River at Cincinnati, Ohio. This canal is about 270 miles long.*
*Map from "The National Map" of the United States Geological Survey.* https://viewer.nationalmap.gov/advanced-viewer/

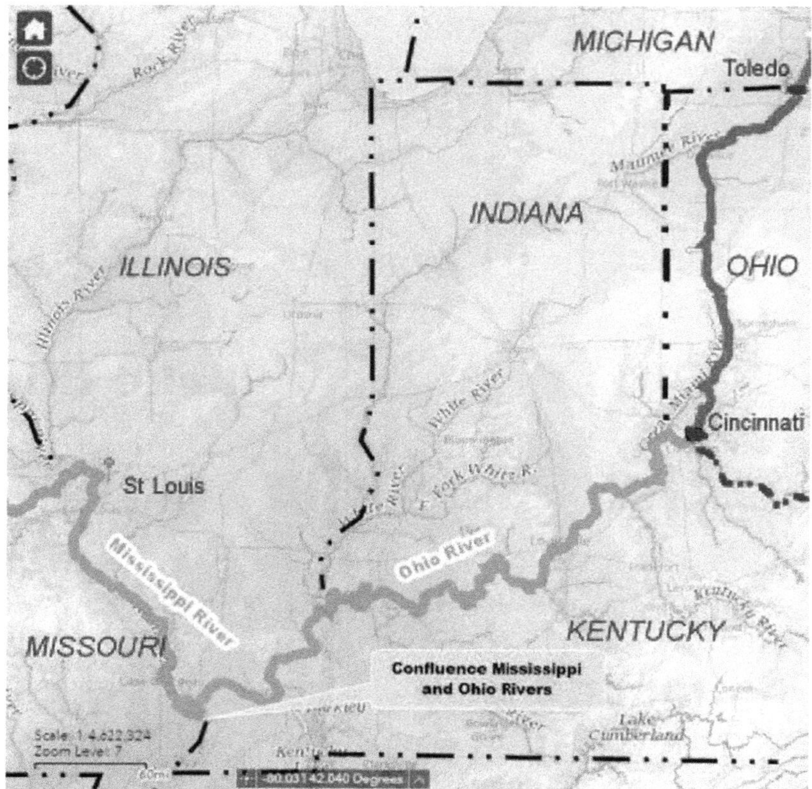


**Map 4**. *From Cincinnati, the family journeyed southwest for over 450 miles on the Ohio River to its confluence with the Mississippi River. Then, they traveled northwest on the Mississippi River for over 180 miles to reach Saint Louis, Missouri.*
*Map from "The National Map" of the United States Geological Survey.*
https://viewer.nationalmap.gov/advanced-viewer/

When they arrived in Saint Louis in the spring of 1847, they were met by friends, Brother and Sister Murray. This was a married couple, but the Mormons call each other Brother and Sister. They had been neighbors in Michigan and attended church together. The Murrays had gone on ahead of the McIntoshes and were there to greet them and help them get settled.

William went to work in the shipyards to earn money for the next part of their journey.

He wrote:

*My health was not very good, but my desire was so great to get along and be with the Church that I spent no idle time.*

Maria was pregnant with their third child, David Hirum, while they journeyed to Saint Louis. He was born on Sunday, September 5, 1847 in Saint Louis. He died of whooping cough two months later, on Tuesday, November 16, 1847. Sadly, it was not unusual for newborns to die of whooping cough in those days.

William wrote:

> *On September the 5th, 1847, David Hirum was born. We lived there and enjoyed ourselves very well till David Hirum got sick. Whopping cough he got and was worse. We did all that we could until he died November the 16th. John Ephraim, then our only child again, we began to think we was going to be bereaved of our children. John got well and we began to overcome our bereavement.*

## Chapter 4

# Saint Louis, Missouri to Jefferson City, Missouri 1848 – 1849

William, Maria and son, John Ephraim would travel further north on the Mississippi River, and then west on the Missouri River. The Missouri River flows into the Mississippi just north of Saint Louis.

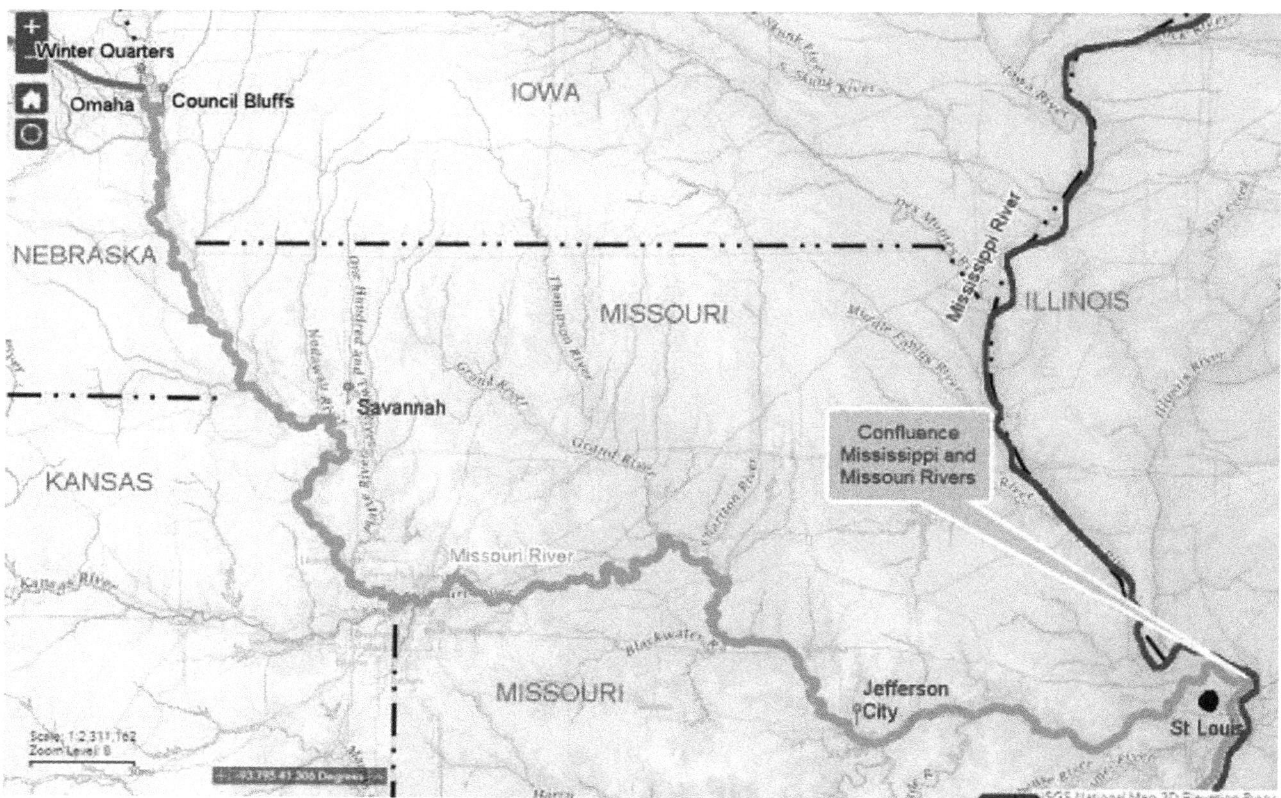


**Map 5.** *Route the family followed on the Missouri River: from Saint Louis, Missouri, to Jefferson City, Missouri; to Savannah, Missouri; to Council Bluffs, Iowa, which is across the river from Winter Quarters, Nebraska. The distance from Saint Louis to Winter Quarters on the river is about 615 miles.*
*Map from "The National Map" of the United States Geological Survey.* https://viewer.nationalmap.gov/advanced-viewer/

William wrote:

*In the summer of 1848, we began to have some thoughts about going to the Valley* [Salt Lake valley in Utah] *and still continue to be industrious and save all the money we could.*

*...about June* [1848], *John McIntosh, my brother, arrived from Michigan and told us that my father and mother and brothers and sisters were all well. Also Maria's father and mother and brothers and sisters were all alive.*

During the winter of 1848, William worked in the shipyards and wrote:

*In the winter I was at work in the shipyard, and I with some others, went down into the river on a flat boat to take the barnacles off the hull of an old steamboat. The ice was running in great pieces in the river. A piece run against our little flat boat and as I was getting out of the way, my foot got caught against the old hull and hurt me very much so that I could not attend to my work. During that time I got sick and I had a very bad time of it. But I was getting better when we started on the steamboat Monroe.* [The Monroe was the ship they booked passage on to take them up the Mississippi River, and then west on the Missouri River to Council Bluffs, Iowa].

*Steamboat similar to "The Steamboat Monroe"*
*Image used with permission of "Dave Thomson Collection at Steamboat.com"*

On Wednesday, April 18, 1849, William Henry was born while they were still living in the Saint Louis area.

John [William's brother] lived with William and Maria and worked in the shipyards. He started for Utah three days after the baby was born.

William continued his narrative:

> *The cholera was very bad in New Orleans at that time and worse on the rivers. That evening we came on board the Monroe Steamer and there was a man taken with the cholera but we did not know what was the matter with him. He was right by us. He complained of cramping in his legs and I rubbed his legs and done the best I could for him. My own health was very poor and had been for some time. In the morning, we started with very good success, and that night also. But the next day the cholera began to visit us. I think it was the steward of the boat that took the cholera first. One after another died till there was not enough hands to manage the boat. We got up the river as far as Jefferson Barracks, the government station, just south of Saint Louis. As soon as the boat was made fast, the people began with all their might to get their goods off the boat, most especially some Californians that was with us. I never seen such a pulling and hauling and scattering of property as there was at that time.*

William is describing the outbreak of cholera on the Mississippi River in 1849. It took the life of former U.S. President James K. Polk after he visited New Orleans. Cholera spread up the Mississippi River system killing over 3,000 people in New Orleans and over 4,500 in Saint Louis. Cholera is generally a disease spread by poor sanitation, resulting in contaminated water supplies.

William made a brief mention of seeing fellow Mormons who were on the way to Winter Quarters, Nebraska.

Mormons from all over the country were traveling to Winter Quarters, Nebraska. The word had spread that Brigham Young had made the first trip to Utah in 1847 and was encouraging the Saints to follow him. They would journey to Utah in organized companies [groups].

William continued:

> *I did not know what was going to become of us. The people was dying in every direction around us and more especially the Californians. Very few of them was left. The captain left the boat and fled for Saint Louis and the cholera cut him down by the way. The authorities of the City deemed it better to move the boat down the river about half a mile. We had not left the boat all this time. There was with us a man and his wife by the*

*name of Melvin with whom we had got acquainted in Saint Louis. They came with us when they moved the boat down under a patch of timber. A good many more went with the boat also. That night we had to stay on the boat. My health was poor. I had not quite recovered from my illness in Saint Louis. We did not get much sleep that night with the crisis of the Brethren and Sisters dying with the cholera. The next morning there was five put into coffins and took away, and the watchmen was crying out. We moved our things that morning into the timber. We had to pack our boxes and many other things up a steep cliff close by the Missouri River. We got our effects moved up there and tried to make ourselves comfortable while the cholera was cutting off our people on the right and on the left. All those circumstances only served to decrease my health and rendered me unfit for the duties that I had to perform.*

*Under the circumstances we was in, it was but a short time before the cholera visited our side. This Melvin and his wife was with us all the time. He began to complain in the afternoon, I think the second day that we were there. He became very sick that night and about daylight he was sick with the cholera. His bowels seemed to run from him like a little brook. He soon became black and all drawn up with cramping. We done the best we could for him. I went down on the bank of the river and got Brother Farnham of Saint Louis who had traveled up the river with us. We administered, but faith was out of the question. It did not seem to have any more effect on him than if we had sprinkled him with water. He left a penniless woman and child to mourn his loss and face a cold and friendless world.*

*I mention this circumstance because we was immediately and closely concerned with it. The bank of the river was a scene of destruction, both of life and property. Feather beds, blankets, etc., were frequently seen with the froth and driftwood floating down the Missouri River, which was full because the warm weather was melting the snow of the mountains.*

*This circumstance so fatigued me that I was nearly confined to my bed. Maria went up into the City to get me some refreshment and to see about getting a coffin for Brother Melvin, who lay close by us, almost as black as a colored man, I mean a Negro. My heart nearly fails me when I undertake to write these things. She succeeded in engaging a coffin, which soon came, and we put him in it and he was soon gone. Maria returned and brought me some milk which done me much good and I began to get better.*

*Soon after this, we thought it best to move into Jefferson City* [west of Saint Louis on the Missouri River; they had not gotten very far from Saint Louis]. *We did so and there witnessed many disagreeable scenes among our Brethren and Sisters. We was detained there eight days when the Steamer Lightfoot came along and we took our passage on it for the Bluffs* [Council Bluffs, Iowa].

## Chapter 5

# Jefferson City, Missouri, to Savannah, Missouri 1849 – 1851

William was now 31; Maria was 26; John Ephraim was 8; and William Henry was 18 months.

William's diary tells us:

*May 1849. But this was not the end of our troubles. The cholera did not like to give us up. Every now and then there was one of our Brethren and Sisters snatched away from us by the cruel monster. We had paid our passage on the Monroe Steamer to the Bluffs, and the expenses that would naturally occur. That, and paying our passage on the Lightfoot to the Bluffs again, very near took all the money that we had.*

*We started up the river very slow. We had what they called the June rise to contend with. They were Missourians I think. I need not further explain their character but I will long remember the conduct of the first mate with the Saints. We arrived at Nodaway, Savannah Landing [Missouri] June the 3rd of 1849.*

*The captain told Schofield, who had chartered the boat, that he could not work and would not take the people any further. So they made it up between them to land the people there for a certain sum of money.*

*Anyhow, I never got any of the money and I don't know that any of the rest got their money. I think this is the truth of the matter. I heard that there was a young Scotch man that crossed the sea with Schofield. He died there in very inhumane circumstances. The people said that Schofield did not pay much attention to him till he died. They said that Schofield took his things, and took his watch from his body and put it on his own body. This is what they said.*

*Nodaway Landing near Savannah, Missouri*
*Picture used with permission of the Library of Congress, Washington, D.C.*

*Area around Savannah, Missouri*
*Picture used with permission of the Library of Congress, Washington, D.C.*

*I went out to the road that led to Savannah. I started on the 4th of June 1849 to go find a place where we could stay till we was able to go further. I over took a man that was hauling a load of goods to Savannah.*

*He asked me if I would come up and ride awhile. I told him I would for I did not feel very well. I asked him if he knew where I could get a house to rent and get into some business for a while. He told me there was a house a little ways ahead that he thought that I could get. It was not long till I found that he was one of the Brethren and that he lived close by. His name was John Freeman.*

*There was a man in company with him who had the care of the house spoken of, and I rented the house right away. I went home with Brother Freeman and got some dinner and I hired him to move us on the morrow.*

*Accordingly, we moved up the sixth day of June when I had a sudden spell of sickness. Only Brother Freeman's folks were friendly to us. Other people were afraid to come near us. They thought we had the cholera. Our health began to increase and we soon felt like living again.*

*The first business that I done was with a man by the name of James Sampson. He heard that I was a mechanic and he wanted some work done. He came to our house and I went with him and commenced to work. I soon was well and able to work. I done his work.*

*I then set up a wagon shop of my own and went to work with all my might. The Lord blessed our labors and we done well. I had all the work I could do and I got the money for it. I labored almost night and day making wagons that winter. We done well till the summer of 1850 when I made a wagon for a man by the name of Willis Web. I done some other work for him, too. The wagon was $25 for the woodwork, and I lent him $15 in money which he agreed to pay in one month. I frequently spoke to him about what he owed me but he never was able to pay me. At last he told me that he did not owe me anything and that I was in his debt. This did not sound good to me, of course, and I sued him. He stood his trial before Squire Bond, or rather appeared there, and brought a lawyer to plead his case. The lawyer found a flaw in some of the doings and had the costs to pay. I did not stop at this; I continued the suit. This took the most part of the summer. The suit came on again, and I got all the evidence I could and went to the Court, seemingly in the midst of my enemies. A good many went to see how the Mormon would get along in Missouri. Some of my neighbors, with whom I had yet to be acquainted were interested in my behalf and went cheerful and wishing me all the good they could.*

*There was a man that told Web that he had better settle with me for he never saw a case more clearly proven in his life. I got judgment against him for the debt, but he had previously put all his property out of his hands, and he was not worth anything. But I found enough to pay the expenses of both Courts and that was all I got. I left the judgment with the judge and he said he would send it to me if he ever got it.*

*Web and his drunken companions set a day when they would come with fifty men and run me and my family out of the place. I told him it would take about that many men like him to mob one Mormon and drive him anywhere. But they never came to mob us. We lived there that winter and I was doing pretty well. I had all the work I could do in my line of business.*

*In the spring of 1851 we were preparing to start for the Valley. We had a new wagon and one yoke of oxen, a pair of steer and two cows for our team, and were pretty well fixed otherwise. And we were all in good health. I acknowledged the blessing of God upon us and around us. He had preserved us from the perils by water and from the perils by land until the time that we was capable of creating better times than we had experienced before. We got ready and took our journey in the company with Brother Freeman for the Valley of the Great Salt Lake, May the 1st, 1851.*

William and Maria had spent from May 1847 to April 1851 living and working in the areas around Saint Louis, Missouri to earn money to continue their journey. They spent part of that money to buy tickets for passage on the Steamboat Monroe to take them up the Mississippi River to the Missouri River to Council Bluffs, Iowa. [Council Bluffs is on the opposite side of the Missouri River from Winter Quarters, Nebraska]. Then, the cholera hit and they had to evacuate the Steamboat Monroe at Jefferson City, Missouri, and lost that money. Then, they spent more money to buy tickets for passage on the Steamboat Lightfoot to Council Bluffs. But due to a quarrel between the Captain of the boat and the passenger's agent, Schofield, everyone was kicked off that steamboat at Savanah, Missouri. Everyone lost their money. William again had to stop their journey to work, for two more years, to earn money to continue their journey. He earned money by building covered wagons for people to continue their trek to Winter Quarters. He also built his family a wagon for their journey.

The family walked from Savannah, Missouri to Council Bluffs, Iowa with their wagon and animals ready for the trip along the Mormon Trail.

*We traveled through the country unmolested. But, of all the times for rain and mud I never saw the like. Our team was strong and able for their load and we trotted along gladly. We camped on the Misquito Creek* [about five miles downstream from Council Bluffs] *one night when we had to stake our wagon down to keep it from being taken away with wind and rain.*

## Chapter 6

# Savannah, Missouri, to Winter Quarters, Nebraska, and to Salt Lake City, Utah 1851

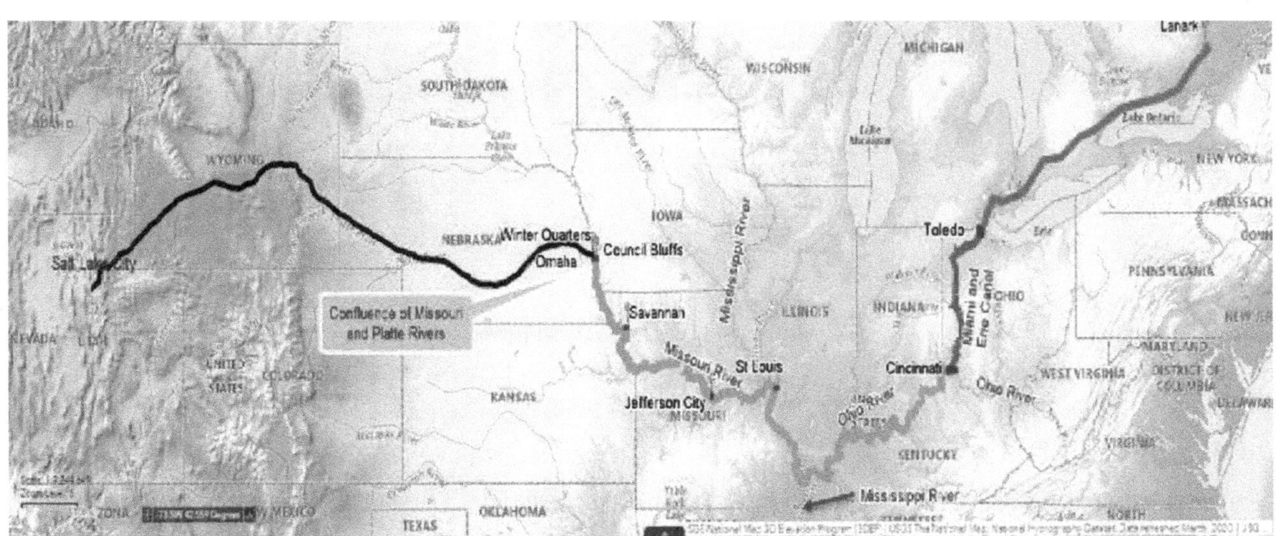


**Map 6.** *William and Maria's entire journey.*
*Map from "The National Map" of the United States Geological Survey.* https://viewer.nationalmap.gov/advanced-viewer/

The Mormon Trail [black line] is the last section of their journey. It goes from Winter Quarters, Nebraska, to Salt Lake City, Utah. The blue line shows their journeys along the Ohio, Mississippi, and Missouri Rivers. The purple line shows their travel along a canal from Toledo to Cincinnati. The red line represents their walk from Lanark, Canada, to Toledo, Ohio, United States.

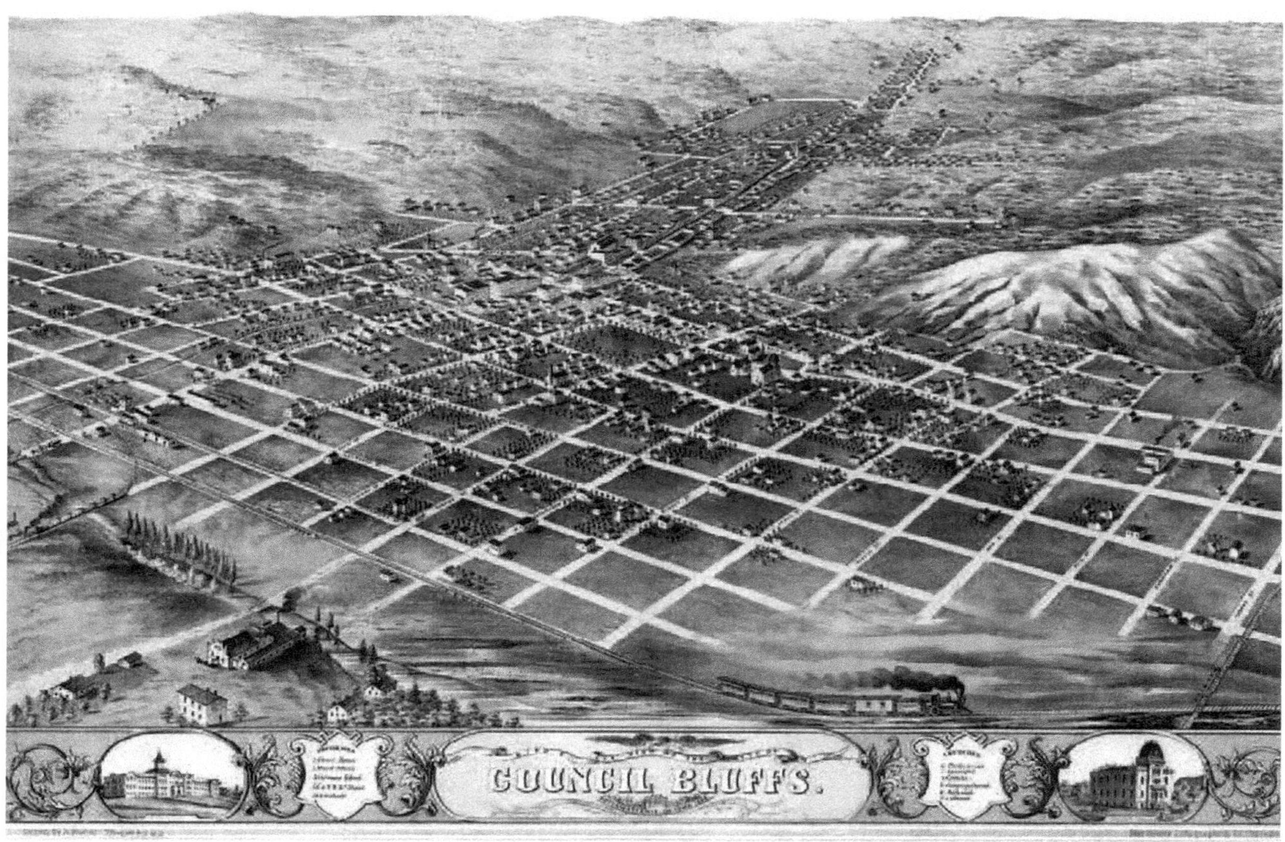


*Council Bluffs, Iowa, circa 1853 (formerly Kanesville)*
*Sketch used with permission of Church of Jesus Christ of Latter-day Saints https://history.churchofjesuschrist.org/*

*We traveled to Council Bluffs* [Iowa] *where we was detained a long time waiting for companies enough to organize to travel to Indian country. The Indians were thought to be very hostile that season.*

*Without being organized, a small company of us crossed the Missouri River and camped near Winter Quarters. I went there frequently, and examined closely the place where my Brethren and Sisters had been banished to.*

*The feelings will not be forgotten, and many other things as well, are stamped vividly in my heart and will stay there until the times of restitution. I feel thankful that the Saints seem to be having a season of rest. But whether the Saints will live their religion as well when they are left alone as when they are driven and smitten, I do not know. But suffice to say, we are going to the Valleys of the Mountains for a season, to try and learn the ways of God that seem strange to us sometimes. But my desire is to go to the Valley that I may be faithful to the religion that I have, even to the end of my calling.*

Council Bluffs, Iowa was known as Kanesville until about 1853. It was named for benefactor Thomas L. Kane, who helped negotiate federal permission for the Mormons to use Indian land along the Missouri for their winter encampment. Kanesville became the main outfitting point for the Mormon exodus to Utah, and it is the recognized as the start of the Mormon Trail.

Beginning in 1846, there was a large influx of Latter-day Saints into the area. But, during the winter of 1847–1848, most Latter-day Saints crossed to the Nebraska side of the Missouri River. They set up camp there and called it Winter Quarters.

As the Mormons gathered at Winter Quarters, the people were organized into companies of one hundred, each company bearing the name of its leader. The one hundred people were further subdivided into groups of fifty; then the fifty people were divided into groups of ten people, with a leader for each grouping.

*Winter Quarters, location of present-day Omaha, Nebraska*
*Sketch used with permission of Church of Jesus Christ of Latter-day Saints* https://history.churchofjesuschrist.org/

Winter Quarters was an instant city on the plains. By Christmas 1846, church members had built a large stockade and about 700 homes, ranging from solid, two-story structures to simple dugouts in the bluffs. It served as church headquarters before the leadership moved west to Utah in 1847.

The next part of the journey would take the Saints through the area that later became Nebraska and Wyoming. They would finish their journey in the Salt Lake valley in present-day Utah. The early groups [such as this one] used covered wagons, pulled by oxen to carry their supplies. Some of the groups were assigned to stop along the way to establish settlements to plant and harvest crops to feed the follow-on pioneers. Some later groups would use hand carts, which did not prove to be very safe or efficient. Eventually pioneers would travel by railroad.

*Covered wagon used by the Utah Pioneers as they crossed the Mormon Trail.*
*Picture used with permission of Church of Jesus Christ of Latter-day Saints* https://history.churchofjesuschrist.org/

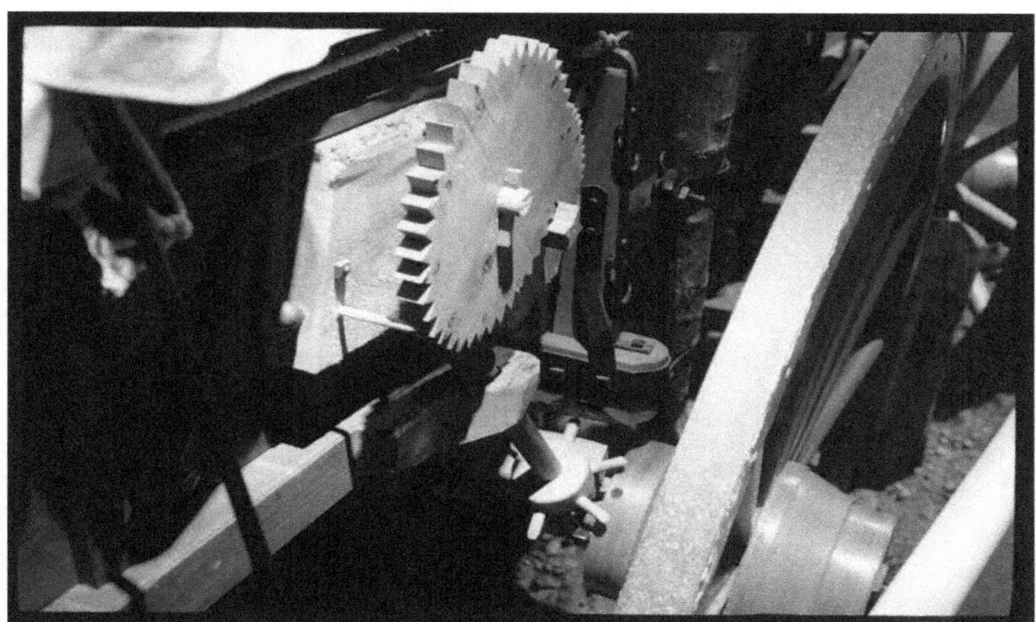

*Replica of the odometer which permitted the pioneers to accurately measure distances. It was attached to the wagon wheel as it traveled. About 360 rotations of the wagon wheel equaled one mile. The pioneers made roughly two miles per hour. This odometer was developed by William Clayton, Mormon pioneer. He published a booklet that provided incredible details to pioneers who used the trail over the next several years, i.e., how far it was to the next camping spot and watering hole.*
*Picture used with permission of Church of Jesus Christ of Latter-day Saints* https://history.churchofjesuschrist.org/

William wrote:

*We stopped in Omaha, Nebraska two or three weeks and endured many heavy rainstorms. We got organized. John Smith was a captain of a hundred. David L. Lewis was captain of ten.* [Actually, David Lewis was the captain of fifty].

*We traveled till we came to the Horn [Elkhorn River].*

The ferry at the Elkhorn River was the first major river crossing west of the Missouri River. They had to cross the Elkhorn River to reach the Platte River. The pioneers would follow the Platte River across Nebraska and Wyoming for hundreds of miles.

*Elkhorn River*
*Picture used with permission of the Library of Congress, Washington, D.C.*

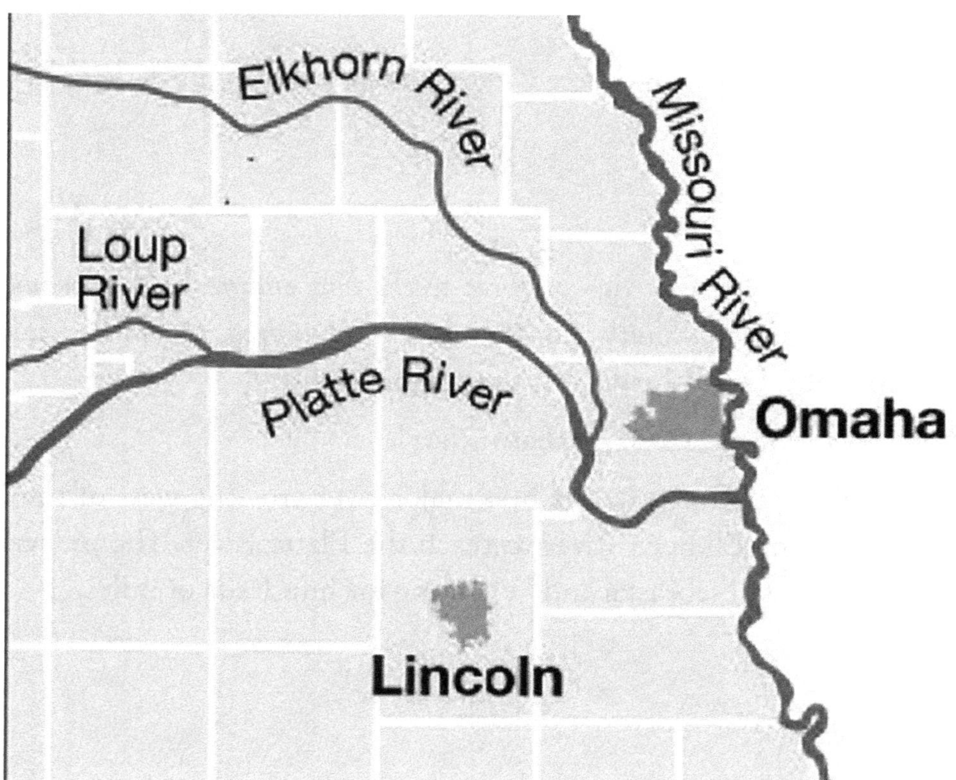


**Map 7**. *Elkhorn River to Platte River from Winter Quarters, Nebraska [Omaha, Nebraska-]*
*Map used with permission of the Library of Congress, Washington, D.C.*

*We found its waters so wide that we could not ford it. We remained there for several days to see if the waters would fall but it rather increased. We did not have money enough to pay our ferriage* [on the Elkhorn River Ferry]. *Therefore we concluded we would go up the Horn till we could ford it. Consequently we took our journey and traveled many days without seeing many prospects of crossing the Horn. We became weary.*

*We came to a place where there was a little island in the middle of the river where we thought we could put a bridge across the river. We done so, and all crossed the river. I think the next evening there came a rain and in the morning the bridge was gone, but we was on the other side of the river.*

*We was very suspicious of the Indians and our suspicions was without a cause altogether. Although we did not know the danger we was in at that time. The only reason we had for suspicion was that four or five Indians came to our camp a few days previous. They had the appearance of warriors. We fed them and they went away. And that was all we seen of them. I suppose they thought our company rather large to meddle with.*

*We resumed our journey over the plains and through the sandy bluffs and to many dangerous roads where we seen plenty of buffalo grazing on their land. Soon we came in sight of the Platte River which was a sight of rejoicing to us for we had been a long time wandering in the mountains. It was not but a few days after we came to the Platte River that we was over taken by Orson Hyde and Judge Brookers and some others was with them. They had been plundered and robbed of nearly all that they had by the Indians. This accounted for some of our fears.*

*At the bridge, we furnished them some things. I let Brookers have a bed quilt and that was the last of it.*

*I should have wrote that David L. Lewis was our chief captain and pilot while we was in the mountains. Much credit is due him for his perseverance and services to the companies in unknown places. We all arrived safe on the Platte, and then we journeyed along with better courage. We did have some difficulties to settle as we went along, but I will not stop to mention them here.*

*North Platte River crossing*
*Sketch used with permission of Church of Jesus Christ of Latter-day Saints* https://history.churchofjesuschrist.org/

*We traveled for several days along the Platte River till for some reason that I do not know, some of the hindmost teams got frightened and ran with the other teams. Suddenly all the teams in the company was running with all their might. I was standing at the head of my team but it was as much as I could do to get away from the wheels of the wagon. As they passed swiftly along, our team did not run very far when the lead cow fell and the wagon was soon on him. I got there soon. Maria was out of the wagon when I got up there. We got the children out of the wagon and got the ox from under it but his horn was broke off and part of his skull with it and it was with some difficulty that we kept him from bleeding to death. That was not all the damage that was done. There was not many hurt there. There was some wagon wheels broke down, wagon beds run off, and we soon gathered our things together again and camped for the night.*

*Pioneers camping in covered wagons on the Mormon Trail*
*Sketch used with permission of Church of Jesus Christ of Latter-day Saints* https://history.churchofjesuschrist.org/

*I was very much concerned about my steer, for I did not know whether he would live or not, knowing that I had not team enough without him to haul my wagon. But Henry Nilson* [Nelson] *voluntarily offered me a good strong cow to work in place of my steer which I thankfully accepted. It was more than I expected from a man that I was so little acquainted with.*

*That night, the sound of the ax, hammer and saw was heard nearly all night. Next morning in good season we all rolled out but my ox was not more than able to follow us. Still we continued our journey, and he began to mend, and in about eight days we put him in the team again and was thankful to Brother Nilson.*

*In consequence of our long trip around the Horn, some were out of provisions. Shortly after we left Laramie* [Fort Laramie, Wyoming] *we had enough and some to spare.*

Fort Laramie, Wyoming maintained food and other supplies to furnish the pioneers for the last part of their journey to Utah.

*Fort Laramie, Wyoming, where wagon trains were resupplied.*
*Sketch used with permission of Church of Jesus Christ of Latter-day Saints https://history.churchofjesuschrist.org/*

*In all these things I feel to acknowledge the Lord and His goodness in sending to us the Gospel of Salvation.*

*While we traveled the weather was generally good after we came to the Platte, but the feed for our animals was very scarce. We got tired of traveling in so large a company and some eight or ten wagons of us, with Captain David L. Lewis, set out for the Valley. We met a good many of our Brethren that were going out to meet the companies with flour and vegetables. We traveled with very good success and arrived in Great Salt Lake City, September the 9th of 1851.*

*Mormon pioneer wagon train driving through Echo Canyon to Salt Lake City, Utah [See* **Map 9***]*
*Sketch used with permission of Church of Jesus Christ of Latter-day Saints https://history.churchofjesuschrist.org/*

## Chapter 7

# Life in Utah 1851

William and Maria, with their sons John Ephraim and William Henry arrived in Utah on Tuesday, September 9, 1851. William was 32; Maria was 27, and pregnant; John Ephraim was 9; and William Henry was 2. William and Maria had left their home in Lanark, Canada, in September 1841. Their journey to Utah had taken ten years and covered 3,100 miles.

The last leg of their journey, as part of the Mormon pioneer company, had taken three months and one week. They traveled 1,032 miles from Winter Quarters, Nebraska, to Salt Lake City, Utah at an average of 15 miles a day.

*Sessions Settlement, now known as Bountiful, Utah.*
*Sketch used with permission of Church of Jesus Christ of Latter-day Saints https://history.churchofjesuschrist.org/*

James Franklin was born on January 8, 1852 in Sessions Settlement, Utah [later Bountiful].

William and Maria would live in Utah with the Saints for the rest of their lives–which would be 48 years, almost another lifetime. During that time, they would make homesteads in seven locations throughout the Utah Territory [see **Map 8**]. They would live a purposeful life devoted to their church and their family.

William's diary tells us:

*My brother, John McIntosh, had come out to meet us and he was with us that night in the city. He had been living up north, and consequently, we went up there with him. We stayed there about three weeks.*

*During that time I done some work for Brother Holbrook and got flour for it. The North Canyon Ward [also called Sessions Settlement, later called Bountiful] looked to me like a fine flourishing settlement and I was desirous to settle there if I could. Although my means was limited and land was very high, I bought a farm from Orson Taylor about a mile south of Sessions and took possession October the 5th, 1851.*

*I plowed about six acres and put in wheat and got my wood out of the canyon. That about completed my fall work. We had a pleasant warm fall. The weather was good and I was glad that we was in the Valleys of the Mountains with the Saints. This was a consolation to me.*

*And on Thursday, January the 8th, 1852, James Franklin McIntosh was born. We enjoyed ourselves very well that winter. It was not a very hard one and when the 6th day of April came, I laid aside all my business and attended the Conference till it was over.*

General Conference is a gathering of members of The Church of Jesus Christ of Latter-day Saints, held every April and October in Salt Lake City, Utah.

*We done the best we could and raised our bread. Although our farm proved to be not a very good one, we felt well and glad that we was with the Saints. That being the first time that we was with the Church. We lived in that place till November 15th, 1853, just over 2 years.*

**Map 8**. *Locations [red] where William and Maria lived within Utah; and other locations [black] that are mentioned in his diary.*
*Map from "The National Map" of the United States Geological Survey.* https://viewer.nationalmap.gov/advanced-viewer/

## Chapter 8

# Bountiful, Utah to West Jordan, Utah 1853 - 1859

Meanwhile, Maria's family, the Caldwell's, had journeyed to the valley. John McIntosh, William's father, travelled with them. They had left Winter Quarters, Nebraska, on Monday, May 16, 1853, and arrived in Salt Lake City, Utah on Saturday, September 17, 1853. They traveled the same 1,032 miles. Their trip took 4 months and 1 day.

William continued writing.

*That fall of 1853, my father* [John McIntosh], *and Maria's mother* [Mary Ann Caldwell], *and three of her brothers* [David Henry, Abraham Vaughn and Isaac James Caldwell], *and her sister Caroline* [also Caroline's son Isaac Neddo], *and two grandchildren* [Anne and David Henry Leonard], *son and daughter of Jane Caldwell* [Jane Cooper Caldwell Leonard died in Monroe, Michigan] *who was married to James Leonard as we have mentioned already—wanted to find a place to settle on where they could make a living. We heard that there was a good chance to make a settlement over in Jordan. Consequently, I sold our farm in Sessions and moved to the west side of Jordan as there was great inducements held out for a flourishing settlement.*

*But we had to get our water from the Jordan Mills place, and they took the water from us several times and our crops dried up. They told us that we had no right in the ditch. After we had made about five miles of a water section through steep banks and bad places, in good faith, he told us we had no right to the water. We had also done our portion in the mill. It was provoking. The mill was run by Daniel R. Allen. This being done several times, it injured our settlement very much. A portion of this was done in the summer of 1857.*

*That summer we managed to raise our bread to do us that season. It is a very dry place. Over Jordan, as it is called, is not very good farming country. A hard place to raise bread stuff. All these things is a school of experience to me. I came to the Valleys of the*

*Mountains to learn to do the Will of God and I guess that, and many other things that I have seen and experienced, will learn me a little more knowledge.*

*I will here write, although I had intended not to write, that in the summer of 1856, I fenced 20 acres of land, broke ten and planted it to wheat and corn and put in some on shares. In all, I had seventeen acres in crops and so had David H. Caldwell and his two brothers, Isaac J. and Abraham V.* [Maria's brothers], *and many others. But through mismanagement in the matter, we lost our crops and had to throw up our improvement, also. I could say more about it but it is of no use.*

*I left in August* [1856] *in company with David H. and A.V. Caldwell and went up north and run a thrashing machine. I left home in August and with what I earned and bought, we had enough grain to do us till another harvest.*

*There are many other things that I say little about. I will write that in the summer of 1855 there was a great difficulty about the Bingham Creek water. There was a good*

*Jordan Valley, Utah*
*Used with permission of the Library of Congress, Washington, D.C.*

*many shareholders that brought the water out in the first place. I will mention a few of their names. There was Joseph Harker, Bishop and, John Bennion, First Councilor.*

*Previous to this time, I had been appointed in the* [West Jordan] *Branch* [by the LDS Church]*, and it became my duty to attend to a great many things as well as be Teacher in the Branch. I generally met with good success.*

*February the 24th,* [1857] *I was sent by the Bishop Joseph Harker, in company with Brother John Bennion, the Bishop's First Councilor, to the Point of the Mountain on West Jordan* [River]*. We got there about 4:00 in the afternoon. We attended to some business that evening and stayed all night with Brother Pond, and in the morning we continued our labors. We had some difficulty to settle with the Brethren and Sisters. We then went down to the water and I baptized Brother Emlay and three of his children. We then confirmed them into the Church of Jesus Christ of Latter Day Saints. This was in the reformation. We told them to try and live at peace with one another and live their religion. We ate with Brother and Sister Emlay and started for home.*

*Jordan River at the Point of the Mountain*
*Picture used with permission of the Library of Congress, Washington, D.C.*

*I am water master and J. K. Butterfield is quarreling and raising hell about the water. But all that I ask for is to have the Spirit of God to direct me in all circumstances and honor my calling in this world. I have been watering my crops. I was up all night. It is hard work attending the water especially in the night and I feel the effects of it yet. This is a very warm day.*

The Mormon Reformation was a period of renewed emphasis on spirituality within the LDS Church. It took place from 1856 to 1857 and was under the direction of Brigham Young, President of the LDS Church. During the Reformation, Brigham Young sent his Counselor, Jedediah M. Grant, and other church leaders, to preach to the people throughout the Utah Territory and surrounding Mormon communities. They had the goal of inspiring the church members to reject sin and turn towards spiritual pursuits. As a result of the Reformation, almost all active or involved LDS Church members were rebaptized as a symbol of their commitment.

During this same time period, several sermons were delivered by other church leaders, Willard Richards and George A. Smith, that touched on the concept of blood atonement. They suggested that apostates [those who renounced Mormonism] and those who committed certain other sins, such as murder, were beyond the saving power of the blood of Christ and could atone for these sins only by being killed in a way that allowed their blood to be shed upon the ground as a sacrificial offering. The belief in blood atonement was never widely accepted by church members, but it became part of the public image of the church and was attacked in Eastern newspapers, along with the practice of polygamy.

William and his family had moved to West Jordan, Utah looking for better farmland and were sorely disappointed. As with all farmland, water is critical and always involved in controversy. They lived there six years before moving on again. While there, they had two more children. Melissa Jane McIntosh was born on Tuesday, June 27, 1854. Alice Maria McIntosh was born on Thursday, September 16, 1858.

## Chapter 9

# The Utah War
# 1857-1858

Trouble was brewing between the Mormons and the United States government. Utah had been created as a Territory of the United States on September 9, 1850. It was one of several territories that were acquired after the Mexican American War in 1848.

It was also part of the Compromise of 1850 [also known as the Missouri Compromise]. This act was passed by Congress to defuse a political confrontation between slave and free states, over whether the new territories should allow slavery or be declared free from slavery. Congress faced another issue regarding Utah. Utah was inhabited largely by Mormons whose practice of polygamy was unpopular in the United States.

During the Presidential election of 1856, a key plank of the platform of the newly formed Republican Party, was a pledge "to prohibit in the territories those twin relics of barbarism: polygamy and slavery". Additionally, presidential candidate James Buchanan was concerned with the threat of a theocratic (religious) state in the union, i.e., political dominance by the LDS Church in the Utah Territory.

At this same time, trouble broke out. It was called the Utah War.

The Utah War was a costly, disruptive and unnecessary confrontation between the Mormon people in the Utah Territory and the government and the Army of the United States. It resulted from misunderstandings that transformed a simple decision to give Utah Territory a new governor into a year-long comedy of errors with a tragic potential. What has been referred to as "Buchanan's Blunder", almost certainly would not have occurred had there been transcontinental telegraphic communications.

Sensitive to Republican charges that Democrats favored the "twin relics of barbarism—polygamy and slavery," President James Buchanan moved quickly after his inauguration to find a non-Mormon governor for Utah. Then, apparently influenced by reports from Judge W. W. Drummond and other former Utah territorial officials, he and his cabinet decided that the Mormons would resist the replacement of Governor Brigham Young. So, without investigation, the contract for mail service to Utah was canceled and a 2,500-man military force was ordered to accompany Alfred Cumming, the newly appointed governor, to Great Salt Lake City.

In the absence of formal notification of the administration's intentions, Brigham Young and other Mormon leaders interpreted the army's coming as religious persecution and adopted a defensive posture. Under his authority as the current governor, Brigham Young declared martial law and deployed the local militia, the Nauvoo Legion, to delay the Federal troops. Harassing actions included burning supply trains and driving hundreds of government cattle to the Great Salt Lake Valley from Wyoming.

Brigham Young's replacement as governor of Utah territory was Alfred Cumming. He was escorted by a contingent of Federal troops led by General Albert Sidney Johnston. It was called the Utah Expedition. Since resistance by the Mormons was expected, the army's orders were to support the installment of the new governor, using force, as necessary.

The "scorched earth" tactics of the Mormons forced General Johnston's Utah Expeditionary Army and the accompanying civil officials to improvise. They set-up winter quarters at Camp Scott and Eckelsville, Wyoming, near the burned-out Fort Bridger to wait out the winter. The nation feared the worst.

The Mormon communities in Utah were called upon to equip a thousand men for defensive duty in the one hundred miles of mountains that separated Camp Scott, Wyoming and Great Salt Lake City, Utah.

Despite his belligerent public posture, Brigham Young never intended to force a showdown with the U.S. Army. But he and other leaders frequently spoke of putting homes to the torch and fleeing into the mountains rather than permitting their enemies to take over their property. Memories of earlier persecutions were invoked to build morale and prepare the people for possible further sacrifices.

That Brigham Young hoped for a diplomatic solution is clear from his early appeal to Thomas L. Kane, the influential Pennsylvanian who had for ten years been a friend of the Mormons; the same Thomas L. Kane who helped establish the head of the Mormon Trail. However, communications and personal problems delayed Kane's approach to President Buchanan, and not until after Christmas did he receive permission to go to Utah as an unofficial emissary. He reached Salt Lake City late in February, via Panama and California. He found the Mormon leadership ready for peace, but doubtful about its feasibility.

On March 23, 1857, Brigham Young announced that the time had come to implement the "Sebastopol" policy, a plan named after a strategic Russian retreat during the Crimean War, 1853-1856. All the Mormon settlements in northern Utah must be abandoned and prepared for burning. Initially conceived as permanent, the evacuation began to be seen by the Mormon leadership as tactical and temporary. Word came that Thomas L. Kane was bringing the new governor, Alfred Cumming, to Salt Lake City without the army. Still, it was a relocation that dwarfed the earlier flights from Missouri and Illinois; approximately 30,000 people moved fifty miles or more to Provo and the other towns in central and southern Utah. There they remained in shared and improvised housing while the outcome of the Utah War was being determined.

During the winter, both sides strengthened their forces.

With the Army leaving Fort Leavenworth, Kansas, in September, they would be crossing the mountains in the winter. Travel would be difficult through the deep snow.

*U.S. Army marching during winter.*
*Sketch used with permission of Church of Jesus Christ of Latter-day Saints https://history.churchofjesuschrist.org/*

Thomas L. Kane and Alfred Cumming arrived in Salt Lake City, Utah in early April 1858. Brigham Young immediately surrendered the gubernatorial title and soon established a comfortable working relationship with his successor. However, neither of the two non-Mormons, Kane or Cumming, would encourage Young's hope that the army might be persuaded to go away, nor could they give him convincing assurance that Johnston's troops would come in peacefully. So, the move south continued.

Meanwhile, President Buchanan responded to rising criticism by publicly appointing two commissioners, Lazarus Powell and Ben McCulloch, to carry an amnesty proclamation to the Mormons. Upon reaching Utah in early June, they found Brigham Young and his colleagues willing to accept forgiveness for past offenses in exchange for accepting Alfred Cumming as the new governor, and the establishment of an army garrison in the territory. When Johnston's army marched through a deserted Salt Lake City on June 26, 1858, and then went on to build Camp Floyd forty miles to the southwest, the Utah War was over.

Here are William's experiences during the Utah War.

There are two pages missing from William's diary here, so we do not know the exact date when he was writing, but it would have been sometime in October 1857.

William was concerned about:

*Going out at that season of the year to oppose the United States Army. I suppose it was all right, but I would have told them to go home and let the younger men face the Army.* [William was 38].

*We started early in the morning and traveled nearly to Weber* [River] *and camped at Batys Station. And from there we went to the mouth of Echo Canyon* [east and a little north of Salt Lake City], *where we halted till we got our orders to march up into the canyon nearer our enemies. I don't know, but some of us almost imagined we seen them on some of the bluffs as we marched along. Be this as it may, we all seemed to be in good spirits. We soon joined the main body of* [our] *Army in Echo Canyon. And I was appointed to look out for our ten in the company with Brother Barrons of Fort Merriman.*

*We went to work and soon built us a wickiup, a frame hut covered with bark or rush. We had many duties to perform to defend ourselves against the band that had arrayed themselves against us. We had not been long there when I got sick. I suppose it was on account of exposure and unclean habits that I got sick. I suffered much but finally I got better. We was there about two weeks.*

*We got home the first Thursday in November [1857]. So you see, we did not have to fight any of the Army, nor did the band of men come to molest us. And I was glad of it. I thought of all Mormonism out there, as well as at home or at a Conference. It was the Will of God, I believe, that we should be there.*

**Map 9.** *Route from Fort Bridger, Wyoming to Salt Lake City, Utah through Echo Canyon*
*Map from "The National Map" of the United States Geological Survey. https://viewer.nationalmap.gov/advanced-viewer/*

William and his family were part of the exodus to flee south.

William continued:

*Since that time I have been at home, attending to duties as they came along, and now the word is to fit up your wagons and teams and start for the southern part of the valley or country. Consequently I went to work to fit up ourselves but I soon found that I was getting crowded with work for other of the Brethren that was in a hurry to get away. I done the best I could about their work, and my own also, and got away as soon as I could.*

*It has been very stormy weather for the two weeks, bad for the Saints to be moving. Many of them are almost destitute of clothing and not a covered wagon to shelter them from the snow and wind and rain at this cold season of the year. And some with a cart and cow or an ox to haul it and getting along almost every way a person could think of. It was the hardest time for the Saints that I have been eye witness.*

On June 26, 1858, Army troops under Colonel Albert Sidney Johnston, known as Johnston's Army, entered the Salt Lake valley, unhindered, riding through the still empty streets of Salt Lake City. As already mentioned, they set up their camp about 40 miles southwest of Salt Lake City and named it Camp Floyd.

*Johnston's Army marching through Salt Lake City, Utah, June 1858.*
*Sketch used with permission of Church of Jesus Christ of Latter-day Saints https://history.churchofjesuschrist.org/*

In early July 1858, the Mormons began to return to their homes after it was clear that no military reinforcements were being sent to Utah. Johnston's Army settled in Camp Floyd. It was in a valley 40 miles southwest of Salt Lake City. This remote location, neighbored by only a few farms and ranches, was chosen to decrease friction between Army troops and Mormons. The Army and the Mormons continued in a fragile co-existence until the troops left in 1861. They were called back for service in the American Civil War.

Journals and diaries of the people from those "few farms and ranches" around Camp Floyd mention trading with the U.S. Army—hay and food supplies for money. Our McIntosh and Caldwell ancestors were part of this trading partnership.

*Camp Floyd, Utah, March 1860*
*Sketch used with permission of the Library of Congress, Washington, D.C.*

## Chapter 10

# West Jordan, Utah to Rush Valley, Utah 1859 - 1860

*Monday, June 27, 1859. West Jordan where we now live is a hard place to get a living. There is so much work to do for little pay. I think I will try farming somewhere else before long.*

*I have sent my son John and a team to Rush Valley to fence a piece of ground and I think we will better our condition at the present to move there as there is a better chance in that place for farming than here.*

*Sunday, August 7, 1859. I have not written anything for several weeks. I have been gone to Rush Valley to cut hay as I intend to move there this fall. I have been gone several weeks and during that time our crops has almost dried up in consequence of our water ditch breaking and other things. Our crops are spoiled. It will take more than one week to straighten matters again. We are well used to having our crops dried up on West Jordan and I think we will try to make a living in Rush Valley for the present. We had good* [Church] *Meetings in Rush Valley and I enjoyed myself very much. We do not have any Meetings here on West Jordan. A great many goes to the city* [Salt Lake City] *to Meeting. The weather has been good and the Saints are as yet enjoying peace and many of the blessings of the Kingdom of God for which I feel thankful.*

*Tuesday and Wednesday, September 27-28, 1859. Preparing to go to Rush Valley to get out our house logs. My son John and I started on Thursday and got to Rush Valley on Friday the 30th. We went to work and got our house logs and polls for corrals.*

William was 40; Maria was 35; John was 17; William Henry was 10; James Franklin was 5; Melissa Jane was 3; Alice Maria was 1. And Maria was pregnant with their next child.

*Rush Valley, Utah*
*Picture from private collection of Beverly McIntosh Brown*

*We had quite a snowstorm on Sunday the 16th of October [*1859*]. We got home [*to West Jordan*] on Wednesday the 19th. All safe. On Thursday morning we commenced digging our potatoes. We finished digging them on Saturday the 22nd.*

*Friday, November 11, 1859. At home today making a broom. A good deal of rain fell last night and a good deal of snow fell today. Still stormy and cold. I have been very busily engaged for some time preparing to move to Rush Valley. The weather is so bad that it seems to be uphill business.*

*On Friday [*November*] the 18th, 1859. I started with my son John and three yoke of oxen and two wagons. We went as far as the point of the mountain [*about half-way to Rush Valley*] and camped for the night. We started in the morning and traveled till we came to the soldiers bridge and camped there about 12 miles from the settlement [*Saint John is in Rush Valley*]. We got there about 3:00 on Sunday. About the first news I* *heard was that John, my brother, was laying at the point of death. We unyoked our oxen and I went to see him and found it true. He could hardly speak to me. His complaint is the inflammation on his lungs and a cold.*

*Wednesday, November 23, 1859. We started back with all the speed we could to send him some medicine from the city. We got home on Thursday through much snow and rain and mud. We lost our way a good many times in the storm. We got home about midnight I think.*

*Friday, November 25, 1859. I went to the city to get John [*William's brother*] his medicine. And I could hardly find my way home through the storm. I got home about bedtime.*

*Saturday, November 26, 1859. John [*William's son*] went on the prairie to hunt a horse to take his uncle's medicine to him. He did not come in until evening with the horses.*

*Sunday, November 27, 1859. He [*John Ephraim*] started for Rush Valley. Plenty of mud and snow.*

*Thursday, December 8, 1859. The weather is more favorable and I think that we will start tomorrow. I am in a hurry to get to Rush Valley for my brother John is very sick and I hardly expect to see him alive.*

*My father left here [*West Jordan*] the first day of December and took with him some medicine that I brought from the city. I will here rectify this mistake: My father left here then, but I had sent the medicine with my son John previously. John returned with David Henry, his cousin, and brought a horse intended for me to ride in haste back to Rush Valley to see John before he died. But my father wished to see his son once more and we set him upon the horse and sent him away. I think on the first day of December. The weather is very stormy this morning.*

*Friday December 9, 1859. We are just ready to start. Annie Trimmer is going to Rush Valley with us on a visit to see her uncles and aunts. When we left, Brother Mantle, one of our neighbors, and E.W. Trimmer, came with us about a mile through the snow in token of their respect for us. That evening we came to the point of the west mountains and stopped overnight with Brother and Sister Early. One of our oxen was very lame and we were obliged to take him out of the team. We traveled that day through much frost and snow and got to Tooele [*16 miles north of Rush Valley*] about 8:00.*

*December 10, 1859. We met two men that afternoon that told us that John had died last Tuesday morning. We pursued our journey as quickly as we could. We found comfortable lodging at Tooele with Brother Gilespie's folks.*

*The next day we arrived at Rush Valley a little while after dark and found that John was buried and his wife and four children left to mourn his loss. He died on Tuesday morning the 6th of December and was buried on Friday between 3 and 4:00 on the 9th day of December 1859. John was a piety man. Mormonism was his one delight under all circumstances as far as I know. Caroline, his wife, told me that he was very desirous to see me before he died. He admonished his wife and friends around him to do well, refrain from evil and live their religion. He died in the faith of a glorious resurrection with the just. His wife and children mourn his loss very much.*

*Monday, December 12, 1859. We find ourselves in Rush Valley. Our folks are all pretty well. The thrashing machine was in the settlement and I went to work with the help of D.H and I.J. Caldwell [*Maria's brothers*] and thrashed my brother's wheat. That was the first work I done. This is about all I have to say about John at present.*

*We are building a house in Shambip [*also known as Saint John, one of the settlements in Rush Valley*] settlement.*

## Chapter 11

# Living in Rush Valley, Utah 1860

*Monday, January 2, 1860. I am engaged in preparing a granary to put John's wheat in. There is a party in the schoolhouse this evening and some of our folk have gone to it. Isaac J. Caldwell just came in from the party and told me that I was well-engaged. I was writing a few things.*

*This week I.J. Caldwell and I have been engaged in cleaning John's wheat. The weather has been very good. I.J. Caldwell has been faithful with me in thrashing and cleaning John's wheat. There is over 200 bushels of his wheat and all taken care of. He has not a great many debts to pay off as far as I know. Fifteen or 20 bushels of wheat would pay all his debts. He has left a wife and four children. They are at present living with David H. Caldwell* [William's brother-in-law]*. They had just moved to Rush Valley and raised a crop and had not yet built a house. He left 10 acres of land under cultivation and some hay ground, a yoke of oxen and four milk cows, I think, and some young stock. Also some 5 or 6 sheep, a wagon and some other things to keep house with. We have not got a house built yet. We are living in the house with Isaac J. Caldwell which is a great accommodation to us at this season of the year.*

*Sunday, January 8, 1860. Went to Meeting and heard some good instruction from Brothers Russell and Burridge and President Miller. I always enjoy myself when I am with the Saints. When I attend Meeting, and strive to do my duty and strive to refrain from anger and govern myself, and have all my weaknesses in subjection to the law of Christ. I am busied about a good many things around home. The boys are going to school. My father is teaching school here at the present time and I want my children to get as good an education as possible, even when it will be a very limited one. We have to labor under many disadvantages here in the Valleys of the Mountains. Still if we are faithful we shall overcome all these for the Lord has said the Saints shall inherit the earth and I believe they will before long.*

*Monday morning, January 17, 1860. I went to work in the schoolhouse making benches and seats. I worked there for 5 days, until Saturday when I went to work preparing hay racks to take a load of hay to Camp Floyd for myself and one for Caroline. We put on our loads that evening. Sunday we went to Meeting and enjoyed ourselves very well. Monday morning I and my son John started for the Camp with the hay. We got in Camp on Tuesday morning. My wagon broke with me and gave me some trouble. We sold our hay and got $46.50. Caroline's hay came to $21.50 which I gave her when we got home.*

*Tuesday, February 1, 1860. I have laid the foundation of our house today. The weather is pleasant, only hard frost at night.*

*Sunday, February 19, 1860. It has been two weeks since I have written anything as I have been busy at work and nothing strange has taken place.*

*Sunday, February 26, 1860. I have been to Meeting this morning and heard some good instruction from the Brethren that spoke. We are striving to build our house as the weather permits. I find that it is very inconvenient, especially at this season of the year, to be without a house. Although I. J. Caldwell and his wife have been very kind to us with their house.*

*Sunday, March 4, 1860. Abraham Edward McIntosh was born. [*He was their eighth child*].*

*Saturday, April 9, 1860. Today we are moving into our new house that we have been building.*

*Sunday, April 10, 1860. We find ourselves very comfortable in our new house for the present. I have been to Meeting this morning. Caroline has moved in with us.*

*Sunday, April 22, 1860. We have pretty much all gone to Meeting this morning. There are a good many of us living together. There are nine of our own family and Caroline, my brother's wife, and her four children. Our house is pretty large and we get along quite well as yet. We are pretty well satisfied as yet with our move from West Jordan, and I think if we live humble and prayerful that God will be with us and bless us. We have been busy this week getting in our crops and we have not got done yet. The weather is very cold.*

*House built by William McIntosh, Saint John, Utah*
*Picture from the private collection of Beverly McIntosh Brown*

*Sunday, May 20, 1860. I have been herding sheep this forenoon and went to Meeting in the afternoon. This is a pleasant day. There is nothing very different taking place these days with regard to Mormonism. Only they are trying to put an end to polygamy. If at first they don't succeed, they may try, try again. I believe all is well in Mormonism if we will do well. I think I will stop writing at present as I have to work too hard to write. My hand is very unsteady.*

*Sunday, June 27, 1860. I have been herding the sheep this forenoon and went to Meeting in the afternoon. We had a good Meeting. The crops here in Rush Valley this season do not appear to be very good. The weather is cold and not good for crops. The weather continues to be cold and windy. Not very favorable for the crops. We are still permitted to live in a measure of peace here in the Valleys of the Mountains. How long this will be the case, I do not know. Neither am I much concerned about it. God is at the helm and all is right. I have been in the mountains this week. My health is not very good and has not been for some time.*

*Monday, July 9, 1860. There was a Meeting in the schoolhouse. This for the purpose of taking into the best way to save our hay as the gentiles is trespassing upon our rights. James J. Steele and David H. Caldwell* [William's brother-in-law] *and myself were appointed as a committee to see to that matter.*

*Sunday, July 15, 1860. I have not been to Meeting today. I have been herding sheep today. We have about 320 sheep to herd and it takes a good deal of care every day that we live in this probation, it brings its cares and its disappointments with it. We need to have the spirit of God with us all the time to direct us in all circumstances that we may be able to live our religion and live at peace with all persons if possible.*

*We are annoyed a good deal with thieves stealing our cattle. Our boys have been out twice in the mountains bringing back the stolen cattle. We are living here upon the frontier portion of the settlements and we are subject to these kind of deprivations both by Indians and white people thieves. The Rush Valley Indians, the Goshutes, are troublesome about begging but they do not steal much. We get along very well with them.*

*Sunday, September 2, 1860. I have been to Meeting today. Tomorrow is the sitting of the probate court in Shambip County* [now Tooele County]. *Perhaps I will have something to say about it after this. There was a petition presented to the Court by the people requesting a grant. A grant of the creek which we have been using with its tributaries which was not granted. There were several other petitions presented to the Court but were overruled by the people. I think we should be more united for our mutual interest than to do business like this. I think it will be a good while before we will come to a unity of opinion. There was a man by the name John Mosman that was fined $500 for selling whiskey to the Indians which had a bad effect among them. Three was shot.*

*Thursday, September 6, 1860. We are preparing to go to the City with a load of pine bark and to do our trading for this season. We got to the City Friday night the 7th. We did our trading on Saturday the 8th. We left the city and came out to Brother Butterfield's and stayed over Sunday.*

*Monday, September 10, 1860. We went to the carding machine with our wool that kept us 3 days longer in getting home. We got home on Friday the 14th and found all pretty well. The Bishop has been over and they made some arrangements about moving our settlement to another place on the same creek where there is better land.*

There was a settlement on Clover Creek called Clover. Church officials wanted the settlers in Clover to move closer to Saint John, where there was more protection from Indian raids. William and his family had lived in Clover, but later moved to Saint John.

*Saturday, September 22, 1860. This is a pleasant morning and the family is all pretty well at present for which I feel thankful. Grandmother Caldwell* [William's mother-in-law] *is sick abed here this morning and unable to go home. Caroline's* [son] *John David is very sick and has come near dying. We have been stacking wheat today.*

*Thursday, October 3, 1860. I started to the Great Salt Lake for a load of salt. We had good luck and got a load and started home on Friday night about 10:00. The rain began to fall and continued to rain till 10:00 on Saturday, the next day. We did not get home till Monday the 7th. When we got home to Shambip, the thrashing machine was in the settlement and we went to work to thrash our wheat.*

*Sunday, November 11, 1860. I have been at Meeting this forenoon. I have been almost crazy with a toothache today. We have been doing a good deal of mountain and canyon work this fall. We have got out some house logs for A.V. Caldwell* [William's brother-in-law] *to build a house for his mother.*

*Friday and Saturday, November 16 and 17, 1860. John, my son, and David Henry, his cousin, went to canyon after a load of straw. They did not get home till daylight on Sunday morning. This is good weather.*

*Thursday, November 21, 1860. This is a very stormy morning. I start to the City* [Salt Lake City] *with a load of tithing wheat in company with David Henry Caldwell* [William's brother-in-law]*. We broke down one wagon by the way which hindered us till we did not get to the City till Saturday the 23rd. We unloaded that day and came out as far as West Jordan and I stayed at Brother Mackey's that night.*

*Sunday, December 9, 1860. I have been at home this last week not doing much. I have a very bad cold. I have not gone to Meeting today. The weather is clear and cold. Today we had a snowstorm. There are some of the folks from this place gone to get their endowments* [from the LDS Church]*. Grandmother and David H. Caldwell, her son, have gone to get their endowments and Caroline has gone to take care of her mother.*

*Monday, December 10, 1860. In the afternoon David and Grandmother, as their children call her, and Caroline came home. Grandmother is my wife's mother. Caroline did not go to get her endowments. I am glad that the ordinances of the House of God are still open to the Saints to receive knowledge and whereby they may be more able to combat with the powers of darkness. We can plainly see that the more the Kingdom of God grows, then the more it drives the world into confusion and despair. I am preparing today to start to mill tomorrow with a grist of wheat for myself and Caroline. This is very cold weather.*

According to the Miriam-Webster Dictionary, an "ordinance" is a prescribed usage, practice, or ceremony. A religious ordinance is a practice that demonstrates the participant's outward expression of faith, which includes sacred rites and ceremonies. Among Christian religions, the most common ordinance is baptism, which is usually the door through which a person becomes a member of a church. For example, one LDS ordinance is the endowment. The endowment consists of a series of covenants [promises to God] that participants make. All LDS Church members who choose to serve as missionaries or participate in a celestial marriage must first complete the endowment ceremony.

*This is the 24th of December, 1860, Monday, the day before Christmas. Our little children are all lively with the expectation of a visit from Christmas Jack with his pies and cakes and candy and ice.*

## Chapter 12

# Living in Rush Valley, Utah 1861

*Friday, January 4, 1861. I have been butchering our hogs today.*

*Monday, January 7, 1861. David Henry Leonard, son of James and Jane Caldwell Leonard, daughter of David and Ann Caldwell, is going to be married this evening with Emma Childs and we are all invited to the wedding. We met together in the evening and the ceremony was preformed and we had a very delicious supper in her father's house and a good dance. But Brother Miller and I were called away to wait on Brother Davis who is very sick. We stayed with him all night. Uncle John Smith, the patriarch, and Lorenso, his brother and the Bishop of this Ward, came here on the evening of the 7th of January and gave out an appointment for a Meeting tomorrow at 10:00.*

*Tuesday, January 15, 1861. This is a very stormy day. We had calculated to go to Tooele with a load of hay and a load of straw.*

*Thursday, January 17, 1861. My son John and I start for Tooele, a distance of about 17 miles. We had a very hard trip. We got home on Friday evening about an hour after dark.*

*Saturday, January 19, 1861. I have been helping David H. Caldwell* [William's brother-in-law] *to cover a coal pit and getting Brother Davis a load of wood. They are expecting Brother Davis to depart this life soon.*

*Friday, January 25, 1861. Brother Davis died about 9:00 in the morning. I went to work with some others and made his coffin.*

*Monday, February 4, 1861. I am calculating to go over to Jordan to settle up some tithing and go up to North Canyon ward to see my father.* [North Canyon Ward is in the area of the current city of Bountiful]. *I have not heard from him for some time.*

*Saturday, February 8, 1861. I arrived in North Canyon and found my father tolerable well at present. He has been sick this winter but is getting well now. He has married a woman suitable for him in his old age. Her name is Finley.* [Temple records show that John married Mary McPherson Findley Ross]. *I stayed with them a few days and done a few chores and then started for home. I did not get back to Rush Valley till Saturday.*

*Monday, February 18, 1861. If I was a good writer there are many things that I would like to write. But one thing I will mention concerning the United States of America, they have had laws which they called the Constitution of the United States. Because of a question in dispute that is about the freedom of colored people, which is best known by the title of the "North and South question of slavery," the Constitution is broken. This took place in the latter part of the year 1860 and I think they will get to war with powder and lead before they quit. And I do not know that I care very much. I, with some others, have been visiting the Rush Valley branch as teachers striving to find out evils that have been among us.*

*Friday, March 1, 1861. I am at Richville Mill this morning getting my grist ground. I think I will be able to start for home about noon. The roads are very bad and I won't get home till Saturday night. I stayed in Tooele tonight.*

*Monday, March 11, 1861. The Kingdom of God is growing and the Saints are gathering and I am satisfied to live in it. We have many difficulties to meet with while we are striving to live our religion, many which I will not mention here. We are doing pretty well in our Branch. I was appointed Teacher* [in the LDS Church] *here sometime ago, though I must say that there is some division among us that causes disorder sometimes.*

*Sunday, March 17, 1861. We have been at Meeting today and in the evening there is a little confusion or misunderstanding with Brother L. Johnston about fixing up a team to go back to the Missouri River to bring on the emigration.*

As the emigrants continued to pour into Utah, Brigham Young established a policy of sending current residents with their horse and oxen teams, loaded with supplies, out to meet the new pioneers. Many families would be low on food, clothing and blankets by the time they neared Utah. The emigrant companies were always scheduled to arrive in September or sometime before winter.

## Chapter 13

# Living in Rush Valley, Utah 1862

*Sunday, September 28, 1862. This is very warm weather for this time of the season. Our garden is quite green yet and growing well. We expect John* [William's son] *back from the States next week.*

John had been out with a team and supplies to help the pioneer companies complete their journey to Salt Lake City. Utah was still a Territory of the United States and the people did not consider themselves part of the United States. So, when they left the boundaries of the Territory of Utah, they consider it "going to the States".

*Wednesday, October 1, 1862. We hear a great many reports about soldiers coming to attend to the Mormon cases* [polygamy] *and to fight and kill off the Indians. There is many reports these days but not much truth.*

*Friday, October 3, 1862. We are very busy hauling our wheat.*

*Saturday, October 4, 1862. John* [William's son] *has returned from the States and accomplished his mission with his team and wagon. All are safe.*

*Sunday, October 5, 1862. I have been driven about with hard work this summer from pillar to post that I have neglected writing a good deal. I have labored too hard but with a call the Lord has blessed my labor and the labor of my two little boys. We raised 350 bushels of wheat. More wheat than we ever raised in one season before. I will say here that when I think of our location in the Valleys of these Mountains I feel truly thankful that I am here with my family in the Kingdom of God. I feel well. I would not exchange my situation with the Queen of England because I know some of what is coming upon the Earth.*

*Friday, December 18, 1862. I was taken with a violent pain in my head and I was obliged to hire a man in my place. The pain in my head got more severe every day for about 5 days when I began to think my disease would prove fatal. I called upon the Elders holding the Priesthood to administer to me which relieved me right off. But no sooner did they leave the house than I was attacked as severe as ever. I continued calling upon the Elders and was served in that way for some time. In the absence of the Elders, I commenced administering to myself and found the same relief as with the Elders and gained the master over the disease that was destroying my body rapidly. I began to gain a little strength very slowly.*

## Chapter 14

# Living in Rush Valley, Utah 1863

*I was hardly able to be out of my bed when Maria my wife was put to bed and on Sunday, January 11, 1863 she bore to me a daughter [*Lillian Elizabeth*]. So you can see that we have had a bothersome time. My health is very poor as yet but I am getting better. Maria does not get strong very fast. She is more weakly than I think is common under similar circumstances. It is pretty hard times for the women just now. I think very few gets along without trouble and pain, and a great many die. I have been sick a good while and have not been writing much. Our children have been sick some also. But I think we are getting a little better. I have been very unwell myself all this winter, hardly able to do any work.*

William was 44; Maria was 39; John was 21; Henry [William Henry] was 14; Frank [James Franklin] was 11; Melissa was 9; Alice was 5; Abe [Abraham Edward] was 3; Lillian was a newborn.

*Monday, March 9, 1863. I am preparing to start for the city [*Salt Lake City*] tomorrow, a distance of about 60 miles. The roads are very bad. When I got to the city I found all in arms in a state of defense because Brigham [*Young*] had been arrested with a United States writ and threats had been made that they were going to take Brigham dead or alive. It is a little band of the United States troops that is camped on the bench just above the city [*Camp Douglas, later Fort Douglas*] that is making all this bother.*

*Thursday, March 12, 1863. I left the city and the excitement was not so great. I think it will soon die away in its own sound because there is not a big enough Army of them to kill us off. That is all that hinders them to try to butcher us at present. I got home on Saturday. All is well and right side up with care.*

*Camp Douglas, Salt Lake City, Utah*
*Used with permission by the Library of Congress, Washington, D.C.*

Camp Douglas was established in October 1862, during the American Civil War, as a small military garrison about three miles east of Salt Lake City. It was located on a rise overlooking the city. One of its missions was to protect the overland mail route and telegraph lines along the Central Overland Route. Its other missions were to keep an eye on the Mormons and any secessionist activities, protect the area from Indians, guard transportation routes crossing Utah, and aid the road survey parties.

*Wednesday, April 1, 1863. I think the soldiers and the Morrisites is about to dirty upon one another and I am glad of it.*

Joseph Morris considered himself a prophet and leader of his newly formed Church of Jesus Christ of Saints of the Most High, commonly called Morrisites. It was founded on April 6, 1861. He and his followers had been excommunicated from the Church of Jesus Christ of Latter-day Saints. He believed in Christ's immediate return and directed his followers to sell all their properties to his church, with himself as the trustee for the Lord. He also told them not to bother planting crops since Christ would be coming soon. Since no one was working, food became scarce. When one of his dissatisfied followers attempted to leave, Morris arrested him and confined him in the Kingston Fort jail in Weber Canyon, just above Ogden, Utah, where the group was located. When word reached the Chief Justice in Salt Lake City that prisoners were being held, a posse was sent to capture Joseph Morris. After some gunfire and a few deaths, including Morris,' seven of the Morrisites were captured and convicted of murder. This happened in March 1863. The Morrisites scattered and were heard of no more.

## Chapter 15

# Living in Rush Valley, Utah
# 1864

*Sunday, June 26, 1864. I am glad that I can say that I feel well and I feel encouraged when I look around me and see the works of God and the Saints gathering to their mountain home. I have no time to feel otherwise. The Bishop and Brother Maessor from the City were over here to Shambip last Sunday and appointed me to take the charge and preside over all church matters. Col. Ross from the City was here at the same time and appointed Brother Burridge as Captain and me as his First Lieutenant, over the military department. So you can see there is enough for me to do.*

*July, Saturday 8th, 1864. I sit down this afternoon to write a few things as I have been to the City and from home a good deal lately. I have not written very much. Indeed there is nothing very new taking place these times. Yet all things are new as for the Lord is making the earth empty and preparing it for the abode of his people. As far as my presiding here in religious and military matters, I do not know that I do preside here yet, but I reckon that I will get the hang of it after a while. I hold the office of Justice of the Peace. The reader can easily see that I have plenty of business on hand in all that I have to do. I have but one objective and that is to do right and keep in view the Kingdom of God.*

*Wednesday. I commenced cutting my hay. A light crop this year. I have been at Meeting this morning. The spirit of the times looks discouraging with regard to some things. I think wicked men seem to stalk abroad at loose ends. When I was about done cutting hay, I took a bad cold and I have been sick ever since. I have the mountain fever.* [He may be referring to Rocky Mountain spotted fever. It is an infectious disease transmitted by ticks].

*August 11, 1864. I am getting a little better although I am very weak. I do not write very much although books might be written.*

## Chapter 16

# Living in Rush Valley, Utah 1865

*Sunday, October 29. As the reader can see it is now more than one year since I have wrote any. It has not been that I am tired of Mormonism or seek to pass over anything that is my duty, I have been as diligent as I could as a President of a little Branch of the Church of Jesus Christ of Latter Day Saints.*

From 1864-1865, William was the Branch President of the Clover Branch of the LDS Church in Clover, Utah.

*In the year 1864, our crops were very light. We did not raise crops enough to sustain ourselves very good. We had some sickness and the water was very scarce, but we had bread enough to eat. We ought never to complain but be thankful that we are as well off as we are located here in the mountains secluded from a great many evils that I need not mention here. Last winter which was the winter of 1865 we enjoyed ourselves very well in worshiping God and singing and dancing till some evil-disposed persons crept in among us and the result was not good. Our peace and comfort was gone. I do not want to say but little about these things. They are not agreeable to write.*

*The winter was a very severe one and we lost some of our cattle and so did the others. This summer has been some better for us. We have raised a pretty good crop and our health has been better. There are many things that I omit writing because I do not write at regular times, hence I labor under a disadvantage. As I have mentioned some things in the former pages of this work about the USA, I will say that they are yet with us and are still waiting to exercise unlawful authority over the Latter Day Saints at the first opportunity they can find. But they are held as with a hook in their jaws and led hither and thither just as the Lord wants them. And we are permitted to live here in the Valleys of the Mountains until now enjoying a considerable degree of peace. I am aware that all will be right with us if we will listen to the requirements of the gospel of Jesus Christ of Latter*

*Day Saints. We are trying to live in Mormonism and do the best we can.*

*John, our oldest son, went back with a team this fall to help to bring in the emigration to help to get them out from the mountains before the snow would come upon them and shut them in.*

*On the first of November 1865 I received a letter from President Brigham Young's office requesting me to go down to southern Utah and help to locate its valleys. That mission relieves me from presiding over this branch. I have watched over this little branch as well as I could. Now my labors is wanted elsewhere.*

Also, on the first of November 1865, Maria gave birth to a daughter they named Caroline Jeanette.

## Chapter 17

# Move from Rush Valley, Utah, to Panaca, Nevada, and back to Utah 1866

William was sent on a mission by the LDS Church to settle an area then called Panaca, Utah. At that time, Utah's western border was much farther west than it is in modern times. So, Panaca was considered to be in Utah when William and his family left on their mission. It would later be included within the border of Nevada.

*Sunday, the 7th [January] 1866. Times seem dull yet. Although we have had one party last week, but a small affair for Christmas and New Year. Today we don't have enough interest in our religion to go to Meeting, hence we have none. My time is occupied a good deal in preparing to go south in the spring.*

*Monday, 8th [January], 1866. I have this day sold my claim to the lower field to Matthew Orr and John Orr for what we called $800: 1 wagon $250 • 2 yokes $400 • 1 colt $100 • with $50 yet remaining to the paid in something. The weather is very severe and the snow is very deep. I want to start for town in the morning, a distance of about fifty miles.*

*Wednesday, 17th [January], 1866. I started for town but I did not get very far on the road. The snow is so deep I could not get through. I got home on Friday evening with my team almost tired out and myself too.*

*Sunday, 21, [January] 1866. The snow is very deep and the rain is falling some and we have no Meeting here on Sunday now. I now sit down to write a few lines. I have not wrote very much lately. My mind has been taken up a good deal about fitting up to go down on the mission that was given me.*

*Saturday, March 10, 1866. We have not lost any time in trying to get things ready for our journey to southern Utah to help strengthen her stakes. We need guns, plenty of powder, lead and caps. These things seem to be the means of our safety in an Indian country. The winter here has been very hard and we have lost some of our cattle and so have a great many others.*

*Today is Sunday the 11th* [March]*, 1866. We are almost ready to start on our journey as soon as the roads is fit to travel on. They are almost impassable at the present time with mud and snow. I think they will be better soon. The season is fast passing away and I feel uneasy least we will not find a place to raise a crop this season.*

*March, the 18th, 1866. Today is Sunday. I have been to Meeting and was listening to Brother Steel preaching the gospel of life and salvation to us if we will obey its requirements. I am going away to southern Utah on my mission and Brother E. Stokey is president now in Shambip. I had calculated to be in Dixie* [southern Utah] *before now but the winter has been so severe that I could not get away. I calculate to go now in a few days.*

*April 9, 1866. Today we have started on our journey and traveled till we came to Camp Floyd. We camped there and the next day pursued our journey to find the feed for our team very scarce.* [William's son, William Henry, took the initial trip with him. They would go back for the rest of the family after they got settled in Panaca].

*We came to Salt Creek and stopped there one day and got some wheat ground.*

*We came to Cores Creek and turned our oxen out and could not find them for two days. When we found them we traveled on.*

*And when we came to Beaver Valley, we took the new road that leads to Meadow Valley by the way of Miners Hill. It is a very hard road to travel. It is nearly a hundred miles over the desert with little water or feed.*

*We arrived in Meadow Valley* [Panaca area] *I think about the first day of May 1866.*

*Two days after we came here I set out for Saint George. When I got there Erastus Snow was holding Conference there with the people and I enjoyed myself very well for a few days. The weather was cold and about the 5th or 6th day of May there fell some snow.*

**Map 10.** *Route [yellow line] taken by William and his son from Saint John to Panaca. Map from "The National Map" of the United States Geological Survey. https://viewer.nationalmap.gov/advanced-viewer/*

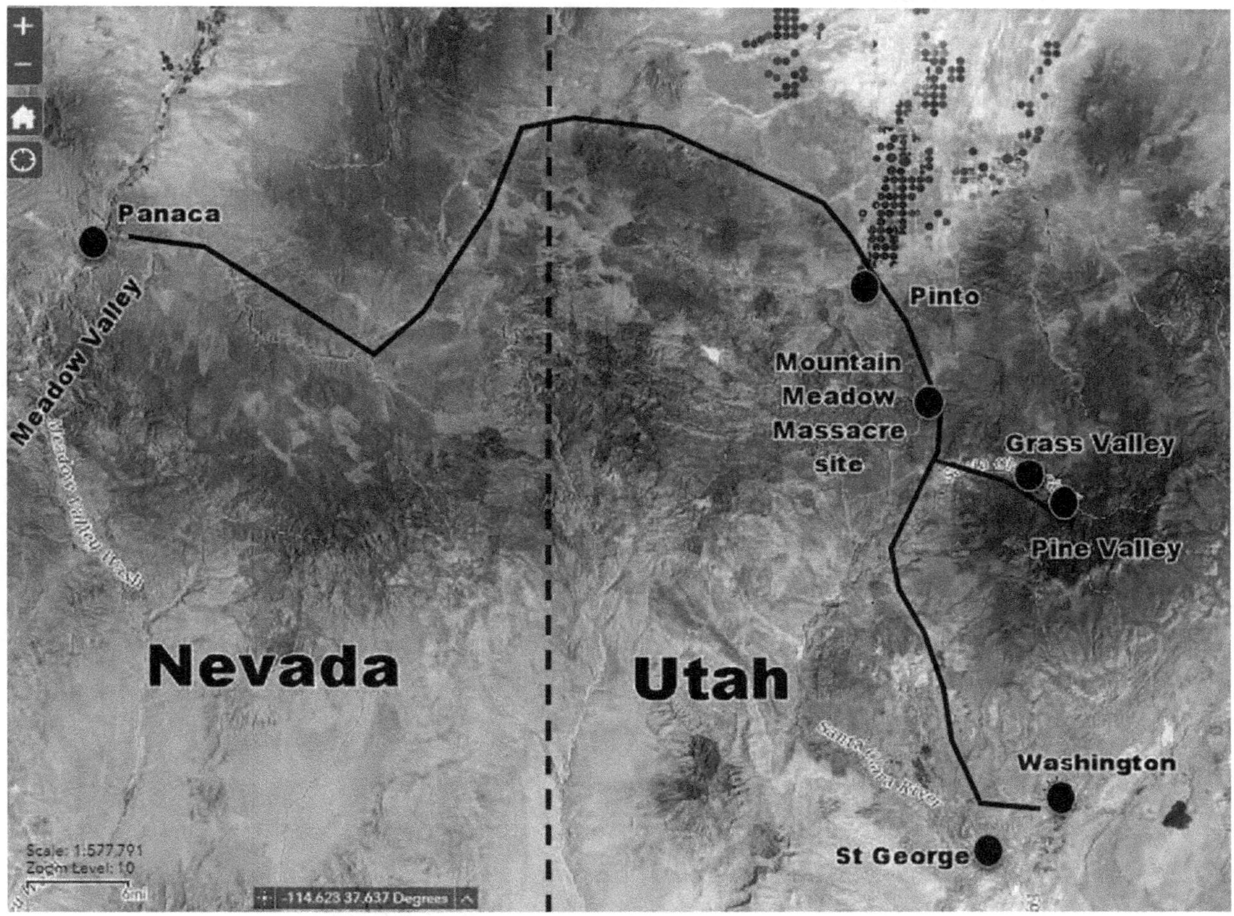


**Map 11**. *William's route [black line] from Panaca to Saint George and back.*
*Map from "The National Map" of the United States Geological Survey. https://viewer.nationalmap.gov/advanced-viewer/*

> *I traveled through the Mountain Meadows and seen the monument made in the memory of those that was murdered there.*

The Mountain Meadows Massacre was a series of attacks on an emigrant wagon train from Arkansas, at Mountain Meadows in southern Utah. The attacks took place from September 7 to September 11, 1857. The result was the mass slaughter of men, women and children. After an attempted cover-up, and an investigation, it was determined that it was conducted by members of the Utah Territorial Militia, together with some Southern Paiute Indians.

*Visited Washington* [town outside of Saint George] *and stayed one night with Woodruff Freeman who treated me kindly.*

*I started again for Meadow Valley and camped that night in the mountains. In the morning we started on our way. Visited Pine Valley and stopped all night with Brother Slade. In the morning resumed our journey and ate dinner with Brother Rencher in Grass Valley.*

*Traveled through Pinto Settlement and came to the desert and camped. That day the Brethrens' team that I traveled with, gave out about 14 miles from Meadow Valley for want of water. And we had to travel that distance in the night without water. It was all we was able to do to get there. Henry* [William's son] *has gone out with Brother Jones today to get the wagon and horses.*

*Today is the 10th day of May 1866. I went out with Brother Mathews, the President of this place, to see some lots. I could have 2 lots. I had a book in which was the particulars of my journey through southern Utah but last night coming down the mountain I lost it.*

*And for the correctness of these things I have to depend on my memory. I am very tired today. Not doing much. We have been very busy engaged in making our fence and putting in our crops and working on ditches and on a schoolhouse and other duties. We have only hauled one load of timber to build a house when we was surprised to hear the news of another move by the Brethren from Saint George. They came to the City of Panaca, Nevada, on the 6th day of June 1866.*

*They went from here to Eagle and Spring Valleys to look for a place suitable for the Latter Day Saints to fort themselves up until this storm will have passed away. I went up with these Brethren to see the country. It is beautifully located. A good grassing country with its washes, creeks and springs, all making their way down to the Colorado River.*

*I got home on the 9th day of June. I was tired and ready for a rest.*

*Monday,* [June] *10. Henry and myself is doing nothing today. Indeed there is not much encouragement to make improvements at this time. Although I feel well knowing that God will do all things right and all will be well with those that will try to do right and not betray His servants into the hands of our enemies. I have found the book that I lost when I was coming from Saint George. Brother Mathews found it and sent it to me. There was nothing much in it but what I had written.*

*Only that morning when we started on the desert, we thought we could get through by evening, about 50 miles, and we did not take much water with us. About noon our horses began to give out. The horses did not drink much water in the morning before we started and the heat of the sun on the desert soon made them wilt for want of water. We got out of the wagon and walked but they would give out anyway. We left the horses and wagon and went down to Panaca afoot. We had walked about 30 miles and when we got to it we was nearly give out. We had nothing to drink all day only about one cup of coffee a piece. We gave what water we had to the horses. We got down home about two o'clock in the morning.*

*June the 12th. I did not say what caused the excitement in 1865 of the move on page 127. The Indian war. The chief cause they were threatening to destroy our settlement and the Brethren from Saint George came to our relief. But we did not have to fort up. The excitement soon died away and soon the people resumed their industry. As I have stated before my son Henry and myself busied ourselves finishing putting in our crop and hauling some timber to build a house. I intended to go back to Tooele as soon as I could and bring my family down to Panaca the same season.*

## Chapter 18

# Panaca, Nevada to Panguitch, Utah, and back to St John, Utah 1867 - 1872

William brought his family to Panaca, Utah in 1867.

In 1866, the border between Utah and Nevada had been officially moved east to include Panaca in Nevada. But, as late as 1870, there was still confusion on where the State borders were. For example, William's family appear twice in the 1870 U.S. Census: once on June 10, 1870, in Panaca, Washington County, Utah; and the second time on July 29, 1870, in Panaca, Lincoln County, Nevada. They had not moved, just the border between the two states.

*Land around Panaca, Nevada*
*Picture from private collection of Beverly McIntosh Brown*

William did not write during the 1870's, but in 1884 he wrote a short summary, in retrospect, of the time from 1871-1872. This is William's recap of his days in Panaca.

> *January 7th, 1884. I will say here that the press of moving and some other reasons which I need not mention here, caused me to neglect writing. Now I wish I had continued to keep a record notwithstanding the many little embarrassments of life. Now I will continue my record on page 135. Days and years flies swift away.*
>
> *I will give a very abridged description of some of my labors in the Dixie country as I have already done about our location in Panaca. We were much molested by the Indians, a tribe called Piutes. They killed many of the miners and some belonging to Pieoch, a little mining town then in the Territory of Utah in 1866. We built up the town of Panaca and we prospered much. We set up a co-op store and I never seen anything like that kind of business prosper as that one did for several years, but it lost sight of right.*

The co-op [co-operative] store was an effort by Brigham Young to encourage Mormon businesses to band together and pool their resources, so they could sell materials and goods exclusively to fellow LDS Church members. This was necessary because some non-Mormon business owners routinely engaged in price gouging on necessities and encouraged boycotting of Mormon businesses. Mormon business owners were routinely charged higher prices by wholesalers when it was discovered they were dealing with Mormons·

> *We got our cattle also but did not get much back. About this time, the State of Nevada extended her state line southeast so far as to take in Pieoch and Panaca and several other little towns. We were all advised to leave the State of Nevada and settle in Utah. This was the council to the Latter Day Saints. I re-located in Panguitch in Utah [1871] but circumstances and sickness in my family caused me to abandon that place and come back to Tooele County [1872] and take care of my wife who was laying sick then and had been sick for some time. These were discouraging times to me but through it all, the gospel and Church of Jesus Christ was the same to me. I did not like to go away from Panaca. That was where I was sent by the first Presidency of the Church of Jesus Christ of Latter Day Saints. But I was anxious to obey Council. I don't think the Bishop was inspired overly much by the good spirit in that move. Nevertheless, the blessing of God was with us if in nothing more, I still find myself steadfast in the Church of Jesus Christ of Latter Day Saints.*

William and Maria's eleventh and last child was born in Panaca in 1869. He was named Joseph Albert. They called him Albert.

## Chapter 19

# Living in Clover, Utah and Saint John, Utah 1884

*March 22, 1884. We have been working on our water ditches preparing them for a free flow of the water for irrigation in the season. With regard to our water dispute, it remains unsettled yet. How it will end I do not know, but one thing I do know, I am tired of it. It has been quite a while since I have wrote anything in this book. There is many obstacles in the way in traveling through this world. Things have prevented me from writing that I will not mention here. I do not think that I am justified in neglecting to keep a record of things as they pass along with me and family.*

*Saint John in Rush Valley, Utah today*
*Picture from private collection of Beverly McIntosh Brown*

## Chapter 20

# Living in Clover, Utah and Saint John, Utah 1889

*Clover Creek in Clover, Utah*
*Picture from private collection of Beverly McIntosh Brown*

*September 24. We were at the Manti Temple* [Manti, Utah] *to do some* [Church] *work for ourselves and for our dead friends.*

Mormons believe in baptism for the dead. They believe baptism is an essential requirement to enter the Kingdom of God, and therefore, offer it by proxy to those who died without the opportunity to receive it.

*That is myself and my wife Maria Caldwell was her maiden name, now Maria McIntosh. We did not accomplish half our work when we received a telegram from Mount Pleasant that our daughter Caroline was dangerously ill at her home in Mount Pleasant, 22 miles north of Manti, Sanpete, Utah. We started from Manti between sundown and dark. Myself and wife and a man I hired to drive my team in the night but we got there too late. She died soon after we arrived there.*

*A short time before this occurrence, I bought a city lot only a street from where Caroline lived, thinking that Caroline and her mother could live close by each other. The reader can see how I have been disappointed. Abraham Edward and family is living on the lot joining. There are many things that transpired in the few years that is gone that I will pass over because I neglected to make a record of them, although there are a few things that I will mention yet.*

In 1889, William and his family suffered another great loss with the death of their eldest child, John Ephraim, in a wagon accident. William copied this article about the accident from a newspaper article.

**Fatal accident at Saint John, Tooele Co., Feb. 8, 1889**

A sad accident resulting in the almost instant death of Brother John E. McIntosh occurred on the Johnson Pass, between Rush and Skull Valleys about 1 mile below the divide at half past four on Saturday the 2nd.

The deceased started from his parent's house on the morning in question to his sheep camp in charge of a team laden with grain and provisions. He was accompanied by Mr. Henry Newman. Arriving on top of the divide and on going down the canyon, the road being very difficult to travel and a considerable downgrade, the team started to run, throwing Brother McIntosh from the wagon.

He fell between the two wheels. The hind wheels passing over his back, fracturing his ribs on both sides and slightly bruising the right side of his head. Mr. Newman stopped the team, assisted the unfortunate man and laid him on some blankets and immediately afterward started down the canyon for help.

He met Mr. S.J. Stookey coming up the canyon on horseback. On returning to the place of the accident, they found him still alive but unable to speak and in about fifteen minutes from the time he received his injuries he breathed his last.

His body was then conveyed to the home of his parents who he had left only a few hours before in good health.

The deceased leaves a widow and three children who reside at Eagle Rock, Idaho [now Idaho Falls, Idaho]. There is also his aged parents, brothers and sisters and a large circle of friends sadly mourn his loss.

He was born in East Toledo, Michigan on June 13, 1842, and was a quiet, inoffensive man and a devoted husband and father.

An inquest on the body of the deceased was held at Saint John precinct before Mr. John McIntosh, J.P. The jurors found as their verdict that the said John E. McIntosh came to his death on Johnson Pass by being accidentally thrown under the wheels of his wagon which passed over his body causing almost instant death. The jurors were David H. Caldwell, David Charles and Nephi Draper. The funeral services were held on Wednesday last at Saint John. C.N. Ahlquist.

Chapter 21

# William's Sons Living in Mount Pleasant, Utah 1890

*It is now Oct.3, 1890. Abraham Edward and James Franklin McIntosh* [William and Maria's sons] *are living there* [Mount Pleasant]*. They have been in the sheep business for several years. Abraham McIntosh quit sheep business this season. James Franklin runs the sheep this season.*

## Chapter 22

# Living in Saint John, Utah 1891

*Today is the 14th of August. After so long a time I thought I would write a few more things. Last year, 1890, has been a year of some trouble to me. Also expensive. My wife has been sorely afflicted with fallen sickness* [epilepsy] *and poor health, and my own health is not good. I have been lame for several years with rheumatism and I am lame now. My hip joint is in bad shape.*

*August 15, 1891. I am not comfortable these times. My health is not very good and I am not able to do any work, but nevertheless the Lord has given us the good things and we have enough to keep us comfortable if we use it right. I feel to give thanks to our Heavenly Father for he is very mercifully and patient with us, patient with the whole Church of Jesus Christ of Latter Day Saints. Especially in conducting political things; it now seems like the enemies of the Kingdom of God are going to be supreme, but difficulty is warded off at this time. Times here in Saint John are very dull. There has been no teacher at my house for a long time. I suppose we might say, as with the people so with the priests, and as with the priests so with the people.*

The following entries are not in chronological order, for reasons unknown.

*October 20, 1891. Albert McIntosh* [Joseph Albert, son] *has worked my farm this year. He is married, has a wife and two children. We are still located in Saint John. We have had trouble and death in our family the last few years. Our oldest son John Ephraim was killed when thrown off a wagon March 2, 1890.* [Actually, the date was February 2, 1889.] *And still more, Sept. 25,* [1889] *our daughter Caroline died.* [Actually, the date was September 26, 1889]. *She was married to Joseph Jordan. She had two children. She died in Mount Pleasant.*

*October 3, 1891. Of late, there has been several deaths in our little town of Saint John. Brother Thomas L. Burridge died April 12, 1891. He was the husband of my daughter Alice. Died George W. Burridge, father of Thomas L. Burridge, Sept 26, 1891.*

*September 10, 1891. Caroline E. McIntosh died.* [The wife of William's brother John. She died in 1891 in Saint John. However, her gravestone reads that she died in 1885; but that is the date her daughter Mary Ann McIntosh Davis died]. *A woman that will be very missed especially with the younger women. She was kind and good among the sick. I will make one or two statements with regard to Bishop George W. Burridge. He has been Bishop in Saint John for over 20 years, and he was faithful to his trust.*

*October 4, 1891. I don't pretend to do any labor. I will soon be 72 years of age. I will say here that T.L. Burridge* [Thomas Lorenzo, husband of his daughter Alice] *was an honest industrious man respected by all his acquaintances.*

*October 14, 1891. I am not very well in health these times. Albert* [Joseph Albert], *my son, is working on the thrashing machine. We are getting our grain thrashed.*

*October 15, 1891. Today is Sunday. The time seems long and lonesome. I used to go to Meeting all the time, but I have not been to Meeting for quite a while. Sickness and other things preventing me from going. This don't seem good. Alice and her four children are living with us yet. John David McIntosh* [son of William's brother, John and Caroline Caldwell McIntosh] *will soon have his house finished, then she will move into the house and lot that she bought from him. The lot being situated in Saint John, Tooele Co., Utah.*

## Chapter 23

# Living in Mount Pleasant, Utah 1892

*In the summer of 1892 in Saint John where we lived formerly we had a severe trouble about our water ditches. We had it before arbitration and before the High Council three times and it is not truly settled yet. And I am sorry that I was one of that party. It is better to suffer wrong than to do wrong.*

*November 15, 1892, we moved to Mount Pleasant where I had previously bought a city lot with an orchard on it. We moved into a new house that I had built December 10, 1891.*

*Main Street, Mount Pleasant, Utah, circa 1910.*
*Picture used with permission of the Library of Congress, Washington, D. C.*

*Typical house in Mount Pleasant, Utah*
*Picture from private collection of Beverly McIntosh Brown*

## Chapter 24

# Living in Mount Pleasant, Utah
# 1893

*May 6. This will show that I have not written anything for quite a while but I will try and write a few things as correct as I can reflect since about 1891.*

*My wife has had very poor health. Consequently times have not been very pleasant. In the summer of 1892, she was tolerably well and in the summer or rather in November 15, 1892, we moved to Mount Pleasant where I had previously bought* [1889] *a city lot with an orchard on it. We moved into a new house that I had built December 10th, 1891. Our house has been comfortable for us this winter but my wife's sickness still lingers with her. I have done all I knowed to do for her comfort but her health is not good.*

*Today is the Sabbath day May 6, 1893. My own health is nothing to brag of, still it is no use to complain. I am too old, that's what is the matter. I will be 72 years this fall September 1893.*

*May, 1893. I took my wife up to Mary McIntosh's house. She lives on the lot above us in the same block. She is A.E McIntosh's* [William's son] *wife. I am alone writing.*

*This is a very backward spring. A great many people went to the dedication of the Temple in Salt Lake City but my wife's health prevented us from going to the dedication. There are other things I would like to speak about but I will not say much about it.*

*Myself and wife got our* [LDS Church] *recommends from the Saint John's Branch to the Mount Pleasant Branch, Sanpete, Utah.*

A Temple Recommend is a card from a Bishop attesting to the holder's adherence to LDS Church principles and practices. It allows a person to enter an LDS Temple, which believers consider to be "the House of the Lord." Members of the Church of Jesus Christ of Latter-day Saints go to the Temple to participate in religious ceremonies, including eternal marriages and to receive instructions on the purpose of life. In this case, it was used to transfer William and Maria from one Church location to another, attesting to their good character.

*May 15, 1893, Monday. Doctor Stiner from the valley is here today. He came here to see my wife. She is sick and has been sick a long time. We were in hopes he would benefit her but I don't know. We try to do for the best. This thing is kind of discouraging but we must be patient under all circumstances.*

*Elisa Wise is taking care of my wife and doing our housework.*

*May 16. Doctor Stiner left here today for Salina.*

*May 18, Thursday. There was a very destructive fire in Mount Pleasant. Mr. Wise and Mr. Fount received much damage. Mr. Fount had all his effects destroyed by the fire. There was much alarm.*

*May 23. I feel very lonesome today. My wife was taken sick yesterday and she is in bed today. I have been trying to do a little work today.*

*May 23. Brother Lund and Brother Clark were here today and administered to my wife. She rested fairly well last night. Yesterday was Sunday.*

*May 24. My wife feels a little better.*

*June 12, 1893. Sunday my wife was sick quite suddenly and rested quite poorly all night. This morning she is a little better but poorly yet.*

*Today I am going to write a letter to W. McIntosh* [his son, William Henry, in Junction City, Utah].

*I have paid Doctor Stiner of Salina $30 and I do not see much good for it.*

*June 18, Sunday. I have paid Elisa Wise $16. She does our housework. My wife is unable to do any work. We pay Elisa $2 a week. Now we live in Mount Pleasant.*

*June 24. My wife still continues in poor health. Frank* [James Franklin] *and Abe* [Abraham Edward] *McIntosh* [sons] *came in from the sheep tending last week but they are gone again.*

*June 26. We had a letter from Alice Burridge* [daughter] *last week. Her and family are well. She has four boys and one girl. She is our daughter. She lives in Saint John.*

*June 27. We had a letter from Lillian McBride. She is our daughter. She lives in Idaho. They are well.*

*August 15, 1893. My wife is a little better now. I took her to the Manti Temple to be baptized for health. Annie McIntosh, Frank* [James Franklin] *McIntosh's wife, and Mary McIntosh, Abe's*[Abraham Edward McIntosh] *wife, went with us.*

*September 6, 1893. She is now able to be about and live a little.*

*September 8. My own health is tolerable good for my age. We are living now in Mount Pleasant, Sanpete. I am 74 years of age this month. My hand is not as steady as when I was young. I, William McIntosh, do not enjoy myself now as well as I did when I was younger.*

*September 10, Sunday. Today I feel lonesome. I will have to try and go to Meeting. I am not able to do much work. We are expecting Alice* [daughter] *and Albert* [Joseph Albert, son] *from Saint John to make us a visit soon. I have been writing to all our children to come and go to the Temple with us and do all the* [LDS Church] *work that we can do for both the living and the dead before it is too late. Life is uncertain.*

*September 19. I have now come in from walking in the orchard and looking at the different kinds of apples and taken a bite of each one. I am alone a few hours, a little before sundown. I must try and go to Meeting more than I have done for some time. We have been to the Temple in Manti August 1893 and calculate to go again in a few days if the Lord is willing.*

*September 25. J.F. McIntosh* [son] *sends one hundred head of sheep to the eastern market. A.E. McIntosh* [son] *has given over his sheep herd to James Gilman, September 25, 1893.*

*October 2, 1893. We have quite a snowstorm for this time of the year. Of late I have been at work putting up a frame building for an outhouse. My health is not very good. I am too old. I don't complain.*

*Alice Burridge, my daughter, came to visit us about ten days ago, September 25.*

*We have been to the Temple in Manti lately and we calculate to go now and have our children sealed to us but there are many things in the way of doing good. It is difficult to get our children to come to the Temple. They are all married and live so far away but we are patient and do the best we can.*

"Sealing" is an ordinance [ritual] performed in LDS Temples. The purpose is to seal familial relationships, making possible the existence of family relationships throughout eternity. They are typically for sealing spouses to each other and children to their parents.

*We went to the Temple in Manti and done some work for the dead but did not do all we wanted to do. We intend to go next summer and do more, if all is well.*

*I took my horses and buggy and took Alice* [daughter] *home. She lives in Tooele County. While I was in Tooele I stayed some with Joseph Albert, my son. He lives on my farm. I got home again all right. Albert came with me to get some apples to take home to his wife. We live in Mount Pleasant. We have an orchard and plenty of apples.*

*December 26, 1893. The day after Christmas. We eat dinner with Mary McIntosh, A.E* [Abraham Edward, son] *McIntosh's wife. The weather till now has been quite pleasant. Today is a little stormy. Myself and wife has had bad health for about a month but we are better now. Thanks be to God for all his goodness.*

*A.E McIntosh started for Saint John, Tooele Co. a week ago last Wednesday.*

## Chapter 25

# Living in Mount Pleasant, Utah 1894

*Mount Pleasant, January 8, 1894. This is what they call the old New Year.*

*J.F. McIntosh* [son] *is on the desert with the sheep. A.E McIntosh* [son] *is in Tooele County, Saint John. We had Annie, Frank's wife, and Mary, A.E McIntosh's wife, to dinner with us and their folks. We had a good time. Maria, my wife, was sick all night with a pain in her stomach. This morning she is a little better.*

*January 9. The weather is very cold. About half a foot of snow on the ground.*

*I am here alone today. My wife is in bed quite sick. I feel quite lonesome. We try to get along. Hired help is so curious but we need someone with us all the time. Our money is kind of scarce these hard times.*

*February 1, 1894. I sit down to write a few things. The above that I have written is correct as near as I can recollect. My wife and myself are here alone this morning. Our health is not very good but we are around doing our chores. I am not strong; whenever I do any kind of hard work I get sick. I am 74 years of age last September. Notwithstanding, I cannot help being pleased that the Latter Day Saints, through the kindness of God, enjoy a goodly degree of peace at the present time. How long it will last I do not know. The will of God be done.*

*There is nothing of importance for me to write. My son, A.E McIntosh, is working in the mines in Tooele County.*

*February 2, 1894. We, William and Maria McIntosh, are living in Mount Pleasant. Joseph Albert, my son, is living on our farm in Saint John, Tooele County, Utah. Franklin McIntosh, my son, is on the desert with the sheep. William Henry* [son] *is living in Junction, Piute County.*

*February 20, Tuesday. We have had a very fine winter so far. But our time here is a very uneasy, lonesome time. As we make our beds we must lay on them yet. Our health is not very good. I am troubled a good deal with the grip* [influenza], *that filthy disease. It troubles me when I take a little cold. Times are very dull on account of civil legislation. The Democrats have to be crazy. Their laws have killed the silver money and the sheep industry in this western country. These things makes money very scarce.*

The national financial panic of 1893, and subsequent nationwide depression, lasted until 1897. It slowed economic growth, caused mining distress, agricultural depression and unemployment.

*February 20. I am in receipt of letters from Gersey Hinkley and Jennett Woodruff, my two sisters. They are well and comfortable. We are that comfortable that we have enough to eat. Times is hard with regards to money but we are in hopes times will be better soon.*

*March 1, 1894. Today is quite cold and stormy looking. Today is fast day and I hope the Saints are all observing and remembering the same. Myself and wife are here alone today. We do remember the fast day but don't go to the House of Worship. Today we are getting well along in years. I am 74 years old last September. My wife is about four years younger than myself.*

On Fast Sunday, church members are encouraged to fast for two consecutive meals and give the money they save by not eating, as a fast offering. These funds are used by the Church to financially assist those in need. Fast Sunday is usually the first Sunday of each month.

*March 6, 1894. Monday. We are still living in Mount Pleasant. We have had a long hard winter and the air is quite cold. I feel quite lonesome. There is none of the boys here now. J.F. McIntosh* [son] *is out on the desert with the sheep. A.E McIntosh* [son] *is in Skull Valley working in the mines. J.A. McIntosh* [son] *is living on our farm in Saint John with his family. Our health is not very good but we intend going to the Temple in the spring if the Lord willing, and do some work for our friends.*

*March 10, Saturday. Last night we had quite a storm of wind and snow. I am afraid it is hard on the sheep and on the sheep men also. So much snow at this time of the year. J.F. McIntosh* [son] *is out on the desert with my sheep. Cruel legislation has killed the sheep industry in this western country for the present. How long it will last I do not know. We have a letter from Annie McIntosh, J.A. McIntosh's* [Joseph Albert, son] *wife. They are all well. They live in Saint John. We live in Sanpete* [County], *Utah.*

*March 15. We are still enjoying that portion of health that we are on our feet but we are old folks. My wife has gone over to Annie McIntosh's today to while away the time a little and I am here alone in our new house in Mount Pleasant, Sanpete, Utah.*

*March 17. My son, A.E. McIntosh, came from Tooele County where he was at work all winter.*

*March 18. Today is Sabbath day. I would like to go to Meeting. I have been away from Meetings quite a while. I want to try and go soon.*

*March 20. If I go to Meeting regular I may feel better than I have lately. Times is hard and it troubles me likely more than it should. The winter has been quite long and tedious.*

*March 23. There is snow all over the ground and the weather is cold. A.E McIntosh* [son] *has come home from Tooele County.*

*We take the Deseret Sun Weekly News. The news gives a hard account of the legislature in Salt Lake City. Governor West wanted to bond the territory to get money to feed his own kind. There are too many loafers in Salt Lake City that are no friends to Latter Day Saints. There are many in Salt Lake City that outside bummers brought here. Many of them brought in here to out vote the Mormons. Liberals, old power kind of folks.*

*March 31, Saturday. This is the last day of March. We have a few inches of snow this morning. We are still living in Mount Pleasant. We are kind of well and able to be around but my health is not very good. Frank* [son] *has our sheep. He has not come from the desert yet.*

*April 14, 1894, Saturday. Stormy looking today. Franklin McIntosh* [son] *has come from the desert with the sheep. It has been a hard winter. The sheep look pretty well. We are both tolerable well at present. Times is very dull. Cruel legislation has hurt the western country, put a stop to improvements generally. We live in Mount Pleasant, Utah.*

*April 13. Times is full of events these days. Cocky's army, that is the Industrial Army, left Ogden in route for Washington.*

Coxey's Army was a protest march by unemployed workers from all parts of the United States, led by Ohio businessman Jacob Coxey. They marched on Washington, D.C. in 1894. That was the second year of a four-year economic depression that was the worst in United States history up to that time.

*Tonight they will be in Kansas. The people in a measure is in sympathy with them. It means something, I do not know what. It is stated that there is three million going to meet in Washington of the Industrial Army.*

*April 26. Some of the Industrial Army has passed through Utah and there is more coming. Some says they hope they will turn the government upside down. Well, I think it needs reform.*

*James F. McIntosh* [son] *received a bill with regard to his wool business. Last season's wool, 1893, a failure. A bill from old Andress of indebtedness. A great deal of dishonest work is carried on these days.*

*A.E McIntosh* [son] *is putting in his crop on the farm above Milburn. The sheep industry is gone up at present and silver also. Wicked legislation. My wife and myself are still living in Mount Pleasant, Sanpete, Utah, middlin' well.*

*July 3, 1894. I have not written in this book for quite awhile as nothing interesting has come along. My health is not very good.*

*We have James Jordan and family from Tooele County, Utah, visiting his relations living here in Mount Pleasant, Sanpete, Utah. We have had quite a good time.*

James Jordan was the father of Joseph Jordan, who married William's daughter Caroline. She passed away in 1889. Joseph remarried and stayed in Mount Pleasant, Utah.

*July 4, 1894. Independence Day. We, as Latter Day Saints, should remember that day with thankfulness to the Almighty for delivering to us the land where Adam dwelt Adamondiamon.*

In the Book of Mormon, one of the many meanings of Adam-ondi-Ahman is where "the family of mortals had its beginning. It was there that mortal man learned to work by the sweat of his brow. It was there that the first mortal children were born to the first mortal parents. Mortal man first learned to communicate with his God in those valleys." There is a hymn about it, looking forward to the Savior's Second Coming, when Adam-ondi-Ahman would be restored to its former beauty and glory.

*July 20. There has nothing happened the last few days worthy of note but as I am alone today I thought I would write a few lines. I feel lonesome. Anyway, the time seems long, and I have not been to Meeting lately.*

*We hear warning after warning to look and notice the signs in the heavens and on the earth. Also the disturbed state of the country all denotes the coming of the Kingdom of God. I am afraid we will not be faithful enough to stand true-hearted through all. It needs the aid of the Spirit of God to enable us to stand true. We must be prayerful.*

*A.E McIntosh* [son] *is at work on the farm that belongs to him and me. The farm is located above Milburn, Sanpete County. Twelve miles or more north of Mount Pleasant, Utah.*

*July 24, 1894. Today I have been at the celebration of the 24th of July in Mount Pleasant, Sanpete, Utah. It was rather dry for Latter Day Saints. This is the first time that statehood was announced in public meeting to the Latter Day Saints. Some hailed statehood with joy and some did not. All is well if we can get along in peace. The people of the world do not like anything like gospel laws. The devil is not dead yet.*

July 24 is celebrated every year as the day the first Mormon pioneers arrived in the Salt Lake valley. Utah became the 45th state, admitted to the Union on January 4, 1896.

*July 25. Today I feel quite lonesome. The day is very warm. The night quite cool. Statehood don't seem to be much joy to all the inhabitants of Utah. Perhaps it will be all well. God is at the helm. If we do not do the will of God we will be brought into bondage, but not if we keep the commandments of God. If we will keep the statutes that God has given us, all will be well with us. But if we don't -- bondage.*

*August 14, 1894. The weather is very warm now. Harvest will soon begin. We have had our quarterly Conference last Saturday and Sunday. I have been to five Meetings while Conference lasted. We had a good time. President George Q. Cannon was with us at the Conference.*

*September 23, 1894. I have not written since August 14. Today is Sabbath day. I have been at Meeting. Just got home. I have nothing particular to write. The time is passing away and I am growing old. Abe* [Abraham Edward, son] *has gone up to the ranch in Milburn, Sanpete, Utah, this week to thrash his wheat. My wife still keeps tolerable well for her.*

*September 24. I thought I would reserve this page and write a few lines that I think of when I feel troubled. After I came back from my Dixie mission, we lived in what is called Rush Valley, Saint John, Tooele County, Utah. I made me a homestead in that place north of Saint John, a little town and lived there with my family and proved up on my homestead and got the government title and deed to my land. We lived there about twenty years when I began to grow old. I was taken down with the rheumatism and was very lame and was not able to work. I had accumulated a little property besides on my homestead. I had some cattle and horses.*

*In Mount Pleasant, Sanpete, Utah, we had a herd of sheep and some real estate. I got so infirm I was not able to do anything like labor.*

*I was called on the Dixie mission in southern Utah I think about the year '67. Our family numbered eleven in all going to southern Utah on my mission and coming back - it took 10 years of my life. I was about 45 years old. Now I am 74 years old. As above stated, I do not feel able to work any and I wanted to sell all and live on our means which is ample to sustain us in our old days, but my wife would not sign the homestead papers. Now we have to get along the best we can.*

William continues to reminisce.

*We are living in our own new house in Mount Pleasant, Utah. Franklin McIntosh* [James Franklin, son] *and A.E McIntosh* [son] *lives here and their families, but my wife don't like it much. She has no relish for any place but old Saint John. We have a comfortable house but it takes more than world things to create happiness either in families or among neighbors or among any community. It needs the spirit of God, the spirit of love and good will to all God's creation.*

*September 28. We are still living in Mount Pleasant. Our health is not very good.*

*Snow is about two feet deep. A fall of snow came last night. Too much snow for me to go to Meeting. We have good Meetings here. Bishop McLund of Mount Pleasant, Sanpete is our Bishop. Seems to be a very good man. I have been in Mount Pleasant over two years and not bishop yet.*

*November 4, 1894. We have been to the Manti Temple this week and A.E McIntosh* [son] *and Mary, his wife, was married over the altar and had their three children sealed to them. Maria, my wife, done some work for her sister Jane Cooper Caldwell, went through the House of the Lord for her. A.E McIntosh was sealed to his parents, William and Maria McIntosh.*

## Chapter 26

# Living in Mount Pleasant, Utah 1895

*January 18, 1895. I did not go to Meeting today. The snow is quite deep. We are tolerable well today, thank God.*

*A.E McIntosh* [son], *Mary McIntosh, his wife, presented us with a pair of twin boys. Mother and twins doing pretty well. These things happened in Mount Pleasant. This may not be exactly the right date but it is pretty correct. Their names are Franklin Vaughn, and Marinus Vernon.*

The twin boys were born on January 10, 1895. Franklin Vaughn died less than a month later on February 7, 1895. Marinus Vernon survived. He was called Vernon.

*August 18, 1895. Ordinations: I, William McIntosh, have been received into the High Priests Quorum this day under the hands of the Presidency of the Stake of Zion.*

*August 18, 1895. Canute Peterson, President of the Sanpete Stake of Zion. My health is very poor. I will be 76 on September 16.*

*September 17, 1895. I do not feel contended very much today. Maria, my wife, is in bed sick. Mary, the wife of my son W.H* [William Henry] *McIntosh, is here with us. She came on a visit not knowing that my wife was sick. She came in good time to help us a little.*

*September. J.F. McIntosh* [son] *started up to the mountains to dip the sheep. It is raining today.*

*September 20. My wife is somewhat better today.*

*I, William McIntosh, have been close at home for sometime. My wife seems to be a little better today. Times are very curious. I would like to write somewhat about the times but …*

*President F. M. Liman says that now when we are ready to take one another by the throat, we can come into their union. I would bid them good morning.*

*September 23. The weather is very cold for this time of the year. We have had two days snowing a little and the weather is quite cold. My wife's health is poor but on the mend. This is three Sundays I have not been at Meeting on account of my wife being sick but she is a little better today.*

*October 4, 1895. Alice Burridge, our daughter, has been with us a week but she is going home tomorrow with all her children, four boys and a girl. She came on a visit to see her mother. She lives in Tooele County, Utah. We live in Mount Pleasant, Sanpete Co., Utah.*

*October 9. I have been to church today and was called upon to speak to the people which I did to the best of my ability. My wife is in very poor health.*

*We are expecting Jacob Keele and family. His wife is our daughter* [Melissa Jane, called Jane]. *They live in Colorado. They were coming on a visit to see their mother. She is sick. She feels a little better today.*

*October 7, Saturday. A.E. McIntosh* [son] *done his thrashing on the Milburn ranch over six hundred bushels last week. Has been a stormy time, rain and snow.*

*Milburn, Utah, where they wintered their sheep.*
*Picture from private collection of Beverly McIntosh Brown*

*October 14. We have had a letter from Jacob Keele's folks stating that they are disappointed about not getting their money and they cannot at this time come to see us.*

*October 8. Alice Burridge* [daughter] *started home last week. The weather has been good.*

*October 27, Sunday. I have attended a Priesthood Meeting today and was called to speak to the Brethren. We had a good Meeting. The times were principally talked of. There is seemingly a good feeling amongst the people in Mount Pleasant, Sanpete, Utah.*

*October 30. There is a great Republican rally in Mount Pleasant tonight. William Sorenson and Judge Johnston are speakers on politics. Politics all the go now.*

*October 31. My wife is very unwell these times. A good deal confined to her bed. It is pretty tough.*

*This is Monday and last Friday, November 1, Hanna Childs came to stay with us this winter. My wife not being able to do any housework. My health for a long time is poor.*

*November 1, 1895. Yesterday I went to Meeting.*

*Sunday the Bishop advised the people not to vote against statehood being statehood was at our doors. Not to vote against it. The times are queer. I will not write what I think of these times. I don't know as it would be wise.*

*November 4, 1895. This is a very stormy day, about two inches of snow came down last night.*

*November 5, 1895. Today is election. Mount Pleasant is quite lively. It is very disagreeable however under foot, snow and slush. We had quite a snowstorm but all is peaceful.*

*November 8. Aunt Fanny from Saint John, Tooele Co. came to make a visit to her daughters that lives here, David H. Caldwell's wife. They live in Tooele Co. She called to see my wife who is sick.*

*November 16. Election is now all over. Things seem to the quiet. How long it will stay remains to be seen.*

*December 1, 1895. We have had about two weeks of cold weather. My wife still continues to be unable to do any work. Very nervous with constipation and other troubles which prostrates her and disables her from doing any work.*

*December 6. 1895. My wife is a little better this morning. This is a beautiful day for this time of the year.*

*December 1895. Reflections of the Mind: There are many things in my mind that I think about. Sometimes causes me to feel well and sometimes not so well but those times that I do not feel well about, I don't write about. There is one thing I feel well about, unfaithful as I have been, I think I have kept the faith in the Church of Jesus Christ of Latter Day Saints. I never seen anything in the laws of the Church to cause me to find fault with men. Many do wrong but the laws of God are the same. Reflection of the mind reaches away yonder but we are beings that know but very little yet. Our Father in heaven, through his servants, has taught us how to live and how to keep his law and we are not so ignorant after all.*

## Chapter 27

# Living in Mount Pleasant, Utah 1896

*January 1, 1896. This is Christmas day. Good sleighing. The sleighs and horse bells are running plentiful here in Mount Pleasant, Sanpete Co., Utah. I don't enjoy myself but I try to make the best of it. My wife is sick in bed, almost helpless.*

*January 14. Hanna Childs is with us doing housework.*

*January 15. We are invited out to dinner but my wife cannot go. Hanna will go and I will go after and eat dinner. I think it is rather a tough time for me and more tough for her. Epilepsy is the disease she is troubled with. Doctors no good.*

*March 17, 1896. I have not written much for quite awhile but the first part of this winter has been very severe. It was very cold weather and I have attended my wife alone. She has been very sick. Alice Burridge* [daughter] *and her children have been with us for quite awhile. The boys cut my wood and done my chores.*

*My wife is displeased with me. She won't allow me to give her a drink of water.*

*March 21. Alice Burridge* [daughter] *is with us yet. She is washing today and the boys are doing the tilting with the washing machine. She is like me, not very rugged. Although I have kept on my feet all through the trouble, I don't feel to complain if my wife was alright. It is no use to complain anyhow.*

*Reader will see my hand is not very steady. I am growing old. I am 76 years old last September 19th.*

*March 26. I have been to 2 funerals today and heard some good preaching which helps me to bear the battle of life. My wife continues to be very far from good health. The weather is very favorable for this time of the year. My wife seems to be a little better these days. She is talking of going home with Alice, my daughter, to stay awhile at Saint John,*

*Tooele. She doesn't like me but still I think she will come back again. I am alone in the house. Our house is very comfortable. My wife and Alice and her family left here to go to Tooele Co. where my daughter lives, Saint John, Tooele Co., Utah.*

*March 31. I have not heard from them since they went on. They went on the train. Tooele Co. is about one hundred miles from here.*

*April 3, 1896. My health is not good. I am old but I am on my feet. I am lonesome but such is life.*

*April 4. Frank* [son] *has just come in with the sheep from the desert.*

*April 21. I had a letter from my folks a few days ago. They arrived safe at their destination. I am here alone today. I am quite lonesome. The wind sounds lonesome today. Spring has come but the wind blows today.*

*April 22. A.E McIntosh* [son] *and his man, Charley Larson, has come down from Twin Creek Canyon where they have been prospecting for a coal mine. Rather discouraged. I do not know what they will do now.*

*April 24. Sale for wool this year is very discouraging. Only 5 or 6 cents a pound.*

*May 2, 1896. It has become my painful privilege to record the demise of J. F. McIntosh, my son. He died and was buried on Saturday, May 2, Mount Pleasant, Utah. We telegraphed for our people to come to the funeral but they could not get here in time. We were obliged to bury him. He died from liver troubles. Ten days sick. He was born January 8, 1852. He was sick but a short time.*

*His mother is sickly and has been for a long time. She lives at the present time in Saint John, Tooele County. Her daughter Alice who lives in Saint John, Tooele County was here taking care of her mother and she took her mother home with her to Saint John, Tooele Co., Utah, thinking to better her health.*

*May 10. She is there now for her health is not good. I am keeping house alone. Very lonesome.*

*June 1, 1896. I have not heard from my folks for quite a while but the last I heard from them my wife is not improving very fast. I think she would be better at home. Our house and things is comfortable. It is a silly bird that wanders away from its nest.*

*There are many things in this life, while we are traveling through it, that is very disagreeable but we must be patient under all circumstances. We had quite a splutter here yesterday on Arbor Day. A flood that done much damage.*

*June 14. I have heard several times from my wife but she don't improve much. I have been to the High Priest Meeting today. Also to our Ward Meeting and heard the Elders preach. Today is a very warm day.*

*June 15. Today I wrote a letter to Hinkley's folks* [William's sister].

*June 24. I am at home today in my house. It is clean and comfortable. My wife is not here with me. She is over in Tooele County with Alice her daughter and when she will come home I don't know. I have some girls here nearly two weeks at work washing and cleaning the house from one end to another. The house is comfortable with four rooms, buttery and closet. I feel lonesome.*

*June 24. Wrote to Albert* [Joseph Albert, J.A., son in Saint John, Utah].

*July 2, 1896. Wrote to Jacob Keele* [husband of daughter, Malisa, in Colorado].

*July 4. I have been to the celebration today in Mount Pleasant. In our Meeting, Jew and Gentile seems to enjoy themselves. These are the last days. The lamb and the lion shall lie down together. Well, this is more there than mobbing but friendship will not last. The devil is not dead yet nor won't be till he is bound out of the millennium and then he will be let loose again a thousand years or more to try the people, even gog and megog multitudes in the decision.*

From the Book of Mormon, Gog will be the leader of a great army that attacks the land of Israel. Magog seems to refer to the northern barbarians and skilled warriors who will fight Gog.

*July 24, 1896. Wrote to Jacob Keele, and D H Caldwell* [Maria's brother].

*Aug. 20, 1896. Wrote to Hinkley* [William's sister in Ohio]. *Wrote to Jacob Keele.*

*August 21. I have not written any for some time but there has been plenty in my mind to write. I have been passing through the snags and rough places lately but I will try and wear it out after awhile if I live the Lord being my helper.*

*August 18. David Henry Leonard* [son of Jane Caldwell Leonard] *and family, eight in all, stayed here two nights on their way to Castle Valley* [east of Mount Pleasant, near Price, Utah]. *We had a good time.*

*August 25. I am at home today. I have just received a card to attend a wedding party. Eugene Jordan's* [nephew from the Caldwell side of the family] *wedding party. I have written a letter to Alice my daughter. She is sick desiring my wife to come home. I am living in my house in Mount Pleasant. I was to Meeting. I attend to Meeting all the time.*

*August. This is Tuesday. I am still living in my own house in Mount Pleasant, Utah. I am alone. My wife is living with Alice her daughter in Tooele County, Utah.*

*September 22. Nothing of much importance is going on these days. Only the confusion of politics. I will say a few words about the death of J.F. McIntosh* [James Franklin, son]. *His death was very sudden. He had the care of my sheep and died without any warning. Pretty much his business and mine was not canceled. Annie McIntosh, Frank McIntosh's wife, stepped in and said it was her right to continue his business but a woman could not well take care of a flock of sheep. The sheep were not well cared for. I was obliged to take the sheep myself. This caused some trouble but we have got along without any lawsuit.*

*September, 1896. My son, A.E McIntosh, has taken the sheep spoken of. He took them on Sept.15, 1896. He has taken them on shares.*

*September 23. I am still living alone in my own house. It is clean and comfortable but I am alone. My wife is living with my son Albert McIntosh in Tooele Co. on my farm. When she will come home I do not know. This is fruit time here.*

*October 12, 1896. Hana Childs is picking apples here today. I am still living alone. I don't hear from my folks. They don't write to me. They are living in Saint John. Yesterday I have been to the High Priest Meeting and to the Ward Meeting. Good kind of talk at Conference.*

*October 15. It is a very fine day today. Although the air is cold, it is good weather for this time of the year. I am still alone and I am very lonesome. Mary McIntosh, A.E McIntosh's wife, and the children started a week ago last Thursday on a visit to Saint John, Tooele Co. A.E. McIntosh* [son] *stays with me till they come home.*

*October 16. Conference time is over with and the Kingdom of God is spreading and growing stronger, if we will stay with it, we will gain a victory that will stay with us if we prove faithful to the end of our journey in this life is drawing near a close. I have not been faithful enough but I have kept the faith. I have never faltered in my belief of the gospel in the Church of Jesus Christ of Latter Day Saints.*

*October 19. This is a fine day for this time of the year.*

*October 20. I am still alone. My folks don't write to me. My folks fret me all the day long. I don't think my wife is doing right well. She has poor health. She has gone from home and living with her son Albert on my farm in Tooele Co. I think she is better at home. My house is good and comfortable and enough to get along with.*

*October 22. Mary McIntosh came home from her visit to Saint John last Wednesday and I wrote a letter to my wife the next day asking her to come home. That was Thursday morning.*

*October 26. Sunday I have been to Meeting twice today. The weather keeps good.*

*November 3, 1896. Tuesday election day in Mount Pleasant. Quite a cold day. It has been a very interesting time. Feels like winter today. A little snow on the ground.*

*November 10. Last night there fell quite a fall of snow, 6 inches. This evening the weather looks fine. Last Sunday I was at a High Priest Meeting and had a good time and to our Sunday Meeting in the afternoon.*

*November 20. A.E. McIntosh* [son] *started out for the desert with the sheep. It's been rainy weather, not very cold.*

*November 21. The weather is good today. My health is better now than it was two weeks ago. I hope to keep well anyhow according to my age which is 76 last September. My wife has not come home yet. I am looking for the day. Her health is not good. I have lived alone this summer. It is very lonesome. I have been to the High Priest Meeting today. I received a letter from my wife.*

*November 23. She resides in Saint John, Tooele Co., Utah. She left here April 1st, 1896 and has not come back since and wants me to send her money to come home with. I sent her $20 to come home with. Maybe she will come home. She is staying with Albert McIntosh, my son, living on my homestead farm in Saint John, Tooele Co. I have been living alone since April 1st, 1896 in Mount Pleasant.*

*December 6, 1896. Saturday. A.E. McIntosh* [son] *killed hogs yesterday. Tomorrow is fast day also High Priest Meeting.*

*December 13, Sunday. Two inches of snow fell this morning. Looks like stormy weather. A.E McIntosh* [son] *and Peter Jensen started for the desert with the rams. It was storming. The flock of the sheep is out on the desert now.*

## Chapter 28

# Living in Mount Pleasant, Utah 1897

*January 3, 1897. I am expecting my wife home about Wednesday from Tooele Co. where she has been over six months. I did not go to Meeting today. My wife came and feels a little better. She is at home now and has been for several weeks. I have not written for quite awhile.*

*January 12. As you see, I have not written for quite awhile. The Kingdom of God is always bright to me. It is bright and will spread and fill the earth. If we are not up and doing well, it will go too fast for us and grow out of our knowledge and we will be left behind in the dark.*

*January 13. There has been fine weather till now. The winter seems to have set in now. Some snow fell last night. The good weather seems to be broke up now.*

*March 4, 1897. It is some time since I have written anything. We are getting along tolerable well considering. My wife is at home now. Her health is not good and I have to stay in the house nearly all the time. I would like to attend Meetings but I must be patient and do the best I can. Winter is here now but it is not very cold weather. A.E McIntosh* [son] *is out on the desert with the sheep. We expect him home April 1.*

*March 4. Our new President McKinley takes his seat in the White House at Washington town. I don't know whether we will be any better for that or not, but it will be as the Lord wills.*

*March 9. We have had a long spell of stormy weather. Yesterday it snowed all day. A cold night last night. I am very anxious to hear from A.E. McIntosh* [son]. *He is out on the desert with my sheep. He has them on shares this season and perhaps longer. I don't get to go to Church or Meetings. My wife's health is not good and I have to stay with her and I feel lonesome all day on Sundays but I must be patient. Perhaps she will be better soon.*

*March 19. We have a long snow all night last night. I have a flock of sheep on the desert and A.E. McIntosh* [son] *is with them. This stormy weather is hard on the sheep.*

*March 20. The weather is a little better today. My wife is a little better today. She is sewing on the sewing machine. The weather is not good. I feel quite lonesome. I don't like to dwell just us two alone. Well, I rented part of our house to Peter Swenson and his wife but they don't seem to be that much company for us old people. Well, we must not be too old and set in our way. We are living in Mount Pleasant, Sanpete Co. in our house. It is quite comfortable.*

*March 29. There fell last night about 10 inches of snow. The weather today is quite cool. Myself and wife are tolerable well today. We are getting about as well as can be expected. Everything in this world is not all A-OK.*

*March 30. I have been to Meeting yesterday in the M.P.* [Mount Pleasant] *Meeting house. They spoke on charity. We had a good time. This month and part of last month has been stormy.*

*April 4., 1897. This is Sunday. I have not been to any Meeting today. I feel better when I go to Meeting. My wife's health is not good and I have to be with her nearly all the time. We have part of our house rented but they are not much company for us. They are newly married people. March weather is here yet stormy and cold.*

*April 8. The weather is cold, snowing a little. My health is not good at present. My wife is busy hemming dish rags on the sewing machine. Her health is not good but her and myself is still around on our feet as yet. We hear that President Woodruff* [President of the LDS Church] *is not well. How sick he is we don't know, but we hope he will live till after the Jubilee, July 24th.*

William is referring to the celebration of 50 years since the settlement of Utah on July 24, 1847. They call the celebration the Jubilee and is celebrated every year.

*It seems as he was standing at the gate according to his years. I almost feel some as if I was not far from crossing the line and going down the valley, 77 years of age. We have rented part of our house to Peter Swenson for the present.*

*April 10. A.E. McIntosh* [son] *came in from the desert with the sheep. His two children, Elvin and Vernon, are very sick. Elvin dangerously. The weather is not good and unhealthy.*

*April 20. The boys are no better. The doctor is attending them almost night and day. The ailment is membrane croop.* [Croup is a respiratory condition that is usually triggered by an acute viral infection of the upper airway.]

*April 25. The boys are a little better with good care. They may be out of danger.* [Both children survived.] *Myself and wife are old people. Our health is not good.*

*May 10, 1897. This season our sheep have done better.*

*June 1, 1897. We have 10 cents for our wool. I have not attended Meeting of late as well as I would like. My wife her health is very poor and I stay at home a good deal.*

*July 17, 1897. Her health still continues poor. I don't know what will be the result of it. Now for a few days she has been a little better. We are getting along nicely.*

*July 23, 1897. My wife was taken with a cramp in her stomach and that continued with her until July 27 then she died, seemingly unconscious of trouble or pain. She was buried in the Mount Pleasant burying ground, Sanpete Co., Utah.*

*July 24. Passed away in memory of old times.*

*August 2,1897. She was buried.*

*August 13. Now I will relate another circumstance. Sister Ronnow of Panaca was in Salt Lake City at the Jubilee 1897, was taken sick there. She got worse after the doctors visited her. She wanted to come home with Annie McIntosh, my son Frank* [James Franklin] *McIntosh's wife. He died over a year ago. Annie McIntosh was at the Jubliee and Sister Ronnow came home with her and died while here.*

*August 14. Her dead body is here in my house now, Annie not having a convenient place for her.*

*August 15. I had just buried my wife a few days ago when Sister Ronnow was brought to my house and placed in ice to preserve her for burial. The same as my wife was. These seem to be the rough times for me.*

*August 21. I have nothing very cheerful to write about these times. But there is one thing that gives me cheer, when I live close to the Lord and sincerely ask for His spirit to guide me. And strive to do His will in keeping His commandments given unto us to keep and observe. Any other way we cannot enter into His Kingdom, the Kingdom of our Lord Jesus Christ.*

*August 23. Annie McIntosh, my son's wife, is washing for me and straightening up things and she is very kind to me after the trouble and trials we have had as stated on this page. I am staying with A.E. McIntosh* [son] *and Mary McIntosh ever since my wife died July 27, 1897.*

*August 30. Today and for quite a few days, I have been in poor health. Today I am trying to take in to the house. I have had the bed clothing and things outdoors getting the air to refresh them as I have had quite a spell of preserving corpses waiting for burial. My wife first and then Sister Ronnow. It has been tough on me lately. They had her preserved in ice till the friends could get here.*

*August 30. Annie McIntosh* [daughter-in-law] *and Ica* [Annie's daughter] *are washing my house here today. Ica got some dinner. I am very unwell too. I have a bad cold. I don't know how long I will stay on this planet. The will of God be done anyway. I am trying to get my house cleaned up after so much sickness and death that I have had lately in my house, Mount Pleasant, Utah.*

*September 8, 1897. The above stated circumstances left my house all in confusion as stated. Annie McIntosh* [daughter-in-law] *was going to fix up my house but she backed out and I got another two women and they will complete the work. As soon as I get my house righted up, I intend to go to the Manti Temple and try and do some work for the living and the dead, if I am well enough. I don't like to go alone.*

*September 9. A.E. McIntosh* [son] *has gone to the sheep camp. The wind is blowing today. I had a letter from Ohio the other day. My sister and her husband talk of coming out on a visit to see me this fall. Whether they will or not I don't know.*

*September 17. I am not very well today. I have a bad cold. I am still alone. I am very lonesome. The weather begins to get colder. I have not heard from Alice* [daughter] *and Albert* [son] *for a long time. They live in Saint John, Tooele Co. Saint John, Tooele Co. is about 75 miles from here, Mount Pleasant, Sanpete Co., Utah.*

*September 19. I have been to Meeting today and enjoyed a portion of the spirit of the house of worship. Still I feel that this world is a lonesome place. Of course the society of the Saints is good.*

*September 21. This is a very fine day for this time of the year. Well, the winter is coming on and I do not know where I will stay this winter. Providence will open the way before me if I am truehearted and strive to keep His law.*

*September 22, 1897. I left Mount Pleasant and went to City Creek Junction, Piute County to visit .W.H* [William Henry] *and Mary McIntosh. He is my son and Mary is his wife.*

*September 24. While I was there my daughter* [Lillian Elizabeth], *Mrs. McBride, came from Idaho came to Mount Pleasant my home. She came to take me home with her. She sent a message after me and I came to Mount Pleasant and I went with her to Idaho and stayed six months. A distance of about three hundred miles from Mount Pleasant.*

*September27. We started for Oakley, Idaho.*

## Chapter 29

# Living in Mount Pleasant, Utah

### 1898

William seems to be reminiscing again since his dates are not consecutive.

*September 1, 1898. I returned to Mount Pleasant and been living alone, very lonesome till June 1, 1898, when I went to the Manti Temple and done some work for the dead - James McIntosh* [probably William's brother] *and for my great grandfather and for William Hammond and for Fanny Hammond, William Hammond's sister.*

*Sunday today I have been to the High Priest Meeting and Meeting in the afternoon.*

*April 25. I thought I would write a few things. My wife died July 27, 1897, and was buried in the Mount Pleasant burying ground. James Franklin died over a year ago and was buried in the Mount Pleasant burial ground. He is my son. My wife was buried in the Mount Pleasant cemetery July 27, 1897. I have been wandering about some ever since.*

*In April 1897 my daughter Lillian came for me. She lives in Idaho and I went with her to stay the winter. Before she came, I had gone to stay awhile with W.H.* [son] *and Mary McIntosh but she sent for me and I went with her to Idaho. Her and me left Mount Pleasant April 8, 1897. I stayed all winter with her and Heber McBride* [Lillian's husband].

*April 6. I came home and I am very lonely. Can't get along just as I want to. A.E McIntosh* [son] *contract is for 1890 with the sheep. There is war now with United States and Spain* [Spanish-American War, 1898-1899].

*April 26, 1898. I am at home very lonesome.*

*May 6, 1898. I am staying in my own house at present. But where I will stay this winter I do not know as yet. I want to get some good folk to stay with me in my own house and I will stay at home. I am very old.*

*June 18, 1898. I do not care about running about much now. I will be 80 years old in September 1898. I have been to church both Meetings today. Today is Sunday.*

About this same time, William learned of the death of his nephew, John David McIntosh. William copied this obituary article from a newspaper.

**Death of a Mercur Man**

Manager McIntosh of the Mercur Produce Company Passes Away. Mercur, June 18, 1898. J.D. McIntosh manager of the Mercur Meat and Produce Company died suddenly today. He went to the slaughterhouse about a mile above town for a horse on which he intended to ride to Lehi after some beef cattle. This was about 6 a.m. At 7 o'clock Mr. McGee the butcher discovered him in the barn.

*June 24. The 4th of July will soon be here. I am still living alone in my own house. A.E. McIntosh* [son] *and Mary his wife lives in the lot joining me. I go there for my meals. I will do otherwise as soon as I can.*

*November 29, 1898. I have not written as you see. The time has passed. Annie McIntosh, my son Franklin's wife died a year ago this last spring in May.*

Annie did not die until 1920. It was William's son, James Franklin, who died May 2, 1896.

*I have not lived alone very much.*

*He* [James Franklin] *came home from the desert with the sheep seemingly in good health. He was taken sick and died in May 1897. His wife and her daughter lived with me a good part of the summer of 1898 while their own house was being repaired. They have moved to their own house.*

*November 16. My sister and her husband came from Ohio state, Toledo. My sister's maiden name is Girsey. Her husband's name is Henry Hinkley. They have come more than two thousand miles to see me. They don't belong to the Mormon church. I think they will stay with me till spring.*

*December 1. We are getting along nicely. This winter so far has been frosty and cold.*

*December 25. Today is Christmas Sunday. My sister and her husband, Henry Hinkley, is here with me yet. We are getting along nicely. I still live in Mount Pleasant, Sanpete Co.*

William died on May 4, 1899 in Mount Pleasant and was buried in the Mount Pleasant cemetery next to his wife, Maria.

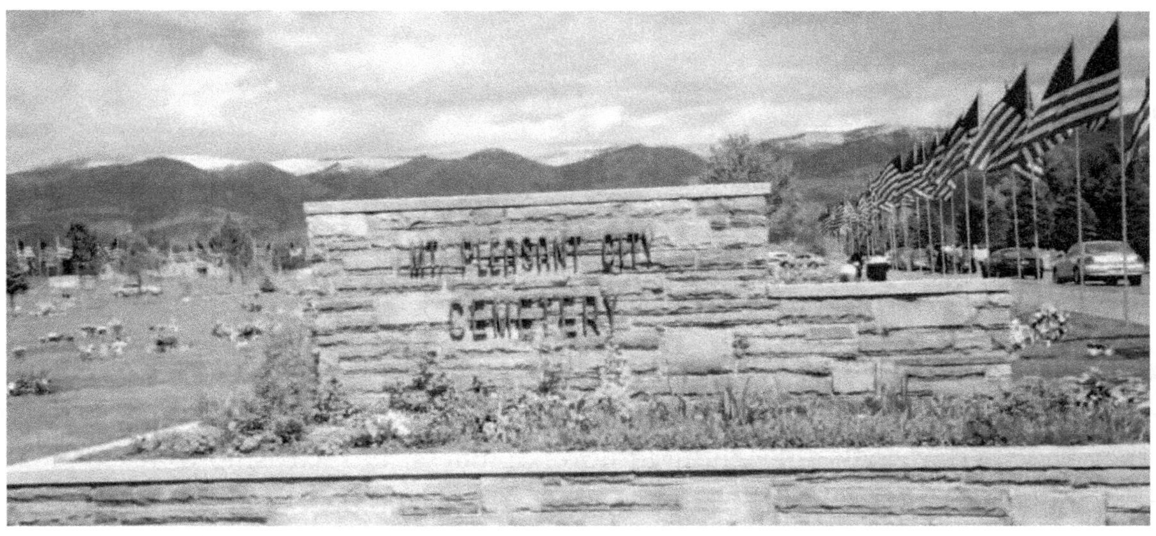


*Mount Pleasant City Cemetery, Utah*
*Picture from the private collection of Beverly McIntosh Brown*

*Headstones of William and Maria Caldwell McIntosh*
*Picture from the private collection of Beverly McIntosh Brown*

## Appendix A

# Legacy of William and Maria Caldwell McIntosh

William and Maria's legacy to us is an example of the meaning of perseverance. They traveled for 10 years to achieve a goal that they chose at the beginning of that time, and they kept to that goal. They endured poverty, illness, and hardship to reach an almost uninhabitable land in which they could be with others who believed as they did. For their descendants, they left proof of what people with a singlemindedness of focus might accomplish. Their beliefs in faith, church, and family provided them with purpose and direction that brought them through every adversity.

The obvious wonder of William's legacy is the existence of the diary itself. William seemed committed to recording a chronicle of his life. And that this chronicle, a diary made of paper, would survive for more than 150 years in a legible format, is simply a miracle. To his later generations and to all who love history, the diary provides firsthand glimpses into everyday life of a previous time. William's reticence to record details of disputes and difficulties – instead simply noting that the matter was resolved – leaves us curious, but also models for us a maturity of outlook not often seen. William's diary illustrates the inner thoughts, strengths, and values of a husband and wife devoted to their faith, their church, their family, and their survival.

As often as people move around, even in the 1850's, most of the descendants of William and Maria stayed in the same area. Two of their children moved away but lived in neighboring states. And another one retired elsewhere but was brought back to Utah to be buried.

In my own case, I grew up in Dugway, Utah, 53 miles west of Saint John, Utah. My grandfather and great-grandfather were both born in Saint John.

My father was born in Mount Pleasant, Utah where William and Maria lived and are buried.

I was born in Provo, Utah, 57 miles north of Mount Pleasant.

One of my brothers settled near West Jordan, Utah and raised his children there. Two of his sons live nearby and are raising their children there. And my brother did not know that his great-great grandfather had lived in West Jordan.

My father's parents lived in Provo, Utah for many years before they retired to Mount Pleasant. Living in Dugway, only 2 ½ hours away, we would visit them almost every weekend. To get to their house, we would drive over Johnson Pass, where John Ephraim died. On the other side of the Pass was Clover and Saint John, which we would drive through. I do not remember my father ever telling us about his family living in Saint John, so we were all surprised to learn the news.

Clover is where William's brother John is buried. He is buried with his wife Caroline Caldwell McIntosh, who was Maria's sister. Maria and Caroline's mother is buried there also, Mary Ann Vaughn Caldwell.

When I first started studying our family history, my father told me that if I wanted to meet the McIntoshes, to go to the Mount Pleasant Cemetery on Memorial Day. Almost my entire pedigree chart on the McIntosh side is buried there and I did meet many cousins there, attending the graves.

Quite a legacy!

William and Maria McIntosh
1819 - 1899 1824 - 1897
The William and Maria Caldwell McIntosh Family, c. 1900
Daughters: Lillian Elizabeth, Alice Maria, Malisa Jane
Sons: Joseph Albert, Abraham Edward, William Henry

*Here is a picture of six of the children of William and Maria Caldwell McIntosh (from the private collection of Beverly McIntosh Brown).*

## Appendix B

# Family Group Records for John and Girsey Rankin McIntosh, Abraham Isaac and Agnes McIntosh Vaughn, William and Maria Caldwell McIntosh, and the eleven children of William and Maria Caldwell McIntosh

# John McIntosh, Sr.

| Husband | John McIntosh Sr.[1,2] | |
|---|---|---|
| Born | 25 Jun 1795 | Croy, Inverness, Scotland, United Kingdom |
| Died | 5 Mar 1875 | Bountiful, Davis, Utah Territory, United States[3] |
| Buried | date: | place: |
| Bapt.(LDS) | 27 Feb 1999 | Bountiful Utah Temple |
| Conf.(LDS) | 27 Feb 1999 | Bountiful Utah Temple |
| Init.(LDS) | 16 May 1860 | Endowment House |
| Endow.(LDS) | 16 May 1860 | Endowment House |
| Father | William McIntosh (1777-1830) | |
| Mother | Isabel McIntosh (1777- ) | |
| SealP (LDS) | 27 Aug 1982 | Provo Utah Temple |
| Marriage | 15 Jun 1817 | Rutherglen, Lanark, Scotland, United Kingdom[4] |
| SealS (LDS) | 16 May 1860 | Endowment House |
| Other Spouse | Mary McPherson (1797-1879) | 16 May 1860 - Bountiful, Davis, Utah, United States |
| SealS (LDS) | 16 May 1860 | Endowment House |

**Events**

1. He witnessed the baptism of his son John.
This is the First Presbyterian Church of Perth, Ontario, Canada Record of Baptisms:
Name: **McIntosh, John**
Spouse: , Grizel
Address: Dalhousie, con.5, lot1
Child: John
Born: 11-14-1821

2. He emigrated in 1821 from Glasgow, Lanark, Scotland, United Kingdom.[5]
page 192: **McIntosh, John, 1799-.** Born Lanarkshire, a son of John and Margaret McIntosh. Ship: Commerce, 1821. Location: West lot 1, con 5, Dalhousie Township.
John McIntosh came here with his wife, Margaret, born 1800, his brother Robert born 1812 and one little girl, possibly a child of John's. Possibly Mrs. Alex Nicholson, nee Janet McIntosh, was a sister. **Rev. William Bell's baptismal records show a baby, John born in November, 1821 to the John McIntosh on this farm, but the mother's name is given as Grizel, so there is a mistake somewhere.** Robert McIntosh married Isabella Easton, daughter of George Easton of the Lesmahagow society. The couple later went to Motherwell, Fullerton Twp, Perth County.
***Apparently there were two John McIntoshes on the ship. The one described above and the one who arrived in Lanark in 1820 and was assigned West lot 1, Con 5; with wife Girzel who gave birth to son John in 1821.***

3. He owned land in 1821 in Lanark, Upper Canada, Canada.[6]
**McIntosh, John**, status is emigrant, received 100 acres in 1821.

4. He owned land in 1821 in Lanark, Upper Canada, Canada.[7]
Origional settler **John McIntosh**, in 1821, located in Dalhousie, concession 5, lot 1W, Comments: Here with family: Small clearing: Broken, rocky lot.

5. He emigrated on 11 May 1821 from Glasgow, Lanark, Scotland, United Kingdom.[8]
Page 202, Line 5811. **McINTOSH, John.** To Quebec on the (ship)Commerce, exited from Greenock (Scotland), 11 May 1821, in assoc with the St Johns Emig Soc. Wife and 2 ch with him. Loc Dalhousie Twp, Lanark Co, ONT. First slmt (settlement) advance to him paid 1 Aug. ICS-2 & 6.

# John McIntosh, Sr.

6. He owned land which he sold in Dalhousie, Concession 05, Lot 01P on 28 Mar 1838 in Dalhousie, Lanark, Ontario, Canada.[9]
Page 8, No. 93, Seller-**McIntosh, John**, Location-Dalh. Con. 05, Lot 01P, Buyer-Matheson, Roderick, Address-Perth, Date-03-28-1838, Price-20, Witness-Matheson, John, Witness-Gray, Peter.

7. Baptism in the Church of Jesus Christ of Latter-day Saints: John McIntosh, in Aug 1838, in Dalhousie, Lanark, Ontario, Canada.

8. He appeared on the census on 6 Aug 1850 in Monroe, Monroe, Michigan, United States.[10]
**Line 22 - John McIntosh, age 55, male, laborer, born in Scotland.**
Line 23 - Geoon McIntosh, age 54, female, born in Scotland.(Girsey)
Line 24 - Issabella McIntosh, age 21, female, born in Canada.
Line 25 - Mary Vagne, age 6, female, born in Michigan, attended school within year. (Mary Vaughn)
Line 26 - Isaac Vagne, age 4, male, born in Michigan. (Isaac Vaughn)
Line 27 - John McIntosh, age 2, male, born in Michigan. (Unidentified person)

9. Migration: Moses Clawson Company/"St Louis Company", Between 16 May and 20 Sep 1853, Salt Lake City, Great Salt Lake, Utah Territory, United States.[11]
295 individuals and 56 wagons were in the company when it began its journey from the outfitting post at Keokuk, Iowa. The company was organized at Kanesville, Iowa (present day Council Bluffs, Iowa).
Company List:
Caldwell, Abraham (age 21)
Caldwell, David Henry (age 25)
Caldwell, Isaac J (age 20)
Caldwell, Mary Ann (age 62)
Leonard, Anne (age 10)
Leonard, David Henry (age 12)
**McIntosh, John (age 57)**
Neddo, Caroline Caldwell (age 26)
Neddo, Isaac James (age 2)

Mormon Pioneer Overland Travel, Moses Clawson Company, 1853, John McIntosh, page 1 of 2

10. Census Index: John McIntosh, 1856, Bountiful, Davis, Utah Territory, United States.[12]

11. Temple Records: Endowment Record, 16 May 1860, Salt Lake City, Great Salt Lake, Utah Territory, United States.[13]
Name-**John McIntosh**, Born-1795, Where born-Croy, Inverness, Scotland, When baptized-Sept 1838, Father-William McIntosh, Mother-Issabelle, Married to Girsey Rankin, Born 1794 in Rutherglin, Lanarkshire, Scotland, When died-Apr 1853 in Origan, Lucas, Ohio, When sealed-16 May 1860 by Brigham Young in Endowment House. WC Slaines. L. Sprague. Sealed For Time-Mary Ross, 1 Mar 1799, Galston, Ayrshire, Scotland. [Note: Mary Ross is a married name for Mary McPherson. She married Findlay, then Ross, then McIntosh].

12. He appeared on the census on 15 Jun 1860 in Bountiful, Davis, Utah Territory, United States.[14]
**Line 4 - Jno. McIntosh, age 62, male, gardner, value of real estate $50, value of personal estate $10, born in Scotland.**
Line 5 - Mary McIntosh, age 62, female, born in Scotland.

13. He appeared on the census on 18 Aug 1870 in Bountiful, Davis, Utah Territory, United States.
**Line 32 - McEntosh, John, age 77, male, white, occupation none, born in Scotland, father and mother of foreign birth.**
Line 33 - McEntosh, Mary, age 72, female, white, keeping house, born in Scotland, father and mother of foreign birth.

14. He signed his will on 10 Feb 1875 in Bountiful, Davis, Utah Territory, United States.
I, **John McIntosh** of Bountiful, County of Davis and Territory of Utah being of sound mind and memory and considering the uncertainty of this frail and transitory life do therefore make public and declare this to be my last Will and Testament that is to say: First I give unto my son **William** my silver watch no. 30895 and my silver mounted horn snuff box for his sole use safe from the control of any person whomsoever. Second, I give devise and bequeath unto my wife **Mary McIntosh** for and during the term of her natural life the dwelling house and land connected therewith which we now occupy as a homestead and all the furniture and all other things used by us in housekeeping in connection with and at her death it is my desire and I direct that all of the said bequeathed property shall be sold by my executor herein

# John McIntosh, Sr.

after named who after he shall have paid the lawful debts of my wife and the expenses of said sale and transfer shall free from the control of anyone, place the remainder of the proceeds of said sale on Zion's Cooperative Mercantile Institution of Bountiful of which, Anson Call is now President, as stock and the interest which from time to time by said Institution shall be declared due thereon shall be paid as often as so declared by the President of said Institution to the indigent of the Town of Bountiful. Third, I hereby appoint my trusty friend **Daniel Davis** of the town aforesaid my executor of this my last Will and Testament hereby revoking all former wills by me made. In witness whereof I have hereto subscribed my name and affixed my seal this tenth day of February in the year of our Lord 1875. **Signed//John McIntosh**. The above written instrument was subscribed by the said John McIntosh in our presence and acknowledged by him to each of us and he at the same time declared the above instrument so subscribed to be his last Will and Testament and we at his request have signed our names as witnesss hereto in his presence and in the prescence of each other and written opposite to our names our respective places of residence. Henry [can't read last name] residing at Bountiful, Davis County, Utah. Israel Call residing at Bountiful, Davis Co., Utah.

15. His obituary was published on 5 Mar 1875 in Bountiful, Davis, Utah Territory, United States.
**OBITUARY, March 5, 1875, Deseret News**
At Bountiful, Davis County, Utah, **John McIntosh**, aged about 82 years. Deceased was born in the Highlands of Scotland, where he immigrated to Canada in year 1824. In the later place he became a member of the Church of Jesus Christ of Latter Day Saints, being baptised in the year 1838 by John E. Page. Leaving there in 1851 he came to Salt Lake City, staying a year or two in Salt Lake City when he moved to Bountiful where he died. For twelve years preceeding his death he had entire charge of the tabernacle at Bountiful, which place he ever kept warm and comfortable for the saints to worship in. He is thus known to many who respect him for his fidelity.

| Wife | Girsel Rankin[2] | |
|---|---|---|
| AKA | Girsey McIntosh, Grace Rankin, Grizel Rankin | |
| Born | 17 Sep 1794 | Old Monkland, Lanark, Scotland, United Kingdom[15] |
| Died | 11 Apr 1853 | Oregon, Lucas, Ohio, United States |
| Buried | 1853 | Oregon, Lucas, Ohio, United States[16] |
| Address | North Oregon Cemetery, Oregon, Ohio, USA | |
| Bapt.(LDS) | 10 Aug 1982 | Provo Utah Temple |
| Conf.(LDS) | 10 Aug 1982 | Provo Utah Temple |
| Init.(LDS) | 26 Mar 1999 | Bountiful Utah Temple |
| Endow.(LDS) | 27 Aug 1982 | Provo Utah Temple |
| Father | John Rankin Sr. (1752- ) | |
| Mother | Agnes Baird (Abt 1755-1855) | |
| SealP (LDS) | 27 Aug 1982 | Provo Utah Temple |

**Events**

1. She emigrated in 1821 from Glasgow, Lanark, Scotland, United Kingdom.[17]
page 192:
McIntosh, John, 1799-
Born Lanarkshire, a son of John and Margaret McIntosh.
Ship: Commerce, 1821
Location: West lot 1, con 5, Dalhousie Township.
John McIntosh came here with his wife, Margaret, born 1800, his brother Robert born 1812 and one little girl, possibly a child of John's. Possibly Mrs. Alex Nicholson, nee Janet McIntosh, was a sister. **Rev. William Bell's baptismal records show a baby, John born in November, 1821 to the John McIntosh on this farm, but the mother's name is given as Grizel, so there is a mistake somewhere.** Robert McIntosh married Isabella Easton, daughter of George Easton of the Lesmahagow society. The couple later whent to Motherwell, Fullerton Twp, Perth County.
2. She emigrated on 11 May 1821 from Glasgow, Lanark, Scotland, United Kingdom.[18]
Page 202, Line 5811. **McINTOSH, John.** To Quebec on the (ship)Commerce, ex Greenock (Scotland), 11 May 1821, in

# John McIntosh, Sr.

assoc with the St Johns Emig Soc. **Wife and 2 ch with him**. Loc Dalhousie Twp, Lanark Co, ONT. First slmt (settlement) advance to him paid 1 Aug. ICS-2 & 6.

3. She appeared on the census on 6 Aug 1850 in Monroe, Monroe, Michigan, United States.[19]
Line 22 - John McIntosh, age 55, male, laborer, born in Scotland.
**Line 23 - Geoon McIntosh, age 54, female, born in Scotland.(Girsey)**
Line 24 - Issabella McIntosh, age 21, female, born in Canada.
Line 25 - Mary Vagne, age 6, female, born in Michigan, attended school within year. (Mary Vaughn)
Line 26 - Isaac Vagne, age 4, male, born in Michigan. (Isaac Vaughn)
Line 27 - John McIntosh, age 2, male, born in Michigan. (Unidentified person)

4. Her obituary was published in 1853.[20]
**Grizel Rankin** married John McIntosh on the 15th of June 1817 in the Barony Parish of Lanark County, Scotland. Their first two children, Agnes and William were born in Bridgeton prior to crossing the Atlantic on the SS Commerce in 1821, true Canadian Pioneers, settling at Dahlhousie in Lanark County, Ontario, where the rest of their children were born. In the 1840s they moved to Monroe, Michigan where they were counted in the 1850 census before moving to Oregon, Ohio where she died and was buried. Her husband went on to the Great Salt Lake Valley and settled near Bountiful, Utah.

5. Temple Records: 1860, Salt Lake City, Great Salt Lake, Utah Territory, United States.[21]
Name-**Rankin-Girsey**, When born-1794, Where born-Rutherglen, Lanark, Scot., When died-Origan, Lucas, Ohio Apr. 1853, When married___ to John McIntosh (Eter), When sealed-16 May 1860.

## Children

| 1 F | **Agnes McIntosh**[22] | |
|---|---|---|
| AKA | Agnes Vaughn | |
| Born | 28 Jan 1818 | Glasgow, Lanark, Scotland, United Kingdom[23] |
| Died | Cir 1847 | Monroe, Michigan, United States |
| Cause of Death | Possibly died in childbirth | |
| Buried | date: | place: |
| Bapt.(LDS) | 12 Feb 1895 | Salt Lake Temple |
| Conf.(LDS) | 28 Dec 1999 | Seattle Washington Temple |
| Init.(LDS) | 7 Jan 2000 | Seattle Washington Temple |
| Endow.(LDS) | 21 May 1971 | Salt Lake Temple |
| SealP (LDS) | 8 Sep 1971 | Salt Lake Temple |
| Spouse | Abraham Isaac Vaughn Jr. (Cir 1783-Bef 1880)[24] | 1846 - Michigan, United States |
| SealS (LDS) | 15 Mar 1995 | Jordan River Utah Temple |

**Events**

1. She emigrated on 11 May 1821 from Glasgow, Lanark, Scotland, United Kingdom.
Page 202, Line 5811. **McINTOSH, John**. To Quebec on the (ship) Commerce, exited Greenock (Scotland), 11 May 1821, in assoc with the St Johns Emig Soc. **Wife and 2 ch with him**. Loc Dalhousie Twp, Lanark Co, ONT. First slmt (settlement) advance to him paid 1 Aug. ICS-2 & 6.

# John McIntosh, Sr.

| Children (cont.) | | | |
|---|---|---|---|
| 2 | M | **William McIntosh** [24,26,27,28] | |
| AKA | | William Gee McIntosh[25] | |
| Born | | 16 Sep 1819 | Barony, Lanarkshire, Scotland, United Kingdom[29,30,31,32] |
| Died | | 4 May 1899 | Mount Pleasant, Sanpete, Utah, United States |
| Cause of Death | | Le Grippe (Influenza) | |
| Buried | | May 1899 | Mount Pleasant, Sanpete, Utah, United States[33] |
| Address | | Mount Pleasant City Cemetery, 900 South 100 East, Mt. Pleasant, Utah 84647, USA | |
| Bapt.(LDS) | | Aug 1838 | Lanark, Ontario, Canada |
| Conf.(LDS) | | 1 Jan 1839 | Lanark, Ontario, Canada |
| Init.(LDS) | | 24 Aug 1861 | Endowment House |
| Endow.(LDS) | | 24 Aug 1861 | Endowment House |
| SealP (LDS) | | 21 Nov 1894 | Manti Utah Temple |
| Spouse | | Maria Caldwell (1824-1897)[34] | 27 Sep 1841 - Bathurst, Lanark, , Canada[35,36,37] |
| SealS (LDS) | | 24 Aug 1861 | Endowment House |

**Events**

1. He emigrated on 11 May 1821 from Lanark, Scotland, United Kingdom.[38]
   Page 202, Line 5811. **McINTOSH, John**. To Quebec on the (ship)Commerce, exited (out of) Greenock (Scotland), 11 May 1821, in assoc with the St Johns Emig Soc. **Wife and 2 ch with him**. Loc Dalhousie Twp, Lanark Co, ONT (Ontario, Upper Canada). First slmt (settlement) advance to him paid 1 Aug.
2. He worked as a sheepman, blacksmith, wagon maker, farmer over his lifetime about 1838 1890.
3. He had a residence from 28 Oct 1841 to Apr 1845 in Toledo, Lucas, Ohio, United States.[38]
   "We came to Toledo, Ohio. We had about 50 cents when we landed at Toledo, as sickly a place as I ever saw. We lived there for several years and suffered much sickness. We came to Toledo on October the 28th, 1841."
4. He had a residence from Apr 1845 to Aug 1845 in Oregon, Lucas, Ohio, United States.[39]
   "In the Spring of 1845, we moved to Oregon, Ohio, and rented a farm about a mile from the Maumee River."
5. He had a residence from Aug 1845 to Apr 1847 in Erie, Monroe, Michigan, United States.
   "We moved to Michigan in 1845."
6. He had a residence from May 1847 to Jun 1849 in Saint Louis, , Missouri, United States.[39]
   "And in the Spring of 1847 we bought a yoke of oxen, a cow and a wagon, about all the property we had. And took our passage on a canal boat at Toledo. We was bound then for St Louis as the Saints were arriving from Nauvoo."

# John McIntosh, Sr.

7. He appeared on the census on 19 Nov 1850 in Jefferson City, Cole, Missouri, United States.[40]
   **Line 40 - William McIntosh, age 31, male, waggon maker, born in LC. (Unknow location).**
   Line 41 - Meoriah McIntosh, age 27, female, born in LC. (Maria) (Unknown location).
   Line 42 - John McIntosh, age 6, male, born in O (Ohio), attended school within the year.
   Line 1 (next page) - William H McIntosh, age 1, male, born in Mo. (Missouri).

8. Migration: David Lewis Company, Between 1 May 1851 and 9 Sep 1851, Salt Lake City, Great Salt Lake, Utah Territory, United States.[41]
   Company List:
   McIntosh, John Ephraim (age 9)
   McIntosh, Maria Caldwell (age 27)
   **McIntosh, William (age 32)**
   McIntosh, William Henry (age 2)

Mormon Pioneer Overland Travel, David Lewis Company, 1851, William McIntosh & family page 1 of 2

9. He resided at North Kanyon Ward 1852 To 1853 in Bountiful, Davis, Utah Territory, United States.[42]

10. He received a Patriarchal blessing.[43]
    No. 385. Great Salt Lake City, July 4th 1852
    A Blessing by John Smith Patriarch, upon the head of **William McIntosh** a son of John and Girsey McIntosh, born Sept. 16th 1819. Scotland. Br William in the Name of Jesus of Nazareth I place my hands upon thy head, Seal upon you the blessings of a Father. I seal upon you all the blessings of the New and Everlasting Covenant. I seal upon you the blessings of health. You shall be able by the power of faith to overcome disease in others. Do any miracles for the prosperity of Zion. Thou art of Blood and Lineage of Ephraim and an heir to all the blessings of the Priesthood. Thou shalt have an inheritance in the Land of Zion. Your posterity shall spread upon the Mountains like Jacob, and become numerous as the Stars. It is your lot to preach the Gospel and it is left to thy choice to say in what part of the Earth you shall preach. Thousands shall obey thy voice, and thou shalt baptize and lead them to Zion with vast stores of riches. No power shall stay your hand. You shall live if you desire it to see the seas roll back to the North Country; Mount Zion and Jerusalem become one land, and Israel gathered from all the Earth and be satisfied, and I seal you up to Eternal lives in the name of Jesus Christ, Amen.

11. Census Index: William McIntosh, 1856, West Jordan, Great Salt Lake, Utah Territory, United States.[44]

12. He was St John LDS Branch President in 1859 in Rush Valley, Shambip, Utah Territory.

13. He appeared on the census on 11 Oct 1860 in Clover, Shambip, Utah Territory, United States.[45]
    Line 25) **Wm McIntosh, age 40, male, farmer, born in Scotland**
    Line 26) Maria McIntosh, age 36, female, born in Canada
    Line 27) Jno E McIntosh, age 18, male, born in Ohio
    Line 28) Wm. H McIntosh, age 11, male, born in Missouri, in school
    Line 29) Jas F McIntosh, age 8, male, born in Utah Territory, in school
    Line 30) Malissa J McIntosh, age 6, female, born in Utah Territory, in school
    Line 31) Alice M McIntosh, age 3, female, born in Utah Territory
    Line 32) Abm E McIntosh, age 6/12, male, born in Utah Territory

14. He was President of Clover Branch, Tooele Stake, Utah between 1864 and 1865 in Clover, Shambip, Utah Territory, United States.[28]

15. He served a mission from Apr 1866 to 1871 in Panaca, Lincoln, Nevada, United States.

16. He appeared on the census on 10 Jun 1870 in Panaca, Washington, Utah Territory.[46]
    **Line 20 - McIntosh, William age 49, male, white, day laborer, value of personal estate 200, born in Scotland, father and mother foreign born, male over 21.**
    Line 21 - McIntosh, Marie, age 45, female, white, keeping house, born in Canada, father and mother foreign born.
    Line 22 - McIntosh, William, age 20, male, white, teamster, born in Missouri, father and mother foreign born.
    Line 23 - McIntosh, Frank, age 18, male, white, work on farm, born in Utah, father and mother foreign born.
    Line 24 - McIntosh, Jane, age 15, female, white, born in Utah, father and mother foreign born, attended school.
    Line 25 - McIntosh, Allice, age 12, female, white, born in Utah, father and mother foreign born, attended school.
    Line 26 - McIntosh, Abraham, age 10, male, white, born in Utah, father and mother foreign born, attended school.

# John McIntosh, Sr.

Line 27 - McIntosh, Lilly, age 7, female, white, born in Utah, father and mother foreign born.
Line 28 - McIntosh, Caroline, age 4, female, white, born in Utah, father and mother foreign born.
Line 29 - McIntosh, Albert, age 1, male, white, born in Utah, father and mother foreign born.

17. He appeared on the census on 28 Jul 1870 in Meadow Valley, Lincoln, Nevada, United States.[47]
**Line 22 - McIntosh, Wm age 50, male, white, farming, value of real estate 300, value of personal estate 800, born in Scotland, father and mother foreign born, male over 21.**
Line 23 - McIntosh, Maria, age 45, female, white, keeping house, born in Canada, father and mother foreign born.
Line 24 - McIntosh, Wm H, age 21, male, white, farming, born in Missouri, father and mother foreign born, male over 21.
Line 25 - McIntosh, Frank, age 18, male, white, farming, born in Utah, father and mother foreign born.
Line 26 - McIntosh, Jane, age 16, female, white, at home, born in Utah, father and mother foreign born, attended school.
Line 27 - McIntosh, Alice, age 12, female, white, school, born in Utah, father and mother foreign born, attended school.
Line 28 - McIntosh, Abe, age 10, male, white, school, born in Utah, father and mother foreign born, attended school.
Line 29 - McIntosh, Lilly, age 7, female, white, school, born in Utah, father and mother foreign born.
Line 30 - McIntosh, Caroline, age 4, female, white, school, born in Utah, father and mother foreign born.
Line 31 - McIntosh, Albert, age 1, male, white, school, born in Nevada, father and mother foreign born.

18. He served a mission between 1871 and 1872 in Panguitch, Iron, Utah Territory, United States.[48]

19. He worked as a Day Laborer between 1871 and 1872 in Panaca, Washington, Utah, United States.

20. He owned land NE 1/4 x SW 1/4 and N 1/2 x SE 1/4, Section 19, Township 5-S, Range 5-W (containing 120 acres) on 27 Jul 1872 in Saint John, Tooele, Utah Territory, United States.[49]
Homestead Proof. Testimony of Claimant.
**William McIntosh** being called as a witness in his own support of his homestead entry for NE1/4 x SW 1/4 & N1/2 x SE 1/4, Sec 19, Township 5 South, Range 5 West.
Ques 1 - What is your name? Ans - William McIntosh
Ques 2 - What is your age? Ans - Sixty years old.
Ques 3 - Are you the head of a family...? Ans - Yes, wife and nine children.
Ques 4 - Are you a native-born citizen of the US? Ans - I am a naturalized citizen of the United States.
Ques 7 - What is your post-office address? Ans - St Johns, Tooele Co. U.T.
Ques 8 - Have you ever made a homestead entry except for this land, No. 1706? Ans - I made a mistake at first and the Commissioner allowed me to amend my entry "C" July 28, 1876.
Ques 11 - When did you first make settlement on the said land? Ans - July 27th, 1872.
Ques 16 - ...did your family reside thereon? Ans - I have a family and they live on the land with me.
Ques 17 - What improvements have you made or do you possess on the land? Ans - I have a house, stable, corrall, black smith shop, well, water ditches, fences.
Ques 18 - When was your house built? Ans - July 1872
Ques 19 - What is the total value of said improvements? Ans - from four to five thousand dollars.
Ques 20 - For what purpose have you used the land? Ans - for farming.
Ques 21 - How much of the land have you broken and cultivated, and what crops, if any, have you raised? Ans - About twenty acres and have raised wheat, oats, potatoes and garden crops.

21. Tax Rolls: 1873, Tooele, Utah Territory, United States.[50]
**McIntosh, William**, Residence- St.J., Valuation of Land Claims and Improvements-250, Number of Cattle-8, Value-140, Number of Horses-2, Value-150, Number of Vehicles-1, Value-75, Value of Merchandise-100, Value of Taxable Property Not Enumerated-50, Total Value-465.

22. Tax Rolls: 1874, Tooele, Utah Territory, United States.[51]
Names of Owners or Possessors-**McIntosh, Wm.**, Residence-St. J., Valuation of Land Claims and Improvements-250, Number of Cattle-8, Value-150, Number of Horses-1, Value-50, Number of Mules-1, Value-95, Number of Swine-2, Value-10, Number of Vehicles-2, Value-100, Value of Merchandise-100, Value of Taxable Property Not Enumerated-100, Total Value-835.

23. Marks and Brands: Place of Brand - Left hip or thigh, 4 Jun 1875, Saint John, Tooele, Utah Territory, United States.[52]
**William McIntosh** was given authorization to use this mark or brand on his herd animals.

24. He submitted an amendment of his application no. 1706.[53]
STATEMENT of Oliver A. Patton, Register, Salt Lake City, Utah Land Office:
...but upon a careful survey of this said land it was found that his said homestead application No. 1706 of July 27th 1872 did not embrace but one hundred and twenty acres. Therefore on the 1st day of June 1875 he again applied at this district

# John McIntosh, Sr.

land office at Salt Lake and was permitted to file his additional farm Homestead (No. 2267) to his original H.E. 1410 application and was soon thereafter notified that the Hon. Commissioner of the General Land Office declined to allow this said last mentioned entry but held it for cancellation after sixty days notice to him of said **McIntosh**. The affidavit says that his original entry was a mistake and accident that it was his intention to enter 160 acres of land as he was advised by his said Surveyor, but which he soon found to be an error and endeavored to correct this error by filing an adjoining farm homestead which he was advised he was entitled to under the 2289th Section Statutes....

STATEMENT BY **ISAAC NEDOW** being duly sworn according to law deposes and says that he is well acquainted with the patch of land imbraced in H.E. No. 1706 - of **William McIntosh-** also with the NE 1/4 of SW 1/4 of Section 19, Township 5 South of Range 5 West; that the said William McIntosh has exclusive and valuable improvements upon said patch, consisting of 20 acres of land, well fenced, and under cultivation, the greatest part of it in wheat, has 2 1/2 story house, shingle roof, lumber floor dwelling house, has 2 rooms and is a comfortable house to live in. This house has also a small adjoining house shingle roof, lumber floor, has a good cellar, lumber on the ground for constructing a stable that has a good granary built out of sawed lumber that he has a good well; that he has hog pens, corralls in fact that he has all the appliances and conveniences of a home upon said land.

STATEMENT OF **JOHN MCINTOSH** being duly sworn according to law deposes and says that he has heard the above affidavit of Isaac Nedow read and that he knows the same to be true; that **William McIntosh** has improvements upon the NE 1/4 of the SW 1/4 of Section 19 in Township 5 South of Range 5 West to the value of about $2000; that he has about 20 acres under fence and cultivation, planted in wheat at present, and a good dwelling house of two rooms in which the said William McIntosh lives; that he has a well, lumber on said land for the purpose of constructing a stable; that he has a corrall; that in fact he is surrounded with all the appliances and comforts of a home.

There was also a question on his first application that his citizenship was illegal, so he was not qualified for homestead land. (He later became a citizen and his citizenship papers were found in the land papers).

See Homestead Certificate 4170 dated 29 Nov 1889. This was finally sorted out and **William McIntosh** received the patent for the land he bought in 1872.

25. He received his Citizenship Certificate found in land records citizenship on 24 Jul 1877 in Tooele, Utah Territory, United States.[54]

Certificate of Citizenship

**UNITED STATES OF AMERICA, TERRITORY OF UTAH--SS.**

**BE IT REMEMBERED,** That on the 26 day of July in the year of our Lord, One Thousand Eight Hundred and Seventy-seven, **William McIntosh** late of Scotland, in the Kingdom of Great Britain at present of Tooele Co. in the Territory aforesaid, appeared in the 3rd Judicial District Court of the United States, in and for Utah Territory, and applied to the said Court to be admitted to become a Citizen of the United States of America, pursuant to the directions and requirements of the several Acts of Congress in relation thereto. And the said William McIntosh, having thereupon produced to the Court such evidence, made such declaration and renunciation, and taken such oath as are by the said Acts required; thereupon it was ordered by the said Court that the said William McIntosh be admitted, and he was accordingly admitted by the said Court to be a **CITIZEN OF THE UNITED STATES OF AMERICA.**

**In Testimony Whereof**, the Seal of the said Court is hereunto affixed, this 26 day of July in the year One Thousand Eight Hundred and Seventy-seven and in the year of our Independence the One Hundred and Second ./s/ C.S. Hill, Clerk. By the Court, U.S. Land Office, Salt Lake City, Utah, September 9, 1879. I hereby certify this is a true and correct copy. /s/ Moses M. Barn

26. He appeared on the census on 12 Jun 1880 in Clover, Tooele, Utah Territory, United States.[55]

**Line 19 - Mackintosh, William, white, male, age 60, head, married, laborer, born in Canada, father born in Canada, mother born Canada.**

Line 20 - Mackintosh, Caroline, white, female, age 53, wife, married, keeping house, born in Canada, father born in Canada, mother born in Canada. (Maria)

Line 21 - Mackintosh, Alice, white, female, age 22, daughter, single, teaching school, born in Utah, father born in Canada, Mother born in Canada.

Line 22 - Mackintosh, Abraham, white, male, age 20, son, single, working on farm, born in Utah, father born in Canada, mother born in Canada.

Line 23 - Mackintosh, Lillian, white, female, age 18, daughter, single, studying at home, attended school, born in Utah, father born in Canada, mother born in Canada.

# John McIntosh, Sr.

Line 24 - Mackintosh, Caroline, white, female, age 15, daughter, single, studying at home, attended school, born in Utah, father born in Canada, mother born in Canada.
Line 25 - Mackintosh, Albert, white, male, age 11, son, single, working on farm, attended school, born in Utah, father born in Canada, mother born in Canada.

27. He had health issues about 1886 in Saint John, Tooele, Utah Territory, United States.[56]
"Today is the 14th of August. After so long a time I thought I would write a few more things. Last year, 1890, has been a year of some trouble to me. Also expensive. My wife has been sorely afflicted with falen sickness [epilepsy] and poor health, and my own health is not good. I have been lame for several years with rheumatism and I am lame now. My hip joint is in bad shape".

28. Witness to a land sale: Section 19, Township 5-S, Range 5-W for Caroline Caldwell McIntosh, on 19 Jul 1888, in Saint John, Tooele, Utah Territory, United States.[57]
This is a statement of **David H Caldwell** on behalf of his sister **Caroline Elisabeth McIntosh** in relation to her purchese of land:
Question 1. -- What is your true name, given in full, your age, residence, and present post-office address? (Give description of land on which you reside, quarter section, township and range.) Ans. David H. Caldwell, 59 years of age, St John Tooele Co Utah Territory, SW 1/4, NW 1/4, Sec 30, Tp(township) 5S, R(range) 5W.
Question 2. -- What is your present occupation...? Ans.-- Farmer, worked for myself, not imployed by anyone.
Question 3. -- Are you related to claimant? I am her Brother, am not in any way interested in this claim.
Question 4. -- How far from the residence of claimant, on said tract, do you reside...? Ans.--About a mile, lived there ten years.
Ques. 5 -- Give the names and residences of two or more persons living nearer to the claimant of this tract than yourself? Ans.-- **Wm McIntosh, & Thomas L Burridge, both live on Sec 19, T 5S, R5W.**
Ques. 21 -- State in detail the character of the improvements... Ans.--Log house 16 x 18, one story, one window, board floors and roof, ... House was built by I.J. Nedow, also the fencing was made by I.J. Nedow.
Ques. 23. -- What is this land worth ...? Ans.--$1.25 per acre.
Ques. 24 -- When did claimant commence living upon this land? Ans.--Dec 22d 1887.

29. He owned land SW 1/4 x NE 1/4, Sec 19, Twp 5-S, Range 5-W, containing 40 acres. on 29 Nov 1889 in Saint John, Tooele, Utah Territory, United States.[58]
Affidavit for Additional Homestead Entry witnessed by Isaac J. Nedow and Geo. E. Dymock.

30. Patent: 10 Dec 1890, in Saint John, Tooele, Utah Territory, United States.[59]
Certif. # 4170
Application # 8552
**William McIntosh**
So. West quarter of the North E. quarter of Section 19
in township five South of Range 5 West of Salt Lake Meridian in Utah Territory containing Forty acres-
10th Dec 1890- 115th year independance
Benjamin Harrison
President, United States of America

31. He had a residence from 15 Nov 1892 to 4 May 1899 in Mount Pleasant, Sanpete, Utah, United States.[60]

32. He was ordained a High Priest by Canute Peterson, Stake President on 18 Aug 1895 in Mount Pleasant, Sanpete, Utah Territory, United States.[61]
Ordination
I, **William McIntosh**, have been received into the High Priests Quorum this day under the hand of the Presidency of the Stake of Zion, August 18, 1895.
Canute Peterson, President of the Sanpete Stake of Zion

# John McIntosh, Sr.

| Children (cont.) | | |
|---|---|---|
| 3 M | **John McIntosh** | |
| Born | 14 Nov 1821 | Dalhousie, Lanark, Ontario, Canada[62,63,64] |
| Died | Cir 1822 | Dalhousie, Lanark, Ontario, Canada |
| Buried | date: | place: |
| Bapt.(LDS) | Child | |
| Conf.(LDS) | Child | |
| Init.(LDS) | Child | |
| Endow.(LDS) | Child | |
| SealP (LDS) | 1 Dec 1989 | Denver Colorado Temple |
| Spouse | This person had no known marriage and no known children | |

| 4 M | **John McIntosh Jr.** [66] | |
|---|---|---|
| AKA | John F. Ginsey McIntosh[65] | |
| Born | 17 Aug 1824 | Dalhousie, Lanark, Upper Canada, Canada[31] |
| Died | 6 Dec 1859 | Clover, Shambip, Utah Territory, United States[67] |
| Cause of Death | Pneumonia | |
| Buried | 9 Dec 1859 | Clover, Shambip, Utah Territory, United States[68] |
| Address | Clover Cemetery, Johnson Lane & Hwy 199, Rush Valley (Clover), Utah 84069, USA | |
| Bapt.(LDS) | 21 Mar 1857 | |
| Conf.(LDS) | 21 Mar 1857 | |
| Init.(LDS) | 20 Sep 1888 | |
| Endow.(LDS) | 20 Sep 1888 | |
| SealP (LDS) | 27 Aug 1982 | Provo Utah Temple |
| Spouse | Caroline Elizabeth Caldwell (1827-1891)[69,70,71,72] | |
| Marr. Date | 9 Dec 1854 - Saint John, Tooele, Utah Territory, United States. (Death of one spouse) | |
| SealS (LDS) | 20 Sep 1888 | Manti Utah Temple |

**Events**

1. He emigrated on 24 Sep 1841 from Toronto, , Ontario, Canada.[38] to the United States.

# John McIntosh, Sr.

2. Migration: Mormon Pioneer Overland Travel, 1847.[73] **McIntosh, John**
Birth Date: 17 Aug 1824
Death Date: 9 May 1859
Gender: Male
Age: 23
Company: 1847-1868 (Unknown Year of Travel)
Pioneer Information: He came to Utah in either 1848 or 1849. He likely came in 1849, as he received a patriarchal blessing in November 1849 and his name didn't appear on the list of those receiving property in Salt Lake in 1848.

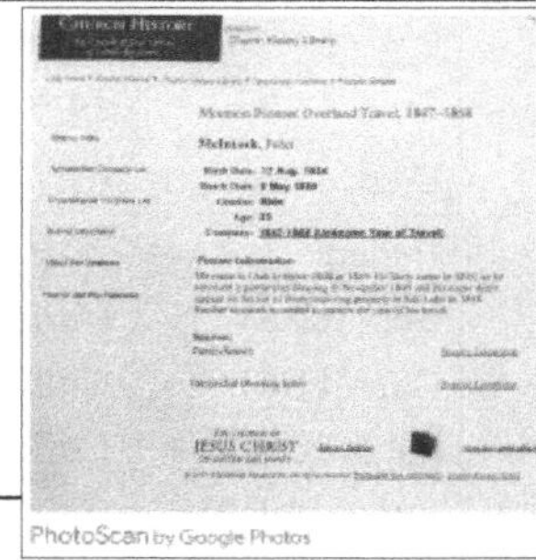
Mormon Pioneer Overland Travel, 1847-1868 - John McIntosh

3. He resided at the home of Joseph Holbrook in Jul 1849 in Antelope Island, Great Salt Lake, Utah Territory.[74] From the Joseph Holbrook Diary: "I was elected first lieutenant in a company of mounted riflemen of the Nauvoo Legion in the summer of 1849. At harvest time I became quite feeble and was unable to work, so my neighbor, **John McIntosh,** cut and cradled my wheat for one-half bushel if I would board him."
4. He appeared on the census on 1 Jun 1850 in Davis, Utah, United States.[75]
**Line 9-John McIntosh, age 25, male, farmer, born in Canada.**
5. Census Index: John McIntosh, 1856, West Jordan, Great Salt Lake, Utah Territory, United States.[76]
6. He worked as a School Teacher from 1858 to 1859 in Saint John, Shambip, Utah Territory, United States.[24]
7. He died on 6 Dec 1859 in Saint John, Shambip, Utah Territory, United States.[24] "By permission I write a few lines in memory of my dear departed husband. **(John McIntosh)** He died on the 6th of December Tuesday morning at 8 o'clock and was buried in Rush Valley burying ground. The severity of the weather not permitting me to have him taken to the city according to my desire. John was good kind husband and I believe had as faithful a heart as ever beat in human breast. He was very fond of his children and very kind to them. In losing him we have lost the best and most faithful friend we ever had. He died faithful to his religion. He said to me he was going to prepare a place for me and if he was counted worthy he would have his wife and children again which I pray for. He may want that the time was come. He left a charge with me to get sealed to him whenever an opportunity offered; likewise to keep away from the gentile race. He greatly desired to see his brother towards the last. I inquired what he had to say to him. He replied, I want to give him my woman and children, tell him, said he, to remember to keep them for me. I am very sorry to think he had but one brother in the valley and was denied the privilege of seeing him. His aged father came to him 2 days before he died; father, said he, you have found your boy very low. Shortly after we called the Elders together and had his father bestow upon him a father blessing. I had the clerk record it in the church records. John was quite a young man. His age was 36 years 3 month and 11 days. He was quite sensible to the last. His last words were, yes put me in the bed. He died quietly as one going to sleep. The last end of the righteous his peace...."
8. He was buried Clover Cemetery on 9 Dec 1859 in Clover, Shambip, Utah Territory, United States.[77]

| 5 M | **James McIntosh** [78] | |
|---|---|---|
| Born | Cir 1825 | Dalhousie, Lanark, Ontario, Canada |
| Died | Aug 1844 | Monroe, Michigan, United States[79] |
| Buried | 1844 | Monroe, Monroe, Michigan, United States |
| Address | La Salle Township Cemetery, La Salle, Michagan, USA | |
| Bapt.(LDS) | 23 Sep 1889 | Manti Utah Temple |
| Conf.(LDS) | 23 Sep 1889 | Manti Utah Temple |
| Init.(LDS) | 2 Feb 1916 | Manti Utah Temple |
| Endow.(LDS) | 2 Feb 1916 | Manti Utah Temple |
| SealP (LDS) | 27 Aug 1982 | Provo Utah Temple |
| Spouse | This person had no known marriage and no known children | |

# John McIntosh, Sr.

| Children (cont.) | | |
|---|---|---|
| 6 F | **Isabel McIntosh** [78] | |
| AKA | Isabella McIntosh | |
| Born | Cir 1829 | Dalhousie, Lanark, Ontario, Canada |
| Died | After 1860 | place: |
| Buried | date: | place: |
| Bapt.(LDS) | 10 Aug 1982 | Provo Utah Temple |
| Conf.(LDS) | 10 Aug 1982 | Provo Utah Temple |
| Init.(LDS) | 11 Aug 2010 | Fresno California Temple |
| Endow.(LDS) | 9 Sep 1982 | Provo Utah Temple |
| SealP (LDS) | 7 Dec 1982 | Provo Utah Temple |
| Spouse | Jacob Simkus (Abt 1835- ) | 12 Dec 1856 - Lucas, Ohio, United States[80,81] |
| SealS (LDS) | 14 Apr 1976 | Manti Utah Temple |

**Events**

1. She appeared on the census on 6 Aug 1850 in Monroe, Monroe, Michigan, United States.[82]
   Line 22 - John McIntosh, age 55, male, laborer, born in Scotland.
   Line 23 - Geoon McIntosh, age 54, female, born in Scotland. (Girsey)
   **Line 24 - Issabella McIntosh, age 21, female, born in Canada.**
   Line 25 - Mary Vagne, age 6, female, born in Michigan, attended school within year. (Mary Vaughn)
   Line 26 - Isaac Vagne, age 4, male, born in Michigan. (Isaac Vaughn)
   Line 27 - John McIntosh, age 2, male, born in Michigan. (Unidentified person).
2. She appeared on the census on 21 Jun 1860 in Toledo, Lucas, Ohio, United States.[83]
   Line 6 - Jacob Simkus, age 25, male, laborer, born in Scotland.
   **Line 7 - Isabela Simkus, age 31, female, born in Ohio.**
   Line 8 - Lena Simkus, age 2, female, born in Preussen. (Ohio?)
   Line 9 - Margaret Simkus, age 69, female, born Preussen.

| 7 F | **Jennette McIntosh** [78,84] | |
|---|---|---|
| AKA | Jennett Campbell, Genett McIntosh, Jeanett McIntosh, Jenett McIntosh, Janet Woodruff, Jannett Woodruff | |
| Born | 22 Apr 1830 | Dalhousie, Lanark, Ontario, Canada[85] |
| Died | 22 Aug 1908 | Toledo, Lucas, Ohio, United States[85] |
| Buried | 1908 | Oregon, Lucas, Ohio, United States[86] |
| Address | Willow Cemetery, 1961 Pickle Road, Oregon, Ohio, USA | |
| Notes | Plot: South-79-6 | |
| Bapt.(LDS) | 10 Aug 1982 | Provo Utah Temple |
| Conf.(LDS) | 10 Aug 1982 | Provo Utah Temple |
| Init.(LDS) | 20 Nov 1998 | Los Angeles California Temple |
| Endow.(LDS) | 21 Aug 1982 | Los Angeles California Temple |
| SealP (LDS) | 27 Aug 1982 | Provo Utah Temple |
| Spouse | Charles Campbell (1829-After 1858)[87] | Abt 1850 - Waterville, Lucas, Ohio, United States[88] |
| SealS (LDS) | 7 Feb 1996 | Jordan River Utah Temple |
| Spouse | Elijah Judd Woodruff (1802-1904)[89,90] | 31 Dec 1866 - Toledo, Lucas, Ohio, United States[91] |
| SealS (LDS) | 15 Mar 1995 | Jordan River Utah Temple |

**Events**

1. She appeared on the census on 15 Oct 1850 in Waterville, Lucas, Ohio, United States.[92]

# John McIntosh, Sr.

1 - Charles Campbell, age 21, male, boatman, born in New York, married within the year.
**2 - Jennette Campbell, age 20, female, born in Canada, married within the year.**

2. She appeared on the census on 24 Jun 1860 in Toledo, Lucas, Ohio, United States.[93]
Line 21 - F Kingsly, age 41, male, , value of real estate $2500, value of personal estate $2000, born in N.B.
**Line 25 - Jenette Campbell, lodger, age 30, female, born in Scotland.**
Line 26 - Ellen Campbell, lodger, age 3, female, born in Ohio.

3. She appeared on the census on 12 Jul 1870 in Toledo, Lucas, Ohio, United States.[94]
Line 4 - Woodruff, H.A., age 67, male, white, merchant, value of real estate $1500, born in Connecticut, eligible to vote.
**Line 5 - Woodruff, J, age 40, female, white, keeping house, born in Canada, father and mother foreign born.**
Line 6 - Woodruff, Alace, age 12, female, white, born in Ohio, mother foreign born.

4. She appeared on the census on 4 Jun 1880 in Toledo, Lucas, Ohio, United States.[95]
Line 3 - Woodruff, A.D, white, male, age 78, head, married, farmer, born in Connecticut, father born in Connecticut, mother born in Connecitcut.
**Line 4 - Woodruff, Genett, white, female, age 50, wife, married, house keeper, born in Canada, father born in Scotland, mother born in Scotland.**

5. She appeared on the census on 1 Jun 1900 in Toledo, Lucas, Ohio, United States.[96]
Line 19 - Woodruff, Elijah, head, white, male, born Sept 1802, age 97, married for 33 years, born in Connecticut, father born in Connecticut, mother born in Connecticut, landlord, able to read, write and speak english, owns mortgage free a home.
**Line 20- Woodruff, Janette, wife, white, female born April 1830, age 70, married for 33 years, had 2 children, 0 living, born in Canada, father born in Scotland, mother born in Scotland, immigrated to US in 1850, been in the US 50 years, able to read, write and speak english.**

| 8 F | **Girsey McIntosh** [78] | |
|---|---|---|
| AKA | Grizel McIntosh | |
| Born | 21 May 1832 | Dalhousie, Lanark, Ontario, Canada[97] |
| Died | 28 Oct 1914 | Toledo, Lucas, Ohio, United States |
| Buried | 31 Oct 1914 | Toledo, Lucas, Ohio, United States |
| Address | Woodlawn Cemetery, 1502 West Central Avenue, Toledo, Ohio 43606, USA | |
| Bapt.(LDS) | 10 Aug 1982 | Provo Utah Temple |
| Conf.(LDS) | 10 Aug 1982 | Provo Utah Temple |
| Init.(LDS) | Completed | Provo Utah Temple |
| Endow.(LDS) | 9 Sep 1982 | Provo Utah Temple |
| SealP (LDS) | 7 Dec 1982 | Provo Utah Temple |
| Spouse | Henry Hinckley (1832-1899) | 3 Apr 1852 - Toledo, Lucas, Ohio, United States[98,99,100] |
| SealS (LDS) | 14 Apr 1976 | Manti Utah Temple |

**Events**

1. She appeared on the census on 9 Aug 1850 in Toledo, Lucas, Ohio, United States.[101]
page 67B, Line 27 - Rocileus C Connele, age 25, male, carpenter, born in Ohio.
**page 68, Line 9 - Girsey McIntosh, age 18, female, born in Canada.**
**(Lots of people lived there like it was a boarding house).**

2. She appeared on the census on 14 Jul 1860 in Perrysburg, Wood, Ohio, United States.[102]
Line 6 - Henry Hinkle, age 28, male, laborer, value of real estate $1400, value of personal estate $300, born in New York, attended school within year.
**Line 7 - Gerzel Hinke, age 28, male, born in Canada. (Girsey)**
Line 8 - Edwin Hinkle, age 8, male, born in Ohio.
Line 9 - Hariet Hinkle, age 7, female, born in Ohio.
Line 10 - Nenit Hinkle, age 3, female, born in Ohio. (Nettie)
Line 11- Theodore Hinkle, age 1, male, born in Ohio.

# John McIntosh, Sr.

3. She appeared on the census on 28 Jul 1870 in Perrysburg, Wood, Ohio, United States.[103]
   Line 22 - Hinkley, Henry, age 38, male, white, farmer, value of real estate $66, born in New York, eligble to vote.
   **Line 23 - Hinkley, Girsy, age 37, female, white, keeping house, born in Canada, father and mother foreign born.**
   Line 24 - Hinkley, Edwin, age 18, male, white, at home, born in Ohio, mother foreign born, attended school within year.
   Line 25 - Hinkley, Harriet, age 17, female, white, at home, born in Ohio, mother foreign born, attended school within year.
   Line 26 - Hinkley, Nettie, age 12, female, white, at home, born in Ohio, mother foreign born, attended school within year.
   Line 27 - Hinkley, Theodore, age 11, male, white, at home, born in Ohio, mother foreign born, attended school within year.
   Line 28 - Hinkley, Charles, age 5, male, white, at home, born in Ohio, mother foreign born.
4. She appeared on the census on 22 Jun 1880 in Rose, Carroll, Ohio, United States.[104]
   Line 26 - Hinckley, Henry, white, male age 48, head, married, farmer, born in New York, father born in New York, mother born in New York.
   **Line 27 - Hinckley, Gersey, white, female age 48, wife, married, keeping house, born in Canada, father born in Scotland, mother born in Scotland.**
   Line 28 - Hinckley, Nettie, white, female, age 23, daughter, single, at home, born in Ohio, father born in New York, mother born in Canada.
   Line 29 - Hinckley, Theodore, white, male, age 20, son, single, farm laborer, born in Ohio, father born New York, mother born in Canada.
   Line 30 - Hinckley, Charles, white, male, age 15, son, single, farm laborer, born in Ohio, father born in New York, mother born in Canada.
5. She appeared on the census on 1 Jun 1900 in Toledo, Lucas, Ohio, United States.[105]
   **Line 75 - Hinckley, Girsey, head, white, female, born Mar 1832, age 68, widowed, had 5 children, 4 living, born in Canada, father born in Scotland, mother born in Scotland, immigrated to US in 1840, lived in US 60 years, able to read, write and speak english, owns mortgage free a home.**
   Line 76 - Hinckley, Charles, son, white, male, born Mar 1863, age 37, single, born in Ohio, father born in New York, mother born in Canada, blacksmith, 0 months out of work, able to read, write and speak english.
6. She appeared on the census on 18 Apr 1910 in Toledo, Lucas, Ohio, United States.[106]
   Line 7 - Webb, Wm. S, head, male, white, age 62, married once for 37 years, born in Ohio, father born in New York, mother born in Ohio, speaks english, carpenter-home, wage worker, not out of work on Apr 15, 1910, 0 weeks out of work in 1909, able to read and write, owns mortgage free a home.
   Line 8 - Webb, Harriet A, wife, female, white, age 57, married once for 37 years, had 4 children, 1 living, born in Ohio, father born in New York, mother born in Canada-english, speaks englsih, no occupation, able to read and write.
   **Line 9 - Hinckley, Girsey, mother-in-law, female, white, age 77, widowed, had 5 children, 4 living, born in Canada-english, father born in Scotland-gaelic, mother born in Scotland-gaelic, immigrated to US in 1840, speaks english, no occupation, able to read and write.**

| 9 | M | **David McIntosh**[107,108] | |
|---|---|---|---|
| Born | | Cal 1834 | Dalhousie, Lanark, Ontario, Canada |
| Died | | 17 Apr 1865 | Andersonville, , Georgia, United States |
| Cause of Death | | Probably died in the Civil War | |
| Buried | | date: | place: |
| Bapt.(LDS) | | 11 Jun 1959 | |
| Conf.(LDS) | | 11 Jun 1959 | |
| Init.(LDS) | | 12 Feb 1936 | |
| Endow.(LDS) | | 9 Sep 1982 | |
| SealP (LDS) | | 26 Oct 1959 | Salt Lake Temple |
| Spouse | | Mary Landis (Cal 1833- )[109] | Cal 1856[110] |
| SealS (LDS) | | 22 Mar 2011 | Salt Lake Temple |

**Events**

1. He appeared on the census in 1860 in Toledo, Lucas, Ohio, United States.[111]
   **Line 34, David McIntosh, age 26, male, laborer, born in Canada.**

# John McIntosh, Sr.

Line 35, Mary McIntosh, age 27, female, born in Pennsylvania.
Line 36, Lilly McIntosh, age 3, female, born in Ohio.

2. David served in the military between 6 Feb 1863 and 27 Jun 1865 in Cleveland, Cuyahoga, Ohio, United States: Civil War.[112]

Research

Our David McIntosh remains elusive.

Beverly McIntosh Brown 24 Apr 2017
He is mentioned in William's Diary in his entry for 1841: "...my father and mother left on their journey with three of their sons - John, James and David - and four daughters - Agnes, Isabell, Jennet and Gersy."
He mentions David again in his entry for summer of 1848 (David would be 14): "John McIntosh told us that my father and mother were well and that they were living pretty much alone. They still had a desire to come to the Valley and be with the Saints. They had four children round them there, when John left, but they were not all at home. There was Isabell, Jennet, Gersy and David nearly all growed up to men and women. There was none of them married only Jennet."

We have found a David McIntosh in the 1860 US Census for Toledo, Lucas, Ohio. He is the right age, was born in Canada and living in the same town as his parents did in 1853 when his mother, Gersey, died and his father left for Utah. None of our researching cousins has found a better match anywhere else.
But this doesn't prove he's our David. There is no David McIntosh in any US Census after 1860 matching ours. We can't find a marriage, death or burial record for him.

There is a Willis D. McIntosh who has a father named David and a mother named Mary Landis. But none of his records help tie David to our line.

9 Jun 2017 Beverly McIntosh Brown. I have found a Civil War Pension Application Request filed by Mary A. Landis McIntosh on 26 Sep 1889; filed because her husband David McIntosh died during the War. Here are the facts:

According to Mary's brother Michael Landis of Toledo, county of Lucas, state of Ohio, in his sworn statement dated 4 Feb 1890, David McIntosh and Mary A Landis were married on 15 May 1854 in his father's house in Perry Township, Wood County, Ohio.

According to Mary's sister Hannah Mowser of Ithaca, county of Gratiot state of Mich, in her sworn statement dated 4 Jan 1890, David McIntosh and Mary A Landis were married on 15 May 1854 in her father's house in Perry Township, Wood County, Ohio.

Mary's own sworn statement dated 26 Sep 1889 stated she was married to David McIntosh on 15 May 1848. But that can't be right. David would only be 14. It sure looks like 1848 but it really could be anything; even 1854!?!

In the 1860 US Census for Toledo, Lucas, Ohio, there is a David McIntosh with wife Mary and daughter Lilly age 3.

David McIntosh enlisted in Company E, 6th Regiment of the Ohio Cavalry on 6 Feb 1863 at Cleveland, Ohio.

It was alleged that David McIntosh died in Andersonville Prison April 17,1865 of [typhoid] fever.

But in the same file, it said David McIntosh was mustered out of the Army on 27 Jun 1865.

In the 1870 US Census for Toledo, Lucas, Ohio there is a Mary McIntosh, listed as a widow, with son Willis age 9.

Mary A McIntosh, living in Indiana, County of Steuben, on 26 Sep 1889, filed her application for David McIntosh's pension.. Jacob Landis residing (illegible), Indiana was a witness to her statement. Is he her father or another brother? Unfortunately she does not mention the names of her children.

# John McIntosh, Sr.

Children (cont.)

Conclusion: He could be our David McIntosh but not definitively. We do know that a David McIntosh and Mary Landis married and had two children. The girl Lilly was not in the 1870 census so she may have died. Their son Willis D. married and had a son Robert. He probably is our David but not enough facts yet.[110]

Produced by: Beverly McIntosh Brown, 15933 W Silver Breeze Dr, Surprise, AZ 85374, 623-584-0440, starfighteraz@gmail.com : 29 Jun 2021

# Source Citations


1. Church of Jesus Christ of Latter-day Saints,*Patriarchal Blessing,* "...William McIntosh son of John and Girsey McIntosh..."

2. Brown, Beverly McIntosh and Marsha Lee McIntosh,*William McIntosh Diary, abridgement* (Self-published, Surprise, AZ. June 2002).

3. "John McIntosh (died 5 Mar 1875)," *The Deseret News*; digital images.

4. Scotland (Edinburgh, Scotland), "Parochial Registers, Co. of Lanark, Barony, M. 1778-1819; D. 1805-1819," June 1817; McIntosh - 15 - John McIntosh, Dyer, Bridgeland, Grizel Rankin in the parish of Rutherglen; FHL microfilm 1,041,478 and 6,900,812.

5. Carol Bennett, *The Lanark Society Settlers, 1820-1821* (Renfrew, Ontario, Canada: Juniper Books, 1991), 192. Repository: Family History Library, 35 North West Temple Street, Salt Lake City, Utah 84150-3400, USA, Call Number: 971.382 W2; From the Public Archives of Canada/Memorandum:
It may be of interest that the Bridgetown Transatlantic Society was one of the emigrating societies which had been formed among the weavers of Glasgow, Hamilton, Paisley and Lanark, Scotland for the purpose of sponsoring a settlement of their members in Canada. In a dispatch of 6 May 1820, the Earl of Bathurst outlined the plan to settle about 1,200 Scotsmen on the newly opened Township of Lanark, Canada with the status of Military Settlement. Each family was to be granted 100 acres of land, and a loan of about L.10 per capita. The plan was accepted, and in June 1820 the settlers, grouped under the names of their sponsoring societies set sail for Canada. Upon their arrival they were allotted land in the Lanark Military settlement, and placed under the control of the Quartermaster-General's Department. Captain William Marshall was named the Superintendent and Secretary as well as the Storekeeper of the settlement. Eventually the individual settlers fulfilled their settlement duties and became eligible for deeds to their land.
The earliest settlers were unemployed Scots who left the overpopulated areas of Glasgow and Lanarkshire, following the Napoleonic war. In 1820, approximately 400 families arrived in Lanark, Canada, bringing with them skills in cotton weaving, carpentry, blacksmithing and shoemaking. A similar influx of Irish settlers arrived during the 1830's and 1840's. However, the growth of the area was somewhat impeded by the muddy, rocky terrain and steep slopes, which prevented easy travel.
Of the settlers who did arrive in Lanark, all males over 21 years of age were granted 100 acres divided up using the traditional grid system. Although the intention of the original settlers was to farm each parcel of land, it soon became apparent that the only lands that could be cultivated were those located in floodplains, along rivers or adjacent to lakes. Consequently, most settlers opted to perform timber-related activities instead. Others left the area for Western Canada or the United States.

6. Ontario Genealogical Society, Kingston Branch, editor,*1820 Canadian Location Report, Lanark County* (Kingston, Ontario, Canada: n.p., 1987). Repository: Family History Library, 35 North West Temple Street, Salt Lake City, Utah 84150-3400, USA, Call Number: 971.382 R2sr.

7. Robert E. Sargeant and J.R. Ernest Miller, editors,*Early Settlers & Col. Marshall's 1834 Report on Conditions 1820-1822.* (N.p.: n.p., 1987), 4, 11/26/87. Repository: Family History Library, 35 North West Temple Street, Salt Lake City, Utah 84150-3400, USA, Call Number: 971.382 R2m; Col. Marshall's 1834 Report of Lots Settled in 1820-21.

8. Donald Whyte,*A Dictionary of Scottish Emigrants to Canada before Confederation*, 4 Volumns (Toronto, Ontario, Canada: Ontario Genealogical Society, c1986-C2005), v. 2: 202. Repository: Family History Library, 35 North West Temple Street, Salt Lake City, Utah 84150-3400, USA, Call Number: 971 F2wd v.1.

9. Sargeant, Robert, extracted this information from the county register, J.R. Ernest Miller, compiler*Lanark County Land Transactions 1820-1847 Volume One 4 April 1820 - 8 February 1840* (Kingston, Ontario, Canada, Ontario Genealogical Society, 1991), Repository: Family History Library, 35 North West Temple Street, Salt Lake City, Utah 84150-3400, USA, Call Number: 971.382 R2s V.1.

10. 1850 U.S. census, Monroe, Michigan, population schedule, Monroe, p. 709, dwelling 137, family 140, John McIntosh; digital images, *ancestry.com*; citing National Archives and Records Administration microfilm M432.

11. Church of Jesus Christ of Latter-day Saints, "Mormon Pioneer Overland Travel, 1847-1868," database (www.lds.org/churchhistory/library/pioneercompany), McIntosh, John in the 1853 Moses Clawson Company.

12. Utah State Census Index, 1856, Utah, population schedule; HISTORICAL BACKGROUND
Utah pioneers petitioned for statehood for the second time in 1856. To show that Utah Territory held enough population to become a state, a census was taken in January and February of that year. In December, a disappointed Governor Brigham Young reported to the territorial legislature that the petition had been rejected. The following passage from that report shows Governor Young was anxious to suggest Utah had a large population. "The enumeration of the inhabitants showed a population of near 77,000 in this territory, and it is presumed that the addition to our numbers, since that was taken, would amount to about twenty thousand. This gives an aggregate equal to or exceeding the ratio of representation for congressmen, removing every objection, if any were made, to our admission, on the score of insufficient population." (Brigham Young, "Governor's Message," Deseret News [Salt Lake City, Utah], December 24, 1856, p. 333, col. 2).
In fact, there is reason to believe the territorial population was considerably less than presented in the Governor's report. The 1850/1851 census of Utah showed only 11,380 residents. The 1860 census showed 40,273. Thus, the 77,000 figure appears to be far too large, and Govenor Young's estimate that 20,000 people entered the territory in one year also seems exaggerated.
Indeed, some names on the 1856 census seem to be fictitious, repeated, or those of non-residents of Utah Territory. For example, ....
A striking feature of the census and further evidence of padding is that virtually every page and most columns begins with a different surname from that ending the previous one; the last family in each column has exactly enough members to reach the last available line.
Index Publishing presents this index for genealogists, historians, demographers, and other researachers who wish to quickly determine where specific individuals are located on the 1856 census of Utah Territory. (Compiled by Bryan Lee Dilts, Index Publishing, PO Box 11476, SLC, UT 1983).

# Source Citations


13. Church of Jesus Christ of Latter-day Saints, Temple Records Index Bureau (Salt Lake City, Utah, United States of America), Salt Lake Temple Endowments 22 Nov 1861 to 22 Dec 1866, Book C, Page 424 or 429, FHL Microfilm 1149514.

14. 1860 U.S. census, Davis, Utah Territory, population schedule, Bountiful, p. 19, dwelling 124, family 115, Jno. McIntosh; digital images, *ancestry.com*; citing National Archives and Records Administration microfilm M653.

15. Scotland, Lanark, *Old Parochial Registers,* Girsel Ranken, FHL Film 1,066,602, arranged chronologicall y by birth/christening date. Repository: Family History Library, 35 North West Temple Street, Salt Lake City, Utah 84150-3400, USA, Call Number: FHL Film 1,066,602. "1794 - Sept 17 - Girsel - John Ranken Coollier Lasher - Agnes Baird."

16. "Find A Grave," database (www.findagrave.com), Grizel "Girsey" Rankin McIntosh.

17. Bennett, Carol, *Lanark Society Settlers, 1820-1821.* (Renfrew, Ontario, Canada: Juniper Books, 1991.), page 192. Repository: Family History Library, 35 North West Temple Street, Salt Lake City, Utah 84150-3400, USA, Call Number: 971.382 W2. From the Public Archives of Canada/Memorandum:
It may be of interest that the Bridgetown Transatlantic Society was one of the emigrating societies which had been formed among the weavers of Glasgow, Hamilton, Paisley and Lanark, Scotland for the purpose of sponsoring a settlement of their members in Canada. In a dispatch of 6 May 1820, the Earl of Bathurst outlined the plan to settle about 1,200 Scotsmen on the newly opened Township of Lanark, Canada with the status of Military Settlement. Each family was to be granted 100 acres of land, and a loan of about L.10 per capita. The plan was accepted, and in June 1820 the settlers, grouped under the names of their sponsoring societies set sail for Canada. Upon their arrival they were allotted land in the Lanark Military settlement, and placed under the control of the Quartermaster-General's Department. Captain William Marshall was named the Superintendent and Secretary as well as the Storekeeper of the settlement. Eventually the individual settlers fulfilled their settlement duties and became eligible for deeds to their land.
The earliest settlers were unemployed Scots who left the overpopulated areas of Glasgow and Lanarkshire, following the Napoleonic war. In 1820, approximately 400 families arrived in Lanark, Canada, bringing with them skills in cotton weaving, carpentry, blacksmithing and shoemaking. A similar influx of Irish settlers arrived during the 1830's and 1840's. However, the growth of the area was somewhat impeded by the muddy, rocky terrain and steep slopes, which prevented easy travel. Although the intention of the original settlers was to farm each parcel of land, it soon became apparent that the only lands that could be cultivated were those located in floodplains, along rivers or adjacent to lakes. Consequently, most settlers opted to perform timber-related activities instead. Others left the area for Western Canada or the United States.

18. Donald Whyte, *A Dictionary of Scottish Emigrants to Canada before Confederation*, 4 Volumns (Toronto, Ontario, Canada: Ontario Genealogical Society, c1986-C2005). Repository: Family History Library, 35 North West Temple Street, Salt Lake City, Utah 84150-3400, USA, Call Number: 971 F2wd v.1.

19. 1850 U.S. census, Monroe, Michigan, population schedule, Monroe, p. 709, dwelling 137, family 140, Grove (Girsey) McIntosh; digital images, *ancestry.com*; citing National Archives and Records Administration microfilm M432.

20. "Find A Grave," database (www.findagrave.com), Girsel Ranken McIntosh.

21. Church of Jesus Christ of Latter-day Saints, Temple Records Index Bureau (Salt Lake City, Utah, United States of America), "Temple Records Index Bureau," item Index Card To Endowment House Temple Records, No. 2857, Book C-S 1g, Page 424.

22. Brown, Beverly McIntosh and Marsha Lee McIntosh,*William McIntosh Diary, abridgement* (Self-published, Surprise, AZ. June 2002), "My oldest sister Agnes...".

23. Scotland Church of Scotland, 23 microfilm rolls; 35 mm vols. Parish registers for Barony, 1672-1854 (Births, Baptisms, Marriages), (Ancestry.com, ), Agnes McIntosh; FHL microfilm 1041477; January 1818
John McIntosh, dyer, Bridgeton and Grace Rankin had their 1st child, born 28th January, baptized 8th February, named Agnes. Witnesses were John Montgomery and William McIntosh, wit.

24. Brown, Beverly McIntosh and Marsha McIntosh, editors,*William McIntosh Diary 1857-1898, Abridgement* (Surprise, AZ: Self-published, June 2002).

25. Daughters of the Utah Pioneers, *History of Tooele County - Old Manuscript* (Salt Lake City, Utah: Publishers Press, 1961), 537.

26. Daughters of Utah Pioneers, *Our Pioneer Heritage* (Salt Lake City, UT: Infobases, Inc., 1996), 19: 422. Repository: Family History Library, 35 North West Temple Street, Salt Lake City, Utah 84150-3400, USA, Call Number: 979.2 H2.

27. Frank Esshorn, editor, *Pioneers and Prominent Men of Utah comprising Photographs-Genealogies-Biographies. Pioneers are those men and women who came to Utah by wagon, hand cart or afoot, between July 24, 1847 and December 30, 1868, before the railroad. Prominent Men are stake presidents, ward bishops, governors, members of the bench, etc., who came to Utah after the coming of the railroad. The early history of the Church of Jesus Christ of Latter-Day Saints. In One Volume, Illustrated* (Salt Lake City, Utah: Utah Pioneers Book Publishing Company, 1913), McIntosh, William: 331 and 1059. Repository: Family History Library, 35 North West Temple Street, Salt Lake City, Utah 84150-3400, USA, Call Number: 979.2 D3e.

28. Andrew Jenson, editor, *Latter-day Saint Biographical Encyclopedia: A Compilation of Biographical Sketches of Prominent Men and Women in The Church of Jesus Christ of Latter-day Saints*, 4 v.: ports. (Salt Lake City, Utah: Western Epics, 1971), William McIntosh: V 4, page 647. Repository: Family History Library, 35 North West Temple Street, Salt Lake City, Utah 84150-3400, USA, Call Number: 920.0792.

29. Brown, Beverly McIntosh and Marsha Lee McIntosh,*William McIntosh Diary, abridgement* (Self-published, Surprise, AZ. June 2002), p 80

# Source Citations

March 1 [1894].
... Today we are getting well along in years. I am 74 years old last September. My wife is about four years younger than myself.

30. Church of Jesus Christ of Latter-day Saints, *Patriarchal Blessing,* William McIntosh.

31. Brown, Beverly McIntosh and Marsha McIntosh, editors, *William McIntosh Diary 1857-1898, Abridgement* (Surprise, AZ: Self-published, June 2002), J-4.

32. Scotland, Church of Scotland (Glasgow, Lanarkshire, Scotland), "Parish registers for Barony, 1672-1854," McIntosh, William; FHL microfilm 1041478; "1819 - McIntosh - John McIntosh grocer Bridgeton & Grizel Rankin had their 2nd child born 16th Sept named William -Witnesses- James Rankin - James McIntosh"

33. Utah Division of State History, "Cemetery & Burial Database," database (https://heritage.utah.gov/history/cemeteries), William McIntosh.

34. International Society of Daughters of Utah Pioneers, editor, *Pioneer Women of Faith and Fortitude*, Volume III (Salt Lake City, Utah: Publishers Press, 1998), Maria Caldwell McIntosh: page 1946. Repository: Family History Library, 35 North West Temple Street, Salt Lake City, Utah 84150-3400, USA, Call Number: 979 D36.

35. McIntosh Reunion Descendants, McIntosh - Descendants of John & Girsey (Grace) (Grizel) Rankin McIntosh (Attachment to Aug 17, 1958 Newsletter - copy in Collection of Bonnie S. Williams), Repository: Bonnie S. Williams, RR 1 Box 247, N Hwy 2, Wilburton, Oklahoma, USA.
William (son of John McINTOSH & Girsey RANKIN) md. Maria CALDWELL
Children:
John Ephraim
Mary Ann
David Hyrum
William Henry md. Mary Elizabeth KEELE
James F. md. Ann JORDAN
Millisa Jane md. Jacob KEELE
Alice Maria md. Thomas L. BURRIDGE
Abram E. md. Mary Louise GUHL
L. Elizabeth md. Heber McBRIDE
Caroline J. md. Joseph JORDAN
Joseph Albert md. Ann RUSSELL.
This single page attachment indicates that the parents of John McIntosh are William McIntosh & Isabell and is indicative of what our side of the family knew of our McIntosh cousins at that time in August 1958.

36. Canada, Ontario. Marriage Registers of Upper Canada/Canada West, Volume 5: Page 59; Family History Library, Salt Lake City; William McIntosh, of Dalhousie, to Maria Caldwell, of Lanark. 27 Sept. 1841. Rev. Macalister. Wit. David Caldwell and John Barrowman.

37. Robert Sergeant and J.R. Ernest Miller, editors, *Some Early Lanark County Marriages 1830-1869* (Kingston, Ontario, Canada: Ontario Genealogical Society, 1993), Bathurst District Marriages 1830-1857: Page 4. Repository: Family History Library, 35 North West Temple Street, Salt Lake City, Utah 84150-3400, USA, Call Number: 911.382 K29s;
Caldwell, Maria, address Lanark, date 09-27-1841, spouse McIntosh, William, address Dalousie, minister McAlister.
Page 19 - McIntosh, William, address Dalhousie, date 09-27-1841, spouse Caldwell, Maria, address Lanark, minister McAlister.

38. Brown, Beverly McIntosh and Marsha McIntosh, editors, *William McIntosh Diary 1857-1898, Abridgement* (Surprise, AZ: Self-published, June 2002), J-1.

39. Brown, Beverly McIntosh and Marsha McIntosh, editors, *William McIntosh Diary 1857-1898, Abridgement* (Surprise, AZ: Self-published, June 2002), J-2.

40. 1850 U.S. census, Andrew, Missouri, population schedule, Jefferson, p. 8, dwelling 801, family 781, William McIntosh; digital images, *ancestry.com*; citing National Archives and Records Administration microfilm M432.

41. Church of Jesus Christ of Latter-day Saints, "Mormon Pioneer Overland Travel, 1847-1868," database (www.lds.org/churchhistory/library/pioneercompany : accessed 22 Dec 2014), William McIntosh travelled with the David Lewis Comnpany in 1851.

42. Church of Jesus Christ of Latter-day Saints, Registry of Names of Persons Residing in the Various Wards as to Bishop's Reports (Salt Lake City, Utah, United States of America), McIntosh, William, North Kanyon Ward (Bountiful); Family History Library, Salt Lake City.

43. Church of Jesus Christ of Latter-day Saints, *Patriarchal Blessing,* William McIntosh by John Smith, No. 385.

44. Utah State Census Index, 1856, Utah, population schedule.

45. 1860 U.S. census, Shambip, Utah, population schedule, Clover, p. 450, dwelling 4028, family 3104, Wm McIntosh; digital images, *ancestry.com*; citing National Archives and Records Administration microfilm M653.

46. 1870 U.S. census, Washington, Utah, population schedule, Panaca, p. 7, dwelling 54, family 48, McIntosh, William; digital images,

# Source Citations

*ancestry.com*; citing National Archives and Records Administration microfilm M593.

47. 1870 U.S. census, Lincoln, Nevada, population schedule, Meadow Valley, p. 186, dwelling 66-68, family 45, McIntosh, Wm; digital images, *ancestry.com*; citing National Archives and Records Administration microfilm M593.

48. Kate B. Carter, editor, *Our Pioneer Heritage*, 20 v.: ill., maps, ports. (Salt Lake City, Utah: Daughters of Utah Pioneers, 1958-1977). Repository: Family History Library, 35 North West Temple Street, Salt Lake City, Utah 84150-3400, USA, Call Number: 979.2 H2.

49. Bureau of Land Management, Record Group 49, *United States. General Land Office.* (Washington, D.C.: The National Archives), Date of Sale 27 Jul 1872; Homestead Application No. 1706; Final Cert No. 1137 dated 9 Sep 1879.

50. Tooele, Utah, United States of America, 1873 Tax Book, entry for McIntosh, William; FHL microfilm 482,525.

51. Tooele, Utah, United States of America, 1874 Tax Book, entry for McIntosh, Wm; FHL microfilm 482,525.

52. Utah, Record of Marks and Brands for the State of Utah, Embracing all the Marks and Brands Recorded from December 9, 1847 to December 31, 1884, 43: Wm. McIntosh, June 4, 1875, St. John's,Tooele Co; Utah State Archives and Record Service, Salt Lake City.

53. Bureau of Land Management, Record Group 49, *United States. General Land Office.* (Washington, D.C.: The National Archives), amendment to application no. 1706.

54. Utah. Court (U.S. Land Office). Salt Lake City, *Certificate of Citizenship* (U.S. Land Office, Salt Lake City, Utah, 1877), "...said Court that the said William McIntosh be admitted , and he was accordingly admitted by the said Court to b e a CITIZEN OF THE UNITED STATES OF AMERICA."

55. 1880 U.S. census, Tooele, Utah Territory, population schedule, Clover, enumeration district (ED) 79, p. 6C, Mackintosh, William; digital images, *ancestry.com*; citing National Archives and Records Administration microfilm T9.

56. Brown, Beverly McIntosh and Marsha Lee McIntosh, *William McIntosh Diary, abridgement* (Self-published, Surprise, AZ. June 2002), p.71 1891 - 14 August.

57. Bureau of Land Management, Record Group 49, *United States. General Land Office.* (Washington, D.C.: The National Archives), Testimony by David H Caldwell on behalf of Caroline E McIntosh mentions Wm McIntosh and Thomas Burridge.

58. Bureau of Land Management, Record Group 49, *United States. General Land Office.* (Washington, D.C.: The National Archives), Application No. 8552; Addition to Homestead No. 1706; Final Homestead Certificate No. 1137 dated 9 Sep 1879.

59. Utah, Tooele County, *Patent Record Book, #* 1, page 185.

60. Brown, Beverly McIntosh and Marsha McIntosh, editors, *William McIntosh Diary 1857-1898, Abridgement* (Surprise, AZ: Self-published, June 2002), pages 73, 80, 83.

61. Brown, Beverly McIntosh and Marsha McIntosh, editors, *William McIntosh Diary 1857-1898, Abridgement* (Surprise, AZ: Self-published, June 2002), page 85.

62. Bell, William Bell, ; compiled by J.R. Ernest Miller, Baptisms, First Presbterian Church Perth, By Rev. William Bell, 1817-1857, compiled by J.R. Ernest Miller from Church Records 1986, Repository: Family History Library, 35 North West Temple Street, Salt Lake City, Utah 84150-3400, USA, Call Number: 971.382/Pl, K29m. Name-McIntosh, John; Spouse-Grizel; Address-Dalhousie, con. 5.lot 1; Child-John; Born-11-14-1821. John and Grizel's baby, John, was baptized.

63. Bennett, Carol, *Lanark Society Settlers, 1820-1821.* (Renfrew, Ontario, Canada: Juniper Books, 1991.), page 192. Repository: Family History Library, 35 North West Temple Street, Salt Lake City, Utah 84150-3400, USA, Call Number: 971.382 W2. page 192:
**McIntosh, John, 1799-**
Born Lanarkshire, a son of John and Margaret McIntosh.
Ship: Commerce, 1821
Location: West lot 1, con 5, Dalhousie Township.
John McIntosh came here with his wife, Margaret, born 1800, his brother Robert born 1812 and one little girl, possibly a child of John's. Possibly Mrs. Alex Nicholson, nee Janet McIntosh, was a sister. **Rev. William Bell's baptismal records show a baby, John born in November, 1821 to the John McIntosh on this farm, but the mother's name is given as Grizel, so there is a mistake somewhere.** Robert McIntosh married Isabella Easton, daughter of George Easton of the Lesmahagow society. The couple later whent to Motherwell, Fullerton Twp, Perth County.

64. Canada Church of England in Canada, Parish register no. 1 of St. Paul's Church, London, Upper Canada, 1829-1846, ( ), John McIntosh; FHL microfilm 928965, on 1 microfilm reel; 35 mm; John, son of John McIntosh, and Grizel, his wife, born 14th Nov. 1821, and baptised 4th February 1822. (No1, in the 5th Concession of Dalhousie).

65. Church of Jesus Christ of Latter-day Saints, Early Church Information File, 1830-1900 (Salt Lake City, Utah, United States of America), McIntosh, John F. Ginsey; FHL microfilm 889368.

66. McIntosh Reunion Descendants, McIntosh - Descendants of John & Girsey (Grace) (Grizel) Rankin McIntosh (Attachment to Aug 17, 1958 Newsletter - copy in Collection of Bonnie S. Williams), Repository: Bonnie S. Williams, RR 1 Box 247, N Hwy 2, Wilburton, Oklahoma, USA. John

# Source Citations

(son of John McINTOSH & Girsey RANKIN) md. C. E. CALDWELL
Children:
Mary Ann md. Samuel DAVIS
John David md. Thirza E. NAY
William Abram md. Nancy Lean GUHL.


67. Brown, Beverly McIntosh and Marsha McIntosh, editors,*William McIntosh Diary 1857-1898, Abridgement* (Surprise, AZ: Self-published, June 2002), pages 20, 21, 22, 25, 26.

68. Utah State Historical Society, "Utah, Cemetery Inventory, 1847-2000," database(https://www.ancestry.com/search/collections/utahburials/), John McIntosh.

69. Daughters of Utah Pioneers, *History of Tooele County* (Salt Lake City, Utah: Publisher's Press, 1961), page 457, Caroline Elizabeth Caldwell (Neddo) (McIntosh) Dymock.

70. John W. McIntosh, *Sketch of the Life of my Grandmother, Caroline Elizabeth Calwell McIntosh*; PDF download, *Henderson Project* (www.hendersonproject.net/Caroline_history_by_John_W_McIntosh.html).

71. Ann Neddo, *Caroline Elizabeth Caldwell* (N.p.: Self, n.d.), This is a short biography self published by Ann Neddo and distributed to interested family members.

72. Daughters of the Utah Pioneers, *History of Tooele County - Old Manuscript* (Salt Lake City, Utah: Publishers Press, 1961), 457.

73. Church of Jesus Christ of Latter-day Saints, "Mormon Pioneer Overland Travel, 1847-1868," database (www.lds.org/churchhistory/library/pioneercompany), McIntosh, John.

74. Daughters of the Utah Pioneers, *East of Antelope Island* (Davis County, Utah: North Davis County Company, 1971), John McIntosh. Repository: Family History Library, 35 North West Temple Street, Salt Lake City, Utah 84150-3400, USA, Call Number: 979.227 H2d.

75. 1850 U.S. census, Davis, Utah Territory, population schedule, Davis County, dwelling 111, family Joseph Holbrook (farmer), John McIntosh (farmer; boarder), age 25, male, born in Canada; NARA microfilm publication M432, roll Film 025,540. Repository: Family History Center, 41 South Hobson, Mesa, AZ, USA, Call Number: Film 025,540;
The first settlement of Utah was in Salt Lake County July 1847. The Territory of Utah was organized by act of Congress 9 September 1850, but official news did not reach Utah until January 1851. An enumeration of the inhabitants of the new Territory was made previous to 1 July 1851, but it included only the population of counties, as follows: Great Salt Lake, Davis, Weber, Utah, Sanpete, Iron, Tooele, Green River Precinct. Subsequently, the regular census was taken, in 1851, following the plan of the United States Census for 1850.

76. Utah State Census Index, 1856, Utah, population schedule, John McIntosh.

77. Utah Division of State History, "Cemetery & Burial Database," database (https://heritage.utah.gov/history/cemeteries), John McIntosh, Clover Cemetery grave Old Section, #19.

78. Brown, Beverly McIntosh and Marsha Lee McIntosh,*William McIntosh Diary, abridgement* (Self-published, Surprise, AZ. June 2002), page 10.

79. Brown, Beverly McIntosh and Marsha Lee McIntosh,*William McIntosh Diary, abridgement* (Self-published, Surprise, AZ. June 2002), "In the year 1845 we moved to Michigan....My brother James took sick in Michigan died there about eight miles from Monroe City towards Toledo. We lived there until the spring of 1846."

80. Lucas, Ohio, Marriage Licenses, McIntosh-Sonkas/Soukas/Sankas; FHL microfilm 317434; McIntosh, Isabella m. Jacob Sankas Dec 12, 1857

81. Walter H. McIntosh, *McIntosh-MacIntosh Families of the United States and Canada*, v.5 (Topsfield, Massachusetts: Self-published, 1985). Repository: Family History Library, 35 North West Temple Street, Salt Lake City, Utah 84150-3400, USA, Call Number: 929.273 M189.

82. 1850 U.S. census, Monroe, Michigan, population schedule, Monroe, p. 709, dwelling 137, family 140, Issabella McIntosh; digital images, *ancestry.com*; citing National Archives and Records Administration microfilm M432.

83. Ohio. Lucas County, *1860 U.S. Census, population schedule* (Washington D.C.: The National Archives), Jacob Simkus household, town of Toledo, Toledo post office, dwelling 1671, family 1627.

84. "Ohio, Deaths 1908-1953," database, Alice Belle Moag names her mother as Janet McIntosh.

85. "Find A Grave," database (www.findagrave.com), Jannette McIntosh Woodruff.

86. "Find A Grave," database (www.findagrave.com), Jannett McIntosh Woodruff.

87. Brown, Beverly McIntosh and Marsha Lee McIntosh,*William McIntosh Diary, abridgement* (Self-published, Surprise, AZ. June 2002), "Jennet married a man by the name of Campbell. That is all I know about him.. Only that he died and left her a widow with two children."

# Source Citations

88. Ohio. Lucas County, 1850 U.S. Census, population schedule, Washington, District of Columbia : The National Archives, 1964, Charles Campbell household, 1850 U.S. census, Lucas County , Ohio, population schedule, Waterville township, page 130 , dwelling 1891, family 1887; Ancestry.com.

89. Brown, Beverly McIntosh and Marsha Lee McIntosh,*William McIntosh Diary, abridgement* (Self-published, Surprise, AZ. June 2002), "Feb 20, 1894. I am in receipt of letters from Girsey Hinckly and Jennett Woodruff, my two sisters."

90. "Ohio, Deaths 1908-1953," database, Alice Belle Moag names her father as Elijah Woodruff (he's her step-father), born in Connecticut.

91. Ohio, Marriages, 1789-2013, Elijah J. Woodruff married Jennett Campbell on 31 Dec 1866; FHL microfilm 912-940.

92. Ohio. Lucas County, 1850 U.S. Census, population schedule, Washington, District of Columbia : The National Archives, 1964, Charles Campbell household, 1850 U.S. census, Lucas County , Ohio, population schedule, Waterville township, page 130 , dwelling 1891, family 1887.

93. Ohio. Lucas County,*1860 U.S. Census, population schedule* (Washington D.C.: The National Archives), F Kingsly household, town of Toledo, Toledo post office, pa ge 226, dwelling 2088, family 2034.

94. *1870 U.S. Census. Ohio, Lucas, Toledo,* H.A. Woodruff household, town of Toledo, Toledo post office , page 18, dwelling 126, family 123. Repository: Family History Library, 35 North West Temple Street, Salt Lake City, Utah 84150-3400, USA, Call Number: 552736.

95. Ohio. Lucas County,*1880 U.S. Census, population schedule* (Washington D.C.: The National Archives), I. Woodruff household, town of Toledo, enumeration distric t [ED] 42, supervisor's district [SD] 1, page 15, dwellin g 142, family 145.

96. Ohio. Lucas County,*1900 U.S. Census, population schedule* (Washington D.C.: The National Archives), Elijah Woodruff household, town of Toledo, enumeration dist rict [ED] 50, supervisor's district [SD] 8, sheet 20 A, dwe lling 415, family 471.

97. Ohio, Wood County. 1860 U.S. Census, Repository: Ancestry.com, http://www.Ancestry.com.

98. Lucas, Ohio, Marriage Licenses, McIntosh-Hinckley; FHL microfilm 317434; McIntosh, Girsey m. Henry Hinckley Feb. 3, 1852.

99. Ohio, Marriages, 1789-2013, Hinckley-McIntosh; FHL microfilm 912-940; Henry Hinckley to Girsey McIntosh. Received May first AD 1852 a certificate of the marriage of Henry Hinckley to Girsey McIntosh on the Third day of April 1852 by Edward D. Sargent Justice of the Peace.

100. Northwestern Ohio Genealogical Society, editor,*Lucas County, Ohio Marriage Records, 1835-1858* (Toledo, Ohio: n.p., 1984). Repository: Family History Library, 35 North West Temple Street, Salt Lake City, Utah 84150-3400, USA, Call Number: 977.112 V2L.

101. Ohio. Lucas County,*1850 U.S. Census, population schedule* (Washington D.C.: The National Archives), Rocileus C Connele household, town of Toledo, dwelling 906 , family 929, page 67B and 68.

102. Ohio. Wood County,*1860 U.S. Census, population schedule* (Washington D.C.: The National Archives), Henry Hinkle household, town of Perrysburg, Perrysburg pos t office, page 191, dwelling 1374, family 1351.

103. Ohio. Wood County,*1870 U.S. Census, population schedule* (Washington D.C.: The National Archives), Henry Hinkley household, town of Perrysburg, Woodville Sand usky Co. post office, page 12, dwelling 89, family 89.

104. Ohio. Wood County,*1880 U.S. Census, population* (Washington D.C.: The National Archives), Henry Hinckley household, town of Rose, enumeration distric t [ED] 104, supervisor's district [SD] 1, page 5B, dwellin g 82, family 83.

105. Ohio. Lucas County,*1900 U.S. Census, population schedule* (Washington D.C.: The National Archives), Girsey Hinckley household, town of Toledo, enumeration dist rict [ED] 50, supervisor's district [SD] 8, sheet 20 B, dwe lling 428, family 485.

106. *1910 U.S. Census. Ohio, Lucas, Toledo,* William Webb household, town of Toledo, enumeration distric t [ED] 149, supervisor's district [SD] 8, sheet 6A, dwellin g 118, family 126.

107. Brown, Beverly McIntosh and Marsha Lee McIntosh,*William McIntosh Diary, abridgement* (Self-published, Surprise, AZ. June 2002), Pages J1 and J4.

108. "Ohio, Deaths 1908-1953," database, Willis D. McIntosh names his father as David McIntosh, birthplace unknown.

109. "Ohio, Deaths 1908-1953," database, Willis D. McIntosh names his mother as Mary Landis, birthplace unknown.

110. Lucas, Ohio, File Number: 000409704, David McIntosh and Mary Landis (child: Willis D. McIntosh; digital images, ancestry.com*Ohio, County Marriages, 1774-1993* .

111. Ohio. Lucas County,*1860 U.S. Census, population schedule* (Washington D.C.: The National Archives), Roll: M653_1003; Page 248; Image: 500.

112. David McIntosh and Mary A. Landis McIntosh; U.S., Civil War Soldier Records and Profiles, 1861-1865; National Archives and Records Administration, Washington.

Produced by: Beverly McIntosh Brown, 15933 W Silver Breeze Dr, Surprise, AZ 85374, 623-584-0440, starfighteraz@gmail.com : 29 Jun 2021



Produced by Legacy

# Abraham Isaac Vaughn, Jr. and Agnes McIntosh

| **Husband** | **Abraham Isaac Vaughn Jr.**[1] | |
|---|---|---|
| AKA | Abram Vaughn | |
| Born | Cir 1783 | Lanark, , Scotland, United Kingdom |
| Died | Bef 1880 | place: |
| Buried | date: | place: |
| Bapt.(LDS) | 1850 | Lanark, , Ontario, Canada |
| Conf.(LDS) | 16 Mar 1995 | Jordan River Utah Temple |
| Init.(LDS) | 31 May 1995 | Jordan River Utah Temple |
| Endow.(LDS) | 24 Jun 1897 | Manti Utah Temple |
| Father | Abraham Isaac Vaughn Sr. (Cir 1762-1795) | |
| Mother | Jane Cooper (1763- )[2] | |
| SealP (LDS) | 28 Apr 1990 | Jordan River Utah Temple |
| Marriage | 1846 | Michigan, United States |
| SealS (LDS) | 15 Mar 1995 | Jordan River Utah Temple |
| Other Spouse | Mary Thomson ( - ) | |
| SealS (LDS) | | |

**Events**

1. He has conflicting birth information of 1809 and Scotland, United Kingdom.
2. He appeared on the census in 1851 in Bathurst, Lanark, Ontario, Canada.[3]
   Line 35 - **Abram Vaughan**, laborer, born in Scotland, Mormon, age 42, male, single.
3. He appeared on the census on 25 Jun 1860 in Erie, Monroe, Michigan, United States.
   Line 35 - Stephen Tuttle, age 46, male, farmer, value of real estate $4000, value of personal estate $1000, born in [can't read[.
   **Line 40 - Abraham Vaughn, age 51, male, laborer, born in Scotland.**
4. He appeared on the census on 9 Aug 1870 in Frenchtown, Monroe, Michigan, United States.[4]
   Line 22 - Stewart, Mary, age 54, female, white, keeping house, born in Scotland, father and mother foreign born.
   Line 23 - Stewart, David, age 28, male, white, farmer, value of real estate 4500, value of personal estate 800, born in Canada, father and mother foreign born, male over 21.
   Line 24 - Stewart, Alexander, age 26, male, white, farmer, value of real estate 4500, value of personal estate 800, born in Canada, father and mother foreign born, male over 21.
   **Line 25 - Vaughn, Abram, age 60, male, white, laborer, born in Scotland, father and mother foreign born, male over 21.**

| **Wife** | **Agnes McIntosh**[5] | |
|---|---|---|
| AKA | Agnes Vaughn | |
| Born | 28 Jan 1818 | Glasgow, Lanark, Scotland, United Kingdom[6] |
| Died | Cir 1847 | Monroe, Michigan, United States |
| Cause of Death | Possibly died in childbirth | |
| Buried | date: | place: |
| Bapt.(LDS) | 12 Feb 1895 | Salt Lake Temple |
| Conf.(LDS) | 28 Dec 1999 | Seattle Washington Temple |
| Init.(LDS) | 7 Jan 2000 | Seattle Washington Temple |
| Endow.(LDS) | 21 May 1971 | Salt Lake Temple |
| Father | John McIntosh Sr. (1795-1875)[7,8] | |
| Mother | Girsel Rankin (1794-1853)[8] | |
| SealP (LDS) | 8 Sep 1971 | Salt Lake Temple |

# Abraham Isaac Vaughn, Jr. and Agnes McIntosh

**Events**

1. She emigrated on 11 May 1821 from Glasgow, Lanark, Scotland, United Kingdom.
   Page 202, Line 5811. **McINTOSH, John**. To Quebec on the (ship) Commerce, exited Greenock (Scotland), 11 May 1821, in assoc with the St Johns Emig Soc. **Wife and 2 ch with him**. Loc Dalhousie Twp, Lanark Co, ONT. First slmt (settlement) advance to him paid 1 Aug. ICS-2 & 6.

## Children

| 1 | F | **Mary Vaughn** |
|---|---|---|
| Born | Cir 1846 | Michigan, United States |
| Died | date: | place: |
| Buried | date: | place: |
| Bapt.(LDS) | 22 Nov 2008 | Billings Montana Temple |
| Conf.(LDS) | 22 Nov 2008 | Billings Montana Temple |
| Init.(LDS) | 11 Dec 2008 | Billings Montana Temple |
| Endow.(LDS) | 11 Dec 2008 | Billings Montana Temple |
| SealP (LDS) | 23 Apr 2009 | Billings Montana Temple |
| Spouse | | |

**Events**

1. She appeared on the census on 6 Aug 1850 in Monroe, Monroe, Michigan, United States.[9] Line 22 - John McIntosh, age 55, male, laborer, born in Scotland.
   Line 23 - Geoon McIntosh, age 54, female, born in Scotland.(Girsey)
   Line 24 - Issabella McIntosh, age 21, female, born in Canada.
   **Line 25 - Mary Vagne, age 6, female, born in Michigan, attended school within year. (Mary Vaughn)**
   Line 26 - Isaac Vagne, age 4, male, born in Michigan. (Isaac Vaughn)
   Line 27 - John McIntosh, age 2, male, born in Michigan. (Unidentified person)

| 2 | M | **Isaac Vaughn** |
|---|---|---|
| Born | 29 Jan 1847 | Michigan, United States |
| Died | Bef 1870 | place: |
| Buried | date: | place: |
| Bapt.(LDS) | 27 May 1998 | Jordan River Utah Temple |
| Conf.(LDS) | 1 Aug 1998 | Jordan River Utah Temple |
| Init.(LDS) | 12 Sep 1998 | Jordan River Utah Temple |
| Endow.(LDS) | 4 Aug 1999 | Jordan River Utah Temple |
| SealP (LDS) | 11 Aug 1999 | Idaho Falls Idaho Temple |
| Spouse | | |

**Events**

1. He appeared on the census on 6 Aug 1850 in Monroe, Monroe, Michigan, United States.[10]
   Line 22 - John McIntosh, age 55, male, laborer, born in Scotland.
   Line 23 - Geoon McIntosh, age 54, female, born in Scotland.(Girsey)
   Line 24 - Issabella McIntosh, age 21, female, born in Canada.
   Line 25 - Mary Vagne, age 6, female, born in Michigan, attended school within year. (Mary Vaughn)
   **Line 26 - Isaac Vagne, age 4, male, born in Michigan. (Isaac Vaughn)**
   Line 27 - John McIntosh, age 2, male, born in Michigan. (Unidentified person)

2. He appeared on the census on 11 Jul 1860 in Frenchtown, Monroe, Michigan, United States.[11]
   Line 11 - John Stuart, age 49, male, farmer, value of real estate 2500, value of personal estate 1,000, born in Scotland.
   Line 12 - Mary Stuart, age 45, female, born in Scotland.
   Line 13 - William Stuart, age 22, male, born in Canada W.

# Abraham Isaac Vaughn, Jr. and Agnes McIntosh

Line 14 - Anna Stuart, age 20, female, born in Canada W.
Line 15 - David Stuart, age 18, male, born in Canada W.
Line 16 - Alexander Stuart, age 16, male, born in Canada W.
**Line 17 - Isaac Vaughn, age 14, male, born in Michigan.**
Line 18 - Chas Kelly, age 6, male, born in Michigan.

Produced by: Beverly McIntosh Brown, 15933 W Silver Breeze Dr, Surprise, AZ 85374, 623-584-0440, starfighteraz@gmail.com : 29 Jun 2021

# Source Citations

1. Brown, Beverly McIntosh and Marsha McIntosh, editors,*William McIntosh Diary 1857-1898, Abridgement* (Surprise, AZ: Self-published, June 2002).

2. Pedigree Resource File CD 26, (Salt Lake City, UT: Intellectual Reserve, Inc., 2001).

3. 1851 census of Canada East, Canada West, New Brunswick, and Nova Scotia, Canada West (Ontario), Lanark County, district 19, sub-district 173, Bathurst, p. 101, Abram Vaughn; RG 31; digital images, ancestry.com.

4. 1870 U.S. census, Monroe, Michigan, population schedule, Frenchtown, p. 41, dwelling 295, family 296, Vaughn, Abram; digital images (ancestry.com); citing National Archives and Records Administration microfilm M593.

5. Brown, Beverly McIntosh and Marsha Lee McIntosh,*William McIntosh Diary, abridgement* (Self-published, Surprise, AZ. June 2002), "My oldest sister Agnes...".

6. Scotland Church of Scotland, 23 microfilm rolls; 35 mm vols. Parish registers for Barony, 1672-1854 (Births, Baptisms, Marriages), (Ancestry.com, ), Agnes McIntosh; FHL microfilm 1041477; January 1818
John McIntosh, dyer, Bridgeton and Grace Rankin had their 1st child, born 28th January, baptized 8th February, named Agnes. Witnesses were John Montgomery and William McIntosh, wit.

7. Church of Jesus Christ of Latter-day Saints,*Patriarchal Blessing,* "...William McIntosh son of John and Girsey McIntosh..."

8. Brown, Beverly McIntosh and Marsha Lee McIntosh,*William McIntosh Diary, abridgement* (Self-published, Surprise, AZ. June 2002).

9. 1850 U.S. census, Monroe, Michigan, population schedule, Monroe, p. 709, dwelling 137, family 140, Mary Vogue (Vaughn); digital images, *ancestry.com*; citing National Archives and Records Administration microfilm M432.

10. 1850 U.S. census, Monroe, Michigan, population schedule, Monroe, p. 709, dwelling 137, family 140, Isaac Vogue (Vaughn); digital images, *ancestry.com*; citing National Archives and Records Administration microfilm M432.

11. 1860 U.S. census, Monroe, Michigan, population schedule, Frenchtown, p. 123, dwelling 948, family 947, Isaac Vaughn; digital images (ancestry.com); citing National Archives and Records Administration microfilm M653.

# Maria Caldwell McIntosh



| | | | | Sex: | F |
|---|---|---|---|---|---|
| **Name:** | **Maria Caldwell** [1] | | | | |
| **AKA:** | Maria McIntosh | | | | |
| **Birth Date:** | 17 Feb 1824 | | | | |
| **Place:** | Lanark, Lanark, Upper Canada, Canada [2,3,4,5,6] | | | | |
| **Death Date:** | 27 Jul 1897 | **Place:** | Mount Pleasant, Sanpete, Utah, United States [7,8] | | |

| | | | |
|---|---|---|---|
| **Burial Date:** | 2 Aug 1897 | **Place:** | Mount Pleasant, Sanpete, Utah, United States [9] |
| **Cause of Death:** | Epilepsy/Old Age | | |
| **Bapt.(LDS):** | 2 Jan 1837 | **Place:** | , Lanark, Ontario, Canada |
| **Conf.(LDS):** | 2 Jan 1837 | **Place:** | , Lanark, Ontario, Canada |
| **Init.(LDS):** | 24 Aug 1861 | **Temple:** | Endowment House |
| **Endow.(LDS):** | 24 Aug 1861 | **Temple:** | Endowment House |

**Events**

1. She had a residence from 28 Oct 1841 to Apr 1845 in Toledo, Lucas, Ohio, United States.[10]
2. She had a residence from Apr 1845 to Aug 1845 in Oregon, Lucas, Ohio, United States.[11]
3. She had a residence from Aug 1845 to Apr 1847 in Erie, Monroe, Michigan, United States.[12]
4. She had a residence from May 1847 to 1851 in Saint Louis, , Missouri, United States.[13]
5. She appeared on the census on 19 Nov 1850 in Jefferson City, Cole, Missouri, United States.[14]
6. Migration: David Lewis Company, Between 1 May 1851 and 9 Sep 1851, Salt Lake City, Great Salt Lake, Utah Territory, United States.[15]
7. Patriarchal Blessing: 4 Jul 1852, Salt Lake City, Great Salt Lake, Utah Territory, United States.[16]
8. She appeared on the census on 11 Oct 1860 in Clover, Shambip, Utah Territory, United States.[17]
9. She appeared on the census on 10 Jun 1870 in Panaca, Washington, Utah Territory.[18]
10. She appeared on the census on 28 Jul 1870 in Meadow Valley, Lincoln, Nevada, United States.[19]
11. She had a residence from 1872 to 1882 in Saint John, Tooele, Utah Territory, United States.[20]
12. She appeared on the census on 12 Jun 1880 in Clover, Tooele, Utah Territory, United States.[21]
13. She received medical attention for Falling sickness - Epilepsy in 1890 in Saint John, Tooele, Utah Territory, United States.[22]
14. She had a residence on 26 Mar 1896 in Saint John, Tooele, Utah, United States.[23]
15. She had a residence on 23 Sep 1896 in Saint John, Tooele, Utah, United States.[24,25]
16. She had a residence on 6 Jan 1897 in Mount Pleasant, Sanpete, Utah, United States.[26]

Mormon Pioneer Overland Travel, 1847-1868

David Lewis Company (1851)

Departure: 1 May 1851
Arrival in Salt Lake Valley: 9 September 1851

David Lewis

PhotoScan by Google Photos

Mormon Pioneer Overland Travel - David Lewis Company, 1851, Maria Caldwell McIntosh, page 1 of 2

# Maria Caldwell McIntosh



| (cont. for Maria Caldwell) | | | |
|---|---|---|---|
| **Father:** | David Caldwell (1781-1849)[27,28,29] | | |
| **Mother:** | Mary Ann Vaughn (1791-1868)[28,30,31,32] | | |
| **SealP (LDS):** | 11 Oct 1893 | **Temple:** | Manti Utah Temple |
| **Spouse:** | ***William McIntosh (16 Sep 1819 - 4 May 1899)**[12,33,34,35,36,37,38,39] | | |
| **Marr. Date:** | 27 Sep 1841 | | |
| **Place:** | Bathurst, Lanark, , Canada [40,41,42] | | |
| **SealS (LDS):** | 24 Aug 1861 | **Temple:** | Endowment House |

# Source Citations




1. International Society of Daughters of Utah Pioneers, editor,*Pioneer Women of Faith and Fortitude*, Volume III (Salt Lake City, Utah: Publishers Press, 1998), Maria Caldwell McIntosh: page 1946. Repository: Family History Library, 35 North West Temple Street, Salt Lake City, Utah 84150-3400, USA, Call Number: 979 D36.

2. Church of Jesus Christ of Latter-day Saints, Patron sheets, 1969-1991 (Salt Lake City: Filmed by the Genealogical Society of Utah, 1970-1991), Batch 5003057, Sheet 22, Film 1553185.
Maria CALDWELL
Sex: F
Event(s):
Birth: 17 Feb 1824, Lanark, Lanark, Ontario
Parents:
Father: David CALDWELL
Mother: Mary Ann VAUGHAN.

3. Brown, Beverly McIntosh and Marsha Lee McIntosh,*William McIntosh Diary, abridgement* (Self-published, Surprise, AZ. June 2002), J-3 Maria's family.

4. Brown, Beverly McIntosh and Marsha Lee McIntosh,*William McIntosh Diary, abridgement* (Self-published, Surprise, AZ. June 2002), p 80 March 1, 1894.

5. Church of Jesus Christ of Latter-day Saints,*Patriarchal Blessing,* "...Maria McIntosh...born February 17th, 1824, Landrick County, Upper Canada." (Lanark County).

6. J.R. Ernest Miller,*Scottish Settlers to Bathurst Area for Bathurst District: includes Lanark, Leeds, Carleton, Frontenac, and Renfrew settlers. Extracted from Dictionary of Scottish Settlers and other Sources. Includes "Supplement to Scottish Settlers to Bathurst Area for Bathurst District: includes Perth and area settlers with spouses & or children / extracted from various sources by J.R. Ernest Miller, 1987".* (Kingston, Ontario, Canada: Ontario Genealogical Society, 1987), page 2. Repository: Family History Library, 35 North West Temple Street, Salt Lake City, Utah 84150-3400, USA, Call Number: 971.3 W2m.

7. Brown, Beverly McIntosh and Marsha Lee McIntosh,*William McIntosh Diary, abridgement* (Self-published, Surprise, AZ. June 2002), p 96 & 97 July 23, 1897. "My wife was taken with a cramp in her stomach and that continued with her until July 27, 1897 then she died, seemingly unconscious of trouble or pain. She was buried in the Mt. Pleasant burying ground, Sanpete Co., Utah. August 23, she was buried".

8. Utah State Historical Society, "Utah, Cemetery Inventory, 1847-2000," database(https://www.ancestry.com/search/collections/utahburials/), Maria Caldwell McIntosh.

9. Utah Division of State History, "Cemetery & Burial Database," database (https://heritage.utah.gov/history/cemeteries), Maria Caldwell McIntosh.

10. Brown, Beverly McIntosh and Marsha Lee McIntosh,*William McIntosh Diary, abridgement* (Self-published, Surprise, AZ. June 2002), page J-1 Toledo, Ohio 1841.

11. Brown, Beverly McIntosh and Marsha Lee McIntosh,*William McIntosh Diary, abridgement* (Self-published, Surprise, AZ. June 2002), page J-2 Oregon, Ohio.

12. Brown, Beverly McIntosh and Marsha McIntosh, editors,*William McIntosh Diary 1857-1898, Abridgement* (Surprise, AZ: Self-published, June 2002).

13. Brown, Beverly McIntosh and Marsha Lee McIntosh,*William McIntosh Diary, abridgement* (Self-published, Surprise, AZ. June 2002), page J-2 Start for St Louis, 1847.

14. 1850 U.S. census, Andrew, Missouri, population schedule, Jefferson, p. 8A, dwelling 801, family 781, Moriah McIntosh; digital images, *ancestry.com*; citing National Archives and Records Administration microfilm M432.

15. Church of Jesus Christ of Latter-day Saints, "Mormon Pioneer Overland Travel, 1847-1868," database (www.lds.org/churchhistory/library/pioneercompany : accessed 22 Dec 2014), Maria Caldwell McIntosh travelled with the David Lewis Comnpany in 1851.

16. Church of Jesus Christ of Latter-day Saints,*Patriarchal Blessing,* Maria McIntosh by John Smith, Patriarch, No 386.

17. 1860 U.S. census, Shambip, Utah, population schedule, Clover, p. 450, dwelling 4028, family 3104, Maria McIntosh; digital images, *ancestry.com*; citing National Archives and Records Administration microfilm M653.

18. 1870 U.S. census, Washington, Utah, population schedule, Panaca, p. 7, dwelling 54, family 48, McIntosh, Marie; digital images, *ancestry.com*; citing National Archives and Records Administration microfilm M593.

19. 1870 U.S. census, Lincoln, Nevada, population schedule, Meadow Valley, p. 186, dwelling 66-68, family 45, McIntosh, Maria; digital images, *ancestry.com*; citing National Archives and Records Administration microfilm M593.

20. Brown, Beverly McIntosh and Marsha Lee McIntosh,*William McIntosh Diary, abridgement* (Self-published, Surprise, AZ. June 2002), p 83 September 24.

21. 1880 U.S. census, Tooele, Utah Territory, population schedule, Clover, enumeration district (ED) 79, p. 6C, Mackintosh, Caroline (Maria); digital images, *ancestry.com*; citing National Archives and Records Administration microfilm T9.

# Source Citations




22. Brown, Beverly McIntosh and Marsha Lee McIntosh,*William McIntosh Diary, abridgement* (Self-published, Surprise, AZ. June 2002), p.71, 14 August 1894.

23. Brown, Beverly McIntosh and Marsha Lee McIntosh,*William McIntosh Diary, abridgement* (Self-published, Surprise, AZ. June 2002), p 89 & 90, March 26, 1896.

24. Brown, Beverly McIntosh and Marsha Lee McIntosh,*William McIntosh Diary, abridgement* (Self-published, Surprise, AZ. June 2002), p 91, September 23, 1896.

25. Brown, Beverly McIntosh and Marsha Lee McIntosh,*William McIntosh Diary, abridgement* (Self-published, Surprise, AZ. June 2002), p 92, October 20, 1896.
"I am still alone. My folks don't write to me. My folks fret me all the day long. I don't think my wife is doing right well. She has poor health. She has gone from home and living with her son Albert on my farm in Tooele Co. I think she is better at home. My house is good and comfortable and enough to get along with."

26. Brown, Beverly McIntosh and Marsha Lee McIntosh,*William McIntosh Diary, abridgement* (Self-published, Surprise, AZ. June 2002), p 95, January 3, 1897.

27. *Scotland, Lanark, Glasgow, St. Andrews-by-the-Green Episopal Church, Baptisms 1812-1821,* Correspondence from researcher James A. Thompson letter dated March 9, 1974-Research by Hazel Weight
Ann 25 Jul 1813 Glasgow
Mary 19 March 1815 Glasgow
John 17 Jun 1817
Jane 20 July 1819 Glasgow.

28. Church of Jesus Christ of Latter-day Saints,*Patriarchal Blessing,* "...Maria McIntosh daughter of David & Ann Caldwell..."

29. ""Caldwells Maintain Family Legacy",*"(Tooele) Tooele Transcript/Bulletin.*

30. Harrison, Susan Eileen nee Ross,*McIntosh Ahnentafel Chart from Wm Alvin GEDCOM* (Collection of Bonnie Shields Williams GEDCOM on Floppy Diskette postmarked Aug 06, 2001), McIntosh Diskette. Repository: Bonnie S. Williams, RR 1 Box 247, N Hwy 2, Wilburton, Oklahoma, USA.
Fourth Generation

11. Mary Ann VAUGHN was born on 12 Jun 1791 in Perkers, Glascow, Scotland. She died on 22 Dec 1868 in St. John, Tooele, Ut and was buried in Clover, Tooele, Ut. She was sealed to her parents on 17 Jun 1994 in the Jordan River Utah temple. Mary was baptized in 1847. She was endowed on 8 Dec 1860 in the Endowment House.

31. International Society of Daughters of Utah Pioneers, editor,*Pioneer Women of Faith and Fortitude*, Volume III (Salt Lake City, Utah: Publishers Press, 1998), Mary Ann Vaughan Caldwell: 474. Repository: Family History Library, 35 North West Temple Street, Salt Lake City, Utah 84150-3400, USA, Call Number: 979 D36.

32. ""Caldwells maintain family legacy",*"(Tooele) Tooele Transcript/Bulletin.*

33. Daughters of Utah Pioneers, *Our Pioneer Heritage* (Salt Lake City, UT: Infobases, Inc., 1996), 19: 422. Repository: Family History Library, 35 North West Temple Street, Salt Lake City, Utah 84150-3400, USA, Call Number: 979.2 H2.

34. Frank Esshorn, editor, *Pioneers and Prominent Men of Utah comprising Photographs-Genealogies-Biographies. Pioneers are those men and women who came to Utah by wagon, hand cart or afoot, between July 24, 1847 and December 30, 1868, before the railroad. Prominent Men are stake presidents, ward bishops, governors, members of the bench, etc., who came to Utah after the coming of the railroad. The early history of the Church of Jesus Christ of Latter-Day Saints. In One Volume, Illustrated* (Salt Lake City, Utah: Utah Pioneers Book Publishing Company, 1913), McIntosh, William: 331 and 1059. Repository: Family History Library, 35 North West Temple Street, Salt Lake City, Utah 84150-3400, USA, Call Number: 979.2 D3e.

35. Andrew Jenson, editor, *Latter-day Saint Biographical Encyclopedia: A Compilation of Biographical Sketches of Prominent Men and Women in The Church of Jesus Christ of Latter-day Saints*, 4 v.: ports. (Salt Lake City, Utah: Western Epics, 1971), William McIntosh: V 4, page 647. Repository: Family History Library, 35 North West Temple Street, Salt Lake City, Utah 84150-3400, USA, Call Number: 920.0792.

36. Brown, Beverly McIntosh and Marsha Lee McIntosh,*William McIntosh Diary, abridgement* (Self-published, Surprise, AZ. June 2002), p 80 March 1 [1894].
... Today we are getting well along in years. I am 74 years old last September. My wife is about four years younger than myself.

37. Church of Jesus Christ of Latter-day Saints,*Patriarchal Blessing,* William McIntosh.

38. Brown, Beverly McIntosh and Marsha McIntosh, editors,*William McIntosh Diary 1857-1898, Abridgement* (Surprise, AZ: Self-published, June 2002), J-4.

39. Scotland, Church of Scotland (Glasgow, Lanarkshire, Scotland), "Parish registers for Barony, 1672-1854," McIntosh, William; FHL microfilm 1041478; "1819 - McIntosh - John McIntosh grocer Bridgeton & Grizel Rankin had their 2nd child born 16th Sept named William -Witnesses- James Rankin - James McIntosh"

40. McIntosh Reunion Descendants, McIntosh - Descendants of John & Girsey (Grace) (Grizel) Rankin McIntosh (Attachment to Aug 17, 1958

# Source Citations



Newsletter - copy in Collection of Bonnie S. Williams), Repository: Bonnie S. Williams, RR 1 Box 247, N Hwy 2, Wilburton, Oklahoma, USA.
William (son of John McINTOSH & Girsey RANKIN) md. Maria CALDWELL
Children:
John Ephraim
Mary Ann
David Hyrum
William Henry md. Mary Elizabeth KEELE
James F. md. Ann JORDAN
Millisa Jane md. Jacob KEELE
Alice Maria md. Thomas L. BURRIDGE
Abram E. md. Mary Louise GUHL
L. Elizabeth md. Heber McBRIDE
Caroline J. md. Joseph JORDAN
Joseph Albert md. Ann RUSSELL.
This single page attachment indicates that the parents of John McIntosh are William McIntosh & Isabell and is indicative of what our side of the family knew of our McIntosh cousins at that time in August 1958.

41. Canada, Ontario. Marriage Registers of Upper Canada/Canada West, Volume 5: Page 59; Family History Library, Salt Lake City; William McIntosh, of Dalhousie, to Maria Caldwell, of Lanark. 27 Sept. 1841. Rev. Macalister. Wit. David Caldwell and John Barrowman.

42. Robert Sergeant and J.R. Ernest Miller, editors,*Some Early Lanark County Marriages 1830-1869* (Kingston, Ontario, Canada: Ontario Genealogical Society, 1993), Bathurst District Marriages 1830-1857: Page 4. Repository: Family History Library, 35 North West Temple Street, Salt Lake City, Utah 84150-3400, USA, Call Number: 911.382 K29s;
Caldwell, Maria, address Lanark, date 09-27-1841, spouse McIntosh, William, address Dalousie, minister McAlister.
Page 19 - McIntosh, William, address Dalhousie, date 09-27-1841, spouse Caldwell, Maria, address Lanark, minister McAlister.

# William McIntosh

Page 1

| | | | |
|---|---|---|---|
| **Name:** | **William McIntosh** [1,2,3,4] | **Sex:** | M |
| **AKA:** | William Gee McIntosh [5] | | |

| | | | |
|---|---|---|---|
| **Birth Date:** | 16 Sep 1819 | | |
| **Place:** | Barony, Lanarkshire, Scotland, United Kingdom [6,7,8,9] | | |
| **Death Date:** | 4 May 1899 | **Place:** | Mount Pleasant, Sanpete, Utah, United States |
| **Burial Date:** | May 1899 | **Place:** | Mount Pleasant, Sanpete, Utah, United States [10] |
| **Cause of Death:** | Le Grippe (Influenza) | | |
| **Bapt.(LDS):** | Aug 1838 | **Place:** | , Lanark, Ontario, Canada |
| **Conf.(LDS):** | 1 Jan 1839 | **Place:** | , Lanark, Ontario, Canada |
| **Init.(LDS):** | 24 Aug 1861 | **Temple:** | Endowment House |
| **Endow.(LDS):** | 24 Aug 1861 | **Temple:** | Endowment House |

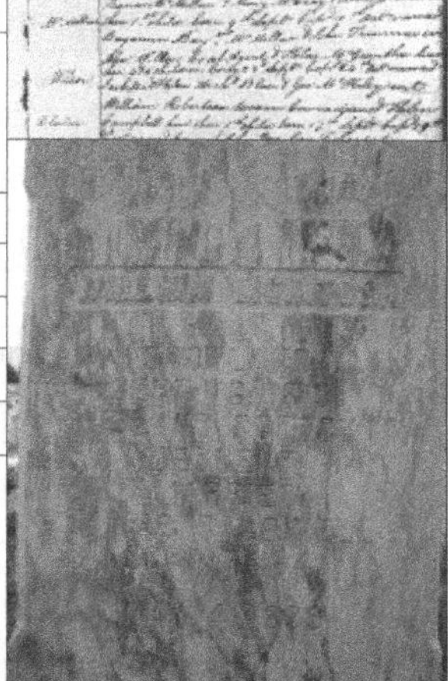

**Events**

1. He emigrated on 11 May 1821 from , Lanark, Scotland, United Kingdom.[11]
2. He worked as a sheepman, blacksmith, wagon maker, farmer over his lifetime about 1838 1890.
3. He had a residence from 28 Oct 1841 to Apr 1845 in Toledo, Lucas, Ohio, United States.[11]
4. He had a residence from Apr 1845 to Aug 1845 in Oregon, Lucas, Ohio, United States.[12]
5. He had a residence from Aug 1845 to Apr 1847 in Erie, Monroe, Michigan, United States.
6. He had a residence from May 1847 to Jun 1849 in Saint Louis, , Missouri, United States.[12]
7. He appeared on the census on 19 Nov 1850 in Jefferson City, Cole, Missouri, United States.[13]

# William McIntosh



8. Migration: David Lewis Company, Between 1 May 1851 and 9 Sep 1851, Salt Lake City, Great Salt Lake, Utah Territory, United States.[14]
9. He resided at North Kanyon Ward 1852 To 1853 in Bountiful, Davis, Utah Territory, United States.[15]
10. He received a Patriarchal blessing.[16]
11. Census Index: William McIntosh, 1856, West Jordan, Great Salt Lake, Utah Territory, United States.[17]
12. He was St John LDS Branch President in 1859 in Rush Valley, Shambip, Utah Territory.
13. He appeared on the census on 11 Oct 1860 in Clover, Shambip, Utah Territory, United States.[18]
14. He was President of Clover Branch, Tooele Stake, Utah between 1864 and 1865 in Clover, Shambip, Utah Territory, United States.[4]

Mormon Pioneer Overland Travel, David Lewis Company, 1851, William McIntosh & family page 1 of 2

15. He served a mission from Apr 1866 to 1871 in Panaca, Lincoln, Nevada, United States.
16. He appeared on the census on 10 Jun 1870 in Panaca, Washington, Utah Territory.[19]
17. He appeared on the census on 28 Jul 1870 in Meadow Valley, Lincoln, Nevada, United States.[20]
18. He served a mission between 1871 and 1872 in Panguitch, Iron, Utah Territory, United States.[21]
19. He worked as a Day Laborer between 1871 and 1872 in Panaca, Washington, Utah, United States.
20. He owned land NE 1/4 x SW 1/4 and N 1/2 x SE 1/4, Section 19, Township 5-S, Range 5-W (containing 120 acres) on 27 Jul 1872 in Saint John, Tooele, Utah Territory, United States.[22]
21. Tax Rolls: 1873, , Tooele, Utah Territory, United States.[23]
22. Tax Rolls: 1874, , Tooele, Utah Territory, United States.[24]
23. Marks and Brands: Place of Brand - Left hip or thigh, 4 Jun 1875, Saint John, Tooele, Utah Territory, United States.[25]
24. He submitted an amendment of his application no. 1706.[26]
25. He received his Citizenship Certificate found in land records citizenship on 24 Jul 1877 in , Tooele, Utah Territory, United States.[27]
26. He appeared on the census on 12 Jun 1880 in Clover, Tooele, Utah Territory, United States.[28]
27. He had health issues about 1886 in Saint John, Tooele, Utah Territory, United States.[29]
28. Witness to a land sale: Section 19, Township 5-S, Range 5-W for Caroline Caldwell McIntosh, on 19 Jul 1888, in Saint John, Tooele, Utah Territory, United States.[30]
29. He owned land SW 1/4 x NE 1/4, Sec 19, Twp 5-S, Range 5-W, containing 40 acres. on 29 Nov 1889 in Saint John, Tooele, Utah Territory, United States.[31]
30. Patent: 10 Dec 1890, in Saint John, Tooele, Utah Territory, United States.[32]
31. He had a residence from 15 Nov 1892 to 4 May 1899 in Mount Pleasant, Sanpete, Utah, United States.[33]
32. He was ordained a High Priest by Canute Peterson, Stake President on 18 Aug 1895 in Mount Pleasant, Sanpete, Utah Territory, United States.[34]

| | | | |
|---|---|---|---|
| **Father:** | John McIntosh Sr. (1795-1875)[35,36] | | |
| **Mother:** | Girsel Rankin (1794-1853)[36] | | |
| **SealP (LDS):** | 21 Nov 1894 | **Temple:** | Manti Utah Temple |
| **Spouse:** | ***Maria Caldwell (17 Feb 1824 - 27 Jul 1897)**[37,38,39,40,41,42,43,44] | | |
| **Marr. Date:** | 27 Sep 1841 | | |
| **Place:** | Bathurst, Lanark, , Canada [45,46,47] | | |
| **SealS (LDS):** | 24 Aug 1861 | **Temple:** | Endowment House |

# Source Citations




1. Brown, Beverly McIntosh and Marsha McIntosh, editors,*William McIntosh Diary 1857-1898, Abridgement* (Surprise, AZ: Self-published, June 2002).

2. Daughters of Utah Pioneers,*Our Pioneer Heritage* (Salt Lake City, UT: Infobases, Inc., 1996), 19: 422. Repository: Family History Library, 35 North West Temple Street, Salt Lake City, Utah 84150-3400, USA, Call Number: 979.2 H2.

3. Frank Esshorn, editor,*Pioneers and Prominent Men of Utah comprising Photographs-Genealogies-Biographies. Pioneers are those men and women who came to Utah by wagon, hand cart or afoot, between July 24, 1847 and December 30, 1868, before the railroad. Prominent Men are stake presidents, ward bishops, governors, members of the bench, etc., who came to Utah after the coming of the railroad. The early history of the Church of Jesus Christ of Latter-Day Saints. In One Volume, Illustrated* (Salt Lake City, Utah: Utah Pioneers Book Publishing Company, 1913), McIntosh, William: 331 and 1059. Repository: Family History Library, 35 North West Temple Street, Salt Lake City, Utah 84150-3400, USA, Call Number: 979.2 D3e.

4. Andrew Jenson, editor,*Latter-day Saint Biographical Encyclopedia: A Compilation of Biographical Sketches of Prominent Men and Women in The Church of Jesus Christ of Latter-day Saints*, 4 v.: ports. (Salt Lake City, Utah: Western Epics, 1971), William McIntosh: V 4, page 647. Repository: Family History Library, 35 North West Temple Street, Salt Lake City, Utah 84150-3400, USA, Call Number: 920.0792.

5. Daughters of the Utah Pioneers,*History of Tooele County - Old Manuscript* (Salt Lake City, Utah: Publishers Press, 1961), 537.

6. Brown, Beverly McIntosh and Marsha Lee McIntosh,*William McIntosh Diary, abridgement* (Self-published, Surprise, AZ. June 2002), p 80 March 1 [1894].
... Today we are getting well along in years. I am 74 years old last September. My wife is about four years younger than myself.

7. Church of Jesus Christ of Latter-day Saints,*Patriarchal Blessing,* William McIntosh.

8. Brown, Beverly McIntosh and Marsha McIntosh, editors,*William McIntosh Diary 1857-1898, Abridgement* (Surprise, AZ: Self-published, June 2002), J-4.

9. Scotland, Church of Scotland (Glasgow, Lanarkshire, Scotland), "Parish registers for Barony, 1672-1854," McIntosh, William; FHL microfilm 1041478; "1819 - McIntosh - John McIntosh grocer Bridgeton & Grizel Rankin had their 2nd child born 16th Sept named William -Witnesses- James Rankin - James McIntosh"

10. Utah Division of State History, "Cemetery & Burial Database," database (https://heritage.utah.gov/history/cemeteries), William McIntosh.

11. Brown, Beverly McIntosh and Marsha McIntosh, editors,*William McIntosh Diary 1857-1898, Abridgement* (Surprise, AZ: Self-published, June 2002), J-1.

12. Brown, Beverly McIntosh and Marsha McIntosh, editors,*William McIntosh Diary 1857-1898, Abridgement* (Surprise, AZ: Self-published, June 2002), J-2.

13. 1850 U.S. census, Andrew, Missouri, population schedule, Jefferson, p. 8, dwelling 801, family 781, William McIntosh; digital images, *ancestry.com*; citing National Archives and Records Administration microfilm M432.

14. Church of Jesus Christ of Latter-day Saints, "Mormon Pioneer Overland Travel, 1847-1868," database (www.lds.org/churchhistory/library/pioneercompany : accessed 22 Dec 2014), William McIntosh travelled with the David Lewis Comnpany in 1851.

15. Church of Jesus Christ of Latter-day Saints, Registry of Names of Persons Residing in the Various Wards as to Bishop's Reports (Salt Lake City, Utah, United States of America), McIntosh, William, North Kanyon Ward (Bountiful); Family History Library, Salt Lake City.

16. Church of Jesus Christ of Latter-day Saints,*Patriarchal Blessing,* William McIntosh by John Smith, No. 385.

17. Utah State Census Index, 1856, Utah, population schedule; HISTORICAL BACKGROUND
Utah pioneers petitioned for statehood for the second time in 1856. To show that Utah Territory held enough population to become a state, a census was taken in January and February of that year. In December, a disappointed Governor Brigham Young reported to the territorial legislature that the petition had been rejected. The following passage from that report shows Governor Young was anxious to suggest Utah had a large population. "The enumeration of the inhabitants showed a population of near 77,000 in this territory, and it is presumed that the addition to our numbers, since that was taken, would amount to about twenty thousand. This gives an aggregate equal to or exceeding the ratio of representation for congressmen, removing every objection, if any were made, to our admission, on the score of insufficient population." (Brigham Young, "Governor's Message," Deseret News [Salt Lake City, Utah], December 24, 1856, p. 333, col. 2).
In fact, there is reason to believe the territorial population was considerably less than presented in the Governor's report. The 1850/1851 census of Utah showed only 11,380 residents. The 1860 census showed 40,273. Thus, the 77,000 figure appears to be far too large, and Govenor Young's estimate that 20,000 people entered the territory in one year also seems exaggerated.
Indeed, some names on the 1856 census seem to be fictitious, repeated, or those of non-residents of Utah Territory. For example, ....
A striking feature of the census and further evidence of padding is that virtually every page and most columns begins with a different surname from that ending the previous one; the last family in each column has exactly enough members to reach the last available line.
Index Publishing presents this index for genealogists, historians, demographers, and other researachers who wish to quickly determine where specific individuals are located on the 1856 census of Utah Territory. (Compiled by Bryan Lee Dilts, Index Publishing, PO Box 11476, SLC, UT 1983).

18. 1860 U.S. census, Shambip, Utah, population schedule, Clover, p. 450, dwelling 4028, family 3104, Wm McIntosh; digital images, *ancestry.com*; citing National Archives and Records Administration microfilm M653.

# Source Citations




19. 1870 U.S. census, Washington, Utah, population schedule, Panaca, p. 7, dwelling 54, family 48, McIntosh, William; digital images, *ancestry.com*; citing National Archives and Records Administration microfilm M593.

20. 1870 U.S. census, Lincoln, Nevada, population schedule, Meadow Valley, p. 186, dwelling 66-68, family 45, McIntosh, Wm; digital images, *ancestry.com*; citing National Archives and Records Administration microfilm M593.

21. Kate B. Carter, editor, *Our Pioneer Heritage*, 20 v.: ill., maps, ports. (Salt Lake City, Utah: Daughters of Utah Pioneers, 1958-1977). Repository: Family History Library, 35 North West Temple Street, Salt Lake City, Utah 84150-3400, USA, Call Number: 979.2 H2.

22. Bureau of Land Management, Record Group 49, *United States. General Land Office.* (Washington, D.C.: The National Archives), Date of Sale 27 Jul 1872; Homestead Application No. 1706; Final Cert No. 1137 dated 9 Sep 1879.

23. Tooele, Utah, United States of America, 1873 Tax Book, entry for McIntosh, William; FHL microfilm 482,525.

24. Tooele, Utah, United States of America, 1874 Tax Book, entry for McIntosh, Wm; FHL microfilm 482,525.

25. Utah, Record of Marks and Brands for the State of Utah, Embracing all the Marks and Brands Recorded from December 9, 1847 to December 31, 1884, 43: Wm. McIntosh, June 4, 1875, St. John's,Tooele Co; Utah State Archives and Record Service, Salt Lake City.

26. Bureau of Land Management, Record Group 49, *United States. General Land Office.* (Washington, D.C.: The National Archives), amendment to application no. 1706.

27. Utah. Court (U.S. Land Office). Salt Lake City, *Certificate of Citizenship* (U.S. Land Office, Salt Lake City, Utah, 1877), "...said Court that the said William McIntosh be admitted , and he was accordingly admitted by the said Court to b e a CITIZEN OF THE UNITED STATES OF AMERICA."

28. 1880 U.S. census, Tooele, Utah Territory, population schedule, Clover, enumeration district (ED) 79, p. 6C, Mackintosh, William; digital images, *ancestry.com*; citing National Archives and Records Administration microfilm T9.

29. Brown, Beverly McIntosh and Marsha Lee McIntosh, *William McIntosh Diary, abridgement* (Self-published, Surprise, AZ. June 2002), p.71 1891 - 14 August.

30. Bureau of Land Management, Record Group 49, *United States. General Land Office.* (Washington, D.C.: The National Archives), Testimony by David H Caldwell on behalf of Caroline E McIntosh mentions Wm McIntosh and Thomas Burridge.

31. Bureau of Land Management, Record Group 49, *United States. General Land Office.* (Washington, D.C.: The National Archives), Application No. 8552; Addition to Homestead No. 1706; Final Homestead Certificate No. 1137 dated 9 Sep 1879.

32. Utah, Tooele County, *Patent Record Book,* # 1, page 185.

33. Brown, Beverly McIntosh and Marsha McIntosh, editors, *William McIntosh Diary 1857-1898, Abridgement* (Surprise, AZ: Self-published, June 2002), pages 73, 80, 83.

34. Brown, Beverly McIntosh and Marsha McIntosh, editors, *William McIntosh Diary 1857-1898, Abridgement* (Surprise, AZ: Self-published, June 2002), page 85.

35. Church of Jesus Christ of Latter-day Saints, *Patriarchal Blessing,* "...William McIntosh son of John and Girsey McIntosh..."

36. Brown, Beverly McIntosh and Marsha Lee McIntosh, *William McIntosh Diary, abridgement* (Self-published, Surprise, AZ. June 2002).

37. International Society of Daughters of Utah Pioneers, editor, *Pioneer Women of Faith and Fortitude*, Volume III (Salt Lake City, Utah: Publishers Press, 1998), Maria Caldwell McIntosh: page 1946. Repository: Family History Library, 35 North West Temple Street, Salt Lake City, Utah 84150-3400, USA, Call Number: 979 D36.

38. Church of Jesus Christ of Latter-day Saints, Patron sheets, 1969-1991 (Salt Lake City: Filmed by the Genealogical Society of Utah, 1970-1991), Batch 5003057, Sheet 22, Film 1553185.
Maria CALDWELL
Sex: F
Event(s):
Birth: 17 Feb 1824, Lanark, Lanark, Ontario
Parents:
Father: David CALDWELL
Mother: Mary Ann VAUGHAN.

39. Brown, Beverly McIntosh and Marsha Lee McIntosh, *William McIntosh Diary, abridgement* (Self-published, Surprise, AZ. June 2002), J-3 Maria's family.

40. Brown, Beverly McIntosh and Marsha Lee McIntosh, *William McIntosh Diary, abridgement* (Self-published, Surprise, AZ. June 2002), p 80 March 1, 1894.

41. Church of Jesus Christ of Latter-day Saints, *Patriarchal Blessing,* "...Maria McIntosh...born February 17th, 1824, Landrick County, Upper Canada." (Lanark County).

# Source Citations



42. J.R. Ernest Miller, *Scottish Settlers to Bathurst Area for Bathurst District: includes Lanark, Leeds, Carleton, Frontenac, and Renfrew settlers. Extracted from Dictionary of Scottish Settlers and other Sources. Includes "Supplement to Scottish Settlers to Bathurst Area for Bathurst District: includes Perth and area settlers with spouses & or children / extracted from various sources by J.R. Ernest Miller, 1987".* (Kingston, Ontario, Canada: Ontario Genealogical Society, 1987), page 2. Repository: Family History Library, 35 North West Temple Street, Salt Lake City, Utah 84150-3400, USA, Call Number: 971.3 W2m.

43. Brown, Beverly McIntosh and Marsha Lee McIntosh, *William McIntosh Diary, abridgement* (Self-published, Surprise, AZ. June 2002), p 96 & 97 July 23, 1897. "My wife was taken with a cramp in her stomach and that continued with her until July 27, 1897 then she died, seemingly unconscious of trouble or pain. She was buried in the Mt. Pleasant burying ground, Sanpete Co., Utah. August 23, she was buried".

44. Utah State Historical Society, "Utah, Cemetery Inventory, 1847-2000," database(https://www.ancestry.com/search/collections/utahburials/), Maria Caldwell McIntosh.

45. McIntosh Reunion Descendants, McIntosh - Descendants of John & Girsey (Grace) (Grizel) Rankin McIntosh (Attachment to Aug 17, 1958 Newsletter - copy in Collection of Bonnie S. Williams), Repository: Bonnie S. Williams, RR 1 Box 247, N Hwy 2, Wilburton, Oklahoma, USA.
William (son of John McINTOSH & Girsey RANKIN) md. Maria CALDWELL
Children:
John Ephraim
Mary Ann
David Hyrum
William Henry md. Mary Elizabeth KEELE
James F. md. Ann JORDAN
Millisa Jane md. Jacob KEELE
Alice Maria md. Thomas L. BURRIDGE
Abram E. md. Mary Louise GUHL
L. Elizabeth md. Heber McBRIDE
Caroline J. md. Joseph JORDAN
Joseph Albert md. Ann RUSSELL.
This single page attachment indicates that the parents of John McIntosh are William McIntosh & Isabell and is indicative of what our side of the family knew of our McIntosh cousins at that time in August 1958.

46. Canada, Ontario. Marriage Registers of Upper Canada/Canada West, Volume 5: Page 59; Family History Library, Salt Lake City; William McIntosh, of Dalhousie, to Maria Caldwell, of Lanark. 27 Sept. 1841. Rev. Macalister. Wit. David Caldwell and John Barrowman.

47. Robert Sergeant and J.R. Ernest Miller, editors, *Some Early Lanark County Marriages 1830-1869* (Kingston, Ontario, Canada: Ontario Genealogical Society, 1993), Bathurst District Marriages 1830-1857: Page 4. Repository: Family History Library, 35 North West Temple Street, Salt Lake City, Utah 84150-3400, USA, Call Number: 911.382 K29s;
Caldwell, Maria, address Lanark, date 09-27-1841, spouse McIntosh, William, address Dalousie, minister McAlister.
Page 19 - McIntosh, William, address Dalhousie, date 09-27-1841, spouse Caldwell, Maria, address Lanark, minister McAlister.

# John Ephraim McIntosh and Margaret Smith

| **Husband** | **John Ephraim McIntosh**[1,2] | |
|---|---|---|
| Born | 13 Jun 1842 | Toledo, Lucas, Ohio, United States[3,4,5] |
| Died | 2 Feb 1889 | Saint John, Tooele, Utah Territory, United States[6,7] |
| Address | Johnson's Pass, Utah, USA | |
| Cause of Death | Accidentally fell under wheels of his wagon on steep pass | |
| Buried | 1889 | Rush Valley, Tooele, Utah, United States |
| Notes | Beverly Brown has been unable to locate John's grave as of Aug 2007, but assumes it is in the St. John City Cemetery. She has declared one of the illegibly marked graves as John's, since no one has been able to find his grave. He died in St. John, why wouldn't he buried here? | |
| Bapt.(LDS) | 1 Jan 1852 | |
| Conf.(LDS) | 1 Jan 1852 | |
| Init.(LDS) | 16 Sep 1865 | Endowment House |
| Endow.(LDS) | 16 Sep 1865 | Endowment House |
| Father | William McIntosh (1819-1899) [8,9,10,11] | |
| Mother | Maria Caldwell (1824-1897) [12] | |
| SealP (LDS) | 11 Oct 1893 | Manti Utah Temple |
| Marriage | Cir 1864 | Saint John, Tooele, Utah Territory, United States[13] |
| SealS (LDS) | 24 May 1995 | Jordan River Utah Temple |

**Events**

1. He was a member of The Church of Jesus Christ of Latter-day Saints.[14]
2. He had a residence from 13 Jun 1842 to Apr 1845 in Toledo, Lucas, Ohio, United States.[15]
   "We came to Toledo, Ohio. We had about 50 cents when we landed at Toledo, as sickly a place as I ever saw."
3. He had a residence from Apr 1845 to Aug 1845 in Oregon, Lucas, Ohio, United States.[16,17]
   Spring - William and his family moved to Oregon, Ohio, just south of Toledo.
4. He had a residence from Aug 1845 to Apr 1847 in Erie, Monroe, Michigan, United States.[16]
   1845 Fall - William and his family moved to Michigan where his parents lived.
5. He had a residence from May 1847 to 1851 in Saint Louis, , Missouri, United States.[18]
   "And in the Spring of 1847 we bought a yoke of oxen, a cow and a wagon, about all the property we had. And took our passage on a canal boat at Toledo. We was bound then for St Louis as the Saints were arriving from Nauvoo."
6. He appeared on the census on 19 Nov 1850 in Jefferson City, Cole, Missouri, United States.[19]
   Line 40 - William McIntosh, age 31, male, waggon maker, born in LC. (LC is an unknown location)
   Line 41 - Meoriah McIntosh, age 27, female, born in LC. (Maria) (LC is an unknown location)
   **Line 42 - John McIntosh, age 6, male, born in O (Ohio), attended school within the year.**
   Line 1 (next page) - William H McIntosh, age 1, male, born in Mo. (Missouri)

# John Ephraim McIntosh and Margaret Smith

7. Migration: David Lewis Company, Between 1 May 1851 and 9 Sep 1851, Salt Lake City, Great Salt Lake, Utah Territory, United States.[20]
   Company List:
   **McIntosh, John Ephraim (age 9)**
   McIntosh, Maria Caldwell (age 27)
   McIntosh, William (age 32)
   McIntosh, William Henry (age 2)

Mormon Pioneer Overland Travel, David Lewis Company, 1851, John Ephraim McIntosh, page 1 of 2

8. He appeared on the census on 11 Oct 1860 in Clover, Shambip, Utah Territory, United States.[21]
   Line 25) Wm McIntosh, age 40, male, farmer, born in Scotland
   Line 26) Maria McIntosh, age 36, female, born in Canada
   Line 27) **Jno E McIntosh, age 18, male, born in Ohio**
   Line 28) Wm. H McIntosh, age 11, male, born in Missouri, in school
   Line 29) Jas F McIntosh, age 8, male, born in Utah Territory, in school
   Line 30) Malissa J McIntosh, age 6, female, born in Utah Territory, in school
   Line 31) Alice M McIntosh, age 3, female, born in Utah Territory
   Line 32) Abm E McIntosh, age 6/12, male, born in Utah Territory

9. Witness to a land sale: between Abraham V. Caldwell and George Dymock, on 10 May 1872, in Saint John, Tooele, Utah, United States.

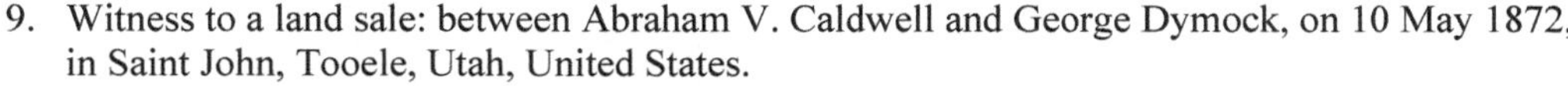

10. He appeared on the census on 12 Jun 1880 in Panaca, Lincoln, Nevada, United States.[22]
    **Line 47 - McIntosh, John, white, male, age 38, head, married, laborer, born in Ohio, father born in Scotland, mother born in Canada.**
    Line 48 - McIntosh, Margaret, white, female, age 31, wife, married, keeping house, born in Scotland, father born in Scotland, mother born in Scotland.
    Line 49 - McIntosh, John, white, male, age 2, son, single, born in Nevada, father born in Ohio, mother born in Scotland.
    Line 50 - McIntosh, Mary, white, female, age 4/12, Jan, daughter, single, born in Nevada, father born in Ohio, mother born in Scotland.

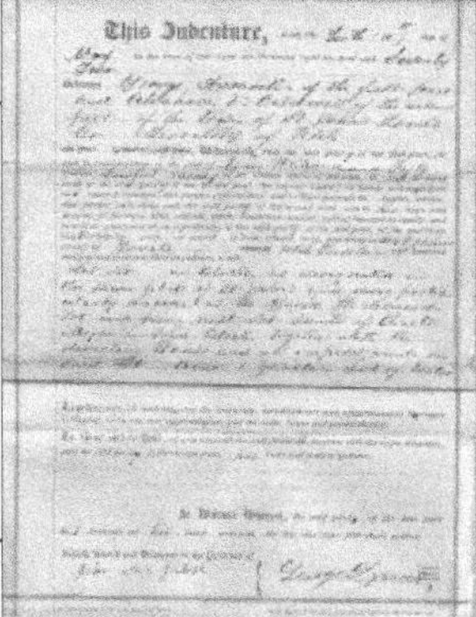
This Indenture,

John McIntosh, witness to sale of land between Abraham V. Caldwell and George Dymock

11. His obituary was published on 8 Feb 1889 in Saint John, Tooele, Utah Territory, United States. William copied the newspaper article of his son's accident and death.

**Fatal accident at St. John**
**St. John, Tooele, Co., Feb. 8, 1889**

A sad accident resulting in the almost instant death of Brother John E. McIntosh occurred on the Johnson Pass, between Rush and Skull Valleys about 1 mile below the divide at half past four on Saturday the 2nd.

The deceased started from his parent's house on the morning in question to his sheep camp in charge of a team laden with grain and provisions. He was accompanied by Mr. Henry Newman. Arriving on top of the divide and on going down the canyon, the road being very difficult to travel and a considerable downgrade, the team started to run, throwing Brother McIntosh from the wagon.

He fell between the two wheels. The hind wheels passing over his back, fracturing his ribs on both sides and slightly brusing the right side of his head. Mr. Newman stopped the team, assisted the unfortunate man and laid him on some blankets and immediately afterward started down the canyon for help.

He met Mr. S. J. Stookey coming up the canyon on horseback. On returning to the place of the accident, they found him still alive but unable to speak and in about fifteen minutes from the time he received his injuries he breathed his last.

His body was then conveyed to the home of his parents who he had left only a few hours before in good health.

The deceased leaves a widow and three children who reside at Eagle Rock, Idaho. There is also his aged parents, brothers and sisters and a large circle of friends sadly mourn his loss.

He was born in East Toledo, Michigan on June 13, 1842, and was a quiet, inoffensive man and devoted husband and father.

An inquest on the body of the deceased was held at St. John precinct before Mr. John McIntosh, J.P. The jurors found as their verdict that the said John E. McIntosh came to his death on Johnson Pass by being accidentally thrown under the wheels of his wagon which passed over his body causing almost instant death.

The jurors were David H. Caldwell, David Charles and Nephi Draper. The funeral services were held on Wednesday last at St. John. C. N. Ahlquist.

# John Ephraim McIntosh and Margaret Smith

| Wife | Margaret Smith | |
|---|---|---|
| AKA | Mary McIntosh, Margaret Miller, Mary Smith, Mary Margaret Smith | |
| Born | Cal 1849 | Scotland, United Kingdom |
| Died | date: | place: |
| Buried | date: | place: |

**Events**

1. She has conflicting birth information of 1849 and Ireland.
2. She appeared on the census on 12 Jun 1880 in Panaca, Lincoln, Nevada, United States.[23]
   Line 47 - McIntosh, John, white, male, age 38, head, married, laborer, born in Ohio, father born in Scotland, mother born in Canada.
   **Line 48 - McIntosh, Margaret, white, female, age 31, wife, married, keeping house, born in Scotland, father born in Scotland, mother born in Scotland.**
   Line 49 - McIntosh, John, white, male, age 2, son, single, born in Nevada, father born in Ohio, mother born in Scotland.
   Line 50 - McIntosh, Mary, white, female, age 4/12, Jan, daughter, single, born in Nevada, father born in Ohio, mother born in Scotland.
3. She had a residence on 2 Feb 1898 in Eagle Rock, Bingham, Idaho, United States.[24]
4. She had a residence in 1915 in Pocatello, Bannock, Idaho, United States.[25] McIntosh, Margaret, (wid John E), r 436 N Main.

**Events: Marriage**

1. Alt Marriage: 1871 1877, Panaca, Lincoln, Nevada, United States.[26]
2. They have conflicting marriage information of Margaret Miller.

## Children

| 1 M | John McIntosh | |
|---|---|---|
| Born | Cal 1878 | Panaca, Lincoln, Nevada, United States |
| Died | date: | place: |
| Buried | date: | place: |
| Bapt.(LDS) | 7 Jun 2003 | Provo Utah Temple |
| Conf.(LDS) | 7 Jun 2003 | Provo Utah Temple |
| Init.(LDS) | 27 Dec 2003 | Guatemala City Guatemala Temple |
| Endow.(LDS) | 27 Jan 2004 | Guatemala City Guatemala Temple |
| SealP (LDS) | 26 Feb 2004 | Guatemala City Guatemala Temple |
| Spouse | | |

**Events**

1. He appeared on the census on 12 Jun 1880 in Panaca, Lincoln, Nevada, United States.[23]
   Line 47 - McIntosh, John, white, male, age 38, head, married, laborer, born in Ohio, father born in Scotland, mother born in Canada.
   Line 48 - McIntosh, Margaret, white, female, age 31, wife, married, keeping house, born in scotland, father born in Scotland, mother born in Scotland.
   **Line 49 - McIntosh, John, white, male, age 2, son, single, born in Nevada, father born in Ohio, mother born in Scotland.**
   Line 50 - McIntosh, Mary, white, female, age 4/12, Jan, daughter, single, born in Nevada, father born in Ohio, mother born in Scotland.

# John Ephraim McIntosh and Margaret Smith

| Children (cont.) | | |
|---|---|---|
| 2 F | **Mary McIntosh** | |
| Born | Jan 1880 | Panaca, Lincoln, Nevada, United States |
| Died | date: | place: |
| Buried | date: | place: |
| Bapt.(LDS) | 23 Sep 2003 | Louisville Kentucky Temple |
| Conf.(LDS) | 23 Sep 2003 | Louisville Kentucky Temple |
| Init.(LDS) | 12 Mar 2004 | Louisville Kentucky Temple |
| Endow.(LDS) | 26 Mar 2004 | Louisville Kentucky Temple |
| SealP (LDS) | 27 Mar 2004 | Louisville Kentucky Temple |
| Spouse | | |

**Events**

1. She appeared on the census on 12 Jun 1880 in Panaca, Lincoln, Nevada, United States.[23]
   Line 47 - McIntosh, John, white, male, age 38, head, married, laborer, born in Ohio, father born in Scotland, mother born in Canada.
   Line 48 - McIntosh, Margaret, white, female, age 31, wife, married, keeping house, born in scotland, father born in Scotland, mother born in Scotland.
   Line 49 - McIntosh, John, white, male, age 2, son, single, born in Nevada, father born in Ohio, mother born in Scotland.
   **Line 50 - McIntosh, Mary, white, female, age 4/12, Jan, daughter, single, born in Nevada, father born in Ohio, mother born in Scotland.**

# Source Citations


1. Brown, Beverly McIntosh and Marsha Lee McIntosh,*William McIntosh Diary, abridgement* (Self-published, Surprise, AZ. June 2002).

2. McIntosh Reunion Descendants, McIntosh - Descendants of John & Girsey (Grace) (Grizel) Rankin McIntosh (Attachment to Aug 17, 1958 Newsletter - copy in Collection of Bonnie S. Williams), Repository: Bonnie S. Williams, RR 1 Box 247, N Hwy 2, Wilburton, Oklahoma, USA. John Ephraim (son of William [McIntosh] & Maria CALDWELL). John Ephraim McINTOSH is a Grandson of John McIntosh & Girsey RANKIN.

This single page attachment indicates that the parents of John McIntosh are William McIntosh & Isabell and is indicative of what our side of the family knew of our McIntosh cousins at that time in August 1958.

3. Brown, Beverly McIntosh and Marsha Lee McIntosh,*William McIntosh Diary, abridgement* (Self-published, Surprise, AZ. June 2002), Toledo was part of Michigan until after the "Ohio-Michigan War" in 1836.

4. Church of Jesus Christ of Latter-day Saints, Record of members, 1852-1941; annual genealogical report, Form E, 1907-1948. West Jordan Ward (Utah). ([Salt Lake City, Utah: Filmed by the Genealogical Society of Utah, 1950]; 3 microfilm reels; 35 mm. Record of members 1852-1923; Family History Library; Film 27416.).

5. Church of Jesus Christ of Latter-day Saints, Early Church Information File, 1830-1900 (Salt Lake City, Utah, United States of America), MacIntosh, John Ephraim; FHL microfilm 889368, item 817; Name: MacIntosh - John Ephraim.
Historians Office, Patriarchal Blessings, Vol. 26, page 98

6. Brown, Beverly McIntosh and Marsha Lee McIntosh,*William McIntosh Diary, abridgement* (Self-published, Surprise, AZ. June 2002), pages 67 and 68.

7. Brown, Beverly McIntosh and Marsha Lee McIntosh,*William McIntosh Diary, abridgement* (Self-published, Surprise, AZ. June 2002), p 71, October 20 , 1891.

8. Brown, Beverly McIntosh and Marsha McIntosh, editors,*William McIntosh Diary 1857-1898, Abridgement* (Surprise, AZ: Self-published, June 2002).

9. Daughters of Utah Pioneers, *Our Pioneer Heritage* (Salt Lake City, UT: Infobases, Inc., 1996), 19: 422. Repository: Family History Library, 35 North West Temple Street, Salt Lake City, Utah 84150-3400, USA, Call Number: 979.2 H2.

10. Frank Esshorn, editor, *Pioneers and Prominent Men of Utah comprising Photographs-Genealogies-Biographies. Pioneers are those men and women who came to Utah by wagon, hand cart or afoot, between July 24, 1847 and December 30, 1868, before the railroad. Prominent Men are stake presidents, ward bishops, governors, members of the bench, etc., who came to Utah after the coming of the railroad. The early history of the Church of Jesus Christ of Latter-Day Saints. In One Volume, Illustrated* (Salt Lake City, Utah: Utah Pioneers Book Publishing Company, 1913), McIntosh, William: 331 and 1059. Repository: Family History Library, 35 North West Temple Street, Salt Lake City, Utah 84150-3400, USA, Call Number: 979.2 D3e.

11. Andrew Jenson, editor, *Latter-day Saint Biographical Encyclopedia: A Compilation of Biographical Sketches of Prominent Men and Women in The Church of Jesus Christ of Latter-day Saints*, 4 v.: ports. (Salt Lake City, Utah: Western Epics, 1971), William McIntosh: V 4, page 647. Repository: Family History Library, 35 North West Temple Street, Salt Lake City, Utah 84150-3400, USA, Call Number: 920.0792.

12. International Society of Daughters of Utah Pioneers, editor,*Pioneer Women of Faith and Fortitude*, Volume III (Salt Lake City, Utah: Publishers Press, 1998), Maria Caldwell McIntosh: page 1946. Repository: Family History Library, 35 North West Temple Street, Salt Lake City, Utah 84150-3400, USA, Call Number: 979 D36.

13. McIntosh Reunion Descendants, McIntosh - Descendants of John & Girsey (Grace) (Grizel) Rankin McIntosh (Attachment to Aug 17, 1958 Newsletter - copy in Collection of Bonnie S. Williams), Repository: Bonnie S. Williams, RR 1 Box 247, N Hwy 2, Wilburton, Oklahoma, USA.
Descendants of John McIntosh
1. John McIntosh (b.25 Jun 1795-Croy,Invernesshire,Scotland;d.5 Mar 1875-Bountiful,Davis,Utah)
sp: Girsey Rankin (b.1794-Rutherglen,Lanarkshire,Scotland;m.15 Jun 1817;d.Apr 1853-Origan,Lucas,Ohio)...
2. William McIntosh (b.16 Sep 1819-Bridgeton,Lanark,Scotland;d.5 May 1899-Mt. Pleasant,Sanpete,Utah)
sp: Maria Caldwell (b.17 Feb 1824-Lanark,Upper Canada;m.26 Sep 1841;d.27 Jul 1897-Mt Pleasant,San Pete,Utah)
3. John Ephraim McIntosh (b.13 Jun 1844-East Toledo,Ohio;d.2 Feb 1889)
sp: Mary Smith.

14. Susan Easton Black, Brigham Young University Religious Studies Center, "Membership of the Church of Jesus Christ of Latter-day Saints, 1830-1848," database, ancestry.com, John Ephriam McIntosh.

15. Brown, Beverly McIntosh and Marsha Lee McIntosh,*William McIntosh Diary, abridgement* (Self-published, Surprise, AZ. June 2002), page J-1 Toledo, Ohio 1841.

16. Brown, Beverly McIntosh and Marsha Lee McIntosh,*William McIntosh Diary, abridgement* (Self-published, Surprise, AZ. June 2002), Highlights 1.

17. Brown, Beverly McIntosh and Marsha Lee McIntosh,*William McIntosh Diary, abridgement* (Self-published, Surprise, AZ. June 2002), page J-2 Oregon, Ohio.

18. Brown, Beverly McIntosh and Marsha Lee McIntosh,*William McIntosh Diary, abridgement* (Self-published, Surprise, AZ. June 2002), page

# Source Citations

J-2.

19. 1850 U.S. census, Andrew, Missouri, population schedule, Jefferson, p. 8A, dwelling 801, family 781, John McIntosh; digital images, *ancestry.com*; citing National Archives and Records Administration microfilm M432.

20. Church of Jesus Christ of Latter-day Saints, "Mormon Pioneer Overland Travel, 1847-1868," database (www.lds.org/churchhistory/library/pioneercompany), John Ephraim McIntosh travelled with the David Lewis Comnpany in 1851.

21. 1860 U.S. census, Shambip, Utah, population schedule, Clover, p. 450, dwelling 4028, family 3104, Jno E McIntosh; digital images, *ancestry.com*; citing National Archives and Records Administration microfilm M653.

22. *1880 U.S. Census. Nevada-Panaca, Lincoln,* John McIntosh household, 1880 U.S. census, Lincoln County , Nevada, population schedule, town of Panaca, enumeration district [ED] 30, supervisor's district [SD] blank, page 6B, dwelling 16, family 16.

23. *1880 U.S. Census. Nevada-Panaca, Lincoln,* John McIntosh household, 1880 U.S. census, Lincoln County , Nevada, population schedule, town of Panaca, enumeratio n district [ED] 30, supervisor's district [SD] blank, pag e 6B, dwelling 16, family 16.

24. Brown, Beverly McIntosh and Marsha Lee McIntosh,*William McIntosh Diary, abridgement* (Self-published, Surprise, AZ. June 2002), pages 67 and 68.
[Note: It appears that William copied this article from a newspaper.]
Fatal accident at St. John
St. John, Tooele, Co., Feb. 8, 1889

A sad accident resulting in the almost instant death of Brother John E. McIntosh occurred on the Johnson Pass, between Rush and Skull Valleys about 1 mile below the divide at half past four on Saturday the 2nd.

The deceased started from his parent's house on the morning in question to his sheep camp in charge of a team laden with grain and provisions. He was accompanied by Mr. Henry Newman. Arriving on top of the divide and on going down the canyon, the road being very difficult to travel and a considerable downgrade, the team started to run, throwing Brother McIntosh from the wagon.

He fell between the two wheels. The hind wheels passing over his back, fracturing his ribs on both sides and slightly brusing the right side of his head. Mr. Newman stopped the team, assisted the unfortunate mand and laid him on some blankets and immediately afterward started down the canyon for help.

He met Mr. S. J. Stookey coming up the canyon on horseback. On returning to the place of the accident, they found him still alive but unable to speak and in about fifteen minutes from the time he received his injuries he breathed his last.

His body was then conveyed to the home of his parents who he had left only a few hours before in good health.

The deceased leaves a widow and three children who reside at Eagle Rock, Idaho. There is also his aged parents, brothers and sisters and a large circle of friends sadly mourn his loss.

He was born in East Toledo, Michigan on June 13, 1842, and was a quiet, inoffensive man and devoted husband and father.

An inquest on the body of the deceased was held at St. John precinct before Mr. John McIntosh, J.P. The jurors found as their verdict that the said John E. McIntosh came to his death on Johnson Pass by being accidentally thrown under the wheels of his wagon which passed over his body causing almost instant death.

The jurors were David H. Caldwell, David Charles and Nephi Draper. The funeral services were held on Wednesday last at St. John. C. N. Ahlquist. William had copied the newspaper article of his son's accident and death

*** Left Widow and 3 children in Eagle Rock, Idaho *** Bev Brown heard it was in Bingham County from someone who had hunted there.

25. *U.S., City Directories, 1822-1995*, Pocatello, Idaho, City Directory, 1916:, 117; digital images,*ancestry.com* ; McIntosh, Margaret (wid John E), r 436 N Main.

26. McIntosh Reunion Descendants, McIntosh - Descendants of John & Girsey (Grace) (Grizel) Rankin McIntosh (Attachment to Aug 17, 1958 Newsletter - copy in Collection of Bonnie S. Williams), Repository: Bonnie S. Williams, RR 1 Box 247, N Hwy 2, Wilburton, Oklahoma, USA.
Descendants of John McIntosh
Page 1, 24 Aug 2001
1. John McIntosh (b.25 Jun 1795-Croy,Invernesshire,Scotland;d.5 Mar 1875-Bountiful,Davis,Utah)
sp: Girsey Rankin (b.1794-Rutherglen,Lanarkshire,Scotland;m.15 Jun 1817;d.Apr 1853-Origan,Lucas,Ohio)...
2. William McIntosh (b.16 Sep 1819-Bridgeton,Lanark,Scotland;d.5 May 1899-Mt. Pleasant,Sanpete,Utah)
sp: Maria Caldwell (b.17 Feb 1824-Lanark,Upper Canada;m.26 Sep 1841;d.27 Jul 1897-Mt Pleasant,San Pete,Utah)
3. John Ephraim McIntosh (b.13 Jun 1844-East Toledo,Ohio;d.2 Feb 1889)
sp: Mary Smith.

# Mary Ann McIntosh

| **Father** | | |
|---|---|---|
| Born | date: | place: |
| Died | date: | place: |
| Buried | date: | place: |
| **Mother** | **Mary Ann McIntosh**[1,2] | |
| Born | 27 Jul 1845 | Oregon, Lucas, Ohio, United States[3,4] |
| Died | 9 Feb 1847 | Monroe, Monroe, Michigan, United States[5] |
| Cause of Death | Died as a child from burns eight days after her clothing caught fire | |
| Buried | Abt 12 Feb 1847 | La Salle, Monroe, Michigan, United States |
| Bapt.(LDS) | Child | |
| Conf.(LDS) | Child | |
| Init.(LDS) | Child | |
| Endow.(LDS) | Child | |
| Father | William McIntosh (1819-1899) [6,7,8,9] | |
| Mother | Maria Caldwell (1824-1897) [10] | |
| SealP (LDS) | 11 Oct 1893 | Manti Utah Temple |
| Marriage | This person had no known marriage and no known children | place: |

**Events**

1. She had a residence from 27 Jul 1845 to Aug 1845 in Oregon, Lucas, Ohio, United States.[11]
   1845 Spring - William and his family moved to Oregon, Ohio, just south of Toledo.

2. She had a residence from Aug 1845 to 9 Feb 1847 in Erie, Monroe, Michigan, United States.[11]
   1845 Fall - William and his family moved to Michigan where his parents lived.

## Children

# Source Citations

1. Brown, Beverly McIntosh and Marsha Lee McIntosh,*William McIntosh Diary, abridgement* (Self-published, Surprise, AZ. June 2002), "..we had two children John E and Maryan.."

2. McIntosh Reunion Descendants, McIntosh - Descendants of John & Girsey (Grace) (Grizel) Rankin McIntosh (Attachment to Aug 17, 1958 Newsletter - copy in Collection of Bonnie S. Williams), Repository: Bonnie S. Williams, RR 1 Box 247, N Hwy 2, Wilburton, Oklahoma, USA. Descendants of John McIntosh Page 1, 24 Aug 2001
1. John McIntosh (b.25 Jun 1795-Croy,Invernesshire,Scotland; d.5 Mar 1875-Bountiful,Davis,Utah)
sp: Girsey Rankin (b.1794-Rutherglen,Lanarkshire,Scotland; m.15 Jun 1817; d.Apr 1853-Origan,Lucas,Ohio)...
2. William McIntosh (b.16 Sep 1819-Bridgeton,Lanark,Scotland; d.5 May 1899-Mt. Pleasant,Sanpete,Utah)
sp: Maria Caldwell (b.17 Feb 1824-Lanark,Upper Canada; m.26 Sep 1841; d.27 Jul 1897-Mt Pleasant,San Pete,Utah)...
3. Mary Ann McIntosh (b.27 Jul 1845-East Toledo,Ohio; d.9 Feb 1847).
This single page attachment indicates that the parents of John McIntosh are William McIntosh & Isabell and is indicative of what our side of the family knew of our McIntosh cousins at that time in August 1958.

3. Brown, Beverly McIntosh and Marsha Lee McIntosh,*William McIntosh Diary, abridgement* (Self-published, Surprise, AZ. June 2002), Highlights 1. July 27, 1845 - William and Maria's daughter Mary Ann was born in Oregon, Ohio.

4. Brown, Beverly McIntosh and Marsha Lee McIntosh,*William McIntosh Diary, abridgement* (Self-published, Surprise, AZ. June 2002), page J-2 Oregon, Ohio.

5. Brown, Beverly McIntosh and Marsha Lee McIntosh,*William McIntosh Diary, abridgement* (Self-published, Surprise, AZ. June 2002), "John had called to me that sissey's, Maryan's, clothes was on fire...we all did the best we could but all seemed of no use. She died in the eighth day of her illness...This was in the 9th of February 1847."

6. Brown, Beverly McIntosh and Marsha McIntosh, editors,*William McIntosh Diary 1857-1898, Abridgement* (Surprise, AZ: Self-published, June 2002).

7. Daughters of Utah Pioneers, *Our Pioneer Heritage* (Salt Lake City, UT: Infobases, Inc., 1996), 19: 422. Repository: Family History Library, 35 North West Temple Street, Salt Lake City, Utah 84150-3400, USA, Call Number: 979.2 H2.

8. Frank Esshorn, editor, *Pioneers and Prominent Men of Utah comprising Photographs-Genealogies-Biographies. Pioneers are those men and women who came to Utah by wagon, hand cart or afoot, between July 24, 1847 and December 30, 1868, before the railroad. Prominent Men are stake presidents, ward bishops, governors, members of the bench, etc., who came to Utah after the coming of the railroad. The early history of the Church of Jesus Christ of Latter-Day Saints. In One Volume, Illustrated* (Salt Lake City, Utah: Utah Pioneers Book Publishing Company, 1913), McIntosh, William: 331 and 1059. Repository: Family History Library, 35 North West Temple Street, Salt Lake City, Utah 84150-3400, USA, Call Number: 979.2 D3e.

9. Andrew Jenson, editor, *Latter-day Saint Biographical Encyclopedia: A Compilation of Biographical Sketches of Prominent Men and Women in The Church of Jesus Christ of Latter-day Saints*, 4 v.: ports. (Salt Lake City, Utah: Western Epics, 1971), William McIntosh: V 4, page 647. Repository: Family History Library, 35 North West Temple Street, Salt Lake City, Utah 84150-3400, USA, Call Number: 920.0792.

10. International Society of Daughters of Utah Pioneers, editor,*Pioneer Women of Faith and Fortitude*, Volume III (Salt Lake City, Utah: Publishers Press, 1998), Maria Caldwell McIntosh: page 1946. Repository: Family History Library, 35 North West Temple Street, Salt Lake City, Utah 84150-3400, USA, Call Number: 979 D36.

11. Brown, Beverly McIntosh and Marsha Lee McIntosh,*William McIntosh Diary, abridgement* (Self-published, Surprise, AZ. June 2002).

Produced by: Beverly McIntosh Brown, 15933 W Silver Breeze Dr, Surprise, AZ 85374, 623-584-0440, starfighteraz@gmail.com : 29 Jun 2021



Produced by Legacy

# David Hirum McIntosh

| Father | David Hirum McIntosh[1,2] | |
|---|---|---|
| Born | 5 Sep 1847 | Saint Louis, , Missouri, United States[3,4] |
| Died | 16 Nov 1847 | Saint Louis, , Missouri, United States[5] |
| Cause of Death | King's Cough - Whooping Cough | |
| Buried | date: | place: |
| Bapt.(LDS) | Child | |
| Conf.(LDS) | Child | |
| Init.(LDS) | Child | |
| Endow.(LDS) | Child | |
| Father | William McIntosh (1819-1899) [6,7,8,9] | |
| Mother | Maria Caldwell (1824-1897) [10] | |
| SealP (LDS) | 11 Oct 1893 | Manti Utah Temple |

**Events**

1. He had a residence from 5 Sep 1847 to 16 Nov 1847 in Saint Louis, , Missouri, United States.[11]
   "And in the Spring of 1847 we bought a yoke of oxen, a cow and a wagon, about all the property we had. And took our passage on a canal boat at Toledo. We was bound then for St Louis as the Saints were arriving from Nauvoo."
   "On September the 5th, 1847, David Hirum was born. We lived there and enjoyed ourselves very well till David Hirum got sick. Whopping cough he got and was worse. We did all that we could until he died November the 16th. John, then our only child again, was very sick and came near dying. We began to think we was going to be bereaved of our children. John got well and we began to overcome our bereavement."

| Mother | | |
|---|---|---|
| Born | date: | place: |
| Died | date: | place: |
| Buried | date: | place: |

**Children**

Produced by: Beverly McIntosh Brown, 15933 W Silver Breeze Dr, Surprise, AZ 85374, 623-584-0440, starfighteraz@gmail.com : 29 Jun 2021

# Source Citations


1. Brown, Beverly McIntosh and Marsha Lee McIntosh,*William McIntosh Diary, abridgement* (Self-published, Surprise, AZ. June 2002), "On Sept the 5th, 1847, David Hirum was born."

2. McIntosh Reunion Descendants, McIntosh - Descendants of John & Girsey (Grace) (Grizel) Rankin McIntosh (Attachment to Aug 17, 1958 Newsletter - copy in Collection of Bonnie S. Williams), Repository: Bonnie S. Williams, RR 1 Box 247, N Hwy 2, Wilburton, Oklahoma, USA.
Descendants of John McIntosh Page 1, 24 Aug 2001
1. John McIntosh (b.25 Jun 1795-Croy,Invernesshire,Scotland;d.5 Mar 1875-Bountiful,Davis,Utah)
sp: Girsey Rankin (b.1794-Rutherglen,Lanarkshire,Scotland;m.15 Jun 1817;d.Apr 1853-Origan,Lucas,Ohio)...
2. William McIntosh (b.16 Sep 1819-Bridgeton,Lanark,Scotland;d.5 May 1899-Mt. Pleasant,Sanpete,Utah)
sp: Maria Caldwell (b.17 Feb 1824-Lanark,Upper Canada;m.26 Sep 1841;d.27 Jul 1897-Mt Pleasant,San Pete,Utah)...
3. David Hyrum McIntosh (b.5 Sep 1847-St. Louis,St. Louis,Missouri;d.16 Nov 1847).
This single page attachment indicates that the parents of John McIntosh are William McIntosh & Isabell and is indicative of what our side of the family knew of our McIntosh cousins at that time in August 1958.

3. Brown, Beverly McIntosh and Marsha Lee McIntosh,*William McIntosh Diary, abridgement* (Self-published, Surprise, AZ. June 2002), "On Sept the 5th, 1847, David Hirum was born. We lived there (St Louis, MO)..."

4. Brown, Beverly McIntosh and Marsha Lee McIntosh,*William McIntosh Diary, abridgement* (Self-published, Surprise, AZ. June 2002), J-3 St. Louis, 1847.

5. Brown, Beverly McIntosh and Marsha Lee McIntosh,*William McIntosh Diary, abridgement* (Self-published, Surprise, AZ. June 2002), "On Sept the 5th, 1847, David Hirum was born. We lived there (St. Louis, MO) and enjoyed ourselves very well till David Hirum got sick, whopping cough he got and was worse, all that we could do until he died Nov the 16th."

6. Brown, Beverly McIntosh and Marsha McIntosh, editors,*William McIntosh Diary 1857-1898, Abridgement* (Surprise, AZ: Self-published, June 2002).

7. Daughters of Utah Pioneers,*Our Pioneer Heritage* (Salt Lake City, UT: Infobases, Inc., 1996), 19: 422. Repository: Family History Library, 35 North West Temple Street, Salt Lake City, Utah 84150-3400, USA, Call Number: 979.2 H2.

8. Frank Esshorn, editor,*Pioneers and Prominent Men of Utah comprising Photographs-Genealogies-Biographies. Pioneers are those men and women who came to Utah by wagon, hand cart or afoot, between July 24, 1847 and December 30, 1868, before the railroad. Prominent Men are stake presidents, ward bishops, governors, members of the bench, etc., who came to Utah after the coming of the railroad. The early history of the Church of Jesus Christ of Latter-Day Saints. In One Volume, Illustrated* (Salt Lake City, Utah: Utah Pioneers Book Publishing Company, 1913), McIntosh, William: 331 and 1059. Repository: Family History Library, 35 North West Temple Street, Salt Lake City, Utah 84150-3400, USA, Call Number: 979.2 D3e.

9. Andrew Jenson, editor, *Latter-day Saint Biographical Encyclopedia: A Compilation of Biographical Sketches of Prominent Men and Women in The Church of Jesus Christ of Latter-day Saints*, 4 v.: ports. (Salt Lake City, Utah: Western Epics, 1971), William McIntosh: V 4, page 647. Repository: Family History Library, 35 North West Temple Street, Salt Lake City, Utah 84150-3400, USA, Call Number: 920.0792.

10. International Society of Daughters of Utah Pioneers, editor,*Pioneer Women of Faith and Fortitude*, Volume III (Salt Lake City, Utah: Publishers Press, 1998), Maria Caldwell McIntosh: page 1946. Repository: Family History Library, 35 North West Temple Street, Salt Lake City, Utah 84150-3400, USA, Call Number: 979 D36.

11. Brown, Beverly McIntosh and Marsha Lee McIntosh,*William McIntosh Diary, abridgement* (Self-published, Surprise, AZ. June 2002), page J-2, Start for St Louis, 1847.

# William Henry McIntosh, Sr. and Mary Elizabeth Keele

| **Husband** | **William Henry McIntosh Sr.**[1,2,3,4,5] | |
|---|---|---|
| AKA | Henry McIntosh | |
| Born | 18 Apr 1849 | Saint Louis, , Missouri, United States[1,6,7] |
| Died | 28 Apr 1901 | Junction, Piute, Utah, United States[7] |
| | | |
| Buried | 1901 | Junction, Piute, Utah, United States[7] |
| Address | Junction Field Cemetery, Highway 89, South of town across road from the Hill Cemetery, J~ | |
| Bapt.(LDS) | 22 Mar 1857 | |
| Conf.(LDS) | 22 Mar 1857 | |
| Init.(LDS) | 29 Mar 1878 | St. George Utah Temple |
| Endow.(LDS) | 29 Mar 1878 | St. George Utah Temple |
| Father | William McIntosh (1819-1899) [8,9,10,11] | |
| Mother | Maria Caldwell (1824-1897) [12] | |
| SealP (LDS) | 24 Mar 1909 | Manti Utah Temple |
| Marriage | 18 Apr 1871 | Panaca, Lincoln, Nevada, United States |
| SealS (LDS) | 29 Mar 1878 | St. George Utah Temple |

**Events**

1. He has conflicting birth information of 18 Apr 1849 and Independence, Jackson, Missouri, United States.[1]
2. He had a residence from 18 Apr 1849 to 1851 in Saint Louis, , Missouri, United States.[13]
"And in the Spring of 1847 we bought a yoke of oxen, a cow and a wagon, about all the property we had. And took our passage on a canal boat at Toledo. We was bound then for St Louis as the Saints were arriving from Nauvoo."
3. He appeared on the census on 19 Nov 1850 in Jefferson City, Cole, Missouri, United States.[14]
Line 40 - William McIntosh, age 31, male, waggon maker, born in LC. (LC is an unknown location)
Line 41 - Meoriah McIntosh, age 27, female, born in LC. (LS is an unknown location)
Line 42 - John McIntosh, age 6, male, born in O (Ohio), attended school within the year.
**Line 1 (next page) - William H McIntosh, age 1, male, born in Mo. (Missouri)**
4. Migration: David Lewis Company, Between 1 May 1851 and 9 Sep 1851, Salt Lake City, Great Salt Lake, Utah Territory, United States.[15]
Company List:
McIntosh, John Ephraim (age 9)
McIntosh, Maria Caldwell (age 27)
McIntosh, William (age 32)
**McIntosh, William Henry (age 2)**

Mormon Pioneer Overland Travel, 1847-1868
David Lewis Company (1851)
Departure: 1 May 1851
Arrival in Salt Lake Valley: 9 September 1851
David Lewis
JESUS CHRIST
PhotoScan by Google Photos


Mormon Pioneer Overland Travel, David Lewis Company, 1851, William Henry McIntosh, page 1 of 2

5. He appeared on the census on 11 Oct 1860 in Clover, Shambip, Utah Territory, United States.[16]
Line 25) Wm McIntosh, age 40, male, farmer, born in Scotland
Line 26) Maria McIntosh, age 36, female, born in Canada
Line 27) Jno E McIntosh, age 18, male, born in Ohio
Line 28) **Wm. H McIntosh, age 11, male, born in Missouri, in school**
Line 29) Jas F McIntosh, age 8, male, born in Utah Territory, in school
Line 30) Malissa J McIntosh, age 6, female, born in Utah Territory, in school
Line 31) Alice M McIntosh, age 3, female, born in Utah Territory
Line 32) Abm E McIntosh, age 6/12, male, born in Utah Territory
6. He appeared on the census on 10 Jun 1870 in Panaca, Washington, Utah Territory.[17]
Line 20 - McIntosh, William age 49, male, white, day laborer, value of personal estate $200, born in Scotland, father and mother foreign born, male over 21.

# William Henry McIntosh, Sr. and Mary Elizabeth Keele

Line 21 - McIntosh, Marie, age 45, female, white, keeping house, born in Canada, father and mother foreign born.
**Line 22 - McIntosh, William, age 20, male, white, teamster, born in Missouri, father and mother foreign born.**
Line 23 - McIntosh, Frank, age 18, male, white, work on farm, born in Utah, father and mother foreign born.
Line 24 - McIntosh, Jane, age 15, female, white, at home, born in Utah, father and mother foreign born, attended school.
Line 25 - McIntosh, Allice, age 12, female, white, born in Utah, father and mother foreign born, attended school.
Line 26 - McIntosh, Abraham, age 10, male, white, born in Utah, father and mother foreign born, attended school.
Line 27 - McIntosh, Lilly, age 7, female, white, born in Utah, father and mother foreign born.
Line 28 - McIntosh, Caroline, age 4, female, white, born in Utah, father and mother foreign born.
Line 29 - McIntosh, Albert, age 1, male, white, born in Utah, father and mother foreign born.

7. He appeared on the census on 28 Jul 1870 in Meadow Valley, Lincoln, Nevada, United States.[18]
Line 22 - McIntosh, Wm age 50, male, white, farming, value of real estate $300, value of personal estate 800, born in Scotland, father and mother foreign born, male over 21.
Line 23 - McIntosh, Marie, age 45, female, white, keeping house, born in Canada, father and mother foreign born.
**Line 24 - McIntosh, Wm H, age 21, male, white, farming, born in Missouri, father and mother foreign born, male over 21.**
Line 25 - McIntosh, Frank, age 18, male, white, farming, born in Utah, father and mother foreign born.
Line 26 - McIntosh, Jane, age 16, female, white, at home, born in Utah, father and mother foreign born, attended school.
Line 27 - McIntosh, Alice, age 12, female, white, school, born in Utah, father and mother foreign born, attended school.
Line 28 - McIntosh, Abe, age 10, male, white, school, born in Utah, father and mother foreign born, attended school.
Line 29 - McIntosh, Lilly, age 7, female, white, school, born in Utah, father and mother foreign born.
Line 30 - McIntosh, Caroline, age 4, female, white, school, born in Utah, father and mother foreign born.
Line 31 - McIntosh, Albert, age 1, male, white, school, born in Nevada, father and mother foreign born.

8. He appeared on the census on 4 Jun 1880 in Meadow Valley, Lincoln, Nevada, United States.[19]
**Line 11 - McIntosh, William, white, male, age 31, head, married, farmer, born in Missouri, father born in Scotland, mother born in Canada.**
Line 12 - McIntosh, Mary, white, female, age 24, wife, married, keeping house, born in Utah, father born in Tennessee, mother born in Pennsylvania.
Line 13 - McIntosh, Mary E, white, female, age 8, daughter, single, born in Nevada, father born in Missouri, mother born in Utah.
Line 14 - McIntosh, William H, white, male, age 6, son, single, born in Nevada, father born in Missouri, mother born in Utah.
Line 15 - McIntosh, Anna M, white, female, age 2, daughter, single, born in Nevada, father born in Missouri, mother born in Utah.

9. He was employed on 5 Nov 1887 in Junction, Piute, Utah Territory, United States.[20]
Appointed appraiser of estate of Alva Harris.

10. He worked as a Justice of the Peace on 23 May 1889 in Junction, Piute, Utah Territory, United States.[20]
Justice of the peace: performed wedding of William J. Heki and Leolettie Petersen, at Junction.

11. He was employed on 15 Nov 1891 in Junction, Piute, Utah Territory, United States.[20]
Justice of the Peace: performed the wedding of Edgar N. Layton and Maud Spencer at Junction.

12. He was employed on 2 Jun 1892 in Junction, Piute, Utah Territory, United States.[20]
Justice of Peace: performed the wedding of James S. Hilend and Phoebe S. Howes, at Junction.

13. He had a residence in Feb 1894 in Junction, Piute, Utah Territory, United States.[21,22]
"We, William and Maria McIntosh, are living in Mt. Pleasant.
Joseph Albert, my son, is living on our farm in St. John, Tooele County, Utah.
Franklin McIntosh, my son, is on the desert with the sheep.
William Henry [son] is living in Junction, Piute County."
"I left Mt. Pleasant and went to City Creek Junction, Piute County to visit W. H. and Mary McIntosh. He is my son and Mary is his wife."

14. He appeared on the census on 5 Jun 1900 in Junction, Piute, Utah, United States.[23]

# William Henry McIntosh, Sr. and Mary Elizabeth Keele

**Line 67 - McIntosh, William H, head, white, male, born Apr 1849, age 51, married 29 years, born in Missouri, father born in Scotland, mother born in Canada, farmer, 0 months unemployed, can read, write and speak english, owns, mortgage free, farm #22.**
Line 68 - McIntosh, Mary, wife, white, female, born May 1855, age 45, married 29 years, had 9 children, 7 living, born in Utah, father born in Tennessee, mother born in Pennsylvania, can read, write and speak english.
Line 69 - McIntosh, Olive, daughter, white, female, born Mar 1884, age 16, single, born in Nevada, father born in Missouri, mother born in Utah, in school, can read, write and speak english.
Line 70 - McIntosh, Elsie, daughter, white, female, born Mar 1887, age 13, single, born in Utah, father born in Missouri, mother born in Utah, in school, can read, write and speak english.
Line 71 - McIntosh, Raymond, son, white, male, born July 1899, age 10/12, single, born in Utah, father born in Missouri, mother born in Utah.

| **Wife** | **Mary Elizabeth Keele**[24,25,26] | |
|---|---|---|
| AKA | Mary Empy, Elizabeth Keele, Mary McIntosh | |
| Born | 29 May 1856 | Farmington, Davis, Utah Territory, United States[7] |
| Died | 26 Feb 1916 | Henderson, Garfield, Utah, United States[7] |
| Cause of Death | Probably pneumonia//Broken leg | |
| Buried | 3 Mar 1916 | Junction, Piute, Utah, United States[27] |
| Address | Junction Field Cemetery, Highway 89, South of town across road from the Hill Cemete~ | |
| Bapt.(LDS) | 8 Nov 1984 | Idaho Falls Idaho Temple |
| Conf.(LDS) | 8 Nov 1984 | Idaho Falls Idaho Temple |
| Init.(LDS) | 29 Mar 1873 | |
| Endow.(LDS) | 29 Mar 1878 | Idaho Falls Idaho Temple |
| Father | Samuel Keele Sr. (1816-1897)[28] | |
| Mother | Ann Elizabeth Hess (1829-1880)[29] | |
| SealP (LDS) | 15 Jun 1881 | St. George Utah Temple |
| Other Spouse | James Hyrum Fielding Empey (1857-1943) | 15 Jul 1909 - Manti, Sanpete, Utah, United States (Divorced) |
| SealS (LDS) | 15 Jul 1909 | Manti Utah Temple |

Mary Elizabeth Keele

**Events**

1. She appeared on the census on 11 Jul 1860 in North Bend, Sanpete, Utah Territory.
   Line 19 - Dwelling 755, House 683, Saml Keel, age 45, male, farmer, worth of retail estate $200, worth of personal property $375, born in Tennessee.
   Line 20 - Anna E Keel, age 31, female, born in Pennsylvania.
   Line 21 - Jacob Keel, age 10, male, born in Iowa, attending school.
   Line 22 - Samuel Keel, age 9, male, born in Iowa, attending school.
   Line 23 - David Keel, age 6, male, born in Utah.
   **Line 24 - Mary Keel, age 4, female, born in Utah.**
   Line 25 - Wm Keel, age 2, male, born in Utah.
   Line 26 - Emma Keel, age 6/12, female, born in Utah.

2. She appeared on the census on 15 Jun 1870 in Panaca, Washington, Utah Territory.
   Line 17 - Samuel Keel, m, age 55, farmer, born in Tennessee, real estate worth $500, personal property worth $800.
   Line 18 - Anne E. Keel, f, age 41, keeping house, born in Pennsylvania.
   Line 19 - Jacob Keel, m, age 21, works on farm, born in Iowa.
   Line 20 - David Keel, m, age 10, works on farm, born in Utah.

# William Henry McIntosh, Sr. and Mary Elizabeth Keele

**Line 21 - Mary Keel, f, age 15, at home, born in Utah.**
Line 22 - William Keel, m, age 11, born in Utah.
Line 23 - Emma Keel, f, age 10, born in Utah.
Line 24 - Haerett Keel, f, age 5, born in Utah.
Line 25 - Sarah Keel, f, age 1, born in Utah.

3. She appeared on the census on 4 Jun 1880 in Meadow Valley, Lincoln, Nevada, United States.[31]
Line 11 - McIntosh, William, white, male, age 31, head, married, farmer, born in Missouri, father born in Scotland, mother born in Canada.
**Line 12 - McIntosh, Mary, white, female, age 24, wife, married, keeping house, born in Utah, father born in Tennessee, mother born in Pennsylvania.**
Line 13 - McIntosh, Mary E, white, female, age 8, daughter, single, born in Nevada, father born in Missouri, mother born in Utah.
Line 14 - McIntosh, William H, white, male, age 6, son, single, born in Nevada, father born in Missouri, mother born in Utah.
Line 15 - McIntosh, Anna M, white, female, age 2, daughter, single, born in Nevada, father born in Missouri, mother born in Utah.

4. She appeared on the census on 5 Jun 1900 in Junction, Piute, Utah, United States.[32]
Line 67 - McIntosh, William H, head, white, male, born Apr 1849, age 51, married 29 years, born in Missouri, father born in Scotland, mother born in Canada, farmer, 0 months unemployed, can read, write and speak english, owns, mortgage free, farm #22.
**Line 68 - McIntosh, Mary, wife, white, female, born May 1855, age 45, married 29 years, had 9 children, 7 living, born in Utah, father born in Tennessee, mother born in Pennsylvania, can read, write and speak english.**
Line 69 - McIntosh, Olive, daughter, white, female, born Mar 1884, age 16, single, born in Nevada, father born in Missouri, mother born in Utah, in school, can read, write and speak english.
Line 70 - McIntosh, Elsie, daughter, white, female, born Mar 1887, age 13, single, born in Utah, father born in Missouri, mother born in Utah, in school, can read, write and speak english.
Line 71 - McIntosh, Raymond, son, white, male, born July 1899, age 10/12, single, born in Utah, father born in Missouri, mother born in Utah.

5. She appeared on the census on 10 Apr 1910 in Junction, Piute, Utah, United States.[33]
Line 4 - Empy, James H, head, male, white, age 52, married 2x, present marriage for 0 years, born in Utah, father born in Canada, speaks english, mother born in England, speaks english, farmer, farm, works on own account, can read and write and speak english, owns farm mortgage free, farm #2.
**Line 5 - Empy, Mary E, wife, female, white, age 53, married x2, present marriage for 0 years, had 9 children, 7 living, born in Utah, father born in Tennessee, mother born in Pennsylvania, speaks english, no occupation. can read and write.**
Line 6 - Empy, Hyrum L, son, male, white, age 16, single, born in Nevada, father born in Utah, mother born in Utah, speaks english, no occupation, attended school, can read and write.
Line 7 - Empy, Inezettie, daughter, female, white, age 15, single, born in Nevada, father born in Utah, mother born in Utah, speaks english, no occupation, attended school, can read and write.
Line 8 - Empy, Elsie D, daughter, female, white, age 10, single, born in Nevada, father born in Utah, mother born in Utah, speaks english, no occupation, attended school, can read and write.
Line 9 - Empy, Ivan H., son, male, white, age 5, single, born in Nevada, father born in Utah, mother born in Utah, no occupation.
Line 10 - McIntosh, Raymond, step-son, male, white, age 10, single, born in Utah, father born in Canada, speaks english, mother born in Utah, speaks english, no occupation, attended school, can read and write.

**Events: Marriage**

1. Alt Marriage: 29 Mar 1878, Saint George, Washington, Utah, United States.

# William Henry McIntosh, Sr. and Mary Elizabeth Keele

## Children

| 1 | F | **Mary Elizabeth McIntosh**[35,36] | |
|---|---|---|---|
| AKA | | Elizabeth Cowdell, Lizzie Cowdle,[34] Lizzie McIntosh | |
| Born | | 2 Feb 1872 | Panaca, Lincoln, Nevada, United States |
| Died | | 22 Jan 1962 | Los Angeles, Los Angeles, California, United States[37] |
| Buried | | 26 Jan 1962 | Inglewood, Los Angeles, California, United States[38] |
| Address | | Inglewood Park Cemetery, Inglewood, California, USA | |
| Bapt.(LDS) | | 7 May 1881 | |
| Conf.(LDS) | | 7 May 1881 | |
| Init.(LDS) | | 18 Jul 1945 | St. George Utah Temple |
| Endow.(LDS) | | 18 Jul 1945 | St. George Utah Temple |
| SealP (LDS) | | 29 Mar 1878 | St. George Utah Temple |
| Spouse | | James Ernest Cowdell (1868-1947)[35] | 8 Jan 1894 - Junction, Piute, Utah Territory, United States[39,40] |
| SealS (LDS) | | 18 Jul 1945 | St. George Utah Temple |

**Events**

1. She appeared on the census on 4 Jun 1880 in Meadow Valley, Lincoln, Nevada, United States.[41]
   Line 11 - McIntosh, William, white, male, age 31, head, married, farmer, born in Missouri, father born in Scotland, mother born in Canada.
   Line 12 - McIntosh, Mary, white, female, age 24, wife, married, keeping house, born in Utah, father born in Tennessee, mother born in Pennsylvania.
   **Line 13 - McIntosh, Mary E, white, female, age 8, daughter, single, born in Nevada, father born in Missouri, mother born in Utah.**
   Line 14 - McIntosh, William H, white, male, age 6, son, single, born in Nevada, father born in Missouri, mother born in Utah.
   Line 15 - McIntosh, Anna M, white, female, age 2, daughter, single, born in Nevada, father born in Missouri, mother born in Utah.
2. She appeared on the census on 11 Apr 1930 in Los Angeles, Los Angeles, California, United States.[42]
   Line 12 - Cowdell, James E, head, owns home, value of home $8,000, owns a radio set, male, white, age 60, married at age 24, did not attend school within year, able to read and write, born in Utah, father born in England, mother born in England, able to speak english, cabinet maker, furniture store, wage worker, actually at work, not a veteran.
   **Line 13 - Cowdell, Mary E, wife, female, white, age 58, married at age 22, did not attend school within year, able to read and write, born in Nevada, father born in Missouri, mother born in Utah, able to speak english, no occupation.**
   Line 14 - Cowdell, Wallace H, son, male, white, age 28, single, did not attend school within year, able to read and write, born in Utah, father born in Utah, mother born in Nevada, able to speak english, salesman, auto parts store, wage worker, actually at work, not a veteran.
   Line 15 - Cowdell, Ernest, son, male, white, age 35, married at age 21, did not attend school within year, able to read and write, born in Utah, father born in Utah, mother born in Nevada, able to speak english, barber at a beauty shop, wage worker, actually at work, not a veteran.
   Line 16 - Cowdell, Imogene, daughter-in-law, female, white, age 32, married at age 18, did not attend school within year, able to read and write, born in Utah, father born in Utah, mother born in Utah, able to speak english, no occupation.
   Line 17 - Cowdell, Marguerite, granddaughter, female, white, age 12, single, attended school within year, able to read and write, born in Utah, father born in Utah, mother born in Utah, able to speak english, no occupation.
   Line 18 - Cowdell, H. Carol, granddaughter, female, white, age 9, single, did attend school within year, born in Utah, father born in Utah, mother born in Utah, no occupation.
   Line 19 - Cowdell, Jesse L, son, male, white, age 26, married at age 23, did not attend school within year, able to read and write, born in Utah, father born in Utah, mother born in Utah, able to speak english, book keeper, auto parts store, wage worker, actually at work, not a veteran.
   Line 20 - Cowdell, Virginia, daughter-in-law, female, white, age 25, married at age 22, did not attend school within year, able to read and write, born in Utah, father born in Utah, mother born in Utah, able to speak english, sales lady, ready to wear shop, wage worker, actually at work.
3. She had a residence on 24 Jul 1931 in California, United States.[34]

# William Henry McIntosh, Sr. and Mary Elizabeth Keele

| Children (cont.) | | |
|---|---|---|
| **2** | **M** | **William Henry McIntosh Jr.** [44,45] |
| AKA | Will McIntosh[43] | |
| Born | 30 Jun 1873 | Saint John, Tooele, Utah Territory, United States[43] |
| Died | 18 May 1942 | Junction, Piute, Utah, United States[43,46] |
| Cause of Death | Broncho-pneumonia[43,46] | |
| Buried | 21 May 1942 | Junction, Piute, Utah, United States[43,47,48] |
| Address | Junction Hill Cemetery, Highway 89, South of town on the big hill, Junction, Utah, US~ | |
| Bapt.(LDS) | 29 Apr 2000 | Oakland California Temple |
| Conf.(LDS) | 1 Jan 1883 | |
| Init.(LDS) | 18 Apr 1894 | Manti Utah Temple |
| Endow.(LDS) | 18 Apr 1894 | Manti Utah Temple |
| SealP (LDS) | 29 Mar 1878 | St. George Utah Temple |
| Spouse | Nora May Morrill (1875-1959)[49,50] | 18 Apr 1894 - Manti, Sanpete, Utah Territory, United States[51,52] |
| SealS (LDS) | 18 Apr 1894 | Manti Utah Temple |

**Events**

1. He was ordained an elder.[43]
2. He appeared on the census on 4 Jun 1880 in Meadow Valley, Lincoln, Nevada, United States.[41]
   Line 11 - McIntosh, William, white, male, age 31, head, married, farmer, born in Missouri, father born in Scotland, mother born in Canada.
   Line 12 - McIntosh, Mary, white, female, age 24, wife, married, keeping house, born in Utah, father born in Tennessee, mother born in Pennsylvania.
   Line 13 - McIntosh, Mary E, white, female, age 8, daughter, single, born in Nevada, father born in Missouri, mother born in Utah.
   **Line 14 - McIntosh, William H, white, male, age 6, son, single, born in Nevada, father born in Missouri, mother born in Utah.**
   Line 15 - McIntosh, Anna M, white, female, age 2, daughter, single, born in Nevada, father born in Missouri, mother born in Utah.
3. Newspaper: 23 Aug 1897, Junction, Piute, Utah, United States.[43]
   Summoned as member of pool of potential jurors in State vs Harry Mills (murder trial); not called as member of actual jury.
4. He appeared on the census on 7 Jun 1900 in Junction, Piute, Utah, United States.[53]
   **Line 35 - McIntosh, William, head, white, male, born June 1873, age 26, married 6 years, born in Utah, father born in (unk), mother born in (unk), farm laborer, 6 months unemployed within year, can read, write and speak english, owns, mortgage free, house.**
   Line 36 - McIntosh, Nora M, wife, white, female, born July 1875, age 24, married 6 years, had 2 children, 2 living, born in Utah, father born in Utah, mother born in Utah, can read, write and speak english.

# William Henry McIntosh, Sr. and Mary Elizabeth Keele

Line 37 - McIntosh, Maynard, son, white, male, born Feb 1895, age 5, single, born in Utah, father born in Utah, mother born in Utah.
Line 38 - McIntosh, Fauntel, daughter, white, female, born Mar 1898, age 2, single, born in Utah, father born in Utah, mother born in Utah.

5. Newspaper: 7 Jul 1905, Junction, Piute, Utah, United States.[43]
Subscriber of City Creek Irrigation Company, named in Articles of Incorporation.

6. He appeared on the census on 19 Apr 1910 in Junction, Piute, Utah, United States.[54]
**Line 24 - McIntosh, William H, head, male, white, age 36, married once for 15 years, born in Utah, father born in Missouri, mother born in Nevada, speaks english, farmer, farm, works on own account, can read and write, owns mortgage free, house.**
Line 25 - McIntosh, Nora M, wife, female, white, age 34, married once for 15 years, had 4 children, 3 living, born in Utah, father born in Utah, mother born in Utah, speaks english, no occupation, can read and write.
Line 26 - McIntosh, Maynard J, son, male, white, age 15, single, born in Utah, father born in Utah, mother born in Utah, speaks english, no occupation, can read and write, attended school.
Line 27 - McIntosh, Fauntel, daughter, female, white, age 12, single, born in Utah, father born in Utah, mother born in Utah, speaks english, no occupation, can read and write, attended school.
Line 28 - McIntosh, Lamar, son, male, white, age 4, single, born in Utah, father born in Utah, mother born in Utah, no occupation.

7. He was employed between 1911 and 1912 in Junction, Piute, Utah, United States.[43]
Farming 40 acres (value: $320), at Junction.

8. He was employed between 1916 and 1917 in Junction, Piute, Utah, United States.[43]
Farming 55 acres (value $545), at Junction.

9. Tax Rolls: 14 Dec 1916, Junction, Piute, Utah, United States.[43]
On delinquent tax list. Per the Piute County News.

10. He was employed between 1918 and 1919 in Junction, Piute, Utah, United States.[43]
Farming 40 acres (value: $1425) at Junction.

11. Draft Registration: 12 Sep 1918, Junction, Piute, Utah, United States.[43]
Registered for the draft. Farmer, working for himself. Medium height, medium build, blue eyes, light hair.

12. Draft Registration: 19 Sep 1918, Junction, Piute, Utah, United States.[43]
Patriotic Men Make Response to Call/Responding to the call of the Nation for recruits for the army, the loyal citizens of Piute county between the ages of 18 and 45, both inclusive, flocked to the registration places last Thursday and when the totals had been counted in the several registration offices throughout the county, 297 names had been recorded. The county fell short just forty names, according to the number allotted. Piute county had been set aside to furnish 337, but only 297 men were registered. The officers have announced that a close canvas will be made and the county thoroughly "combed" for any slacker and should any be found they will be made to suffer the penalty as prescribed for failing to register. / Reports from all the registration offices throughout the county are to the effect that the work was done expeditiously and that there was not the least semblance of disorder. The day had been declared a holiday and all business houses were closed for the occasion. / The following is a list of the men registered: / ... Junction ... **William Henry McIntosh**, 57... Of Junction; appears on list of "persons whose registration cards are in the possession of "Piute County Draft Board, WWI-era.

13. Newspaper: 13 Feb 1919, Junction, Piute, Utah, United States.[43]
County Clerk W.S. Price, J.T. Woods, William McIntosh and G.M. Beebe of Junction were visitors here for a few hours yesterday. Per the Piute Chieftain.

14. He had a residence Dec 1919 to 1921 in Driggs, Teton, Idaho, United States.[43]

15. He was employed between 1920 and 1921 in Junction, Piute, Utah, United States.[43]
Farming 40 acres (value: $1425) at Junction.

16. He appeared on the census on 6 Jan 1920 in Driggs, Teton, Idaho, United States.[55]
**Line 93 - McIntosh, William H., head, owns house with a mortgage, male, white, age 46, married, can read, write and speak english, born in Utah, father born in Missouri, mother born in Utah, farmer on general farm, works on own account, farm #31.**
Line 94 - McIntosh, Nora M., wife, female, white, age 44, married, can read, write and speak english, born in Utah,

# William Henry McIntosh, Sr. and Mary Elizabeth Keele

father born in Utah, mother born in Utah.
Line 95 - McIntosh, Maynard, son, male, white, age 24, single, can read, write and speak english, born in Utah, father born in Utah, mother born in Utah.
Line 96 - McIntosh, Lamar, son, male, white, age 14, single, in school, can read, write and speak english, born in Utah, father born in Utah, mother born in Utah.
Line 97 - McIntosh, Leila, daughter, female, white, age 8, single, in school, can read, write and speak english, born in Utah, father born in Utah, mother born in Utah.
Line 98 - McIntosh, Ramona, daughter, female, white, age 4, single, born in Utah, father born in Utah, mother born in Utah.
Line 99 - Gilger, Hugh, son-in-law, male, white, age 24, widowed, can read, write and speak english, born in Utah, father born in USA, mother born in Germany, farm laborer on farm, wage worker.
Line 100 - Gilger, Freda, granddaughter, female, white, age 1 10/12, born in Utah, father born in Utah, mother born in Utah.

17. He worked as a garageman between 1924 and 1931 in Junction, Piute, Utah, United States.[43]

18. Civic duty: City councilman, Between 1930 and 1931, Junction, Piute, Utah, United States.[43]

19. He appeared on the census on 3 Apr 1930 in Junction, Piute, Utah, United States.[56]
**Line 34 - McIntosh, William H, head, owns home, value of home $500, does not live on a farm, male, white, age 56, married at age 20, did not attend school within year, can read and write, born in Utah, father born in Missouri, mother born in Utah, able to speak english, mechanic, garage, works on own account, actually at work, not a veteran.**
Line 35 - McIntosh, Nora M, wife, female, white, age 54, married at age 18, did not attend school within year, can read and write, born in Utah, father born in Utah, mother born in Utah, able to speak english, no occupation.
Line 36 - McIntosh, Leila, daughter, female, white, age 19, single, did not attend school within year, can read and write, born in Utah, father born in Utah, mother born in Utah, able to speak english, no occupation.
Line 37 - McIntosh, Ramona, daughter, female, white, age 14, single, did attend school within year, can read and write, born in Utah, father born in Utah, mother born in Utah, able to speak english, no occupation.

20. Newspaper: 6 Feb 1931, Junction, Piute, Utah, United States.[43]
Mr. and Mrs. M. Reed, Gilbert Beebe, Mr. and Mrs. Donald McIntosh, Mr. and Mrs. J.H. Empey, Mr. and Mrs. Joseph Ipson, William and Leila McIntosh and Elizabeth Barnson all attended the funeral services of Mr. Benj. Lewis in Circleville held on Wednesday. Per the Piute County News.

21. Newspaper: 10 Jul 1931, Junction, Piute, Utah, United States.[43]
Rainbow Trout Planted in City Creek / 10,500 rainbow trout, obtained from the government hatcheries in Springville, were planted in the south fork of City Creek by members of the local Rod and Gun Club. Soon we will have fishing in our own grounds and it will be unnecessary to go far away to get a fish for breakfast and bunches of enterprising and sport loving fellows of Junction got busy and secured some thirty cans of fingerling rainbow trout to plant in the south fork of City Creek / I don't know just who counted them but they claim 10,500 fish were planted, enough to give us all several fries. / The following men and boys went up with trucks to plant the fish last Wednesday morning: Lars C. Peterson, **W.H. McIntosh**, Cal Price, Gene Carson, Lester Barnson, Ferral Barlow, Elwin Robinson and H. Earl Bay went up to see that the fish were planted right. Per the Piute County News.

22. Newspaper: 24 Jul 1931, Junction, Piute, Utah, United States.[43]
Mrs. Lizzie Cowdle of California is here visiting at the home of her brothers and sister, W.H. and Abe McIntosh and Mrs. Elsie Ackerman. Lizzie has many friends here who are extending the hand of welcome and hope she will remain long enough to visit with us all. Per the Piute County News.

23. Newspaper: 18 Sep 1931, Junction, Piute, Utah, United States.[43]
Miss Fredia Gilger of Parowan is here to spend the winter with her grandparents, Mr. and Mrs. W.H. McIntosh. She will attend school in Junction. She returned with her grandparents last Thursday when they came back from Parowan where they had spent the day on business. Per the Piute County News.

24. He was elected to office on 23 Oct 1931 in Junction, Piute, Utah, United States.[43]
Republican Name Candidates for Municipal Election / At a Republican primary held in Junction Saturday evening, October 17, the following candidates were nominated to be voted on at the municipal election to be held "Tuesday, November 3rd, 1931: / Town president, McKinley Morrill. / City councilmen: Joseph Ipson, incumbent; **W.H. McIntosh**, incumbent; Luther Moore, incumbent; and John H. Luke. Per the Piute County News.

25. Newspaper: 25 Oct 1940, Junction, Piute, Utah, United States.[43]
Freeda Talbot and small son of Panguitch are visiting at the home of Mr. and Mrs. Will McIntosh [Junction] for a short

# William Henry McIntosh, Sr. and Mary Elizabeth Keele

time. Per the Piute County News.

26. Newspaper: 10 Apr 1942, Junction, Piute, Utah, United States.[43]
Ramona Proctor and children and Freeda Talbot and son of Panguitch are at the home of Mr. and Mrs. William McIntosh, assisting to care for Mr. McIntosh, who is very ill with pneumonia. Mrs. McIntosh is also confined to her bed with a broken hip, received last January. Per Piute County News.

27. His obituary was published on 18 May 1942 in Junction, Piute, Utah, United States.[43]
**Lifetime resident of Utah**. Farmer. Died at home. Funeral services held 21 May 1942 at Junction chapel, conducted by Bishop Applegate.
Prominent Resident of Junction Called to Reward: William H. McIntosh, Jr. Passes at Junction Monday of This Week. / William H. McIntosh, Jr., 69, a resident of Junction for about 58 years, passed away at his home Monday morning, May 18, of pneumonia and complicaions. He was ill for several weeks, but was seemingly on the road to recovery, being able to get up and around he house a little, when he took a relapse and in spite of everything possible being done for him, he grew rapidly worse. His life was prolonged by the use of an oxygen tank, but all to no avail. / He was born April 30, 1873 at Saint Johns, Tooele county, Utah, to William Henry and Mary Keele McIntosh. The family moved to Panaca, Nevada when he was a small child, and from there to Junction, when "Will" was eleven years old. / On April 18, 1894, he married Nora May Morrill in the temple. To them were born six children, two of who preceded him in death. / In December, 1919, the family moved to Driggs, Idaho, where they remained for about two years and then returned to Junction, where they have since resided. / Mr. McIntosh has held a number of civil positions here, being a member of the town board for many years past, until his death. He has been a school board member, an officer in different water companies and other organizations. He was an elder in the church. He was a good neighbor and friend and will be greatly missed in our community. / Besides his widow, he is survived by four children, Maynard McIntosh, Lamar McIntosh, and Mrs. Lelia Gardiner, all of Junction; and Mrs. Ramona Proctor, of Panguitch. Eleven grandchildren and two great-grandchildren also survive.
29 May 1942: Funeral services were held May 22nd for William McIntosh, who died the first of the week. Bishop Jay W. Applegate was in charge of the services. The speakers were Pres. W. Ellis Bay of Kingston, Barlo T. Luke and Bishop Jay W. Applegate. Special musical numbers were: piano solo, Helen Morrill; songs by Phyllis Jackman and Ora Nell Greenhalgh, Nola Whittaker, accompanied by Judd Haycock and Bruce Betenson. Burial was in the City cemetery.
All per the Piute County News.

28. Newspaper: 29 May 1942, Junction, Piute, Utah, United States.[43]
Mrs. Ramona Proctor and family of Panguitch, who have been here the past number of weeks at the bedside of her father, William McIntosh left last week. Per the Piute County News,

29. Newspaper: 29 May 1942, Junction, Piute, Utah, United States.[43]
Dr. Joseph Sudweeks of Provo and his mother, Sarah Sudweeks of Kimberley, Idaho, spent Thursday and part of Friday here, where they attended the funeral services for William McIntosh, Thursday. Per the Piute County News.

| 3 | M | **Samuel John McIntosh** | |
|---|---|---|---|
| Born | | 26 Mar 1874 | Panaca, Lincoln, Nevada, United States |
| Died | | 18 Oct 1877 | place: |
| Buried | | date: | place: |
| Bapt.(LDS) | | Child | |
| Conf.(LDS) | | Child | |
| Init.(LDS) | | Child | |
| Endow.(LDS) | | Child | |
| SealP (LDS) | | 29 Mar 1878 | St. George Utah Temple |
| Spouse | | This person had no known marriage and no known children | |

Produced by: Beverly McIntosh Brown, 15933 W Silver Breeze Dr, Surprise, AZ 85374, 623-584-0440, starfighteraz@gmail.com : 29 Jun 2021

# William Henry McIntosh, Sr. and Mary Elizabeth Keele

| Children (cont.) | | |
|---|---|---|
| 4 F | **Alice Maria McIntosh** | |
| Born | 9 Apr 1875 | Saint John, Tooele, Utah Territory, United States |
| Died | 10 Feb 1878 | place: |
| Buried | date: | place: |
| Bapt.(LDS) | Child | |
| Conf.(LDS) | Child | |
| Init.(LDS) | Child | |
| Endow.(LDS) | Child | |
| SealP (LDS) | 29 Mar 1878 | St. George Utah Temple |
| Spouse | This person had no known marriage and no known children | |
| 5 F | **Anna Mae McIntosh** [57] | |
| AKA | Anna May Black, Anna Dunsire, Anna Lester, Annie May McIntosh,[57] Mamie Ann McIntosh, Anna Sprague | |
| Born | 26 Nov 1878 | Panaca, Lincoln, Nevada, United States[58] |
| Died | 22 Nov 1956 | Ely, White Pine, Nevada, United States[59] |
| Buried | 1956 | Ely, White Pine, Nevada, United States[60] |
| Address | Ely City Cemetery, Ely, Nevada, USA | |
| Bapt.(LDS) | 6 Sep 1891 | |
| Conf.(LDS) | 6 Sep 1891 | |
| Init.(LDS) | 27 Aug 1999 | Seattle Washington Temple |
| Endow.(LDS) | 6 Apr 1992 | St. George Utah Temple |
| SealP (LDS) | BIC | |
| Spouse | Daniel Lester Sprague (1874-1918)[61] | |
| Marr. Date | 21 Nov 1895 - Junction, Piute, Utah Territory, United States. (Divorced before 29 Apr 1910)[62] | |
| SealS (LDS) | 12 Jan 1996 | Provo Utah Temple |
| Spouse | Sidney Nephi Albert Black (1868-1928) | 2 Jul 1918 - Richfield, Sevier, Utah, United States[63,64] |
| SealS (LDS) | 5 May 1999 | Mesa Arizona Temple |
| Spouse | David J. Dunsire (1862-1928) | 27 Feb 1928 - Sevier, Sevier, Utah, United States |
| SealS (LDS) | 13 Nov 2012 | Rexburg Idaho Temple |

**Events**

1. She appeared on the census on 4 Jun 1880 in Meadow Valley, Lincoln, Nevada, United States.[41]
   Line 11 - McIntosh, William, white, male, age 31, head, married, farmer, born in Missouri, father born in Scotland, mother born in Canada.
   Line 12 - McIntosh, Mary, white, female, age 24, wife, married, keeping house, born in Utah, father born in Tennessee, mother born in Pennsylvania.
   Line 13 - McIntosh, Mary E, white, female, age 8, daughter, single, born in Nevada, father born in Missouri, mother born in Utah.
   Line 14 - McIntosh, William H, white, male, age 6, son, single, born in Nevada, father born in Missouri, mother born in Utah.
   **Line 15 - McIntosh, Anna M, white, female, age 2, daughter, single, born in Nevada, father born in Missouri, mother born in Utah.**
2. She appeared on the census on 5 Jun 1900 in Junction, Piute, Utah, United States.
   Line 92 - Sprague, Daniel, head, white, male, born July 1874, age 25, married for 5 years, born in Utah, father born in Ohio, mother born in Iowa, day laborer, can read, write and speak english, owns home.
   **Line 93 - Sprague, Annie M, wife, white, female, born Nov 1878, age 21, married 5 years, had 2 children, none living, born in Nevada, father born in Missouri, mother born in Utah, can read, write and speak english.**
3. She appeared on the census on 28 Apr 1910 in Junction, Piute, Utah, United States.

# William Henry McIntosh, Sr. and Mary Elizabeth Keele

**Line 17 - Sprague, Annie M., head, female, white, age 31, divorced, had 6 children, 3 living, born in Nevada, father born in Utah, mother born in Utah, can read, write and speak english, housekeeper in a boarding house, wage worker, owns home.**
Line 18 - Sprague, Rose, daughter, female, white, age 9, single, born in Utah, father born in Utah, mother born in Nevada.
Line 19 - Sprague, Calvin, son, male, white, age 6, single, born in Utah, father born in Utah, mother born in Nevada.
Line 20 - Sprague, Irma, daughter, female, white, age 3, single, born in Utah, father born in Utah, mother born in Nevada.

4. She appeared on the census on 28 Jan 1920 in Marysvale, Piute, Utah, United States.
Line 74 - Black, Sidney, head, rents home, male, white, age 51, married, can read, write and speak english, born in Utah, father born in Ireland, speaks Irish, mother born in Illinois, miner in a gold mine, wage worker.
**Line 75 - Black, Annie M., wife, female, white, age 48, married, can read, write and speak english, born in Nevada, father born in US, mother born in Utah.**
Line 76 - Sprague, Erma S., step-daughter, female, white, age 13, single, in school, born in Utah, both parents born in Utah.
Line 77 - Sprague, Calvin, step-son, female, white, age 15, single, in school, born in Utah, both parents born in Utah.

5. She appeared on the census on 4 Apr 1930 in Garfield, Salt Lake, Utah, United States.
**Line 71 - Dunsire, Annie M., boarder, female, white, age 50, widowed, can read, write and speak english, born in Nevada, father born in Utah, mother born in Nevada, no occupation.**

| 6 | M | **Abram McIntosh** [65,66,67] | |
|---|---|---|---|
| AKA | | Abe McIntosh, Abraham McIntosh[65] | |
| Born | | 13 Mar 1882 | Panaca, Lincoln, Nevada, United States[68] |
| Died | | 4 Mar 1947 | Junction, Piute, Utah, United States[68,69] |
| Cause of Death | | Cerebral hemorrhage due to hypertension[68] | |
| Buried | | 8 Mar 1947 | Junction, Piute, Utah, United States[68,70] |
| Address | | Junction Hill Cemetery, Highway 89, South of town on the big hill, Junction, Utah, US~ | |
| Notes | | His tombstone ways he was born in 1882, whereas his death certificate shows he was born in 1879; whereas his obituary shows he was born in 1882; whereas his draft registration card shows he was born in 1880. US~ | |
| Bapt.(LDS) | | 6 Sep 1891 | |
| Conf.(LDS) | | 6 Sep 1891 | |
| Init.(LDS) | | 4 Dec 1951 | Salt Lake Temple |
| Endow.(LDS) | | 4 Dec 1951 | Salt Lake Temple |
| SealP (LDS) | | BIC | |
| Spouse | | Elizabeth Hanna Barnson (1884-1976) | |
| Marr. Date | | 29 Mar 1900 - Junction, Piute, Utah, United States. (Divorced on 24 Oct 1902)[71] | |

# William Henry McIntosh, Sr. and Mary Elizabeth Keele

| Children (cont.) | | |
|---|---|---|
| SealS (LDS) | 10 May 1978 | Provo Utah Temple |
| Spouse | Charlotte Ann Davis (1884-1939)[72] | 3 Aug 1904 - Junction, Piute, Utah, United States[73] |
| SealS (LDS) | 4 Jun 1954 | Salt Lake Temple |

**Events**

1. He worked as a mechanic, as reported on his death certificate.[74]
2. Baptism in the Church of Jesus Christ of Latter-day Saints: and Confirmation by John Morrill, on 6 Sep 1891.[69]
3. He appeared on the census on 5 Jun 1900 in Junction, Piute, Utah, United States.[75]
   **Line 94 - McIntosh, Abram, head, white, male, born Mar 1881, age 19, married within the year, born in Nevada, father born in Missouri, mother born in Utah, day laborer, 0 months unemployed, can read, write and speak english, rents house.**
   Line 95 - McIntosh, Elizabeth, wife, white, female, born 1884, age 15, married within the year, 0 children, 0 living, born in Utah, father born in Denmark, mother born in England, can read, write and speak english.
4. Directory: Registered a Ford touring car (22 horsepower) with the state, 10 Aug 1914, Junction, Piute, Utah, United States.[69]
5. He worked as a farmer on 15 acres (value: $145) between 1916 and 1917 in Junction, Piute, Utah, United States.[69]
6. Tax Rolls: on delinquent tax list, 14 Dec 1916, Junction, Piute, Utah, United States.[69]
7. Tax Rolls: real property on delinquent tax list to be redeemed or sold on 16 December 1918, Junction, Piute, Utah, United States.[69]
8. Draft Registration: for World War I, 12 Sep 1918, Junction, Piute, Utah, United States.[69]
   He reported his birth date at 1880 instead of 1879 or 1881 or 1882.
   Occupation as working for himself in automobile passenger and repair work.
   Medium height, stout build; blue eyes, dark brown hair.
9. Draft Registration: 19 Sep 1918, Junction, Piute, Utah, United States.[69]
   Patriotic Men Make Response to Call/Responding to the call of the Nation for recruits for the army, the loyal citizens of Piute county between the ages of 18 and 45, both inclusive, flocked to the registration places last Thursday and when the totals had been counted in the several registration offices throughout the county, 297 names had been recorded. The county fell short just forty names, according to the number allotted. Piute county had been set aside to furnish 337, but only 297 men were registered. The officers have announced that a close canvas will be made and the county thoroughly "combed" for any slacker and should any be found they will be made to suffer the penalty as prescribed for failing to register. / Reports from all the registration offices throughout the county are to the effect that the work was done expeditiously and that there was not the least semblance of disorder. The day had been declared a holiday and all business houses were closed for the occasion. / The following is a list of the men registered: / ... Junction ... Abram McIntosh, 209... Of Junction; appears on list of "persons whose registration cards are in the possession of "Piute County Draft Board, WWI-era.
10. He appeared on the census on 3 Jan 1920 in Junction, Piute, Utah, United States.[69]
    **Line 66 - McIntosh, Abram, head, owns home mortagage free, male, white, age 39, married, can read, write and speak english, born in Nevada, father born in Utah, mother born in Nevada, laborer, wage worker.**
    Line 67 - McIntosh, Charlotte, wife, female, white, age 33, married, can read, write and speak english, born in Utah, father born in Utah, mother born in Utah.
    Line 68 - McIntosh, Donald, son, male, white, age 14, single in school, born in Utah, father born in Nevada, mother born in Utah.
    Line 69 - McIntosh, Arlean, daughter, female, white, age 12, single, in school, born in Utah, father born in Nevada, mother born in Utah.
    Line 70 - McIntosh, Claron, son, male, white, age 8, single, in school, born in Utah, father born in Nevada, mother born in Utah.
    Line 71 - McIntosh, Wilda, daughter, female, white, age 6, single, in school, born in Utah, father born in Nevada, mother born in Utah.
    Line 72 - McIntosh, Glen D, son, male, white, age 1 3/12, single, born in Utah, father born in Nevada, mother born in Utah.

# William Henry McIntosh, Sr. and Mary Elizabeth Keele

11. He appeared on the census on 4 Apr 1930 in Junction, Piute, Utah, United States.[76]
**Line 76 - McIntosh, Abram, head, owns home, value of home $550, does not live on farm, male, white, age 49, married at age 28, did not attend school within year, can read and write, born in Nevada, father born in United States, mother born in Nevada, able to speak english, miner, mines, works on own account, actually at work, not a veteran.**
Line 77 - McIntosh, Charlotte A, wife, female, white, age 44, married at age 19, did not attend school within year, can read and write, born in Utah, father born in Utah, mother born in Nevada, able to speak english, no occupation.
Line 78 - McIntosh, Claron, son, male, white, age 18, single, did attend school within year, can read and write, born in Utah, father born in Nevada, mother born in Utah, able to speak english, no occupation.
Line 79 - McIntosh, Wilda, daughter, female, white, age 16, single, did attend school within year, can read and write, born in Utah, father born in Nevada, mother born in Utah, able to speak english, no occupation.
Line 80 - McIntosh, Glen D, son, male, white, age 10, single, did attend school within year, can read and write, born in Utah, father born in Nevada, mother born in Utah, able to speak english, no occupation.
Line 81 - McIntosh, Dell, son, male, white, age 5, single, did not attend school within year, born in Utah, father born in Nevada, mother born in Utah, no occupation.

12. He was employed on 22 May 1931 in Junction, Piute, Utah, United States.[69]
Messsrs. Abe and Don McIntosh of Junction and Ray McIntosh and Ernest Johnson of Marysvale went to Grand Canyon and secured employment. They intend moving their families down there for the summer.

13. He was employed on 3 Jul 1931 in Junction, Piute, Utah, United States.[69]
Abe McIntosh has returned from Bryce Canyon where he went to find work. We understand that several of the fellows who went from here got on and the others were promised work in the next ten days.

14. Newspaper: 3 Jul 1931, Junction, Piute, Utah, United States.[69]
Mrs. Arlene Snow and two children of Manti were visiting at the home of Arlene's parents, Mr. and Mrs. Abe McIntosh on Saturday and Sunday. When she returned home she was accompanied by her sister, Wilda, who will visit there for a couple ofweeks.

15. Newspaper: 24 Jul 1931, Junction, Piute, Utah, United States.[69]
Mrs. Lizzie Cowdle of California is here visiting at the home of her brothers and sister, W.H. and Abe McIntosh and Mrs. Elsie Ackerman. Lizzie has many friends here who are extending the hand of welcome and hope she will remain long enough to visit with us all.

16. Newspaper: 18 Sep 1931, Junction, Piute, Utah, United States.[77]
Mr. and Mrs. Don McIntosh have moved into the house just west of Don's parents, Mr. and Mrs. Abe McIntosh, for the winter.

17. He appeared on the census on 24 Apr 1940 in Junction, Piute, Utah, United States.
**Line 16 - McIntosh, Abram, head, male, white, age 58, widowed, finished 8th grade, born in Utah, lived in same house in 1935, not employed, has other source of income.**
Line 17 - McIntosh, Dell, son, male, white, age 16, single, in high school, born in Utah, lived in same house in 1935, no occupation.

18. Newspaper: 14 Feb 1947, Junction, Piute, Utah, United States.[69]
Mr. and Mrs. Dell McIntosh of Tooele, were visiting over the weekend with their parents, Mr. Abe McIntosh and Mr. and Mrs. Melvin Price. They were accompanied by Dell's sister, Mrs. Arlene Snow, of Salt Lake City.

19. His obituary was published on 21 Mar 1947 in Junction, Piute, Utah, United States.[69]
**Last Rites Conducted For Abram McIntosh** / Funeral services for Abram McIntosh, 65, Junction, who died March 4 following a lingering illness, were conducted March 8 at 2 o'clock p.m. in the Junction L.D.S. Ward Chapel by Armond Luke. / Song, "Sometime Somewhere", by Myrtle and Rexine Anderson, accompanied by Bessie Greenhalgh. / Prayer, Morrill Ipson. / Talk, Martel Anderson. / Trio, "Nearer My God To Thee", Delois Jensen, Thelda Thompson and Alice Zabriskie, accompanied by Bessie Greehalgh. / Talk, J.W. Applegate / Violin solo, "Perfect Day", by Judd Haycock, Circleville. / Talk, Armond Luke. / Song, "Sweet Rest in Heaven", Junction choir. / Benediction, Edward Davis, of Circleville. / Dedication, Devalson Allen. / Abram McIntosh was born in Panaca, Nevada, March 13, 1882, a son of Wm. Henry and Mary Keele McIntosh. He married Charlotte Anne Davis in Junction August 3, 1904. She died in 1939. / Mr. McIntosh was a mechanic and a member of the Church of Jesus Christ of Latter-day Saints. / Surviving are five sons and daughters: Donald McIntosh, Junction; Dell McIntosh, Sevier; Arlene Snow, Salt Lake City; Wilda Olive Lund, Salt Lake City; Lizzie Cowdell and Annie May Sprague, Los Angeles, California. / Among those from out of town who came for the funeral besides his children, were two of his sisters, Lizzie and Olive; Mr. and Mrs. Luther Davis, Mr. and Mrs. Edward

# William Henry McIntosh, Sr. and Mary Elizabeth Keele

Davies, Mr. and Mrs. Ezra Bird, Mr. and Mrs. Geo. Bird and Mrs. Vera Nay of Circleville; Mr. and Mrs. Wilford Davies, Mr. and Mrs. Jay Davies, Antimony; Mr. and Mrs. Archie Gleaves, Mr. and Mrs. Gerold LeFevre and Mrs. Maudie Dickenson, Panguitch; Mrs. Karl Norton and Mr. and Mrs. Ralph Frederick, Marysvale; Mr. and Mrs. Chesney Snow, Kingston; Mr. and Mrs Argie McIntosh, Tooele, Mr. and Mrs. Lester Brown [sic] and Mr. and Mrs. Miles Stoker, Koosharem.

| 7 F | **Olive McIntosh** | |
|---|---|---|
| AKA | Olive Johnson, Olive Lund | |
| Born | 25 Mar 1884 | Panaca, Lincoln, Nevada, United States[78] |
| Died | 8 Jun 1955 | Salt Lake City, Salt Lake, Utah, United States[78] |
| Cause of Death | Cerebral hemorrhage//Senility[78] | |
| Buried | 11 Jun 1955 | Millcreek, Salt Lake, Utah, United States[78,79] |
| Address | Elysian Burial Gardens, 1075 East College St (4580 South), Millcreek, Utah 84117, U~ | |
| Notes | Plot: A-38-2 | U~ |
| Bapt.(LDS) | 6 Jul 1875 | |
| Conf.(LDS) | 6 Jul 1895 | |
| Init.(LDS) | 15 Jan 2008 | Washington D.C. Temple |
| Endow.(LDS) | 1 Apr 1992 | St. George Utah Temple |
| SealP (LDS) | 3 Apr 1998 | Las Vegas Nevada Temple |
| Spouse | Joseph Sylvester Johnson (1881-1959) | 15 Aug 1901 - Junction, Piute, Utah, United States[80] |
| SealS (LDS) | 5 Sep 1992 | Provo Utah Temple |
| Spouse | Louis William Lund (1878-1962)[81] | |
| Marr. Date | 9 Jun 1919 - Mount Pleasant, Sanpete, Utah, United States. (Death of one spouse)[82] | |
| SealS (LDS) | 7 May 2013 | Manti Utah Temple |

**Events**

1. She appeared on the census on 5 Jun 1900 in Junction, Piute, Utah, United States.[83]
   Line 67 - McIntosh, William H, head, white, male, born Apr 1849, age 51, married 29 years, born in Missouri, father born in Scotland, mother born in Canada, farmer, 0 months unemployed, can read, write and speak english, owns, mortgage free, farm #22.
   Line 68 - McIntosh, Mary, wife, white, female, born May 1855, age 45, married 29 years, had 9 children, 7 living, born in Utah, father born in Tennessee, mother born in Pennsylvania, can read, write and speak english.
   **Line 69 - McIntosh, Olive, daughter, white, female, born Mar 1884, age 16, single, born in Nevada, father born in Missouri, mother born in Utah, in school 4 months, can read, write and speak english.**
   Line 70 - McIntosh, Elsie, daughter, white, female, born Mar 1887, age 13, single, born in Utah, father born in Missouri, mother born in Utah, in school 4 months, can read, write and speak english.
   Line 71 - McIntosh, Raymond, son, white, male, born July 1899, age 10/12, single, born in Utah, father born in Missouri, mother born in Utah.
2. She appeared on the census on 26 Apr 1910 in Junction, Piute, Utah, United States.
   Sheet No. 4A, Line 50 - Johnson, Joseph S., head, male, white, age 28, married twice, married for 4 years, born in Utah, father born in Utah, mother born in Utah, can read, write and speak english, farmer on own farm #33.
   Sheet No. 4B, **Line 51 - Johnson, Olive, wife, female, white, age 26, married twice, married 4 years, had one child,**

# William Henry McIntosh, Sr. and Mary Elizabeth Keele

**one living, born in Nevada, father born in Vermont, mother born in Nevada, can read, write and speak english.**
Line 52 - Johnson, Joseph E., son, male, white, age 7, single, born in Utah, father born in Utah, mother born in Nevada, in school.

3. She appeared on the census on 28 Jan 1920 in Marysvale, Piute, Utah, United States.
Line 71 - Lund, William, head, rents house, male, white, age 39, married, can read, write and speak english, born in Utah, parents both from Denmark and speak danish, works as manager for a restaurant on own account.
**Line 72 - Lund, Olive, wife, female, white, age 36, married, can read, write and speak english, born in Nevada, father born in U.S., mother born in U.S.**
Line 73 - Johnson, Ernest, step-son, male, white, age 17, single, can read, write and speak english, born in Utah, father born in Utah, mother born in Nevada, no occupation.
4. She appeared on the census on 2 Apr 1930 in Salt Lake City, Salt Lake, Utah, United States.
Line 40 - Lund, William L, head, rents home for $20, male, white, age 49, married at age 22, can read, write and speak english, born in Utah, both parents born in Denmark, janitor at a hotel.
**Line 41 - Lund, Olive, wife, female, white, age 45, married at age 17, can read, write and speak english, born in Nevada, father born in Utah, mother born in Nevada, cook at a hotel.**
5. She appeared on the census on 8 Apr 1940 in Salt Lake City, Salt Lake, Utah, United States.
Line 21 - Lund, William, head, male, white, age 61, married, finished high school, born in Utah, lived in same place in 1935, not employed, has another source of income.
**Line 22 - Lund, Olive, wife, female, white, age 56, married, finished 6th grade, born in Nevada, lived in same place in 1935, no occupation.**

| 8 | F | **Elsie McIntosh** [84,85] |
|---|---|---|
| Born | 3 Mar 1887 | Junction, Piute, Utah Territory, United States[85] |
| Died | 28 Jan 1963 | Panguitch, Garfield, Utah, United States[85] |
| Cause of Death | Heart Attack | |
| Buried | 31 Jan 1963 | Junction, Piute, Utah, United States[85] |
| Address | Junction Hill Cemetery, Highway 89, South of town on the big hill, Junction, Utah, US~ | |
| Bapt.(LDS) | 1 Aug 1895 | |
| Conf.(LDS) | 1 Aug 1895 | |
| Init.(LDS) | 24 Mar 1909 | Manti Utah Temple |
| Endow.(LDS) | 24 Mar 1909 | Manti Utah Temple |
| SealP (LDS) | BIC | |
| Spouse | Joseph Jochein Ackerman (1885-1979) | 7 Feb 1907 - Junction, Piute, Utah, United States[85,86] |
| SealS (LDS) | 24 Mar 1909 | Manti Utah Temple |

**Events**

1. Blessing in the Church of Jesus Christ of Latter-day Saints: by John Morrill, on 5 May 1887.[85]
2. Baptism in the Church of Jesus Christ of Latter-day Saints: by Horace Morrill, on 1 Aug 1895.[85]
3. She appeared on the census on 5 Jun 1900 in Junction, Piute, Utah, United States.[87]
Line 67 - McIntosh, William H, head, white, male, born Apr 1849, age 51, married 29 years, born in Missouri, father born in Scotland, mother born in Canada, farmer, 0 months unemployed, can read, write and speak english, owns, mortgage free, farm #22.
Line 68 - McIntosh, Mary, wife, white, female, born May 1855, age 45, married 29 years, had 9 children, 7 living, born in Utah, father born in Tennessee, mother born in Pennsylvania, can read, write and speak english.

# William Henry McIntosh, Sr. and Mary Elizabeth Keele

Line 69 - McIntosh, Olive, daughter, white, female, born Mar 1884, age 16, single, born in Nevada, father born in Missouri, mother born in Utah, in school 4 months, can read, write and speak english.
**Line 70 - McIntosh, Elsie, daughter, white, female, born Mar 1887, age 13, single, born in Utah, father born in Missouri, mother born in Utah, in school 4 months, can read, write and speak english.**
Line 71 - McIntosh, Raymond, son, white, male, born July 1899, age 10/12, single, born in Utah, father born in Missouri, mother born in Utah.

4. She appeared on the census on 16 Jan 1920 in Fort Duchesne, Uintah, Utah, United States.[88]
Line 35 - Ackerman, Joseph, head, rents house, male, white, age 34, married, can read, write and speak english, born in Utah, father born in Holland, speaks Dutch, mother born in Holland, speaks Dutch, laborer on a farm, wage worker.
**Line 36 - Ackerman, Elsie, wife, female, white, age 33, married, can read, write and speak english, born in Utah, father born in Utah, mother born in Nevada.**
Line 37 - Ackerman, Velda, daughter, female, white, age 9, single, in school, can read, write and speak english, born in Utah, father born in Utah, mother botn in Utah.
Line 38 - Ackerman, Marion, son, male, white, age 7, single, in school, can read, write and speak english, born in Utah, father born in Utah, mother born in Utah.
Line 39 - Ackerman, Fern, daughter, female, white, age 5, single, born in Utah, father born in Utah, mother born in Utah.
Line 40 - Ackerman, Racola, daughter, female, white, age 2, single, born in Utah, father born in Utah, mother born in Utah.

5. She had a residence on 19 Mar 1926 in Antimony, Garfield, Utah, United States.[85]
"Mr. and Ms. Joseph Ackerman of Antimony have moved to their home here which they recently purchassed. Welcome to our midst, folks, hope you will not be disappointed with us." Piute Chieftain.

6. She appeared on the census on 8 Apr 1930 in Junction, Piute, Utah, United States.[89]
Line 7 - Ackerman, Joseph, head, owns home, lives on a farm, male, white, age 45, married at age 22, did not attend school within year, able to read and write, born in Utah, father born in Holland, mother born in Holland, speaks english, farmer on a general farm, owner, actually at work, not a veteran, farm #2.
**Line 8 - Ackerman, Elsie, wife, female, white, age 43, married at age 19, did not attend school within year. able to read and write, born in Utah, father born in Missouri, mother born in Utah, speaks english, no occupation.**
Line 9 - Ackerman, Velda, daughter, female, white, age 19, single, did not attend school within year, able to read and write, born in Utah, father born in Utah, mother born in Utah, speaks english, no occupation.
Line 10 - Ackerman, Marion W, son, male, white, age 17, single, attended school within year, able to read and write, born in Utah, father born in Utah, mother born in Utah, speaks english, no occupation.
Line 11 - Ackerman, Dortha F, daughter, female, white, age 17, single, attended school within year, able to read and write, born in Utah, father born in Utah, mother born in Utah, speaks english, no occupation.
Line 12 - Ackerman, Racola, daughter, female, white, age 12, single, attended school within year, able to read and write, born in Utah, father born in Utah, mother born in Utah, speaks english, no occupation.
Line 13 - Ackerman, Joseph V, son, male, white, age 9, single attended school within year, able to read and write, born in Utah, father born in Utah, mother born in Utah, no occupation.
Line 14 - Ackerman, Leah, daughter, female, white, age 7, single, attended school within year, born in Utah, father born in Utah, mother born in Utah, no occupation.
Line 15 - Ackerman, Vila L, daughter, female, white, age 5/12, single, did not attend school within year, born in Utah, father born in Utah, mother born in Utah, no occupation.

7. Newspaper: 24 Jul 1931, Junction, Piute, Utah, United States.[85]
Mrs. Lizzie Cowdle of California is here visiting at the home of her brothers and sister, W.H. and Abe McIntosh and Mrs. Elsie Ackerman. Lizzie has many friends here who are extending the hand of welcome and hope she will remain long enough to visit with us all. Per the Piute County News.

8. Her obituary was published on 31 Jan 1963 in Junction, Piute, Utah, United States.[90]
**Elsie M. Ackerman**. Services Today in Junction Ward / Funeral services for Mrs. Elsie McIntosh Ackerman, 75, who died Monday evening in a Panguitch hospital of a heart attack, will be held Friday at 1 p.m. in the Junction Ward Chapel. / She was born March 3, 1887, a daughter of William Henry and Mary Keele McIntosh. She was married to Joseph Ackerman, Feb. 7, 1907 at Junction, later solemnized in the Manti LDS Temple March 24, 1909. / Survivors include husband, Junction; two sons, four daughters, Mrs. Carl (Velda) Norton, Marion W., both of Marysvale; Mrs. T.F. (Racola) LeFevre, Magna; J. Voyle, Junction; Mrs. LaNoy (Leah) Christensen, Ogden; Mrs. Donald C. (Vila) Whittaker,

# William Henry McIntosh, Sr. and Mary Elizabeth Keele

Circleville; 16 grandchildren, three great grandchildren. / Friends may call at the family home Thursday evening and Friday prior to services. Burial will be in the Junction Cemetery by Neal S. Magleby Mortuary, Richfield.

| 9 | M | **Raymond U. McIntosh** [91,92] | |
|---|---|---|---|
| Born | | 30 Jul 1899 | Junction, Piute, Utah, United States[92] |
| Died | | 3 Feb 1954 | East Ely, White Pine, Nevada, United States[93] |
| Cause of Death | | Coronary artery disease//Diabetes | |
| Buried | | 6 Feb 1954 | Ely, White Pine, Nevada, United States[94] |
| Address | | Ely City Cemetery, Ely, Nevada, USA | |
| Bapt.(LDS) | | 2 Jul 1910 | |
| Conf.(LDS) | | 2 Jul 1910 | |
| Init.(LDS) | | 11 Feb 1955 | Salt Lake Temple |
| Endow.(LDS) | | 11 Feb 1955 | Salt Lake Temple |
| SealP (LDS) | | BIC | |
| Spouse | | Telma Clara Anderton (1905-1976)[95] | 24 Mar 1920 - Sevier, Sevier, Utah, United States[96,97] |
| SealS (LDS) | | 11 Feb 1955 | Salt Lake Temple |

FATHER
RAYMOND MCINTOSH
1899 — 1954

**Events**

1. He appeared on the census on 5 Jun 1900 in Junction, Piute, Utah, United States.[98]
2. He appeared on the census on 10 Apr 1910 in Junction, Piute, Utah, United States.[99]
3. Draft Registration: 19 Sep 1918, Junction, Piute, Utah, United States.[92]
   Patriotic Men Make Response to Call/Responding to the call of the Nation for recruits for the army, the loyal citizens of Piute county between the ages of 18 and 45, both inclusive, flocked to the registration places last Thursday and when the totals had been counted in the several registration offices throughout the county, 297 names had been recorded. The county fell short just forty names, according to the number allotted. Piute county had been set aside to furnish 337, but only 297 men were registered. The officers have announced that a close canvas will be made and the county thoroughly "combed" for any slacker and should any be found they will be made to suffer the penalty as prescribed for failing to register. / Reports from all the registration offices throughout the county are to the effect that the work was done expeditiously and that there was not the least semblance of disorder. The day had been declared a holiday and all business houses were closed for the occasion. / The following is a list of the men registered: / ... Junction ... Ray McIntosh, 13... Of Junction; appears on list of "persons whose registration cards are in the possession of "Piute County Draft Board, WWI-era.
4. Draft Registration: WWI, 26 Sep 1918, Piute, Utah, United States.[92]
   Tram operator for Mineral Products Corporation at Alunite. Next of kin is sister, at Junction. Medium height, medium build; blue eyes, brown hair.
5. He had a residence on 3 Apr 1920 in Marysvale, Piute, Utah, United States.[92]
6. He appeared on the census on 2 Apr 1930 in Salt Lake City, Salt Lake, Utah, United States.
   **Line 92 - McIntosh, Ray, head, rents home for $25, male, white, age 30, married at age 20, can read, write and speak english, born in Utah, both parents born in Tennessee, laborer at odd jobs.**
   Line 93 - McIntosh, Telma, wife, female, white, age 24, married at age 15, can read, write and speak english, born in Utah, father born in Pennsylvania, mother born in Utah.
   Line 94 - McIntosh, Marjorie, daughter, female, white, age 9, single, in school, born in Utah, parents born in Utah.
   Line 95 - McIntosh, Marion, son, male, white, age 7, single, in school, born in Utah, parents born in Utah.
   Line 96 - McIntosh, Arnold, son, male, white, age 5, single, born in Utah, parents born in Utah.

# William Henry McIntosh, Sr. and Mary Elizabeth Keele

Line 97 - McIntosh, Gile, son, male, white, age 2 7/12, single, born in Utah, parents born in Utah.

7. He was employed on 22 May 1931 in Junction, Piute, Utah, United States.[92]
Messrs. Abe and Don McIntosh of Junction and **Ray McIntosh** and Ernest Johnson of Marysvale went to Grand Canyon and secured employment. They intend moving their families down there for the summer. Per the Piute County News.

8. Newspaper: 24 Jul 1931, Junction, Piute, Utah, United States.[92]
Ray McIntosh of Marysvale was visiting relatives in Junction Saturday evening. Per Piute County News.

9. Newspaper: 18 Sep 1931, Junction, Piute, Utah, United States.[92]
Ray McIntosh, Wesley Anderton and Auer Peterson of Marysvale were business visitors in Junction one day last week. Per the Piute County News.

10. He worked as a patrolman for city police.

11. He worked as a tram operator for Mineral Products Corporation in Alunite, Piute, Utah, United States.[92]

12. He appeared on the census on 22 Apr 1940 in Monroe, Sevier, Utah, United States.
**Line 35 - McIntosh, Ray, head, male, white, age 40, married, finished 8th grade, born in Utah, in 1935 lived in Richfield, Piute, Utah, farmer on own farm #7.**
Line 36 - McIntosh, Telma, wife, female, white, age 34, married, finished 7th grade, born in Utah, in 1935 lived in Richfield, Piute, Utah.
Line 37 - McIntosh, Marion, son, male, white, age 17, single, finished high school, born in Utah, in 1935 lived in Richfield, Piute, Utah, farm laborer on farm.
Line 38 - McIntosh, Arnold, son, male, white, age 15, single, in 7th grade, born in Utah, in 1935 lived in Richfield, Piute, Utah.
Line 39 - McIntosh, Gile, son, male, white, age 12, in 4th grade, born in Utah, in 1935 lived in Richfield, Piute, Utah.
Line 40 - McIntosh, Donald, son, male, white, age 10, single, in 2nd grade, born in Utah, in 1935 lived in Richfield, Piute, Utah.
Next page
Line 41 - McIntosh, James K, son, male, white, age 1, single, born in Utah.

# Source Citations


1. Brown, Beverly McIntosh and Marsha Lee McIntosh,*William McIntosh Diary, abridgement* (Self-published, Surprise, AZ. June 2002), "Willaim Henry was born April the 18th, 1849."

2. McIntosh Reunion Descendants, McIntosh - Descendants of John & Girsey (Grace) (Grizel) Rankin McIntosh (Attachment to Aug 17, 1958 Newsletter - copy in Collection of Bonnie S. Williams), Repository: Bonnie S. Williams, RR 1 Box 247, N Hwy 2, Wilburton, Oklahoma, USA.
William Henry (son of William [McINTOSH] & Maria CALDWELL) md. Mary Elizabeth KEELE
Children:
 1. Elizabeth
 2. William
 3. Mame Annie
 4. Abraham
 5. Elsie
 6. Raymond.
David Hyrum McINTOSH is a Grandson of John McINTOSH & Girsey RANKIN
died as an infant, so no marriage.
This single page attachment indicates that the parents of John McIntosh are William McIntosh & Isabell and is indicative of what our side of the family knew of our McIntosh cousins at that time in August 1958.

3. Utah, State Department of Health, Certificate of Death, death certificate state file no. 55181116; registrar's no. 1100 (1955), Olive McIntosh Lund names her father as Henry McIntosh born in Missouri.

4. Utah, State Department of Health, Certificate of Death, death certificate state file no. 4; registrar's no. 8 (1947), Abram McIntosh names his father as William Henary McIntosh born in St. Louis, Mo.

5. Utah, State Department of Health, Certificate of Death, death certificate state file no. 2; registrar's no. 2 (1942), William Henry McIntosh names his father as William H. McIntosh born in USA.

6. *Rootsweb.com. Interment Records,* William Henry McIntosh, Sr. Repository: Rootsweb.com.

7. Dortha B. Davenport, *History of Junction and Its People* (Junction, Utah: Dortha B. Davenport, 2005), page 12. Repository: Family History Library, 35 North West Temple Street, Salt Lake City, Utah 84150-3400, USA, Call Number: 979.253/J1 H2d.

8. Brown, Beverly McIntosh and Marsha McIntosh, editors,*William McIntosh Diary 1857-1898, Abridgement* (Surprise, AZ: Self-published, June 2002).

9. Daughters of Utah Pioneers, *Our Pioneer Heritage* (Salt Lake City, UT: Infobases, Inc., 1996), 19: 422. Repository: Family History Library, 35 North West Temple Street, Salt Lake City, Utah 84150-3400, USA, Call Number: 979.2 H2.

10. Frank Esshorn, editor, *Pioneers and Prominent Men of Utah comprising Photographs-Genealogies-Biographies. Pioneers are those men and women who came to Utah by wagon, hand cart or afoot, between July 24, 1847 and December 30, 1868, before the railroad. Prominent Men are stake presidents, ward bishops, governors, members of the bench, etc., who came to Utah after the coming of the railroad. The early history of the Church of Jesus Christ of Latter-Day Saints. In One Volume, Illustrated* (Salt Lake City, Utah: Utah Pioneers Book Publishing Company, 1913), McIntosh, William: 331 and 1059. Repository: Family History Library, 35 North West Temple Street, Salt Lake City, Utah 84150-3400, USA, Call Number: 979.2 D3e.

11. Andrew Jenson, editor, *Latter-day Saint Biographical Encyclopedia: A Compilation of Biographical Sketches of Prominent Men and Women in The Church of Jesus Christ of Latter-day Saints*, 4 v.: ports. (Salt Lake City, Utah: Western Epics, 1971), William McIntosh: V 4, page 647. Repository: Family History Library, 35 North West Temple Street, Salt Lake City, Utah 84150-3400, USA, Call Number: 920.0792.

12. International Society of Daughters of Utah Pioneers, editor,*Pioneer Women of Faith and Fortitude*, Volume III (Salt Lake City, Utah: Publishers Press, 1998), Maria Caldwell McIntosh: page 1946. Repository: Family History Library, 35 North West Temple Street, Salt Lake City, Utah 84150-3400, USA, Call Number: 979 D36.

13. Brown, Beverly McIntosh and Marsha Lee McIntosh,*William McIntosh Diary, abridgement* (Self-published, Surprise, AZ. June 2002), page J-2 Start for St Louis, 1847.

14. 1850 U.S. census, Andrew, Missouri, population schedule, Jefferson, p. 8B, dwelling 801, family 781, William H McIntosh; digital images, *ancestry.com*; citing National Archives and Records Administration microfilm M432.

15. Church of Jesus Christ of Latter-day Saints, "Mormon Pioneer Overland Travel, 1847-1868," database (www.lds.org/churchhistory/library/pioneercompany : accessed 22 Dec 2014), William Henry McIntosh travelled with the David Lewis Comnpany in 1851.

16. 1860 U.S. census, Shambip, Utah, population schedule, Clover, p. 450, dwelling 4028, family 3104, Wm H McIntosh; digital images, *ancestry.com*; citing National Archives and Records Administration microfilm M653.

17. 1870 U.S. census, Washington, Utah, population schedule, Panaaca, p. 7, dwelling 54, family 48, McIntosh, William; digital images, *ancestry.com*; citing National Archives and Records Administration microfilm M593.

18. 1870 U.S. census, Lincoln, Nevada, population schedule, Meadow Valley, p. 186, dwelling 66-68, family 45, McIntosh, Wm H; digital

# Source Citations


images, *ancestry.com*; citing National Archives and Records Administration microfilm M593.

19. Nevada, Lincoln County, *1880 U.S. Census, population schedule* (Washington [District of Columbia]: The National Archives), William McIntosh household, 1880 U.S. census, Lincoln Count y, Nevada, population schedule, town of Meadow Valley Wash , enumeration district [ED] 80, supervisor's district [SD ] blank, sheet 2, dwelling 13, family 13.

20. Ardis E. Parshall, *Historical Directory of Piute County, Utah* (Provo, Utah: unpublished manuscript, work-in-progress, n.d.), William Henry McIntosh, Sr.

21. Brown, Beverly McIntosh and Marsha Lee McIntosh,*William McIntosh Diary, abridgement* (Self-published, Surprise, AZ. June 2002), p 80 February 2 [1894].

22. Brown, Beverly McIntosh and Marsha Lee McIntosh,*William McIntosh Diary, abridgement* (Self-published, Surprise, AZ. June 2002), p 98 September 2 [1897].

23. 1900 U.S. census, Piute, Utah, population schedule, Junction, enumeration district (ED) 114, sheet 2B, dwelling 37, family 37, McIntosh, William H; digital images,*ancestry.com*; citing National Archives and Records Administration microfilm T623.

24. Utah, State Department of Health, Certificate of Death, death certificate state file no. 55181116; registrar's no. 1100 (1955), Olive McIntosh Lund names her mother as Mary E. Kell born in Utah.

25. Utah, State Department of Health, Certificate of Death, death certificate state file no. 4; registrar's no. 8 (1947), Abram McIntosh names his mother as Mary Keele born in Farmington, Utah.

26. Utah, State Department of Health, Certificate of Death, death certificate state file no. 2; registrar's no. 2 (1942), William Henry McIntosh names his mother as Mary Keele born in USA.

27. Dortha B. Davenport, *History of Junction and Its People* (Junction, Utah: Dortha B. Davenport, 2005), page 13. Repository: Family History Library, 35 North West Temple Street, Salt Lake City, Utah 84150-3400, USA, Call Number: 979.253/J1 H2d.

28. Colorado Department of Public Health and Environment, death certificate 7657 (1926), Jacob Keele names his father as Samuel Keele.

29. Colorado Department of Public Health and Environment, death certificate 7657 (1926), Jacob Keele names his mother's maiden name as Hess.

30. Brigham Young University-Idaho, "Western States Marriage Index," database (http://abish.byui.edu/specialCollections/westernStates/search.cfm), Mary E McIntosh and James H Empy.

31. Nevada, Lincoln County, *1880 U.S. Census, population schedule* (Washington [District of Columbia]: The National Archives), William McIntosh household, 1880 U.S. census, Lincoln County, Nevada, population schedule, town of Meadow Valley, Wash, enumeration district [ED] 80, supervisor's district [SD ] blank, sheet 2, dwelling 13, family 13.

32. 1900 U.S. census, Piute, Utah, population schedule, Junction, enumeration district (ED) 114, sheet 2B, dwelling 37, family 37, McIntosh, Mary; digital images, *ancestry.com*; citing National Archives and Records Administration microfilm T623.

33. 1910 U.S. census, Piute, Utah, population schedule, Junction, enumeration district (ED) 71, sheet 1A, p. 31, dwelling 2, family 2, Empy, Mary E; digital images, *ancestry.com*; citing National Archives and Records Administration microfilm T624.

34. Ardis E. Parshall, *Historical Directory of Piute County, Utah* (Provo, Utah: unpublished manuscript, work-in-progress, n.d.), Mary McIntosh Cowdell.

35. Birth Certificates for James Ernest Cowdell and Mary Elizabeth McIntosh, Birth Certificate said to be in possession of Mrs. Rula Marquerite Cowdell Walker, 3449 Roxanne, Long Beach, CA (info as of 1979).

36. McIntosh Reunion Descendants, McIntosh - Descendants of John & Girsey (Grace) (Grizel) Rankin McIntosh (Attachment to Aug 17, 1958 Newsletter - copy in Collection of Bonnie S. Williams), Repository: Bonnie S. Williams, RR 1 Box 247, N Hwy 2, Wilburton, Oklahoma, USA.
Elizabeth - daughter of William Henry [McINTOSH] & Mary Elizabeth KEELE.
Elizabeth McINTOSH is a Great-Granddaughter of John McINTOSH & Girsey RANKIN and Granddaughter of William McINTOSH & Maria CALDWELL.

37. California State Department of Health Services, Center for Health Statistics, "California. Death Index, 1940-1997," database, Mary Elizabeth McIntosh Cowdell.

38. "Find A Grave," database (www.findagrave.com), Mary Elizabeth McIntosh Cowdell.

39. Marriage Certificate of James Ernest Cowdell and Mary Elizabeth McIntosh, Marriage Certificate said to be in possession of Mrs. Rula Marquerite Cowdell Walker, 3449 Roxanne, Long Beach, CA (info as of 1979).

40. "Utah, Select County Marriages, 1887-1937," database, Mary E McIntosh married James E Cowdell on 8 Jan 1894 in Piute County, Utah.

41. Nevada, Lincoln County, *1880 U.S. Census, population schedule* (Washington [District of Columbia]: The National Archives), William

# Source Citations

McIntosh household, 1880 U.S. census, Lincoln County, Nevada, population schedule, town of Meadow Valley Wash, enumeration district [ED] 80, supervisor's district [SD ] blank, sheet 2, dwelling 13, family 13.

42. California. Los Angeles County, *1930 U.S. Census, population schedule* (Washington D.C.: The National Archives), James E Cowdell household, 1930 U.S. census, Los Angeles County, California, population schedule, town of Los Angeles, enumeration district [ED] 19-258, supervisor's district [ SD] 17, sheet 48A, dwelling 272, family 213.

43. Ardis E. Parshall, *Historical Directory of Piute County, Utah* (Provo, Utah: unpublished manuscript, work-in-progress, n.d.), William Henry McIntosh, Jr.

44. McIntosh - Family record of William and Nora Morrill McIntosh, Family records in possession of Ramona McIntosh Proctor 115 N 3 W Panguitch, Utah.

45. McIntosh Reunion Descendants, McIntosh - Descendants of John & Girsey (Grace) (Grizel) Rankin McIntosh (Attachment to Aug 17, 1958 Newsletter - copy in Collection of Bonnie S. Williams), Repository: Bonnie S. Williams, RR 1 Box 247, N Hwy 2, Wilburton, Oklahoma, USA.
William - son of William Henry [McINTOSH] & Mary Elizabeth KEELE.
William McINTOSH is a Great-Grandson of John McINTOSH & Girsey RANKIN and Grandson of William McINTOSH & Maria CALDWELL
no further information.

46. Utah, State Department of Health, Certificate of Death, death certificate state file no. 2; registrar's no. 2 (1942), William Henry McIntosh, born 30 Jun 1873, died 18 May 1942.

47. Utah, State Department of Health, Certificate of Death, Death certificate state file no. 2; registrar's no. 2 (1942), William Henry McIntosh, born 30 Jun 1873, died 18 May 1942.

48. Utah Division of State History, "Cemetery & Burial Database," database (https://heritage.utah.gov/history/cemeteries), William Henry McIntosh.

49. Utah, State Department of Health, Certificate of Death, death certificate state file no. 2; registrar's no. 2 (1942), William Henry McIntosh names his wife as Nora M. Morrill.

50. Ardis E. Parshall, *Historical Directory of Piute County, Utah* (Provo, Utah: unpublished manuscript, work-in-progress, n.d.), Nora May Morill.

51. Brigham Young University-Idaho, "Western States Marriage Index," database (http://abish.byui.edu/specialCollections/westernStates/search.cfm), William H. McIntosh Jr. and Nora M. Morrill.

52. Ardis E. Parshall, *Historical Directory of Piute County, Utah* (Provo, Utah: unpublished manuscript, work-in-progress, n.d.), William Henry McIntosh, Jr. and Nora May Morrill.

53. 1900 U.S. census, Piute, Utah, population schedule, Junction, enumeration district (ED) 114, sheet 1A, p. 229, dwelling 7, family 7, McIntosh, William; digital images, *ancestry.com*; citing National Archives and Records Administration microfilm T623.

54. 1910 U.S. census, Piute, Utah, population schedule, Junction, enumeration district (ED) 71, sheet 2A, p. 32, dwelling 21, family 22, McIntosh, William H.; digital images, *ancestry.com*; citing National Archives and Records Administration microfilm T624.

55. 1920 U.S. census, Teton, Idaho, population schedule, Driggs, enumeration district (ED) 233, sheet 2B, p. 161, dwelling 37, family 39, McIntosh, William H.; digital images (ancestry.com); citing National Archives and Records Administration microfilm T625.

56. 1930 U.S. census, Piute, Utah, population schedule, Junction, enumeration district (ED) 16-4, sheet 2A, p. 156, dwelling 28, family 29, McIntosh, William H.; digital images (ancestry.com); citing National Archives and Records Administration microfilm T626.

57. McIntosh Reunion Descendants, McIntosh - Descendants of John & Girsey (Grace) (Grizel) Rankin McIntosh (Attachment to Aug 17, 1958 Newsletter - copy in Collection of Bonnie S. Williams), Repository: Bonnie S. Williams, RR 1 Box 247, N Hwy 2, Wilburton, Oklahoma, USA.
Mame Annie - daughter of William Henry [McINTOSH] & Mary Elizabeth KEELE.
Mame Annie McINTOSH is a Great-Granddaughter of John McINTOSH & Girsey RANKIN and Granddaughter of William McINTOSH & Maria CALDWELL
no further information.

58. *1880 U.S. Census. Nevada-Panaca, Lincoln,* Place: Meadow Valley Wash, Lincoln, Nevada
Anna M., age 2, birthplace, Nevada.

59. "U.S., Social Security Death Index, 1935-2014," database, Anna May McIntosh Black.

60. "Find A Grave," database (www.findagrave.com), Annie M. Sprague.

61. Ardis E. Parshall, *Historical Directory of Piute County, Utah* (Provo, Utah: unpublished manuscript, work-in-progress, n.d.), Daniel Lester Sprague.

62. Brigham Young University-Idaho, "Western States Marriage Index," database (http://abish.byui.edu/specialCollections/westernStates/search.cfm), Daniel Lester Sprague and Annie May McIntosh.

# Source Citations


63. Brigham Young University-Idaho, "Western States Marriage Index," database (http://abish.byui.edu/specialCollections/westernStates/search.cfm), Annie M. Sprague and Sidney Black.

64. Ardis E. Parshall, *Historical Directory of Piute County, Utah* (Provo, Utah: unpublished manuscript, work-in-progress, n.d.), Sidney Black.

65. McIntosh Reunion Descendants, McIntosh - Descendants of John & Girsey (Grace) (Grizel) Rankin McIntosh (Attachment to Aug 17, 1958 Newsletter - copy in Collection of Bonnie S. Williams), Repository: Bonnie S. Williams, RR 1 Box 247, N Hwy 2, Wilburton, Oklahoma, USA. Abraham - son of William Henry [McINTOSH] & Mary Elizabeth KEELE.
Abraham McINTOSH is a Great-Grandson of John McINTOSH & Girsey RANKIN and Grandson of William McINTOSH & Maria CALDWELL no further information.

66. Records for Abram and Charlottie Davis McIntosh, Sources of Information:
Presiding Bishops Office 40 North Main St Salt Lake City, Utah
Personal records of Arlene McIntosh Snow 802 Jefferson St Salt Lake City, Utah.

67. Utah, State Department of Health, Certificate of Death, death certificate state file no. 3 (1939), Charlotte Ann Davis McIntosh names her husband as Abraham McIntosh.

68. Utah, State Department of Health, Certificate of Death, death certificate state file no. 4; registrar's no. 8 (1947), Abram McIntosh, born 13 Mar 1879, died 4 Mar 1947.

69. Ardis E. Parshall, *Historical Directory of Piute County, Utah* (Provo, Utah: unpublished manuscript, work-in-progress, n.d.), Abram McIntosh.

70. Utah Division of State History, "Cemetery & Burial Database," database (https://heritage.utah.gov/history/cemeteries), Abram McIntosh.

71. Ardis E. Parshall, *Historical Directory of Piute County, Utah* (Provo, Utah: unpublished manuscript, work-in-progress, n.d.), Abram McIntosh married Elizabeth Barnson.

72. Utah, State Department of Health, Certificate of Death, death certificate state file no. 4; registrar's no. 8 (1947), Abram McIntosh names his wife as Charlotte Davis.

73. Ardis E. Parshall, *Historical Directory of Piute County, Utah* (Provo, Utah: unpublished manuscript, work-in-progress, n.d.), Abram McIntosh married Charlotte Anne Davies 3 Aug 1904.

74. Utah, State Department of Health, Certificate of Death, death certificate state file no. 4; registrar's no. 8 (1947), Abram McIntosh.

75. 1900 U.S. census, Piute, Utah, population schedule, Junction, enumeration district (ED) 114, sheet 2B, p. 230, dwelling 39, family 39, McIntosh, Abram; digital images,*ancestry.com*; citing National Archives and Records Administration microfilm T623.

76. 1930 U.S. census, Piute, Utah, population schedule, Junction, enumeration district (ED) 16-4, sheet 2B, p. 156, dwelling 35, family 36, McIntosh, Abram; digital images (ancestry.com); citing National Archives and Records Administration microfilm T626.

77. Ardis E. Parshall, *Historical Directory of Piute County, Utah* (Provo, Utah: unpublished manuscript, work-in-progress, n.d.), Abe McIntosh.

78. Utah, State Department of Health, Certificate of Death, death certificate state file no. 55181116; registrar's no. 1100 (1955), Olive McIntosh Lund.

79. "Find A Grave," database (www.findagrave.com), Olive McIntosh Johnson.

80. Brigham Young University-Idaho, "Western States Marriage Index," database (http://abish.byui.edu/specialCollections/westernStates/search.cfm), Joseph Sylvester Johnson married Olive McIntosh on 15 Aug 1901 in Junction, Utah.

81. Utah, State Department of Health, Certificate of Death, death certificate state file no. 55181116; registrar's no. 1100 (1955), Olive McIntosh Lund names her husband as Louis William Lund.

82. Brigham Young University-Idaho, "Western States Marriage Index," database (http://abish.byui.edu/specialCollections/westernStates/search.cfm), Lewis E. Lund and Olive Johnson.

83. 1900 U.S. census, Piute, Utah, population schedule, Junction, enumeration district (ED) 114, sheet 2B, dwelling 37, family 37, McIntosh, Olive; digital images, *ancestry.com*; citing National Archives and Records Administration microfilm T623.

84. McIntosh Reunion Descendants, McIntosh - Descendants of John & Girsey (Grace) (Grizel) Rankin McIntosh (Attachment to Aug 17, 1958 Newsletter - copy in Collection of Bonnie S. Williams), Repository: Bonnie S. Williams, RR 1 Box 247, N Hwy 2, Wilburton, Oklahoma, USA. Elsie - daughter of William Henry [McINTOSH] & Mary Elizabeth KEELE.
Elsie McINTOSH is a Great-Granddaughter of John McINTOSH & Girsey RANKIN and Granddaughter of William McINTOSH & Maria CALDWELL.

85. Ardis E. Parshall, *Historical Directory of Piute County, Utah* (Provo, Utah: unpublished manuscript, work-in-progress, n.d.), Elsie McIntosh.

# Source Citations

86. Brigham Young University-Idaho, "Western States Marriage Index," database (http://abish.byui.edu/specialCollections/westernStates/search.cfm), Elsie McIntosh and Joseph Ackerman.

87. 1900 U.S. census, Piute, Utah, population schedule, Junction, enumeration district (ED) 114, sheet 2B, dwelling 37, family 37, McIntosh, Elsie; digital images, *ancestry.com*; citing National Archives and Records Administration microfilm T623.

88. 1920 U.S. census, Uintah, Utah, population schedule, Fort Duchesne, enumeration district (ED) 131, sheet 13A, p. 36, dwelling 8, family 8, Ackerman, Elsie; digital images, *ancestry.com*; citing National Archives and Records Administration microfilm T625.

89. 1930 U.S. census, Piute, Utah, population schedule, Junction, enumeration district (ED) 16-5, sheet 1A, p. 159, dwelling 2, family 2, Ackerman, Elsie; digital images (ancestry.com); citing National Archives and Records Administration microfilm T626.

90. Ardis E. Parshall, *Historical Directory of Piute County, Utah* (Provo, Utah: unpublished manuscript, work-in-progress, n.d.), Elsie McIntosh Ackerman.

91. McIntosh Reunion Descendants, McIntosh - Descendants of John & Girsey (Grace) (Grizel) Rankin McIntosh (Attachment to Aug 17, 1958 Newsletter - copy in Collection of Bonnie S. Williams), Repository: Bonnie S. Williams, RR 1 Box 247, N Hwy 2, Wilburton, Oklahoma, USA.
Raymond - son of William Henry [McINTOSH] & Mary Elizabeth KEELE.
Raymond McINTOSH is a Great-Grandson of John McINTOSH & Girsey RANKIN and Grandson of William McINTOSH & Maria CALDWELL no further information.

92. Ardis E. Parshall, *Historical Directory of Piute County, Utah* (Provo, Utah: unpublished manuscript, work-in-progress, n.d.), Raymond U. McIntosh.

93. "U.S., Social Security Death Index, 1935-2014," database, Raymond U. McIntosh.

94. "Find A Grave," database (www.findagrave.com), Raymond McIntosh.

95. Records for Raymond and Telma Anderton McIntosh. Mrs Marjorie McIntosh Pope 11 Reno Rd Box 816 Ely, Nevada

96. Ardis E. Parshall, *Historical Directory of Piute County, Utah* (Provo, Utah: unpublished manuscript, work-in-progress, n.d.), Raymond U. McIntosh and Thelma Clara Anderton; 3 Apr 1920: Marriage license: Ray McIntosh, age 21, and Thelma Clara Anderton, age 20, both of Marysvale...went to Manti to be married in the temple. Per the Richfield Reaper.

97. "Utah, Select County Marriages, 1887-1937," database, Ray Mcintosh and Telma Clara Anderton.

98. 1900 U.S. census, Piute, Utah, population schedule, Junction, enumeration district (ED) 114, sheet 2B, dwelling 37, family 37, McIntosh, Raymond; digital images, *ancestry.com*; citing National Archives and Records Administration microfilm T623.

99. 1910 U.S. census, Piute, Utah, population schedule, Junction, enumeration district (ED) 71, sheet 1A, p. 31, dwelling 2, family 2, McIntosh, Raymond; digital images, *ancestry.com*; citing National Archives and Records Administration microfilm T624.

# James Franklin McIntosh and Anne Mae Jordan

| **Husband** | **James Franklin McIntosh**[1] | |
|---|---|---|
| AKA | Frank McIntosh | |
| Born | 8 Jan 1852 | Bountiful, Davis, Utah Territory, United States[2] |
| Died | 2 May 1896 | Mount Pleasant, Sanpete, Utah, United States[1] |
| Cause of Death | Liver failure | |
| Buried | 2 May 1896 | Mount Pleasant, Sanpete, Utah, United States[3] |
| Address | Mount Pleasant City Cemetery, 900 South 100 East, Mt. Pleasant, Utah 84647, USA | |
| Notes | Plot: A-115-1-4 | |
| Bapt.(LDS) | 1 Jan 1860 | |
| Conf.(LDS) | 1 Jan 1860 | |
| Init.(LDS) | 29 Mar 1878 | St. George Utah Temple |
| Endow.(LDS) | 29 Mar 1878 | St. George Utah Temple |
| Father | William McIntosh (1819-1899) [1,4,5,6] | |
| Mother | Maria Caldwell (1824-1897) [7] | |
| SealP (LDS) | 11 Oct 1893 | Manti Utah Temple |
| Marriage | 29 Mar 1878 | Saint George, Washington, Utah Territory, United States |
| SealS (LDS) | 29 Mar 1878 | St. George Utah Temple |

**Events**

1. He was born in 1852.
   Bountiful was previously known as Session's Settlement.

2. Census Index: James Franklin McIntosh, 1856, West Jordan, Great Salt Lake, Utah Territory, United States.[8]

3. He appeared on the census on 11 Oct 1860 in Clover, Shambip, Utah Territory, United States.[9]
   Line 25 - Wm McIntosh, age 40, male, farmer, born in Scotland
   Line 26 - Maria McIntosh, age 36, female, born in Canada
   Line 27 - Jno E McIntosh, age 18, male, born in Ohio
   Line 28 - Wm. H McIntosh, age 11, male, born in Missouri, in school
   **Line 29 - Jas F McIntosh, age 8, male, born in Utah Territory, in school**
   Line 30 - Malissa J McIntosh, age 6, female, born in Utah Territory, in school
   Line 31 - Alice M McIntosh, age 3, female, born in Utah Territory
   Line 32 - Abm E McIntosh, age 6/12, male, born in Utah Territory

4. He appeared on the census on 10 Jun 1870 in Panaca, Washington, Utah Territory.[10]
   Line 20 - McIntosh, William age 49, male, white, day laborer, value of personal estate $200, born in Scotland, father and mother foreign born, male over 21.
   Line 21 - McIntosh, Marie, age 45, female, white, keeping house, born in Canada, father and mother foreign born.
   Line 22 - McIntosh, William, age 20, male, white, teamster, born in Missouri, father and mother foreign born.
   **Line 23 - McIntosh, Frank, age 18, male, white, work on farm, born in Utah, father and mother foreign born.**
   Line 24 - McIntosh, Jane, age 15, female, white, at home, born in Utah, father and mother foreign born, attended school.
   Line 25 - McIntosh, Allice, age 12, female, white, born in Utah, father and mother foreign born, attended school.
   Line 26 - McIntosh, Abraham, age 10, male, white, born in Utah, father and mother foreign born, attended school.
   Line 27 - McIntosh, Lilly, age 7, female, white, born in Utah, father and mother foreign born.
   Line 28 - McIntosh, Caroline, age 4, female, white, born in Utah, father and mother foreign born.
   Line 29 - McIntosh, Albert, age 1, male, white, born in Utah, father and mother foreign born.

5. He appeared on the census on 28 Jul 1870 in Meadow Valley, Lincoln, Nevada, United States.[11]
   Line 22 - McIntosh, Wm age 50, male, white, farming, value of real estate $300, value of personal estate $800, born in Scotland, father and mother foreign born, male over 21.
   Line 23 - McIntosh, Marie, age 45, female, white, keeping house, born in Canada, father and mother foreign born.
   Line 24 - McIntosh, Wm H, age 21, male, white, farming, born in Missouri, father and mother foreign born, male over 21.
   **Line 25 - McIntosh, Frank, age 18, male, white, farming, born in Utah, father and mother foreign born.**

# James Franklin McIntosh and Anne Mae Jordan

Line 26 - McIntosh, Jane, age 16, female, white, at home, born in Utah, father and mother foreign born, attended school.
Line 27 - McIntosh, Alice, age 12, female, white, school, born in Utah, father and mother foreign born, attended school.
Line 28 - McIntosh, Abe, age 10, male, white, school, born in Utah, father and mother foreign born, attended school.
Line 29 - McIntosh, Lilly, age 7, female, white, school, born in Utah, father and mother foreign born.
Line 30 - McIntosh, Caroline, age 4, female, white, school, born in Utah, father and mother foreign born.
Line 31 - McIntosh, Albert, age 1, male, white, school, born in Nevada, father and mother foreign born.

6. He appeared on the census on 12 Jun 1880 in Panaca, Lincoln, Nevada, United States.[12]
**Line 45 - McIntosh, Franklin, white, male age 27, head, married, teamster, born in Missouri, father born in Scotland, mother born in Canada.**
Line 46 - McIntosh, Anna, white, female, age 23, wife, married, keeping house, born in Utah, father born in England, mother born in England.
7. He worked as a sheep raiser from 1890 to 1894 in Saint John, Tooele, Utah, United States.[13]
8. He had a residence from 1892 to 2 May 1896 in Mount Pleasant, Sanpete, Utah, United States.[14]
9. His obituary was published after 2 May 1896 in Mount Pleasant, Sanpete, Utah, United States.[1]
Extracted from the Diary of William McIntosh. This is his son James Frankling.
May 2, 1896. It has become my painful privilege to record the demise of J F McIntosh, my son. He died and was buried on Saturday May 2, Mount Pleasant, Utah. The son of William and Maria McIntosh of Mount Pleasant. We telegraphed for our people to come to the funeral but they could not get here in time for the funeral. We was obliged to bury him. He died from liver troubles. Ten days sick. He was born January 8, 1852. He was sick but a short time. His mother is sickly and has been for a long time. She lives at the present time in St. John, Tooele County. Her daughter Alice who lives in St. John, Tooele County was here taking care of her mother and she took her mother home with her to St. John, Tooele Co., Utah, thinking to better her health.

| **Wife** | **Anne Mae Jordan** | |
|---|---|---|
| AKA | Ann Jordan, Anna Mae Jordan, Annie McIntosh | |
| Born | 25 Oct 1857 | West Jordan, Great Salt Lake, Utah Territory, United States[15] |
| Died | 27 Sep 1920 | Mount Pleasant, Sanpete, Utah, United States[15] |
| Cause of Death | Cerebral Apoplexy (stroke)//Arteriosclerosis[15] | |
| Buried | 30 Sep 1920 | Mount Pleasant, Sanpete, Utah, United States[15,16] |
| Address | Mount Pleasant City Cemetery, 900 South 100 East, Mt. Pleasant, Utah 84647, USA | |
| Notes | Mt Pleasant Cemetery, grave location A-115-1-3. | |
| Bapt.(LDS) | 20 Oct 1967 | |
| Conf.(LDS) | 1 Jan 1864 | |
| Init.(LDS) | 9 Sep 1872 | Endowment House |
| Endow.(LDS) | 9 Sep 1872 | Endowment House |
| Father | James Francis Jordan (1824-1900) [17,18,19] | |
| Mother | Sarah Canon (1820-1890) [20,21,22] | |
| SealP (LDS) | 6 Feb 1968 | Manti Utah Temple |

**Events**

1. She appeared on the census on 11 Oct 1860 in Clover, Shambip, Utah Territory, United States.[23]
Line 36) Ja Jordan, age 35, male, farmer, born in England.
Line 37) Sarah Jordan, age 38, female, born in England.
Line 38) Leonard J Jordan, age 12, male, born in England.

# James Franklin McIntosh and Anne Mae Jordan

Line 39) Mary J Jordan, age 9, female, born in England, in school.
Line 40) Fanny Jordan, age 7, female, born in England, in school.
**Line 1) Anna Jordan, age 4, female, born in Utah Territory.**
Line 2) Emeline Jordan, age 1, female, born in Utah Territory.

2. She appeared on the census on 20 Aug 1870 in Salt Lake City, Salt Lake, Utah, United States.
James Jordan, age 44
Sarah Jordon, age 45
Mary Jordon, age 19
**Annie Jordon, age 14**
Joseph Jordon, age 7
Mary Decker, age 65

3. She appeared on the census on 12 Jun 1880 in Panaca, Lincoln, Nevada, United States.[12]
Line 45 - McIntosh, Franklin, white, male age 27, head, married, teamster, born in Missouri, father born in Scotland, mother born in Canada.
**Line 46 - McIntosh, Anna, white, female, age 23, wife, married, keeping house, born in Utah, father born in England, mother born in England.**

4. Marks and Brands: Marks in Ears, 20 Sep 1899, Mount Pleasant, Sanpete, Utah, United States.[24]
Annie received authorization to use certain marks and brands on her herd animals.

5. She appeared on the census on 21 Jun 1900 in Mount Pleasant, Sanpete, Utah, United States.[25]
**Line 60 - McIntosh, Ann, head, white, female, born Oct 1856, age 43, widowed, had 0 children, 0 living, born in Utah, father born in England, mother born in England, can read, write and speak english, owns, mortgage free, farm #143.**
Line 61 - Johanson, Kimball, son-in-law, white, male, born Sept 1873, age 26, married 1 year, born in Utah, father born in Denmark, mother born in Denmark, sheep herder, can read, write and speak english, owns, farm # 144.
Line 62 - Johanson, Ica, daughter, white, female, born Nov 1879, age 20, married 1 year, had 0 children, 0 living, born in Utah, father born in California, mother born in Califormia, can read, write and speak english.

6. She appeared on the census on 5 May 1910 in Mount Pleasant, Sanpete, Utah, United States.[26]
**Line 8 - McIntosh, Anna, head, female, white, age 52, widowed, born in Utah, father born in England-English, mother born in England-English, speaks english, no occupation, can read and write, owns, mortgage free, house.**

7. Marks and Brands: 4 May 1912, Mount Pleasant, Sanpete, Utah, United States.[27]
Annie received authorization to use certain marks and brands on her herd animals.

8. She appeared on the census on 24 Jan 1920 in Mount Pleasant, Sanpete, Utah, United States.[28]
Line 27 - Johansen, Kimbal, head, owns home, mortgage free, male, white, age 48, married, can read and write, born in Utah, father born in Denmark-speaks Danish, mother born in Denmark-speaks Danish, speaks english, farmer, general farm, works on own account, farm #120.
Line 28 - Johansen, Ica, wife, female, white, age 40, married, can read and write, born in Nevada, father born in Nevada, mother born in Nevada, speaks english, no occupation.
Line 29 - Johansen, Vera, daughter, female, white, age 14, single, attended school, can read and write, born in Utah, father born in Utah, mother born in Utah, speaks english, no occupation.
Line 30 - Johansen, Tanetta, daughter, female, white, age 12, single, attended school, can read and write, born in Utah, father born in Utah, mother born in Utah, speaks english, no occupation.
Line 31 - Johansen, Neils, son, male, white, age 6, single, did not attend school, can read and write, born in Utah, father born in Utah, mother born in Utah, no occupation.
Line 32 - Johansen, Carlyle, son, male, white, age 3 8/12, single, born in Utah, father born in Utah, mother born in Utah, no occupation.
**Line 33 - McIntosh, Annie, mother-in-law, female, white, age 63, widowed, born in Utah, father born in England-speaks English, mother born in England-speaks English, speaks english, no occupation.**

9. Her obituary was published on 1 Oct 1920 in Mount Pleasant, Sanpete, Utah, United States.
**Funeral Held for Annie McIntosh**
Funeral services were held Thursday at 2 o'clock at the South Ward chapel for Mrs. Annie McIntosh, age 63 years, who died Monday, Sept. 27th in this city following three years illness with paralysis. Bishop A.E. McIntosh conducted the services. The opening prayer was offered by Hans Lund, and the closing prayer by Chris Johansen. The speakers were Pres. C.N. Lund and Bishop McIntosh. The grave was dedicated by Bishop McIntosh. The choir furnished appropriate

# James Franklin McIntosh and Anne Mae Jordan

hymns for the services.
Mrs. McIntosh was born at Taylorsville on October 25, 1856. She is survived by a brother, Joseph Jordan of this city, and three sisters, Mrs. Fannie Rigby of Fairview, Mrs. Mary Jane Tanner of Clover, Utah and Mrs. Emma Talman of Van Couver, Canada.
Those who came here to attend the funeral were Mrs. Tanner and son, Azel of Clover, Mrs. Ellen Jordan, Mrs. Ellen Davis and son, John S. of Tooele, Utah and the Rigby family of Fairview and Clear Creek.
*Mt. Pleasant Pyramid*

## Children

| 1 | F | **Ica Minda Crow McIntosh** [29,30,31] | |
|---|---|---|---|
| AKA | | Ica Minda Crow, Isamina Crow, Ica M Johansen | |
| Born | | 7 Nov 1879 | Panaca, , Nevada, United States[32,33] |
| Died | | 3 Sep 1943 | Delta, Millard, Utah, United States[33,34] |
| Cause of Death | | Cardio nephritis[34] | |
| Buried | | 6 Sep 1943 | Mount Pleasant, Sanpete, Utah, United States[33,35,36] |
| Address | | Mount Pleasant City Cemetery, 900 South 100 East, Mt. Pleasant, Utah 84647, USA | |
| Status | | Adopted | |
| Child-Par.Rel. | | Father: Adopted, Mother: Adopted | |
| Bapt.(LDS) | | 20 Oct 1888 | |
| Conf.(LDS) | | 20 Oct 1888 | |
| Init.(LDS) | | 7 Jun 1899 | Manti Utah Temple |
| Endow.(LDS) | | 7 Jun 1899 | Manti Utah Temple |
| SealP (LDS) | | 22 Dec 2016 | Billings Montana Temple |
| Spouse | | Kimball Johansen (1870-1953)[37] | 7 Jun 1899 - Manti, Sanpete, Utah, United States[38,39] |
| SealS (LDS) | | 7 Jun 1899 | Manti Utah Temple |

JOHANSEN
ICA M. 1879 — 1943
KIMBALL 1870 — 1953

**Events**

1. She appeared on the census on 26 Jun 1880 in Clover Valley, Lincoln, Nevada, United States.[40]
   Line 49 - Crow, William H., white, male, age 30, head, married, farmer, born in California, father born in Missouri, mother born England.
   Line 50 - Crow, Martha A., white, female, age 28, wife, married, keeping house, born in Iowa, father born in England, mother born in Canada.
   Next Page
   Line 1 - Crow, George E., white, male, age 7, single, born in Nevada, father born in California, mother born in Iowa.
   Line 2 - Crow, Joseph E., white, male, age 4, son, single, born in Nevada, father born in California, mother born in Iowa.
   Line 3 - Crow, Martha J., white, female, age 2, daughter, single, born in Nevada, father born in California, mother born in Iowa.
   **Line 4 - Crow, Icamina, white, female, age 7/12, born in November, daughter, single, born in Nevada, father born in California, mother born in Iowa.**

2. Adopted: 1882, Panaca, , Nevada, United States.
   Extracted from a memoir written by Ica's older sister:
   ***Mr. and Mrs. Frank McIntosh came to see if Dad would give them one of us girls. They didn't have any children so Dad let them have my sister just older than me. They were well off, so my sister had a good home.***

   ***On 7 June 1899 he was married to Ica Minda Crowe in the Manti Temple. She was the daughter of William and***

# James Franklin McIntosh and Anne Mae Jordan

***Martha Crowe of Clover Valley, Nevada. Her mother died when she was only two and when she was three, her father could no longer provide for his six small children and sent her to live with Frank and Annie Jordon McIntosh in 1882; they had no other children. They later moved to Mt. Pleasant where she met Kimball.***

3. She appeared on the census on 21 Jun 1900 in Mount Pleasant, Sanpete, Utah, United States.[41]
Line 60 - McIntosh, Ann, head, white, female, born Oct 1856, age 43, widowed, had 0 children, 0 living, born in Utah, father born in England, mother born in England, can read, write and speak english, owns, mortgage free, farm #143.
Line 61 - Johanson, Kimball, son-in-law, white, male, born Sept 1873, age 26, married 1 year, born in Utah, father born in Denmark, mother born in Denmark, sheep herder, can read, write and speak english, owns, farm # 144.
**Line 62 - Johanson, Ica, daughter, white, female, born Nov 1879, age 20, married 1 year, had 0 children, 0 living, born in Utah, father born in California, mother born in Califormia, can read, write and speak english.**

4. She appeared on the census on 4 May 1910 in Mount Pleasant, Sanpete, Utah, United States.[42]
Line 81 - Johansen, Kimball, head, male, white, age 39, married (M1) for 12 years, born in Utah, father born in Denmark-Danish, mother born in Denmark-Danish, speaks english, farmer, general farm, working on own account, can read and write, owns, mortgage free, house.
**Line 82 - Johansen, Ica R Minda, wife, female, white, age 30, married (M1) for 12 years, had 3 children, 2 living, born in Nevada, father born in Nevada, mother born in Nevada, speaks english, no occupation, can read and write.**
Line 83 - Johansen, Vera R Minda, daughter, female, white, age 3, single, born in Utah, father born in Utah, mother born in Nevada, no occupation.
Line 84 - Johansen, Anna Janetta, female, white, age 1 8/12, single, born in Utah, father born in Utah, mother born in Nevada, no occupation.

5. She appeared on the census on 24 Jan 1920 in Mount Pleasant, Sanpete, Utah, United States.[43]
Line 27 - Johansen, Kimbal, head, owns home, mortgage free, male, white, age 48, married, can read and write, born in Utah, father born in Denmark-Danish, mother born in Denmark-Danish, speaks english, farmer, general farm, works on own account, farm #120.
**Line 28 - Johansen, Ica, wife, female, white, age 40, married, can read and write, born in Nevada, father born in Nevada, mother born in Nevada, speaks english, no occupation.**
Line 29 - Johansen, Vera, daughter, female, white, age 14, single, attended school, can read and write, born in Utah, father born in Utah, mother born in Utah, speaks english, no occupation.
Line 30 - Johansen, Tanetta, daughter, female, white, age 12, single, attended school, can read and write, born in Utah, father born in Utah, mother born in Utah, speaks english, no occupation.
Line 31 - Johansen, Neils, son, male, white, age 6, single, did not attend school, can read and write, born in Utah, father born in Utah, mother born in Utah, no occupation.
Line 32 - Johansen, Carlyle, son, male, white, age 38/12, single, born in Utah, father born in Utah, mother born in Utah, no occupation.
Line 33 - McIntosh, Annie, mother-in-law, female, white, age 63, widowed, born in Utah, father born in England-English, mother born in England-English, speaks english, no occupation.

6. She appeared on the census on 18 Apr 1930 in Sutherland, Millard, Utah, United States.[44]
Line 60 - Johansen, Kimball, head, owns house, on a farm, male, white, age 59, married, age 28 at first marriage, can read, write and speak english, born in Utah, father born in Denmark, mother born in Denmark, farmer on a general farm, works on own account, employed, not a veteran, farm #61.
**Line 61 - Johansen, Ica, wife, female, white, age 51, married at age 20, can read, write and speak english, born in Nevada, father born in US, mother born in Nevada.**
Line 62 - Johansen, Niels F., son, male, white, age 17, single, in school, can read, write and speak english, born in Utah, father born in Utah, mother born in Nevada.
Line 63 - Johansen, Carlyle D., son, male, white, age 14, single, in school, can read, write and speak english, born in Utah, father born in Utah, mother born in Nevada.

7. She had a residence in 1940 in Woodrow, Millard, Utah, United States.

8. She appeared on the census on 17 Apr 1940 in Sutherland, Millard, Utah, United States.
Line 56 - Johansen, Kimball, head, male, white, age 69, married, finished 8th grade, born in Utah, lived in same house in 1935, farmer on own farm #83.
**Line 57 - Johansen, Ica, wife, female, white, age 59, married, finished one year high school, born in Nevada, lived in same house in 1935.**
Line 58 - Johansen, Caryle, son, male, white, age 23, single, finished one year high school, born in Utah, lived in same

# James Franklin McIntosh and Anne Mae Jordan

house in 1935, working on family farm.

9. Her obituary was published after 3 Sep 1943.
**MRS. ICA C. JOHANSEN DIES AT HOME IN DELTA**
Mrs. Ica Crowe Johansen, 64, wife of Kimball Johansen, died at her home in Delta Friday at 5:20 p.m. Mrs. Johansen was born on November 7, 1878 at Panaca, Nevada, a daughter of William and Martha Crowe. She attended school in Mt. Pleasant and in 1899 was married to Kimball Johansen in the Manti Temple. They resided in Mt. Pleasant until 1921 when the family moved to Delta. She is survived by her husband and the following children; Mrs. Vera Barney, Mrs. Tavetta Sorensen, and Don C. Johansen; seven grandchildren; two sisters, Mrs. Lizzie Burgess of Salt Lake and Mrs. Jenney Langdon of Oregon and one brother, George Crowe of Caliente, Nevada. Funeral services were held in the Sutherland Church house, Monday morning at 10 a.m. Services and burials at Mt. Pleasant on Monday at 4 p.m

# Source Citations


1. Brown, Beverly McIntosh and Marsha McIntosh, editors,*William McIntosh Diary 1857-1898, Abridgement* (Surprise, AZ: Self-published, June 2002).

2. Brown, Beverly McIntosh and Marsha McIntosh, editors,*William McIntosh Diary 1857-1898, Abridgement* (Surprise, AZ: Self-published, June 2002), J-10.

3. "Find A Grave," database (www.findagrave.com), James Franklin McIntosh.

4. Daughters of Utah Pioneers, *Our Pioneer Heritage* (Salt Lake City, UT: Infobases, Inc., 1996), 19: 422. Repository: Family History Library, 35 North West Temple Street, Salt Lake City, Utah 84150-3400, USA, Call Number: 979.2 H2.

5. Frank Esshorn, editor, *Pioneers and Prominent Men of Utah comprising Photographs-Genealogies-Biographies. Pioneers are those men and women who came to Utah by wagon, hand cart or afoot, between July 24, 1847 and December 30, 1868, before the railroad. Prominent Men are stake presidents, ward bishops, governors, members of the bench, etc., who came to Utah after the coming of the railroad. The early history of the Church of Jesus Christ of Latter-Day Saints. In One Volume, Illustrated* (Salt Lake City, Utah: Utah Pioneers Book Publishing Company, 1913), McIntosh, William: 331 and 1059. Repository: Family History Library, 35 North West Temple Street, Salt Lake City, Utah 84150-3400, USA, Call Number: 979.2 D3e.

6. Andrew Jenson, editor, *Latter-day Saint Biographical Encyclopedia: A Compilation of Biographical Sketches of Prominent Men and Women in The Church of Jesus Christ of Latter-day Saints*, 4 v.: ports. (Salt Lake City, Utah: Western Epics, 1971), William McIntosh: V 4, page 647. Repository: Family History Library, 35 North West Temple Street, Salt Lake City, Utah 84150-3400, USA, Call Number: 920.0792.

7. International Society of Daughters of Utah Pioneers, editor,*Pioneer Women of Faith and Fortitude*, Volume III (Salt Lake City, Utah: Publishers Press, 1998), Maria Caldwell McIntosh: page 1946. Repository: Family History Library, 35 North West Temple Street, Salt Lake City, Utah 84150-3400, USA, Call Number: 979 D36.

8. Utah State Census Index, 1856, Utah, population schedule; HISTORICAL BACKGROUND
Utah pioneers petitioned for statehood for the second time in 1856. To show that Utah Territory held enough population to become a state, a census was taken in January and February of that year. In December, a disappointed Governor Brigham Young reported to the territorial legislature that the petition had been rejected. The following passage from that report shows Governor Young was anxious to suggest Utah had a large population. "The enumeration of the inhabitants showed a population of near 77,000 in this territory, and it is presumed that the addition to our numbers, since that was taken, would amount to about twenty thousand. This gives an aggregate equal to or exceeding the ratio of representation for congressmen, removing every objection, if any were made, to our admission, on the score of insufficient population." (Brigham Young, "Governor's Message," Deseret News [Salt Lake City, Utah], December 24, 1856, p. 333, col. 2).
In fact, there is reason to believe the territorial population was considerably less than presented in the Governor's report. The 1850/1851 census of Utah showed only 11,380 residents. The 1860 census showed 40,273. Thus, the 77,000 figure appears to be far too large, and Govenor Young's estimate that 20,000 people entered the territory in one year also seems exaggerated.
Indeed, some names on the 1856 census seem to be fictitious, repeated, or those of non-residents of Utah Territory. For example, ....
A striking feature of the census and further evidence of padding is that virtually every page and most columns begins with a different surname from that ending the previous one; the last family in each column has exactly enough members to reach the last available line.
Index Publishing presents this index for genealogists, historians, demographers, and other researachers who wish to quickly determine where specific individuals are located on the 1856 census of Utah Territory. (Compiled by Bryan Lee Dilts, Index Publishing, PO Box 11476, SLC, UT 1983).

9. 1860 U.S. census, Shambip, Utah, population schedule, Clover, p. 450, dwelling 4028, family 3104, Jas F McIntosh; digital images, *ancestry.com*; citing National Archives and Records Administration microfilm M653.

10. 1870 U.S. census, Washington, Utah, population schedule, Panaca, p. 7, dwelling 54, family 48, McIntosh, Frank; digital images, *ancestry.com*; citing National Archives and Records Administration microfilm M593.

11. 1870 U.S. census, Lincoln, Nevada, population schedule, Meadow Valley, p. 186, dwelling 66-68, family 45, McIntosh, Frank; digital images, *ancestry.com*; citing National Archives and Records Administration microfilm M593.

12. *1880 U.S. Census. Nevada-Panaca, Lincoln,* Franklin McIntosh household, 1880 U.S. census, Lincoln Coun ty, Nevada, population schedule, town of Panaca, enumeratio n district [ED] 30, supervisor's district [SD] blank, pag e 6B, dwelling 15, family 15.

13. Brown, Beverly McIntosh and Marsha McIntosh, editors,*William McIntosh Diary 1857-1898, Abridgement* (Surprise, AZ: Self-published, June 2002), pages 69 and 80.

14. Brown, Beverly McIntosh and Marsha McIntosh, editors,*William McIntosh Diary 1857-1898, Abridgement* (Surprise, AZ: Self-published, June 2002), pages, 76, 80, 83.

15. Utah, State Department of Health, Certificate of Death, death certificate state file no. 253 (1920), Annie McIntosh.

16. "Find A Grave," database (www.findagrave.com), Annie McIntosh.

17. Utah, State Department of Health, Certificate of Death, death certificate state file no. 113 (1919), Leonard James Jordan names his father as James F. Jordan born in England.

18. Utah, State Department of Health, Certificate of Death, death certificate state file no. 78; registrar's no. 28 (1939), Joseph Clark Jordan names

# Source Citations

his father as James F. Jordan born in England.

19. Utah, State Department of Health, Certificate of Death, death certificate state file no. 253 (1920), Annie McIntosh names her father as James Jordan born in England.

20. Utah, State Department of Health, Certificate of Death, death certificate state file no. 113 (1919), Leonard James Jordan names his mother as Sarah Cannon born in England.

21. Utah, State Department of Health, Certificate of Death, death certificate state file no. 78; registrar's no. 28 (1939), Joseph Clark Jordan names his mother as Sarah Cannon born in England.

22. Utah, State Department of Health, Certificate of Death, death certificate state file no. 253 (1920), Annie McIntosh names her mother as Sarah Cannon born in USA.

23. 1860 U.S. census, Shambip, Utah, population schedule, Clover, p. 452, dwelling 4038, family 3114, Anna Jordan; digital images, *ancestry.com*; citing National Archives and Records Administration microfilm M653.

24. Utah, Record of Marks and Brands for the State of Utah; Utah State Archives and Record Service, Salt Lake City.

25. 1900 U.S. census, Sanpete, Utah, population schedule, MT Pleasant, enumeration district (ED) 128, sheet 16B, p. 192, dwelling 329, family 333, McIntosh, Annie; digital images,*ancestry.com*; citing National Archives and Records Administration microfilm T623.

26. 1910 U.S. census, Sanpete, Utah, population schedule, Mt Pleasant, enumeration district (ED) 156, sheet 12A, p. 164, dwelling 205, family 215, McIntosh, Anna; digital images,*ancestry.com*; citing National Archives and Records Administration microfilm T624.

27. Utah, Record of Marks and Brands for the State of Utah, Embreacing all Marks and Brands of Record to October 1st, 1912, 360:Annie McIntosh, May 4th, 1912, Mt. Pleasant, Sanpete Co; Utah State Archives and Record Service, Salt Lake City.

28. 1920 U.S. census, Sanpete, Utah, population schedule, Mount Pleasant, enumeration district (ED) 110, sheet 14A, p. 241, dwelling 302, family 307, McIntosh, Annie; digital images (ancestry.com); citing National Archives and Records Administration microfilm T625.

29. McIntosh Reunion Descendants, McIntosh - Descendants of John & Girsey (Grace) (Grizel) Rankin McIntosh (Attachment to Aug 17, 1958 Newsletter - copy in Collection of Bonnie S. Williams), Repository: Bonnie S. Williams, RR 1 Box 247, N Hwy 2, Wilburton, Oklahoma, USA.
Ica (adopted child of James F. [McINTOSH] & Ann JORDAN.
Ica McINTOSH (adopted) Great-Grandchild of John McIntosh & Girsey RANKIN
and Grandchild of William McINTOSH & Maria CALDWELL
no other information included.
This single page attachment indicates that the parents of John McIntosh are William McIntosh & Isabell and is indicative of what our side of the family knew of our McIntosh cousins at that time in August 1958.

30. Brown, Beverly McIntosh and Marsha Lee McIntosh,*William McIntosh Diary, abridgement* (Self-published, Surprise, AZ. June 2002), p 97 August 30 [1897].
"Annie McIntosh and Ica, are washing my house here today. Ica got some dinner. I am very unwell too. I have a bad cold. I don't know how long I will stay on this planet. The will of God be done anyway."

31. Utah, State Department of Health, Certificate of Death, death certificate state file no. 95 (1931), Neils Franklin Johansen names his mother as Ica McIntosh born in Panaca, Nevada.

32. Utah, State Department of Health, Certificate of Death, death certificate state file no. __; registrar's no. 3 (1943), Ica M. Johansen.

33. "Find A Grave," database (www.findagrave.com), Ica Crowe Johansen.

34. Utah, State Department of Health, Certificate of Death, death certificate state file no. 52180533; registrar's no. 423 (1943), Ica M. Johansen.

35. Utah, State Department of Health, Certificate of Death, death certificate state file no. 52180533; registrar's no. 423 (1942), Ica M. Johansen.

36. Utah State Historical Society, "Utah, Cemetery Inventory, 1847-2000," database(https://www.ancestry.com/search/collections/utahburials/), Ica McIntosh Johansen, grave A-32-3-7.

37. Utah, State Department of Health, Certificate of Death, death certificate state file no. 95 (1931), Neils Franklin Johansen names his father as Kimball Johansen born in Mt Pleasant, Utah.

38. "Utah, Select County Marriages, 1887-1937," database, Kimball Johansen and Ica R Minda Crane (Crow).

39. Brigham Young University-Idaho, "Western States Marriage Index," database (http://abish.byui.edu/specialCollections/westernStates/search.cfm), Kimball Johansen and Ica R Minda Crane (Crow).

40. 1880 U.S. census, Lincoln, Nevada, population schedule, Clover Valley, enumeration district (ED) 30, p. 17D, dwelling 9, family 9, Crow, Isamina; digital images,*ancestry.com*; citing National Archives and Records Administration microfilm T9.

# Source Citations

41. 1900 U.S. census, Sanpete, Utah, population schedule, MT Pleasant, enumeration district (ED) 128, sheet 16B, p. 192, dwelling 329, family 333, Johanson, Ica; digital images, *ancestry.com*; citing National Archives and Records Administration microfilm T623.

42. 1910 U.S. census, Sanpete, Utah, population schedule, Mt Pleasant, enumeration district (ED) 156, sheet 10B, p. 162, dwelling 173, family 183, Johansen, Ida R. Minda; digital images, *ancestry.com*; citing National Archives and Records Administration microfilm T624.

43. 1920 U.S. census, Sanpete, Utah, population schedule, Mount Pleasant, enumeration district (ED) 110, sheet 14A, p. 241, dwelling 302, family 307, Johansen, Ica; digital images (ancestry.com); citing National Archives and Records Administration microfilm T625.

44. 1930 U.S. census, Millard, Utah, population schedule, Southerland, enumeration district (ED) 14-31, sheet 4B, p. 110, dwelling 66, family 66, Johansen, Ica; digital images, *ancestry.com*; citing National Archives and Records Administration microfilm T626.

# Melissa Jane McIntosh and Jacob Keele

| Husband | Jacob Keele | |
|---|---|---|
| AKA | Jacob Charles Keele | |
| Born | 9 May 1847 | Council Bluffs, , Iowa, United States[1,2] |
| Died | 2 Aug 1926 | Grand Junction, Mesa, Colorado, United States[1,2] |
| Cause of Death | Apoplexy; Stroke[1] | |
| | | |
| Buried | 4 Aug 1926 | Grand Junction, Mesa, Colorado, United States[1] |
| Address | Orchard Mesa Cemetery (now Municipal Cemetery), Grand Junction, Colorado 81501, US~ | |
| Bapt.(LDS) | 11 Mar 1995 | Jordan River Utah Temple |
| Conf.(LDS) | 30 Jun 1999 | Seattle Washington Temple |
| Init.(LDS) | 10 Oct 1872 | Endowment House |
| Endow.(LDS) | 10 Oct 1872 | Endowment House |
| Father | Samuel Keele Sr. (1816-1897) [3] (Relationship: Family member ) | |
| Mother | Ann Elizabeth Hess (1829-1880) [4] (Relationship: Family member ) | |
| SealP (LDS) | 15 Apr 1953 | Salt Lake Temple |
| Marriage | 10 Oct 1872 | Salt Lake City, Great Salt Lake, Utah Territory, United States[5,6] |
| SealS (LDS) | 10 Oct 1872 | Endowment House |
| Other Spouse | Rachel Emily Amelia Tuttle (1858-1935) | |
| Date | 5 Nov 1902 - Salt Lake City, Salt Lake, Utah, United States (Divorced on 19 Oct 1904) | |
| SealS (LDS) | 11 May 1993 | Logan Utah Temple |
| Other Spouse | Fannie Evelyn Booton (1856-1921) | 13 Dec 1905 - Red Lodge, Carbon, Montana, United States |
| SealS (LDS) | 14 May 2013 | Bogotá Colombia Temple |

JACOB KEELE
MAY 9, 1847
AUGUST 2, 1926

**Events**

1. He appeared on the census on 8 Oct 1850 in Pottawattamie, Iowa, United States.
   Line 26 - Samuel Reel (Keele), age 33, male, no occupation, born in Tennessee.
   Line 26 - Ann Reel (Keele), age 21, female, born in Tennessee.
   **Line 27 - Jacob Reel (Keele) age 1, male, born in Iowa.**
2. Migration: with the Henry Bryant Manning Jolley Company, 15 Sep 1852.[9]
   Keele, Annie Elizabeth Hess (23)
   Keele, Dabney Uel (26)
   **Keele, Jacob (3)**
   Keele, Mary Angeline Jolley (18)
   Keele, Nancy Eleanor McCullough (64)
   Keele, Richard John (65)
   Keele, Samuel (36)
   Keele, Samuel (1)
   Keele, Thomas Henery (23)

   Mormon Pioneer Overland Travel, 1847–1868
   Henry Bryant Manning Jolley Company (1852)

   Mormon Pioneer Overland Travel, Henry Bryant Manning Jolley Company, 1852, Jacob Keele, page 1 of 2
3. He appeared on the census on 11 Jul 1860 in North Bend, Sanpete, Utah Territory.
4. He worked as a farmer.[1]
5. He appeared on the census on 15 Jun 1870 in Panaca, Washington, Utah Territory.
   Line 17 - Samuel Keel (Keele), male, age 55, farmer, born in Tennessee, real estate worth $500, personal property worth $800.
   Line 18 - Anne E. Keel, female, age 41, keeping hours, born in Pennsylvania.
   **Line 19 - Jacob Keel, male, age 21, works on farm, born in Iowa.**
   Line 20 - David Keel, male, age 10, works on farm, born in Utah.
   Line 21 - Mary Keel, female, age 15, at home, born in Utah.

# Melissa Jane McIntosh and Jacob Keele

Line 22 - William Keel, male, age 11, born in Utah.
Line 23 - Emma Keel, female, age 10, born in Utah.
Line 24 - Haerett Keel, female, age 5, born in Utah.
Line 25 - Sarah Keel, female, age 1, born in Utah.

6. He appeared on the census on 12 Jun 1880 in Panaca, Lincoln, Nevada, United States.[10]
**Line 1 - Keele, Jacob, white, male, age 31, head, married, laborer, born in Missouri, father born in Tennessee, mother born in Pennsylvania.**
Line 2 - Keele, Mellissa, white, female, age 25, wife, married, keeping house, born in Utah, father born in Scotland, mother born in Canada.
Line 3 - Keele, Maria E., white, female, age 6, daughter, single, born in Nevada, father born in Missouri, mother born in Utah.
Line 4 - Keele, Alice M., white, female, age 5, daughter, single, born in Nevada, father born in Missouri, mother born in Utah.
Line 5 - Keele, Jacob, white, male, age 2, son, single, born in Nevada, father born in Missouri, mother born in Utah.
Line 6 - Keele, William W., white, male, age 2/12, son, single, born in Nevada, father born in Missouri, mother born in Utah.

7. He had a residence in 1887 in Fruita, Mesa, Colorado, United States.
Their last three children were born in Fruita.

8. He had a residence in Oct 1895 in Colorado, United States.[11]

9. He had a residence in 1900 in Burlington, Big Horn, Wyoming, United States.[12]
In 1900, William Abram McIntosh with his Johnson nephews and a few others, moved to Burlington, Wyoming. While getting settled,
"they stayed with Jake Keele's family." Roah said, "We lived with the Keele's about a week and I think we about drove Mrs. Keele crazy." [Mrs. Keele was William's cousin. See Christopherson history.]

10. He appeared on the census on 12 Jan 1920 in Fruita, Mesa, Colorado, United States.
Line 37 - Dwelling 202, House 208, Keele, Thomas, head, rents home, male, white, age 42, married, can read and write, born in Utah, father born in Utah, mother born in Utah, speaks english, miner in a coal mine, wage earner.
Line 38 - Keele, Jane, wife, female, white, age 32, married, can read and write, born in Utah, father born in Utah, mother in Utah, no occupation, speaks english.
Line 39 - Keele, Thomas Jr, son, male, white, age 14, single, in school, can read and write, born in Utah, father born in Utah, mother born in Utah, speaks english.
Line 40 - Keele, Sarah, daughter, female, white, age 12, single, in school, can read and write, born in Utah, father born in Utah, mother born in Utah, speaks english.
Line 41 - Keele, Benata, daughter, female, white, age 10, single, in school, can read and write, born in Utah, father born in Utah, mother born in Utah, speaks english.
Line 42 - Keele, Deloria, daughter, female, white, age 8, single, in school, born in Utah, father born in Utah, mother born in Utah, speaks english.
Line 43 - Keele, Virgil, son, male, white, age 5, single, not in school, born in Utah, father born in Utah, mother born in Utah.
Line 44 - Keels, Naomi, daughter, female, white, age 1 9/12, single, born in Utah, father born in Utah, mother born in Utah.
**Line 45 - Keele, Jacob, cousin, male, white, age 70, widowed, can read and write, born in Iowa, father born in Tennessee, mother born in Pennslyvania, speaks english, no occupation.**
Line 46 - Keele, Fanny, cousin, female, white, age 62, widowed, can read and write, born in Iowa, father born in Virginia, mother born in New York, speaks english, no occupation.

11. His obituary was published on 3 Aug 1926 in Grand Junction, Mesa, Colorado, United States.
**Jacob Keele**, for many years a resident of this city, passed away last evening at his home at the age of 78 years. He had not been in good health for some time, his death coming as a result of a paralytic stroke. The deceased was the father of A.J. Keele, who resides at 1258 Colorado Avenue and who left the city today for De Beque, where he is making the funeral arrangements. The body is at the Krohn Funeral parlor awaiting the completion of the arrangements for the funeral, which will be held within the next few days.

Jacob Keele was born on May 29, 1849, in Council Bluffs, Iowa. His father, Samuel, was 33 and his mother, Ann, was

# Melissa Jane McIntosh and Jacob Keele

20. He married Melissa Jane McIntosh on October 10, 1872, in Salt Lake City, Utah. She died on March 9, 1902 in Burlington, Wyoming. They had nine children in 19 years. He died on August 2, 1926, in Grand Junction, Colorado, at the age of 77.

| **Wife** | **Melissa Jane McIntosh**[13,14,15] | |
|---|---|---|
| AKA | Jane McIntosh, Malisa McIntosh | |
| Born | 27 Jun 1854 | West Jordan, Great Salt Lake, Utah Territory, United States[6,14] |
| Died | 9 Mar 1902 | Burlington, Big Horn, Wyoming, United States[6] |
| Buried | 12 Mar 1902 | Burlington, Big Horn, Wyoming, United States[6,16] |
| Address | Burlington Cemetery, 1 mile north and 1/2 mile east of center of town, Burlington, Wy~ | |
| Bapt.(LDS) | 1 Jan 1867 | |
| Conf.(LDS) | 1 Jan 1867 | |
| Init.(LDS) | 10 Oct 1872 | Endowment House |
| Endow.(LDS) | 10 Oct 1872 | Endowment House |
| Father | William McIntosh (1819-1899) [17,18,19,20] | |
| Mother | Maria Caldwell (1824-1897) [21] | |
| SealP (LDS) | 4 Feb 1915 | Manti Utah Temple |

**Events**

1. She appeared on the census on 11 Oct 1860 in Clover, Shambip, Utah Territory, United States.[22]
   Line 25) Wm McIntosh, age 40, male, farmer, born in Scotland
   Line 26) Maria McIntosh, age 36, female, born in Canada
   Line 27) Jno E McIntosh, age 18, male, born in Ohio
   Line 28) Wm. H McIntosh, age 11, male, born in Missouri, in school
   Line 29) Jas F McIntosh, age 8, male, born in Utah Territory, in school
   **Line 30) Malissa J McIntosh, age 6, female, born in Utah Territory, in school**
   Line 31) Alice M McIntosh, age 3, female, born in Utah Territory
   Line 32) Abm E McIntosh, age 6/12, male, born in Utah Territory

2. She appeared on the census on 10 Jun 1870 in Panaca, Washington, Utah Territory.[23]
   Line 20 - McIntosh, William age 49, male, white, day laborer, value of personal estate 200, born in Scotland, father and mother foreign born, male over 21.
   Line 21 - McIntosh, Marie, age 45, female, white, keeping house, born in Canada, father and mother foreign born.
   Line 22 - McIntosh, William, age 20, male, white, teamster, born in Missouri, father and mother foreign born.
   Line 23 - McIntosh, Frank, age 18, male, white, work on farm, born in Utah, father and mother foreign born.
   **Line 24 - McIntosh, Jane, age 15, female, white, at home, born in Utah, father and mother foreign born, attended school.**
   Line 25 - McIntosh, Allice, age 12, female, white, born in Utah, father and mother foreign born, attended school.
   Line 26 - McIntosh, Abraham, age 10, male, white, born in Utah, father and mother foreign born, attended school, cannot write.
   Line 27 - McIntosh, Lilly, age 7, female, white, born in Utah, father and mother foreign born.
   Line 28 - McIntosh, Caroline, age 4, female, white, born in Utah, father and mother foreign born.
   Line 29 - McIntosh, Albert, age 1, male, white, born in Utah, father and mother foreign born.

3. She appeared on the census on 28 Jul 1870 in Meadow Valley, Lincoln, Nevada, United States.[24]
   Line 22 - McIntosh, Wm age 50, male, white, farming, value of real estate 300, value of personal estate 800, born in Scotland, father and mother foreign born, male over 21.
   Line 23 - McIntosh, Marie, age 45, female, white, keeping house, born in Canada, father and mother foreign born.

# Melissa Jane McIntosh and Jacob Keele

Line 24 - McIntosh, Wm H, age 21, male, white, farming, born in Missouri, father and mother foreign born, male over 21.
Line 25 - McIntosh, Frank, age 18, male, white, farming, born in Utah, father and mother foreign born.
**Line 26 - McIntosh, Jane, age 16, female, white, at home, born in Utah, father and mother foreign born, attended school.**
Line 27 - McIntosh, Alice, age 12, female, white, school, born in Utah, father and mother foreign born, attended school.
Line 28 - McIntosh, Abe, age 10, male, white, school, born in Utah, father and mother foreign born, attended school, cannot write.
Line 29 - McIntosh, Lilly, age 7, female, white, school, born in Utah, father and mother foreign born.
Line 30 - McIntosh, Caroline, age 4, female, white, school, born in Utah, father and mother foreign born.
Line 31 - McIntosh, Albert, age 1, male, white, school, born in Nevada, father and mother foreign born.

4. She appeared on the census on 12 Jun 1880 in Panaca, Lincoln, Nevada, United States.[10]
Line 1 - Keele, Jacob, white, male, age 31, head, married, laborer, born in Missouri, father born in Tennessee, mother born in Pennsylvania.
**Line 2 - Keele, Mellissa, white, female, age 25, wife, married, keeping house, born in Utah, father born in Scotland, mother born in Canada.**
Line 3 - Keele, Maria E., white, female, age 6, daughter, single, born in Nevada, father born in Missouri, mother born in Utah.
Line 4 - Keele, Alice M., white, female, age 5, daughter, single, born in Nevada, father born in Missouri, mother born in Utah.
Line 5 - Keele, Jacob, white, male, age 2, son, single, born in Nevada, father born in Missouri, mother born in Utah.
line 6 - Keele, William W., white, male, age 2/12, Mar, son, single, born in Nevada, father born in Missouri, mother born in Utah.
5. She had a residence between 1887 and 1893 in Fruita, Mesa, Colorado, United States.
Their last 3 children were born in Fruita, Colorado.
6. She had a residence on 9 Oct 1895 in Colorado, United States.[25]
7. She had a residence circa 1900 in Burlington, Big Horn, Wyoming, United States.[26]
"In 1900, William Abram McIntosh with his Johnson nephews and a few others, moved to Burlington, Wyoming. While getting settled."
"they stayed with Jake Keele's family." Roah said, "We lived with the Keele's about a week and I think we about drove Mrs. Keele crazy." [Mrs. Keele was William's cousin. See Christopherson history.]

"Frederick and Maria Keele Robinson came to the basin with Maria's parents, Jacob and Melissa McIntosh Keele."

## Children

| 1 F | **Maria Elizabeth Keele**[27,28] | |
|---|---|---|
| AKA | May Keele, Maria Robinson | |
| Born | 14 Aug 1873 | Panaca, Lincoln, Nevada, United States[29] |
| Died | 7 Dec 1918 | De Beque, Mesa, Colorado, United States[29] |
| Cause of Death | Spanish Flu | |
| Buried | Dec 1918 | De Beque, Mesa, Colorado, United States[29,30] |
| Address | DeBeque Cemetery, DeBeque, Colorado, USA | |
| Bapt.(LDS) | 10 Oct 1903 | |
| Conf.(LDS) | 11 Oct 1903 | |
| Init.(LDS) | 7 Feb 1998 | Las Vegas Nevada Temple |
| Endow.(LDS) | 28 Sep 1938 | Salt Lake Temple |
| SealP (LDS) | 29 Mar 1985 | Idaho Falls Idaho Temple |
| Spouse | Frederick Walker Robinson (1865-1920)[28] | 30 Oct 1892 - Mesa, Colorado, United States[31,32] |
| SealS (LDS) | 28 Sep 1938 | Salt Lake Temple |

# Melissa Jane McIntosh and Jacob Keele

Children (cont.)

**Events**

1. She was described as really black hair with blue, blue eyes.

2. She appeared on the census on 12 Jun 1880 in Panaca, Lincoln, Nevada, United States.[10]
Line 1 - Keele, Jacob, white, male, age 31, head, married, laborer, born in Missouri, father born in Tennessee, mother born in Pennsylvania.
Line 2 - Keele, Mellissa, white, female, age 25, wife, married, keeping house, born in Utah, father born in Scotland, mother born in Canada.
**Line 3 - Keele, Maria E., white, female, age 6, daughter, single, born in Nevada, father born in Missouri, mother born in Utah.**
Line 4 - Keele, Alice M., white, female, age 5, daughter, single, born in Nevada, father born in Missouri, mother born in Utah.
Line 5 - Keele, Jacob, white, male, age 2, son, single, born in Nevada, father born in Missouri, mother born in Utah.
line 6 - Keele, William W., white, male, age 2/12, Mar, son, single, born in Nevada, father born in Missouri, mother born in Utah.

3. She had a residence circa 1900 in Burlington, Big Horn, Wyoming, United States.
"Frederick and Maria Keele Robinson came to the basin with Maria's parents, Jacob and Melissa McIntosh Keele."

4. She had a residence about 1907 in Otto, Big Horn, Wyoming, United States.[33]

5. She appeared on the census on 15 Apr 1910 in Meeteetse, Park, Wyoming, United States.[34]
Line 69 - Robinson, Frew (Fred) W., head, male, white, age 44, married one time, age 17 at first marriage, born in Wisconsin, father born in United States, mother born in United States, can read, write and speak english, teamster in general teaming, wage worker, employed, rents house.
**Line 70 - Robinson, May (Maria) E, wife, female, white, age 37, married one time, age 17 at first marriage, had 6 children, 6 living, born in Nevada, father born in Missouri, mother born in Utah, can read, write and speak english.**
Line 71 - Robinson, Anna J, daughter, female, white, age 16, single, born in Colorado, father born in Wisconsin, mother born in Nevada, in school, can read, write and speak english.
Line 72 - Robinson, Jacob M, son, male, white, age 13, single, born in Colorado, father born in Wisconsin, mother born in Nevada, in school, can read, write and speak english.
Line 73 - Robinson, Donald (Donnell) K, son, male, white, age 11, single, born in Colorado, father born in Wisconsin, mother born in Nevada, in school, can read, write and speak english.
Line 74 - Robinson, Roy (Royal) R, son, male, white, age 9, single, born in Wyoming, father born in Wisconsin, mother born in Nevada, in school, can read, write and speak english.
Line 75 - Robinson, Coral M, daughter, female, white, age 6, single, born in Wyoming, father born in Wisconsin, mother born in Nevada, in school, can read, write and speak english.
Line 76 - Robinson, Evelena, daughter, female, white, age 3, single, born in Wyoming, father born in Wisconsin, mother born in Nevada.

6. She had a residence after 15 Apr 1910 in Fruita, Mesa, Colorado, United States.[33]

# Melissa Jane McIntosh and Jacob Keele

| Children (cont.) | | |
|---|---|---|
| **2** M | **Alma Jacob Keele**[35] | |
| AKA | Jacob Keele, Jake Keele | |
| Born | 2 Feb 1875 | Panaca, Lincoln, Nevada, United States[36,37] |
| Died | 1 Oct 1938 | Salmon, Lemhi, Idaho, United States[38,39,40] |
| Cause of Death | Heart Disease | |
| Buried | 3 Oct 1938 | Salmon, Lemhi, Idaho, United States[36] |
| Address | City Cemetery, Salmon, Idaho, USA | |
| Notes | Plot: E-08-12 | |
| Bapt.(LDS) | 12 Dec 1984 | Idaho Falls Idaho Temple |
| Conf.(LDS) | 12 Dec 1984 | Idaho Falls Idaho Temple |
| Init.(LDS) | 10 Feb 1998 | Las Vegas Nevada Temple |
| Endow.(LDS) | 9 Jan 1985 | Idaho Falls Idaho Temple |
| SealP (LDS) | 29 Mar 1985 | Idaho Falls Idaho Temple |
| Spouse | Dollie Coral Garner (1885-1975) | 31 Dec 1901 - Burlington, Big Horn, Wyoming, United States[41] |
| SealS (LDS) | 13 Jul 1994 | Idaho Falls Idaho Temple |

**Events**

1. He worked as a blacksmith.
2. He appeared on the census on 12 Jun 1880 in Panaca, Lincoln, Nevada, United States.[10]
   Line 1 - Keele, Jacob, white, male, age 31, head, married, laborer, born in Missouri, father born in Tennessee, mother born in Pennsylvania.
   Line 2 - Keele, Mellissa, white, female, age 25, wife, married, keeping house, born in Utah, father born in Scotland, mother born in Canada.
   Line 3 - Keele, Maria E., white, female, age 6, daughter, single, born in Nevada, father born in Missouri, mother born in Utah.
   Line 4 - Keele, Alice M., white, female, age 5, daughter, single, born in Nevada, father born in Missouri, mother born in Utah.
   **Line 5 - Keele, Jacob, white, male, age 2, son, single, born in Nevada, father born in Missouri, mother born in Utah.**
   line 6 - Keele, William W., white, male, age 2/12, Mar, son, single, born in Nevada, father born in Missouri, mother born in Utah.

| | | |
|---|---|---|
| **3** F | **Alice Melissa Keele**[42] | |
| AKA | Alice Burkett | |
| Born | 16 Oct 1875 | Panaca, Lincoln, Nevada, United States[43] |
| Died | 29 Jan 1920 | Fruita, Mesa, Colorado, United States[43] |
| Buried | 1 Feb 1920 | Fruita, Mesa, Colorado, United States[43] |
| Address | Elmwood Cemetery, Fruita, Colorado, USA | |
| Notes | Plot: Blck 4, Row 7 | |
| Bapt.(LDS) | 8 Nov 1984 | Idaho Falls Idaho Temple |
| Conf.(LDS) | 4 Feb 1998 | Las Vegas Nevada Temple |
| Init.(LDS) | 7 Feb 1998 | Las Vegas Nevada Temple |
| Endow.(LDS) | 8 Nov 1984 | Idaho Falls Idaho Temple |
| SealP (LDS) | 29 Mar 1985 | Idaho Falls Idaho Temple |
| Spouse | Richard Burkitt (1871-1939) | 30 Oct 1892 - Fruita, Mesa, Colorado, United States[44,45,46] |
| SealS (LDS) | 1 May 1998 | |

# Melissa Jane McIntosh and Jacob Keele

| | Las Vegas Nevada Temple |
|---|---|

**Events**

1. She appeared on the census on 12 Jun 1880 in Panaca, Lincoln, Nevada, United States.[10]
Line 1 - Keele, Jacob, white, male, age 31, head, married, laborer, born in Missouri, father born in Tennessee, mother born in Pennsylvania.
Line 2 - Keele, Mellissa, white, female, age 25, wife, married, keeping house, born in Utah, father born in Scotland, mother born in Canada.
Line 3 - Keele, Maria E., white, female, age 6, daughter, single, born in Nevada, father born in Missouri, mother born in Utah.
**Line 4 - Keele, Alice M., white, female, age 5, daughter, single, born in Nevada, father born in Missouri, mother born in Utah.**
Line 5 - Keele, Jacob, white, male, age 2, son, single, born in Nevada, father born in Missouri, mother born in Utah.
line 6 - Keele, William W., white, male, age 2/12, son, single, born in Nevada, father born in Missouri, mother born in Utah.

2. She appeared on the census on 11 May 1910 in Rhone, Mesa, Colorado, United States.[47]
Line 37 - Burkitt, Richard, head, male, white, age 38, married once for 17 years, born in Iowa, father born in Illinois, mother born in Illinois, speaks english, farmer, general farm, works on own account, able to read and write, owns with a mortgage farm # 305.
**Line 38 - Burkitt, Alise, wife, female, white, age 34, married once for 17 years, had 4 children, 3 living, born in Nevada, father born in Utah, mother born in Utah, speaks english, no occupation, able to read and write.**
Line 39 - Burkitt, Edith M., daughter, female, white, age 15, single, born in Iowa, father born in Iowa, mother born in Nevada, speaks english, no occupation, able to read and write, attended school within year.
Line 40 - Burkitt, Madge, daughter, female, white, age 7, single, born in Colorado, father born in Iowa, mother born in Nevada, no occupation, able to read and write, attended school within year.
Line 41 - Burkitt, Richard R., son, male, white, age 4, single, born in Colorado, father born in Iowa, mother born in Nevada, no occupation.

3. She appeared on the census on 11 Jan 1920 in Muddy, Montrose, Colorado, United States.
Alice didn't die until 29 Jan 1920 but for some reason, she was not included in the Census.

| 4 M | **William Wallace Keele**[48] | |
|---|---|---|
| AKA | Wallace Keele | |
| Born | Apr 1880 | Panaca, Lincoln, Nevada, United States |
| Died | Abt 1884 | Huntington, Emery, Utah, United States |
| Buried | date: | place: |
| Bapt.(LDS) | Child | |
| Conf.(LDS) | Child | |
| Init.(LDS) | Child | |
| Endow.(LDS) | Child | |
| SealP (LDS) | 15 Oct 1998 | Las Vegas Nevada Temple |
| Spouse | This person had no known marriage and no known children | |

**Events**

1. He appeared on the census on 12 Jun 1880 in Panaca, Lincoln, Nevada, United States.[10] Line 1 - Keele, Jacob, white, male, age 31, head, married, laborer, born in Missouri, father born in Tennessee, mother born in Pennsylvania.
Line 2 - Keele, Mellissa, white, female, age 25, wife, married, keeping house, born in Utah, father born in Scotland, mother born in Canada.
Line 3 - Keele, Maria E., white, female, age 6, daughter, single, born in Nevada, father born in Missouri, mother born in Utah.
Line 4 - Keele, Alice M., white, female, age 5, daughter, single, born in Nevada, father born in Missouri, mother born in Utah.
Line 5 - Keele, Jacob, white, male, age 2, son, single, born in Nevada, father born in Missouri, mother born in Utah.
**line 6 - Keele, William W., white, male, age 2/12, son, single, born in Nevada, father born in Missouri, mother born in Utah.**

# Melissa Jane McIntosh and Jacob Keele

| Children (cont.) | | | |
|---|---|---|---|
| 5 | F | **Annie Estella Keele** [49] | |
| AKA | | Anna Keele, Stella Keele | |
| Born | | 2 Aug 1883 | Huntington, Emery, Utah Territory, United States[50] |
| Died | | 26 Apr 1965 | Fortuna, Humboldt, California, United States[50] |
| Buried | | 28 Apr 1965 | Eureka, Humboldt, California, United States[50] |
| Address | | Sunset Memorial Park, Eureka, California, USA | |
| Bapt.(LDS) | | 14 Oct 1995 | Ogden Utah Temple |
| Conf.(LDS) | | 14 Oct 1995 | Ogden Utah Temple |
| Init.(LDS) | | 9 Oct 1997 | Ogden Utah Temple |
| Endow.(LDS) | | 21 Oct 1997 | Ogden Utah Temple |
| SealP (LDS) | | 3 Apr 1998 | Las Vegas Nevada Temple |
| Spouse | | Calvin Huston Kendall Sr. (1875-1952) | 25 Dec 1899 - Fruita, Mesa, Colorado, United States[51,52] |
| SealS (LDS) | | 6 Nov 1997 | Ogden Utah Temple |

**Events**

1. She appeared on the census on 26 Apr 1910 in Ogden, Weber, Utah, United States.
   Line 8 - Kendall, C Husten, head, male, white, age 35, married once for ten years, born in Missouri, father born in Wisconsin, mother born in Mississippi, speaks english, black smith, wage worker, can read and write, rents home,
   **Line 9 - Kendall, Stella, wife, female, white, age 26, married once for ten years, had 4 children, 4 living, born in Nevada, father born in Pennsylvania, mother born in Scotland, can read, write and speak english.**
   Line 10 - Kendall, Pearl, daughter, female, white, age 8, single, born in Wyoming, father born in Missouri, mother born in Nevada, in school.
   Line 11 - Kendall, Maude, daughter, female, white, age 6, single, born in Wyoming, father born in Missouri, mother born in Nevada, in school.
   Line 12 - Kendall, William, son, male, white, age 4, single, born in Colorado, father born in Missouri, mother born in Nevada.
   Line 13 - Kendall, Ruby, daughter, female, white, age 1 7/12, single, born in Colorado, father born in Missouri, mother born in Nevada.

2. She appeared on the census on 13 Feb 1920 in Manville, Niobrara, Wyoming, United States.
   Line 76 - Kendall, Houston, head, rents home, male, white, age 44, married, can read, write and speak english, born in Missouri, father born in Missouri, mother born in Missour, blacksmith, wage worker.
   **Line 77 - Kendall, Estella, wife, female, white, age 36, married, can read, write and speak english, born in Utah, father born in Nevada, mother born in Nevada.**
   Line 78 - Kendall, William, son, male, white, age 12, single, in school, born in Colorado, father born in Missouri, mother born in Utah.
   Line 79 - Kendall, Ruby, daughter, female, white, age 10, single, in school, born in Colorado, father born in Missouri, mother born in Utah.
   Line 80 - Kendall,Thelma, daughter, female, white, age 8, single, in school, born in Utah, father born in Missouri, mother born in Utah.
   Line 81 - Kendall, Cecil, son, male, white, age 6, single, in school, born in Colorado, father born in Missouri, mother born in Utah.
   Line 82 - Kendall, Houston, son, male, white, age 1 3/12, single, born in Colorado, father born in Missouri, mother born in Utah.

3. She appeared on the census on 3 Apr 1930 in Twin Falls, Twin Falls, Idaho, United States.
   Line 50 - Kendall, Calvin H., head, rents home for $20, not a farm, male, white, age 54, married at age 24, can read, write and speak english, born in Missouri, father born in Indiana, mother born in Arkansas, laborer, odd jobs, wage worker, not a veteran.
   Next Page
   **Line 51 - Kendall, Annie E., wife, female, white, age 46, married at age 16, can read, write and speak english, born in Utah, father born in Pennsylvania, mother born in Scotland.**

# Melissa Jane McIntosh and Jacob Keele

Line 52 - Kendall, Cecil C, son, male, white, age 16 single, can read, write and speak english, born in Colorado, father born in Missouri, mother born in Utah, laborer on a farm, wage worker.
Line 53 - Kendall, Calvin H, son, male, white, age 11, single, in school, born in Wyming, father born in Missouri, mother born in Utah.
Line 54 - Halstead, Pearl E., daughter, female, white, age 28, divorced, was age 16 at first marriage, born in Wyoming, father born in Missouri, mother born in Utah, worker at odd jobs.
Line 55 - Halstead, Husten, H., grandson, male, white, age 11, single, in school, born in Wyoming, father born in Nebraska, mother born in Wyoming.
Line 56 - Halstead, Ferne V, granddaughter, female, white, age 7, single, born in California, father born in Nebraska, mother born in Wyoming.
Line 57 - Halstead, Eugene P., grandson, male, white, age 4, single, born in California, father born in Nebraska, mother born in Wyoming.

4. She appeared on the census on 4 Apr 1940 in Eureka, Humboldt, California, United States.
Line 68 - Kendall, Calvin H, head, male, white, age 65, married, finished 6th grade, born in Missouri, lived in same place in 1935, not employed, has other source of income.
**Line 69 - Kendall, Annie S, wife, female, white, age 56, married, finished 7th grade, born in Utah, lived in same place in 1935.**

| 6 | F | **Lillian Janette Keele** [53] | |
|---|---|---|---|
| AKA | | Nettie Armstrong, Nettie Keele, Nettie Weir | |
| Born | | 25 Dec 1885 | Huntington, Emery, Utah Territory, United States[54] |
| Died | | 8 Aug 1963 | Delta, Delta, Colorado, United States[54] |
| Buried | | Aug 1963 | Delta, Delta, Colorado, United States[54] |
| Address | | Mesa View Cemetery, Delta, Colorado, USA | |
| Notes | | Plot: Christus 31 B 3 | |
| Bapt.(LDS) | | 29 May 1898 | Scotland, United Kingdom |
| Conf.(LDS) | | 29 May 1898 | |
| Init.(LDS) | | 8 Nov 1984 | |
| Endow.(LDS) | | 8 Nov 1984 | Las Vegas Nevada Temple |
| SealP (LDS) | | 29 Mar 1985 | Idaho Falls Idaho Temple |
| Spouse | | David Weir (Cir 1881-Cir 1950) | 20 Apr 1903 - Big Horn, Wyoming, United States. (Divorced)[55] |
| SealS (LDS) | | 1 May 1998 | Las Vegas Nevada Temple |
| Spouse | | David Marion Armstrong (1876-1935) | |
| Marr. Date | | 20 Sep 1907 - Vernal, Uintah, Utah, United States. (Divorced before 1930)[56] | |
| SealS (LDS) | | 1 May 1998 | Las Vegas Nevada Temple |
| Spouse | | Arvid Wiik (1899-1995)[57] | 1 May 1935 - Gardnerville, Douglas, Nevada, United States |
| SealS (LDS) | | 25 Jan 2019 | Vernal Utah Temple |

**Events**

1. She appeared on the census on 28 Apr 1910 in De Beque, Mesa, Colorado, United States.
Line 19 - Armstrong, David, head, male, white, age 34, married once for 7 years, born in Missouri, laborer on farm.
**Line 20 - Armstrong, Nettie, wife, female, white, age 23, married once for 7 years, had 3 children, 3 living, born in Utah.**
Line 21 - Armstrong, Grace, daughter, female, white, age 6, single, born in Wyoming.
Line 22 - Armstrong, May, daughter, female, white, age 3, single, born in Utah.
Line 23 - Armstrong, Frank, son, male, white, age 3/12, single, born in Colorado.

2. She appeared on the census on 22 Apr 1940 in Reno, Washoe, Nevada, United States.
Line 33 - Wiik, Arvid, head, male, white, age 40, married, finished 4th grade, born in Finland, lived in same place in

# Melissa Jane McIntosh and Jacob Keele

1935, employed as cement mixer at cement plant, earned $2160 last year.
**Line 34 - Wiik, Nettie, wife, female, white, age 57, married, finished 8th grace, born in Nevada, lived in same place in 1935.**

| 7 | M | **Abraham Deloss Keele** [58] |
|---|---|---|
| AKA | Abraham Pelora Keele, Delos A. Keele | |
| Born | 1887 | Fruita, Mesa, Colorado, United States |
| Died | After 1910 | place: |
| Buried | date: | place: |
| Bapt.(LDS) | 4 Feb 1998 | Las Vegas Nevada Temple |
| Conf.(LDS) | 4 Feb 1998 | Las Vegas Nevada Temple |
| Init.(LDS) | 10 Feb 1998 | Las Vegas Nevada Temple |
| Endow.(LDS) | 6 May 1998 | Las Vegas Nevada Temple |
| SealP (LDS) | 15 Oct 1998 | Las Vegas Nevada Temple |
| Spouse | This person had no known marriage and no known children | |

**Events**

1. He appeared on the census on 12 May 1910 in Meeteetse, Park, Wyoming, United States.
   **Line 14 - Keele, Delliss A, hired man, male, white, age 20, single, born in Colorado, father born in Missouri, mother born in Scotland, speaks english, sheep shearer in a sheep camp, can read, write and speak english.**

| 8 | F | **Jennie May Keele** [59] |
|---|---|---|
| Born | Cir 1890 | Fruita, Mesa, Colorado, United States |
| Died | 1890 | Fruita, Mesa, Colorado, United States |
| Buried | date: | place: |
| Bapt.(LDS) | Child | |
| Conf.(LDS) | Child | |
| Init.(LDS) | Child | |
| Endow.(LDS) | Child | |
| SealP (LDS) | 14 Sep 1984 | Idaho Falls Idaho Temple |
| Spouse | This person had no known marriage and no known children | |

| 9 | M | **Virgil Vaughn Keele** [60] |
|---|---|---|
| Born | 27 Jul 1893 | Fruita, Mesa, Colorado, United States[61] |
| Died | 18 Sep 1965 | Anaconda, Deer Lodge, Montana, United States[61,62,63] |
| Cause of Death | Heart Disease | |
| Buried | 23 Sep 1965 | Humphrey, Clark, Idaho, United States[61] |
| Address | Humphrey Cemetery, Humphrey, Idaho, USA | |
| Bapt.(LDS) | 1 Jun 1935 | |
| Conf.(LDS) | 2 Jun 1935 | |
| Endow.(LDS) | 9 Jan 1985 | Idaho Falls Idaho Temple |
| SealP (LDS) | 29 Mar 1985 | Idaho Falls Idaho Temple |
| Spouse | Claire Florence Robbins (1913-2002) | 3 Jul 1930 - Saint Anthony, Fremont, Idaho, United States[64,65] |
| SealS (LDS) | 17 Mar 2011 | St. George Utah Temple |

**Events**

1. Military Draft Registration: World War I.[66]
2. He worked as a smelterman.

# Melissa Jane McIntosh and Jacob Keele

3. He had a residence on 3 Jul 1930 in Cody, Park, Wyoming, United States.

# Source Citations

1. Colorado Department of Public Health and Environment, death certificate 7657 (1926), Jacob Keele.

2. "Find A Grave," database (www.findagrave.com), Jacob Keele.

3. Colorado Department of Public Health and Environment, death certificate 7657 (1926), Jacob Keele names his father as Samuel Keele.

4. Colorado Department of Public Health and Environment, death certificate 7657 (1926), Jacob Keele names his mother's maiden name as Hess.

5. McIntosh Reunion Descendants, McIntosh - Descendants of John & Girsey (Grace) (Grizel) Rankin McIntosh (Attachment to Aug 17, 1958 Newsletter - copy in Collection of Bonnie S. Williams), Page 1. Repository: Bonnie S. Williams, RR 1 Box 247, N Hwy 2, Wilburton, Oklahoma, USA.
Descendants of John McIntosh
Page 1. 24 Aug 2001
1. John McIntosh (b.25 Jun 1795-Croy,Invernesshire,Scotland;d.5 Mar 1875-Bountiful,Davis,Utah)
sp: Girsey Rankin (b.1794-Rutherglen,Lanarkshire,Scotland;m.15 Jun 1817;d.Apr 1853-Origan,Lucas,Ohio)...
2. William McIntosh (b.16 Sep 1819-Bridgeton,Lanark,Scotland;d.5 May 1899-Mt. Pleasant,Sanpete,Utah)
sp: Maria Caldwell (b.17 Feb 1824-Lanark,Upper Canada;m.26 Sep 1841;d.27 Jul 1897-Mt Pleasant,San Pete,Utah)...
3. Melissa Jane McIntosh (b.27 Jun 1853-West Jordan,Salt Lake,Utah)
sp: Jacob Keele (b.29 May 1847;d.Sep 1925-Grand Junction,Mesa,Colorado)
4. Maria Elizabeth Keele (b.14 Aug 1873-Panaca,Lincoln,Nevada;d.Dec 1918)
sp: Frederick Walker Robinson (m.10 Nov 1892)
4. Alice Melissa Keele (b.16 Oct 1874-Panaca,Lincoln,Nevada;d.1919)
sp: Richard Burkett
4. Alma Jacob Keele (b.2 Feb 1876-Panaca,Lincoln,Nevada;d.1941)
sp: Dollie C. Garner
4. Wallace Keele (b.1879-Panaca,Lincoln,Nevada;d.Abt 1881)
4. Annie Estella Keele (b.2 Aug 1883-Huntington,Emery,Utah)
sp: Calvin Husten Kendall
4. Lettie Keele (b.25 Dec 1885-Panaca,Lincoln,Nevada)
sp: Orvid Welk
4. Delos A. Keele (b.1887-Fruita,Mesa,Colorado)
4. Jennie May Keele (b.Abt 1890-Fruita,Mesa,Colorado)
4. Virgil Vaughn Keele (b.26 Jul 1893-Fruita,Mesa,Colorado)
sp: Claire Robbins.
all nine children listed, no grandchildren listed.
This single page attachment indicates that the parents of John McIntosh are William McIntosh & Isabell and is indicative of what our side of the family knew of our McIntosh cousins at that time in August 1958.

6. "Find A Grave," database (www.findagrave.com), Melissa Jane McIntosh Keele.

7. Brigham Young University-Idaho, "Western States Marriage Index," database(http://abish.byui.edu/specialCollections/westernStates/search.cfm), Jacob Keele and Rachel A.T. Briggs.

8. All Counties, Montana, Marriages, 1865-1987 page 736, Keele, Jacob of Burlington, Woming-Jones, Fannie E of Red Lodge, Montana, 1905; digital images, ancestry.com.

9. Church of Jesus Christ of Latter-day Saints, "Mormon Pioneer Overland Travel, 1847-1868," database (www.lds.org/churchhistory/library/pioneercompany), Keele, Jacob.

10. *1880 U.S. Census. Nevada-Panaca, Lincoln,* Jacob Keele household, 1880 U.S. census, Lincoln County, Ne vada, population schedule, town of Panaca, enumeration dist rict [ED] 30, supervisor's district [SD] blank, page 7C, dw elling 17, family 17.

11. Brown, Beverly McIntosh and Marsha Lee McIntosh,*William McIntosh Diary, abridgement* (Self-published, Surprise, AZ. June 2002), page 85.

12. Loveland, Carla Neves,*Sagebrush and Roses, A History of Otto and Burlington Wyoming* (Lindon, Utah, Alexander's Digital Printing, 2003), pages 347, 359. Repository: Family History Library, 35 North West Temple Street, Salt Lake City, Utah 84150-3400, USA, Call Number: 978.733 H2. Includes history of county and genealogy of residents.
Includes: Dobson, Hibbert, Neves, Reid, Riley, Tolman, and Yorgason.

13. McIntosh Reunion Descendants, McIntosh - Descendants of John & Girsey (Grace) (Grizel) Rankin McIntosh (Attachment to Aug 17, 1958 Newsletter - copy in Collection of Bonnie S. Williams), Repository: Bonnie S. Williams, RR 1 Box 247, N Hwy 2, Wilburton, Oklahoma, USA.
Millisa Jane (daughter of William [McINTOSH] & Maria CALDWELL) md. Jacob KEELE
Children:
1. Maria
2. Alice
3. Alma J.
4. Estella
5. Wallace
6. Jennett
7. Delos

# Source Citations

8. Virgil Vaughn.
Millisa Jane McINTOSH is a Granddaughter of John McINTOSH & Girsey RANKIN.

14. Brown, Beverly McIntosh and Marsha Lee McIntosh,*William McIntosh Diary, abridgement* (Self-published, Surprise, AZ. June 2002), "Malisa Jane was born June 27th, 1853."

15. Roberts, Barbara (editor), *McIntosh Clan 5th Annual Reunion Report* (Newsletter of 4 July 1960 in Collection of Bonnie S. Williams), Repository: Bonnie S. Williams, RR 1 Box 247, N Hwy 2, Wilburton, Oklahoma, USA.

REUNION REPORT...

3. Sketches of the activities of the descendants of the following persons during the last fifty years:
   a. Descendants of William McIntosh:
      1. William Henry McIntosh ---
         by Boyd McIntosh, Kearns, Utah
      2. Malissa Jan McIntosh Keele ---
         no representative
      3. Alice Maria McIntosh Burridge ---
         by Wanda Burridgs
      4. Abraham E. McIntosh ---
         by Fern Jacobs
      5. Lillian Elisabeth McIntosh McBride ---
         no representative
      6. Joseph Albert McIntosh ---
         by Michael McIntosh
   b. Descendants of John McIntosh:
      1. John David McIntosh ---
         by Deon Hitchcock
      2. William Abram McIntosh ---
         by Lena Donaldson...

FAMILY REPRESENTATIVES...

The family representatives are as follows:

1. Family of William Henry McIntosh --
   Boyd McIntosh, Kearns, Utah
2. Melissa Jane McIntosh Keele --
   Keele Family, Anaconda, Montana
3. Alice Maria McIntosh Burridge --
   Wanda Burridge, Nephi, Utah
4. Abraham E. McIntosh --
   Fern Jacobs, Mt. Pleasant, Utah
5. Lillian Elizabeth McIntosh McBride --
   J. W. McBride, Tremonton, Utah
6. Joseph Albert McIntosh --
   To be appointed by Don McIntosh
7. John David McIntosh --
   Annie Algets, Las Vegas, Nevada
8. William Abram McIntosh --
   Roah Dunsworth. The 5th Annual Reunion was held at Provo Park on 12 Jun 1960. Newsletter dated July 4, 1960.

16. Paul Christiansen, US GenWeb, "Big Horn County Cemeteries," database,*WYGenWebProject* (rootsweb.ancestry.com/~wybighor/cemeteries.html).

17. Brown, Beverly McIntosh and Marsha McIntosh, editors,*William McIntosh Diary 1857-1898, Abridgement* (Surprise, AZ: Self-published, June 2002).

18. Daughters of Utah Pioneers, *Our Pioneer Heritage* (Salt Lake City, UT: Infobases, Inc., 1996), 19: 422. Repository: Family History Library, 35 North West Temple Street, Salt Lake City, Utah 84150-3400, USA, Call Number: 979.2 H2.

19. Frank Esshorn, editor, *Pioneers and Prominent Men of Utah comprising Photographs-Genealogies-Biographies. Pioneers are those men and women who came to Utah by wagon, hand cart or afoot, between July 24, 1847 and December 30, 1868, before the railroad. Prominent Men are stake presidents, ward bishops, governors, members of the bench, etc., who came to Utah after the coming of the railroad. The early history of the Church of Jesus Christ of Latter-Day Saints. In One Volume, Illustrated* (Salt Lake City, Utah: Utah Pioneers Book Publishing Company, 1913), McIntosh, William: 331 and 1059. Repository: Family History Library, 35 North West Temple Street, Salt Lake City, Utah 84150-3400, USA, Call Number: 979.2 D3e.

20. Andrew Jenson, editor, *Latter-day Saint Biographical Encyclopedia: A Compilation of Biographical Sketches of Prominent Men and Women in The Church of Jesus Christ of Latter-day Saints*, 4 v.: ports. (Salt Lake City, Utah: Western Epics, 1971), William McIntosh: V 4, page 647. Repository: Family History Library, 35 North West Temple Street, Salt Lake City, Utah 84150-3400, USA, Call Number: 920.0792.

21. International Society of Daughters of Utah Pioneers, editor,*Pioneer Women of Faith and Fortitude*, Volume III (Salt Lake City, Utah: Publishers Press, 1998), Maria Caldwell McIntosh: page 1946. Repository: Family History Library, 35 North West Temple Street, Salt Lake City, Utah 84150-3400, USA, Call Number: 979 D36.

# Source Citations


22. 1860 U.S. census, Shambip, Utah, population schedule, Clover, p. 450, dwelling 4028, family 3104, Malissa J McIntosh; digital images, *ancestry.com*; citing National Archives and Records Administration microfilm M653.

23. 1870 U.S. census, Washington, Utah, population schedule, Panaaca, p. 7, dwelling 54, family 48, McIntosh, Jane; digital images, *ancestry.com*; citing National Archives and Records Administration microfilm M593.

24. 1870 U.S. census, Lincoln, Nevada, population schedule, Meadow Valley, p. 186, dwelling 66-68, family 45, McIntosh, Jane; digital images, *ancestry.com*; citing National Archives and Records Administration microfilm M593.

25. Brown, Beverly McIntosh and Marsha Lee McIntosh,*William McIntosh Diary, abridgement* (Self-published, Surprise, AZ. June 2002).

26. Loveland, Carla Neves,*Sagebrush and Roses, A History of Otto and Burlington Wyoming* (Lindon, Utah, Alexander's Digital Printing, 2003), pages 359 and 449. Repository: Family History Library, 35 North West Temple Street, Salt Lake City, Utah 84150-3400, USA, Call Number: 978.733 H2.

27. McIntosh Reunion Descendants, McIntosh - Descendants of John & Girsey (Grace) (Grizel) Rankin McIntosh (Attachment to Aug 17, 1958 Newsletter - copy in Collection of Bonnie S. Williams), Repository: Bonnie S. Williams, RR 1 Box 247, N Hwy 2, Wilburton, Oklahoma, USA.
Maria (daughter of Millisa Jane [McINTOSH] & Jacob KEELE).
Maria KEELE is a Great-Granddaughter of John McINTOSH & Girsey RANKIN
and a Granddaughter of William McINTOSH & Maria CALDWELL
no further information.

28. Carla Neves Loveland,*Sagebrush and Roses: A History of Otto and Burlington Wyoming*, One Volume (Lindon, Utah: Alexander's Digital Printing, 2003), 449.

29. "Find A Grave," database (www.findagrave.com), Maria Elizabeth Keele Robinson.

30. Utah Division of State History, "Cemetery & Burial Database," database (https://heritage.utah.gov/history/cemeteries), Maria Elizabeth Keele Robinson.

31. McIntosh Reunion Descendants, McIntosh - Descendants of John & Girsey (Grace) (Grizel) Rankin McIntosh (Attachment to Aug 17, 1958 Newsletter - copy in Collection of Bonnie S. Williams), Page 1. Repository: Bonnie S. Williams, RR 1 Box 247, N Hwy 2, Wilburton, Oklahoma, USA.
Descendants of John McIntosh
Page 1 24 Aug 2001
1. John McIntosh (b.25 Jun 1795-Croy,Invernesshire,Scotland;d.5 Mar 1875-Bountiful,Davis,Utah)
sp: Girsey Rankin (b.1794-Rutherglen,Lanarkshire,Scotland;m.15 Jun 1817;d.Apr 1853-Origan,Lucas,Ohio)...
2. William McIntosh (b.16 Sep 1819-Bridgeton,Lanark,Scotland;d.5 May 1899-Mt. Pleasant,Sanpete,Utah)
sp: Maria Caldwell (b.17 Feb 1824-Lanark,Upper Canada;m.26 Sep 1841;d.27 Jul 1897-Mt Pleasant,San Pete,Utah)...
3. Melissa Jane McIntosh (b.27 Jun 1853-West Jordan,Salt Lake,Utah)
sp: Jacob Keele (b.29 May 1847;d.Sep 1925-Grand Junction,Mesa,Colorado)
4. Maria Elizabeth Keele (b.14 Aug 1873-Panaca,Lincoln,Nevada;d.Dec 1918)
sp: Frederick Walker Robinson (m.10 Nov 1892).
no children listed.

32. "Colorado, Marriages, 1859-1900," database, Maria E. Keele and Fred W. Robinson.

33. Carla Neves Loveland,*Sagebrush and Roses: A History of Otto and Burlington Wyoming*, One Volume (Lindon, Utah: Alexander's Digital Printing, 2003), page 449.

34. 1910 U.S. census, Park, Wyoming, population schedule, Meeteetse, enumeration district (ED) 29, sheet 1B, p. 138, dwelling 16, family 16, Robinson, May (Maria) E; digital images,*ancestry.com*; citing National Archives and Records Administration microfilm T624.

35. McIntosh Reunion Descendants, McIntosh - Descendants of John & Girsey (Grace) (Grizel) Rankin McIntosh (Attachment to Aug 17, 1958 Newsletter - copy in Collection of Bonnie S. Williams), Repository: Bonnie S. Williams, RR 1 Box 247, N Hwy 2, Wilburton, Oklahoma, USA.
Alma J. (son of Millisa Jane [McINTOSH] & Jacob KEELE).
Alma J. KEELE is a Great-Grandson of John McINTOSH & Girsey RANKIN
and a Grandson of William McINTOSH & Maria CALDWELL
no further information.

36. "Find A Grave," database (www.findagrave.com), Alma Jacob Keele.

37. Idaho Department of Public Welfare, Bureau of Vital Statistics, death certificate 110972 (1938), Alma Jacob Keele; digital image, ancestry.com.

38. "Find A Grave," database (www.findagrave.com), Alma Jacob Keele, born 2 Feb 1875; died 1 Oct 1938.

39. Idaho Department of Public Welfare, Bureau of Vital Statistics, death certificate 110972 (1938), Alma Jacob Keele, born 2 Feb 1875; died 1 Oct 1938; digital image, ancestry.com.

40. "Idaho, Death Index, 1890-1964," database, Alma Jacob Keele, born 2 Feb 1875; died 1 Oct 1938.

# Source Citations

41. McIntosh Reunion Descendants, McIntosh - Descendants of John & Girsey (Grace) (Grizel) Rankin McIntosh (Attachment to Aug 17, 1958 Newsletter - copy in Collection of Bonnie S. Williams), Page 1. Repository: Bonnie S. Williams, RR 1 Box 247, N Hwy 2, Wilburton, Oklahoma, USA.
Descendants of John McIntosh
24 Aug 2001
1. John McIntosh (b.25 Jun 1795-Croy,Invernesshire,Scotland;d.5 Mar 1875-Bountiful,Davis,Utah)
sp: Girsey Rankin (b.1794-Rutherglen,Lanarkshire,Scotland;m.15 Jun 1817;d.Apr 1853-Origan,Lucas,Ohio)...
2. William McIntosh (b.16 Sep 1819-Bridgeton,Lanark,Scotland;d.5 May 1899-Mt. Pleasant,Sanpete,Utah)
sp: Maria Caldwell (b.17 Feb 1824-Lanark,Upper Canada;m.26 Sep 1841;d.27 Jul 1897-Mt Pleasant,San Pete,Utah)...
3. Melissa Jane McIntosh (b.27 Jun 1853-West Jordan,Salt Lake,Utah)
sp: Jacob Keele (b.29 May 1847;d.Sep 1925-Grand Junction,Mesa,Colorado)
4. Alma Jacob Keele (b.2 Feb 1876-Panaca,Lincoln,Nevada;d.1941)
sp: Dollie C. Garner
...
no children listed.

42. McIntosh Reunion Descendants, McIntosh - Descendants of John & Girsey (Grace) (Grizel) Rankin McIntosh (Attachment to Aug 17, 1958 Newsletter - copy in Collection of Bonnie S. Williams), Repository: Bonnie S. Williams, RR 1 Box 247, N Hwy 2, Wilburton, Oklahoma, USA.
Alice (daughter of Millisa Jane [McINTOSH] & Jacob KEELE).
Alice KEELE is a Great-Granddaughter of John McINTOSH & Girsey RANKIN
and a Granddaughter of William McINTOSH & Maria CALDWELL
no further information.

43. "Find A Grave," database (www.findagrave.com), Alice Melissa Burkitt.

44. McIntosh Reunion Descendants, McIntosh - Descendants of John & Girsey (Grace) (Grizel) Rankin McIntosh (Attachment to Aug 17, 1958 Newsletter - copy in Collection of Bonnie S. Williams), Page 1. Repository: Bonnie S. Williams, RR 1 Box 247, N Hwy 2, Wilburton, Oklahoma, USA.
Descendants of John McIntosh
24 Aug 2001
1. John McIntosh (b.25 Jun 1795-Croy,Invernesshire,Scotland;d.5 Mar 1875-Bountiful,Davis,Utah) sp: Girsey Rankin (b.1794-Rutherglen,Lanarkshire,Scotland;m.15 Jun 1817;d.Apr 1853-Origan,Lucas,Ohio)2. William McIntosh (b.16 Sep 1819-Bridgeton,Lanark,Scotland;d.5 May 1899-Mt. Pleasant,Sanpete,Utah)
sp: Maria Caldwell (b.17 Feb 1824-Lanark,Upper Canada;m.26 Sep 1841;d.27 Jul 1897-Mt Pleasant,San Pete,Utah)
3. Melissa Jane McIntosh (b.27 Jun 1853-West Jordan,Salt Lake,Utah)
sp: Jacob Keele (b.29 May 1847;d.Sep 1925-Grand Junction,Mesa,Colorado)
4. Alice Melissa Keele (b.16 Oct 1874-Panaca,Lincoln,Nevada;d.1919)
sp: Richard Burkett.
no children listed.

45. Select Counties, Colorado, Select County Marriages, 1863-2018 page 110, Richard Burkitt of Fruita-Keele, Alice M. of Fruita, 1892; digital images, ancestry.com.

46. "Colorado, Mesa, Arapahoe and Boulder Counties, Compiled Marriages, 1859-1900," database, Richard Burkett and Alice M. Kaele married on 30 Oct 1892 in Mesa County, Colorado.

47. 1910 U.S. census, Mesa, Colorado, population schedule, Rhone, enumeration district (ED) 89, sheet 17A84, p. 9, dwelling 9, family Burkitt, Alice; digital images, *ancestry.com*; citing National Archives and Records Administration microfilm T624.

48. McIntosh Reunion Descendants, McIntosh - Descendants of John & Girsey (Grace) (Grizel) Rankin McIntosh (Attachment to Aug 17, 1958 Newsletter - copy in Collection of Bonnie S. Williams), Repository: Bonnie S. Williams, RR 1 Box 247, N Hwy 2, Wilburton, Oklahoma, USA.
Wallace (son of Millisa Jane [McINTOSH] & Jacob KEELE).
Wallace KEELE is a Great-Grandson of John McINTOSH & Girsey RANKIN
and a Grandson of William McINTOSH & Maria CALDWELL
no further information.

49. McIntosh Reunion Descendants, McIntosh - Descendants of John & Girsey (Grace) (Grizel) Rankin McIntosh (Attachment to Aug 17, 1958 Newsletter - copy in Collection of Bonnie S. Williams), Repository: Bonnie S. Williams, RR 1 Box 247, N Hwy 2, Wilburton, Oklahoma, USA.
Estella (daughter of Millisa Jane [McINTOSH] & Jacob KEELE).
Estella KEELE is a Great-Granddaughter of John McINTOSH & Girsey RANKIN
and a Granddaughter of William McINTOSH & Maria CALDWELL
no further information.

50. "Find A Grave," database (www.findagrave.com), Annie Estella Keele Kendall.

51. McIntosh Reunion Descendants, McIntosh - Descendants of John & Girsey (Grace) (Grizel) Rankin McIntosh (Attachment to Aug 17, 1958 Newsletter - copy in Collection of Bonnie S. Williams), Page 1. Repository: Bonnie S. Williams, RR 1 Box 247, N Hwy 2, Wilburton, Oklahoma, USA.
Descendants of John McIntosh
24 Aug 2001
1. John McIntosh (b.25 Jun 1795-Croy,Invernesshire,Scotland;d.5 Mar 1875-Bountiful,Davis,Utah)
sp: Girsey Rankin (b.1794-Rutherglen,Lanarkshire,Scotland;m.15 Jun 1817;d.Apr 1853-Origan,Lucas,Ohio)...
2. William McIntosh (b.16 Sep 1819-Bridgeton,Lanark,Scotland;d.5 May 1899-Mt. Pleasant,Sanpete,Utah)

# Source Citations

sp: Maria Caldwell (b.17 Feb 1824-Lanark,Upper Canada;m.26 Sep 1841;d.27 Jul 1897-Mt Pleasant,San Pete,Utah)...
3. Melissa Jane McIntosh (b.27 Jun 1853-West Jordan,Salt Lake,Utah)
sp: Jacob Keele (b.29 May 1847;d.Sep 1925-Grand Junction,Mesa,Colorado)...
4. Annie Estella Keele (b.2 Aug 1883-Huntington,Emery,Utah)
sp: Calvin Husten Kendall.
no children listed.

52. "Colorado, Mesa County, Marriage Index, 1883-2010," database, Husten Kendall married Annie Estella Keele on 28 Dec 1899 in Mesa, Colorado.

53. McIntosh Reunion Descendants, McIntosh - Descendants of John & Girsey (Grace) (Grizel) Rankin McIntosh (Attachment to Aug 17, 1958 Newsletter - copy in Collection of Bonnie S. Williams), Repository: Bonnie S. Williams, RR 1 Box 247, N Hwy 2, Wilburton, Oklahoma, USA.
Jennett (daughter of Millisa Jane [McINTOSH] & Jacob KEELE).
Jennett KEELE is a Great-Granddaughter of John McINTOSH & Girsey RANKIN
and a Granddaughter of William McINTOSH & Maria CALDWELL
no further information.

54. "Find A Grave," database (www.findagrave.com), Lillian Jenette Keele Wiik.

55. Brigham Young University-Idaho, "Western States Marriage Index," database (http://abish.byui.edu/specialCollections/westernStates/search.cfm), David Weir and Lillie Jennett Keele.

56. Brigham Young University-Idaho, "Western States Marriage Index," database (http://abish.byui.edu/specialCollections/westernStates/search.cfm), Lillian J. Weir and David M. Armstrong.

57. "Find A Grave," database (www.findagrave.com), Arvid Wiik.

58. McIntosh Reunion Descendants, McIntosh - Descendants of John & Girsey (Grace) (Grizel) Rankin McIntosh (Attachment to Aug 17, 1958 Newsletter - copy in Collection of Bonnie S. Williams), Repository: Bonnie S. Williams, RR 1 Box 247, N Hwy 2, Wilburton, Oklahoma, USA.
Delos (son of Millisa Jane [McINTOSH] & Jacob KEELE).
Delos KEELE is a Great-Grandson of John McINTOSH & Girsey RANKIN
and a Grandson of William McINTOSH & Maria CALDWELL
no further information.

59. McIntosh Reunion Descendants, McIntosh - Descendants of John & Girsey (Grace) (Grizel) Rankin McIntosh (Attachment to Aug 17, 1958 Newsletter - copy in Collection of Bonnie S. Williams), Page 1. Repository: Bonnie S. Williams, RR 1 Box 247, N Hwy 2, Wilburton, Oklahoma, USA.
Descendants of John McIntosh
24 Aug 2001
1. John McIntosh (b.25 Jun 1795-Croy,Invernesshire,Scotland;d.5 Mar 1875-Bountiful,Davis,Utah)
sp: Girsey Rankin (b.1794-Rutherglen,Lanarkshire,Scotland;m.15 Jun 1817;d.Apr 1853-Origan,Lucas,Ohio)...
2. William McIntosh (b.16 Sep 1819-Bridgeton,Lanark,Scotland;d.5 May 1899-Mt. Pleasant,Sanpete,Utah)
sp: Maria Caldwell (b.17 Feb 1824-Lanark,Upper Canada;m.26 Sep 1841;d.27 Jul 1897-Mt Pleasant,San Pete,Utah)...
3. Melissa Jane McIntosh (b.27 Jun 1853-West Jordan,Salt Lake,Utah)
sp: Jacob Keele (b.29 May 1847;d.Sep 1925-Grand Junction,Mesa,Colorado)...
4. Jennie May Keele (b.Abt 1890-Fruita,Mesa,Colorado).
no spouse or children listed, this is all the information on her.

60. McIntosh Reunion Descendants, McIntosh - Descendants of John & Girsey (Grace) (Grizel) Rankin McIntosh (Attachment to Aug 17, 1958 Newsletter - copy in Collection of Bonnie S. Williams), Repository: Bonnie S. Williams, RR 1 Box 247, N Hwy 2, Wilburton, Oklahoma, USA.
Virgil Vaughn (son of Millisa Jane [McINTOSH] & Jacob KEELE).
Virgil Vaughn KEELE is a Great-Grandson of John McINTOSH & Girsey RANKIN
and a Grandson of William McINTOSH & Maria CALDWELL
no further information.

61. "Find A Grave," database (www.findagrave.com), Virgil Vaughn Keele.

62. *Montana Death Index, 1907-2002* (http://www.ancestry.com/), Virgil Vaughn Keele. Repository: Montana Office of Vital Statistics.

63. Social Security Death Index (Online publication - Provo, UT, USA: Ancestry.com Operations Inc, 2009.Original data), Virgil Vaughn Keele.

64. Brigham Young University-Idaho, "Western States Marriage Index," database (http://abish.byui.edu/specialCollections/westernStates/search.cfm), Virgil V. Keele and Clara Robbins.

65. "Find A Grave," database (www.findagrave.com), Virgil Vaughn Keele and Claire Robbins.

66. *U.S., World War I Draft Registration Cards,* Virgil Vaughn Keele.

# Alice Maria McIntosh and Thomas Lorenzo Burridge

| **Husband** | **Thomas Lorenzo Burridge**[1,2,3,4] | |
|---|---|---|
| Born | 2 Dec 1853 | Valletta, , , Malta[5] |
| Died | 12 Apr 1891 | Saint John, Tooele, Utah Territory, United States[6] |
| Buried | 14 Apr 1891 | Rush Valley, Tooele, Utah, United States[7] |
| Address | St. John Cemetery, East on Main Street to Cemetery Road, Rush Valley, Utah 84069, USA | |
| Bapt.(LDS) | 25 Mar 1862 | |
| Conf.(LDS) | 25 Mar 1862 | |
| Init.(LDS) | 6 Jan 1881 | Endowment House |
| Endow.(LDS) | 6 Jan 1881 | Endowment House |
| Father | George Wilcox Burridge (1813-1891) [8] | |
| Mother | Hannah Jane Shaw (1827-1909) [9,10] | |
| SealP (LDS) | 22 Jan 1886 | Logan Utah Temple |
| Marriage | 6 Jan 1881 | Salt Lake City, Great Salt Lake, Utah Territory, United States |
| SealS (LDS) | 6 Jan 1881 | Endowment House |

**Events**

1. He emigrated on 22 Apr 1855 from Liverpool, Lancaster, England, United Kingdom.
2. He immigrated on 22 May 1855 to New York, New York, New York, United States.[11]
3. He immigrated Milo Andrus Company between 4 Aug and 24 Oct 1855 to Salt Lake City, Great Salt Lake, Utah Territory, United States.[12]
   461 individuals were in the company when it began its journey from the outfitting post at Mormon Grove, Kansas (Near Atchison). This was a Perpetual Emigration Fund Company.
   Company List:
   Burridge, Charlotte Hannah (age 4)
   Burridge, George Wilcox (age 42)
   Burridge, Hannah Jane (age 37)
   **Burridge, Thomas Lorenzo (age 2)**

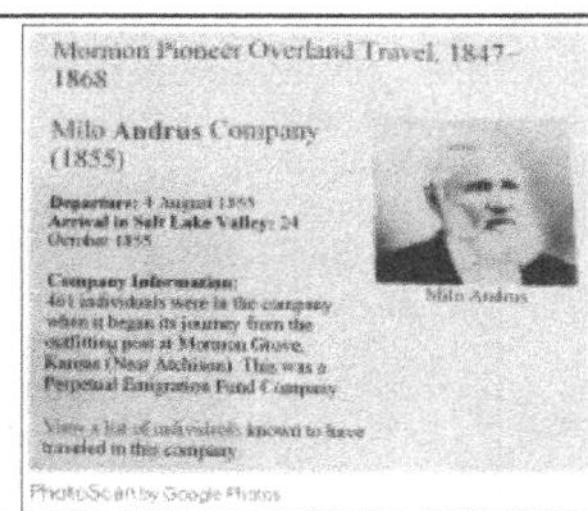

Mormon Pioneer Overland Travel, 1847-1868
Milo Andrus Company (1855)
Company Information:
Milo Andrus
PhotoScan by Google Photos


Mormon Pioneer Overland Travel, Milo Andrus Company, Thomas Lorenzo Burridge, page 1 of 2

4. He appeared on the census on 11 Oct 1860 in Clover, Shambip, Utah Territory, United States.[13]
   Line 1) Geo Burridge, age 48, male, farmer, born in England
   Line 2) Hannah Burridge, age 33, female, born in Scotland
   Line 3) Cht Burridge, age 9, female, born in Scotland, in school
   Line 4) **Thos Burridge, age 7, male, born in Scotland, in school**
   Line 5) Paulina Burridge, age 3, female, born in Utah Territor
5. He appeared on the census on 2 Jun 1870 in Saint John, Tooele, Utah Territory, United States.[14]
   Line 21 - Burridge, George, age 52, male, white, farmer, value of real estate 1000, value of personal estate 300, born in Denmark, father & mother foreign born yes.
   Line 22 - Burridge, Hannah, age 42, female, white, keeping house, born in Scotland, father & mother foreign yes.
   **Line 23 - Burridge, Thomas, age 16, male, white, at home, born in England, father & mother foreign born yes.**
   Line 24 - Burridge, Pauline, age 12, female, white, at home, born in Utah, father & mother foreign born yes, cannot read or write.
6. He appeared on the census on 12 Jun 1880 in Clover, Tooele, Utah Territory, United States.[15]
   Line 4 - Burridge, George, white, male, age 67, head, married, retail grocer, born in England, father born in England, mother born in England.
   Line 5 - Burridge, Anna, white, female, age 52, wife, married, keeping house, born in Scotland, father born in Scotland, mother born in Scotland.

# Alice Maria McIntosh and Thomas Lorenzo Burridge

Line 6 - Burridge, Ella, white, female, age 31, daughter, single, keeping house, born in England, father born in England, mother born in Scotland.
**Line 7 - Burridge, Thomas L., white, male, age 27, son, single, born in England, father born in England, mother born in Scotland.**

7. Witness to a land sale: for Caroline Caldwell McIntosh, on 19 Jul 1888, in Saint John, Tooele, Utah Territory, United States.[16]

| **Wife** | **Alice Maria McIntosh**[17,18,19,20,21] | |
|---|---|---|
| AKA | Alice Marie McIntosh, Maria McIntosh | |
| Born | 26 Sep 1857 | West Jordan, Great Salt Lake, Utah Territory, United States[22] |
| Died | 31 Oct 1914 | Provo, Utah, Utah, United States[22] |
| Address | Provo General Hospital, Provo, Utah, USA | |
| Cause of Death | Duodenal ulcer[23] | |
| Buried | 3 Nov 1914 | Provo, Utah, Utah, United States[23,24,25] |
| Address | Provo City Cemetery, 610 South State, Provo, Utah 84606, USA | |
| Notes | Block 9, Lot 105 | |
| Bapt.(LDS) | 1 Jan 1867 | |
| Conf.(LDS) | 1 Jan 1867 | |
| Init.(LDS) | 6 Jan 1881 | Endowment House |
| Endow.(LDS) | 6 Jan 1881 | Endowment House |
| Father | William McIntosh (1819-1899) [26,27,28,29] | |
| Mother | Maria Caldwell (1824-1897) [30] | |
| SealP (LDS) | 11 Oct 1893 | Manti Utah Temple |

St. John Cemetery

**Events**

1. She appeared on the census on 11 Oct 1860 in Clover, Shambip, Utah Territory, United States.[31]
   Line 25) Wm McIntosh, age 40, male, farmer, born in Scotland
   Line 26) Maria McIntosh, age 36, female, born in Canada
   Line 27) Jno E McIntosh, age 18, male, born in Ohio
   Line 28) Wm. H McIntosh, age 11, male, born in Missouri, in school
   Line 29) Jas F McIntosh, age 8, male, born in Utah Territory, in school
   Line 30) Malissa J McIntosh, age 6, female, born in Utah Territory, in school
   Line 31) **Alice M McIntosh, age 3, female, born in Utah Territory**
   Line 32) Abm E McIntosh, age 6/12, male, born in Utah Territory
2. She appeared on the census on 10 Jun 1870 in Panaca, Washington, Utah Territory.[32]
   Line 20 - McIntosh, William age 49, male, white, day laborer, value of personal estate 200, born in Scotland, father and mother foreign born, male over 21.
   Line 21 - McIntosh, Marie, age 45, female, white, keeping house, born in Canada, father and mother foreign born.
   Line 22 - McIntosh, William, age 20, male, white, teamster, born in Missouri, father and mother foreign born.
   Line 23 - McIntosh, Frank, age 18, male, white, work on farm, born in Utah, father and mother foreign born.
   Line 24 - McIntosh, Jane, age 15, female, white, at home, born in Utah, father and mother foreign born, attended school.
   **Line 25 - McIntosh, Allice, age 12, female, white, born in Utah, father and mother foreign born, attended school.**
   Line 26 - McIntosh, Abraham, age 10, male, white, born in Utah, father and mother foreign born, attended school, cannot write.
   Line 27 - McIntosh, Lilly, age 7, female, white, born in Utah, father and mother foreign born.
   Line 28 - McIntosh, Caroline, age 4, female, white, born in Utah, father and mother foreign born.
   Line 29 - McIntosh, Albert, age 1, male, white, born in Utah, father and mother foreign born.
3. She appeared on the census on 28 Jul 1870 in Meadow Valley, Lincoln, Nevada, United States.[33]

# Alice Maria McIntosh and Thomas Lorenzo Burridge

Line 22 - McIntosh, Wm age 50, male, white, farming, value of real estate 300, value of personal estate 800, born in Scotland, father and mother foreign born, male over 21.
Line 23 - McIntosh, Marie, age 45, female, white, keeping house, born in Canada, father and mother foreign born.
Line 24 - McIntosh, Wm H, age 21, male, white, farming, born in Missouri, father and mother foreign born, male over 21.
Line 25 - McIntosh, Frank, age 18, male, white, farming, born in Utah, father and mother foreign born.
Line 26 - McIntosh, Jane, age 16, female, white, at home, born in Utah, father and mother foreign born, attended school.
**Line 27 - McIntosh, Alice, age 12, female, white, school, born in Utah, father and mother foreign born, attended school.**
Line 28 - McIntosh, Abe, age 10, male, white, school, born in Utah, father and mother foreign born, attended school, cannot write.
Line 29 - McIntosh, Lilly, age 7, female, white, school, born in Utah, father and mother foreign born.
Line 30 - McIntosh, Caroline, age 4, female, white, school, born in Utah, father and mother foreign born.
Line 31 - McIntosh, Albert, age 1, male, white, school, born in Nevada, father and mother foreign born.

4. She appeared on the census on 12 Jun 1880 in Clover, Tooele, Utah Territory, United States.[34]
Line 19 - Mackintosh, William, white, male, age 60, head, married, laborer, born in Canada, father born in Canada, mother born Canada.
Line 20 - Mackintosh, Caroline, white, female, age 53, wife, married, keeping house, born in Canada, father born in Canada, mother born in Canada.
**Line 21 - Mackintosh, Alice, white, female, age 22, daughter, single, teaching school, born in Utah, father born in Canada, Mother born in Canada.**
Line 22 - Mackintosh, Abraham, white, male, age 20, son, single, working on farm, born in Utah, father born in Canada, mother born in Canada.
Line 23 - Mackintosh, Lillian, white, female, age 18, daughter, single, studying at home, attended school, born in Utah, father born in Canada, mother born in Canada.
Line 24 - Mackintosh, Caroline, white, female, age 15, daughter, single, studying at home, attended school, born in Utah, father born in Canada, mother born in Canada.
Line 25 - Mackintosh, Albert, white, male, age 11, son, single, working on farm, attended school, born in Utah, father born in Canada, mother born in Canada.

5. She had a residence in Oct 1891 in Saint John, Tooele, Utah, United States.[35,36]
"... Alice and her four children are living with us yet."
"We had a letter from Alice Burridge last week. Her and family are well. She has four boys and one girl. She is our daughter. She lives in St. John."

6. She appeared on the census on 29 Jun 1900 in Saint John, Tooele, Utah, United States.[37]
**Line 69 - Burridge, Alice, head, white, female, born, Sept 1858, age 41, widowed, had 6 children, 4 living, born in Utah, father born in Scotland, mother born in Canada, able to read, write and speak english, owns, mortgage free, farm #22.**
Line 70 - Burridge, George T, son, white, male, born June 1882, age 19, single, born in Idaho, father born in England, mother born in Utah, farm laborer, 2 months unemployed within year, able to read, write and speak english.
Line 71 - Burridge, William M, son, white, male, born Oct 1883, age 16, single, born in Utah, father born in England, mother born in Utah, farm laborer, 0 months unemployed, able to read, write and speak english.
Line 72 - Burridge, Franklin D, son, white, male, born Dec 1885, age 14, single, born in Utah, father born in England, mother born in Utah, farm laborer, 0 months unemployed, able to read, write and speak english.
Line 73 - Burridge, Theol L, son, white, male, born Nov 1891, age 8, single, born in Utah, father born in England, mother born in Utah, at school 7 months.

7. She appeared on the census on 27 Apr 1910 in Provo, Utah, Utah, United States.[38]
**Line 56 - Burridge, Alice, head, female, white, age 52, widowed, had 6 children, 3 living, born in Utah, father born in Scotland, speaks Scotch, mother born in Canada, speaks english, speaks english, occupation-keeps (can't read it), works on own account, can read and write, owns mortgage free house.**
Line 57 - Burridge, Franklin, son, male, white, age 24, single, born in Utah, father born on Island of Malta, mother born in Utah, speaks english, occupation is mason, brickyard, wage worker, not out of work on 15 Apr 1910, can read and write.

# Alice Maria McIntosh and Thomas Lorenzo Burridge

Line 58 - Burridge, Theol, son, male, white, age 18, single, born in Utah, father born on Island of Malta, mother born in Utah, speaks english, no occupation, can read and write, attended school within year.

8. Her obituary was published after 31 Oct 1914 in Provo, Utah, Utah, United States.
   **Alice Maria McIntosh** by Wanda Burridge:
   Alice Maria McIntosh was born Sep. 16, 1858 in West Jordan, Utah, to William and Maria Caldwell McIntosh. She was married Jan. 6, 1881 to Thomas Lorenzo Burridge. He was the son of George Wilcox and Hannah Shaw Burridge. Alice was left a widow in April 1891 with five small children and in November, 1891 her sixth child was born, being Theo Lorenzo. He was the husband of Wanda Christison. Alice worked very hard to support her six children. She would ride in a white top buggy from St. John all over Tooele County to sell milk, ice, cream, yeast, etc. In 1900 she moved to educate her boys, two of whom were already attending BYU. Alice was an ambitious and wonderful mother. She lived to see four of her children laid to rest. She died in Provo in October 1914. Theo, the youngest, lived to the age of 41 and was the father of the only grandchildren of four girls and two boys. There are now thirteen great grand children from the marriage of Alice Maria McIntosh and Thomas Lorenzo Burridge.

## Children

| 1 | M | **George Thomas Burridge** [39] | |
|---|---|---|---|
| Born | | 19 Jun 1882 | Iona, Bonneville, Idaho, United States[40,41] |
| Died | | 10 Jul 1911 | Provo, Utah, Utah, United States[41] |
| Cause of Death | | Orchitis (inflammation of the testicles) resulting from groin injury[42] | |
| Buried | | 12 Jul 1911 | Provo, Utah, Utah, United States[42,43] |
| Address | | Provo City Cemetery, 610 South State, Provo, Utah 84606, USA | |
| Notes | | Plot: Block 9, Lot 105 | |
| Bapt.(LDS) | | 9 Aug 1891 | |
| Conf.(LDS) | | 9 Aug 1891 | |
| Init.(LDS) | | 25 Feb 1937 | Endowment House |
| Endow.(LDS) | | 25 Feb 1937 | Endowment House |
| SealP (LDS) | | 5 Apr 2016 | Provo Utah Temple |
| Spouse | | This person had no known marriage and no known children | |

**Events**

1. He worked as a civil engineer.
2. He appeared on the census on 29 Jun 1900 in Saint John, Tooele, Utah, United States.[44]
   Line 69 - Burridge, Alice, head, white, female, born, Sept 1858, age 41, widowed, had 6 children, 4 living, born in Utah, father born in Scotland, mother born in Canada, able to read, write and speak english, owns, mortgage free, farm #22.
   **Line 70 - Burridge, George T, son, white, male, born June 1882, age 19, single, born in Idaho, father born in England, mother born in Utah, farm laborer, 2 months unemployed within year, able to read, write and speak english.**
   Line 71 - Burridge, William M, son, white, male, born Oct 1883, age 16, single, born in Utah, father born in England, mother born in Utah, farm laborer, 0 months unemployed, able to read, write and speak english.
   Line 72 - Burridge, Franklin D, son, white, male, born Dec 1885, age 14, single, born in Utah, father born in England, mother born in Utah, farm laborer, 0 months unemployed, able to read, write and speak english.
   Line 73 - Burridge, Theol L, son, white, male, born Nov 1891, age 8, single, born in Utah, father born in England, mother born in Utah, at school 7 months.

Medical
Inflamation of the testis

# Alice Maria McIntosh and Thomas Lorenzo Burridge

Children (cont.)

| 2 | M | **William McIntosh Burridge** [45] |
|---|---|---|
| Born | 4 Oct 1883 | Saint John, Tooele, Utah Territory, United States[46] |
| Died | 29 Nov 1905 | Mapleton, Utah, Utah, United States[46] |
| Cause of Death | Heart disease[46] | |
| Buried | 3 Dec 1905 | Provo, Utah, Utah, United States[47] |
| Address | Provo City Cemetery, 610 South State, Provo, Utah 84606, USA | |
| Bapt.(LDS) | 23 Aug 1896 | |
| Conf.(LDS) | 23 Aug 1896 | |
| Init.(LDS) | 25 Apr 1938 | Manti Utah Temple |
| Endow.(LDS) | 25 Apr 1938 | Manti Utah Temple |
| SealP (LDS) | 5 Apr 2016 | Provo Utah Temple |
| Spouse | This person had no known marriage and no known children | |

**Events**

1. He was blessed.[48]
   Name - Burridge, William M.; Parents - Thomas L., Alice McIntosh; Date and Place of Birth - 4 Oct 1883 in St. John, (record difficult to read).

2. He appeared on the census on 29 Jun 1900 in Saint John, Tooele, Utah, United States.[49]
   Line 69 - Burridge, Alice, head, white, female, born, Sept 1858, age 41, **widowed**, had 6 children, 4 living, born in Utah, father born in Scotland, mother born in Canada, able to read, write and speak english, owns, mortgage free, farm #22.
   Line 70 - Burridge, George T, son, white, male, born June 1882, age 19, single, born in Idaho, father born in England, mother born in Utah, farm laborer, 2 months unemployed within year, able to read, write and speak english.
   **Line 71 - Burridge, William M, son, white, male, born Oct 1883, age 16, single, born in Utah, father born in England, mother born in Utah, farm laborer, 0 months unemployed, able to read, write and speak english.**
   Line 72 - Burridge, Franklin D, son, white, male, born Dec 1885, age 14, single, born in Utah, father born in England, mother born in Utah, farm laborer, 0 months unemployed, able to read, write and speak english.
   Line 73 - Burridge, Theol L, son, white, male, born Nov 1891, age 8, single, born in Utah, father born in England, mother born in Utah, at school 7 months.

Medical
"Believed to be disease of heart. Sudden death Found dead in wagon which he was driving. Reported history of stomach trouble."

| 3 | M | **Franklin Dennis Burridge** [50] |
|---|---|---|
| AKA | Frank Burridge | |
| Born | 6 Dec 1885 | Saint John, Tooele, Utah Territory, United States[51,52] |
| Died | 20 Dec 1922 | Provo, Utah, Utah, United States[52,53] |
| Address | State Mental Hospital, Provo, Utah, USA | |
| Cause of Death | Cerebral Hemorrhage[52] | |
| Buried | 1922 | Beaver, Beaver, Utah, United States[52,53] |
| Address | Mountain View Cemetery, 450 North 600 East, Beaver, Utah 84713, USA | |
| Notes | Plot: B-170-1 | |
| Bapt.(LDS) | 23 Aug 1896 | |
| Conf.(LDS) | 23 Aug 1896 | |
| Init.(LDS) | 3 Apr 1934 | St. George Utah Temple |
| Endow.(LDS) | 3 Apr 1934 | St. George Utah Temple |
| SealP (LDS) | 5 Apr 2016 | Provo Utah Temple |
| Spouse | Lurena Farrer (1893-1974) | 23 Jun 1920 - Beaver, Beaver, Utah, United States |

# Alice Maria McIntosh and Thomas Lorenzo Burridge

| Children (cont.) | | |
|---|---|---|
| SealS (LDS) | 3 Apr 1934 | St. George Utah Temple |

**Events**

1. He was blessed.[48]
   Name - Burridge, Franklin Dennis; Parents - Thomas L., Alice McIntosh; Date and Place of Birth - 7 Dec 1885 in St. John, (record difficult to read).
2. He worked as a brick mason.[52]
3. He appeared on the census on 29 Jun 1900 in Saint John, Tooele, Utah, United States.[54]
   Line 69 - Burridge, Alice, head, white, female, born, Sept 1858, age 41, **widowed**, had 6 children, 4 living, born in Utah, father born in Scotland, mother born in Canada, able to read, write and speak english, owns, mortgage free, farm #22.
   Line 70 - Burridge, George T, son, white, male, born June 1882, age 19, single, born in Idaho, father born in England, mother born in Utah, farm laborer, 2 months unemployed within year, able to read, write and speak english.
   Line 71 - Burridge, William M, son, white, male, born Oct 1883, age 16, single, born in Utah, father born in England, mother born in Utah, farm laborer, 0 months unemployed, able to read, write and speak english.
   **Line 72 - Burridge, Franklin D, son, white, male, born Dec 1885, age 14, single, born in Utah, father born in England, mother born in Utah, farm laborer, 0 months unemployed, able to read, write and speak english.**
   Line 73 - Burridge, Theol L, son, white, male, born Nov 1891, age 8, single, born in Utah, father born in England, mother born in Utah, at school 7 months.
4. He appeared on the census on 27 Apr 1910 in Provo, Utah, Utah, United States.[55]
   Line 56 - Burridge, Alice, head, female, white, age 52, **widowed**, had 6 children, 3 living, born in Utah, father born in Scotland, speaks Scotch, mother born in Canada, speaks english, speaks english, occupation-keeps (can't read it), works on own account, can read and write, owns mortgage free house.
   **Line 57 - Burridge, Franklin, son, male, white, age 24, single, born in Utah, father born on Island of Malta, mother born in Utah, speaks english, occupation is mason, brickyard, wage worker, not out of work on 15 Apr 1910, can read and write.**
   Line 58 - Burridge, Theol, son, male, white, age 18, single, born in Utah, father born on Island of Malta, mother born in Utah, speaks english, no occupation, can read and write, attended school within year.
5. He died State Mental Hospital on 20 Dec 1922 in Provo, Utah, Utah, United States.[52]

Medical
He had "acute mania for 14 days before his death, which was instantaneous".

| 4 F | **Alice Marie Burridge** [56] | |
|---|---|---|
| AKA | Alice Mariah Burridge[48] | |
| Born | 1 Jan 1888 | Saint John, Tooele, Utah Territory, United States[57] |
| Died | 12 May 1896 | Saint John, Tooele, Utah, United States[58] |
| Buried | 1896 | Saint John, Tooele, Utah, United States[59] |
| Address | St. John Cemetery, East on Main Street to Cemetery Road, Rush Valley, Utah 84069, USA | |
| Bapt.(LDS) | 27 Oct 1896 | Salt Lake Temple |
| Conf.(LDS) | 1 Jan 1896 | Salt Lake Temple |
| Init.(LDS) | 13 Nov 1913 | Salt Lake Temple |
| Endow.(LDS) | 13 Nov 1913 | Salt Lake Temple |
| SealP (LDS) | 31 May 1995 | Jordan River Utah Temple |
| Spouse | This person had no known marriage and no known children | |

**Events**

1. She was blessed.[48]
   Name - Burridge, Alic Mariah; Parents - Thomas L., Alice McIntosh; Date and Place of Birth - 1 Jan 1888 in St. John, (record difficult to read).

| Children (cont.) | | | |
|---|---|---|---|
| 5 | M | **Jared Burridge**[60] | |
| Born | | 2 Feb 1890 | Saint John, Tooele, Utah Territory, United States[61] |
| Died | | 17 Sep 1890 | Saint John, Tooele, Utah Territory, United States[61] |
| Buried | | Sep 1890 | Saint John, Tooele, Utah Territory, United States[62] |
| Address | | St. John Cemetery, East on Main Street to Cemetery Road, Rush Valley, Utah 84069, ~ | |
| Bapt.(LDS) | | Child | |
| Conf.(LDS) | | Child | |
| Init.(LDS) | | Child | |
| Endow.(LDS) | | Child | |
| SealP (LDS) | | 11 Nov 2005 | |
| Spouse | | This person had no known marriage and no known children | |

**Events**

1. He was blessed.[48] Name - Burridge, Jared; Parents - Thomas L., Alice McIntosh; Date and Place of Birth - 2 Feb 1890 in St. John, (record difficult to read).

| 6 | M | **Theol Lorenzo Burridge Sr.**[63,64] | |
|---|---|---|---|
| Born | | 18 Nov 1891 | Saint John, Tooele, Utah Territory, United States[65,66,67] |
| Died | | 17 Feb 1933 | Salt Lake City, Salt Lake, Utah, United States[67,68] |
| Address | | Veterans Hospital, Salt Lake City, Utah, USA | |
| Cause of Death | | Burns, third degree//Psychosis, manic type[69] | |
| Buried | | 19 Feb 1933 | Nephi, Juab, Utah, United States[69,70] |
| Address | | Vine Bluff Cemetery, 1250 North 400 East, Nephi, Utah 84648, USA | |
| Notes | | Plot: A4-18-5 | |
| Bapt.(LDS) | | 23 Jun 1900 | |
| Conf.(LDS) | | 23 Jun 1900 | |
| Init.(LDS) | | 6 Jul 1922 | Manti Utah Temple |
| Endow.(LDS) | | 6 Jul 1922 | Manti Utah Temple |
| SealP (LDS) | | 5 Apr 2016 | |
| Spouse | | Wanda Jane Christison (1893-1986)[71,72] | 15 Oct 1919 - Salt Lake City, Salt Lake, Utah, United States[73] |
| SealS (LDS) | | 7 Jul 1922 | Manti Utah Temple |

**Events**

1. He was blessed.[48]
   Name - Burridge, Theol; Parents - Thomas L., Alice McIntosh; Date and Place of Birth - (can't read it) in St John (record diffcult to read).
2. He worked as a carpenter/builder/contractor.[69]
3. He appeared on the census on 29 Jun 1900 in Saint John, Tooele, Utah, United States.[74]
   Line 69 - Burridge, Alice, head, white, female, born, Sept 1858, age 41, **widowed**, had 6 children, 4 living, born in Utah, father born in Scotland, mother born in Canada, able to read, write and speak english, owns, mortgage free, farm # 22.
   Line 70 - Burridge, George T, son, white, male, born June 1882, age 19, single, born in Idaho, father born in England, mother born in Utah, farm laborer, 2 months unemployed within year, able to read, write and speak english.
   Line 71 - Burridge, William M, son, white, male, born Oct 1883, age 16, single, born in Utah, father born in England, mother born in Utah, farm laborer, 0 months unemployed, able to read, write and speak english.
   Line 72 - Burridge, Franklin D, son, white, male, born Dec 1885, age 14, single, born in Utah, father born in England, mother born in Utah, farm laborer, 0 months unemployed, able to read, write and speak english.

# Alice Maria McIntosh and Thomas Lorenzo Burridge

**Line 73 - Burridge, Theol L, son, white, male, born Nov 1891, age 8, single, born in Utah, father born in England, mother born in Utah, at school 7 months.**

4. He appeared on the census on 27 Apr 1910 in Provo, Utah, Utah, United States.[75]
   Line 56 - Burridge, Alice, head, female, white, age 52, **widowed**, had 6 children, 3 living, born in Utah, father born in Scotland, speaks Scotch, mother born in Canada, speaks english, speaks english, occupation-keeps (can't read it), works on own account, can read and write, owns mortgage free house.
   Line 57 - Burridge, Franklin, son, male, white, age 24, single, born in Utah, father born on Island of Malta, mother born in Utah, speaks english, occupation is mason, brickyard, wage worker, not out of work on 15 Apr 1910, can read and write.
   **Line 58 - Burridge, Theol, son, male, white, age 18, single, born in Utah, father born on Island of Malta, mother born in Utah, speaks english, no occupation, can read and write, attended school within year.**
5. Military Draft Registration: World War I, 5 Jun 1917, Roosevelt, Duchesne, Utah, United States.[76] He was tall but stout; had brown eyes with auburn hair.
6. He served in the military US Navy, Fireman 3d Class between 27 Nov 1917 and 28 May 1919.[77]
7. He appeared on the census on 12 Jan 1920 in Castle Gate, Carbon, Utah, United States.
   **Line 63 - Burridge, Theol L, head, rents home, male, white, age 28, married, born in Utah, father born in Malta, mother born in Utah, guard at a mining site.**
   Line 64 - Burridge, Wanda, wife, female, white, age 25, married, born in Utah, father born in Utah, mother born in Utah.
8. He appeared on the census on 2 Apr 1930 in Castle Gate, Carbon, Utah, United States.
   **Line 40 - Burridge, Theo L., head, rents home for $17.50, has a radio, male, white, age 38, married at age 26, can read, write and speak english, born in Utah, father born on Ile of Malta, mother born in Scotland, carpenter in coal mining industry.**
   Line 41 - Burridge, Jane W., wife, female, white, age 32, married at age of 23, can read, write and speak english, born in Utah, father born in Utah, mother born in Utah.
   Line 42 - Burridge, Alice J, daughter, female, white, age 9, single in school, born in Utah, father and mother born in Utah.
   Line 43 - Burridge, Barbara, daughter, female, white, age 8, single, in school, born in Utah, father and mother in Utah.
   Line 44 - Burridge, Elaine, daughter, female, white, age 6, single, in school, born in Utah, father and mother in Utah.
   Line 45 - Burridge, Kathryn, daughter, female, white, age 6, single, not in school, born in Utah, father and mother in Utah.
   Line 46 - Burridge, Theo L, Jr, son, male, white, age 2, single, not in school, born in Utah, father and mother born in Utah.

Medical

The doctor made notes on the reverse side of the death certificate:
About last of Nov or first of December began to show some mental disturbance. While working on prospect in mountains on Feb. 4, 1933 he became greatly disturbed and jumped into a fire then ran away from camp during the very cold weather. This caused some freezing of toes and fingers. Burns, 3rd degree hands, feet, left leg, left arm, less extensive burns on neck and back.[73]

# Source Citations

1. Frank Esshorn, editor, *Pioneers and Prominent Men of Utah comprising Photographs-Genealogies-Biographies. Pioneers are those men and women who came to Utah by wagon, hand cart or afoot, between July 24, 1847 and December 30, 1868, before the railroad. Prominent Men are stake presidents, ward bishops, governors, members of the bench, etc., who came to Utah after the coming of the railroad. The early history of the Church of Jesus Christ of Latter-Day Saints. In One Volume, Illustrated* (Salt Lake City, Utah: Utah Pioneers Book Publishing Company, 1913), Thomas Lorenzo Burridge: 783. Repository: Family History Library, 35 North West Temple Street, Salt Lake City, Utah 84150-3400, USA, Call Number: 979.2 D3e.

2. Utah, State Department of Health, Certificate of Death, death certificate State File No. 415 (1905), William M. Burridge names his father as Thomas born at Isle of Malta.

3. Utah, State Department of Health, Certificate of Death, death certificate State File No. 567 (1922), Frank Dennis Burridge names his father as George Burridge born in Utah. (This is wrong as his father's name was Thomas).

4. Utah, State Department of Health, Certificate of Death, death certificate psychosis, manic type (1933), Theol Lorenzo Burridge names his father as Thomas Lorenzo Burridge born in the Isle of Malta.

5. Utah, State Department of Health, Certificate of Death, death certificate State File No. 226 (1911), George Thomas Burridge names his father as Thomas L Burridge born in Malta.

6. Brown, Beverly McIntosh and Marsha McIntosh, editors, *William McIntosh Diary 1857-1898, Abridgement* (Surprise, AZ: Self-published, June 2002), 71,72.

7. Hickman, Connie, Sexton records, *Utah, Tooele, St John Cemetery,* North Section. Repository: St. John Cemetery, Cemetery Road, Rush Valley, UT 84069. Burial Information Burridge, Thomas
Birth 0/0/1853
Death 0/0/1891
Burial 0/0/0
Grave Location St. John Cemetery, North Section
Source Connie Hickman
Comments
Relatives Hannah Burridge (Mother)
George Burridge (Father).

8. Utah, State Department of Health, Certificate of Death, death certificate State File No 123 (1940), Pauline Burridge Neddo father is George Wilcox Burridge born in England.

9. Utah, State Department of Health, Certificate of Death, death certificate State File No 123 (1940), Pauline Burridge Neddo mother is Hannah Jane Shaw born in Huntley, Scotland.

10. George Wilcox Burridge, "Diaries of George Wilcox Burridge" (MS 8667, Salt Lake City, Utah, 1867-1891), p. 17; digital images, Church of Jesus Christ of Latter-day Saints, *Church History* (https://catalog.churchofjesuschrist.org/assets?id=fe8860f7-c0b1-480c-9054-2a371a6cc3f4&crate=0&index=9).

11. *Mormon Immigration Index: Voyages* ([S.I. " s.n.], 2001 by Intellectual Reserve, Inc.).

12. Church of Jesus Christ of Latter-day Saints, "Mormon Pioneer Overland Travel, 1847-1868," database (www.lds.org/churchhistory/library/pioneercompany), Burridge, Thomas Lorenzo travelled with the Milo Andrus Company 1855.

13. 1860 U.S. census, Shambip, Utah, population schedule, Clover, p. 451, dwelling 4031, family 3107, Thos Burridge; digital images, *ancestry.com*; citing National Archives and Records Administration microfilm M653.

14. 1870 U.S. census, Tooele, Utah, population schedule, St Johns, p. 3, dwelling 20, family 20, Burridge, Thomas; digital images*ancestry.com*; citing National Archives and Records Administration microfilm M593.

15. 1880 U.S. census, Tooele, Utah Territory, population schedule, Clover, enumeration district (ED) 79, p. 5 or 102, Burridge, Thomas L; digital images, *ancestry.com*; citing National Archives and Records Administration microfilm T9.

16. Bureau of Land Management, Record Group 49, *United States. General Land Office.* (Washington, D.C.: The National Archives), Statement by David H Caldwell on behalf of Caroline E McIntosh, mentions Wm McIntosh and Thomas Burridge.

17. McIntosh Reunion Descendants, McIntosh - Descendants of John & Girsey (Grace) (Grizel) Rankin McIntosh (Attachment to Aug 17, 1958 Newsletter - copy in Collection of Bonnie S. Williams), Repository: Bonnie S. Williams, RR 1 Box 247, N Hwy 2, Wilburton, Oklahoma, USA.
Alice Maria (daughter of William [McINTOSH] & Maria CALDWELL) md. Thomas L. BURRIDGE
Children:
1. George Thomas
2. William M.
3. Franklin Dennis
4. Alice Marie
5. Jared
6. Theol Lorenzo.

# Source Citations

Alice Maria McINTOSH is a Granddaughter of John McINTOSH & Girsey RANKIN.
This single page attachment indicates that the parents of John McIntosh are William McIntosh & Isabell and is indicative of what our side of the family knew of our McIntosh cousins at that time in August 1958.

18. Utah, State Department of Health, Certificate of Death, death certificate State File No. 226 (1911), George Thomas Burridge names his mother as Alice McIntosh.

19. Utah, State Department of Health, Certificate of Death, death certificate State File No. 415 (1905), William M. Burridge names his mother as Alice McIntosh born in Salt Lake Co, Utah.

20. Utah, State Department of Health, Certificate of Death, death certificate State File No. 567 (1922), Frank Dennis Burridge names his mother as Alice McIntosh born in Utah.

21. Utah, State Department of Health, Certificate of Death, death certificate psychosis, manic type (1933), Theol Lorenzo Burridge names his mother as Alice Maria MacIntosh born in West Jordan, Utah.

22. Utah, State Department of Health, Certificate of Death, death certificate State File No. 317 (1914), Alice M. Burridge, born 26 Sep 1857, died 31 Oct 1914.

23. Utah, State Department of Health, Certificate of Death, death certificate State File No. 317 (1914), Alice M. Burridge.

24. Utah State Historical Society, "Utah, Cemetery Inventory, 1847-2000," database(https://www.ancestry.com/search/collections/utahburials/), Alice Maria McIntosh Burridge, Block 9, Lot 105.

25. Utah Division of State History, "Cemetery & Burial Database," database (https://heritage.utah.gov/history/cemeteries), Alice Maria McIntosh Burridge, Block 9, Lot 105.

26. Brown, Beverly McIntosh and Marsha McIntosh, editors,*William McIntosh Diary 1857-1898, Abridgement* (Surprise, AZ: Self-published, June 2002).

27. Daughters of Utah Pioneers, *Our Pioneer Heritage* (Salt Lake City, UT: Infobases, Inc., 1996), 19: 422. Repository: Family History Library, 35 North West Temple Street, Salt Lake City, Utah 84150-3400, USA, Call Number: 979.2 H2.

28. Frank Esshorn, editor, *Pioneers and Prominent Men of Utah comprising Photographs-Genealogies-Biographies. Pioneers are those men and women who came to Utah by wagon, hand cart or afoot, between July 24, 1847 and December 30, 1868, before the railroad. Prominent Men are stake presidents, ward bishops, governors, members of the bench, etc., who came to Utah after the coming of the railroad. The early history of the Church of Jesus Christ of Latter-Day Saints. In One Volume, Illustrated* (Salt Lake City, Utah: Utah Pioneers Book Publishing Company, 1913), McIntosh, William: 331 and 1059. Repository: Family History Library, 35 North West Temple Street, Salt Lake City, Utah 84150-3400, USA, Call Number: 979.2 D3e.

29. Andrew Jenson, editor, *Latter-day Saint Biographical Encyclopedia: A Compilation of Biographical Sketches of Prominent Men and Women in The Church of Jesus Christ of Latter-day Saints*, 4 v.: ports. (Salt Lake City, Utah: Western Epics, 1971), William McIntosh: V 4, page 647. Repository: Family History Library, 35 North West Temple Street, Salt Lake City, Utah 84150-3400, USA, Call Number: 920.0792.

30. International Society of Daughters of Utah Pioneers, editor,*Pioneer Women of Faith and Fortitude*, Volume III (Salt Lake City, Utah: Publishers Press, 1998), Maria Caldwell McIntosh: page 1946. Repository: Family History Library, 35 North West Temple Street, Salt Lake City, Utah 84150-3400, USA, Call Number: 979 D36.

31. 1860 U.S. census, Shambip, Utah, population schedule, Clover, p. 450, dwelling 4028, family 3104, Alice M McIntosh; digital images, *ancestry.com*; citing National Archives and Records Administration microfilm M653.

32. 1870 U.S. census, Washington, Utah, population schedule, Panaca, p. 7, dwelling 54, family 48, McIntosh, Allice; digital images, *ancestry.com*; citing National Archives and Records Administration microfilm M593.

33. 1870 U.S. census, Lincoln, Nevada, population schedule, Meadow Valley, p. 186, dwelling 66-68, family 45, McIntosh, Alice; digital images, *ancestry.com*; citing National Archives and Records Administration microfilm M593.

34. 1880 U.S. census, Tooele, Utah Territory, population schedule, Clover, enumeration district (ED) 79, p. 6C, Mackintosh, Alice; digital images, *ancestry.com*; citing National Archives and Records Administration microfilm T9.

35. Brown, Beverly McIntosh and Marsha Lee McIntosh,*William McIntosh Diary, abridgement* (Self-published, Surprise, AZ. June 2002), page 72 October 15, 1891.

36. Brown, Beverly McIntosh and Marsha Lee McIntosh,*William McIntosh Diary, abridgement* (Self-published, Surprise, AZ. June 2002), p 76 June 26 [1893].

37. 1900 U.S. census, Tooele, Utah, population schedule, St. John, enumeration district (ED) 147, sheet 5B, p. 253, dwelling 93, family 93, Burridge, Alice; digital images,*ancestry.com*; citing National Archives and Records Administration microfilm T623.

38. 1910 U.S. census, Utah, Utah, population schedule, Provo, enumeration district (ED) 196, sheet 19B, p. 122, dwelling 148, family 155,

# Source Citations

Burridge, Alice; digital images, *ancestry.com*; citing National Archives and Records Administration microfilm T624.

39. McIntosh Reunion Descendants, McIntosh - Descendants of John & Girsey (Grace) (Grizel) Rankin McIntosh (Attachment to Aug 17, 1958 Newsletter - copy in Collection of Bonnie S. Williams), Repository: Bonnie S. Williams, RR 1 Box 247, N Hwy 2, Wilburton, Oklahoma, USA.
George Thomas (son of Alice Maria [McINTOSH] & Thomas L. BURRIDGE).
George Thomas BURRIDGE is a Great-Grandson of John McINTOSH & Girsey RANKIN
and a Grandson of William McINTOSH & Maria CALDWELL.

40. Frank Esshorn, editor, *Pioneers and Prominent Men of Utah comprising Photographs-Genealogies-Biographies. Pioneers are those men and women who came to Utah by wagon, hand cart or afoot, between July 24, 1847 and December 30, 1868, before the railroad. Prominent Men are stake presidents, ward bishops, governors, members of the bench, etc., who came to Utah after the coming of the railroad. The early history of the Church of Jesus Christ of Latter-Day Saints. In One Volume, Illustrated* (Salt Lake City, Utah: Utah Pioneers Book Publishing Company, 1913), George Thomas Burridge: 783. Repository: Family History Library, 35 North West Temple Street, Salt Lake City, Utah 84150-3400, USA, Call Number: 979.2 D3e.

41. Utah, State Department of Health, Certificate of Death, death certificate State File No. 226 (1911), George Thomas Burridge, born 19 Jun 1882, died 10 Jul 1911.

42. Utah, State Department of Health, Certificate of Death, death certificate State File No. 226 (1911), George Thomas Burridge.

43. Utah State Historical Society, "Utah, Cemetery Inventory, 1847-2000," database(https://www.ancestry.com/search/collections/utahburials/), George T. Burridge, block 9, lot 105.

44. 1900 U.S. census, Tooele, Utah, population schedule, St. John, enumeration district (ED) 147, sheet 5B, p. 253, dwelling 93, family 93, Burridge George T.; digital images, *ancestry.com*; citing National Archives and Records Administration microfilm T623.

45. McIntosh Reunion Descendants, McIntosh - Descendants of John & Girsey (Grace) (Grizel) Rankin McIntosh (Attachment to Aug 17, 1958 Newsletter - copy in Collection of Bonnie S. Williams), Repository: Bonnie S. Williams, RR 1 Box 247, N Hwy 2, Wilburton, Oklahoma, USA.
William M. (son of Alice Maria [McINTOSH] & Thomas L. BURRIDGE).
William M. BURRIDGE is a Great-Grandson of John McINTOSH & Girsey RANKIN
and a Grandson of William McINTOSH & Maria CALDWELL.

46. Utah, State Department of Health, Certificate of Death, death certificate State File No. 415 (1905), William M. Burridge.

47. Utah State Historical Society, "Utah, Cemetery Inventory, 1847-2000," database(https://www.ancestry.com/search/collections/utahburials/), William McIntosh Burridge, block 9, lot 105.

48. Church of Jesus Christ of Latter-day Saints, *Saint John, Utah Ward Records,* Repository: Family History Library, 35 North West Temple Street, Salt Lake City, Utah 84150-3400, USA, Call Number: FHL Film 27,317.

49. 1900 U.S. census, Tooele, Utah, population schedule, St. John, enumeration district (ED) 147, sheet 5B, p. 253, dwelling 93, family 93, Burridge, William M.; digital images, *ancestry.com*; citing National Archives and Records Administration microfilm T623.

50. McIntosh Reunion Descendants, McIntosh - Descendants of John & Girsey (Grace) (Grizel) Rankin McIntosh (Attachment to Aug 17, 1958 Newsletter - copy in Collection of Bonnie S. Williams), Repository: Bonnie S. Williams, RR 1 Box 247, N Hwy 2, Wilburton, Oklahoma, USA.
Franklin Dennis (son of Alice Maria [McINTOSH] & Thomas L. BURRIDGE).
Franklin Dennis BURRIDGE is a Great-Grandson of John McINTOSH & Girsey RANKIN
and a Grandson of William McINTOSH & Maria CALDWELL.

51. Frank Esshorn, editor, *Pioneers and Prominent Men of Utah comprising Photographs-Genealogies-Biographies. Pioneers are those men and women who came to Utah by wagon, hand cart or afoot, between July 24, 1847 and December 30, 1868, before the railroad. Prominent Men are stake presidents, ward bishops, governors, members of the bench, etc., who came to Utah after the coming of the railroad. The early history of the Church of Jesus Christ of Latter-Day Saints. In One Volume, Illustrated* (Salt Lake City, Utah: Utah Pioneers Book Publishing Company, 1913), Franklin Dennis Burridge: 783. Repository: Family History Library, 35 North West Temple Street, Salt Lake City, Utah 84150-3400, USA, Call Number: 979.2 D3e.

52. Utah, State Department of Health, Certificate of Death, death certificate State File No. 567 (1922), Frank Dennis Burridge.

53. Utah State Historical Society, "Utah, Cemetery Inventory, 1847-2000," database(https://www.ancestry.com/search/collections/utahburials/), Franklin Dennis Burridge.

54. 1900 U.S. census, Tooele, Utah, population schedule, St. John, enumeration district (ED) 147, sheet 5B, p. 253, dwelling 93, family 93, Burridge, Franklin D.; digital images, *ancestry.com*; citing National Archives and Records Administration microfilm T623.

55. 1910 U.S. census, Utah, Utah, population schedule, Provo, enumeration district (ED) 196, sheet 19B, p. 122, dwelling 148, family 155, Burridge, Franklin; digital images, *ancestry.com*; citing National Archives and Records Administration microfilm T624.

56. McIntosh Reunion Descendants, McIntosh - Descendants of John & Girsey (Grace) (Grizel) Rankin McIntosh (Attachment to Aug 17, 1958 Newsletter - copy in Collection of Bonnie S. Williams), Repository: Bonnie S. Williams, RR 1 Box 247, N Hwy 2, Wilburton, Oklahoma, USA.
Alice Marie (daughter of Alice Maria [McINTOSH] & Thomas L. BURRIDGE).

# Source Citations

Alice Marie BURRIDGE is a Great-Granddaughter of John McINTOSH & Girsey RANKIN
and a Granddaughter of William McINTOSH & Maria CALDWELL.

57. Frank Esshorn, editor, *Pioneers and Prominent Men of Utah comprising Photographs-Genealogies-Biographies. Pioneers are those men and women who came to Utah by wagon, hand cart or afoot, between July 24, 1847 and December 30, 1868, before the railroad. Prominent Men are stake presidents, ward bishops, governors, members of the bench, etc., who came to Utah after the coming of the railroad. The early history of the Church of Jesus Christ of Latter-Day Saints. In One Volume, Illustrated* (Salt Lake City, Utah: Utah Pioneers Book Publishing Company, 1913), Alice Marie Burridge: 783. Repository: Family History Library, 35 North West Temple Street, Salt Lake City, Utah 84150-3400, USA, Call Number: 979.2 D3e.

58. Frank Esshorn, editor, *Pioneers and Prominent Men of Utah comprising Photographs-Genealogies-Biographies. Pioneers are those men and women who came to Utah by wagon, hand cart or afoot, between July 24, 1847 and December 30, 1868, before the railroad. Prominent Men are stake presidents, ward bishops, governors, members of the bench, etc., who came to Utah after the coming of the railroad. The early history of the Church of Jesus Christ of Latter-Day Saints. In One Volume, Illustrated* (Salt Lake City, Utah: Utah Pioneers Book Publishing Company, 1913), Alice Marie Burridge: 783. Repository: Family History Library, 35 North West Temple Street, Salt Lake City, Utah 84150-3400, USA, Call Number: 979.2 D3e; BURRIDGE, THOMAS LORENZO (son of George Wilcox Burridge and Hannah Shaw). Born Dec. 2, 1853, Valetta, Isle of Malta. Came to Utah with parents.

Married Alice Maria McIntosh Jan. 8, 1881, Salt Lake City (daughter of William McIntosh and Maria Caldwell of St. John, Utah, pioneers 1852). She was born Sept. 16, 1858.
Their children: George Thomas b. Jan. 19, 1882; William McIntosh b. Oct. 6, 1883, d. Nov. 30, 1903; Franklin Dennis b. Dec. 7, 1885;**Alice Marie b. Jan. 1, 1888, d. May 12, 1896**; Jared b. Jan. 2, 1890, d. Sept. 15, 1890; Theol Lorenzo b. Nov. 18, 1891. Family home St. John.

Seventy; ward teacher; assistant Sunday school superintendent St. John ward. Justice of peace. Pioneer to Cottonwood Creek. Farmer and sheepraiser. Died April 12, 1891.

59. Hickman, Connie, Sexton records, *Utah, Tooele, St John Cemetery,* North Section. Repository: St. John Cemetery, Cemetery Road, Rush Valley, UT 84069. Burial Information Burridge, Alice
Birth 0/0/0
Death 0/0/1898
Burial 0/0/0
Grave Location St. John Cemetery, North Section
Source Connie Hickman
Comments Primary President. the comment "Primary President" is referring to her mother Alice Maria McINTOSH Burridge, died 31 Oct 1914, buried in the Provo City Cemetery.

60. McIntosh Reunion Descendants, McIntosh - Descendants of John & Girsey (Grace) (Grizel) Rankin McIntosh (Attachment to Aug 17, 1958 Newsletter - copy in Collection of Bonnie S. Williams), Repository: Bonnie S. Williams, RR 1 Box 247, N Hwy 2, Wilburton, Oklahoma, USA.
Jared (son of Alice Maria [McINTOSH] & Thomas L. BURRIDGE).
Jared BURRIDGE is a Great-Grandson of John McINTOSH & Girsey RANKIN
and a Grandson of William McINTOSH & Maria CALDWELL.

61. Frank Esshorn, editor, *Pioneers and Prominent Men of Utah comprising Photographs-Genealogies-Biographies. Pioneers are those men and women who came to Utah by wagon, hand cart or afoot, between July 24, 1847 and December 30, 1868, before the railroad. Prominent Men are stake presidents, ward bishops, governors, members of the bench, etc., who came to Utah after the coming of the railroad. The early history of the Church of Jesus Christ of Latter-Day Saints. In One Volume, Illustrated* (Salt Lake City, Utah: Utah Pioneers Book Publishing Company, 1913), Jared Burridge: 783. Repository: Family History Library, 35 North West Temple Street, Salt Lake City, Utah 84150-3400, USA, Call Number: 979.2 D3e.

62. Hickman, Connie, Sexton records, *Utah, Tooele, St John Cemetery,* North Section. Repository: St. John Cemetery, Cemetery Road, Rush Valley, UT 84069. Burial Information Burridge, Jared
Birth 0/0/1890
Death 0/0/1890
Burial 0/0/0
Grave Location St. John Cemetery, North Section
Source Connie Hickman
Comments.

63. McIntosh Reunion Descendants, McIntosh - Descendants of John & Girsey (Grace) (Grizel) Rankin McIntosh (Attachment to Aug 17, 1958 Newsletter - copy in Collection of Bonnie S. Williams), Repository: Bonnie S. Williams, RR 1 Box 247, N Hwy 2, Wilburton, Oklahoma, USA.
Theol Lorenzo (son of Alice Maria [McINTOSH] & Thomas L. BURRIDGE).
Theol Lorenzo BURRIDGE is a Great-Grandson of John McINTOSH & Girsey RANKIN
and a Grandson of William McINTOSH & Maria CALDWELL.

64. Utah, State Department of Health, Certificate of Death, death certificate state file no. 50-250462; registrars no. 82 (1950), The father of Theol Lorenzo Burridge, Jr. is named as Theol Lorenzo Burridge, Sr. born in St John, Utah.

65. Frank Esshorn, editor, *Pioneers and Prominent Men of Utah comprising Photographs-Genealogies-Biographies. Pioneers are those men and women who came to Utah by wagon, hand cart or afoot, between July 24, 1847 and December 30, 1868, before the railroad. Prominent Men are*

# Source Citations

*stake presidents, ward bishops, governors, members of the bench, etc., who came to Utah after the coming of the railroad. The early history of the Church of Jesus Christ of Latter-Day Saints. In One Volume, Illustrated* (Salt Lake City, Utah: Utah Pioneers Book Publishing Company, 1913), Theo Lorenzo Burridge: 783. Repository: Family History Library, 35 North West Temple Street, Salt Lake City, Utah 84150-3400, USA, Call Number: 979.2 D3e.

66. Utah, State Department of Health, Certificate of Death, death certificate State File no. 273 (1933), Theol Lorenzo Burridge, born 18 Nov 1891, died 17 Feb 1933.

67. Utah State Historical Society, "Utah, Cemetery Inventory, 1847-2000," database(https://www.ancestry.com/search/collections/utahburials/), Theol Lorenzo Burridge.

68. Utah, State Department of Health, Certificate of Death, death certificate State File no. 273 (1933), Theol Lorenzo Burridge, born 18 Nov 1891, died, 17 Feb 1933.

69. Utah, State Department of Health, Certificate of Death, death certificate State File no. 273 (1933), Theol Lorenzo Burridge.

70. "Find A Grave," database (www.findagrave.com), Theol Lorenzo Burridge, St. John Cemetery, Utah.

71. Utah, State Department of Health, Certificate of Death, death certificate psychosis, manic type (1933), Theol Lorenzo Burridge names his wife as Wanda (Christison) Burridge.

72. Utah, State Department of Health, Certificate of Death, death certificate state file no. 50-250462; registrars no. 82 (1950), Theol Lorenzo Burridge named his mother as Wanda Christison born in Nephi, Utah.

73. "Utah, Select Marriages, 1887-1966," database, Theol Lorenzo Burridge and Wanda Christison married 15 Oct 1919 in Salt Lake City Utah.

74. 1900 U.S. census, Tooele, Utah, population schedule, St. John, enumeration district (ED) 147, sheet 5B, p. 253, dwelling 93, family 93, Burridge, Theol L; digital images,*ancestry.com*; citing National Archives and Records Administration microfilm T623.

75. 1910 U.S. census, Utah, Utah, population schedule, Provo, enumeration district (ED) 196, sheet 19B, p. 122, dwelling 148, family 155, Burridge, Theol; digital images,*ancestry.com*; citing National Archives and Records Administration microfilm T624.

76. "U.S., World War I Draft Registration Cards, 1917-1918," database, Theol Lorenzo Burridge.

77. Ancestry.com, "Utah, Veterans with Federal Service Buried in Utah, Territorial to 1966," database, Theol Lorenzo Burridge, USS Dearsarge, Navy, WWI.

# Abraham Edward McIntosh and Mary Louise Guhl

| **Husband** | **Abraham Edward McIntosh**[1,2,3,4] | |
|---|---|---|
| AKA | A. E. McIntosh, Abe McIntosh, Abram McIntosh | |
| Born | 4 Mar 1860 | Clover, Shambip, Utah Territory, United States[5] |
| Died | 16 Oct 1943 | Mount Pleasant, Sanpete, Utah, United States[6] |
| Cause of Death | Chronic Myocarditis[5] | |
| Buried | 20 Oct 1943 | Mount Pleasant, Sanpete, Utah, United States[5,7] |
| Address | Mount Pleasant City Cemetery, 900 South 100 East, Mt. Pleasant, Utah 84647, USA | |
| Bapt.(LDS) | 1 Jan 1868 | |
| Conf.(LDS) | 1 Jan 1868 | |
| Init.(LDS) | 21 Nov 1894 | Manti Utah Temple |
| Endow.(LDS) | 21 Nov 1894 | Manti Utah Temple |
| Father | William McIntosh (1819-1899) [8,9,10,11] | |
| Mother | Maria Caldwell (1824-1897) [12] | |
| SealP (LDS) | 21 Nov 1894 | Manti Utah Temple |
| Marriage | 1 Jan 1884 | Saint John, Tooele, Utah Territory, United States[13,14,15,16] |
| SealS (LDS) | 21 Nov 1894 | Manti Utah Temple |
| Other Spouse | Lenora Marie Monsen (1877-1954)[17] | 30 Jun 1937 - Manti, Sanpete, Utah, United States |
| SealS (LDS) | 1 Nov 1994 | Salt Lake Temple |

**Events**

1. He received a Patriarchial blessing from William McBride.
2. He worked as a farmer & stock raiser.[19]
3. He appeared on the census on 11 Oct 1860 in Clover, Shambip, Utah Territory, United States.[20]
   Line 25) Wm McIntosh, age 40, male, farmer, born in Scotland
   Line 26) Maria McIntosh, age 36, female, born in Canada
   Line 27) Jno E McIntosh, age 18, male, born in Ohio
   Line 28) Wm. H McIntosh, age 11, male, born in Missouri, in school
   Line 29) Jas F McIntosh, age 8, male, born in Utah Territory, in school
   Line 30) Malissa J McIntosh, age 6, female, born in Utah Territory, in school
   Line 31) Alice M McIntosh, age 3, female, born in Utah Territory
   Line 32) **Abm E McIntosh, age 6/12, male, born in Utah Territory**
4. He was ordained a Seventies - High Priest - Bishop between 1868 and 1924 in Mount Pleasant, Sanpete, Utah Territory, United States.[4]
   "Abraham was baptized when about eight years old, and ordained successively to the offices of Deacon, Teacher, Priest, Elder and Seventy....In 1913 he was ordained a High Priest by James E. Talmage and set apart as first counselor to Bishop Adolph Merz; he served in that capacity until Sept. 13, 1914, when he was ordained a Bishop by Francis M. Lyman and set apart to preside over the Mt. Pleasant South Ward."
5. He appeared on the census on 10 Jun 1870 in Panaca, Washington, Utah Territory.[21]
   Line 20 - McIntosh, William age 49, male, white, day laborer, value of personal estate $200, born in Scotland, father and

# Abraham Edward McIntosh and Mary Louise Guhl

mother foreign born, male over 21.
Line 21 - McIntosh, Marie, age 45, female, white, keeping house, born in Canada, father and mother foreign born.
Line 22 - McIntosh, William, age 20, male, white, teamster, born in Missouri, father and mother foreign born.
Line 23 - McIntosh, Frank, age 18, male, white, work on farm, born in Utah, father and mother foreign born.
Line 24 - McIntosh, Jane, age 15, female, white, at home, born in Utah, father and mother foreign born, attended school.
Line 25 - McIntosh, Allice, age 12, female, white, born in Utah, father and mother foreign born, attended school.
**Line 26 - McIntosh, Abraham, age 10, male, white, born in Utah, father and mother foreign born, attended school.**
Line 27 - McIntosh, Lilly, age 7, female, white, born in Utah, father and mother foreign born.
Line 28 - McIntosh, Caroline, age 4, female, white, born in Utah, father and mother foreign born.
Line 29 - McIntosh, Albert, age 1, male, white, born in Utah, father and mother foreign born.

6. He appeared on the census on 28 Jul 1870 in Meadow Valley, Lincoln, Nevada, United States.[22]
Line 22 - McIntosh, Wm, age 50, male, white, farming, value of real estate $300, value of personal estate $800, born in Scotland, father and mother foreign born, male over 21.
Line 23 - McIntosh, Marie, age 45, female, white, keeping house, born in Canada, father and mother foreign born.
Line 24 - McIntosh, Wm H, age 21, male, white, farming, born in Missouri, father and mother foreign born, male over 21.
Line 25 - McIntosh, Frank, age 18, male, white, farming, born in Utah, father and mother foreign born.
Line 26 - McIntosh, Jane, age 16, female, white, at home, born in Utah, father and mother foreign born, attended school.
Line 27 - McIntosh, Alice, age 12, female, white, in school, born in Utah, father and mother foreign born, attended school.
**Line 28 - McIntosh, Abe, age 10, male, white, in school, born in Utah, father and mother foreign born, attended school.**
Line 29 - McIntosh, Lilly, age 7, female, white, in school, born in Utah, father and mother foreign born.
Line 30 - McIntosh, Caroline, age 4, female, white, born in Utah, father and mother foreign born.
Line 31 - McIntosh, Albert, age 1, male, white, school, born in Nevada, father and mother foreign born.

7. He appeared on the census on 12 Jun 1880 in Clover, Tooele, Utah Territory, United States.[23]
Line 19 - Mackintosh, William, white, male, age 60, head, married, laborer, born in Canada, father born in Canada, mother born Canada.
Line 20 - Mackintosh, Caroline, white, female, age 53, wife, married, keeping house, born in Canada, father born in Canada, mother born in Canada. (Marie, not Caroline who was living there as a guest).
Line 21 - Mackintosh, Alice, white, female, age 22, daughter, single, teaching school, born in Utah, father born in Canada, Mother born in Canada.
**Line 22 - Mackintosh, Abraham, white, male, age 20, son, single, working on farm, born in Utah, father born in Canada, mother born in Canada.**
Line 23 - Mackintosh, Lillian, white, female, age 18, daughter, single, studying at home, attended school, born in Utah, father born in Canada, mother born in Canada.
Line 24 - Mackintosh, Caroline, white, female, age 15, daughter, single, studying at home, attended school, born in Utah, father born in Canada, mother born in Canada.
Line 25 - Mackintosh, Albert, white, male, age 11, son, single, working on farm, attended school, born in Utah, father born in Canada, mother born in Canada.

8. Marks and Brands: Place of Brand - left hip or thigh, 24 Oct 1885, Saint John, Tooele, Utah Territory, United States.[24]
(The date is hard to read).
Abraham Edward McIntosh had authorization to use certain marks and brands on this herd animals

9. Marks and Brands: Marks Connected With Swallowfork in Left Ear, 12 Feb 1887, Saint John, Tooele, Utah Territory, United States.[25]
"Swallowfork in left ear, hole in same, and under slope off right ear; February 12, 1887; A.E. McIntosh, St. Johns, Tooele Co."

10. Marks and Brands: Marks Connected with Swallowfork in Right Ear, 12 Feb 1887, Saint John, Tooele, Utah Territory, United States.[25]
"Swallowfork in right ear, hole in same, and under slope off left ear; February 12, 1887; A.E. McIntosh; St. Johns, Tooele Co."

11. He worked as a rancher & stock raiser in 1889.[26]
"They came to Mt. Pleasant in 1889, where Mr. McIntosh engaged in sheep and cattle raising. For years he has been one

# Abraham Edward McIntosh and Mary Louise Guhl

of the foremost breeders of purebred Rambouillets in the state."

12. He had a residence on 24 Sep 1889 in Mount Pleasant, Sanpete, Utah Territory, United States.[27,28,29,30,31,32]
... Mt. Pleasant ... I bought a city lot only a street from where Caroline lived ... Abraham Edward and family is living on the lot joining.
It is now Oct. 3, 1890. Abraham Edward and James Franklin McIntosh [William's sons] are living there [Mt. Pleasant]. They have been in the sheep business for several years. Abraham McIntosh quit sheep business this season. James Franklin runs the sheep this season.
Frank and Abe McIntosh [sons] came in from the sheep tending last week but they are gone again.
My son, A. E. McIntosh came from Tooele County where he was at work all winter.
23rd - There is snow all over the ground and the weather is cold. A. E. [William's son] McIntosh has come home from Tooele County.
[William continues to reminisce] 1892. We are living in our own new house in Mt. Pleasant, Utah. Franklin McIntosh [William's son] and A.E. [son] McIntosh lives here and their families, but my wife don't like it much. She has no relish for any place but old St. John. ...
The 4th of July will soon be here. I am still living alone in my own house. A. E. McIntosh [son] and Mary his wife lives in the lot joining me. I go there for my meals. I will do otherwise as soon as I can."

13. He worked as a miner from Nov 1893 to Mar 1894 in Skull Valley, Tooele, Utah Territory.[33]

14. Temple Records: 1894, Manti, Sanpete, Utah Territory, United States.[34]
Name in full-McIntosh-Abraham Edward, When born-4 March 1860, Where born-St. Johns, Tooele, Utah, Father-William McIntosh, Mother-Maria Caldwell, When Married-1 Jan 1884 to Mary Louisa Guhl, Heir-Self, When baptized-1868, When endowed-21 Nov 1894, When sealed to wife-21 Nov 1894.

15. He worked as a farmer on 20 Jul 1894 in Milburn, Sanpete, Utah Territory.[35,36]

16. He appeared on the census on 25 Jun 1900 in Mount Pleasant, Sanpete, Utah, United States.[37]
**Line 7 - McIntosh, Abe, head, white, male, born Mar 1860, age 40, married 16 years, born in Utah, father born in Canada, mother born in Canada, sheep raiser, can read, write and speak english, owns, mortgage free, farm, #197.**
Line 8 - McIntosh, Mary L, wife, white, female, born May 1862, age 38, married 16 years, had 6 children, 4 living, born in Utah, father born in Denmark, mother born in Denmark, can read, write and speak english.
Line 9 - McIntosh, A. Vance, son, white, male, born Apr 1885, age 15, single, born in Utah, father born in Utah, mother born in Utah, at school, can read, write and speak english.
Line 10 - McIntosh, Estelle A, daughter, white, female, born Dec 1880, age 10, single, born in Utah, father born in Utah, mother born in Utah, at school, can read, write and speak english.
Line 11 - McIntosh, Evin P, son, white, male, born June 1892, age 7, single, born in Utah, father born in Utah, mother born in Utah, at school, can read, write and speak english.
Line 12 - McIntosh, Vernon M, son, white, male, born Jan 1895, age 5, single, born in Utah, father born in Utah, mother born in Utah, cannot read or write, can speak english.

17. Marks and Brands: Position 10, 26 Jul 1900, Mount Pleasant, Sanpete, Utah, United States.[38]

18. Marks and Brands: Marks in Ears, 27 Jul 1900, Mount Pleasant, Sanpete, Utah, United States.[25]

19. Marks and Brands: Marks in Ears, 27 Jul 1900, Mount Pleasant, Sanpete, Utah, United States.[25]

20. Civic duty: City Councilman, from 1904 to 1905, Mount Pleasant, Sanpete, Utah, United States.[39]

21. He was ordained on 13 Sep 1904 in Mount Pleasant, Sanpete, Utah, United States.[40]
No. 1898...At Mt. Pleasant, Utah...September 13, 1904. To whom it may concern: This Certifies that I have this day ordained Abraham E. McIntosh of Mt. Pleasant, Utah a Bishop of South Ward in the Church of Jesus Christ of Latter-day Saints. Signed Francis M. Lyman

22. He served a mission to the Eastern States from 1905 to 1907.[41]

23. He appeared on the census on 15 May 1910 in Mount Pleasant, Sanpete, Utah, United States.[42]
**Line 22 - McIntosh, Abram E, head, male, white, age 50, married once for 26 years, born in Utah, father born in Scotland-speaks English, mother born in Scotland-speaks English, speaks english, farmer/sheep raiser, general farm, employer, can read and write, owns, mortgage free, house.**
Line 23 - McIntosh, Mary Louise, wife, female, white, age 47, married once for 26 years, had 7 children, 5 living, born

# Abraham Edward McIntosh and Mary Louise Guhl

in Utah, father born in Denmark-speaks Danish, mother born in Denmark-speaks Danish, speaks english, no occupation, can read and write.
Line 24 - McIntosh, Abram Vance, son, male, white, age 25, single, born in Utah, father born in Utah, mother born in Utah, speaks english, laborer, farm, employee, can read and write.
Line 25 - McIntosh, Anna Estella, daughter, female, white, age 20, single, born in Utah, father born in Utah, mother born in Utah, speaks english, dressmaker, at home, works on own account, can read and write.
Line 26 - McIntosh, Elvin Peter, son, male, white, age 17, single, born in Utah, father born in Utah, mother born in Utah, speaks english, no occupation, can read and write, attended school during the year.
Line 27 - McIntosh, Vernon Marinous, son, male, white, age 15, single, born in Utah, father born in Utah, mother born in Utah, speaks english, no occupation, can read and write, attended school during the year.
Line 28 - McIntosh, Grace Maria, daughter, female, white, age 6, single, born in Utah, father born in Utah, mother born in Utah, speaks english, no occupation, attended school during the year.
Line 29 - Christensen, Marimous, brother-in-law, male, white, age 55, single, born in Denmark-speaks Danish, father born in Denmark-speaks Danish, mother born in Denmark-speaks Danish, also speaks english, laborer, sheep herd, employee, not out of work on Apr 15, 1910, 0 weeks unemployed in 1909, can read and write.

24. Civic duty: City Councilman, from 1912 to 1913, Mount Pleasant, Sanpete, Utah, United States.[39]

25. Marks and Brands: 9 May 1912, Mount Pleasant, Sanpete, Utah, United States.[43]
Page 350
Illustration of cow or sheep head with large ears. The marks are indicated on the illustration. A.E. McIntosh, Mt. Pleasant, Sanpete Co., May 9, 1912.

26. Marks and Brands: 9 May 1912, Mount Pleasant, Sanpete, Utah, United States.[25]

27. Civic duty: City Councilman, 1916, Mount Pleasant, Sanpete, Utah, United States.[39]

28. He owned land N 1/2 x SW 1/4 and W 1/2 x SE 1/4, Section 18, Township 12 South, Range 5 East, Salt Lake Meridan, State of Utah, containing 160 acres, at the rate of $3.50 per acre, Serial No. 018118 on 12 Dec 1919 in Mount Pleasant, Sanpete, Utah, United States.[44]
Department of the Interior. Isolated Tract. Application and Affidavit. Witness: Vance A. McIntosh (son of Abraham E McIntosh). Original signatures of both men are on the document.
Land was good for grazing and some dry farming.

29. He appeared on the census on 24 Jan 1920 in Mount Pleasant, Sanpete, Utah, United States.[45]
**Line 34 - McIntosh, A.E., head, owns home, mortgage free, male, white, age 59, married, can read and write, born in Utah, father born in Scotland-speaks Scotch, mother born in Scotland-speaksScotch, speaks english, farmer, general farm, works on own account, farm #121.**
Line 35 - McIntosh, Mary L, wife, female, white, age 57, married, can reaad and write, born in Utah, father born in Denmark-speaks Danish, mother born in Denmark-speaks Danish, speaks english, no occupation.
Line 36 - McIntosh, Alvin, son, male, white, age 27, single, can read and write, born in Utah, father born in Utah, mother born in Utah, speaks english, farmer, general farm, employee.
Line 37 - McIntosh, Vernon, son, male, white, age 25, single, can read and write, born in Utah, father born in Utah, mother born in Utah, speaks english, farmer, general farm, employee.
Line 38 - McIntosh, Grace M, daughter, female, white, age 16, single, attended school, can read and write, born in Utah, father born in Utah, mother born in Utah, speaks english, no occupation.

30. He appeared on the census on 4 Apr 1930 in Milburn, Sanpete, Utah, United States.[46]
**Line 11 - McIntosh, Abraham E, head, owns home, lives on a farm, male, white, age 69, married at age 23, can read, write and speak english, born in Utah, father born in Scotland, mother born in Scotland, farmer on a general farm, # 20, not a veteran.**
Line 12 - McIntosh, Vance, son, owns home, lives on a farm, male, white, age 45, married at age 29, did not attend school within year, can read and write, born in Utah, father born in Utah, mother born in Utah, able to speak english, farmer, general farm, works on own account, actually at work, not a veteran, farm #21.
Line 13 - Johnson, Lester, laborer, male, white, age 21, single, did not attend school within year, can read and write, born in Utah, father born in Utah, mother born in Denmark, able to speak english, laborer, farm, wage worker, actually at work, not a veteran.

31. He appeared on the census on 10 Apr 1930 in Mount Pleasant, Sanpete, Utah, United States.[47]
**Line 52 - McIntosh, Abraham E, head, owns home, value of home $3000, does not live on farm, male, white, age 70,**

# Abraham Edward McIntosh and Mary Louise Guhl

**married at age 24, did not attend school within year, can read and write, born in Utah, father born in Scotland, mother born in Canada-speaks English, able to speak english, farmer, general farm, works on own account.**
Line 53 - McIntosh, wife, female, white, age 67, married at age 22, did not attend school within year, can read and write, born in Utah, father born in Denmark, mother born in Denmark, able to speak english, no occupation.

32. He appeared on the census on 7 Apr 1940 in Mount Pleasant, Sanpete, Utah, United States.[48]
**Line 25 - 308 South State St, owns house worth $1500, not a farm, McIntosh, A.E., head, male, white, age 80, married, finished 2 years high school, born in Utah, lived in same house in 1935, not employed, has other source of income.**
Line 26 - McIntosh, Nora M., wife, female, white, age 62, married, finished 9th grade, born in Utah, lived in same place in 1935, not employed, has other source of income.

33. His obituary was published after 16 Oct 1943.
**Active Career Comes To End--Abraham Edward McIntosh Passes Away at Family Home--**Abraham Edward McIntosh, 83, prominent sheep raiser, farmer, politician and Church leader, died here at his home Saturday afternoon following a lingering illness. Mr. McIntosh was born March 4, 1860 at Clover Creek, a son of William and Maria Caldwell McIntosh. His family made their home in St. John where he spent his boyhood and early manhood. He was married to Louise Guhl of St. John in January 1884. In 1889, they moved to Mt. Pleasant where he had since made his home. To them were born seven children. Mrs. McIntosh died here August 22, 1936. Mr. McIntosh has been prominent in civic affairs of this city. He served as city councilman for six years and was active in every progressive movement in the city. Mr. McIntosh was a leader in the Church of Jesus Christ of Latter-day Saints. He filled a mission to the Eastern States from 1905-1907. He served as a counselor to Bishop Adolph Merz and when Bishop Merz resigned he was made bishop in the Mt. Plesant South Ward, which position he held for more than 13 years. Mr. McIntosh was a large property holder, sheep raiser and farmer. He operated a large sheep plant and cattle ranch at Milburn for 55 years. He was one of the oldest sheep raisers in the valley. June 30, 1937, he was married to Nora M. Beckstrom in the Manti Temple. He is survived by his widow, two sons: Vance McIntosh, Mt. Pleasant and Elvin McIntosh, Los Angeles; two daughters, Mrs. Estella Schofield and Mrs. Grace Burns, Los Angeles, Calif.; one brother, Albert McIntosh, Los Angeles; six step-children, Mrs. Myrtle Johansen, Castle Dale; Orald Beckstrom, Mount Pleasant; Mable Household, Bingham Canyon; Guy Beckstrom, Bingham Canyon; Harold Beckstrom, West Jordan; Mrs. Beth Jolley, Lehi; 11 grandchildren, and three great-grandchildren. Funeral services were conducted Wednesday at 2 pm at the South Ward Chapel by J. Seymour Jensen, bishop. The grave in the City cemetery was dedicated by John Monsen and burial was under direction of the Jacobs Mortuary. Among those from California who came to attend the service were Mr. and Mrs. Joseph Schofield, Mr. and Mrs. Elvin McIntosh, Mrs. Bert Burns and children, and Mrs. Maxine Hood, all of Los Angeles.

| Wife | Mary Louise Guhl[49,50,51] | |
|---|---|---|
| AKA | Mary Louisa Guhl, Mary McIntosh | |
| Born | 27 May 1862 | Weber Canyon, Weber, Utah Territory, United States[52] |
| Died | 21 Aug 1936 | Mount Pleasant, Sanpete, Utah, United States[16,52] |
| Cause of Death | Chronic Myocarditis & Chronic arthritis[52] | |
| Buried | 24 Aug 1936 | Mount Pleasant, Sanpete, Utah, United States[52,53] |
| Address | Mount Pleasant City Cemetery, 900 South 100 East, Mt. Pleasant, Utah 84647, USA | |
| Bapt.(LDS) | 1 Jan 1873 | |
| Conf.(LDS) | 1 Jan 1873 | |
| Init.(LDS) | 21 Nov 1894 | |

# Abraham Edward McIntosh and Mary Louise Guhl

| | | |
|---|---|---|
| | Manti Utah Temple | |
| Endow.(LDS) | 21 Nov 1894 | Manti Utah Temple |
| Father | Soren Peter Guhl (1821-1883) | |
| Mother | Mariane Madsen (1824-1904) [54] | |
| SealP (LDS) | BIC | |

**Events**

1. She appeared on the census on 2 Jun 1870 in Saint John, Tooele, Utah Territory, United States.[55]
2. Baptism in the Church of Jesus Christ of Latter-day Saints: baptized by Francis De St. Jeor, in 1873.
3. She had a residence about 1876 in Clover, Tooele, Utah Territory, United States.[56]
4. Patriarchal Blessing: 3 Jul 1879, Johnson Settlement, Tooele, Utah Territory.[57]
   Johnson Settlement July 3rd 1879.
   Church of Jesus Christ of Latter-day Saints
   A blessing given by Wm. McBride, Patriarch, Upon the head of Mary Louisa Guhl, daughter of Peter and Mary Ann Peterson Guhl. Born May 27th 1862, Weber County Utah.
5. She appeared on the census on 12 Jun 1880 in Clover, Tooele, Utah Territory, United States.[58]
   Line 47 - Gould, Mary A, white, female, age 56, widow, born in Denmark, father born in Denmark, mother born in Denmark.
   Line 48 - Gould, Christian, white, male, age 30, son, single, laborer, born in Denmark, father born in Denmark, mother born in Denmark.
   Line 49 - Gould, Marinus, white, male, age 26, son, single, laborer, born in Denmark, father born in Denmark, mother born in Denmark.
   Line 50 - Gould, Peter, white, male, age 24, son, single, laborer, born in Denmark, father born in Denmark, mother born in Denmark.
   **Line 1 - Gould, Mary, white, female, age 18, daughter, single, born in Utah, father born in Denmark, mother born in Denmark.**
   Line 2 - Gould, Aleissa, white, female, age 16, daughter, single, attended shcool, born in Utah, father born in Denmark, mother born in Denmark.
6. She was relief society teacher in 1889 in Mount Pleasant, Sanpete, Utah Territory, United States.[16]
7. She had a residence on 6 May 1893 in Mount Pleasant, Sanpete, Utah Territory, United States.[59]
   "I took my wife up to Mary McIntosh's house. She lives on the lot above us in the same block. She is A. E. McIntosh's [William's son] wife. I am alone writing."
8. She appeared on the census on 25 Jun 1900 in Mount Pleasant, Sanpete, Utah, United States.[60]
9. She appeared on the census on 10 May 1910 in Mount Pleasant, Sanpete, Utah, United States.[61]
   Line 22 - McIntosh, Abram E, head, male, white, age 50, married once for 26 years, born in Utah, father born in Scotland-speaks English, mother born in Scotland-speaks English, speaks english, farmer/sheep raiser, general farm, employer, can read and write, owns, mortgage free, house.
   **Line 23 - McIntosh, Mary Louise, wife, female, white, age 47, married once for 26 years, had 7 children, 5 living, born in Utah, father born in Denmark-speaks Danish, mother born in Denmark-speaks Danish, speaks english, no occupation, can read and write.**
   Line 24 - McIntosh, Abram Vance, son, male, white, age 25, single, born in Utah, father born in Utah, mother born in Utah, speaks english, laborer, farm, employee, can read and write.
   Line 25 - McIntosh, Anna Estella, daughter, female, white, age 20, single, born in Utah, father born in Utah, mother born in Utah, speaks english, dressmaker, at home, works on own account, can read and write, did not attend school during the year.
   Line 26 - McIntosh, Elvin Peter, son, male, white, age 17, single, born in Utah, father born in Utah, mother born in Utah, speaks english, no occupation, can read and write, attended school within the year.
   Line 27 - McIntosh, Vernon Marinous, son, male, white, age 15, single, born in Utah, father born in Utah, mother born in Utah, speaks english, no occupation, can read and write, attended school within the year.
   Line 28 - McIntosh, Grace Maria, daughter, female, white, age 6, single, born in Utah, father born in Utah, mother born in Utah, speaks english, no occupation, attended school within the year.

# Abraham Edward McIntosh and Mary Louise Guhl

Line 29 - Christensen, Marimous, brother-in-law, male, white, age 55, single, born in Denmark-speaks Danish, father born in Denmark-speaks Danish, mother born in Denmark-speaks Danish, also speaks english, laborer, sheep herd, employee, not out of work on Apr 15, 1910, 0 weeks unemployed in 1909, can read and write.

10. She appeared on the census on 24 Jan 1920 in Mount Pleasant, Sanpete, Utah, United States.[62]
Line 34 - McIntosh, A.E., head, owns home, mortgage free, male, white, age 59, married, can read and write, born in Utah, father born in Scotland-speaks Scotch, mother born in Scotland-speaks Scotch, speaks english, farmer, general farm, works on own account, farm #121.
**Line 35 - McIntosh, Mary L, wife, female, white, age 57, married, can read and write, born in Utah, father born in Denmark-speaks Danish, mother born in Denmark-speaks Danish, speaks english, no occupation.**
Line 36 - McIntosh, Alvin, son, male, white, age 27, single, can read and write, born in Utah, father born in Utah, mother born in Utah, speaks english, farmer, general farm, employee.
Line 37 - McIntosh, Vernon, son, male, white, age 25, single, can read and write, born in Utah, father born in Utah, mother born in Utah, speaks english, farmer, general farm, employee.
Line 38 - McIntosh, Grace M, daughter, female, white, age 16, single, attended school, can read and write, born in Utah, father born in Utah, mother born in Utah, speaks english, no occupation.

11. She appeared on the census on 10 Apr 1930 in Mount Pleasant, Sanpete, Utah, United States.[63]
Line 52 - McIntosh, Abraham E, head, owns home, value of home $3000, does not live on farm, male, white, age 70, married at age 24, did not attend school within year, can read and write, born in Utah, father born in Scotland, mother born in Canada-English, able to speak english, farmer, general farm, works on own account.
**Line 53 - McIntosh, wife, female, white, age 67, married at age 22, did not attend school within year, can read and write, born in Utah, father born in Denmark, mother born in Denmark, able to speak english, no occupation.**

**Events: Marriage**

1. Marriage Fact: Married by George Burridge.

## Children

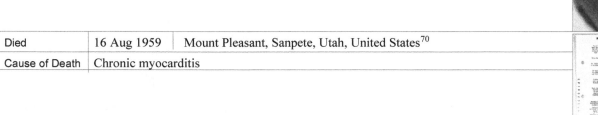

| 1 | M | **Abraham Vance McIntosh** [64,65,66,67,68] | |
|---|---|---|---|
| AKA | A. Vance McIntosh, A. V. McIntosh, Abram Vance McIntosh, Vance A. McIntosh | | |
| Born | 26 Apr 1885 | Saint John, Tooele, Utah Territory, United States[69,70] | |
| Died | 16 Aug 1959 | Mount Pleasant, Sanpete, Utah, United States[70] | |
| Cause of Death | Chronic myocarditis | | |
| Buried | 19 Aug 1959 | Mount Pleasant, Sanpete, Utah, United States[70,71,72] | |
| Address | Mount Pleasant City Cemetery, 900 South 100 East, Mt. Pleasant, Utah 84647, USA | | |
| Notes | Plot: B-6-2-4 | | |
| Bapt.(LDS) | 2 Aug 1894 | | |
| Conf.(LDS) | 2 Aug 1894 | | |
| Init.(LDS) | 24 Jun 1909 | Manti Utah Temple | |
| Endow.(LDS) | 24 Jun 1909 | Manti Utah Temple | |
| SealP (LDS) | 21 Nov 1894 | Manti Utah Temple | |

# Abraham Edward McIntosh and Mary Louise Guhl

| Children (cont.) | | |
|---|---|---|
| Spouse | Florence Karna Monsen (1887-1966)[73,74,75,76] | 15 Oct 1913 - Salt Lake City, Salt Lake, Utah, United States[77,78] |
| SealS (LDS) | 15 Oct 1913 | Salt Lake Temple |

**Events**

1. He worked as a rancher and sheepman.[70]

2. Religion and Education: Between 1885 and 1959. His name is variously spelled Abraham and Abram.

   Abram was blessed on 2 Aug 1883 by David H. Caldwell, his grandfather. He was an Elder, Seventies for the LDS Church. He went on a mission for the LDS Church to the Central States from 19 July 1909 to 14 Nov 1911. He began schooling Sept 1891 and graduated May 1904. He went to Ephraim to high school and later to Provo to Brigham Young High School. While there he contracted typhoid fever.

3. Baptism in the Church of Jesus Christ of Latter-day Saints: 2 Aug 1894.[69] by Levi B. Reynolds.

4. He appeared on the census on 25 Jun 1900 in Mount Pleasant, Sanpete, Utah, United States.[79]
   Line 7 - McIntosh, Abe, head, white, male, born Mar 1860, age 40, married 16 years, born in Utah, father born in Canada, mother born in Canada, sheep raiser, can read, write and speak english, owns, mortgage free, farm, #197.
   Line 8 - McIntosh, Mary L, wife, white, female, born May 1862, age 38, married 16 years, had 6 children, 4 living, born in Utah, father born in Denmark, mother born in Denmark, can read, write and speak english.
   **Line 9 - McIntosh, A. Vance, son, white, male, born Apr 1885, age 15, single, born in Utah, father born in Utah, mother born in Utah, at school, can read, write and speak english.**
   Line 10 - McIntosh, Estelle A, daughter, white, female, born Dec 1880, age 10, single, born in Utah, father born in Utah, mother born in Utah, at school, can read, write and speak english.
   Line 11 - McIntosh, Evin P, son, white, male, born June 1892, age 7, single, born in Utah, father born in Utah, mother born in Utah, at school, can read, write and speak english.
   Line 12 - McIntosh, Vernon M, son, white, male, born Jan 1895, age 5, single, born in Utah, father born in Utah, mother born in Utah, cannot read or write, can speak english.

5. Correspondence: from Vance McIntosh to Florence Monsen, 20 Feb 1903, Black Hills, , Utah, United States. Black Hills, Utah
   Feb.20th, 1903
   Miss Florence Monsen
   Mt. Pleasant, Ut.
   Dearest friend,
   You should see me now. Say but this is a wicked wicked world.
   Haven't seen but two persons for a week, but am going visiting tomorrow and perhaps will get a chance to send this to Black Rock.
   Say but it has been busy times out here since I blew in, no snow except in the tops of the mountains and couldn't drive to it with a wagon, and no springs. But we are in clover now. Have about 4 inches of snow.
   Say I haven't kept my part of the bargain of writing twice a week. I didn't see the use of writing when there was no chance of getting it mailed (do you). Well I will tell it all to you this time.
   Say but we had some wind hear the other nite it filled the back of the bed, the toe pan and piled up all over the stove, thought it would sure blow us out of bed but we held her down.
   We are in a pretty place (that is to look at), are camped about a half a mile from Severe lake on the east bench of the black hills, the lake is certainly pretty, there is about a block of hard-pan all around the edge and then about a block of dark green looking mud or sky and then the water. Don't suppose you know what a hard-pan is, it is a light colored clay formation, level as a floor and so hard that yoiu can't make a track in it without you kick and there isn't a shrub or any knid of plant growing on them in some some places they go for miles where they are in the bottom of a basin or valley they hold water and make shallow ponds. (So much for the hard-pan)
   They say you can't get to the water of Severe Lake because of it being so swampy or a kind of bottomless mud. I was going down today and explore but find myself to lazy. Will tell you more after the investigation.
   Well Florence how are you. Suppose every thing is as lively as ever, it is sure the opposite out here, but a person can't have all sunshine.
   When I think of all the good times we had together I kind o' long to get home again. But theres allways sunshine after darkness.
   Had better cut this out or I will be weeping and wake Eck. up, he is snooring so loud that it shakes the wagon.

# Abraham Edward McIntosh and Mary Louise Guhl

Well the clock says quiting time, and I am going to move tomorrow early so had better saw off and you must be getting tired of this junk.
Say did Ole get home all right. I haven't got mail nor heard a word from home since I left.
Well dear be good and write to me often.
Yours with love
Vance

6. Temple Records: 1909, Manti, Sanpete, Utah Territory, United States.[80]
Name in full-McIntosh-Abraham Vance, When born-26 Apr 1885, Where born-St. John, Tooele, Utah, Father-Abraham E. McIntosh, Mother-Mary Louisa Guhl, Heir-Self, When baptized-1893, When endowed-24 June 1909.

7. Blessing in the Church of Jesus Christ of Latter-day Saints: Patriarchal Blessing, on 18 Jul 1909, in Mount Pleasant, Sanpete, Utah, United States.[81] Brother McIntosh, in the name of the Lord Jesus, I lay my hands on your head to give unto you a patriarchal blessing which shall be a comfort and consolation unto you. The Lord is very pleased with you because from your childhood you have kept yourself pure and holy and tried to do what you have considered right according to your best knowledge. You have honored your father and your mother and the promises to you that you shall live long and do a great and a mighty work. To your own satisfaction, you shall do a great work both for the living and for the dead. You shall be a David on Mt. Zion. You shall be prepared to meet the Lord in the clouds of heaven and have the privilege to reign with him through the millennium as a king and a ruler. But before that day you will have the privilege to receive a companion whom the Lord has selected for you and she will be one with you and follow you as you follow the Lord. The Lord will bless you with many children and because you and your wife will make your house a house of prayer. Spirit of prayer shall be given unto your children and never leave them. You shall have great knowledge, wisdom and understanding. Both you and your wife will train them in the fear and knowledge of God. You rejoiced in that knowledge before the foundation of the earth was laid. You had a privilege granted unto you to come to the earth in these the later days through parents who would train you in such a way that you might be strengthened in your young days in your desire to serve God. Also at that time you had the privilege given to you to choose your companion and the children that the Lord will give unto you. You desired very much to have the privilege to receive tabernacles through you and your companion. The Lord will give unto you the same blessing that he gave to Abraham that your children or posterities shall be enumerable as the stars of heaven. You belong to the tribe of Joseph who was sold into Egypt and as he was pure of heart so are you and the day will come that you shall see God Your Heavenly Father. You were born in the lineage of Ephraim and you were one with him to fight the great battle in heaven. Like him, you were faithful. It was then he told you that through all eternity you shall be one with him and reign with him in the celestial glory under the presidency of him who is the lamb, slain from before the foundation of the earth was laid. Your understanding was so great in regard to what the Lord had appointed for you that you felt willing to come here and follow him no matter, life or death in order to be worthy of the crown laid up in store for you. That spirit will rest upon you from now on until you are in greater mass than before. So, you will always say in your heart I will do thy will and do all I can for the salvation of the human family. May the Lord protect you. Your days shall be lengthened out so you will be able to labor and do good for the human family even through the millennium. The angels of God will be around you and the spirit of God within you whereby you will be strengthened to fulfill the mission you are appointed to do. Your tongue shall be loosened and your voice shall be powerful and it shall penetrate the hearts of the people to hear. You shall bear your testimony and some of them shall be frightened in their hearts and ask you what they shall do for their salvation. Many people will be filled with great love for you and try to do all the good they can. When you shall return home from your mission some of them will cry because you will have to leave them. Your enemies shall have no power over you and some of them will be your real friends. The Lord will protect you from all destruction from land and sea which shall go over the earth in these the later days. Everything your heart can desire from prayer and prestige in righteousness shall be given unto you.
These blessing I lay upon you by virtue of the holy priesthood upon condition of your own faithfulness in the name of the Lord Jesus. Amen

8. Mission with the Church of Jesus Christ of Latter-day Saints: to the Central States, from 19 Jul 1909 to 14 Nov 1911.
Central States Mission
Honorable Release
Church of Jesus Christ of Latter Day Saints.
Independence, Mo., November 1, 1911
Elder A. Vance McIntosh
Dear Brother:

# Abraham Edward McIntosh and Mary Louise Guhl

This will notify you that you are *Honorable Released from your labors in the Central States Mission of the Church of Jesus Christ of Latter-Day Saints*, to return home to your friends and the association of your family and the Saints of God. We commend you for your faithfulness and devotion to the work of the Master while in the mission field and trust that in returning home you will continue in the cause you have so loyally represented, which brings salvation to the living and redemption to the dead. Cease not to be faithful, strengthen the weak; stimulate the faltering ones with noble ambitions, pointing the youth of Israel to lives of usefulness and stations of honor in this dispensation. Ever listen to the promptings of the Spirit of Truth, yield implicit obedience to the authority of the Lord Jesus, and sustain the priesthood with unfaltering fidelity, that your name may be written in the Lamb's Book of Life, and your deeds may live when you are not. May your homeward journey be a safe and pleasant one, and may peace and prosperity attend all your righteous endeavors throughout life. With kindest personal regards, believe me,
Your Brother.,
/s/ S.O. Bennion
President

9. He appeared on the census on 10 May 1910 in Mount Pleasant, Sanpete, Utah, United States.[82]
Line 22 - McIntosh, Abram E, head, male, white, age 50, married (M1) for 26 years, born in Utah, father born in Scotland-English, mother born in Scotland-English, speaks english, farmer/sheep raiser, general farm, employer, can read and write, owns, mortgage free, house.
Line 23 - McIntosh, Mary Louise, wife, female, white, age 47, married (M1) for 26 years, had 7 children, 5 living, born in Utah, father born in Denmark-Danish, mother born in Denmark-Danish, speaks english, no occupation, can read and write.
**Line 24 - McIntosh, Abram Vance, son, male, white, age 25, single, born in Utah, father born in Utah, mother born in Utah, speaks english, laborer, farm, employee, can read and write.**
Line 25 - McIntosh, Anna Estella, daughter, female, white, age 20, single, born in Utah, father born in Utah, mother born in Utah, speaks english, dressmaker, at home, works on own account, can read and write, did not attend school.
Line 26 - McIntosh, Elvin Peter, son, male, white, age 17, single, born in Utah, father born in Utah, mother born in Utah, speaks english, no occupation, can read and write, attended school.
Line 27 - McIntosh, Vernon Marinous, son, male, white, age 15, single, born in Utah, father born in Utah, mother born in Utah, speaks english, no occupation, can read and write, attended school.
Line 28 - McIntosh, Grace Maria, daughter, female, white, age 6, single, born in Utah, father born in Utah, mother born in Utah, speaks english, no occupation, attended school.
Line 29 - Christensen, Marimous, brother-in-law, male, white, age 55, single, born in Denmark-Danish, father born in Denmark-Danish, mother born in Denmark-Danish, speaks english, laborer, sheep herd, employee, not out of work on Apr 15, 1910, 0 weeks unemployed in 1909, can read and write.

10. He was ordained a Seventy on 26 Nov 1911.[69]
By Rulon S. Wells.
"To Whom It May Concern: This certifies that **A.Vance McIntosh** is a member of the **Sixty Sixth Quorum of Seventy**, in the Mt. Pleasant South Ward of the North Sanpete Stake of Zion of the Church of Jesus Christ of Latter-day Saints, and is hereby recommended to any Quorum with which he may desire to unite. He has removed to Payson Ward. /s/Henry Hasler In behalf of the Presidents of 66 Quorum."

**SEVENTY'S GENEALOGY**
Name in full: A. Vance McIntosh
Father's Name: Abraham E. McIntosh
Mother's maiden name: Mary L. Guhl
Born at: St. John, Tooele Co., Utah, 26 April 1885.
Baptized by: Levi B. Reynolds, 2 Aug 1894
Ordained a Seventy by Rulon S. Wellls, 26 Nov 1911
**I certify** that above is a correct transcript of the entries in the record of members.
/s/ Henry Hasler, Secretary
Removed to Payson, Ward, Stake, Cause of leaving:

11. He worked as an electrician on 16 Mar 1917 in Mount Pleasant, Sanpete, Utah, United States.[83]

12. Draft Registration: World War I, 12 Sep 1918, Manti, Sanpete, Utah, United States.[84] **Abraham Vance McIntosh**

# Abraham Edward McIntosh and Mary Louise Guhl

Occupation: Supt. Water Works; Asst. Electrician in Mt. Pleasant, Sanpete, Utah.
Nearest Relative: Florence M. McIntosh (wife) in Mt. Pleasant, Utah.
Description: white, male, medium height, medium build, blue eyes, brown hair.

13. He worked as a Supt. Water Works, Asst. Electrician on 12 Sep 1918 in Mount Pleasant, Sanpete, Utah, United States.[84]

14. He was described as medium height, medium build, blue eyes, brown hair on 12 Sep 1918 in Manti, Sanpete, Utah, United States.[84]

15. He appeared on the census on 26 Jan 1920 in Mount Pleasant, Sanpete, Utah, United States.[85]
**Line 56 - McIntosh, Vance, head, owns home, mortgage free, male, white, age 34, married, can read and write, born in Utah, father born in Utah, mother born in Denmark-speaks Danish, speaks english, farmer.**
Line 57 - McIntosh, Florence, wife, female, white, age 32, married, can read and write, born in Utah, father born in Utah, mother born in Utah, speaks english, no occupation.
Line 58 - McIntosh, Fern, daughter, female, white, age 34/12, single, born in Utah, father born in Utah, mother born in Utah, no occupation.
Line 59 - McIntosh, Edwin, son, male, white, age 5/12, single, born in Utah, father born in Utah, mother born in Utah, no occupation.

16. He appeared on the census on 4 Apr 1930 in Milburn, Sanpete, Utah, United States.[86] Line 11 - McIntosh, Abraham E, head, owns home, lives on a farm, male, white, age 69, married at age 23, can read, write and speak english, born in Utah, father born in Scotland, mother born in Scotland, farmer on a general farm, #20, not a veteran.
**Line 12 - McIntosh, Vance, son, owns home, lives on a farm, male, white, age 45, married at age 29, did not attend school within year, can read and write, born in Utah, father born in Utah, mother born in Utah, able to speak english, farmer, general farm, works on own account, actually at work, not a veteran, farm #21.**
Line 13 - Johnson, Lester, laborer, male, white, age 21, single, did not attend school within year, can read and write, born in Utah, father born in Utah, mother born in Denmark, able to speak english, laborer, farm, wage worker, actually at work, not a veteran.

17. He appeared on the census on 24 Apr 1930 in Mount Pleasant, Sanpete, Utah, United States.[87]
**Line 4 - McIntosh, A. Vance, head, owns home, value of home $3000, does not live on a farm, male, white, age 44, married at age 28, did not attend school within year, can read and write, born in Utah, father born in Utah, mother born in Utah, able to speak english, farmer, general farm, employer, actually at work, not a veteran, farm # 106A.**
Line 5 - McIntosh, Florence M, wife, female, white, age 42, married at age 26, did not attend school within year, can read and write, born in Utah, father born in Utah, mother born in Utah, no occupation.
Line 6 - McIntosh, F. Fern, daughter, female, white, age 13, single, did attend school within year, can read and write, born in Utah, father born in Utah, mother born in Utah, able to speak english, no occupation.
Line 7 - McIntosh, J. Edwin, son, male, white, age 10, single, did attend school within year, can read and write, born in Utah, father born in Utah, mother born in Utah, able to speak english, no occupation.
Line 8 - McIntosh, Jean A, daughter, female, white, age 3 10/12, single, did not attend school within year, born in Utah, father born in Utah, mother born in Utah, no occupation.
Line 9 - Neilson, Neils A, uncle, male, white, age 58, single, did not attend school within year, can read and write, born in Utah, father born in Sweden, mother born in Sweden, able to speak english, farmer, general farm, employer, actually at work, not a veteran, farm #107A

18. He had a residence from 1934 to May 1957 in Provo, Utah, Utah, United States.
In the 1950 Provo City Directory, his address was:
721 (From 760 North 700 East to North 800 East, east and north (formerly Timp Way).

19. He appeared on the census on 13 Apr 1940 in Mount Pleasant, Sanpete, Utah, United States.[88]
Line 3 - 109 South 3rd West, owns house worth $3000, Monsen, Annette, head, female, white, age 75, widowed, finished 8th grade, born in Utah, lived in same house in 1935, not employed, has another source of income.
Line 4 - McIntosh, Florence, daughter, female, white, age 52, married, finished 1 year college, born in Utah, lived in same house in 1935, not employed, no other source of income.
**Line 5 - McIntosh, Vance, son-in-law, male, white, age 53, married, finished 4 years high school, born in Utah, lived in same house in 1935, employed as a farmer on a farm, worked 60 hours the week before the census, works on own account, worked 52 weeks in 1939, earned nothing, has another source of income, Farm #21.**
Line 6 - McIntosh, Edwin, son, male, white, age 20, single, in school, 2nd year of college, born in Utah, lived in same house in 1935, farm helper on family farm, has another source of income.
Line 7 - McIntosh, Jean, daughter, female, white, age 13, single, in school, 7th grade, born in Utah, lived in same house

# Abraham Edward McIntosh and Mary Louise Guhl

in 1935.
Line 8 - McIntosh, Don, son, male, white, age 9, single, in school, 2nd grade, born in Utah, lived in same house in 1935.
Line 9 - Jacobs, Fern, grand-daughter, female, white, age 23, married, finished 2 years college, born in Utah, lived in same house in 1935.
Line 10 - Jacobs, Chariton, grandson-in-law, male, white, age 27, male, in school 3rd year of college, born in Utah, lived in same house in 1935, assistant funeral director at funeral home, private work, worked 12 weeks in 1939, earned $180, has other source of income.
Line 11 - Jacobs, Karen, great-granddaughter, female, white, age 1/12, single, born in Utah.

20. He worked as a maintenance man at Utah Valley Hospital 1950's in Provo, Utah, Utah, United States.
**"PERSONALITY OF THE MONTH**
**UTAH VALLEY HOSPITAL**
**Mr. Vance McIntosh** was born in St. John, Tooele County, Utah in 1885. He attended Mt. Pleasant elementary schools, and high school. He then went to the Brigham Young University for three years in 1902 1903, and I904. He filled a two year mission for the L.D.S. Church in the Central States. In 1911 Mr. McIntosh married Florence Monson, and they made their home in Mt. Pleasant, Sanpete County, where he was engaged in raising registered horses and sheep.
They have four children, two boys and two girls. They have all attended the Brigham Young University.
The McIntosh family later moved to Provo and "Mac" worked at Geneva for three years before coming to the Utah Valley Hospital. Mr. McIntosh has been with the Utah Valley Hospital for eight years working with the Maintenance Department and as Storeroom Clerk. His hobbies are all kind of sports in which he was very active in his youth. He likes prospecting, and has a beautiful rock collection. He also likes hunting and fishing.
Mr. McIntosh represents the Maintenance Department in the Employees Council.

21. He had a residence from May 1957 to 16 Aug 1959 in Mount Pleasant, Sanpete, Utah, United States.

22. His obituary was published on 18 Aug 1959.
**Abram Vance Mcintosh**, 74, died at his home of a heart ailment. Born April 26, 1885, Mt. Pleasant, to Abram E. and Louise Guhl Mcintosh. Married Florence Monsen Oct 15, Salt Lake LDS Temple. Missionary, rancher and sheepman. Survivors; Wife; two sons, Edwin J., Dugway; Don V., American Fork; two daughters, Mrs. Chariton (Fern) Jacobs, Mt. Pleasant; Mrs. William (Jean) Kennedy, Berkeley, Calif.; seven grandchildren; two sisters.
Funeral services were held Wednesday afternoon, August 19, in the Mt. Pleasant Second-Third Ward Chapel for **A. Vance McIntosh**, 74, who died Sunday at 6:15pm at his home in Mt. Pleasant of heart trouble and complications. Burial was in Mt. Pleasant cemetery directed by Jacobs Mortuary. Mr. McIntosh was born April 26, 1885, in St. Johns, Utah, a son of A. E. and Mary Louise Guhl McIntosh. He attended public schools here and Brigham Young University for three years. He served a mission to the Central States for the LDS Church. October 15, 1913, he married Florence Monsen in the Salt Lake Temple. He was a rancher and a sheepman for many years. He and his father were some of the first to bring registered Rambouillet into prominence in this community. In 1934 he moved to Provo where he was employed at the Utah Valley Hospital until retiring two years ago. They moved back to Mt. Pleasant last year in May. Surviving are his widow, two sons and two daughters: Edwin J. McIntosh, Dugway; Don V. McIntosh, American Fork; Mrs. Chariton (Fern)Jacobs, Mt. Pleasant; Mrs. Willliam (Jean) Kennedy, Berkeley, California; seven grandchildren; two sisters, Mrs. Joseph (Stella) Schofield; and Mrs. Robert (Grace) Burns, Los Angeles, California.
**Salt Lake Tribune (UT) August 18, 1959**

# Abraham Edward McIntosh and Mary Louise Guhl

| Children (cont.) | | |
|---|---|---|
| **2 M** | **William Edward McIntosh** [89,90] | |
| Born | 25 Feb 1887 | Saint John, Tooele, Utah Territory, United States |
| Died | 20 Dec 1891 | Mount Pleasant, Sanpete, Utah Territory, United States |
| Buried | Dec 1891 | Mount Pleasant, Sanpete, Utah Territory, United States[91] |
| Address | Mount Pleasant City Cemetery, 900 South 100 East, Mt. Pleasant, Utah 84647, USA | |
| Notes | Plot: A-99-3-1 | |
| Bapt.(LDS) | Child | |
| Conf.(LDS) | Child | |
| Init.(LDS) | Child | |
| Endow.(LDS) | Child | |
| SealP (LDS) | 21 Nov 1894 | Manti Utah Temple |
| Spouse | This person had no known marriage and no known children | |
| **3 F** | **Anna Estelle McIntosh** | |
| AKA | Annie Estelle McIntosh,[92] Estella Anna McIntosh, Stella McIntosh, Stele Schofield | |
| Born | 24 Dec 1889 | Mount Pleasant, Sanpete, Utah Territory, United States |
| Died | 13 Jan 1973 | Los Angeles, California, United States[93] |
| Buried | Jan 1973 | Whittier, Los Angeles, California, United States[94] |
| Address | Rose Hills Memorial Park, 3888 Workman Mill Road, Whittier, California, USA | |
| Bapt.(LDS) | 18 Jul 1898 | |
| Conf.(LDS) | 18 Jul 1898 | |
| Init.(LDS) | 2 Oct 1912 | Salt Lake Temple |
| Endow.(LDS) | 2 Oct 1912 | Salt Lake Temple |
| SealP (LDS) | 21 Nov 1894 | Manti Utah Temple |
| Spouse | Joseph William Schofield (1887-1974) | 2 Nov 1912 - Salt Lake City, Salt Lake, Utah, United States[95,96] |
| SealS (LDS) | 2 Oct 1912 | Salt Lake Temple |

**Events**

1. She appeared on the census on 25 Jun 1900 in Mount Pleasant, Sanpete, Utah, United States.[97]
   Line 7 - McIntosh, Abe, head, white, male, born Mar 1860, age 40, married 16 years, born in Utah, father born in Canada, mother born in Canada, sheep raiser, can read, write and speak english, owns, mortgage free, farm, #197.
   Line 8 - McIntosh, Mary L, wife, white, female, born May 1862, age 38, married 16 years, had 6 children, 4 living, born in Utah, father born in Denmark, mother born in Denmark, can read, write and speak english.
   Line 9 - McIntosh, A. Vance, son, white, male, born Apr 1885, age 15, single, born in Utah, father born in Utah, mother born in Utah, at school, can read, write and speak english.
   **Line 10 - McIntosh, Estelle A, daughter, white, female, born Dec 1880, age 10, single, born in Utah, father born in Utah, mother born in Utah, at school, can read, write and speak english.**
   Line 11 - McIntosh, Elvin P, son, white, male, born June 1892, age 7, single, born in Utah, father born in Utah, mother born in Utah, at school, can read, write and speak english.
   Line 12 - McIntosh, Vernon M, son, white, male, born Jan 1895, age 5, single, born in Utah, father born in Utah, mother born in Utah, cannot read or write, can speak english.
2. She appeared on the census on 10 May 1910 in Mount Pleasant, Sanpete, Utah, United States.[98]
   Line 22 - McIntosh, Abram E, head, male, white, age 50, married once for 26 years, born in Utah, father born in Scotland-English, mother born in Scotland-English, speaks english, farmer/sheep raiser, general farm, employer, can read and write, owns, mortgage free, house.
   Line 23 - McIntosh, Mary Louise, wife, female, white, age 47, married once for 26 years, had 7 children, 5 living, born in Utah, father born in Denmark-speaks Danish, mother born in Denmark-speaks Danish, speaks english, no occupation, can read and write.

# Abraham Edward McIntosh and Mary Louise Guhl

Line 24 - McIntosh, Abram Vance, son, male, white, age 25, single, born in Utah, father born in Utah, mother born in Utah, speaks english, laborer, farm, employee, can read and write.
**Line 25 - McIntosh, Anna Estella, daughter, female, white, age 20, single, born in Utah, father born in Utah, mother born in Utah, speaks english, dressmaker, at home, works on own account, can read and write, did not attend school within the year.**
Line 26 - McIntosh, Elvin Peter, son, male, white, age 17, single, born in Utah, father born in Utah, mother born in Utah, speaks english, no occupation, can read and write, attended school.
Line 27 - McIntosh, Vernon Marinous, son, male, white, age 15, single, born in Utah, father born in Utah, mother born in Utah, speaks english, no occupation, can read and write, attended school.
Line 28 - McIntosh, Grace Maria, daughter, female, white, age 6, single, born in Utah, father born in Utah, mother born in Utah, speaks english, no occupation, attended school.
Line 29 - Christensen, Marimous, brother-in-law, male, white, age 55, single, born in Denmark-speaks Danish, father born in Denmark-speaksDanish, mother born in Denmark-speaks Danish, speaks english, laborer, shepherd, employee, not out of work on Apr 15, 1910, 0 weeks unemployed in 1909, can read and write.

3. Temple Records: 1912, Salt Lake City, Salt Lake, Utah, United States.[99]
Name in full-McIntosh-Annie Estelle, When born-24 Dec 1889, Where born-Mt. Pleasant, Sanpete, Utah, Father-Abraham E. McIntosh, Mother-Mary L. Guhl, Heir-self, When baptized-1898, When endowed-2 Oct 1912.

4. She appeared on the census on 24 Jan 1920 in Mount Pleasant, Sanpete, Utah, United States.[100]
Line 43 - Scofield, Joseph, head, rents home, male, white, age 32, married, can read and write, born in Utah, father born in Utah, mother born in Utah, speaks english, laborer, farm, employee.
**Line 44 - Scofield, Annie, wife, female, white, age 30, married, attended school, cannot read or write, born in Utah, father born in Utah, mothr born in Utah, speaks english, no occupation.**
Line 45 - Scofield, Louise, daughter, female, white, age 6, single, born in Utah, father born in Utah, mother born in Utah, no occupation.
Line 46 - Scofield, Maxine, daughter, female, white, age 33/12, single, born in Utah, father born in Utah, mother born in Utah, no occupation.
Line 47 - Scofield, Gwen, daughter, female, white, age 1/12, single, born in Utah, father born in Utah, mother born in Utah, no occupation.

5. She appeared on the census on 5 Apr 1930 in Salt Lake City, Salt Lake, Utah, United States.[101]
Line 92 - Schofield, Joseph, head, rents home, $35 monthly rental, does not live on a farm, male, white, age 42, married at age 25, did not attend school within year, can read and write, born in Utah, father born in Utah, mother born in Utah, able to speak english, clerk, department store, wage worker, actually at work, not a veteran.
**Line 93 - Schofield, Stelle, wife, female, white, age 40, married at age 23, did not attend school within year, can read and write, born in Utah, father born in Utah, mother born in Utah, able to speak english, no occupation.**
Line 94 - Schofield, Louise, daughter, female, white, age 16, single, did attend school within year, can read and write, born in Utah, father born in Utah, mother born in Utah, able to speak english, no occupation.
Line 95 - Schofield, Maxine, daughter, female, white, age 14, single, did attend school within year, can read and write, born in Utah, father born in Utah, mother born in Utah, able to speak english, no occupation.
Line 96 - Schofield, Gwendelyn, daughter, female, white, age 10, single, did attend school within year, can read and write, born in Utah, father born in Utah, mother born in Utah, able to speak english, no occupation.

6. She appeared on the census on 3 Apr 1940 in Montebello, Los Angeles, California, United States.[102]
Line 4 - 570 Kern St., rents house for $26, not a farm, Schofield, Joseph W., head, male, white, age 52, married, finished 2 years high school, born in Utah, in 1935 lived in Mt. Pleasant, San Pete, Utah, salesman for retail merchandise, private work, worked 36 hours the week before the census, worked 26 weeks in 1939, earned $400, no other source of income.
**Line 5 - Schofield, Estelle, wife, female, white, age 50, married, finished 2 years high school, born in Utah, in 1935 lived in Mt. Pleasant, San Pete, Utah, not employed.**
Line 6 - Lasson, Mary Louise, daughter, female, white, age 26, divorced, finished 4 years high school, born in Utah, in 1935 lived in Mt. Pleasant, San Pete Utah, at private work, worked 48 hours week prior to census, saleslady for retail merchandise store, worked 52 weeks in 1939, earned $884, has other source of income.
Line 7 - Schofield, Maxine, daughter, female, white, age 24, single, finished 4 years high school, born in Utah, in 1935 lived in Mt. Pleasant, San Pete Utah, at private work, worked 48 hours week prior to census, saleslady for retail merchandise store, worked 52 weeks in 1939, earned $936, has no other source of income.
Line 8 - Lasson, Alan, grandson, male, white, age 7, single, in school 1st grade, born in Utah, in 1935 lived in Mt. Pleasant San Pete Utah.

# Abraham Edward McIntosh and Mary Louise Guhl

| 4 | M | **Elvin Peter McIntosh** [103] | |
|---|---|---|---|
| Born | | 28 Jun 1892 | Saint John, Tooele, Utah Territory, United States |
| Died | | 18 Mar 1958 | Los Angeles, Los Angeles, California, United States[104] |
| Cause of Death | | Bronchopneumonia | |
| Buried | | 21 Mar 1958 | Glendale, Los Angeles, California, United States |
| Address | | Forest Lawn Memorial Park, 1712 S. Glendale Avenue, Glendale, California 91205, USA | |
| Notes | | Plot: Brotherly Love, Lot 1871, Space 2 | |
| Bapt.(LDS) | | 9 Jun 1903 | |
| Conf.(LDS) | | 9 Jun 1903 | |
| Init.(LDS) | | 7 Feb 1917 | Manti Utah Temple |
| Endow.(LDS) | | 7 Feb 1917 | Manti Utah Temple |
| SealP (LDS) | | 21 Nov 1894 | Manti Utah Temple |
| Spouse | | Anna Muriel Vadis McArthur (1901-1965) | 27 Nov 1923 - Provo, Utah, Utah, United States[105] |
| SealS (LDS) | | 15 Sep 2001 | Provo Utah Temple |

**Events**

1. He appeared on the census on 25 Jun 1900 in Mount Pleasant, Sanpete, Utah, United States.[106]
   Line 7 - McIntosh, Abe, head, white, male, born Mar 1860, age 40, married 16 years, born in Utah, father born in Canada, mother born in Canada, sheep raiser, can read, write and speak english, owns, mortgage free, farm, #197.
   Line 8 - McIntosh, Mary L, wife, white, female, born May 1862, age 38, married 16 years, had 6 children, 4 living, born in Utah, father born in Denmark, mother born in Denmark, can read, write and speak english.
   Line 9 - McIntosh, A. Vance, son, white, male, born Apr 1885, age 15, single, born in Utah, father born in Utah, mother born in Utah, at school, can read, write and speak english.
   Line 10 - McIntosh, Estelle A, daughter, white, female, born Dec 1880, age 10, single, born in Utah, father born in Utah, mother born in Utah, at school, can read, write and speak english.
   **Line 11 - McIntosh, Evin P, son, white, male, born June 1892, age 7, single, born in Utah, father born in Utah, mother born in Utah, at school, can read, write and speak english.**
   Line 12 - McIntosh, Vernon M, son, white, male, born Jan 1895, age 5, single, born in Utah, father born in Utah, mother born in Utah, cannot read or write, can speak english.

2. He appeared on the census on 10 May 1910 in Mount Pleasant, Sanpete, Utah, United States.[107]
   Line 22 - McIntosh, Abram E, head, male, white, age 50, married once for 26 years, born in Utah, father born in Scotland-speaks English, mother born in Scotland-speaks English, speaks english, farmer/sheep raiser, general farm, employer, can read and write, owns, mortgage free, house.
   Line 23 - McIntosh, Mary Louise, wife, female, white, age 47, married once for 26 years, had 7 children, 5 living, born in Utah, father born in Denmark-speaks Danish, mother born in Denmark-speaks Danish, speaks english, no occupation, can read and write.
   Line 24 - McIntosh, Abram Vance, son, male, white, age 25, single, born in Utah, father born in Utah, mother born in Utah, speaks english, laborer, farm, employee, can read and write.
   Line 25 - McIntosh, Anna Estella, daughter, female, white, age 20, single, born in Utah, father born in Utah, mother born in Utah, speaks english, dressmaker, at home, works on own account, can read and write.
   **Line 26 - McIntosh, Elvin Peter, son, male, white, age 17, single, born in Utah, father born in Utah, mother born in Utah, speaks english, no occupation, can read and write, attended school.**
   Line 27 - McIntosh, Vernon Marinous, son, male, white, age 15, single, born in Utah, father born in Utah, mother born in Utah, speaks english, no occupation, can read and write, attended school.
   Line 28 - McIntosh, Grace Maria, daughter, female, white, age 6, single, born in Utah, father born in Utah, mother born in Utah, speaks english, no occupation, attended school.
   Line 29 - Christensen, Marimous, brother-in-law, male, white, age 55, single, born in Denmark-speaks Danish, father born in Denmark-speaks Danish, mother born in Denmark-speaks Danish, speaks english, laborer, sheep herd, employee, not out of work on Apr 15, 1910, 0 weeks unemployed in 1909, can read and write.

# Abraham Edward McIntosh and Mary Louise Guhl

3. Temple Records: 1917, Manti, Sanpete, Utah, United States.[108]
   Name in full-McIntosh-Elvin Peter, When born 28 Jun 1892, Where born-Mt. Pleasant, Utah, Father-Abraham E. McIntosh, Mother-Mary L. Gould, Heir-self, When baptized 9 Jun 1903, When endowed-7 Feb 1917.
4. He worked as an aluminum inspector for Alcoa Aluminum Company.
5. He appeared on the census on 24 Jan 1920 in Mount Pleasant, Sanpete, Utah, United States.[109]
   Line 34 - McIntosh, A.E., head, owns home, mortgage free, male, white, age 59, married, can read and write, born in Utah, father born in Scotland-Scotch, mother born in Scotland-Scotch, speaks english, farmer, general farm, works on own account, farm #121.
   Line 35 - McIntosh, Mary L, wife, female, white, age 57, married, can reaad and write, born in Utah, father born in Denmark-DAnish, mother born in Denmark-Danish, speaks english, no occupation.
   **Line 36 - McIntosh, Alvin, son, male, white, age 27, single, can read and write, born in Utah, father born in Utah, mother born in Utah, speaks english, farmer, general farm, employee.**
   Line 37 - McIntosh, Vernon, son, male, white, age 25, single, can read and write, born in Utah, father born in Utah, mother born in Utah, speaks english, farmer, general farm, employee.
   Line 38 - McIntosh, Grace M, daughter, female, white, age 16, single, attended school, can read and write, born in Utah, father born in Utah, mother born in Utah, speaks english, no occupation.
6. He appeared on the census on 11 Apr 1930 in Salt Lake City, Salt Lake, Utah, United States.[110]
   **Line 46 - McIntosh, Elvin, head, rents home, $15 monthly rental, does not live on a farm, male, white, age 37, married at age 31, did not attend school within year, can read and write, born in Utah, father born in Utah, mother born in Utah, able to speak english, salesman, vacuum company, wage worker, actually at work, not a veteran.**
   Line 47 - McIntosh, Muriel, wife, female, white, age 28, married at age 22, did not attend school within year, can read and write, born in Utah, father born in Utah, mother born in Utah, able to speak english, no occupation.
   Line 48 - McIntosh, Vernon, son, male, white, age 1 6/12, single, did not attend school within year, born in Utah, father born in Utah, mother born in Utah, no occupation.
7. He appeared on the census on 23 Apr 1940 in Los Angeles, Los Angeles, California, United States.[111]
   **Line 6 - 1369 West 24th St, rents house for $20, not a farm, McIntosh, Elvin, head, male, white, age 47, married, finished 4 years high school, born in Utah, lived in same place in 1935, crossing guard at S.R.A., worked 39 weeks in 1939, earned $585, no other source of income.**
   Line 7 - McIntosh, Muriel, wife, female, white, age 38, married, finished 1 year high school, born in Utah, lived in same place in 1935, not employed.
   Line 8 - McIntosh, Vernon R., son, male, white, age 11, single, in school 6th grade, born in Utah, lived in same place in 1935.
   Line 9 - McArthur, Philena, mother-in-law, female, white, age 65, widowed, finished 8th grade, born in Utah, lived in same place in 1935, not employed, has other source of income.

| 5 M | **Franklin Vaughn McIntosh** [112] | |
|---|---|---|
| AKA | Vaughn McIntosh | |
| Born | 10 Jan 1895 | Mount Pleasant, Sanpete, Utah Territory, United States[113] |
| Died | 7 Feb 1895 | Mount Pleasant, Sanpete, Utah Territory, United States |
| Buried | Feb 1895 | Mount Pleasant, Sanpete, Utah Territory, United States |
| Address | Mount Pleasant City Cemetery, 900 South 100 East, Mt. Pleasant, Utah 84647, USA | |
| Status | Twin | |
| Bapt.(LDS) | Child | |
| Conf.(LDS) | Child | |
| Init.(LDS) | Child | |
| Endow.(LDS) | Child | |
| SealP (LDS) | BIC | |
| Spouse | This person had no known marriage and no known children | |

# Abraham Edward McIntosh and Mary Louise Guhl

| Children (cont.) | | |
|---|---|---|
| 6 M | **Vernon Marenus McIntosh** [115] | |
| AKA | Marinus Vernon McIntosh,[114] Vernon Marines McIntosh | |
| Born | 10 Jan 1895 | Mount Pleasant, Sanpete, Utah Territory, United States[116,117] |
| Died | 17 Oct 1922 | Mount Pleasant, Sanpete, Utah, United States[117] |
| Cause of Death | Diabetes//His obituary says he died of complications of tonsilitis. Another obituary says when he had his tonsilectomy, they could bare[118] | |
| Buried | 20 Oct 1922 | Mount Pleasant, Sanpete, Utah, United States[117,119] |
| Address | Mount Pleasant City Cemetery, 900 South 100 East, Mt. Pleasant, Utah 84647, USA | |
| Status | Twin | |
| Bapt.(LDS) | 9 Jun 1903 | |
| Conf.(LDS) | 9 Jun 1903 | |
| Init.(LDS) | 7 Feb 1924 | Manti Utah Temple |
| Endow.(LDS) | 7 Feb 1924 | Manti Utah Temple |
| SealP (LDS) | BIC | |
| Spouse | This person had no known marriage and no known children | |

**Events**

1. He worked as a farmer.[118]
2. He appeared on the census on 25 Jun 1900 in Mount Pleasant, Sanpete, Utah, United States.[120]
   Line 7 - McIntosh, Abe, head, white, male, born Mar 1860, age 40, married 16 years, born in Utah, father born in Canada, mother born in Canada, sheep raiser, can read, write and speak english, owns, mortgage free, farm, #197.
   Line 8 - McIntosh, Mary L, wife, white, female, born May 1862, age 38, married 16 years, had 6 children, 4 living, born in Utah, father born in Denmark, mother born in Denmark, can read, write and speak english.
   Line 9 - McIntosh, A. Vance, son, white, male, born Apr 1885, age 15, single, born in Utah, father born in Utah, mother born in Utah, at school, can read, write and speak english.
   Line 10 - McIntosh, Estelle A, daughter, white, female, born Dec 1880, age 10, single, born in Utah, father born in Utah, mother born in Utah, at school, can read, write and speak english.
   Line 11 - McIntosh, Evin P, son, white, male, born June 1892, age 7, single, born in Utah, father born in Utah, mother born in Utah, at school, can read, write and speak english.
   **Line 12 - McIntosh, Vernon M, son, white, male, born Jan 1895, age 5, single, born in Utah, father born in Utah, mother born in Utah, cannot read or write, can speak english.**
3. He appeared on the census on 10 May 1910 in Mount Pleasant, Sanpete, Utah, United States.[121]
   Line 22 - McIntosh, Abram E, head, male, white, age 50, married (M1) for 26 years, born in Utah, father born in Scotland-English, mother born in Scotland-English, speaks english, farmer/sheep raiser, general farm, employer, can read and write, owns, mortgage free, house.
   Line 23 - McIntosh, Mary Louise, wife, female, white, age 47, married (M1) for 26 years, had 7 children, 5 living, born in Utah, father born in Denmark-Danish, mother born in Denmark-Danish, speaks english, no occupation, can read and write.
   Line 24 - McIntosh, Abram Vance, son, male, white, age 25, single, born in Utah, father born in Utah, mother born in Utah, speaks english, laborer, farm, employee, can read and write.

# Abraham Edward McIntosh and Mary Louise Guhl

Line 25 - McIntosh, Anna Estella, daughter, female, white, age 20, single, born in Utah, father born in Utah, mother born in Utah, speaks english, dressmaker, at home, works on own account, can read and write, did not attend school.
Line 26 - McIntosh, Elvin Peter, son, male, white, age 17, single, born in Utah, father born in Utah, mother born in Utah, speaks english, no occupation, can read and write, attended school.
**Line 27 - McIntosh, Vernon Marinous, son, male, white, age 15, single, born in Utah, father born in Utah, mother born in Utah, speaks english, no occupation, can read and write, attended school.**
Line 28 - McIntosh, Grace Maria, daughter, female, white, age 6, single, born in Utah, father born in Utah, mother born in Utah, speaks english, no occupation, attended school.
Line 29 - Christensen, Marimous, brother-in-law, male, white, age 55, single, born in Denmark-Danish, father born in Denmark-Danish, mother born in Denmark-Danish, speaks english, laborer, sheep herd, employee, not out of work on Apr 15, 1910, 0 weeks unemployed in 1909, can read and write.

4. Draft Registration: World War I, 5 Jun 1917, Sanpete, Utah, United States.[122]
   Occupation: Farmer in Milburn Precinct.
   Description: short height, medium build, blue eyes, light color hair.

5. He appeared on the census on 19 Jan 1920 in Scofield, Carbon, Utah, United States.[123]
   Line 39 - Neilson, Adolph, head, home owned, male, white, age 32, married, did not attend school within year, can read and write,born in Utah, father born in Denmark, speaks Danish, mother born in Denmark, speaks Danish, speaks english, blacksmith, mine, wage worker.
   **Line 49 - McIntosh, Vernon, boarder, male, white, age 25, single, can read and write, born in Utah, father born in Utah, mother born in Utah, can speak english, miner, coal, wage worker.**

6. He appeared on the census on 24 Jan 1920 in Mount Pleasant, Sanpete, Utah, United States.[124]
   Line 34 - McIntosh, A.E., head, owns home, mortgage free, male, white, age 59, married, can read and write, born in Utah, father born in Scotland-Scotch, mother born in Scotland-Scotch, speaks english, farmer, general farm, works on own account, farm #121.
   Line 35 - McIntosh, Mary L, wife, female, white, age 57, married, can reaad and write, born in Utah, father born in Denmark-DAnish, mother born in Denmark-Danish, speaks english, no occupation.
   Line 36 - McIntosh, Alvin, son, male, white, age 27, single, can read and write, born in Utah, father born in Utah, mother born in Utah, speaks english, farmer, general farm, employee.
   **Line 37 - McIntosh, Vernon, son, male, white, age 25, single, can read and write, born in Utah, father born in Utah, mother born in Utah, speaks english, farmer, general farm, employee.**
   Line 38 - McIntosh, Grace M, daughter, female, white, age 16, single, attended school, can read and write, born in Utah, father born in Utah, mother born in Utah, speaks english, no occupation.

7. He received The State of Utah Certificate of Acknowledgement of Service on 11 Nov 1920 in Salt Lake City, Salt Lake, Utah, United States.
   "The State of Utah in grateful acknowledgement of the sacrifices and devoted services of her sons in the military and naval forces of the United States in the war with Germany and her allies issues this certificate in the name of VERNON MCINTOSH as a testimonial to his valor, fidelity and patriotic service in the Great World Conflict for the preservation of Liberty, Popular Gevernment and Civilization. Given at Salt Lake City, this 11th day of November 1920 by virtue of an act of the Legislature of the State of Utah, approved March 20, 1919. Signed by the Govenor,"

8. His obituary was published in the "Salt Lake Telegram" on 18 Oct 1922 in Salt Lake City, Salt Lake, Utah, United States.

   **Tonsilitis Proves Fatal to M'Intosh**
   Mount Pleasant, Oct, 18 - Vernon, the 21-year-old son of Bishop and Mrs. A.E. McIntosh, died at his home here yesterday from complications following tonsilitis. He is survived by his parents and two brothers, Elvin and Vance and two sisters, Mrs. Joseph Scofield and Grace McIntosh, all of this place.

   **Vernon McIntosh Dies Suddenly at Mt. Pleasant**
   Special to The Tribune.
   Mt. Pleasant, Oct. 17.--Vernon McIntosh, 35 years of age, youngest son of Bishop and Mrs. A. E. McIntosh died suddenly this morning from diabetes. The young man was operated upon for the removal of his tonsils about a month ago and was seriously ill from severe hemorrhages at that time.
   After several blood transfusions had been resorted to, he began improving and was nearly well when he became suddenly ill and died after two day of illness.

# Abraham Edward McIntosh and Mary Louise Guhl

Mr. McIntosh is survived by his parents, two brothers, Vance and Elvin McIntosh and two sisters, Mrs. Joseph Scofield and Miss Grace McIntosh, all of Mt. Pleasant.

9. His obituary was published in the "Salt Lake Tribune" on 18 Oct 1922 in Salt Lake City, Salt Lake, Utah, United States.
**Vernon McIntosh Dies Suddenly at Mt. Pleasant**
Special to The Tribune.
Mt. Pleasant, Oct. 17.--Vernon McIntosh, 35 years of age, youngest son of Bishop and Mrs. A. E. McIntosh died suddenly this morning from diabetes. The young man was operated upon for the removal of his tonsils about a month ago and was seriously ill from severe hemorrhages at that time.
After several blood transfusions had been resorted to, he began improving and was nearly well when he became suddenly ill and died after two day of illness.
Mr. McIntosh is survived by his parents, two brothers, Vance and Elvin McIntosh and two sisters, Mrs. Joseph Scofield and Miss Grace McIntosh, all of Mt. Pleasant.

10. Temple Records: 1924, Manti, Sanpete, Utah, United States.[125]
Name in full-McIntosh-Vernon Marinus, When born-10 Jan 1895, Where born-Mt. Pleasant, Sanpete, Utah, When died-17 Oct 1922, Heir-Abraham E. McIntosh, Relation-Father, When baptized 9 Jun 1903, When endowed-7 Feb 1924

| 7 | F | **Grace Maria McIntosh** [126] | |
|---|---|---|---|
| Born | | 6 Sep 1903 | Mount Pleasant, Sanpete, Utah, United States[127] |
| Died | | 11 May 1993 | Meadow Vista, Placer, California, United States[127] |
| Buried | | 15 May 1993 | Whittier, Los Angeles, California, United States |
| Address | | Rose Hills Memorial Park, 3888 Workman Mill Road, Whittier, California, USA | |
| Bapt.(LDS) | | 13 Mar 1912 | |
| Conf.(LDS) | | 13 Mar 1912 | |
| Init.(LDS) | | 31 Mar 1978 | Oakland California Temple |
| Endow.(LDS) | | 31 Mar 1978 | Oakland California Temple |
| SealP (LDS) | | BIC | |
| Spouse | | Robert Burns Sr. (1902-1962) | 14 Nov 1923 - Provo, Utah, Utah, United States[128,129] |
| SealS (LDS) | | 11 Oct 2008 | Sacramento California Temple |

**Events**

1. She appeared on the census on 10 May 1910 in Mount Pleasant, Sanpete, Utah, United States.[130]
Line 22 - McIntosh, Abram E, head, male, white, age 50, married (M1) for 26 years, born in Utah, father born in Scotland-English, mother born in Scotland-English, speaks english, farmer/sheep raiser, general farm, employer, can read and write, owns, mortgage free, house.
Line 23 - McIntosh, Mary Louise, wife, female, white, age 47, married (M1) for 26 years, had 7 children, 5 living, born in Utah, father born in Denmark-Danish, mother born in Denmark-Danish, speaks english, no occupation, can read and write.
Line 24 - McIntosh, Abram Vance, son, male, white, age 25, single, born in Utah, father born in Utah, mother born in Utah, speaks english, laborer, farm, employee, can read and write.
Line 25 - McIntosh, Anna Estella, daughter, female, white, age 20, single, born in Utah, father born in Utah, mother born in Utah, speaks english, dressmaker, at home, works on own account, can read and write, did not attend school.
Line 26 - McIntosh, Elvin Peter, son, male, white, age 17, single, born in Utah, father born in Utah, mother born in Utah, speaks english, no occupation, can read and write, attended school.
Line 27 - McIntosh, Vernon Marinous, son, male, white, age 15, single, born in Utah, father born in Utah, mother born in Utah, speaks english, no occupation, can read and write, attended school.
**Line 28 - McIntosh, Grace Maria, daughter, female, white, age 6, single, born in Utah, father born in Utah, mother born in Utah, speaks english, no occupation, attended school.**
Line 29 - Christensen, Marimous, brother-in-law, male, white, age 55, single, born in Denmark-Danish, father born in Denmark-Danish, mother born in Denmark-Danish, speaks english, laborer, sheep herd, employee, not out of work on Apr 15, 1910, 0 weeks unemployed in 1909, can read and write.

# Abraham Edward McIntosh and Mary Louise Guhl

2. She appeared on the census on 24 Jan 1920 in Mount Pleasant, Sanpete, Utah, United States.[131]
   Line 34 - McIntosh, A.E., head, owns home, mortgage free, male, white, age 59, married, can read and write, born in Utah, father born in Scotland-Scotch, mother born in Scotland-Scotch, speaks english, farmer, general farm, works on own account, farm #121.
   Line 35 - McIntosh, Mary L, wife, female, white, age 57, married, can reaad and write, born in Utah, father born in Denmark-DAnish, mother born in Denmark-Danish, speaks english, no occupation.
   Line 36 - McIntosh, Alvin, son, male, white, age 27, single, can read and write, born in Utah, father born in Utah, mother born in Utah, speaks english, farmer, general farm, employee.
   Line 37 - McIntosh, Vernon, son, male, white, age 25, single, can read and write, born in Utah, father born in Utah, mother born in Utah, speaks english, farmer, general farm, employee.
   **Line 38 - McIntosh, Grace M, daughter, female, white, age 16, single, attended school, can read and write, born in Utah, father born in Utah, mother born in Utah, speaks english, no occupation.**
3. She appeared on the census on 2 Apr 1930 in Salt Lake City, Salt Lake, Utah, United States.[132]
   Line 47 - Burns, Robert, head, rents home, $22.50 montly rental, owns radio set, does not live on farm, male, white, age 28, maried at age 21, did not attend school within year, can read and write, born in Utah, father born in Utah, mother born in Utah, able to speak english, salesman, bakery, wage worker, actually at work, not a veteran.
   **Line 48 - Burns, Grace M, wife, female, white, age 26, married at age 20, did not attend school within year, can read and write, born in Utah, father born in Utah, mother born in Utah, no occupation.**
   Line 49 - Burns, Kent M, son, male, white, age 2 10/12, single, did not attend school within year, born in Utah, father born in Utah, mother born in Utah, no occupation.
   Line 50 - Burns, Josephine, daughter, female, white, age 10, single, did attend school, can read and write, born in Utah, father born in Utah, mother born in Utah, able to speak english, no occupation.
4. She appeared on the census on 10 Apr 1940 in Montebello, Los Angeles, California, United States.[133]
   Line 80 - 671 Fraser Ave, rents house for $33, Burns, Robert, head, male, white, age 38, married, finished 4 years high school, born in Utah, lived in same place in 1935, in private work, worked 48 hours in week prior to census, truck driver for trucking, worked 52 weeks in 1939, earned $1820, no other source of income.
   Next page
   **Line 1 - Burns, Grace, wife, female, white, age 36, married, finished 4 years high school, born in Utah, lived in same place in 1935, not employed.**
   Line 2 - Burns, Kent M., son, male, white, age 12, single, in school 6th grade, born in Utah, lived in same place in 1935.
   Line 3 - Burns, Danny L., son, male, white, age 3, single, born in California.
   Line 4 - Burns Vyvian P., brother, male, white, age 1, single, born in Utah.

# Source Citations

1. Utah, State Department of Health, Certificate of Death, death certificate (1959), Abram Vance McIntosh names his father as Abram Edward McIntosh.

2. Utah, State Department of Health, Certificate of Death, death certificate state file no. 151 (1922), Varnon Marenous McIntosh names his father as Abraham E. McIntosh born in Utah.

3. Noble Warrum, editor, *Utah Since Statehood, Volumes 1-4*, 4 Volumes (Chicago, IL and Salt Lake City UT: S.J. Clarke Publishing Co., 1919), Volume III, A.E. McIntosh. Repository: Family History Library, 35 North West Temple Street, Salt Lake City, Utah 84150-3400, USA, Call Number: 979.2 H2.

4. Andrew Jenson, editor, *Latter-day Saint Biographical Encyclopedia: A Compilation of Biographical Sketches of Prominent Men and Women in The Church of Jesus Christ of Latter-day Saints*, 4 v.: ports. (Salt Lake City, Utah: Western Epics, 1971), Abraham Edward McIntosh: Vol 2, page 581. Repository: Family History Library, 35 North West Temple Street, Salt Lake City, Utah 84150-3400, USA, Call Number: 920.0792.

5. Utah, State Department of Health, Certificate of Death, death certificate File no. 84; Registrars No. 37 (1943), Abram Edward McIntosh.

6. Utah, State Department of Health, Certificate of Death, death certificate File No. 84; Registrar's No. 37. (1943), Abram Edward McIntosh.

7. Utah Division of State History, "Cemetery & Burial Database," database (https://heritage.utah.gov/history/cemeteries), Abram Edward McIntosh.

8. Brown, Beverly McIntosh and Marsha McIntosh, editors,*William McIntosh Diary 1857-1898, Abridgement* (Surprise, AZ: Self-published, June 2002).

9. Daughters of Utah Pioneers, *Our Pioneer Heritage* (Salt Lake City, UT: Infobases, Inc., 1996), 19: 422. Repository: Family History Library, 35 North West Temple Street, Salt Lake City, Utah 84150-3400, USA, Call Number: 979.2 H2.

10. Frank Esshorn, editor, *Pioneers and Prominent Men of Utah comprising Photographs-Genealogies-Biographies. Pioneers are those men and women who came to Utah by wagon, hand cart or afoot, between July 24, 1847 and December 30, 1868, before the railroad. Prominent Men are stake presidents, ward bishops, governors, members of the bench, etc., who came to Utah after the coming of the railroad. The early history of the Church of Jesus Christ of Latter-Day Saints. In One Volume, Illustrated* (Salt Lake City, Utah: Utah Pioneers Book Publishing Company, 1913), McIntosh, William: 331 and 1059. Repository: Family History Library, 35 North West Temple Street, Salt Lake City, Utah 84150-3400, USA, Call Number: 979.2 D3e.

11. Andrew Jenson, editor, *Latter-day Saint Biographical Encyclopedia: A Compilation of Biographical Sketches of Prominent Men and Women in The Church of Jesus Christ of Latter-day Saints*, 4 v.: ports. (Salt Lake City, Utah: Western Epics, 1971), William McIntosh: V 4, page 647. Repository: Family History Library, 35 North West Temple Street, Salt Lake City, Utah 84150-3400, USA, Call Number: 920.0792.

12. International Society of Daughters of Utah Pioneers, editor,*Pioneer Women of Faith and Fortitude*, Volume III (Salt Lake City, Utah: Publishers Press, 1998), Maria Caldwell McIntosh: page 1946. Repository: Family History Library, 35 North West Temple Street, Salt Lake City, Utah 84150-3400, USA, Call Number: 979 D36.

13. McIntosh Reunion Descendants, McIntosh - Descendants of John & Girsey (Grace) (Grizel) Rankin McIntosh (Attachment to Aug 17, 1958 Newsletter - copy in Collection of Bonnie S. Williams), Repository: Bonnie S. Williams, RR 1 Box 247, N Hwy 2, Wilburton, Oklahoma, USA.
Abram E. (son of William [McINTOSH] & Maria CALDWELL), md. Mary Louise GUHL
Children:
1. Abram Vance
2. William E.
3. Anne Estella
4. Elvin Peter
5. Vernon Marines
6. Vaughn
7. Grace.

Abram E. McINTOSH is a Grandson of John McINTOSH & Girsey RANKIN.
This single page attachment indicates that the parents of John McIntosh are William McIntosh & Isabell and is indicative of what our side of the family knew of our McIntosh cousins at that time in August 1958.

14. Brigham Young University-Idaho, "Western States Marriage Index," database (http://abish.byui.edu/specialCollections/westernStates/search.cfm), Abraham Edward McIntosh and Mary Louisa Guhl.

15. Noble Warrum, editor, *Utah Since Statehood, Volumes 1-4*, 4 Volumes (Chicago, IL and Salt Lake City UT: S.J. Clarke Publishing Co., 1919), III, A.E. McIntosh is named as married to Mary Louise Guhl. Repository: Family History Library, 35 North West Temple Street, Salt Lake City, Utah 84150-3400, USA, Call Number: 979.2 H2.

16. "Mary Louise G. McIntosh,"*Daughters of Utah Pioneers, Obituary Scrapbook, 1933-1939*; digital images. Repository: Ancestry.com, http://www.Ancestry.com.

17. Edmund West compiler, *"Family Data Collection - Individual Records," database, Ancestry.com, Provo, Utah* (2000), accessed 21 May 2004), Maria Leanora Mogensen. Name: Maria Leanora Mogensen, Spouse: , Parents: Peter Monsen Mogensen, Ane Kerstine Christensen, Birth Place: Sanpete, Mount Pleasant, UT, Birth Date: 13 May 1877, Death Place: Castle Dale, Emery, UT, Death Date: 21 April 1954.

Produced by: Beverly McIntosh Brown, 15933 W Silver Breeze Dr, Surprise, AZ 85374, 623-584-0440, starfighteraz@gmail.com : 29 Jun 2021

## Source Citations

18. Brigham Young University-Idaho, "Western States Marriage Index," database (http://abish.byui.edu/specialCollections/westernStates/search.cfm), Abraham E. McIntosh and Nora M. Beckstrom.

19. Utah, State Department of Health, Certificate of Death, death certificate (1943), Abram Edward McIntosh.

20. 1860 U.S. census, Shambip, Utah, population schedule, Clover, p. 450, dwelling 4028, family 3104, Abm E McIntosh; digital images, *ancestry.com*; citing National Archives and Records Administration microfilm M653.

21. 1870 U.S. census, Washington, Utah, population schedule, Panaaca, p. 7, dwelling 54, family 48, McIntosh, Abraham; digital images, *ancestry.com*; citing National Archives and Records Administration microfilm M593.

22. 1870 U.S. census, Lincoln, Nevada, population schedule, Meadow Valley, p. 186, dwelling 66-68, family 45, McIntosh, Abe; digital images, *ancestry.com*; citing National Archives and Records Administration microfilm M593.

23. 1880 U.S. census, Tooele, Utah Territory, population schedule, Clover, enumeration district (ED) 79, p. 6C, Mackintosh, Abraham; digital images, *ancestry.com*; citing National Archives and Records Administration microfilm T9.

24. Utah, Record of Marks and Brands for the State of Utah, December 31, 1884 to December 31, 1888: 44, 164, and 167, A.E. McIntosh, Mt. Pleasant, Sanpete Co; Utah State Archives and Record Service, Salt Lake City.

25. Utah, Record of Marks and Brands for the State of Utah; Utah State Archives and Record Service, Salt Lake City.

26. "Abraham Edward McIntosh," *Daughters of Utah Pioneers, Obituary Scrapbook, 1933-1939*; digital images. Repository: Ancestry.com, http://www.Ancestry.com.

27. Brown, Beverly McIntosh and Marsha Lee McIntosh,*William McIntosh Diary, abridgement* (Self-published, Surprise, AZ. June 2002), p 67 September 24 [1889].

28. Brown, Beverly McIntosh and Marsha Lee McIntosh,*William McIntosh Diary, abridgement* (Self-published, Surprise, AZ. June 2002), p 69 Oct. 3, 1890.

29. Brown, Beverly McIntosh and Marsha Lee McIntosh,*William McIntosh Diary, abridgement* (Self-published, Surprise, AZ. June 2002), p 76 June 24 [1893].

30. Brown, Beverly McIntosh and Marsha Lee McIntosh,*William McIntosh Diary, abridgement* (Self-published, Surprise, AZ. June 2002), p 81 March 17 & March 23 [1894].

31. Brown, Beverly McIntosh and Marsha Lee McIntosh,*William McIntosh Diary, abridgement* (Self-published, Surprise, AZ. June 2002), p 83 September 24 [1894] 1892.

32. Brown, Beverly McIntosh and Marsha Lee McIntosh,*William McIntosh Diary, abridgement* (Self-published, Surprise, AZ. June 2002), p 100 June 24 [1898].

33. Brown, Beverly McIntosh and Marsha Lee McIntosh,*William McIntosh Diary, abridgement* (Self-published, Surprise, AZ. June 2002), p 80 March 6, Monday [1894].
"We are still living in Mount Pleasant. We have had a long hard winter and the air is quite cold. I feel quite lonesome. There is none of the boys here now. J. F. McIntosh [William's son] is out on the desert with the sheep. A. E. McIntosh [son] is in Skull Valley working in the mines. J.A. McIntosh [son] is living on our farm in St. John with his family."
...

34. Church of Jesus Christ of Latter-day Saints, Temple Records Index Bureau (Salt Lake City, Utah, United States of America), McIntosh - Abraham Edward.

35. Brown, Beverly McIntosh and Marsha Lee McIntosh,*William McIntosh Diary, abridgement* (Self-published, Surprise, AZ. June 2002), p 82 July 20 [1894].
"A.E. McIntosh [William's son] is at work on the farm that belongs to him and me. The farm is located above Milburn, Sanpete County. Twelve miles or more north of Mt. Pleasant, Utah."

36. Brown, Beverly McIntosh and Marsha Lee McIntosh,*William McIntosh Diary, abridgement* (Self-published, Surprise, AZ. June 2002), p 82 September 23 [1894].
"Abe [William's son] has gone up to the ranch in Milburn, Sanpete, Utah, this week to thrash his wheat."

37. 1900 U.S. census, Sanpete, Utah, population schedule, Mt. Pleasant, enumeration district (ED) 128, sheet 21A, p. 197, dwelling 441, family 446, McIntosh, Abe; digital images, *ancestry.com*; citing National Archives and Records Administration microfilm T623.

38. Utah, Record of Marks and Brands for the State of Utah, Embracing All Marks ands Brands Recorded to June 1st, 1901, 91:A.E. McIntosh recorded July 26, 1900; 354:A.E. McIntosh recorded July 27, 1900; 320:A.E. McIntosh recorded July 27, 1900; Utah State Archives and Record Service, Salt Lake City.

39. Madsen, Hilda Madsen, compiler, and Mt. Plesant Pioneer Historical Association, "Mount Pleasant 1859-1939" (Salt Lake City, Utah, Stevens

# Source Citations


& Wallis, Inc., 1939), page 237. Repository: Family History Library, 35 North West Temple Street, Salt Lake City, Utah 84150-3400, USA, Call Number: 979.2563/M2 H2.

40. Church of Jesus Christ of Latter-day Saints, *Temple Records Index Bureau,* Salt Lake City, Utah, Church of Jesus Christ of Latter Day Saints, Record of Ordination, Mt. Pleasant, Utah. Repository: Family History Library, 35 North West Temple Street, Salt Lake City, Utah 84150-3400, USA.

41. Andrew Jenson, editor, *Latter-day Saint Biographical Encyclopedia: A Compilation of Biographical Sketches of Prominent Men and Women in The Church of Jesus Christ of Latter-day Saints*, 4 v.: ports. (Salt Lake City, Utah: Western Epics, 1971), Abraham Edward McIntosh: V 2, page 581. Repository: Family History Library, 35 North West Temple Street, Salt Lake City, Utah 84150-3400, USA, Call Number: 920.0792.

42. 1910 U.S. census, Sanpete, Utah, population schedule, Mt. Pleasant, enumeration district (ED) 156, sheet 15A, p. 167, dwelling 270, family 282, McIntosh, Abram E; digital images, *ancestry.com*; citing National Archives and Records Administration microfilm T624.

43. Utah, Record of Marks and Brands for the State of Utah, Embracing All Marks and Brands of Record to October 1st, 1912, 350:A.E. McIntosh recorded May 9, 1912; 343:A.E. McIntosh recorded May 9, 1912; 93:A.E. McIntosh recorded May 9, 1912; Utah State Archives and Record Service, Salt Lake City.

44. Bureau of Land Management, Record Group 49, *United States. General Land Office.* (Washington, D.C.: The National Archives), Patent No. 749034 issued 12 May 1920, Serial No. 018118, Receipt No. 2299229.

45. 1920 U.S. census, Sanpete, Utah, population schedule, Mount Pleasant, enumeration district (ED) 110, sheet 16A, p. 243, dwelling 303, family 308, McIntosh, A. E.; digital images (ancestry.com); citing National Archives and Records Administration microfilm T625.

46. 1930 U.S. census, Sanpete, Utah, population schedule, Milburn, enumeration district (ED) 20-19, sheet 2A, p. 116, dwelling 20, family 20, McIntosh, Abraham E.; digital images (ancestry.com); citing National Archives and Records Administration microfilm T626.

47. 1930 U.S. census, Sanpete, Utah, population schedule, Mount Pleasant, enumeration district (ED) 20-22, sheet 8B, p. 139, dwelling 153, family 156, McIntosh, Abraham E.; digital images (ancestry.com); citing National Archives and Records Administration microfilm T626.

48. 1940 U.S. census, Sanpete, Utah, population schedule, Mount Pleasant, enumeration district (ED) 20-26, sheet 11A, p. 201, household 214, McIntosh, A.E; digital images, *ancestry.com*; citing National Archives and Records Administration microfilm T627.

49. Church of Jesus Christ of Latter-day Saints, *Seventy's Certificate of Transfer with Seventy's Genealogy,* A.Vance McIntosh.

50. Utah, State Department of Health, Certificate of Death, death certificate (1959), Abram Vance McIntosh mother is Mary Guhl McIntosh.

51. Utah, State Department of Health, Certificate of Death, death certificate state file no. 151 (1922), Varnon Marenous McIntosh names his mother as Mary E. Guhl born in Utah.

52. Utah, State Department of Health, Certificate of Death, death certificate File no. 101; Registrar's no. 28 (1936), Mary Louise Guhl McIntosh.

53. Utah Division of State History, "Cemetery & Burial Database," database (https://heritage.utah.gov/history/cemeteries), Mary Louise Guhl McIntosh, A 34 3 2.

54. Utah, State Department of Health, Certificate of Death, death certificate state file no. 333 (1938), Gertrude Christensen Johnson names her mother as Mary Ann Petersen born in Denmark.

55. 1870 U.S. census, Tooele, Utah, population schedule, St Johns, p. 2, dwelling 11, family 11, Gool, Mary; digital images, *ancestry.com*; citing National Archives and Records Administration microfilm M593.

56. Lena McIntosh, Nancy Lena Guhl McIntosh Autobiography, Repository: Bonnie S. Williams, RR 1 Box 247, N Hwy 2, Wilburton, Oklahoma, USA.

57. Church of Jesus Christ of Latter-day Saints, *Patriarchal Blessing.*

58. 1880 U.S. census, Tooele, Utah Territory, population schedule, Clover, enumeration district (ED) 79, Gould, Mary; digital images, *ancestry*; citing National Archives and Records Administration microfilm T9.

59. Brown, Beverly McIntosh and Marsha Lee McIntosh, *William McIntosh Diary, abridgement* (Self-published, Surprise, AZ. June 2002), p 75 May 6 [1893].

60. 1900 U.S. census, Sanpete, Utah, population schedule, Mt. Pleasant, enumeration district (ED) 128, sheet 21A, p. 197, dwelling 441, family 446, McIntosh, Mary; digital images, *ancestry.com*; citing National Archives and Records Administration microfilm T623.

61. 1910 U.S. census, Sanpete, Utah, population schedule, Mt. Pleasant, enumeration district (ED) 156, sheet 15A, p. 167, dwelling 270, family 282, McIntosh, Mary Louise; digital images, *ancestry.com*; citing National Archives and Records Administration microfilm T624.

62. 1920 U.S. census, Sanpete, Utah, population schedule, Mount Pleasant, enumeration district (ED) 110, sheet 16A, p. 243, dwelling 303, family 308, McIntosh, Mary; digital images (ancestry.com); citing National Archives and Records Administration microfilm T625.

# Source Citations

63. 1930 U.S. census, Sanpete, Utah, population schedule, Mount Pleasant, enumeration district (ED) 20-22, sheet 8B, p. 139, dwelling 153, family 156, Mcintosh, Mary Louise; digital images (ancestry.com); citing National Archives and Records Administration microfilm T626.

64. Arizona Department of Health Services - Office of Vital Records, death certificate D-102 (1999), Edwin J. McIntosh, father is Abram Vance McIntosh.

65. Utah, State Department of Health, Certificate of Death, death certificate File no. (blank); Registrar's no. 17 (1966), Florence K. Monsen McIntosh spouse is Abram Vance McIntosh.

66. Utah, State Department of Health, Certificate of Death, death certificate state file no. 298 (1915), Robert Vance McIntosh names his father as Abraham Vance McIntosh born in Utah.

67. Utah State Department of Health, birth certificate Florence Fern McIntosh names her father as A.V. McIntosh and her mother as Florence K. Monsen.

68. Utah State Department of Health, birth certificate Edwin Jospeh McIntosh names his father as Abraham Vance McIntosh.

69. Church of Jesus Christ of Latter-day Saints, *Seventy's Certificate of Transfer with Seventy's Genealogy,* A. Vance McIntosh.

70. Utah, State Department of Health, Certificate of Death, death certificate File no. 59200053; Registrar's no. 24 (1959), Abram Vance McIntosh.

71. Utah Division of State History, "Cemetery & Burial Database," database (https://heritage.utah.gov/history/cemeteries), Abraham Vance McIntosh, grave B-6-2-4.

72. "Find A Grave," database (www.findagrave.com), Abram Vance McIntosh.

73. Arizona Department of Health Services - Office of Vital Records, death certificate D-102 (1999), Edwin J. McIntosh, mother is Florence Karna Monson.

74. Utah, State Department of Health, Certificate of Death, death certificate (1966), Florence Karna Monsen McIntosh spouse is Abram Vance McIntosh.

75. Utah, State Department of Health, Certificate of Death, death certificate state file no. 298 (1915), Robert Vance McIntosh names his mother as Florence Monsen born in Utah.

76. Utah State Department of Health, birth certificate Edwin Joseph McIntosh names his mother as Florence Monsen.

77. McIntosh Reunion Descendants, McIntosh - Descendants of John & Girsey (Grace) (Grizel) Rankin McIntosh (Attachment to Aug 17, 1958 Newsletter - copy in Collection of Bonnie S. Williams), Pages 1-2. Repository: Bonnie S. Williams, RR 1 Box 247, N Hwy 2, Wilburton, Oklahoma, USA.
Descendants of John McIntosh
24 Aug 2001, page 1 of 2
1. John McIntosh (b.25 Jun 1795-Croy,Invernesshire,Scotland;d.5 Mar 1875-Bountiful,Davis,Utah)
sp: Girsey Rankin (b.1794-Rutherglen,Lanarkshire,Scotland;m.15 Jun 1817;d.Apr 1853-Origan,Lucas,Ohio)...
2. William McIntosh (b.16 Sep 1819-Bridgeton,Lanark,Scotland;d.5 May 1899-Mt. Pleasant,Sanpete,Utah)
sp: Maria Caldwell (b.17 Feb 1824-Lanark,Upper Canada;m.26 Sep 1841;d.27 Jul 1897-Mt Pleasant,San Pete,Utah)...
3. Abram Edward McIntosh (b.4 Mar 1860-Clover,Tooele,Utah;d.14 Oct 1913)
sp: Mary Louisa Guhl (b.27 May 1862-Weber Canyon,Weber,Utah;m.1 Jan 1884;d.21 Aug 1936-Mt. Pleasant,S,Utah)
4. Abram Vance McIntosh (b.26 Apr 1885-St. John,Tooele,Utah)
sp: Florence Karma Monson (b.14 Sep 1887-Mt. Pleasant,Sanpete,Utah;m.16 Oct 1913)
5. Florence Fern McIntosh (b.16 Mar 1917-Mt. Pleasant,Sanpete,Utah;d.(See Notes))
sp: H. Chariton Jacobs (m.22 Jun 1939)
5. Joseph Edwin McIntosh (b.1 Sep 1919-Mt. Pleasant,Sanpete,Utah)
5. Jean Annette McIntosh (b.24 Mar 1926-Mt. Pleasant,Sanpete,Utah)
Descendants of John McIntosh
Page 2
24 Aug 2001
5. Donald V. McIntosh (b.30 Aug 1915-Payson,Sanpete,Utah).
4 children listed, no grandchildren listed.

78. Noble Warrum, editor, *Utah Since Statehood, Volumes 1-4*, 4 Volumes (Chicago, IL and Salt Lake City UT: S.J. Clarke Publishing Co., 1919), iii, Abraham Vance McIntosh states he married Florence Karna Monsen. Repository: Family History Library, 35 North West Temple Street, Salt Lake City, Utah 84150-3400, USA, Call Number: 979.2 H2.

79. 1900 U.S. census, Sanpete, Utah, population schedule, Mt. Pleasant, enumeration district (ED) 128, sheet 21A, p. 197, dwelling 441, family 446, McIntosh, A. Vance; digital images, *ancestry.com*; citing National Archives and Records Administration microfilm T623.

80. Church of Jesus Christ of Latter-day Saints, Temple Records Index Bureau (Salt Lake City, Utah, United States of America), McIntosh - Abraham Vance.

# Source Citations

81. Church of Jesus Christ of Latter-day Saints, *Patriarchal Blessing,* Given to Vance McIntosh by Moss Anderson.

82. 1910 U.S. census, Sanpete, Utah, population schedule, Mt. Pleasant, enumeration district (ED) 156, sheet 15A, p. 167, dwelling 270, family 282, McIntosh, Abram Vance; digital images, *ancestry.com*; citing National Archives and Records Administration microfilm T624.

83. Utah State Department of Health, birth certificate Florence Fern McIntosh names her father's occupation as electrician.

84. "U.S., World War I Draft Registration Cards, 1917-1918," database, Abraham Vance McIntosh.

85. 1920 U.S. census, Sanpete, Utah, population schedule, Mount Pleasant, enumeration district (ED) 110, sheet 17B, p. 244, dwelling 306, family 312, McIntosh, A. Vance; digital images (ancestry.com); citing National Archives and Records Administration microfilm T625.

86. 1930 U.S. census, Sanpete, Utah, population schedule, Milburn, enumeration district (ED) 20-19, sheet 2A, p. 116, dwelling 21, family 21, McIntosh, Vance; digital images (ancestry.com); citing National Archives and Records Administration microfilm T626.

87. 1930 U.S. census, Sanpete, Utah, population schedule, Mount Pleasant, enumeration district (ED) 20-22, sheet 18A, p. 149, dwelling 353, family 364, McIntosh, A. Vance; digital images (ancestry.com); citing National Archives and Records Administration microfilm T626.

88. 1940 U.S. census, Sanpete, Utah, population schedule, Mount Pleasant, enumeration district (ED) 20-26, sheet 8A, p. 138, household 146, McIntosh, Vance; digital images, *ancestry.com*; citing National Archives and Records Administration microfilm T627.

89. McIntosh Reunion Descendants, McIntosh - Descendants of John & Girsey (Grace) (Grizel) Rankin McIntosh (Attachment to Aug 17, 1958 Newsletter - copy in Collection of Bonnie S. Williams), Repository: Bonnie S. Williams, RR 1 Box 247, N Hwy 2, Wilburton, Oklahoma, USA.
William E. (son of Abram E. [McINTOSH] & Mary Louise GUHL).
William E. McINTOSH is a Great-Grandson of John McINTOSH & Girsey RANKIN
and is a Grandson of William McINTOSH & Maria CALDWELL
no other information
NOTE: Brother, Abram "Vance" McIntosh was actively involved in the McIntosh Clan and genealogy at this time.

90. McIntosh Reunion Descendants, McIntosh - Descendants of John & Girsey (Grace) (Grizel) Rankin McIntosh (Attachment to Aug 17, 1958 Newsletter - copy in Collection of Bonnie S. Williams), Page 2. Repository: Bonnie S. Williams, RR 1 Box 247, N Hwy 2, Wilburton, Oklahoma, USA. Descendants of John McIntosh
Page 1. 24 Aug 2001
1. John McIntosh (b.25 Jun 1795-Croy,Invernesshire,Scotland;d.5 Mar 1875-Bountiful,Davis,Utah)
sp: Girsey Rankin (b.1794-Rutherglen,Lanarkshire,Scotland;m.15 Jun 1817;d.Apr 1853-Origan,Lucas,Ohio)...
2. William McIntosh (b.16 Sep 1819-Bridgeton,Lanark,Scotland;d.5 May 1899-Mt. Pleasant,Sanpete,Utah)
sp: Maria Caldwell (b.17 Feb 1824-Lanark,Upper Canada;m.26 Sep 1841;d.27 Jul 1897-Mt Pleasant,San Pete,Utah)...
3. Abram Edward McIntosh (b.4 Mar 1860-Clover,Tooele,Utah;d.14 Oct 1913)
sp: Mary Louisa Guhl (b.27 May 1862-Weber Canyon,Weber,Utah;m.1 Jan 1884;d.21 Aug 1936-Mt. Pleasant,S,Utah)...
Descendants of John McIntosh
Page 2
24 Aug 2001...
4. William E. McIntosh (b.25 Feb 1887-St. John,Tooele,Utah;d.20 Dec 1891).
died age 5.

91. Utah Division of State History, "Cemetery & Burial Database," database (https://heritage.utah.gov/history/cemeteries), William Edward McIntosh, Mt. Pleasant City Cemetery grave A-99-3-1.

92. McIntosh Reunion Descendants, McIntosh - Descendants of John & Girsey (Grace) (Grizel) Rankin McIntosh (Attachment to Aug 17, 1958 Newsletter - copy in Collection of Bonnie S. Williams), Repository: Bonnie S. Williams, RR 1 Box 247, N Hwy 2, Wilburton, Oklahoma, USA.
Anne Estella (daughter of Abram E. [McINTOSH] & Mary Louise GUHL).
Anne Estella McINTOSH is a Great-Granddaughter of John McINTOSH & Girsey RANKIN
and is a Granddaughter of William McINTOSH & Maria CALDWELL
no other information
NOTE: Brother, Abram "Vance" McIntosh was actively involved in the McIntosh Clan and genealogy at this time.

93. California State Department of Health Services, Center for Health Statistics, "California. Death Index, 1940-1997," database, Anne Estelle McIntosh Schofield.

94. "Find A Grave," database (www.findagrave.com), Estelle Schofield, 37025159.

95. McIntosh Reunion Descendants, McIntosh - Descendants of John & Girsey (Grace) (Grizel) Rankin McIntosh (Attachment to Aug 17, 1958 Newsletter - copy in Collection of Bonnie S. Williams), Page 2. Repository: Bonnie S. Williams, RR 1 Box 247, N Hwy 2, Wilburton, Oklahoma, USA.
Descendants of John McIntosh
Page 1. 24 Aug 2001
1. John McIntosh (b.25 Jun 1795-Croy,Invernesshire,Scotland;d.5 Mar 1875-Bountiful,Davis,Utah)
sp: Girsey Rankin (b.1794-Rutherglen,Lanarkshire,Scotland;m.15 Jun 1817;d.Apr 1853-Origan,Lucas,Ohio)...
2. William McIntosh (b.16 Sep 1819-Bridgeton,Lanark,Scotland;d.5 May 1899-Mt. Pleasant,Sanpete,Utah)
sp: Maria Caldwell (b.17 Feb 1824-Lanark,Upper Canada;m.26 Sep 1841;d.27 Jul 1897-Mt Pleasant,San Pete,Utah)...

# Source Citations

3. Abram Edward McIntosh (b.4 Mar 1860-Clover,Tooele,Utah;d.14 Oct 1913)
sp: Mary Louisa Guhl (b.27 May 1862-Weber Canyon,Weber,Utah;m.1 Jan 1884;d.21 Aug 1936-Mt. Pleasant,S,Utah)...
Descendants of John McIntosh
Page 2. 24 Aug 2001...
4. Estella Anna McIntosh (b.24 Dec 1889-Mt. Pleasant,San Pete,Utah).
no husband or children listed.

96. "Utah, Select County Marriages, 1887-1937," database, Joseph W Schofield married Annie Estelle McIntosh on 2 Oct 1912 in Salt Lake City, Utah.

97. 1900 U.S. census, Sanpete, Utah, population schedule, Mt. Pleasant, enumeration district (ED) 128, sheet 21A, p. 197, dwelling 441, family 446, McIntosh Estella A; digital images,*ancestry.com*; citing National Archives and Records Administration microfilm T623.

98. 1910 U.S. census, Sanpete, Utah, population schedule, Mt. Pleasant, enumeration district (ED) 156, sheet 15A, p. 167, dwelling 270, family 282, McIntosh, Anna Estella; digital images,*ancestry.com*; citing National Archives and Records Administration microfilm T624.

99. Church of Jesus Christ of Latter-day Saints, Temple Records Index Bureau (Salt Lake City, Utah, United States of America), McIntosh - Annie Estelle.

100. 1920 U.S. census, Sanpete, Utah, population schedule, Mt Pleasant, enumeration district (ED) 110, sheet 16A, dwelling 305, family 310, Schofield, Estelle; digital images (ancestry.com); citing National Archives and Records Administration microfilm T625.

101. 1930 U.S. census, Salt Lake, Utah, population schedule, Salt Lake City, enumeration district (ED) 18-127, sheet 4B, p. 104, dwelling 87, family 93, Schofield, Stella; digital images (ancestry.com); citing National Archives and Records Administration microfilm T626.

102. 1940 U.S. census, Los Angeles, California, population schedule, Montebello, enumeration district (ED) 19-418, sheet 3A, p. 8091, household 53, Schofield, Estelle; digital images,*ancestry.com*; citing National Archives and Records Administration microfilm T627.

103. McIntosh Reunion Descendants, McIntosh - Descendants of John & Girsey (Grace) (Grizel) Rankin McIntosh (Attachment to Aug 17, 1958 Newsletter - copy in Collection of Bonnie S. Williams), Repository: Bonnie S. Williams, RR 1 Box 247, N Hwy 2, Wilburton, Oklahoma, USA.
Elvin Peter (son of Abram E. [McINTOSH] & Mary Louise GUHL).
Elvin Peter McINTOSH is a Great-Grandson of John McINTOSH & Girsey RANKIN
and is a Grandson of William McINTOSH & Maria CALDWELL
no other information
NOTE: Brother, Abram "Vance" McIntosh was actively involved in the McIntosh Clan and genealogy at this time.

104. California State Department of Health Services, Center for Health Statistics, "California. Death Index, 1940-1997," database, Elvin Peter McIntosh, born 28 Jan 1892, died 18 Mar 1958.

105. "Utah, Select County Marriages, 1887-1937," database, Elvin P McIntosh married Muriel McArthur on 27 Nov 1923 in Utah County, Utah.

106. 1900 U.S. census, Sanpete, Utah, population schedule, Mt. Pleasant, enumeration district (ED) 128, sheet 21A, p. 197, dwelling 441, family 446, McIntosh, Elvin P; digital images,*ancestry.com*; citing National Archives and Records Administration microfilm T623.

107. 1910 U.S. census, Sanpete, Utah, population schedule, Mt Pleasant, enumeration district (ED) 156, sheet 15A, p. 167, dwelling 272, family 284, McIntosh, Elvin Peter; digital images,*ancestry.com*; citing National Archives and Records Administration microfilm T624.

108. Church of Jesus Christ of Latter-day Saints, Temple Records Index Bureau (Salt Lake City, Utah, United States of America), McIntosh - Elvin Peter.

109. 1920 U.S. census, Sanpete, Utah, population schedule, Mount Pleasant, enumeration district (ED) 110, sheet 16A, p. 243, dwelling 303, family 308, McIntosh, Alvin; digital images (ancestry.com); citing National Archives and Records Administration microfilm T625.

110. 1930 U.S. census, Salt Lake, Utah, population schedule, Salt Lake City, enumeration district (ED) 18-2, sheet 8A, p. 18, dwelling 189, family 189, McIntosh, Elvin; digital images (ancestry.com); citing National Archives and Records Administration microfilm T626.

111. 1940 U.S. census, Los Angeles, California, population schedule, Los Angeles, enumeration district (ED) 60-847, sheet 16A, p. 16422, household 479, McIntosh, Elvin; digital images,*ancestry.com*; citing National Archives and Records Administration microfilm T627.

112. McIntosh Reunion Descendants, McIntosh - Descendants of John & Girsey (Grace) (Grizel) Rankin McIntosh (Attachment to Aug 17, 1958 Newsletter - copy in Collection of Bonnie S. Williams), Repository: Bonnie S. Williams, RR 1 Box 247, N Hwy 2, Wilburton, Oklahoma, USA.
Vaughn (son of Abram E. [McINTOSH] & Mary Louise GUHL).
Vaughn McINTOSH is a Great-Grandson of John McINTOSH & Girsey RANKIN
and is a Grandson of William McINTOSH & Maria CALDWELL
no other information
NOTE: Brother, Abram "Vance" McIntosh was actively involved in the McIntosh Clan and genealogy at this time.

113. Brown, Beverly McIntosh and Marsha Lee McIntosh,*William McIntosh Diary, abridgement* (Self-published, Surprise, AZ. June 2002), p 85 January 18 [1895]. "A. E. McIntosh [William's son], Mary McIntosh, his wife, presented him with a pair of twin boys. Mother and twins doing pretty well. These things happened in Mt. Pleasant. This may not be exactly the right date but it is pretty correct. Their names are Franklin Vaughn,

# Source Citations

Marinus Vernon. [Note: Franklin Vaughn died Feb 7, 1895]."

114. McIntosh Reunion Descendants, McIntosh - Descendants of John & Girsey (Grace) (Grizel) Rankin McIntosh (Attachment to Aug 17, 1958 Newsletter - copy in Collection of Bonnie S. Williams), Repository: Bonnie S. Williams, RR 1 Box 247, N Hwy 2, Wilburton, Oklahoma, USA.
Vernion Marines (son of Abram E. [McINTOSH] & Mary Louise GUHL). Vernon Marines McINTOSH is a Great-Grandson of John McINTOSH & Girsey RANKIN
and is a Grandson of William McINTOSH & Maria CALDWELL
no other information
NOTE: Brother, Abram "Vance" McIntosh was actively involved in the McIntosh Clan and genealogy at this time.

115. McIntosh Reunion Descendants, McIntosh - Descendants of John & Girsey (Grace) (Grizel) Rankin McIntosh (Attachment to Aug 17, 1958 Newsletter - copy in Collection of Bonnie S. Williams), Repository: Bonnie S. Williams, RR 1 Box 247, N Hwy 2, Wilburton, Oklahoma, USA.
Vernion Marines (son of Abram E. [McINTOSH] & Mary Louise GUHL).
Vernon Marines McINTOSH is a Great-Grandson of John McINTOSH & Girsey RANKIN
and is a Grandson of William McINTOSH & Maria CALDWELL
no other information
NOTE: Brother, Abram "Vance" McIntosh was actively involved in the McIntosh Clan and genealogy at this time.

116. Brown, Beverly McIntosh and Marsha Lee McIntosh,*William McIntosh Diary, abridgement* (Self-published, Surprise, AZ. June 2002), p 85 January 18 [1895].
"A. E. McIntosh [William's son], Mary McIntosh, his wife, presented him with a pair of twin boys. Mother and twins doing pretty well. These things happened in Mt. Pleasant. This may not be exactly the right date but it is pretty correct. Their names are Franklin Vaughn, Marinus Vernon. [Note: Franklin Vaughn died Feb 7, 1895]."

117. Utah, State Department of Health, Certificate of Death, death certificate state file no. 151 (1922), Varnon Marenus McIntosh.

118. Utah, State Department of Health, Certificate of Death, death certificate state file no. 151 (1922), Varnon Marenous McIntosh.

119. "Find A Grave," database (www.findagrave.com), Vernon Marenus McIntosh, 141916.

120. 1900 U.S. census, Sanpete, Utah, population schedule, Mt. Pleasant, enumeration district (ED) 128, sheet 21A, p. 197, dwelling 441, family 446, McIntosh, Vernon M; digital images,*ancestry.com*; citing National Archives and Records Administration microfilm T623.

121. 1910 U.S. census, Sanpete, Utah, population schedule, Mt. Pleasant, enumeration district (ED) 156, sheet 15A, p. 167, dwelling 270, family 282, McIntosh, Vernon Marinous; digital images,*ancestry.com*; citing National Archives and Records Administration microfilm T624.

122. "U.S., World War I Draft Registration Cards, 1917-1918," database, Vernon M. McIntosh.

123. 1920 U.S. census, Carbon, Utah, population schedule, Scofield, enumeration district (ED) 39, sheet 6A, p. 23, dwelling 109, family 110, McIntosh, Vernon; digital images (ancestry.com); citing National Archives and Records Administration microfilm T625.

124. 1920 U.S. census, Sanpete, Utah, population schedule, Mount Pleasant, enumeration district (ED) 110, sheet 16A, p. 243, dwelling 303, family 308, McIntosh, Vernon M.; digital images (ancestry.com); citing National Archives and Records Administration microfilm T625.

125. Church of Jesus Christ of Latter-day Saints, Temple Records Index Bureau (Salt Lake City, Utah, United States of America), McIntosh - Vernon Marinus.

126. McIntosh Reunion Descendants, McIntosh - Descendants of John & Girsey (Grace) (Grizel) Rankin McIntosh (Attachment to Aug 17, 1958 Newsletter - copy in Collection of Bonnie S. Williams), Repository: Bonnie S. Williams, RR 1 Box 247, N Hwy 2, Wilburton, Oklahoma, USA.
Grace (daughter of Abram E. [McINTOSH] & Mary Louise GUHL).
Grace McINTOSH is a Great-Granddaughter of John McINTOSH & Girsey RANKIN
and is a Granddaughter of William McINTOSH & Maria CALDWELL
no other information
NOTE: Brother, Abram "Vance" McIntosh was actively involved in the McIntosh Clan and genealogy at this time.

127. "U.S., Social Security Death Index, 1935-2014," database, Grace M. Burns.

128. McIntosh Reunion Descendants, McIntosh - Descendants of John & Girsey (Grace) (Grizel) Rankin McIntosh (Attachment to Aug 17, 1958 Newsletter - copy in Collection of Bonnie S. Williams), Page 2. Repository: Bonnie S. Williams, RR 1 Box 247, N Hwy 2, Wilburton, Oklahoma, USA.
Descendants of John McIntosh
Page 1. 24 Aug 2001
1. John McIntosh (b.25 Jun 1795-Croy,Invernesshire,Scotland;d.5 Mar 1875-Bountiful,Davis,Utah)
sp: Girsey Rankin (b.1794-Rutherglen,Lanarkshire,Scotland;m.15 Jun 1817;d.Apr 1853-Origan,Lucas,Ohio)...
2. William McIntosh (b.16 Sep 1819-Bridgeton,Lanark,Scotland;d.5 May 1899-Mt. Pleasant,Sanpete,Utah)
sp: Maria Caldwell (b.17 Feb 1824-Lanark,Upper Canada;m.26 Sep 1841;d.27 Jul 1897-Mt Pleasant,San Pete,Utah)...
3. Abram Edward McIntosh (b.4 Mar 1860-Clover,Tooele,Utah;d.14 Oct 1913)
sp: Mary Louisa Guhl (b.27 May 1862-Weber Canyon,Weber,Utah;m.1 Jan 1884;d.21 Aug 1936-Mt. Pleasant,S,Utah)...
Descendants of John McIntosh
Page 2. 24 Aug 2001...

# Source Citations

4. Grace McIntosh (b.6 Sep)
sp: Bert Burns.
no children listed
already found Robert Burns, called "Bert" as husband, from McIntosh Newsletters.

129. "Utah, Select County Marriages, 1887-1937," database, Robert Burns married Grace Maria McIntosh on 14 Nov 1923 in Utah County, Utah.

130. 1910 U.S. census, Sanpete, Utah, population schedule, Mt. Pleasant, enumeration district (ED) 156, sheet 15A, p. 167, dwelling 270, family 282, McIntosh, Grace Maria; digital images,*ancestry.com*; citing National Archives and Records Administration microfilm T624.

131. 1920 U.S. census, Sanpete, Utah, population schedule, Mount Pleasant, enumeration district (ED) 110, sheet 16A, p. 243, dwelling 303, family 308, McIntosh, Grace M.; digital images (ancestry.com); citing National Archives and Records Administration microfilm T625.

132. 1930 U.S. census, Salt Lake, Utah, population schedule, Salt Lake City, enumeration district (ED) 18-6, sheet 2A, p. 96, dwelling 35, family 35, Burns, Grace M.; digital images (ancestry.com); citing National Archives and Records Administration microfilm T626.

133. 1940 U.S. census, Los Angeles, California, population schedule, Montebello, enumeration district (ED) 19-419, sheet 5B, p. 8388, household 137, Burns, Grace; digital images,*ancestry.com*; citing National Archives and Records Administration microfilm T627.

# Lillian Elizabeth McIntosh and Heber Kimball McBride

| **Husband** | **Heber Kimball McBride**[1] | |
|---|---|---|
| Born | 16 May 1857 | Grantsville, Tooele, Utah Territory, United States[2] |
| Died | 14 Oct 1919 | Burley, Cassia, Idaho, United States[2,3] |
| Cause of Death | Nephritis (kidney infection) | |
| Buried | 17 Oct 1919 | Oakley, Cassia, Idaho, United States[4,5] |
| Address | Oakley Cemetery, R22 E Sec 4, Oakley, Idaho, USA | |
| Bapt.(LDS) | 10 Jun 1865 | |
| Conf.(LDS) | 10 Jun 1865 | |
| Init.(LDS) | 9 Oct 1882 | Endowment House |
| Endow.(LDS) | 9 Oct 1882 | Endowment House |
| Father | James John McBride (1818-1881) | |
| Mother | Olive Mehetable Cheney (1817-1904)[6] | |
| SealP (LDS) | BIC | |
| Marriage | 9 Oct 1882 | Salt Lake City, Great Salt Lake, Utah Territory, United States |
| SealS (LDS) | 9 Oct 1882 | Endowment House |

**Events**

1. He appeared on the census on 4 Jun 1900 in Oakley, Cassia, Idaho, United States.[7]
2. He appeared on the census on 29 Apr 1910 in Oakley, Cassia, Idaho, United States.[8]
3. His obituary was published in The South Idaho Press on 17 Oct 1919 in Burley, Cassia, Idaho, United States.[9]
   **Heber K. McBride**
   Heber K. McBride passed away at his home in Burley, Tuesday evening at the age of sixty two years. Funeral services will be held today - Thursday - at Oakley and interment made in the Oakley cemetery.

| **Wife** | **Lillian Elizabeth McIntosh**[10,11] | |
|---|---|---|
| AKA | Lilly McBride, Lilien Elisabeth McIntosh | |
| Born | 11 Jan 1863 | Saint John, Tooele, Utah Territory, United States[12,13,14] |
| Died | 21 May 1943 | Tremonton, Box Elder, Utah, United States[15,16] |
| Cause of Death | Yellow Fever//Senility | |
| Buried | 23 May 1943 | Oakley, Cassia, Idaho, United States |
| Address | Oakley Cemetery, R22 E Sec 4, Oakley, Idaho, USA | |
| Notes | Plot: 147 | |
| Bapt.(LDS) | 31 Aug 1873 | |
| Conf.(LDS) | 31 Aug 1873 | |
| Init.(LDS) | 9 Oct 1882 | Endowment House |
| Endow.(LDS) | 9 Oct 1882 | Endowment House |
| Father | William McIntosh (1819-1899)[17,18,19,20] | |
| Mother | Maria Caldwell (1824-1897)[21] | |
| SealP (LDS) | BIC | |

**Events**

1. She appeared on the census on 10 Jun 1870 in Panaca, Washington, Utah Territory.[22]
2. She appeared on the census on 28 Jul 1870 in Meadow Valley, Lincoln, Nevada, United States.[23]
   Line 22 - McIntosh, Wm age 50, male, white, farming, value of real estate 300, value of personal estate 800, born in Scotland, father and mother foreign born, male over 21.
   Line 23 - McIntosh, Marie, age 45, female, white, keeping house, born in Canada, father and mother foreign born.

Produced by: Beverly McIntosh Brown, 15933 W Silver Breeze Dr, Surprise, AZ 85374, 623-584-0440, starfighteraz@gmail.com : 29 Jun 2021

# Lillian Elizabeth McIntosh and Heber Kimball McBride

Line 24 - McIntosh, Wm H, age 21, male, white, farming, born in Missouri, father and mother foreign born, male over 21.
Line 25 - McIntosh, Frank, age 18, male, white, farming, born in Utah, father and mother foreign born.
Line 26 - McIntosh, Jane, age 16, female, white, at home, born in Utah, father and mother foreign born, attended school.
Line 27 - McIntosh, Alice, age 12, female, white, school, born in Utah, father and mother foreign born, attended school.
Line 28 - McIntosh, Abe, age 10, male, white, school, born in Utah, father and mother foreign born, attended school, cannot write.
**Line 29 - McIntosh, Lilly, age 7, female, white, in school, born in Utah, father and mother foreign born.**
Line 30 - McIntosh, Caroline, age 4, female, white, school, born in Utah, father and mother foreign born.
Line 31 - McIntosh, Albert, age 1, male, white, school, born in Nevada, father and mother foreign born.

3. She appeared on the census on 12 Jun 1880 in Clover, Tooele, Utah Territory, United States.[24]
4. She had a residence on 27 Jun 1893 in Oakley, Cassia, Idaho, United States.[25]
   "We had a letter from Lillian McBride. She is our daughter. She lives in Idaho. They are well."
5. She appeared on the census on 4 Jun 1900 in Oakley, Cassia, Idaho, United States.[26]
6. She appeared on the census on 29 Apr 1910 in Oakley, Cassia, Idaho, United States.[27]
7. She appeared on the census on 6 Jan 1920 in Burley, Cassia, Idaho, United States.[28]
8. She appeared on the census on 15 Apr 1930 in Los Angeles, Los Angeles, California, United States.[29]
9. She appeared on the census on 16 Apr 1940 in Boise, Ada, Idaho, United States.
10. She had a residence 21 May 1942-1943 in Tremonton, Box Elder, Utah, United States. Lived with her daughter Alice Ward.
11. Her obituary was published on 27 May 1943 in Burley, Cassia, Idaho, United States.[30]
    **Lilliam McBride Taken by Death**
    **Pioneer Resident Moved to Oakley in 1883**
    Funeral services for Mrs. Lillian E. McBride, who died May 21 at the home of her daughter, Mrs. Alice L. Ward at Tremonton, Utah, were held May 25 there. The body was taken to Oakley for interment, where graveside services were held at 4 p.m.
    Mrs. McBride was born Jan. 11, 1863, at St. John Utah. She was the daughter of William McIntosh and Maria Caldwell McIntosh.
    She married Heber K. McBride Oct. 9, 1882, in the old Endowment house in Salt Lake City. They moved to Oakley in 1883 and were pioneers of that section of the country.
    Mr. McBride died in 1919 in Burley. Mrs. McBride moved to Boise, where she was matron of the Children's home for six years. Since that time she has spent some time in Texas and California. The last few years whe has lived with her daughter,
    Mrs. Alice Ward of Tremonton.
    Mrs. McBride is survived by the following children: Mrs. Marie Sanford, Boise; J.W. McBride, Brigham City, Utah; E.H. McBride, Provo, Utah; Mrs. Alice Ward, Tremonton, Utah; Mrs. Kathryn Squire, Kansas City, Mo., and Mrs. Leah Collett, Columbus, S.C. She is also survived by 25 grandchildren and 15 great grandchildren.

**Events: Marriage**

1. Marriage Fact: Endowment House.

# Lillian Elizabeth McIntosh and Heber Kimball McBride

## Children

| 1 | F | **Marie McBride** [31,32] | |
|---|---|---|---|
| AKA | | Maria Sanforn | |
| Born | | 1 Aug 1883 | Grantsville, Tooele, Utah Territory, United States |
| Died | | 17 Feb 1967 | Boise, Ada, Idaho, United States |
| Buried | | 1967 | Boise, Ada, Idaho, United States[33] |
| Address | | Cloverdale Memorial Park, Boise, Idaho, USA | |
| Bapt.(LDS) | | 3 Sep 1891 | |
| Conf.(LDS) | | 3 Sep 1891 | |
| Init.(LDS) | | 29 Apr 1909 | Salt Lake Temple |
| Endow.(LDS) | | 29 Apr 1909 | Salt Lake Temple |
| SealP (LDS) | | 18 Mar 1981 | Idaho Falls Idaho Temple |
| Spouse | | Arthur Marion Sanford (1884-1971) | 29 Apr 1909 - Salt Lake City, Salt Lake, Utah, United States[34] |
| SealS (LDS) | | 29 Apr 1909 | Salt Lake Temple |

**Events**

1. She appeared on the census on 4 Jun 1900 in Oakley, Cassia, Idaho, United States.[35]
   Line 39 - McBride, Heber J, head, white, male, born May 1857, age 63, married for 17 years, born in Utah, father born in Ohio, mother born in Vermont, farmer, can read, write and speak english, owns farm mortgage free, form #15.
   Line 40 - McBride, Lillian E, wife, white, female, born Jan 1865, age 37, married 17 years, had 7 children, 6 living, born in Utah, father born in Scotland, mother born in Canada, can read, write and speak english.
   **Line 41 - McBride, Maria, daughter, white, female, born Aug 1883, age 16, single, born in Utah, father born in Utah, mother born in Utah, at school, can read, write and speak english.**
   Line 42 - McBride, James W, son, white, male, born Aug 1885, age 14, single, born in Idaho, father born in Utah, mother born in Utah, at school, can read, write and speak english.
   Line 43 - McBride, Heber E, son, white, male, born in Idaho, father born in Utah, mother born in Utah, at school.
   Line 44 - McBride, Alice S, daughter, white, female, born Nov 1892, age 7, single, born in Idaho, father born in Utah, mother born in Utah, at school.
   Line 45 - McBride, Edward V, son, white, male, born May 1895, age 5, single, born in Idaho, father born in Utah, mother born in Utah.
   Line 46 - McBride, Katherine J, daughter, white, female, born Feb 1898, aage 2, single, born in Idaho, father born in Utah, mother born in Utah.

2. She appeared on the census on 18 Apr 1910 in Locust, Cassia, Idaho, United States.
   Line 9 - Sanford, Arthur, head, male, white, age 26, married this year, born in Idaho, father born in USA, mother born in Utah, can read, write and speak english, farmer.
   **Line 10 - Sanford, Marie, wife, female, white, age 26, married within year, born in Utah, father born in Utah, mother born in Utah.**

3. She appeared on the census on 9 Jan 1920 in Burley, Cassia, Idaho, United States.
   Line 43 - Sanford, Arthur, head, male, white, age 36, married, can read, write and speak english, born in Idaho, father born in Utah, mother born in Utah, not employed.
   **Line 44 - Sanford, Marie, wife, female, white, age 37, married, can read, write and speak english, born in Utah both parents born in Utah.**
   Line 45 - Sanford, Wilma, daughter, female, white, age 10, single, in school, born in Utah, father born in Idaho, mother born in Utah.
   Line 46 - Sanford, Afra, daughter, female, white, age 8, single, in school, born in Idaho, father born in Idaho, mother born in Utah.
   Line 47 - Sanford, Laru, daughter, female, white, age 6, single, born in Idaho, father born in Idaho, mother born in Utah.
   Line 48 - Sanford, Halver, son, male, white, age 4 10/12, single, born in Idaho, father born in Idaho, mother born in Utah.
   Line 49 - Sanford, Lardel, daughter, female, white, age 2, single, born in Idaho, father born in Idaho, mother born in Utah.
   Line 50 - Sanford, Lowel C., brother, male, white, age 16, single, in school, born in Idaho, father born in Utah, mother

# Lillian Elizabeth McIntosh and Heber Kimball McBride

born in Utah.

4. She appeared on the census on 11 Apr 1930 in Boise, Ada, Idaho, United States.
Line 79 - Sanford, Arthur M, head, owns home valued at $2000, male, white, age 45, married at age 23, can read, write and speak english, born in Idaho, father born in Utah, mother born in Utah, employed as a painter.
**Line 80 - Sanford, Marie, wife, female, white, age 46, married at age 24, can read, write and speak english, born in Utah, both parents born in Utah.**
Line 81 - Sanford, Wilma, daughter, female, white, age 20, single, can read, write and speak english, born in Idaho, father born in Idaho, mother born in Utah, employed as stenographer at a department store, wage worker.
Line 82 - Sanford, Afra, daughter, female, white, age 18, single, in school, born in Idaho, father born in Idaho, mother born in Utah.
Line 83 - Sanford, Laru, daughter, female, white, age 16, single in school, born in Idaho, father born in Idaho, mother born in Utah.
Line 84 - Sanford, Lardel, daughter, female, white, age 10, single, in school, born in Idaho, father born in Idaho, mother born in Utah.
Line 85 - Sanford, Halver, son, male, white, age 14, single, in school, born in Idaho, father born in Idaho, mother born in Utah.
Line 86 - Sanford, Junella, daughter, female, white, age 5, single, born in Idaho, father born in Idaho, mother born in Utah.

5. She appeared on the census in Apr 1940 in Boise, Ada, Idaho, United States.
Line 68 - Sanford, AM, head, male, white, age 56, married, finished 2 years high school, born in Idaho, lived in same place in 1935, employed as janitor at cour house, earned $1100 last year.
**Line 69 - Sanford, Marie, wife, female, white, age 56, married, finished one year high school, born in Idaho, lived in same place in 1935.**
Line 70 - Sanford, Laru, daughter, female, white, age 26, single, finished high school, born in Idaho, lived in same place in 1935, employed as receptionist at dentist office, earned $468 last year.
Line 71 - Sanford, Junella, daughter, female, white, age 16, single, in first year high school, born in Idaho, lived in same place in 1935.

6. Her obituary was published in The Idaho Sunday Statesman on 19 Feb 1967 in Boise, Ada, Idaho, United States.
**Mrs. Marie Sanford**
Services for Mrs. Marie McBride Sanford, 83, 3503 State, who died early Friday morning at a Boise nursing home, will be conducted at 2:30 p.m. Monday at Relyea Chapel by Bishop Ronald Carter. Interment will follow at Cloverdale. Contributions to a favorite charity are suggested.
Born Aug. 1, 1883, in Grantsville, Utah, she was married to Arthur M. Sanford on April 29, 1909, in the Salt Lake City LDS Temple. They lived in Boise for many years until 1958, when they moved to Salt Lake City. They returned to Boise two years ago. Mrs. Sanford was a member of the LDS Church and was active in the Relief Society, singing mothers groups, Daughters of Utah Pioneers and the Republican Women's Club in Salt Lake City.
Survivors include her husband, Arthur, and a son, Hal, both of Boise; five daughters, Mrs. Wilma Jorgensen of Ogden, Mrs. Afra Blakeslee of West Covina, Calif., Mrs. Kay Warner of Mesa, Ariz., Mrs. Del Stivision of Boise and Mrs. Junella Couts of Miami, Fla.; three sisters, Mrs. Alice Ward of Salt Lake City, Mrs, Kathryn Squires of Baldwin Park, Calif., and Mrs. Leah Collett of Calgary, Albta., Canada; and 12 grandchildren and nine great-grandchildren.

# Lillian Elizabeth McIntosh and Heber Kimball McBride

| Children (cont.) | | |
|---|---|---|
| 2 M | **James William McBride** [36,37,38,39] | |
| AKA | Will McBride | |
| Born | 1 Aug 1885 | Oakley, Cassia, Idaho Territory, United States[2] |
| Died | 1 Dec 1960 | Tremonton, Box Elder, Utah, United States[2,40] |
| Buried | 3 Dec 1960 | Oakley, Cassia, Idaho, United States[41] |
| Address | Oakley Cemetery, R22 E Sec 4, Oakley, Idaho, USA | |
| Notes | Plot: 224 | |
| Bapt.(LDS) | 3 Aug 1893 | |
| Conf.(LDS) | 3 Aug 1893 | |
| Init.(LDS) | 6 Jul 1905 | Logan Utah Temple |
| Endow.(LDS) | 6 Jul 1905 | Logan Utah Temple |
| SealP (LDS) | 5 May 1981 | Logan Utah Temple |
| Spouse | Julia Maria Smith (1889-1930)[38] | 9 Apr 1909 - Salt Lake City, Salt Lake, Utah, United States[42] |
| SealS (LDS) | 29 Apr 1909 | Salt Lake Temple |
| Spouse | Clotilda Desire Beecher (1882-1960) | 11 Jul 1942 - Preston, Franklin, Idaho, United States |
| SealS (LDS) | 28 Apr 2004 | Logan Utah Temple |

**Events**

1. He appeared on the census on 4 Jun 1900 in Oakley, Cassia, Idaho, United States.[43]
   Line 39 - McBride, Heber J, head, white, male, born May 1857, age 63, married for 17 years, born in Utah, father born in Ohio, mother born in Vermont, farmer, can read, write and speak english, owns farm mortgage free, farm #15.
   Line 40 - McBride, Lillian E, wife, white, female, born Jan 1865, age 37, married 17 years, had 7 children, 6 living, born in Utah, father born in Scotland, mother born in Canada, can read, write and speak english.
   Line 41 - McBride, Maria, daughter, white, female, born Aug 1883, age 16, single, born in Utah, father born in Utah, mother born in Utah, at school, can read, write and speak english.
   **Line 42 - McBride, James W, son, white, male, born Aug 1885, age 14, single, born in Idaho, father born in Utah, mother born in Utah, at school, can read, write and speak english.**
   Line 43 - McBride, Heber E, son, white, male, born in Idaho, father born in Utah, mother born in Utah, at school.
   Line 44 - McBride, Alice S, daughter, white, female, born Nov 1892, age 7, single, born in Idaho, father born in Utah, mother born in Utah, at school.
   Line 45 - McBride, Edward V, son, white, male, born May 1895, age 5, single, born in Idaho, father born in Utah, mother born in Utah.
   Line 46 - McBride, Katherine J, daughter, white, female, born Feb 1898, age 2, single, born in Idaho, father born in Utah, mother born in Utah.

2. He appeared on the census on 27 Apr 1910 in Oakley, Cassia, Idaho, United States.
   **Line 8 - McBride, William J, head, male, white, age 24, single, married one year, born in Idaho, both parents born in Utah, employed as sheep shearer, wage worker, can read, write and speak english, owns house mortgage free.**
   Line 9 - McBride, Julia, wife, female, white, age 20, single, married one year, born in Idaho, both parents born in Utah, can read, write and speak english, not employed.

3. Draft Registration: World War I, 12 Sep 1918, Albion, Cassia, Idaho, United States.[44]
   Occupation: Mgr. Creamery for Mutual Creamery Co. in Burley, Idaho.
   Wife: Julia M. McBride in Burley, Idaho.
   Description: medium height, medium build, blue eyes, light hair.

4. He appeared on the census on 3 Jan 1920 in Burley, Cassia, Idaho, United States.
   **Line 44 - McBride, James, head, rents home, male, white, age 35, married, can read, write and speak english, born in Idaho, both parents born in Utah, employed as salesman for drygoods, wage worker.**

Produced by: Beverly McIntosh Brown, 15933 W Silver Breeze Dr, Surprise, AZ 85374, 623-584-0440, starfighteraz@gmail.com : 29 Jun 2021

# Lillian Elizabeth McIntosh and Heber Kimball McBride

Line 45 - McBride, Julia, wife, female, white, age 29, married, can read, write and speak english, born in Idaho, both parents born in Utah.
Line 46 - McBride, Verda, daughter, female, white, age 9, single, in school, born in Idaho, both parents born in Idaho.
Line 47 - McBride, Asahel, son, male, age 8, single, in school, born in Idaho, both parents born in Idaho.
Line 48 - McBride, Fern, daughter, female, white, age 6, single, in school, born in Idaho, both parents born in Idaho.
Line 49 - McBride, Cleavland, son, male, white, age 2 6/12, single, born in Idaho, both parents born in Idaho.
Line 50 - McBride, Jene, son, male, age 2/12, single, born in Idaho, both parents born in Idaho.

5. He appeared on the census on 4 Apr 1930 in Burley, Cassia, Idaho, United States.
**Line 93 - McBride, J William, head, rents home for $17/month, does not own a radio, male, white, age 44, married at age 23, can read, write and speak english, born in Idaho, both parents born in Utah, employed as truck driver for a laundry, wage worker, not a veteran.**
Line 94 - McBride, Julia, wife, female, white, age 40, married at age 19, can read, write and speak english, born in Idaho, both parents born in Utah.
Line 95 - McBride, Asahel V, son, male, white, age 18, single, in school, born in Idaho, both parents born in Idaho.
Line 96 - McBride, Fern, daughter, female, white, age 16, single, in school, born in Idaho, both parents born in Idaho.
Line 97 - McBride, Cleaveland S., son, male, white, age 13, single, in school, born in Idaho, both parents born in Idaho.
Line 98 - McBride, Harold W., son, male, white, age 9, single, in school, born in Idaho, both parents born in Idaho.
Line 99 - McBride, Wayne S., son, male, white, age 8, single, in school, born in Idaho, both parents born in Idaho.
Line 11 - McBride, Horton D., son, male, white, age 5, single, born in Utah, both parents born in Idaho.

6. He appeared on the census on 22 Apr 1940 in Salt Lake City, Salt Lake, Utah, United States.
**Line 25 - McBride, James W., head, male, white, age 55, widowed, finished 8th grade, born in Idaho, in 1935 lived in Elba, Cassia, Idaho, owns a farm, farmer.**
Line 26 - McBride, Cleveland S., son, male, white, age 22, single, born in Idaho, in 1935, lived in Elba, Cassia, Idaho, laborer on a farm.
Line 27 - McBride, Wayne S., son, male, white, age 18, single, finished 3rd year of high school, born in Idaho, in 1935 lived in Elba, Cassia, Idaho, farm laborer.

7. His obituary was published after 1 Dec 1960.
**OBITUARY OF JAMES WILLIAM MCBRIDE**
James William McBride was born Aug. 1, 1885 at Oakley Idaho to Heber Kimball and Lillian Mcintosh McBride. He married Julia M. Smith April 29, 1909, in the Salt Lake Temple, Church of Jesus Christ of Latter Day Saints. She died July 10, 1930.
He married married Cloe Beecher Ward July 11, 1941 at Preston, Idaho.
He is survived by five sons and two daughters, Asahel V. and Horton D., both Salt Lake City; Harold W. and Mrs. Archie (Verda) Ball, both Blackfoot, Idaho; Capt. Wayne S., U. S. Air Force, Okinawa; Lt. J. Lynn, U. W. Air Force, Spokane, Wash.; and Mrs. Lewis (Fern) Moncur, Aberdeen, Idaho.
Also surviving are 18 grandchildren, a brother, and four sisters.
Funeral services were Saturday, Dec. 5 at 11 a.m. in the Tremonton Second L.D.S. chapel. Burial was in the Oakley. Idaho, Cemetery

# Lillian Elizabeth McIntosh and Heber Kimball McBride

| Children (cont.) | | |
|---|---|---|
| **3 F** | **Olive Marian McBride** [45] | |
| AKA | Mamie McBride | |
| Born | 10 Apr 1888 | Oakley, Cassia, Idaho Territory, United States |
| Died | 9 May 1900 | Oakley, Cassia, Idaho, United States |
| Buried | May 1900 | Oakley, Cassia, Idaho, United States |
| Address | Oakley Cemetery, R22 E Sec 4, Oakley, Idaho, USA | |
| Bapt.(LDS) | 23 Aug 1896 | |
| Conf.(LDS) | 23 Aug 1896 | |
| Init.(LDS) | 30 Jul 1924 | Logan Utah Temple |
| Endow.(LDS) | 30 Jul 1924 | Logan Utah Temple |
| SealP (LDS) | BIC | |
| Spouse | This person had no known marriage and no known children | |
| **4 M** | **Ephraim Heber McBride** [47] | |
| AKA | Edgar McBride,[46] Heber E. McBride | |
| Born | 25 Aug 1890 | Oakley, Cassia, Idaho, United States |
| Died | 16 Nov 1965 | Oakland, Alameda, California, United States[48] |
| Buried | 19 Nov 1965 | Oakland, Alameda, California, United States[49] |
| Address | Evergreen Cemetery, 6450 Camden Street, Oakland, California 94605, USA | |
| Bapt.(LDS) | 6 Aug 1899 | |
| Conf.(LDS) | 6 Aug 1899 | |
| Init.(LDS) | 1 Aug 1923 | Logan Utah Temple |
| Endow.(LDS) | 1 Aug 1923 | Logan Utah Temple |
| SealP (LDS) | BIC | |
| Spouse | Lydia Campbell (1892-1970) | 11 Dec 1911 - Oakley, Cassia, Idaho, United States. (Divorced after 4 Apr 1940) [50] |
| SealS (LDS) | 1 Aug 1923 | |
| Spouse | Estella Mae Bates (1889-1955) | 1 Apr 1945 - Richmond, Contra Costa, California, United States. (Divorced) |
| SealS (LDS) | 5 Jan 1999 | Jordan River Utah Temple |
| Spouse | Bessie Henrietta Hansen (1895-1973) | |
| Marr. Date | 6 Jul 1956 - Oakland, Alameda, California, United States. (Death of one spouse) | |
| SealS (LDS) | 22 Apr 1958 | Los Angeles California Temple |

**Events**

1. He appeared on the census on 4 Jun 1900 in Oakley, Cassia, Idaho, United States.[51]
   Line 39 - McBride, Heber J, head, white, male, born May 1857, age 63, married for 17 years, born in Utah, father born in Ohio, mother born in Vermont, farmer, can read, write and speak english, owns farm mortgage free, form #15.
   Line 40 - McBride, Lillian E, wife, white, female, born Jan 1865, age 37, married 17 years, had 7 children, 6 living, born in Utah, father born in Scotland, mother born in Canada, can read, write and speak english.
   Line 41 - McBride, Maria, daughter, white, female, born Aug 1883, age 16, single, born in Utah, father born in Utah, mother born in Utah, at school, can read, write and speak english.
   Line 42 - McBride, James W, son, white, male, born Aug 1885, age 14, single, born in Idaho, father born in Utah, mother born in Utah, at school, can read, write and speak english.
   **Line 43 - McBride, Heber E, son, white, male, born in Idaho, age 9, father born in Utah, mother born in Utah, at school.**
   Line 44 - McBride, Alice S, daughter, white, female, born Nov 1892, age 7, single, born in Idaho, father born in Utah, mother born in Utah, at school.
   Line 45 - McBride, Edward V, son, white, male, born May 1895, age 5, single, born in Idaho, father born in Utah, mother

Produced by: Beverly McIntosh Brown, 15933 W Silver Breeze Dr, Surprise, AZ 85374, 623-584-0440, starfighteraz@gmail.com : 29 Jun 2021

# Lillian Elizabeth McIntosh and Heber Kimball McBride

born in Utah.
Line 46 - McBride, Katherine J, daughter, white, female, born Feb 1898, aage 2, single, born in Idaho, father born in Utah, mother born in Utah.

2. He appeared on the census on 29 Apr 1910 in Oakley, Cassia, Idaho, United States.[52]
   Line 60 - McBride, Heber K, head, male, white, age 58, married once for 28 years, born in Utah, father born in Ohio, mother born in USA, speaks english, farmer, can read and write, owns farm, mortgage free, farm #15.
   Line 61 - McBride, Lillian E, wife, female, white, age 47, married once for 28 years, had 8 children, 6 living, born in Utah, father born in USA, mother born in USA, speaks english, can read and write.
   **Line 62 - McBride, Heber E, son, male, white, age 19, single, born in Idaho, father born in Utah, mother born in Utah, speaks english, helps on farm, can read and write, in school.**
   Line 63 - McBride, Alice L, daughter, female, white, age 17, single, born in Idaho, father born in Utah, mother born in Utah, speaks english, helps on farm, can read and write in school.
   Line 64 - McBride, Kathryn J, daughter, female, white, age 12, single, born in Idaho, father born in Utah, mother born in Utah, speaks english, can read and write, in school.
   Line 65 - McBride, Leah, daughter, female, white, age 6, single, born in Idaho, father born in Utah, mother born in Utah, speaks english.

3. Draft Registration: World War I, 5 Jun 1917, Oakley, Cassia, Idaho, United States.[53]
   Occupation: farmer.
   Wife and 3 children.
   Description: short height, stout build, blue eyes, brown hair.

4. He appeared on the census on 2 Apr 1930 in Sandy, Salt Lake, Utah, United States.
   **Line 94 - McBride, Edgar (Ephraim), head, rents home for $12/month, male, white, age 36, married at age 21, can read, write and speak english, born in Idaho, both parents born in Utah, laborer at steel mill, not a veteran.**
   Line 95 - McBride, Lydi (Lydia), wife, female, white, age 35, married at age 19, can read, write and speak english, born in Utah, both parents born in Iowa.
   Line 96 - McBride, Ralph, son, male, white, age 17, single, in school, born in Idaho, father born in Idaho, mother born in Utah.
   Line 97 - McBride, Adrin, son, male, white, age 15, single, in school, born in Idaho, father born in Idaho, mother born in Utah.
   Line 98 - McBride, Mateland, son, male, white, age 13, single, in school, born in Idaho, father born in Idaho, mother born in Utah.
   Line 99 - McBride, Wanda, daughter, female, white, age 11, single, in school, born in Idaho, father born in Idaho, mother born in Utah.
   Line 100 - McBride, Leo, son, male, white, age 9, single, in school, born in Idaho, father born in Idaho, mother born in Utah.
   **Note: go to sheet 5, line 96.** (Somehow, Dorothy got separated from her family. She is on sheet 5, line 96).

5. He appeared on the census on 5 Apr 1940 in Provo, Utah, Utah, United States.
   **Line 12 - McBride, Ephraim, head, male, white, age 49, married, finished 2 years high school, born Idaho, lived in same house in 1935, employed as carpenter at finishing company, earned $880 last year.**
   Line 13 - McBride, Lydia, wife, female, white, age 47, married, finished 8 years school, born in Utah, lived in same house in 1935.
   Line 14 - McBride, Adrian E., son, male, white, age 25, single, finished 2 years high school, born in Idaho, lived in same house in 1935, employed as chouffer for a taxi, earned $120 last year.
   Line 15 - McBride, Mateland, son, male, white, age 23, single, finished 2 years college, born in Idaho, lived in same house in 1935, employed as chouffer for a taxi, earned $480 last year.
   Line 16 - McBride, Dorothy, daughter, female, white, age 11, single, in 3rd grade, born in Utah.

# Lillian Elizabeth McIntosh and Heber Kimball McBride

| Children (cont.) | | |
|---|---|---|
| 5 F | **Alice Lillian McBride** [54] | |
| Born | 15 Nov 1892 | Oakley, Cassia, Idaho, United States |
| Died | 29 Mar 1986 | Boise, Ada, Idaho, United States[55] |
| Buried | 1 Apr 1986 | Salt Lake City, Salt Lake, Utah, United States[56] |
| Address | Salt Lake City Cemetery, 200 North (4th Ave) "N" Street, Salt Lake City, Utah 84103, US~ | |
| Notes | Plot: West, 14, 36, 5E | |
| Bapt.(LDS) | 14 Jul 1901 | |
| Conf.(LDS) | 14 Jul 1901 | |
| Init.(LDS) | 12 Nov 1914 | Salt Lake Temple |
| Endow.(LDS) | 12 Nov 1914 | Salt Lake Temple |
| SealP (LDS) | BIC | |
| Spouse | Moroni William Ward (1890-1967) | 12 Nov 1914 - Salt Lake City, Salt Lake, Utah, United States[57,58] |
| SealS (LDS) | 12 Nov 1914 | Salt Lake Temple |

**Events**

1. She appeared on the census on 4 Jun 1900 in Oakley, Cassia, Idaho, United States.[59]
Line 39 - McBride, Heber J, head, white, male, born May 1857, age 63, married for 17 years, born in Utah, father born in Ohio, mother born in Vermont, farmer, can read, write and speak english, owns farm mortgage free, form #15.
Line 40 - McBride, Lillian E, wife, white, female, born Jan 1865, age 37, married 17 years, had 7 children, 6 living, born in Utah, father born in Scotland, mother born in Canada, can read, write and speak english.
Line 41 - McBride, Maria, daughter, white, female, born Aug 1883, age 16, single, born in Utah, father born in Utah, mother born in Utah, at school, can read, write and speak english.
Line 42 - McBride, James W, son, white, male, born Aug 1885, age 14, single, born in Idaho, father born in Utah, mother born in Utah, at school, can read, write and speak english.
Line 43 - McBride, Heber E, son, white, male, born in Idaho, father born in Utah, mother born in Utah, at school.
**Line 44 - McBride, Alice L, daughter, white, female, born Nov 1892, age 7, single, born in Idaho, father born in Utah, mother born in Utah, at school.**
Line 45 - McBride, Edward V, son, white, male, born May 1895, age 5, single, born in Idaho, father born in Utah, mother born in Utah.
Line 46 - McBride, Katherine J, daughter, white, female, born Feb 1898, age 2, single, born in Idaho, father born in Utah, mother born in Utah.

2. She appeared on the census on 29 Apr 1910 in Oakley, Cassia, Idaho, United States.[60]
Line 60 - McBride, Heber K, head, male, white, age 58, married once for 28 years, born in Utah, father born in Ohio, mother born in USA, speaks english, farmer, can read and write, owns farm, mortgage free, farm #15.
Line 61 - McBride, Lillian E, wife, female, white, age 47, married once for 28 years, had 8 children, 6 living, born in Utah, father born in USA, mother born in USA, speaks english, can read and write.
Line 62 - McBride, Heber E, son, male, white, age 19, single, born in Idaho, father born in Utah, mother born in Utah, speaks english, helps on farm, can read and write, in school.
**Line 63 - McBride, Alice L, daughter, female, white, age 17, single, born in Idaho, father born in Utah, mother born in Utah, speaks english, helps on farm, can read and write in school.**
Line 64 - McBride, Kathryn J, daughter, female, white, age 12, single, born in Idaho, father born in Utah, mother born in Utah, speaks english, can read and write, in school.
Line 65 - McBride, Leah, daughter, female, white, age 6, single, born in Idaho, father born in Utah, mother born in Utah, speaks english.

3. She appeared on the census on 6 Mar 1920 in Marchfield, Cassia, Idaho, United States.
Line 51 - Ward, M.W., head, owns home, lives on a farm, male, white, age 29, married, can read, write and speak

# Lillian Elizabeth McIntosh and Heber Kimball McBride

english, born in Idaho, both parents born in Utah, farmer on own farm, farm number 115.
**Line 52 - Ward, Alice L., wife, female, white, age 27, married, can read, write and speak english, born in Idaho, both parents born in Utah.**
Line 53 - Ward, Lorna, daughter, female, white, age 4/12, single, born in Idaho, both parents born in Idaho.

4. She appeared on the census on 22 Apr 1930 in Declo, Cassia, Idaho, United States.
Line 22 - Ward, Moroni W, head, owns home, lives on a farm, male, white, age 39, married at age 25, can read, write and speak english, born in Idaho, both parents born in Utah, farmer on own farm, not a veteran, farm number 37.
**Line 23 - Ward, Alice L, wife, female, white, age 37, married at age 23, can read, write and speak english, born in Idaho, both parents born in Utah,**
Line 24 - Ward, Lorna, daughter, female, white, age 10, single, in school, born in Idaho, both parents born in Utah.

5. She appeared on the census on 16 Apr 1940 in Boise, Ada, Idaho, United States.
Line 29 - Ward, Moroni W, head, male, white, age 50, married, finished high school, born in Idaho, in 1935 lived in Declo, Cassia, Idaho, employed as a barber earned $550 last year.
**Line 30 - Ward, Alice L, wife, female, white, age 47, married, finished high school, born in Idaho, in 1935 lived in Declo, Cassia, Idaho, employed as saleslady in cosmetics.**
Line 31 - McBride, Lillian E., mother-in-law, female, white, age 77, widowed, born in Utah, in 1935 lived in Declo, Cassia, Idaho.

6. She had a residence between 1942 and 1943 in Tremonton, Box Elder, Utah, United States. Her mother died in her home.

7. Her obituary was published.
**Alice Ward**
Boise - Alice Lillian McBride Ward, 93, Boise and former Oakley resident, died March 29 at Boise Samaritan Village. She was born Nov. 15, 1892 at Oakley, the daughter of Heber K. and Lillian McIntosh McBride. She married Moroni W. Ward Nov. 12, 1914, in the Salt Lake LDS Temple. He died in 1967. They had lived in Declo for many years, and had later lived in Boise, Tremonton and Salt Lake City. She had lived in Denver and then Boise after the death of her husband. She had owned and operated a nursing home in Salt Lake; was a retired LPN reflexologist; operated several health salons; and was a member of the LDS Church, serving as a teacher and in various auxiliaries. She is survived by one daughter, Mrs. Neal R. (Lorna) Olson, Salt Lake; one sister, Leah Collett, Canada; four grandchildren; 16 great-grandchildren; and four great-great-grandchildren. The funeral and burial were held in Salt Lake April 1.

| 6 | M | **Edward Vaughn McBride** [61] | |
|---|---|---|---|
| AKA | | E. Vaughn McBride[2] | |
| Born | | 9 May 1895 | Oakley, Cassia, Idaho, United States[2] |
| Died | | 20 Mar 1905 | Oakley, Cassia, Idaho, United States[2] |
| Buried | | Mar 1905 | Oakley, Cassia, Idaho, United States[62] |
| Address | | Oakley Cemetery, R22 E Sec 4, Oakley, Idaho, USA | |
| Notes | | Plot 147 | |
| Bapt.(LDS) | | Child | |
| Conf.(LDS) | | Child | |
| Init.(LDS) | | Child | |
| Endow.(LDS) | | Child | |
| SealP (LDS) | | BIC | |
| Spouse | | This person had no known marriage and no known children | |

**Events**

1. He appeared on the census on 4 Jun 1900 in Oakley, Cassia, Idaho, United States.[63]
Line 39 - McBride, Heber J, head, white, male, born May 1857, age 63, married for 17 years, born in Utah, father born in Ohio, mother born in Vermont, farmer, can read, write and speak english, owns farm mortgage free, form #15.
Line 40 - McBride, Lillian E, wife, white, female, born Jan 1865, age 37, married 17 years, had 7 children, 6 living, born in Utah, father born in Scotland, mother born in Canada, can read, write and speak english.
Line 41 - McBride, Maria, daughter, white, female, born Aug 1883, age 16, single, born in Utah, father born in Utah,

# Lillian Elizabeth McIntosh and Heber Kimball McBride

mother born in Utah, at school, can read, write and speak english.
Line 42 - McBride, James W, son, white, male, born Aug 1885, age 14, single, born in Idaho, father born in Utah, mother born in Utah, at school, can read, write and speak english.
Line 43 - McBride, Heber E, son, white, male, born in Idaho, father born in Utah, mother born in Utah, at school.
Line 44 - McBride, Alice S, daughter, white, female, born Nov 1892, age 7, single, born in Idaho, father born in Utah, mother born in Utah, at school.
**Line 45 - McBride, Edward V, son, white, male, born May 1895, age 5, single, born in Idaho, father born in Utah, mother born in Utah.**
Line 46 - McBride, Katherine J, daughter, white, female, born Feb 1898, aage 2, single, born in Idaho, father born in Utah, mother born in Utah.

| 7 F | **Kathryn Jane McBride**[64] | |
|---|---|---|
| AKA | Kathryn Livingston, Katherine McBride, Kathryn Squire | |
| Born | 2 Feb 1898 | Oakley, Cassia, Idaho, United States |
| Died | 15 Jun 1975 | Baldwin Park, Los Angeles, California, United States[65] |
| Buried | Jun 1975 | Whittier, Los Angeles, California, United States[66] |
| Address | Rose Hills Memorial Park, 3888 Workman Mill Road, Whittier, California, USA | |
| Notes | Plot: Cumorah Lawn, Lot 2212, Grave 4 | |
| Bapt.(LDS) | 19 May 1906 | |
| Conf.(LDS) | 19 May 1906 | |
| Init.(LDS) | 8 Jun 1916 | Salt Lake Temple |
| Endow.(LDS) | 8 Jun 1916 | Salt Lake Temple |
| SealP (LDS) | BIC | |
| Spouse | Leonard Campbell Livingston (1895-1937) | |
| Marr. Date | 7 Jun 1916 - Salt Lake City, Salt Lake, Utah, United States. (Death of one spouse)[67] | |
| SealS (LDS) | 7 Jun 1916 | Salt Lake Temple |
| Spouse | James Squire (1896-1963) | 3 Jul 1941 - Kansas City, Jackson, Missouri, United States[68] |
| SealS (LDS) | 18 Apr 2008 | Jordan River Utah Temple |

**Events**

1. She appeared on the census on 4 Jun 1900 in Oakley, Cassia, Idaho, United States.[69]
Line 39 - McBride, Heber J, head, white, male, born May 1857, age 63, married for 17 years, born in Utah, father born in Ohio, mother born in Vermont, farmer, can read, write and speak english, owns farm mortgage free, form #15.
Line 40 - McBride, Lillian E, wife, white, female, born Jan 1865, age 37, married 17 years, had 7 children, 6 living, born in Utah, father born in Scotland, mother born in Canada, can read, write and speak english.
Line 41 - McBride, Maria, daughter, white, female, born Aug 1883, age 16, single, born in Utah, father born in Utah, mother born in Utah, at school, can read, write and speak english.
Line 42 - McBride, James W, son, white, male, born Aug 1885, age 14, single, born in Idaho, father born in Utah, mother born in Utah, at school, can read, write and speak english.
Line 43 - McBride, Heber E, son, white, male, born in Idaho, father born in Utah, mother born in Utah, at school.
Line 44 - McBride, Alice S, daughter, white, female, born Nov 1892, age 7, single, born in Idaho, father born in Utah, mother born in Utah, at school.
Line 45 - McBride, Edward V, son, white, male, born May 1895, age 5, single, born in Idaho, father born in Utah, mother born in Utah.
**Line 46 - McBride, Katherine J, daughter, white, female, born Feb 1898, age 2, single, born in Idaho, father born in Utah, mother born in Utah.**

# Lillian Elizabeth McIntosh and Heber Kimball McBride

2. She appeared on the census on 29 Apr 1910 in Oakley, Cassia, Idaho, United States.[70]
   Line 60 - McBride, Heber K, head, male, white, age 58, married once for 28 years, born in Utah, father born in Ohio, mother born in USA, speaks english, farmer, can read and write, owns farm, mortgage free, farm #15.
   Line 61 - McBride, Lillian E, wife, female, white, age 47, married once for 28 years, had 8 children, 6 living, born in Utah, father born in USA, mother born in USA, speaks english, can read and write.
   Line 62 - McBride, Heber E, son, male, white, age 19, single, born in Idaho, father born in Utah, mother born in Utah, speaks english, helps on farm, can read and write, in school.
   Line 63 - McBride, Alice L, daughter, female, white, age 17, single, born in Idaho, father born in Utah, mother born in Utah, speaks english, helps on farm, can read and write in school.
   **Line 64 - McBride, Kathryn J, daughter, female, white, age 12, single, born in Idaho, father born in Utah, mother born in Utah, speaks english, can read and write, in school.**
   Line 65 - McBride, Leah, daughter, female, white, age 6, single, born in Idaho, father born in Utah, mother born in Utah, speaks english.

3. She appeared on the census on 3 Jan 1920 in Burley, Cassia, Idaho, United States.
   Line 62 - Livingstone, Lenard, head, owns home, no mortgage, male, white, age 23, married, can read, write and speak english, born in Utah, both parents born in Utah, yard clerk at a freight yard, wage worker.
   **Line 63 - Livingstone, Katheryn, wife, female, white, age 21, married, can read, write and speak english, born in Idaho, both parents born in Utah.**
   Line 64 - Livingstone, Verile, daughter [son], white, age 2 7/12, single, born in Idaho, father born in Utah, mother born in Idaho.
   Line 65 - Livingstone, Lillian, daughter, female, white, age 9/12, single, born in Idaho, father born in Utah, mother born in Idaho.

4. She appeared on the census on 15 Apr 1930 in Los Angeles, Los Angeles, California, United States.[71]
   Line 79 - Livingstone, L.C., head, home rented, rent paid $35 monthly, owns a radio set, does not live on a farm, male, white, age 33, married at 21, did not attend school within year, able to read and write, born in Utah, father born in Utah, mother born in Utah, able to speak english, laborer, Dairy Co, wage worker, actually at work, not a veteran.
   **Line 80 - Livingston, Kathryn, wife, does not live on farm, female, white, age 32, married at 20, did not attend school within year, able to read and write, born in Idaho, father born in Utah, mother born in Utah, able to speak english, saleslady, department store, wage worker, actually at work.**
   Line 81 - Livingstone, Verle, son, does not live on farm, male, white, age 15, single, attended school within year, able to read and write, born in Idaho, father born in Utah, mother born in Idaho, able to speak english, no occupation.
   Line 82 - Livingstone, Lillian, daughter, does not live on farm, female, white, age 11, single, attended school within year, able to read and write, born in Idaho, father born in Utah, mother born in Idaho, able to speak english, no occupation.
   Line 83 - McBride, Lillian, mother-in-law, does not live on farm, female, white, age 67, widowed, did not attend school within year, able to read and write, born in Utah, father born in Scotland, mother born in Scotland, able to speak english, no occupation.

5. She appeared on the census on 3 Apr 1940 in Kansas City, Jackson, Missouri, United States.
   **Line 35 - Livingston, Kathryn, head, female, white, age 42, widowed, finished high school, born in Idaho, lived in Dallas, Texas in 1935, not a farm, at private work, worked 70 hours in week prior to Census, distributor of wholesale cosmetics, works on own account, worked 52 weeks last year, income $0, has other income.**

# Lillian Elizabeth McIntosh and Heber Kimball McBride

| Children (cont.) | | | |
|---|---|---|---|
| 8 F | **Dorcas Leah McBride** [72] | | |
| AKA | Dorcas Collett, Leah Collett, Leah McBride | | |
| Born | 25 Jan 1904 | Oakley, Cassia, Idaho, United States | |
| Died | 18 May 1987 | Calgary, , Alberta, Canada[73] | |
| Buried | 1987 | Calgary, , Alberta, Canada[74] | |
| Address | Mountain View Memorial Gardens, Calgary, Alberta, Canada | | |
| Notes | Plot: Christus | | |
| Bapt.(LDS) | 12 Sep 1912 | | |
| Conf.(LDS) | 12 Sep 1912 | | |
| Init.(LDS) | 7 Jun 1927 | Salt Lake Temple | |
| Endow.(LDS) | 7 Jun 1927 | Salt Lake Temple | |
| SealP (LDS) | BIC | | |
| Spouse | Karl Warren Collett (1898-1956) | 7 Jun 1927 - Salt Lake City, Salt Lake, Utah, United States[75] | |
| SealS (LDS) | 7 Jun 1927 | Salt Lake Temple | |

**Events**

1. She appeared on the census on 29 Apr 1910 in Oakley, Cassia, Idaho, United States.[76]
Line 60 - McBride, Heber K, head, male, white, age 58, married once for 28 years, born in Utah, father born in Ohio, mother born in USA, speaks english, farmer, can read and write, owns farm, mortgage free, farm #15.
Line 61 - McBride, Lillian E, wife, female, white, age 47, married once for 28 years, had 8 children, 6 living, born in Utah, father born in USA, mother born in USA, speaks english, can read and write.
Line 62 - McBride, Heber E, son, male, white, age 19, single, born in Idaho, father born in Utah, mother born in Utah, speaks english, helps on farm, can read and write, in school.
Line 63 - McBride, Alice L, daughter, female, white, age 17, single, born in Idaho, father born in Utah, mother born in Utah, speaks english, helps on farm, can read and write in school.
Line 64 - McBride, Kathryn J, daughter, female, white, age 12, single, born in Idaho, father born in Utah, mother born in Utah, speaks english, can read and write, in school.
**Line 65 - McBride, Leah, daughter, female, white, age 6, single, born in Idaho, father born in Utah, mother born in Utah, speaks english.**

2. She appeared on the census on 6 Jan 1920 in Burley, Cassia, Idaho, United States.[77]
Line 71 - McBride, Lillian, head, owns home, with a mortgage, female, white, age 55, widowed, able to read and write, born in Utah, father born in Scotland-speaks Scottish, mother born in Ohio, able to speak english, nurse, private nursing, wage worker.
**Line 72 - McBride, Lea, daughter, female, white, age 16, single, attended school within year, able to read and write, born in Idaho, father born in Utah, mother born in Utah, able to speak english, no occupation.**

3. She appeared on the census on 16 Apr 1930 in Fort Douglas, Salt Lake, Utah, United States.
Line 96 - Collett, Karl W., head, rents house for $20/month, has a radio, male, white, age 31, married at age 27, can read, write and speak english, born in Utah, both parents born in Utah, employed as superintendent of construction at Fort Douglas, Utah, not a veteran.
**Line 97 - Collett, Leah, wife, female, white, age 25, married at age 21, can read, write and speak english, born in Idaho, both parents born in Utah.**
Line 98 - Collett, La Rae, daughter, female, white, age 2 0/12, single, born in Utah, both parents born in Utah.
Line 99 - Collett, Jolene, daughter, female, white, age 0 6/12, single, born in Utah, both parents born in Utah.
Line 100 - Bosch, Fredrick, lodger, male, white, age 31, married at age 27, can read, write and speak english, born in Minnesota, parents both born in Germany, truck driver in construction.

4. She had a residence in 1935 in Boulder, Clark, Nevada, United States.

5. She appeared on the census on 6 Apr 1940 in Shasta, Shasta, California, United States.
Line 4 - Collett, Karl W., head, male, white, age 42, married, finished 4 years high school, born in Utah, in 1935 lived in Boulder, Clark, Nevada, employed as assistant superintendent.

# Lillian Elizabeth McIntosh and Heber Kimball McBride

**Line 5 - Collett, Leah E, wife, female, white, age 36, married, finished 3 years high school, born in Idaho, in 1935 lived in Boulder, Clark, Nevada.**
Line 6 - Collett, LaRay, daughter, female, white, age 12, single, in school 6th grade, born in Utah, in 1935 lived in Boulder, Clark, Nevada.
Line 7 - Collett, Jolene, daughter, female, white, age 10, single, in school 2nd grade, born in Utah, in 1935 lived in Boulder, Clark, Nevada.

6. Her obituary was published in the Calgary Herald on 21 May 1987 in Calgary, , Alberta, Canada.
**Collett** - Dorcas Leah Collett, aged 83 years of Calgary, passed away at the Calgary General Hospital on May 18,1987. She was born at Oakley, Idaho on January 25, 1904. After marrying Karl Collett on June 7, 1927, she and her husband later lived in the states of Utah, Nevada, Arizona, California, North Carolina and South Carolina before coming to Calgary in 1947. Mrs. Collett is survived by two daughters, LaRae Robertson (Dil) Calgary, and Jolene Terry (Orlyn), Denver, Colorado; seven grandchildren, Rondalee Loosle (Barry), Calgary; Paul Robertson (Lynn), White Rock, B.C., Karl Roberson (Jeanna) Boise, Idaho, Fredric Robertson, Chicago, Illinois, Karlton Terry (Yasmin) and Jubal Terry, both of Denver and Tamara Bryant (Tom), Vale Colorado; eight great-grandchildren and many devoted nieces and nephews. Mrs. Collett was predeceased by her husband Karl who died in a plane accident on December 9, 1956. Services at the Church of Jesus Christ of Latter-day Saints, 14540 Parkland Blvd. S.E. on Friday, May 22 at 10:30 a.m., Bishop William E. Payne officiating. Interment to follow at Mountain View Memorial Gardens. Pierson's Funeral Services, Directors. Phone 235-3602.

# Source Citations

1. Genealogy records-Heber and Lillian McIntosh Kimball, Gen. Soc. film 2520 pt 4 pg 6 Oakley Ward Records.

2. database, *Internment.net-Cemetery Records Online* (http://www.interment.net/data/us/id/cassia/oakley/index.htm, Jan 2010), 12 Jan 2010, Oakley Cemetery, Cassia County, Idaho.

3. Idaho Board of Health, Bureau of Vital Stastitics, death certificate File No. 27723 (1919), Heber K McBride.

4. database, *Internment.net-Cemetery Records Online* (http://www.interment.net/data/us/id/cassia/oakley/index.htm, Jan 2010), 12 Jan 2010, Oakley Cemetery, Cassia County, Idaho, lot 147.

5. "Find A Grave," database (www.findagrave.com), Heber K McBride, 36440870.

6. International Society of Daughters of Utah Pioneers, editor,*Pioneer Women of Faith and Fortitude*, Volume III (Salt Lake City, Utah: Publishers Press, 1998), Olive Mehetable Cheney McBride: 1924. Repository: Family History Library, 35 North West Temple Street, Salt Lake City, Utah 84150-3400, USA, Call Number: 979 D36.

7. 1900 U.S. census, Cassia, Idaho, population schedule, Oakley, enumeration district (ED) 35, sheet 3A, p. 313, dwelling 47, family 49, McBride, Heber; digital images,*ancestry.com*; citing National Archives and Records Administration microfilm T623.

8. 1910 U.S. census, Cassia, Idaho, population schedule, Oakley, enumeration district (ED) 113, sheet 8B, p. 277, dwelling 48, family 50, McBride, Heber K; digital images,*ancestry.com*; citing National Archives and Records Administration microfilm T624.

9. *The South Idaho Press*; digital images.

10. McIntosh Reunion Descendants, McIntosh - Descendants of John & Girsey (Grace) (Grizel) Rankin McIntosh (Attachment to Aug 17, 1958 Newsletter - copy in Collection of Bonnie S. Williams), Repository: Bonnie S. Williams, RR 1 Box 247, N Hwy 2, Wilburton, Oklahoma, USA.
L. Elizabeth (daughter of William [McINTOSH] & Maria CALDWELL) md. Heber McBRIDE
Children:
1. Maria
2. James William
3. Olive Marian
4. Heber Ephraim
5. Alice Lillian
6. Edward Vaughn
7. Kathryn Jane
8. Dorcas Leah.

L. Elizabeth McINTOSH is a Granddaughter of John McINTOSH & Girsey RANKIN.
This single page attachment indicates that the parents of John McIntosh are William McIntosh & Isabell and is indicative of what our side of the family knew of our McIntosh cousins at that time in August 1958.

11. Roberts, Barbara (editor), *McIntosh Clan 5th Annual Reunion Report* (Newsletter of 4 July 1960 in Collection of Bonnie S. Williams), Repository: Bonnie S. Williams, RR 1 Box 247, N Hwy 2, Wilburton, Oklahoma, USA.
REUNION REPORT...

3. Sketches of the activities of the descendants of the following persons during the last fifty years:
   a. Descendants of William McIntosh:
      1. William Henry McIntosh ---
         by Boyd McIntosh, Kearns, Utah
      2. Malissa Jan McIntosh Keele ---
         no representative
      3. Alice Maria McIntosh Burridge ---
         by Wanda Burridgs
      4. Abraham E. McIntosh ---
         by Fern Jacobs
      5. Lillian Elisabeth McIntosh McBride ---
         no representative
      6. Joseph Albert McIntosh ---
         by Michael McIntosh
   b. Descendants of John McIntosh:
      1. John David McIntosh ---
         by Deon Hitchcock
      2. William Abram McIntosh ---
         by Lena Donaldson...

FAMILY REPRESENTATIVES...
The family representatives are as follows:
1. Family of William Henry McIntosh --
   Boyd McIntosh, Kearns, Utah
2. Melissa Jane McIntosh Keele --
   Keele Family, Anaconda, Montana
3. Alice Maria McIntosh Burridge --
   Wanda Burridge, Nephi, Utah

# Source Citations

4. Abraham E. McIntosh --
   Fern Jacobs, Mt. Pleasant, Utah
5. Lillian Elizabeth McIntosh McBride --
   J. W. McBride, Tremonton, Utah
6. Joseph Albert McIntosh --
   To be appointed by Don McIntosh
7. John David McIntosh --
   Annie Algets, Las Vegas, Nevada
8. William Abram McIntosh --
   Roah Dunsworth. The 5th Annual Reunion was held at Provo Park on 12 Jun 1960. Newsletter dated July 4, 1960.

12. Brown, Beverly McIntosh and Marsha Lee McIntosh,*William McIntosh Diary, abridgement* (Self-published, Surprise, AZ. June 2002), p 45 Friday, December 18 [1862].

13. Brown, Beverly McIntosh and Marsha Lee McIntosh,*William McIntosh Diary, abridgement* (Self-published, Surprise, AZ. June 2002), p 47 1863 Highlights.
January. William and Maria's daughter Lillian Elizabeth was born on the 11th in St. John.

14. Utah Department of Commerce, Bureau of the Census, death certificate State File No. 66; Registrar's No. 17 (1943), Lillian E. McBride; digital image, *myheritage.com* .

15. Utah Department of Commerce, Bureau of the Census, death certificate State Fiel No. 66, Registrar's No. 17 (1943), Lillian E. McBride.

16. Utah Department of Commerce, Bureau of the Census, death certificate State File No. 66; Registrat's No. 17 (1943), Lillian E. McBride; digital image, *myheritage.com* .

17. Brown, Beverly McIntosh and Marsha McIntosh, editors,*William McIntosh Diary 1857-1898, Abridgement* (Surprise, AZ: Self-published, June 2002).

18. Daughters of Utah Pioneers, *Our Pioneer Heritage* (Salt Lake City, UT: Infobases, Inc., 1996), 19: 422. Repository: Family History Library, 35 North West Temple Street, Salt Lake City, Utah 84150-3400, USA, Call Number: 979.2 H2.

19. Frank Esshorn, editor, *Pioneers and Prominent Men of Utah comprising Photographs-Genealogies-Biographies. Pioneers are those men and women who came to Utah by wagon, hand cart or afoot, between July 24, 1847 and December 30, 1868, before the railroad. Prominent Men are stake presidents, ward bishops, governors, members of the bench, etc., who came to Utah after the coming of the railroad. The early history of the Church of Jesus Christ of Latter-Day Saints. In One Volume, Illustrated* (Salt Lake City, Utah: Utah Pioneers Book Publishing Company, 1913), McIntosh, William: 331 and 1059. Repository: Family History Library, 35 North West Temple Street, Salt Lake City, Utah 84150-3400, USA, Call Number: 979.2 D3e.

20. Andrew Jenson, editor, *Latter-day Saint Biographical Encyclopedia: A Compilation of Biographical Sketches of Prominent Men and Women in The Church of Jesus Christ of Latter-day Saints*, 4 v.: ports. (Salt Lake City, Utah: Western Epics, 1971), William McIntosh: V 4, page 647. Repository: Family History Library, 35 North West Temple Street, Salt Lake City, Utah 84150-3400, USA, Call Number: 920.0792.

21. International Society of Daughters of Utah Pioneers, editor,*Pioneer Women of Faith and Fortitude*, Volume III (Salt Lake City, Utah: Publishers Press, 1998), Maria Caldwell McIntosh: page 1946. Repository: Family History Library, 35 North West Temple Street, Salt Lake City, Utah 84150-3400, USA, Call Number: 979 D36.

22. 1870 U.S. census, Washington, Utah, population schedule, Panaca, p. 7, dwelling 54, family 48, McIntosh, Lilly; digital images*ancestry.com*; citing National Archives and Records Administration microfilm M593.

23. 1870 U.S. census, Lincoln, Nevada, population schedule, Meadow Valley, p. 186, dwelling 66-68, family 45, McIntosh, Lilly; digital images, *ancestry.com*; citing National Archives and Records Administration microfilm M593.

24. 1880 U.S. census, Tooele, Utah Territory, population schedule, Clover, enumeration district (ED) 79, p. 6C, Mackintosh, Lillian; digital images, *ancestry.com*; citing National Archives and Records Administration microfilm T9.

25. Brown, Beverly McIntosh and Marsha Lee McIntosh,*William McIntosh Diary, abridgement* (Self-published, Surprise, AZ. June 2002), page 76, June 27 [1893].

26. 1900 U.S. census, Cassia, Idaho, population schedule, Oakley, enumeration district (ED) 35, sheet 3A, p. 313, dwelling 47, family 49, McBride, Lillian E; digital images,*ancestry.com*; citing National Archives and Records Administration microfilm T623.

27. 1910 U.S. census, Cassia, Idaho, population schedule, Oakley, enumeration district (ED) 113, sheet 8B, p. 277, dwelling 48, family 50, McBride, Lillian E; digital images,*ancestry.com*; citing National Archives and Records Administration microfilm T624.

28. Idaho. Cassia County, *1920 U.S. Census, population schedule* (Washington D.C.: The National Archives), Lillian McBride household, 1920 U.S. census, Cassia County, Idaho, population schedule, town of Burley, enumeration d istrict [ED] 133, supervisor's district 2, sheet 6B, dwelling 119, family 124.

29. 1930 U.S. census, Los Angeles, California, population schedule, Los Angeles, enumeration district (ED) 19-379, sheet 17B, p. 70, dwelling 374,

# Source Citations

family 425, McBride Lillian; digital images (ancestry.com); citing National Archives and Records Administration microfilm T626.

30. "Lillian McBride Taken by Death," *The Herald-Bulletin*; digital images.

31. McIntosh Reunion Descendants, McIntosh - Descendants of John & Girsey (Grace) (Grizel) Rankin McIntosh (Attachment to Aug 17, 1958 Newsletter - copy in Collection of Bonnie S. Williams), Repository: Bonnie S. Williams, RR 1 Box 247, N Hwy 2, Wilburton, Oklahoma, USA.
Maria (daughter of L. Elizabeth [McINTOSH] & Heber McBRIDE).
Maria McBRIDE is a Great-Granddaughter of John McINTOSH & Girsey RANKIN
and a Granddaughter of William McINTOSH & Maria CALDWELL
no further information.

32. Roberts, Barbara (editor), *McIntosh Clan 5th Annual Reunion Report* (Newsletter of 4 July 1960 in Collection of Bonnie S. Williams), Repository: Bonnie S. Williams, RR 1 Box 247, N Hwy 2, Wilburton, Oklahoma, USA.
NEWS ITEMS
A letter from Marie McBride Sanford tells us that Alice McBride Ward could not attend the reunion, since her husband is in the hospital suffering from his second heart attack. Let us join our prayers with hers for his recovery.

33. "Find A Grave," database (www.findagrave.com), Marie McBride Sanford.

34. "Western States Marriage Index, 1809-2011," database, Arthur M. Sanford married Marie McBride on 29 Apr 1909 in SLC, UT.

35. 1900 U.S. census, Cassia, Idaho, population schedule, Oakley, enumeration district (ED) 35, sheet 3A, p. 313, dwelling 47, family 49, McBride, Maria; digital images, *ancestry.com*; citing National Archives and Records Administration microfilm T623.

36. *McBride - Diary of James McBride, Diary in possession of L. V. Livingston.*

37. McIntosh Reunion Descendants, McIntosh - Descendants of John & Girsey (Grace) (Grizel) Rankin McIntosh (Attachment to Aug 17, 1958 Newsletter - copy in Collection of Bonnie S. Williams), Repository: Bonnie S. Williams, RR 1 Box 247, N Hwy 2, Wilburton, Oklahoma, USA.
James William (son of L. Elizabeth [McINTOSH] & Heber McBRIDE).
James William McBRIDE is a Great-Grandson of John McINTOSH & Girsey RANKIN
and a Grandson of William McINTOSH & Maria CALDWELL
no further information.

38. Records for James & Julia Smith McBride. Information from church records, Treasure of Truth Book submitted by Fern McBride Moncur Box 393 Aberdeen, Idaho.

39. Roberts, Barbara (editor), *McIntosh Clan 5th Annual Reunion Report* (Newsletter of 4 July 1960 in Collection of Bonnie S. Williams), Repository: Bonnie S. Williams, RR 1 Box 247, N Hwy 2, Wilburton, Oklahoma, USA.
FAMILY REPRESENTATIVES...
The family representatives are as follows:
1. Family of William Henry McIntosh --
Boyd McIntosh, Kearns, Utah
2. Melissa Jane McIntosh Keele --
Keele Family, Anaconda, Montana
3. Alice Maria McIntosh Burridge --
Wanda Burridge, Nephi, Utah
4. Abraham E. McIntosh --
Fern Jacobs, Mt. Pleasant, Utah
5. Lillian Elizabeth McIntosh McBride --
J. W. McBride, Tremonton, Utah
6. Joseph Albert McIntosh --
To be appointed by Don McIntosh
7. John David McIntosh --
Annie Algets, Las Vegas, Nevada
8. William Abram McIntosh --
Roah Dunsworth.

40. McIntosh Family Organization, *Newsletter,* Tremonton, Idaho newspaper.

41. database, *Internment.net-Cemetery Records Online* (http://www.interment.net/data/us/id/cassia/oakley/index.htm, Jan 2010), 12 Jan 2010, Oakley Cemetery, Cassia County, Idaho, Lot 224.

42. "Utah, Select Marriages, 1887-1966," database, James William Mcbride married Julia M. Smith on 29 Apr 1909 in Salt Lake, Utah.

43. 1900 U.S. census, Cassia, Idaho, population schedule, Oakley, enumeration district (ED) 35, sheet 3A, p. 313, dwelling 47, family 49, McBride, James; digital images, *ancestry.com*; citing National Archives and Records Administration microfilm T623.

44. "U.S., World War I Draft Registration Cards, 1917-1918," database, James W. McBride.

45. McIntosh Reunion Descendants, McIntosh - Descendants of John & Girsey (Grace) (Grizel) Rankin McIntosh (Attachment to Aug 17, 1958

# Source Citations

Newsletter - copy in Collection of Bonnie S. Williams), Repository: Bonnie S. Williams, RR 1 Box 247, N Hwy 2, Wilburton, Oklahoma, USA.
Olive Marian (daughter of L. Elizabeth [McINTOSH] & Heber McBRIDE).
Olive Marian McBRIDE is a Great-Granddaughter of John McINTOSH & Girsey RANKIN
and a Granddaughter of William McINTOSH & Maria CALDWELL
no further information.

46. 1930 U.S. census, Salt Lake, Utah, population schedule; digital images (ancestry.com); citing National Archives and Records Administration microfilm T626.

47. McIntosh Reunion Descendants, McIntosh - Descendants of John & Girsey (Grace) (Grizel) Rankin McIntosh (Attachment to Aug 17, 1958 Newsletter - copy in Collection of Bonnie S. Williams), Repository: Bonnie S. Williams, RR 1 Box 247, N Hwy 2, Wilburton, Oklahoma, USA.
Heber Ephraim (son of L. Elizabeth [McINTOSH] & Heber McBRIDE).
Heber Ephraim McBRIDE is a Great-Grandson of John McINTOSH & Girsey RANKIN
and a Grandson of William McINTOSH & Maria CALDWELL
no further information.

48. "U.S., Social Security Death Index, 1935-2014," database, Ephriam McBride.

49. "Find A Grave," database (www.findagrave.com), Ephraim Heber McBride, 119238081.

50. Brigham Young University-Idaho, "Western States Marriage Index," database (http://abish.byui.edu/specialCollections/westernStates/search.cfm), Ephraim McBride and Lydia Campbell.

51. 1900 U.S. census, Cassia, Idaho, population schedule, Oakley, enumeration district (ED) 35, sheet 3A, p. 313, dwelling 47, family 49, McBride, Heber E; digital images, *ancestry.com*; citing National Archives and Records Administration microfilm T623.

52. 1910 U.S. census, Cassia, Idaho, population schedule, Oakley, enumeration district (ED) 113, sheet 8B, p. 277, dwelling 48, family 50, McBride, Heber E; digital images, *ancestry.com*; citing National Archives and Records Administration microfilm T624.

53. "U.S., World War I Draft Registration Cards, 1917-1918," database, Ephraim H. McBride.

54. McIntosh Reunion Descendants, McIntosh - Descendants of John & Girsey (Grace) (Grizel) Rankin McIntosh (Attachment to Aug 17, 1958 Newsletter - copy in Collection of Bonnie S. Williams), Repository: Bonnie S. Williams, RR 1 Box 247, N Hwy 2, Wilburton, Oklahoma, USA.
Alice Lillian (daughter of L. Elizabeth [McINTOSH] & Heber McBRIDE).
Alice Lillian McBRIDE is a Great-Granddaughter of John McINTOSH & Girsey RANKIN
and a Granddaughter of William McINTOSH & Maria CALDWELL
no further information.

55. "U.S., Social Security Death Index, 1935-2014," database, Lillian Alice McBride Ward.

56. "Utah, Salt Lake Ciy, Cemetey Records, 1848-1992," database, *ancestry.com* , Lillian Alice McBride Ward, plot 107254, grave W-14-36-E-5.

57. "Utah, Select County Marriages, 1887-1937," database, Moroni Wm. Ward married Alice L. Mcbride on 12 Nov 1914 in SLC, UT.

58. "Western States Marriage Index, 1809-2011," database, Moroni W Ward married Alice L Mcbride on 12 Nov 1914 in SCL, UT.

59. 1900 U.S. census, Cassia, Idaho, population schedule, Oakley, enumeration district (ED) 35, sheet 3A, p. 313, dwelling 47, family 49, McBride, Alice L; digital images, *ancestry.com*; citing National Archives and Records Administration microfilm T623.

60. 1910 U.S. census, Cassia, Idaho, population schedule, Oakley, enumeration district (ED) 113, sheet 8B, p. 277, dwelling 48, family 50, McBride, Alice L; digital images, *ancestry.com*; citing National Archives and Records Administration microfilm T624.

61. McIntosh Reunion Descendants, McIntosh - Descendants of John & Girsey (Grace) (Grizel) Rankin McIntosh (Attachment to Aug 17, 1958 Newsletter - copy in Collection of Bonnie S. Williams), Repository: Bonnie S. Williams, RR 1 Box 247, N Hwy 2, Wilburton, Oklahoma, USA.
Edward Vaughn (son of L. Elizabeth [McINTOSH] & Heber McBRIDE).
Edward Vaughn McBRIDE is a Great-Grandson of John McINTOSH & Girsey RANKIN
and a Grandson of William McINTOSH & Maria CALDWELL
no further information.

62. database, *Internment.net-Cemetery Records Online* (http://www.interment.net/data/us/id/cassia/oakley/index.htm, Jan 2010), 12 Jan 2010, Oakley Cemetery, Cassia County, Idaho, Lot 147.

63. 1900 U.S. census, Cassia, Idaho, population schedule, Oakley, enumeration district (ED) 35, sheet 3A, p. 313, dwelling 47, family 49, McBride, Edward V; digital images, *ancestry.com*; citing National Archives and Records Administration microfilm T623.

64. McIntosh Reunion Descendants, McIntosh - Descendants of John & Girsey (Grace) (Grizel) Rankin McIntosh (Attachment to Aug 17, 1958 Newsletter - copy in Collection of Bonnie S. Williams), Repository: Bonnie S. Williams, RR 1 Box 247, N Hwy 2, Wilburton, Oklahoma, USA.
Kathryn Jane (daughter of L. Elizabeth [McINTOSH] & Heber McBRIDE).
Kathryn Jane McBRIDE is a Great-Granddaughter of John McINTOSH & Girsey RANKIN
and a Granddaughter of William McINTOSH & Maria CALDWELL

# Source Citations

no further information.

65. "U.S., Social Security Death Index, 1935-2014," database, Kathryn Squire.

66. "Find A Grave," database (www.findagrave.com), Katherine Jane "Kathryn" McBride Livingston-Squire, 115334280.

67. "Western States Marriage Index, 1809-2011," database, Leonard C. Livingston married Katheryn J. McBride on 7 Jun 1916 in Salt Lake, Utah.

68. Missouri, Marriage Records, 1805-2002 James Squire married Kathryn Livingston on 30 Jun 1941 in Jackson, Missouri; digital images, ancestry.com.

69. 1900 U.S. census, Cassia, Idaho, population schedule, Oakley, enumeration district (ED) 35, sheet 3A, p. 313, dwelling 47, family 49, McBride, Kathryn J; digital images,*ancestry.com*; citing National Archives and Records Administration microfilm T623.

70. 1910 U.S. census, Cassia, Idaho, population schedule, Oakley, enumeration district (ED) 113, sheet 8B, p. 277, dwelling 48, family 50, McBride, Kathryn J; digital images,*ancestry.com*; citing National Archives and Records Administration microfilm T624.

71. 1930 U.S. census, Los Angeles, California, population schedule, Los Angeles, enumeration district (ED) 19-379, sheet 17B, p. 70, dwelling 374, family 425, Livingstone, Kathryn; digital images (ancestry.com); citing National Archives and Records Administration microfilm T626.

72. McIntosh Reunion Descendants, McIntosh - Descendants of John & Girsey (Grace) (Grizel) Rankin McIntosh (Attachment to Aug 17, 1958 Newsletter - copy in Collection of Bonnie S. Williams), Repository: Bonnie S. Williams, RR 1 Box 247, N Hwy 2, Wilburton, Oklahoma, USA.
Dorcas Leah (daughter of L. Elizabeth [McINTOSH] & Heber McBRIDE).
Dorcas Leah McBRIDE is a Great-Granddaughter of John McINTOSH & Girsey RANKIN
and a Granddaughter of William McINTOSH & Maria CALDWELL
no further information.

73. "U.S., Social Security Death Index, 1935-2014," database, Leah Collette.

74. "Find A Grave," database (www.findagrave.com), Dorcas Leah McBride Collett, 138510435.

75. "Utah, Select County Marriages, 1887-1937," database, Karl Warren Collett married Dorcas Leah Mcbride on 7 Jun 1927 in SLC, UT.

76. 1910 U.S. census, Cassia, Idaho, population schedule, Oakley, enumeration district (ED) 113, sheet 8B, p. 277, dwelling 48, family 50, McBride, Leah D; digital images,*ancestry.com*; citing National Archives and Records Administration microfilm T624.

77. Idaho. Cassia County, *1920 U.S. Census, population schedule* (Washington D.C.: The National Archives), Lillian McBride household, 1920 U.S. census, Cassia County , Idaho, population schedule, town of Burley, enumeration d istrict [ED] 133, supervisor's district 2, sheet 6B, dwelli ng 119, family 124.

# Caroline Jeanette McIntosh and Joseph Clark Jordan

| **Husband** | **Joseph Clark Jordan**[1] | |
|---|---|---|
| AKA | Clark Joseph Jordan, Joseph C. Jordon | |
| Born | 2 Apr 1863 | Saint John, Tooele, Utah Territory, United States[2] |
| Died | 19 Jul 1939 | Mount Pleasant, Sanpete, Utah, United States[2] |
| Cause of Death | Carcinoma of stomach[2] | |
| | | |
| Buried | 22 Jul 1939 | Mount Pleasant, Sanpete, Utah, United States[2,3] |
| Address | Mount Pleasant City Cemetery, 900 South 100 East, Mt. Pleasant, Utah 84647, USA | |
| Bapt.(LDS) | 11 Mar 1995 | Jordan River Utah Temple |
| Conf.(LDS) | 20 Aug 1996 | Ogden Utah Temple |
| Init.(LDS) | 24 Feb 1999 | Provo Utah Temple |
| Endow.(LDS) | 8 Jun 1945 | Logan Utah Temple |
| Father | James Francis Jordan (1824-1900) [4,5,6] | |
| Mother | Sarah Canon (1820-1890) [7,8,9] | |
| SealP (LDS) | 6 Feb 1968 | Manti Utah Temple |
| Marriage | 5 Jan 1887 | Saint John, Tooele, Utah, United States |
| SealS (LDS) | 12 May 1947 | Logan Utah Temple |
| Other Spouse | Lucina Elizabeth Madsen (1862-1944)[10,11] | 23 Oct 1895 - Manti, Sanpete, Utah, United States |
| SealS (LDS) | 21 Jun 1995 | Provo Utah Temple |

**Events**

1. He worked as a farmer.[2]
2. He appeared on the census on 20 Aug 1870 in Salt Lake City, Great Salt Lake, Utah Territory, United States.
3. He appeared on the census on 12 Jun 1880 in Clover, Tooele, Utah Territory, United States.[13]
4. He appeared on the census on 14 Jun 1900 in Mount Pleasant, Sanpete, Utah, United States.[14]
5. He appeared on the census on 24 Apr 1910 in Mount Pleasant, Sanpete, Utah, United States.[15]
6. He appeared on the census on 28 Jan 1920 in Mount Pleasant, Sanpete, Utah, United States.[16]
7. He appeared on the census on 19 Apr 1930 in Mount Pleasant, Sanpete, Utah, United States.[17]
8. His obituary was published after 19 Jul 1939. **Joseph Clark Jordan**
   Mt. Pleasant - Funeral services for Joseph Clark Jordan, 76, who died Wednesday morning, will be conducted by Bishop A.L. Petersen at 2 p.m. Saturday in Mt. Pleasant North ward L.D.S. church. Interment will be in Mt. Pleasant city cemetery, directed by Ursenbach funeral home.

   **Joseph Clark Jordan**
   Mt. Pleasant - Joseph Clark Jordan, 76, prominent farmer, woolgrower and stockman, died at the family home Wednesday morning after a three months' illness from carcinoma.
   Mr. Jordan served several years as a city councilman and also as president of the Sanpete County Woolgrowers' association and had been active in fraternal and civic organizations. He was born in St. John, Tooele county, Utah, April 2, 1863, a son of James F. and Sarah Jordan. He had been a resident of Mt. Pleasant since 1888.
   He married Luzina Madsen Frandsen in Manti L.D.S. temple October 23,1855.
   Surviving are his widow, two sons and two dauthters. Mrs. I.E. Jorgensen of Salt Lake City, James F. and Peter N. Jordan and Mrs. Lorain Beck of Mt. Pleasant; eight grandchildren and four great-grandchildren.
   The body is at Ursenbach Funeral home pending funeral arrangements.

# Caroline Jeanette McIntosh and Joseph Clark Jordan

| Wife | Caroline Jeanette McIntosh[18] | |
|---|---|---|
| AKA | Caroline Jordan, Caroline Gennette McIntosh, Caroline Jennett McIntosh | |
| Born | 1 Nov 1865 | Saint John, Tooele, Utah Territory, United States |
| Died | 26 Sep 1889 | Mount Pleasant, Sanpete, Utah Territory, United States[19,20,21,22] |
| Cause of Death | Possibly from complications of childbirth | |
| Buried | 1889 | Mount Pleasant, Sanpete, Utah Territory, United States |
| Address | Mount Pleasant City Cemetery, 900 South 100 East, Mt. Pleasant, Utah 84647, USA | |
| Bapt.(LDS) | 1 Jan 1873 | |
| Conf.(LDS) | 1 Jan 1873 | |
| Init.(LDS) | 27 Jun 1997 | Portland Oregon Temple |
| Endow.(LDS) | 12 Nov 1914 | Salt Lake Temple |
| Father | William McIntosh (1819-1899) [23,24,25,26] | |
| Mother | Maria Caldwell (1824-1897) [27] | |
| SealP (LDS) | BIC | |

CAROLINE McINTOSH
JORDAN
NOV. 1, 1865
SEPT. 26, 1889

**Events**

1. She appeared on the census on 10 Jun 1870 in Panaca, Washington, Utah Territory.[28]
   Line 20 - McIntosh, William age 49, male, white, day laborer, value of personal estate $200, born in Scotland, father and mother foreign born, male over 21.
   Line 21 - McIntosh, Marie, age 45, female, white, keeping house, born in Canada, father and mother foreign born.
   Line 22 - McIntosh, William, age 20, male, white, teamster, born in Missouri, father and mother foreign born.
   Line 23 - McIntosh, Frank, age 18, male, white, work on farm, born in Utah, father and mother foreign born.
   Line 24 - McIntosh, Jane, age 15, female, white, at home, born in Utah, father and mother foreign born, attended school.
   Line 25 - McIntosh, Allice, age 12, female, white, born in Utah, father and mother foreign born, attended school.
   Line 26 - McIntosh, Abraham, age 10, male, white, born in Utah, father and mother foreign born, attended school, cannot write.
   Line 27 - McIntosh, Lilly, age 7, female, white, born in Utah, father and mother foreign born.
   **Line 28 - McIntosh, Caroline, age 4, female, white, born in Utah, father and mother foreign born.**
   Line 29 - McIntosh, Albert, age 1, male, white, born in Utah, father and mother foreign born.
2. She appeared on the census on 28 Jul 1870 in Meadow Valley, Lincoln, Nevada, United States.[29]
   Line 22 - McIntosh, Wm age 50, male, white, farming, value of real estate $300, value of personal estate $800, born in Scotland, father and mother foreign born, male over 21.
   Line 23 - McIntosh, Marie, age 45, female, white, keeping house, born in Canada, father and mother foreign born.
   Line 24 - McIntosh, Wm H, age 21, male, white, farming, born in Missouri, father and mother foreign born, male over 21.
   Line 25 - McIntosh, Frank, age 18, male, white, farming, born in Utah, father and mother foreign born.
   Line 26 - McIntosh, Jane, age 16, female, white, at home, born in Utah, father and mother foreign born, attended school.
   Line 27 - McIntosh, Alice, age 12, female, white, school, born in Utah, father and mother foreign born, attended school.
   Line 28 - McIntosh, Abe, age 10, male, white, school, born in Utah, father and mother foreign born, attended school, cannot write.
   Line 29 - McIntosh, Lilly, age 7, female, white, school, born in Utah, father and mother foreign born.
   **Line 30 - McIntosh, Caroline, age 4, female, white, school, born in Utah, father and mother foreign born.**
   Line 31 - McIntosh, Albert, age 1, male, white, school, born in Nevada, father and mother foreign born.
3. She appeared on the census on 12 Jun 1880 in Clover, Tooele, Utah Territory, United States.[30]
   Line 19 - Mackintosh, William, white, male, age 60, head, married, laborer, born in Canada, father born in Canada, mother born Canada.
   Line 20 - Mackintosh, Caroline, [Maria] white, female, age 53, wife, married, keeping house, born in Canada, father born in Canada, mother born in Canada.
   Line 21 - Mackintosh, Alice, white, female, age 22, daughter, single, teaching school, born in Utah, father born in Canada, mother born in Canada.
   Line 22 - Mackintosh, Abraham, white, male, age 20, son, single, working on farm, born in Utah, father born in Canada,

# Caroline Jeanette McIntosh and Joseph Clark Jordan

mother born in Canada.
Line 23 - Mackintosh, Lillian, white, female, age 18, daughter, single, studying at home, attended school, born in Utah, father born in Canada, mother born in Canada.
**Line 24 - Mackintosh, Caroline, white, female, age 15, daughter, single, studying at home, attended school, born in Utah, father born in Canada, mother born in Canada.**
Line 25 - Mackintosh, Albert, white, male, age 11, son, single, working on farm, attended school, born in Utah, father born in Canada, mother born in Canada.

**Events: Marriage**

1. Alt Marriage: 16 May 1887, Saint John, Tooele, Utah, United States.

## Children

| 1 F | **Fanny Jordan** [31] | |
|---|---|---|
| Born | 13 Sep 1887 | Mount Pleasant, Sanpete, Utah Territory, United States |
| Died | 19 Mar 1889 | Mount Pleasant, Sanpete, Utah Territory, United States |
| Buried | Mar 1889 | Mount Pleasant, Sanpete, Utah Territory, United States |
| Address | Mount Pleasant City Cemetery, 900 South 100 East, Mt. Pleasant, Utah 84647, USA | |
| Notes | Plot: A-116-2-1a | |
| Bapt.(LDS) | Child | |
| Conf.(LDS) | Child | |
| Init.(LDS) | Child | |
| Endow.(LDS) | Child | |
| SealP (LDS) | 12 May 1947 | Logan Utah Temple |
| Spouse | This person had no known marriage and no known children | |

| 2 F | **Marie Trinite Jordan** | |
|---|---|---|
| Born | 23 Aug 1889 | Mount Pleasant, Sanpete, Utah Territory, United States |
| Died | 15 Nov 1889 | Mount Pleasant, Sanpete, Utah Territory, United States |
| Buried | Nov 1889 | Mount Pleasant, Sanpete, Utah Territory, United States |
| Address | Mount Pleasant City Cemetery, 900 South 100 East, Mt. Pleasant, Utah 84647, USA | |
| Notes | Plot: A-116-2-3 | |
| Status | Twin | |
| Bapt.(LDS) | Child | |
| Conf.(LDS) | Child | |
| Init.(LDS) | Child | |
| Endow.(LDS) | Child | |
| SealP (LDS) | 5 Jul 2011 | San Diego California Temple |
| Spouse | This person had no known marriage and no known children | |

# Caroline Jeanette McIntosh and Joseph Clark Jordan

| Children (cont.) | | |
|---|---|---|
| 3 F | **Anna Janette Jordan** | |
| Born | 23 Aug 1889 | Mount Pleasant, Sanpete, Utah Territory, United States |
| Died | Bef 1896 | place: |
| Buried | date: | Mount Pleasant, Sanpete, Utah Territory, United States |
| Status | Twin | |
| Bapt.(LDS) | Child | |
| Conf.(LDS) | Child | |
| Init.(LDS) | Child | |
| Endow.(LDS) | Child | |
| SealP (LDS) | 12 May 1947 | Logan Utah Temple |
| Spouse | This person had no known marriage and no known children | |

# Source Citations


1. Utah, State Department of Health, Certificate of Death, death certificate state file no. 60; registrar's no. 20 (1944), Lucina E. Madsen names her husband as Joseph Jordan.

2. Utah, State Department of Health, Certificate of Death, death certificate state file no. 78; registrar's no. 28 (1939), Joseph Clark Jordan.

3. "Find A Grave," database (www.findagrave.com), Joseph Clark Jordan, 140658.

4. Utah, State Department of Health, Certificate of Death, death certificate state file no. 113 (1919), Leonard James Jordan names his father as James F. Jordan born in England.

5. Utah, State Department of Health, Certificate of Death, death certificate state file no. 78; registrar's no. 28 (1939), Joseph Clark Jordan names his father as James F. Jordan born in England.

6. Utah, State Department of Health, Certificate of Death, death certificate state file no. 253 (1920), Annie McIntosh names her father as James Jordan born in England.

7. Utah, State Department of Health, Certificate of Death, death certificate state file no. 113 (1919), Leonard James Jordan names his mother as Sarah Cannon born in England.

8. Utah, State Department of Health, Certificate of Death, death certificate state file no. 78; registrar's no. 28 (1939), Joseph Clark Jordan names his mother as Sarah Cannon born in England.

9. Utah, State Department of Health, Certificate of Death, death certificate state file no. 253 (1920), Annie McIntosh names her mother as Sarah Cannon born in USA.

10. Utah, State Department of Health, Certificate of Death, death certificate state file no. 78; registrar's no. 28 (1939), Joseph Clark Jordan names his wife as Lucina Madsen.

11. Utah, State Department of Health, Certificate of Death, death certificate state fiel no. 469; registrar's no. 559 (1944), Hannah Elena Jorgensen names her mother as Lucina Madsen born in Mt. Pleasant, Utah.

12. Brigham Young University-Idaho, "Western States Marriage Index," database (http://abish.byui.edu/specialCollections/westernStates/search.cfm), Joseph C. Jordan and Lucina Frandsen.

13. 1880 U.S. census, Tooele, Utah Territory, population schedule, Clover, enumeration district (ED) 79, p. 6C, Jordan, Joseph; digital images, *ancestry.com*; citing National Archives and Records Administration microfilm T9.

14. 1900 U.S. census, Sanpete, Utah, population schedule, MT Pleasant, enumeration district (ED) 128, sheet 12A, p. 188, dwelling 244, family 247, Jordan, Joseph; digital images, *ancestry.com*; citing National Archives and Records Administration microfilm T623.

15. 1910 U.S. census, Sanpete, Utah, population schedule, Mt Pleasant, enumeration district (ED) 156, sheet 7A, p. 159, dwelling 102, family 106, Jordan, Joseph C.; digital images, *ancestry.com*; citing National Archives and Records Administration microfilm T624.

16. 1920 U.S. census, Sanpete, Utah, population schedule, Mount Pleasant, enumeration district (ED) 110, sheet 19B, p. 246, dwelling 362, family 369, Jordan, Joseph; digital images (ancestry.com); citing National Archives and Records Administration microfilm T625.

17. 1930 U.S. census, Sanpete, Utah, population schedule, Mount Pleasant, enumeration district (ED) 20-22, sheet 14A, p. 145, dwelling 278, family 289, Jordan, Joseph C.; digital images (ancestry.com); citing National Archives and Records Administration microfilm T626.

18. McIntosh Reunion Descendants, McIntosh - Descendants of John & Girsey (Grace) (Grizel) Rankin McIntosh (Attachment to Aug 17, 1958 Newsletter - copy in Collection of Bonnie S. Williams), Repository: Bonnie S. Williams, RR 1 Box 247, N Hwy 2, Wilburton, Oklahoma, USA.
Caroline J. (daughter of William [McINTOSH] & Maria CALDWELL) md. Joseph JORDAN
Children:
1. Fannie
2. Annie Janetta.
Caroline J. McINTOSH is a Granddaughter of John McINTOSH & Girsey RANKIN.
This single page attachment indicates that the parents of John McIntosh are William McIntosh & Isabell and is indicative of what our side of the family knew of our McIntosh cousins at that time in August 1958.

19. Brown, Beverly McIntosh and Marsha Lee McIntosh,*William McIntosh Diary, abridgement* (Self-published, Surprise, AZ. June 2002), "...Sept 25 our daughter Caroline died.....She died in Mt Pleasant (Utah)."

20. Brown, Beverly McIntosh and Marsha Lee McIntosh,*William McIntosh Diary, abridgement* (Self-published, Surprise, AZ. June 2002), p 67 September 24 [1889].
"We were at the Manti Temple to do some work for ourselves and for our dead friends. ... we received a telegram from Mt. Pleasant that our daughter Caroline was dangerously ill at her home in Mt. Pleasant, 22 miles north of Manti, Sanpete, Utah. We started from Manti between sundown and dark. Myself and wife and a man I hired to drive my team in the night but we got there too late. She died soon after we arrived there".

21. Brown, Beverly McIntosh and Marsha Lee McIntosh,*William McIntosh Diary, abridgement* (Self-published, Surprise, AZ. June 2002), "...Sept 25 our daughter Caroline died.....She died in Mount Pleasant (Utah)."

# Source Citations

22. Brown, Beverly McIntosh and Marsha Lee McIntosh,*William McIntosh Diary, abridgement* (Self-published, Surprise, AZ. June 2002), p 71 October 20 [1891].
And still more, Sept. 25, [1889] our daughter Caroline died. She was married to Joseph Jordan. She had two children. She died in Mt. Pleasant.

23. Brown, Beverly McIntosh and Marsha McIntosh, editors,*William McIntosh Diary 1857-1898, Abridgement* (Surprise, AZ: Self-published, June 2002).

24. Daughters of Utah Pioneers,*Our Pioneer Heritage* (Salt Lake City, UT: Infobases, Inc., 1996), 19: 422. Repository: Family History Library, 35 North West Temple Street, Salt Lake City, Utah 84150-3400, USA, Call Number: 979.2 H2.

25. Frank Esshorn, editor,*Pioneers and Prominent Men of Utah comprising Photographs-Genealogies-Biographies. Pioneers are those men and women who came to Utah by wagon, hand cart or afoot, between July 24, 1847 and December 30, 1868, before the railroad. Prominent Men are stake presidents, ward bishops, governors, members of the bench, etc., who came to Utah after the coming of the railroad. The early history of the Church of Jesus Christ of Latter-Day Saints. In One Volume, Illustrated* (Salt Lake City, Utah: Utah Pioneers Book Publishing Company, 1913), McIntosh, William: 331 and 1059. Repository: Family History Library, 35 North West Temple Street, Salt Lake City, Utah 84150-3400, USA, Call Number: 979.2 D3e.

26. Andrew Jenson, editor,*Latter-day Saint Biographical Encyclopedia: A Compilation of Biographical Sketches of Prominent Men and Women in The Church of Jesus Christ of Latter-day Saints*, 4 v.: ports. (Salt Lake City, Utah: Western Epics, 1971), William McIntosh: V 4, page 647. Repository: Family History Library, 35 North West Temple Street, Salt Lake City, Utah 84150-3400, USA, Call Number: 920.0792.

27. International Society of Daughters of Utah Pioneers, editor,*Pioneer Women of Faith and Fortitude*, Volume III (Salt Lake City, Utah: Publishers Press, 1998), Maria Caldwell McIntosh: page 1946. Repository: Family History Library, 35 North West Temple Street, Salt Lake City, Utah 84150-3400, USA, Call Number: 979 D36.

28. 1870 U.S. census, Washington, Utah, population schedule, Panaca, p. 7, dwelling 54, family 48, McIntosh, Caroline; digital images, *ancestry.com*; citing National Archives and Records Administration microfilm M593.

29. 1870 U.S. census, Lincoln, Nevada, population schedule, Meadow Valley, p. 186, dwelling 66-68, family 45, McIntosh Caroline; digital images, *ancestry.com*; citing National Archives and Records Administration microfilm M593.

30. 1880 U.S. census, Tooele, Utah Territory, population schedule, Clover, enumeration district (ED) 79, p. 6C, Mackintosh, Caroline; digital images, *ancestry.com*; citing National Archives and Records Administration microfilm T9.

31. McIntosh Reunion Descendants, McIntosh - Descendants of John & Girsey (Grace) (Grizel) Rankin McIntosh (Attachment to Aug 17, 1958 Newsletter - copy in Collection of Bonnie S. Williams), Repository: Bonnie S. Williams, RR 1 Box 247, N Hwy 2, Wilburton, Oklahoma, USA.
Fannie (daughter of Caroline J. [McINTOSH] & Joseph JORDAN).
Fannie JORDAN is a Great-Granddaughter of John McINTOSH & Girsey RANKIN
and a Granddaughter of William McINTOSH & Maria CALDWELL
no other information.

# Joseph Albert McIntosh and Annie Eliza Russell

| **Husband** | **Joseph Albert McIntosh**[1,2,3,4,5] | |
|---|---|---|
| AKA | Albert McIntosh, J. A. McIntosh, John Albert McIntosh, Joseph Elbert McIntosh | |
| Born | 8 Mar 1869 | Panaca, Washington, Utah Territory, United States |
| Died | 21 Jan 1950 | Los Angeles, Los Angeles, California, United States[6] |
| Cause of Death | Conditions resulting from the car accident that killed his wife | |
| Buried | 24 Jan 1950 | Rush Valley, Tooele, Utah, United States[7] |
| Address | St. John Cemetery, East on Main Street to Cemetery Road, Rush Valley, Utah 84069, USA | |
| Bapt.(LDS) | 1 Jun 1882 | |
| Conf.(LDS) | 1 Jun 1882 | |
| Init.(LDS) | 25 Jun 1924 | Salt Lake Temple |
| Endow.(LDS) | 25 Jun 1924 | Salt Lake Temple |
| Father | William McIntosh (1819-1899) [8,9,10,11] | |
| Mother | Maria Caldwell (1824-1897) [12] | |
| SealP (LDS) | BIC | |
| Marriage | 6 Mar 1888 | Saint John, Tooele, Utah Territory, United States (Death of one spouse)[13] |
| SealS (LDS) | 25 Jun 1924 | Salt Lake Temple |

**Events**

1. He worked as a sheep herder in Utah, Utah, United States.
2. He appeared on the census on 10 Jun 1870 in Panaca, Washington, Utah Territory, United States.[14]
   Line 20 - McIntosh, William age 49, male, white, day laborer, value of personal estate 200, born in Scotland, father and mother foreign born, male over 21.
   Line 21 - McIntosh, Marie, age 45, female, white, keeping house, born in Canada, father and mother foreign born.
   Line 22 - McIntosh, William, age 20, male, white, teamster, born in Missouri, father and mother foreign born.
   Line 23 - McIntosh, Frank, age 18, male, white, work on farm, born in Utah, father and mother foreign born.
   Line 24 - McIntosh, Jane, age 15, female, white, at home, born in Utah, father and mother foreign born, attended school.
   Line 25 - McIntosh, Allice, age 12, female, white, born in Utah, father and mother foreign born, attended school.
   Line 26 - McIntosh, Abraham, age 10, male, white, born in Utah, father and mother foreign born, attended school.
   Line 27 - McIntosh, Lilly, age 7, female, white, born in Utah, father and mother foreign born.
   Line 28 - McIntosh, Caroline, age 4, female, white, born in Utah, father and mother foreign born.
   **Line 29 - McIntosh, Albert, age 1, male, white, born in Utah, father and mother foreign born.**
3. He appeared on the census on 28 Jul 1870 in Meadow Valley, Lincoln, Nevada, United States.[15]
   Line 22 - McIntosh, Wm age 50, male, white, farming, value of real estate 300, value of personal estate 800, born in Scotland, father and mother foreign born, male over 21.
   Line 23 - McIntosh, Marie, age 45, female, white, keeping house, born in Canada, father and mother foreign born.
   Line 24 - McIntosh, Wm H, age 21, male, white, farming, born in Missouri, father and mother foreign born, male over 21.
   Line 25 - McIntosh, Frank, age 18, male, white, farming, born in Utah, father and mother foreign born.
   Line 26 - McIntosh, Jane, age 16, female, white, at home, born in Utah, father and mother foreign born, attended school.
   Line 27 - McIntosh, Alice, age 12, female, white, school, born in Utah, father and mother foreign born, attended school.
   Line 28 - McIntosh, Abe, age 10, male, white, school, born in Utah, father and mother foreign born, attended school.
   Line 29 - McIntosh, Lilly, age 7, female, white, school, born in Utah, father and mother foreign born.
   Line 30 - McIntosh, Caroline, age 4, female, white, school, born in Utah, father and mother foreign born.
   **Line 31 - McIntosh, Albert, age 1, male, white, school, born in Nevada, father and mother foreign born.**
4. He appeared on the census on 12 Jun 1880 in Clover, Tooele, Utah Territory, United States.[16]
   Line 19 - Mackintosh, William, white, male, age 60, head, married, laborer, born in Canada, father born in Canada, mother born Canada.
   Line 20 - Mackintosh, Caroline, white, female, age 53, wife, married, keeping house, born in Canada, father born in

# Joseph Albert McIntosh and Annie Eliza Russell

Canada, mother born in Canada. (Maria)
Line 21 - Mackintosh, Alice, white, female, age 22, daughter, single, teaching school, born in Utah, father born in Canada, Mother born in Canada.
Line 22 - Mackintosh, Abraham, white, male, age 20, son, single, working on farm, born in Utah, father born in Canada, mother born in Canada.
Line 23 - Mackintosh, Lillian, white, female, age 18, daughter, single, studying at home, attended school, born in Utah, father born in Canada, mother born in Canada.
Line 24 - Mackintosh, Caroline, white, female, age 15, daughter, single, studying at home, attended school, born in Utah, father born in Canada, mother born in Canada.
**Line 25 - Mackintosh, Albert, white, male, age 11, son, single, working on farm, attended school, born in Utah, father born in Canada, mother born in Canada.**

5. He had a residence in 1891 in Saint John, Tooele, Utah Territory, United States.[17,18,19,20,21]
"Albert McIntosh [son] has worked my farm this year. He is married, has a wife and two children. We are still located in St. John."
"We, William and Maria McIntosh, are living in Mt. Pleasant.
Joseph Albert, my son, is living on our farm in St. John, Tooele County, Utah."
"We are still living in Mount Pleasant. We have had a long hard winter and the air is quite cold. I feel quite lonesome. There is none of the boys here now. J. F. McIntosh [son] is out on the desert with the sheep. A. E. McIntosh [son] is in Skull Valley working in the mines. J.A. McIntosh [son] is living on our farm in St. John with his family."

6. He appeared on the census on 29 Jun 1900 in Saint John, Tooele, Utah, United States.[22]
**Line 74 - McIntosh, Joseph A, head, white, male, born Mar 1869, age 31, married 16 years, born in Utah, father born in Ohio, mother born in Ohio, farming, 0 months unemployed, able to read, write and speak english, owns, mortgage free, farm #23.**
Line 75 - McIntosh, Liza, wife, white, female, born Oct 1867, age 32, married 16 years, had 6 children, 6 living, born in Utah, father born in England, mother born in England, able to read, write and speak english.
Line 76 - McIntosh, William A, son, white, male, born Nov 1889, age 10, single, born in Utah, father born in Utah, mother born in Utah, at school, able to read, write and speak english.
Line 77 - McIntosh, Emily E, daughter, white, female, born Sept 1891, age 8, single, born in Utah, father born in Utah, mother born in Utah, at school.
Line 78 - McIntosh, Hyrum D, son, white, male, born Oct 1893, age 6, single, born in Utah, father born in Utah, mother born in Utah, at school.
Line 79 - McIntosh, Boyd H, son, white, male, born Jan 1896, age 4, single, born in Utah, father born in Utah, mother born in Utah.
Line 80 - McIntosh, Annie M, daughter, white, female, born Mar 1898, age 2, single, born in Utah, father born in Utah, mother born in Utah.
Line 81 - McIntosh, unnamed, [Alta Grace], daughter, white, female, born April 1900, age 2/12, single, born in Utah, father born in Utah, mother born in Utah.

7. He appeared on the census on 19 Apr 1910 in Provo, Utah, Utah, United States.[23]
**Line 1 - McIntosh, J.A. head, male, white, age 41, married 22 years, born in Nevada, father born in Scotland -Scotch, mother born in Canada-Scotch, speaks english, teamster-freight, employee, out of work on Apr 15, 1910, out of work 8 weeks in 1909, can read and write, owns, house.**
Line 2 - McIntosh, Annie, wife, female, white, age 42, married 22 years, had 9 children, 8 living, born in Utah, father born in England-English, mother born in England-English, speaks english, can read and write.
Line 3 - McIntosh, Albert, son, male, white, age 20, single, born in Utah, father born in Nevada, mother born in Utah, speaks english, teamster, employee, out of work on Apr 15, 1910, out of work 4 weeks in 1909, can read and write.
Line 4 - McIntosh, Emily, daughter, female, white, age 18, single, born in Utah, father born in Nevada, mother born in Utah, speaks english, seamstress, can read and write, attended school since Sept 1, 1909.
Line 5 - McIntosh, Donald, son, male, white, age 16, single, born in Utah, father born in Nevada, mother born in Utah, speaks english, teamster, employee, out of work on Apr 15, 1910, out of work 2 weeks in 1909, can read and write, attended school since Sept 1, 1909.
Line 6 - McIntosh, Basil, son, male, white, age 14, single, born in Utah, father born in Nevada, mother born in Utah, speaks english, can read and write, attended school since Sept 1, 1909.

# Joseph Albert McIntosh and Annie Eliza Russell

Line 7 - McIntosh, Marie, daughter, female, white, age 12, single, born in Utah, father born in Nevada, mother born in Utah, speaks english, can read and write, attended school since Sept 1, 1909.
Line 8 - McIntosh, Kimball, son, male, white, age 8, single, born in Utah, father born in Nevada, mother born in Utah, speaks english.
Line 9 - McIntosh, Kenneth, son, male, white, age 5, single, born in Utah, father born in Nevada, mother born in Utah, speaks english.
Line 10 - McIntosh, Rollo, son, male, white, age 3, single, born in Utah, father born in Nevada, mother born in Utah, speaks english.

8. He appeared on the census on 6 Jan 1920 in Provo, Utah, Utah, United States.[24]
**Line 35 - McIntosh, J.A., head, owns home, mortgage free, male, white, age 52, married, can read and write, born in Utah, father born in Scotland, speaks scotch, mother born in Scotland, speaks Scotch, speaks english, mining, lead mine, wage worker.**
Line 36 - McIntosh, Annie, wife, female, white, age 52, married, can read and write, born in Utah, father born in United States, mother born in United States, speaks english, no occupation.

9. He appeared on the census on 2 Apr 1930 in Provo, Utah, Utah, United States.[25]
**Line 1 - McIntosh, Jos. A., head, owns house valued at $3000, not a farm, male, white, age 62, married at age 21, can read, write and speak english, born in Nevada, father born in Scotland, mother born in Scotland, laborer at ranch, wage worker, employed, not a veteran.**
Line 2 - McIntosh, Annie, wife, female, white, age 62, married at age 21, can read, write and speak english, born in Utah, father born in England, mother born in England.
Line 3 - McIntosh, Fay, daughter, female, white, age 19, single, in school, can read, write and speak english, born in Utah, father born in Nevada, mother born in Utah.

10. He appeared on the census on 18 Apr 1940 in Compton, Los Angeles, California, United States.[26]
**Line 21 - owns house valued at $2500, not a farm, McIntosh, Joseph A., head, male, white, age 71, married, finished 4 years high school, born in Nevada, in 1935 lived in South Gate, Los Angeles, California, no occupation, has another source of income.**
Line 22 - McIntosh, Annie, wife, female, white, age 71, married, finished 4 years high school, born in Utah, in 1935 lived in South Gate, Los Angeles, California.
Line 23 - Garrell, Fay, daughter, female, white, age 28, married, finished 2 years college, born in Utah, in 1935 lived in South Gate, Los Angeles, California, saleslady at drug store.

11. His obituary was published in Jan 1950 in Salt Lake City, Salt Lake, Utah, United States.
**Joseph Albert McIntosh**, 80, died Saturday at 3 a.m. in a Los Angeles Hospital after a lingering illness resulting from an automobile accident eight years ago.
A former Utahn, Mr. McIntosh resided for many years in Provo and St. John, Tooele county. He had been a rancher and sheepman until his retirement to Los Angeles, Cal., 12 years ago.
Mr. McIntosh was born March 8, 1869, in Panaca, Nev., a son of William and Maria Caldwell McIntosh. He came to Utah with his parents as a boy.
He married Annie E. Russell in St. John March 7, 1888. She died in the accident that crippled Mr. McIntosh eight years ago.
Mr. McIntosh was a member of the Church of Jesus Christ of Latter-day Saints and had been active as president of St. John L.D.S. Sunday school when he resided there.
Surviving are six sons, William Albert, Donald H. and Kimball D. McIntosh, Salt Lake City; Basil Hugh, Kenneth Grant McIntosh, Los Angeles, Cal.; Henry Rollo McIntosh, San Francisco, Cal.; a daugthter, Mrs. Fay Maxine Jerrell, Las Vegas, Nev.; 17 grandchildren and 10 great-grandchildren.
Funeral Services will be conducted Tuesday at 2 p.m. in St. John L.D.S. ward chapel by Evan Vaughn Arthur, bishop. Friends may call at Tooele mortuary Tuesday before services. The body is to arrive in St. John Monday night. Burial will be in St. John cemetery.

# Joseph Albert McIntosh and Annie Eliza Russell

| **Wife** | **Annie Eliza Russell**[4,27] | |
|---|---|---|
| AKA | Annie McIntosh, Annie Elizabeth Russell, Elizabeth Russell, Liza Russell, Lizie Russell | |
| Born | 23 Oct 1867 | Saint John, Tooele, Utah Territory, United States |
| Died | 10 Jul 1940 | Barstow, San Bernardino, California, United States |
| Cause of Death | Killed in a car accident | |
| Buried | 1940 | Rush Valley, Tooele, Utah, United States |
| Address | St. John Cemetery, East on Main Street to Cemetery Road, Rush Valley, Utah 84069, USA | |
| Bapt.(LDS) | 1 Aug 1875 | |
| Conf.(LDS) | 1 Aug 1875 | |
| Init.(LDS) | 25 Jun 1924 | Salt Lake Temple |
| Endow.(LDS) | 25 Jun 1924 | Salt Lake Temple |
| Father | William Greenwood Russell Sr. (1812-1872) [28,29,30,31,32,33] | |
| Mother | Elizabeth Vickery (1825-1912) [34] | |
| SealP (LDS) | BIC | |

**Events**

1. She appeared on the census on 2 Jun 1870 in Saint John, Tooele, Utah Territory, United States.[35] [Parents of these children in Stockton (nearby) on this date].
   Line 1 - Russell, Brigham, age 16, male, white, at home, born in Utah, father & mother foreign born yes, male over 21.
   Line 2 - Russell, John, age 14, male, white, at home, born in Utah, father & mother foreign born yes.
   Line 3 - Russell, Joseph, age 12, male, white, at home, born in Utah, father & mother foreign born yes.
   Line 4 - Russell, Heber, age 10, male, white, at home, born in Utah, father & mother foreign born yes.
   Line 5 - Russell, Hiram, age 9, male, white, at home, born in Utah, father & mother foreign born yes.
   Line 6 - Russell, Elizabeth, age 6, female, white, at home, born in Utah, father & mother foreign born yes.
   Line 7 - Russell Daniel, age 4, male, white, at home, born in Utah, father & mother foreign born yes.
   **Line 8 - Russell, Annie E, age 2, female, white, at home, born in Utah, father & mother foreign born yes.**

2. She appeared on the census on 17 Jun 1880 in Rush Lake, Tooele, Utah Territory, United States.[36]
   Line 32, Russell, Elizabeth, white, female, age 52, head, widowed, housekeeping, born in England, father born in England, mother born in England.
   Line 33, Russell, Joseph, white, male, age 22, son, single, herder, attended school within year, born in Utah, father born in England, mother born in England.
   Line 34 - Russell, Heber, white, male, age 20, son, single, wood chopper, attended school within year, born in Utah, father born in England, mother born in England.
   Line 35 - Russell, Hyrum, white, male, age 18, son, single, wood chopper, attended school within year, born in Utah, father born in England, mother born in England.
   Line 36 - Russell, Elizabeth, white, female, age 17, daughter, single, at home, attended school within year, born in Utah, father born in England, mother born in England.
   Line 37 - Russell, Daniel, white, male, age 16, son, single, mail carrier, attended school within year. born in Utah, father born in England, mother born in England.
   **Line 38 - Russell, Anne, white, female, age 12, single, at home, attended school within year, born in Utah, father born in England, mother born in England.**

3. She appeared on the census on 29 Jun 1900 in Saint John, Tooele, Utah, United States.[37]
   Line 74 - McIntosh, Joseph A, head, white, male, born Mar 1869, age 31, married 16 years, born in Utah, father born in Ohio, mother born in Ohio, farming, 0 months unemployed, able to read, write and speak english, owns, mortgage free, farm #23.
   **Line 75 - McIntosh, Liza, wife, white, female, born Oct 1867, age 32, married 16 years, had 6 children, 6 living, born in Utah, father born in England, mother born in England, able to read, write and speak english.**
   Line 76 - McIntosh, William A, son, white, male, born Nov 1889, age 10, single, born in Utah, father born in Utah, mother born in Utah, at school, able to read, write and speak english.

# Joseph Albert McIntosh and Annie Eliza Russell

Line 77 - McIntosh, Emily E, daughter, white, female, born Sept 1891, age 8, single, born in Utah, father born in Utah, mother born in Utah, at school.
Line 78 - McIntosh, Hyrum D, son, white, male, born Oct 1893, age 6, single, born in Utah, father born in Utah, mother born in Utah, at school.
Line 79 - McIntosh, Boyd H, son, white, male, born Jan 1896, age 4, single, born in Utah, father born in Utah, mother born in Utah.
Line 80 - McIntosh, Annie M, daughter, white, female, born Mar 1898, age 2, single, born in Utah, father born in Utah, mother born in Utah.
Line 81 - McIntosh, unnamed, daughter, white, female, born April 1900, age 2/12, single, born in Utah, father born in Utah, mother born in Utah.

4. She appeared on the census on 19 Apr 1910 in Provo, Utah, Utah, United States.[38]
Line 1 - McIntosh, J.A. head, male, white, age 41, married 22 years, born in Nevada, father born in Scotland -Scotch, mother born in Canada-Scotch, speaks english, teamster-freight, employee, out of work on Apr 15, 1910, out of work 8 weeks in 1909, can read and write, owns, house.
**Line 2 - McIntosh, Annie, wife, female, white, age 42, married 22 years, had 9 children, 8 living, born in Utah, father born in England-English, mother born in England-English, speaks english, can read and write.**
Line 3 - McIntosh, Albert, son, male, white, age 20, single, born in Utah, father born in Nevada, mother born in Utah, speaks english, teamster, employee, out of work on Apr 15, 1910, out of work 4 weeks in 1909, can read and write.
Line 4 - McIntosh, Emily, daughter, female, white, age 18, single, born in Utah, father born in Nevada, mother born in Utah, speaks english, seamstress, can read and write, attended school since Sept 1, 1909.
Line 5 - McIntosh, Donald, son, male, white, age 16, single, born in Utah, father born in Nevada, mother born in Utah, speaks english, teamster, employee, out of work on Apr 15, 1910, out of work 2 weeks in 1909, can read and write, attended school since Sept 1, 1909.
Line 6 - McIntosh, Basil, son, male, white, age 14, single, born in Utah, father born in Nevada, mother born in Utah, speaks english, can read and write, attended school since Sept 1, 1909.
Line 7 - McIntosh, Marie, daughter, female, white, age 12, single, born in Utah, father born in Nevada, mother born in Utah, speaks english, can read and write, attended school since Sept 1, 1909.
Line 8 - McIntosh, Kimball, son, male, white, age 8, single, born in Utah, father born in Nevada, mother born in Utah, speaks english.
Line 9 - McIntosh, Kenneth, son, male, white, age 5, single, born in Utah, father born in Nevada, mother born in Utah, speaks english.
Line 10 - McIntosh, Rollo, son, male, white, age 3, single, born in Utah, father born in Nevada, mother born in Utah, speaks english.

5. She appeared on the census on 6 Jan 1920 in Provo, Utah, Utah, United States.[39]
Line 35 - McIntosh, J.A., head, owns home, mortgage free, male, white, age 52, married, can read and write, born in Utah, father born in Scotland, speaks scotch, mother born in Scotland, speaks Scotch, speaks english, mining, lead mine, wage worker.
**Line 36 - McIntosh, Annie, wife, female, white, age 52, married, can read and write, born in Utah, father born in United States, mother born in United States, speaks english, no occupation.**

6. She had a residence on 19 Nov 1929 in Provo, Utah, Utah, United States.

7. She appeared on the census on 2 Apr 1930 in Provo, Utah, Utah, United States.[40]
Line 1 - McIntosh, Jos. A., head, owns house valued at $3000, not a farm, male, white, age 62, married at age 21, can read, write and speak english, born in Nevada, father born in Scotland, mother born in Scotland, laborer at ranch, wage worker, employed, not a veteran.
**Line 2 - McIntosh, Annie, wife, female, white, age 62, married at age 21, can read, write and speak english, born in Utah, father born in England, mother born in England.**
Line 3 - McIntosh, Fay, daughter, female, white, age 19, single, in school, can read, write and speak english, born in Utah, father born in Nevada, mother born in Utah.

8. Alt Death: 10 Jul 1938, Barstow, San Bernardino, California, United States.[41]
Her son, Donald Hyrum, wrote a story about his mother. The last line says: "...she was killed in an automobile accident near Barstow, California on July 10, 1938."

# Joseph Albert McIntosh and Annie Eliza Russell

Her obituary in The Milford News is dated July 14, 1938, and says she died on July 10, 1938.
However, she is listed in the 1940 Census, dated 18 Apr 1940, as living with her husband and youngest daughter.

9. Her obituary was published on 14 Jul 1938.[42]
**Mother Local Man Killed Near Vegas**
Funeral services for Annie Elisabeth McIntosh 71, who was killed in a head-on motor car collision at Las Vegas, Nevada, Sunday, are to be conducted Friday at 1 p.m. at the St. John L.D.S. ward chapel. Interment will be in St. John cemetery. Mrs. McIntosh, with her husband, Joseph Albert McIntosh, and her son, Kimball H. McIntosh, were coming from her home in Los Angeles to Milford, to visit her sons, William Albert McIntosh of Milford and Donald H. McIntosh of East St. Louis, who was visiting in Utah. She was killed instantly when the automobile in which she was riding met head-on with another machine 62 miles west of Las Vegas, and Mr. McIntosh lay critically injured in a Las Vegas hospital for some time.
Born in St. John October 23, 1866, a daughter of William and Elizabeth Vicory Russell, she was married to Mr. McIntosh, also of St. John, and later moved to Provo, where they made their home for 26 years. Four years ago they moved to Los Angeles, where she had since resided.
Surviving are her husband; her sons, William Albert McIntosh of Milford, Donald H. McIntosh of East St. Louis, Ill.; Basil H., Kimball D., Kenneth G. and Henry Rollo McIntosh of Los Angeles, a daughter Mrs. Faye Maxine Burett of Los Angeles, and a brother Heber C. Russell of St. John.

10. She appeared on the census on 18 Apr 1940 in Compton, Los Angeles, California, United States.[43]
Line 21 - owns house valued at $2500, not a **farm,** McIntosh, Joseph A., head, male, white, age 71, married, finished 4 years high school, born in Nevada, in 1935 lived in South Gate, Los Angeles, California, no occupation, has another source of income.
**Line 22 - McIntosh, Annie, wife, female, white, age 71, married, finished 4 years high school, born in Utah, in 1935 lived in South Gate, Los Angeles, California.**
Line 23 - Garrell, Fay, daughter, female, white, age 28, married, finished 2 years college, born in Utah, in 1935 lived in South Gate, Los Angeles, California, saleslady at drug store.

## Children

| 1 | M | **William Albert McIntosh** [4,44] | |
|---|---|---|---|
| AKA | | Albert McIntosh, Bert McIntosh | |
| Born | | 28 Nov 1889 | Saint John, Tooele, Utah Territory, United States[45] |
| Died | | 28 Feb 1952 | Salt Lake City, Salt Lake, Utah, United States[45] |
| Address | | LDS Hospital, 325 8th Avenue, Salt Lake City, Utah 84143, USA | |
| Cause of Death | | Arteriosclerotic heart disease[45] | |
| Buried | | 3 Mar 1952 | Millcreek, Salt Lake, Utah, United States[45] |
| Address | | Wasatch Lawn Memorial Park, 3401 South Highland Drive, Millcreek, Utah, USA | |
| Notes | | We don't have his plot number but his wife Grace Georgia Kirkman McIntosh is in Plot: Glendale 174-2-E. The pictures of their head stones on findagrave.com look alike so he must be next to her. | |
| Bapt.(LDS) | | 17 Sep 1898 | |
| Conf.(LDS) | | 17 Sep 1898 | |
| Init.(LDS) | | Completed | Los Angeles California Temple |
| Endow.(LDS) | | 16 Sep 1960 | Los Angeles California Temple |

Produced by: Beverly McIntosh Brown, 15933 W Silver Breeze Dr, Surprise, AZ 85374, 623-584-0440, starfighteraz@gmail.com : 29 Jun 2021

# Joseph Albert McIntosh and Annie Eliza Russell

| Children (cont.) | | |
|---|---|---|
| SealP (LDS) | 8 Apr 1964 | Salt Lake Temple |
| Spouse | Grace Georgia Kirkman (1898-1972)[46] | 12 Oct 1916 - Nephi, Juab, Utah, United States[47] |
| SealS (LDS) | 16 Sep 1960 | Los Angeles California Temple |

**Events**

1. He worked as a conductor for the Union Pacific Railroad.[45]
2. He worked as a teamster in Utah, Utah, United States.
3. He appeared on the census on 29 Jun 1900 in Saint John, Tooele, Utah, United States.
   Line 74 - McIntosh, Joseph A, head, white, male, born Mar 1869, age 31, married 16 years, born in Utah, father born in Ohio, mother born in Ohio, farming, 0 months unemployed, able to read, write and speak english, owns, mortgage free, farm #23.
   Line 75 - McIntosh, Liza, wife, white, female, born Oct 1867, age 32, married 16 years, had 6 children, 6 living, born in Utah, father born in England, mother born in England, able to read, write and speak english.
   **Line 76 - McIntosh, William A, son, white, male, born Nov 1889, age 10, single, born in Utah, father born in Utah, mother born in Utah, at school, able to read, write and speak english.**
   Line 77 - McIntosh, Emily E, daughter, white, female, born Sept 1891, age 8, single, born in Utah, father born in Utah, mother born in Utah, at school.
   Line 78 - McIntosh, Hyrum D, son, white, male, born Oct 1893, age 6, single, born in Utah, father born in Utah, mother born in Utah, at school.
   Line 79 - McIntosh, Boyd H, son, white, male, born Jan 1896, age 4, single, born in Utah, father born in Utah, mother born in Utah.
   Line 80 - McIntosh, Annie M, daughter, white, female, born Mar 1898, age 2, single, born in Utah, father born in Utah, mother born in Utah.
   Line 81 - McIntosh, unnamed, daughter, white, female, born April 1900, age 2/12, single, born in Utah, father born in Utah, mother born in Utah.
4. He appeared on the census on 19 Apr 1910 in Provo, Utah, Utah, United States.[48]
   Line 1 - McIntosh, J.A. head, male, white, age 41, married 22 years, born in Nevada, father born in Scotland -Scotch, mother born in Canada-Scotch, speaks english, teamster-freight, employee, out of work on Apr 15, 1910, out of work 8 weeks in 1909, can read and write, owns, house.
   Line 2 - McIntosh, Annie, wife, female, white, age 42, married 22 years, had 9 children, 8 living, born in Utah, father born in England-English, mother born in England-English, speaks english, can read and write.
   **Line 3 - McIntosh, Albert, son, male, white, age 20, single, born in Utah, father born in Nevada, mother born in Utah, speaks english, teamster, employee, out of work on Apr 15, 1910, out of work 4 weeks in 1909, can read and write.**
   Line 4 - McIntosh, Emily, daughter, female, white, age 18, single, born in Utah, father born in Nevada, mother born in Utah, speaks english, seamstress, can read and write, attended school since Sept 1, 1909.
   Line 5 - McIntosh, Donald, son, male, white, age 16, single, born in Utah, father born in Nevada, mother born in Utah, speaks english, teamster, employee, out of work on Apr 15, 1910, out of work 2 weeks in 1909, can read and write, attended school since Sept 1, 1909.
   Line 6 - McIntosh, Basil, son, male, white, age 14, single, born in Utah, father born in Nevada, mother born in Utah, speaks english, can read and write, attended school since Sept 1, 1909.
   Line 7 - McIntosh, Marie, daughter, female, white, age 12, single, born in Utah, father born in Nevada, mother born in Utah, speaks english, can read and write, attended school since Sept 1, 1909.
   Line 8 - McIntosh, Kimball, son, male, white, age 8, single, born in Utah, father born in Nevada, mother born in Utah, speaks english.
   Line 9 - McIntosh, Kenneth, son, male, white, age 5, single, born in Utah, father born in Nevada, mother born in Utah, speaks english.
   Line 10 - McIntosh, Rollo, son, male, white, age 3, single, born in Utah, father born in Nevada, mother born in Utah, speaks english.
5. He appeared on the census on 14 Jan 1920 in Pocatello, Bannock, Idaho, United States.[49]
   **Line 34 - McIntosh, William, lodger, male, white, age 30, married, can read, write and speak english, born in Utah, father born in Utah, mother born in Utah, occupation-brakeman on the rail road, wage worker.**
   Line 35 - McIntosh, Grace, lodger, female, white, age 21, married, can read, write and speak english, born in Utah,

# Joseph Albert McIntosh and Annie Eliza Russell

father born in Utah, mother born in Utah, no occupation.

6. He appeared on the census on 10 Apr 1930 in Milford, Beaver, Utah, United States.[50]
**Line 55 - McIntosh, William A, head, home rented, $32 monthly rental, owns radio set, does not live on farm, male, white, age 41, married at age 27, did not attend school within year, can read and write, born in Utah, father born in Utah, mother born in Utah, able to speak english, conductor, railroad, wage worker, actually at work.**
Line 56 - McIntosh, Grace, wife, female, white, age 31, married at age 19, did not attend school within year, can read and write, born in Utah, father born in Utah, mother born in Utah, able to speak english, no occupation.
Line 57 - McIntosh, Patsy J, daughter, female, white, age 8, single, can read and write, born in Utah, father born in Utah, mother born in Utah, no occupation.
Line 58 - McIntosh, Norma M, daughter, female, white, age 4, single, cannot read and write, born in Utah, father born in Utah, mother born in Utah, no occupation.
Line 59 - McIntosh, Joann, daughter, female, white, age 2 9/12, single, cannot read and write, born in Utah, father born in Utah, mother born in Utah, no occupation.

7. He appeared on the census on 4 Apr 1940 in Milford, Beaver, Utah, United States.
**Line 1 - McIntosh, William A., head, male, white, age 50, married, attended high school 2 years, born in Utah, lived in same house in 1935, employed as conductor for steam railroad, wage worker.**
Line 2 - McIntosh, Grace, wife, female, white, age 41, married, attended high school 2 years, born in Utah, lived in same house in 1935, no occupaction, works in household.
Line 3 - McIntosh, Patsy Jean, daughter, female, white, age 18, single attending high school in 3rd year, born in Utah, lived in same house in 1935, student.
Line 4 - McIntosh, Norma, daughter, female, white, age 15, single, attending high school in 1st year, born in Utah, lived in same house in 1935, student.
Line 5 - McIntosh, Joann, daughter, female, white, age 12, single, attending school, grade 6, born in Utah, lived in same house in 1935, student.
Line 6 - McIntosh, Michael, son, male white, age 6, single, in school, born in Utah.

8. His obituary was published in the "The Salt Lake Telegram" on 29 Feb 1952 in Salt Lake City, Salt Lake, Utah, United States.
William Albert McIntosh, 1772 E. 21st South, conductor employed by the Union Pacific Railroad Co. for 35 years, died Thursday at 9:40 a.m. in a Salt Lake hospital of a heart aliment.
A son of Joseph Albert and Anna Elizabeth Russell McIntosh, he was born in St. Johns, Tooele County, Nov. 28, 1889. He married Grace Kirkman in Nephi Oct. 12, 1917.
Survivors include his widow, Salt Lake City; a son, Michael McIntosh; and two daughters, Mrs. Norma Palosky and Mrs. Joann Corbett, Salt Lake City; a third daughter, Mrs. Patricia Atkins, Rchmond, Va.; three grandchildren; four brothers: Donald and Kimball McIntosh, Salt Lake City; Basil and Kenneth McIntosh, Los Angeles, and one sister, Mrs. Faye Jerrill, Las Vegas.
Funeral services will be conducted Monday at 2 p.m. in Rosslyn Heights Ward, Church of Jesus Christ of Latter-day Saints, 1870 Parleys Canyon Blvd., by Claron O. Spencer, bishop.
Friends may call at 36 E. 7th South Sunday from 4 to 8 p.m., and Monday prior to services.

# Joseph Albert McIntosh and Annie Eliza Russell

| Children (cont.) | | |
|---|---|---|
| 2 F | **Emily Elizabeth McIntosh**[4,51] | |
| AKA | Emily Mark, Emily Wymore | |
| Born | 14 Sep 1891 | Saint John, Tooele, Utah Territory, United States |
| Died | 11 Dec 1918 | Medicine Bow, Carbon, Wyoming, United States |
| Cause of Death | Influenza | |
| Buried | 18 Dec 1918 | Rush Valley, Tooele, Utah, United States |
| Address | Saint John Cemetery, Rush Valley, Utah, USA | |
| Bapt.(LDS) | 5 Jul 2017 | Fort Collins Colorado Temple |
| Conf.(LDS) | 5 Jul 2017 | Fort Collins Colorado Temple |
| Init.(LDS) | 11 Jul 2017 | Fort Collins Colorado Temple |
| Endow.(LDS) | 26 Jan 2019 | Provo Utah Temple |
| SealP (LDS) | 19 Jun 2019 | Fort Collins Colorado Temple |
| Spouse | William Roy Wymore (1891-1948) | 29 Dec 1917 - Salt Lake City, Salt Lake, Utah, United States[52,53] |
| SealS (LDS) | 7 Feb 2003 | Los Angeles California Temple |

**Events**

1. She appeared on the census on 29 Jun 1900 in Saint John, Tooele, Utah, United States.
   Line 74 - McIntosh, Joseph A, head, white, male, born Mar 1869, age 31, married 16 years, born in Utah, father born in Ohio, mother born in Ohio, farming, 0 months unemployed, able to read, write and speak english, owns, mortgage free, farm #23.
   Line 75 - McIntosh, Liza, wife, white, female, born Oct 1867, age 32, married 16 years, had 6 children, 6 living, born in Utah, father born in England, mother born in England, able to read, write and speak english.
   Line 76 - McIntosh, William A, son, white, male, born Nov 1889, age 10, single, born in Utah, father born in Utah, mother born in Utah, at school, able to read, write and speak english.
   **Line 77 - McIntosh, Emily E, daughter, white, female, born Sept 1891, age 8, single, born in Utah, father born in Utah, mother born in Utah, at school.**
   Line 78 - McIntosh, Hyrum D, son, white, male, born Oct 1893, age 6, single, born in Utah, father born in Utah, mother born in Utah, at school.
   Line 79 - McIntosh, Boyd H, son, white, male, born Jan 1896, age 4, single, born in Utah, father born in Utah, mother born in Utah.
   Line 80 - McIntosh, Annie M, daughter, white, female, born Mar 1898, age 2, single, born in Utah, father born in Utah, mother born in Utah.
   Line 81 - McIntosh, unnamed, daughter, white, female, born April 1900, age 2/12, single, born in Utah, father born in Utah, mother born in Utah.

2. She appeared on the census on 19 Apr 1910 in Provo, Utah, Utah, United States.[54]
   Line 1 - McIntosh, J.A. head, male, white, age 41, married 22 years, born in Nevada, father born in Scotland -Scotch, mother born in Canada-Scotch, speaks english, teamster-freight, employee, out of work on Apr 15, 1910, out of work 8 weeks in 1909, can read and write, owns, house.
   Line 2 - McIntosh, Annie, wife, female, white, age 42, married 22 years, had 9 children, 8 living, born in Utah, father born in England-English, mother born in England-English, speaks english, can read and write.
   Line 3 - McIntosh, Albert, son, male, white, age 20, single, born in Utah, father born in Nevada, mother born in Utah, speaks english, teamster, employee, out of work on Apr 15, 1910, out of work 4 weeks in 1909, can read and write.
   **Line 4 - McIntosh, Emily, daughter, female, white, age 18, single, born in Utah, father born in Nevada, mother born in Utah, speaks english, seamstress, can read and write, attended school since Sept 1, 1909.**
   Line 5 - McIntosh, Donald, son, male, white, age 16, single, born in Utah, father born in Nevada, mother born in Utah, speaks english, teamster, employee, out of work on Apr 15, 1910, out of work 2 weeks in 1909, can read and write, attended school since Sept 1, 1909.
   Line 6 - McIntosh, Basil, son, male, white, age 14, single, born in Utah, father born in Nevada, mother born in Utah, speaks english, can read and write, attended school since Sept 1, 1909.
   Line 7 - McIntosh, Marie, daughter, female, white, age 12, single, born in Utah, father born in Nevada, mother born in Utah, speaks english, can read and write, attended school since Sept 1, 1909.

# Joseph Albert McIntosh and Annie Eliza Russell

Line 8 - McIntosh, Kimball, son, male, white, age 8, single, born in Utah, father born in Nevada, mother born in Utah, speaks english.
Line 9 - McIntosh, Kenneth, son, male, white, age 5, single, born in Utah, father born in Nevada, mother born in Utah, speaks english.
Line 10 - McIntosh, Rollo, son, male, white, age 3, single, born in Utah, father born in Nevada, mother born in Utah, speaks english.

3. Her obituary was published in The Provo Post on 13 Dec 1918 in Provo, Utah, Utah, United States.
   Mrs. Emily Wymore, wife of William Wymore, died yesterday at Medicine Bow, Wyo., where she had gone to assist her sister to nurse one of her children who was ill from influenza. While there she was attacked and succumbed to the disease. She was 27 years of age, the daughter of Mr. and Mrs. Joseph McIntosh of the Fifth ward. Her husband who is in the military service, reached her bedside just before she died. The body will be brought to Provo for burial.
4. Memorial.
   This was written by Sandra Jerrell about her mother Faye McIntosh Jerrell and her grandmother Annie Eliza Russell McIntosh:
   "Mom remembers how terrible Grandma McIntosh felt when Emily died and how hard it was for her. [Emily's] sister Marie and husband Ralph Lee were both sick in bed with the flu. Emily got time off from teaching school [in Utah] and went to Wyoming to take care of them. She was there three days and then got the flu and died. When the war was over in 1918 Grandma McIntosh was so excited when she heard it that she threw the alarm clock out the window. But that was also a very sad time in her life. When Emily's husband, Bill Wymore, came home he was to find out that Emily had died from the flu epidemic while he was gone. He came to the McIntosh home and stayed for a few months, but he was so heart broken he finally said that he would have to leave."

| 3 M | **Donald Hyrum McIntosh** [4,55,56,57,58] | |
|---|---|---|
| AKA | Don McIntosh, Hyrum D. McIntosh | |
| Born | 1 Oct 1893 | Saint John, Tooele, Utah Territory, United States[59,60] |
| Died | 27 Dec 1976 | Salt Lake City, Salt Lake, Utah, United States[9,60,61,62] |
| Cause of Death | Old age | |
| Buried | 30 Dec 1976 | Provo, Utah, Utah, United States[60,63,64,65] |
| Address | Provo City Cemetery, 610 South State, Provo, Utah 84606, USA | |
| Notes | Block 13, Lot 83 | |
| Bapt.(LDS) | 2 Aug 1902 | |
| Conf.(LDS) | 2 Aug 1902 | |
| Init.(LDS) | 25 Jun 1924 | Salt Lake Temple |
| Endow.(LDS) | 25 Jun 1924 | Salt Lake Temple |
| SealP (LDS) | 25 Jun 1924 | Salt Lake Temple |
| Spouse | Melba C. Cropper (1899-1982) | 2 Aug 1924 - Salt Lake City, Salt Lake, Utah, United States[66] |
| SealS (LDS) | 3 Sep 1924 | Salt Lake Temple |

**Events**

1. He was blessed on 19 Nov 1893 in Saint John, Tooele, Utah Territory, United States.
2. He appeared on the census on 29 Jun 1900 in Saint John, Tooele, Utah, United States.
   Line 74 - McIntosh, Joseph A, head, white, male, born Mar 1869, age 31, married 16 years, born in Utah, father born in Ohio, mother born in Ohio, farming, 0 months unemployed, able to read, write and speak english, owns, mortgage free, farm #23.
   Line 75 - McIntosh, Liza, wife, white, female, born Oct 1867, age 32, married 16 years, had 6 children, 6 living, born in Utah, father born in England, mother born in England, able to read, write and speak english.

# Joseph Albert McIntosh and Annie Eliza Russell

Line 76 - McIntosh, William A, son, white, male, born Nov 1889, age 10, single, born in Utah, father born in Utah, mother born in Utah, at school, able to read, write and speak english.
Line 77 - McIntosh, Emily E, daughter, white, female, born Sept 1891, age 8, single, born in Utah, father born in Utah, mother born in Utah, at school.
**Line 78 - McIntosh, Hyrum D, son, white, male, born Oct 1893, age 6, single, born in Utah, father born in Utah, mother born in Utah, at school.**
Line 79 - McIntosh, Boyd H, son, white, male, born Jan 1896, age 4, single, born in Utah, father born in Utah, mother born in Utah.
Line 80 - McIntosh, Annie M, daughter, white, female, born Mar 1898, age 2, single, born in Utah, father born in Utah, mother born in Utah.
Line 81 - McIntosh, unnamed, daughter, white, female, born April 1900, age 2/12, single, born in Utah, father born in Utah, mother born in Utah.

3. He appeared on the census on 19 Apr 1910 in Provo, Utah, Utah, United States.[67]
Line 1 - McIntosh, J.A. head, male, white, age 41, married 22 years, born in Nevada, father born in Scotland -Scotch, mother born in Canada-Scotch, speaks english, teamster-freight, employee, out of work on Apr 15, 1910, out of work 8 weeks in 1909, can read and write, owns, house.
Line 2 - McIntosh, Annie, wife, female, white, age 42, married 22 years, had 9 children, 8 living, born in Utah, father born in England-English, mother born in England-English, speaks english, can read and write.
Line 3 - McIntosh, Albert, son, male, white, age 20, single, born in Utah, father born in Nevada, mother born in Utah, speaks english, teamster, employee, out of work on Apr 15, 1910, out of work 4 weeks in 1909, can read and write.
Line 4 - McIntosh, Emily, daughter, female, white, age 18, single, born in Utah, father born in Nevada, mother born in Utah, speaks english, seamstress, can read and write, attended school since Sept 1, 1909.
**Line 5 - McIntosh, Donald, son, male, white, age 16, single, born in Utah, father born in Nevada, mother born in Utah, speaks english, teamster, employee, out of work on Apr 15, 1910, out of work 2 weeks in 1909, can read and write, attended school since Sept 1, 1909.**
Line 6 - McIntosh, Basil, son, male, white, age 14, single, born in Utah, father born in Nevada, mother born in Utah, speaks english, can read and write, attended school since Sept 1, 1909.
Line 7 - McIntosh, Marie, daughter, female, white, age 12, single, born in Utah, father born in Nevada, mother born in Utah, speaks english, can read and write, attended school since Sept 1, 1909.
Line 8 - McIntosh, Kimball, son, male, white, age 8, single, born in Utah, father born in Nevada, mother born in Utah, speaks english.
Line 9 - McIntosh, Kenneth, son, male, white, age 5, single, born in Utah, father born in Nevada, mother born in Utah, speaks english.
Line 10 - McIntosh, Rollo, son, male, white, age 3, single, born in Utah, father born in Nevada, mother born in Utah, speaks english.

4. He appeared on the LDS Church Census census in 1920.[68]
Joseph Albert McIntosh, head, male, birthplace North America.
Annie Russell McIntosh, wife, female, birthplace North America.
**Don Hyrum McIntosh, son, male,**
Daniel Kimball McIntosh, son, male,
Kenneth Grant McIntosh, son, male,
Rollo Henry McIntosh, son, male,
Fay Maxine McIntosh, daughter, female, birthplace North America.

5. He appeared on the LDS Church Census census in 1930.[68]
Address: 205 Caroline St., Amarillo, Texas
**1. Donald Hyrum McIntosh-Elder b. 1 Oct 1893, St. John, Tooele, Utah, zinc miner.**
2. Melba Cropper- female b. 19 Aug 1899, Hinckley, Millard, Utah
3. Meldon Joseph McIntosh- male b. 5 July 1925, Murray, Salt Lake, Utah
4. Marilyn Joy McIntosh- female b. 4 Mar 1928, Salt Lake, Salt Lake, Utah

6. He worked as a metallurgy engineer.

7. He appeared on the census on 14 Apr 1930 in Amarillo, Potter, Texas, United States.
**Line 83 - McIntosh, Donald H, head, rents house for $30, not a farm, male, white, age 35, married at age 30, can read,**

# Joseph Albert McIntosh and Annie Eliza Russell

**write and speak english, born in Utah, father born in Utah, mother born in Utah, works as assistant supertintendant at zinc smelter, wage worker, not a veteran.**
Line 84 - McIntosh, Melba C., wife, female, white, age 30, married at age 24, can read,write and speak english, born in Utah, father born in Utah, mother born in Utah.
Line 85 - McIntosh, Meldon J., son, male, white, age 4, single, not in school, born in Utah, father born in Utah, mother born in Utah.
Line 86 - McIntosh, Marilin J., daughter, female, white, age 2, single, born in Utah, father born in Utah, mother born in Utah.

8. He had a residence in 1931 in East Saint Louis, St. Clair, Illinois, United States.
He was living in East St. Louis per his mother's obituary.

9. Draft Registration: World War II, 27 Apr 1942, Corpus Christi, Nueces, Texas, United States.[69] Description of Registrant: white; 5' 11 1/2"; 168 #; brown eyes, black hair, light complexion; middle finger on right hand injured.
Employer's Name and Address: American Smelting and Refining, Corpus Christi, Nueces, Texas.
Age: 48.

10. He appeared on the LDS Church Census census in 1950.[68]
**Donald Hyrum McIntosh, male, birth 1893, birthplace St Johns, Utah.**
Melba Cropper McIntosh, female, born in Hinkley, Utah.
Meldon Joseph McIntosh, male, born in Murray, Utah.
Howard Hugh McIntosh, male, born in Amarillo, Texas.
Hazel Halice McIntosh, female, born in East St Louis, Illinois.
Florence Faye McIntosh, female, born in Hinkley, Utah.
Fred Ferral McIntosh, male, born in Corpus Christi, Texas.

11. His obituary was published in The Daily Herald after 27 Dec 1976 in Provo, Utah, Utah, United States.[70]
Funeral services for **Don Hyrum McIntosh**, 83, of 79 Marrcrest South, Provo, who died of causes incident to age on Monday, Dec. 27, 1976 in the Valley West Hospital in Salt Lake City, will be Thursday a 11 a.m. in the Pleasant View Sixth Ward Chapel, 2445 N. 650 E.
Mr. McIntosh was born Oct.1,1893 in St. John,Tooele County, a son of Joseph A. and Annie E. Russell McIntosh. He married Melba Cropper on Sept. 3, 1924 in the Salt Lake LDS Temple.
A metallurgy engineer, Mr. McIntosh retired in 1959 from American Smelting and Refining Company as the head of the Western Division. He was a star athlete at Brigham Young University and obtained a master's degree in metallurgy from the University of Utah in 1926. He was in "Who's Who in the West".
Active in the LDS Church, Mr. McIntosh was a high priest in the Pleasant View Sixth Ward, had been a branch president in St. Louis, Mo.; Amarillo and Corpus Christi, Tex., and a counselor in a bishopric in El Paso, Tex.
Survivors include his widow; two sons and three daughters, Meldon J. McIntosh, Ogden; Howard H. McIntosh, Brigham City; Mrs. Glen J (Joy) Evans, San Bernardino, Calif.; Mrs. Glen A. (Hazel) Weight, Salt Lake City; Mrs. Harold H. (Faye) Jarvis, San Gabriel, Calif.; 33 grandchildren; one great-grandchild; one brother and one sister, Kenneth G. McIntosh and Mrs. Martin (Faye) Jarrell, both of Hurricane, Washington County.
Friends may call at the Berg Mortuary in Provo, Wednesday from 6 to 8 p.m. or Thursday at the ward chapel prior to services. Burial will be in Provo City Cemetery

# Joseph Albert McIntosh and Annie Eliza Russell

| Children (cont.) | | |
|---|---|---|
| 4 M | **Basil Hugh McIntosh** [4,71] | |
| Born | 6 Jan 1896 | Saint John, Tooele, Utah, United States |
| Died | 28 Aug 1956 | Inglewood, Los Angeles, California, United States[72] |
| Buried | 1956 | Glendale, Los Angeles, California, United States[73] |
| Address | Forest Lawn Memorial Park, 1712 S. Glendale Avenue, Glendale, California 91205, USA | |
| Notes | Grave located in Tranquility, Lot 1041, Space 2. | |
| Bapt.(LDS) | 26 Aug 1904 | |
| Conf.(LDS) | 26 Aug 1904 | |
| Init.(LDS) | Completed | Los Angeles California Temple |
| Endow.(LDS) | 11 Oct 1963 | Los Angeles California Temple |
| SealP (LDS) | 8 Apr 1964 | Salt Lake Temple |
| Spouse | Bernice Christine Oates (1902-1973) | 14 Jun 1919 - Tooele, Tooele, Utah, United States |
| SealS (LDS) | 17 Jun 2003 | Provo Utah Temple |

**Events**

1. He was blessed on 12 Apr 1896 in Saint John, Tooele, Utah, United States.
2. He appeared on the census on 29 Jun 1900 in Saint John, Tooele, Utah, United States.
   Line 74 - McIntosh, Joseph A, head, white, male, born Mar 1869, age 31, married 16 years, born in Utah, father born in Ohio, mother born in Ohio, farming, 0 months unemployed, able to read, write and speak english, owns, mortgage free, farm #23.
   Line 75 - McIntosh, Liza, wife, white, female, born Oct 1867, age 32, married 16 years, had 6 children, 6 living, born in Utah, father born in England, mother born in England, able to read, write and speak english.
   Line 76 - McIntosh, William A, son, white, male, born Nov 1889, age 10, single, born in Utah, father born in Utah, mother born in Utah, at school, able to read, write and speak english.
   Line 77 - McIntosh, Emily E, daughter, white, female, born Sept 1891, age 8, single, born in Utah, father born in Utah, mother born in Utah, at school.
   Line 78 - McIntosh, Hyrum D, son, white, male, born Oct 1893, age 6, single, born in Utah, father born in Utah, mother born in Utah, at school.
   **Line 79 - McIntosh, Boyd H, [Basil], son, white, male, born Jan 1896, age 4, single, born in Utah, father born in Utah, mother born in Utah.**
   Line 80 - McIntosh, Annie M, daughter, white, female, born Mar 1898, age 2, single, born in Utah, father born in Utah, mother born in Utah.
   Line 81 - McIntosh, unnamed, daughter, white, female, born April 1900, age 2/12, single, born in Utah, father born in Utah, mother born in Utah.
3. He appeared on the census on 19 Apr 1910 in Provo, Utah, Utah, United States.[74]
   Line 1 - McIntosh, J.A. head, male, white, age 41, married 22 years, born in Nevada, father born in Scotland -Scotch, mother born in Canada-Scotch, speaks english, teamster-freight, employee, out of work on Apr 15, 1910, out of work 8 weeks in 1909, can read and write, owns, house.
   Line 2 - McIntosh, Annie, wife, female, white, age 42, married 22 years, had 9 children, 8 living, born in Utah, father born in England-English, mother born in England-English, speaks english, can read and write.
   Line 3 - McIntosh, Albert, son, male, white, age 20, single, born in Utah, father born in Nevada, mother born in Utah, speaks english, teamster, employee, out of work on Apr 15, 1910, out of work 4 weeks in 1909, can read and write.
   Line 4 - McIntosh, Emily, daughter, female, white, age 18, single, born in Utah, father born in Nevada, mother born in

# Joseph Albert McIntosh and Annie Eliza Russell

Utah, speaks english, seamstress, can read and write, attended school since Sept 1, 1909.
Line 5 - McIntosh, Donald, son, male, white, age 16, single, born in Utah, father born in Nevada, mother born in Utah, speaks english, teamster, employee, out of work on Apr 15, 1910, out of work 2 weeks in 1909, can read and write, attended school since Sept 1, 1909.
**Line 6 - McIntosh, Basil, son, male, white, age 14, single, born in Utah, father born in Nevada, mother born in Utah, speaks english, can read and write, attended school since Sept 1, 1909.**
Line 7 - McIntosh, Marie, daughter, female, white, age 12, single, born in Utah, father born in Nevada, mother born in Utah, speaks english, can read and write, attended school since Sept 1, 1909.
Line 8 - McIntosh, Kimball, son, male, white, age 8, single, born in Utah, father born in Nevada, mother born in Utah, speaks english.
Line 9 - McIntosh, Kenneth, son, male, white, age 5, single, born in Utah, father born in Nevada, mother born in Utah, speaks english.
Line 10 - McIntosh, Rollo, son, male, white, age 3, single, born in Utah, father born in Nevada, mother born in Utah, speaks english.

4. He served in the military U.S. Navy, World War I between 1917 and 1918.

5. He appeared on the census on 7 Jan 1920 in Lima, Beaverhead, Montana, United States.
   Line 64 - **McIntosh, Basil H., head, rents house, male white, age 23, married, can read, write and speak english, born in Utah, father and mother born in Utah, works as a machinist helper at railroad shop, wage worker.**
   Line 65 - McIntosh, Bernice C., wife, female, white, age 19, married, can read, write and speak english, born in California, father born in England, mother born in Texas.

6. He appeared on the census on 5 Apr 1930 in Inglewood, Los Angeles, California, United States.
   Line 91 - **McIntosh, Basil H., head, owns house valued at $4000, owns a radio, not on a farm, male, white, age 34, married at age 23, can read, write, and speak english, born in Utah, father born in Nevada, mother born in Utah, works as machinist at automatic sprinkler co., wage worker, veteran of WW.**
   Line 92 - McIntosh, Bernice C., wife, female, white, age 27, married at age 17, can read, write and speak english, born in California, father born in England, mother born in Texas,
   Line 93 - McIntosh, Beth, daughter, female, white, age 9, single, in school, born in California, father born in Utah, mother born in California.
   Line 94 - McIntosh, Bonnie, daughter, female, white, age 5, single, in school, born in California, father born in Utah, mother born in California.

7. He appeared on the census on 9 Apr 1940 in South Gate, Los Angeles, California, United States.
   Line 51 - **McIntosh, Basil, head, male, white, age 43, married, finished grade 8, born in Utah, lived in same house in 1935, works as superintendant in pipe shop, worked 52 weeks last year, earned $2400.**
   Line 52 - McIntosh, Bernice, wife, female, white, age 38, married, finished grade 8, born in California, lived in same house in 1935,
   Line 53 -McIntosh, Beth, daughter, female, white, age 19, single, born in California, lived in same house in 1935.
   Line 54 - McIntosh, Bonnie, daughter, female, white, age 15, born in California, lived in same house in 1935.

# Joseph Albert McIntosh and Annie Eliza Russell

| Children (cont.) | | |
|---|---|---|
| 5 F | **Anna Marie McIntosh**[4,75] | |
| AKA | Marie McIntosh | |
| Born | 4 Mar 1898 | Saint John, Tooele, Utah, United States |
| Died | 16 Mar 1930 | Grace, Caribou, Idaho, United States[76] |
| Cause of Death | Uremia from Brights Disease//Influenza. Her obituary states she died of complications from a nervous breakdown. | |
| Buried | 18 Mar 1930 | Rush Valley, Tooele, Utah, United States[77,78] |
| Address | St. John Cemetery, East on Main Street to Cemetery Road, Rush Valley, Utah 84069, USA | |
| Bapt.(LDS) | 15 Jul 1906 | |
| Conf.(LDS) | 15 Jul 1906 | |
| Init.(LDS) | 7 Jan 1920 | Salt Lake Temple |
| Endow.(LDS) | 7 Jan 1920 | Salt Lake Temple |
| SealP (LDS) | 25 Jun 1924 | Salt Lake Temple |
| Spouse | Ralph Lee Sr. (1895-1966) | 6 Nov 1916 - Farmington, Davis, Utah, United States[79,80] |
| SealS (LDS) | 7 Jan 1920 | Salt Lake Temple |

**Events**

1. She appeared on the census on 29 Jun 1900 in Saint John, Tooele, Utah, United States.
   Line 74 - McIntosh, Joseph A, head, white, male, born Mar 1869, age 31, married 16 years, born in Utah, father born in Ohio, mother born in Ohio, farming, 0 months unemployed, able to read, write and speak english, owns, mortgage free, farm #23.
   Line 75 - McIntosh, Liza, wife, white, female, born Oct 1867, age 32, married 16 years, had 6 children, 6 living, born in Utah, father born in England, mother born in England, able to read, write and speak english.
   Line 76 - McIntosh, William A, son, white, male, born Nov 1889, age 10, single, born in Utah, father born in Utah, mother born in Utah, at school, able to read, write and speak english.
   Line 77 - McIntosh, Emily E, daughter, white, female, born Sept 1891, age 8, single, born in Utah, father born in Utah, mother born in Utah, at school.
   Line 78 - McIntosh, Hyrum D, son, white, male, born Oct 1893, age 6, single, born in Utah, father born in Utah, mother born in Utah, at school.
   Line 79 - McIntosh, Boyd H, son, white, male, born Jan 1896, age 4, single, born in Utah, father born in Utah, mother born in Utah.
   **Line 80 - McIntosh, Annie M, daughter, white, female, born Mar 1898, age 2, single, born in Utah, father born in Utah, mother born in Utah.**
   Line 81 - McIntosh, unnamed, daughter, white, female, born April 1900, age 2/12, single, born in Utah, father born in Utah, mother born in Utah.
2. She appeared on the census on 19 Apr 1910 in Provo, Utah, Utah, United States.[81]
   Line 1 - McIntosh, J.A. head, male, white, age 41, married 22 years, born in Nevada, father born in Scotland -Scotch, mother born in Canada-Scotch, speaks english, teamster-freight, employee, out of work on Apr 15, 1910, out of work 8 weeks in 1909, can read and write, owns, house.
   Line 2 - McIntosh, Annie, wife, female, white, age 42, married 22 years, had 9 children, 8 living, born in Utah, father born in England-English, mother born in England-English, speaks english, can read and write.
   Line 3 - McIntosh, Albert, son, male, white, age 20, single, born in Utah, father born in Nevada, mother born in Utah, speaks english, teamster, employee, out of work on Apr 15, 1910, out of work 4 weeks in 1909, can read and write.
   Line 4 - McIntosh, Emily, daughter, female, white, age 18, single, born in Utah, father born in Nevada, mother born in Utah, speaks english, seamstress, can read and write, attended school since Sept 1, 1909.

Produced by: Beverly McIntosh Brown, 15933 W Silver Breeze Dr, Surprise, AZ 85374, 623-584-0440, starfighteraz@gmail.com : 29 Jun 2021

# Joseph Albert McIntosh and Annie Eliza Russell

Line 5 - McIntosh, Donald, son, male, white, age 16, single, born in Utah, father born in Nevada, mother born in Utah, speaks english, teamster, employee, out of work on Apr 15, 1910, out of work 2 weeks in 1909, can read and write, attended school since Sept 1, 1909.
Line 6 - McIntosh, Basil, son, male, white, age 14, single, born in Utah, father born in Nevada, mother born in Utah, speaks english, can read and write, attended school since Sept 1, 1909.
**Line 7 - McIntosh, Marie, daughter, female, white, age 12, single, born in Utah, father born in Nevada, mother born in Utah, speaks english, can read and write, attended school since Sept 1, 1909.**
Line 8 - McIntosh, Kimball, son, male, white, age 8, single, born in Utah, father born in Nevada, mother born in Utah, speaks english.
Line 9 - McIntosh, Kenneth, son, male, white, age 5, single, born in Utah, father born in Nevada, mother born in Utah, speaks english.
Line 10 - McIntosh, Rollo, son, male, white, age 3, single, born in Utah, father born in Nevada, mother born in Utah, speaks english.

3. She appeared on the census on 9 Jan 1920 in Medicine Bow, Carbon, Wyoming, United States.
Line 78 - Lee, Ralph, head, rents house, male, white, age 23, married, can read, write and speak english, born in Utah, both parents born in Utah, worked as machinist in garage, wage worker.
Line 79 **- Lee, Anne M., wife, female, white, age 21, married, can read, write and speak english, born in Utah, both parents born in Utah,**
Line 80 - Lee, Ralph H, son, male, white, age 6/12, single,born in Utah, both parents born in Utah.

4. Her obituary was published on 18 Mar 1930 in Provo, Utah, Utah, United States.
**Lee Services are Thursday**
Funeral services for Mrs. Marie McIntosh Lee, 31, wife of Ralph Lee of Grace, Idaho, daughter of Mr. and Mrs. J.A. McIntosh of 187 East Third North street, Provo, will be held Thursday at 1 p.m. in the Fifth ward chapel. The body may be viewed at the McIntosh residence prior to the services. Following the services, the body will be taken to St. Johns, Utah, for burial.
Mrs. Lee died Sunday at her home in Grace, Idaho, following a two weeks' illness from complications which followed a nervous breakdown. She was born March 4, 1899, in St. Johns, Utah, and came to Provo with her parents when she was nine years of age. She attended the Provo public schools and the B.Y.U., and resided here until her marriage to Ralph Lee of Tooele, when they moved to Grace, Idaho. In addition to her husband and parents, Mrs. Lee is survived by the following children: Ralph, Jr., 11; Maxine, 9, and Jack 5. She also leaves one sister, Fay McIntosh, of Provo, and six brothers: Kimball McIntosh, Provo; Albert McIntosh, Milford; Donald McIntosh, Amarilla, Texas; Basil, Kenneth and Joseph McIntosh, Los Angeles.

| 6 | F | **Alta Grace McIntosh** [4,82] | |
|---|---|---|---|
| Born | | 27 Apr 1900 | Saint John, Tooele, Utah, United States |
| Died | | After 29 Jul 1900 | Saint John, Tooele, Utah, United States[83] |
| Buried | | 1900 | Rush Valley, Tooele, Utah, United States[84] |
| Address | | Saint John Cemetery, Rush Valley, Utah, USA | |
| Bapt.(LDS) | | Child | |
| Endow.(LDS) | | Child | |
| SealP (LDS) | | 25 Jun 1924 | Salt Lake Temple |
| Spouse | | This person had no known marriage and no known children | |

**Events**

1. She appeared on the census on 29 Jun 1900 in Saint John, Tooele, Utah, United States.[85]
Line 74 - McIntosh, Joseph A, head, white, male, born Mar 1869, age 31, married 16 years, born in Utah, father born in Ohio, mother born in Ohio, farming, 0 months unemployed, able to read, write and speak english, owns, mortgage free, farm #23.
Line 75 - McIntosh, Liza, wife, white, female, born Oct 1867, age 32, married 16 years, had 6 children, 6 living, born in Utah, father born in England, mother born in England, able to read, write and speak english.
Line 76 - McIntosh, William A, son, white, male, born Nov 1889, age 10, single, born in Utah, father born in Utah, mother born in Utah, at school, able to read, write and speak english.
Line 77 - McIntosh, Emily E, daughter, white, female, born Sept 1891, age 8, single, born in Utah, father born in

# Joseph Albert McIntosh and Annie Eliza Russell

Utah, mother born in Utah, at school.
Line 78 - McIntosh, Hyrum D, son, white, male, born Oct 1893, age 6, single, born in Utah, father born in Utah, mother born in Utah, at school.
Line 79 - McIntosh, Boyd H, son, white, male, born Jan 1896, age 4, single, born in Utah, father born in Utah, mother born in Utah.
Line 80 - McIntosh, Annie M, daughter, white, female, born Mar 1898, age 2, single, born in Utah, father born in Utah, mother born in Utah.
**Line 81 - McIntosh, unnamed [Alta Grace], daughter, white, female, born April 1900, age 2/12, single, born in Utah, father born in Utah, mother born in Utah.**

2. Alt Death: After 29 Jul 1900, Saint John, Tooele, Utah, United States.[86]
An unnamed girl who was born in Apr 1900 is listed in the 1900 Census on 29 Jul 1900. This has to be Alta Grace McIntosh. Therefore she died sometime after 29 Jul 1900.

| 7 | M | Kimball Daniel McIntosh [4,87,88] | |
|---|---|---|---|
| AKA | | Daniel Kimball McIntosh, Kim McIntosh | |
| Born | | 4 Oct 1901 | Saint John, Tooele, Utah, United States |
| Died | | 17 Dec 1967 | Salt Lake City, Salt Lake, Utah, United States[89] |
| Cause of Death | | Heart Ailment | |
| Buried | | 1967 | Millcreek, Salt Lake, Utah, United States |
| Address | | Wasatch Lawn Memorial Park, 3401 South Highland Drive, Millcreek, Utah, USA | |
| Bapt.(LDS) | | 17 Nov 1911 | |
| Conf.(LDS) | | 17 Nov 1911 | |
| Init.(LDS) | | Completed | Idaho Falls Idaho Temple |
| Endow.(LDS) | | 4 May 1970 | Salt Lake Temple |
| SealP (LDS) | | 11 May 1970 | Salt Lake Temple |
| Spouse | | Pearl Freda Dormet (1912-2003) | 15 Aug 1947 - Reno, Washoe, Nevada, United States |
| SealS (LDS) | | Permission Required | |

**Events**

1. He appeared on the census on 19 Apr 1910 in Provo, Utah, Utah, United States.[90]
Line 1 - McIntosh, J.A. head, male, white, age 41, married 22 years, born in Nevada, father born in Scotland -Scotch, mother born in Canada-Scotch, speaks english, teamster-freight, employee, out of work on Apr 15, 1910, out of work 8 weeks in 1909, can read and write, owns, house.
Line 2 - McIntosh, Annie, wife, female, white, age 42, married 22 years, had 9 children, 8 living, born in Utah, father born in England-English, mother born in England-English, speaks english, can read and write.
Line 3 - McIntosh, Albert, son, male, white, age 20, single, born in Utah, father born in Nevada, mother born in Utah, speaks english, teamster, employee, out of work on Apr 15, 1910, out of work 4 weeks in 1909, can read and write.
Line 4 - McIntosh, Emily, daughter, female, white, age 18, single, born in Utah, father born in Nevada, mother born in Utah, speaks english, seamstress, can read and write, attended school since Sept 1, 1909.
Line 5 - McIntosh, Donald, son, male, white, age 16, single, born in Utah, father born in Nevada, mother born in Utah, speaks english, teamster, employee, out of work on Apr 15, 1910, out of work 2 weeks in 1909, can read and write, attended school since Sept 1, 1909.
Line 6 - McIntosh, Basil, son, male, white, age 14, single, born in Utah, father born in Nevada, mother born in Utah, speaks english, can read and write, attended school since Sept 1, 1909.
Line 7 - McIntosh, Marie, daughter, female, white, age 12, single, born in Utah, father born in Nevada, mother born in Utah, speaks english, can read and write, attended school since Sept 1, 1909.
**Line 8 - McIntosh, Kimball, son, male, white, age 8, single, born in Utah, father born in Nevada, mother born in Utah, speaks english.**

# Joseph Albert McIntosh and Annie Eliza Russell

Line 9 - McIntosh, Kenneth, son, male, white, age 5, single, born in Utah, father born in Nevada, mother born in Utah, speaks english.
Line 10 - McIntosh, Rollo, son, male, white, age 3, single, born in Utah, father born in Nevada, mother born in Utah, speaks english.

2. He appeared on the LDS Church Census census in 1920.[68] Joseph Albert McIntosh, head, male, birthplace North America.
Annie Russell McIntosh, wife, female, birthplace North America.
Don Hyrum McIntosh, son, male,
**Daniel Kimball McIntosh, son, male,**
Kenneth Grant McIntosh, son, male,
Rollo Henry McIntosh, son, male,
**Fay Maxine McIntosh, daughter, female**

3. He appeared on the census on 13 Apr 1930 in Eureka, Juab, Utah, United States.
Line 43 - **McIntosh, Kimball D., head, rents house for $10, no radio, not on a farm, male, white, age 27, divorced, not in school, can read and write, born in Utah, father born in Utah, mother born in Utah, teacher at a high school, not a veteran.**

4. He appeared on the LDS Church Census census in 1955.[68]
**Kimball Daniel McIntosh, head, male, born in St. John, Utah.**
Pearl Freda Dormet McIntosh, wife, female, born in McGill, Nevada.
Mary Kim McIntosh, daughter, female, born in Salt Lake, Utah.

5. His obituary was published on 19 Dec 1967 in Salt Lake City, Salt Lake, Utah, United States.
**Kimball Daniel McIntosh**, 66, 1467 E. 1700 South, died of a heart ailment Dec. 17 at home. Born Oct. 4, 1901, St. Johns, Tooele County, to Joseph Albert and Annie Russell McIntosh. Married Pearl Dormet, Aug 15, 1947, Reno, Nev. Member, LDS Church. Graduate Brigham Young University. Retired employee American Smelting and Refining Co. research department. Survivors: widow; daughter, Mary, Salt Lake City; brothers, sister, Donald H., Provo; Kenneth G., Southgate, Calif.; Mrs. Faye Jarrell, Las Vegas, Nev. Funeral, Thursday noon, 260 E. South Temple where friends call one hour prior to services. Burial, Wasatch Lawn Memorial Park.

| 8 | M | **Kenneth Grant McIntosh**[4,91] | |
|---|---|---|---|
| Born | | 29 Jul 1904 | Saint John, Tooele, Utah, United States[92,93,94] |
| Died | | 17 Feb 1997 | Hurricane, Washington, Utah, United States[92,93,94] |

| | | |
|---|---|---|
| Buried | 20 Feb 1997 | Hurricane, Washington, Utah, United States[94,95] |
| Address | Hurricane Cemetery, 600 North 200 East, Hurricane, Utah 84737, USA | |
| Bapt.(LDS) | 25 Jun 1916 | |
| Conf.(LDS) | 25 Jun 1916 | |
| Init.(LDS) | 24 Mar 1962 | Los Angeles California Temple |
| Endow.(LDS) | 24 Mar 1962 | Los Angeles California Temple |
| SealP (LDS) | 25 Jun 1924 | Salt Lake Temple |
| Spouse | Grace Chloe Roberts (1909-1984) | 23 Jun 1939 - Compton, Los Angeles, California, United States[96,97] |
| SealS (LDS) | 24 Mar 1962 | Los Angeles California Temple |

**Events**

1. He was blessed on 6 Nov 1904 in Saint John, Tooele, Utah, United States.
2. He appeared on the census on 19 Apr 1910 in Provo, Utah, Utah, United States.[98]

# Joseph Albert McIntosh and Annie Eliza Russell

Line 1 - McIntosh, J.A. head, male, white, age 41, married 22 years, born in Nevada, father born in Scotland -Scotch, mother born in Canada-Scotch, speaks english, teamster-freight, employee, out of work on Apr 15, 1910, out of work 8 weeks in 1909, can read and write, owns, house.
Line 2 - McIntosh, Annie, wife, female, white, age 42, married 22 years, had 9 children, 8 living, born in Utah, father born in England-English, mother born in England-English, speaks english, can read and write.
Line 3 - McIntosh, Albert, son, male, white, age 20, single, born in Utah, father born in Nevada, mother born in Utah, speaks english, teamster, employee, out of work on Apr 15, 1910, out of work 4 weeks in 1909, can read and write.
Line 4 - McIntosh, Emily, daughter, female, white, age 18, single, born in Utah, father born in Nevada, mother born in Utah, speaks english, seamstress, can read and write, attended school since Sept 1, 1909.
Line 5 - McIntosh, Donald, son, male, white, age 16, single, born in Utah, father born in Nevada, mother born in Utah, speaks english, teamster, employee, out of work on Apr 15, 1910, out of work 2 weeks in 1909, can read and write, attended school since Sept 1, 1909.
Line 6 - McIntosh, Basil, son, male, white, age 14, single, born in Utah, father born in Nevada, mother born in Utah, speaks english, can read and write, attended school since Sept 1, 1909.
Line 7 - McIntosh, Marie, daughter, female, white, age 12, single, born in Utah, father born in Nevada, mother born in Utah, speaks english, can read and write, attended school since Sept 1, 1909.
Line 8 - McIntosh, Kimball, son, male, white, age 8, single, born in Utah, father born in Nevada, mother born in Utah, speaks english.
**Line 9 - McIntosh, Kenneth, son, male, white, age 5, single, born in Utah, father born in Nevada, mother born in Utah, speaks english.**
Line 10 - McIntosh, Rollo, son, male, white, age 3, single, born in Utah, father born in Nevada, mother born in Utah, speaks english.

3. He appeared on the LDS Church Census census in 1920.[68]
Joseph Albert McIntosh, head, male, birthplace North America.
Annie Russell McIntosh, wife, female, birthplace North America.
Don Hyrum McIntosh, son, male,
Daniel Kimball McIntosh, son, male,
**Kenneth Grant McIntosh, son, male,**
Rollo Henry McIntosh, son, male,
Fay Maxine McIntosh, daughter, female, birthplace North America.

4. He appeared on the census on 4 Apr 1930 in Los Angeles, Los Angeles, California, United States.
**Line 11 - McIntosh, Kenneth G., head, rents house for $30, does not own radio, male, white, age 25, single, born in Utah, father born in Nevada, mother born in Utah, checker at plumbing store, wage worker, not a veteran.**
Line 12 - McIntosh, Rollo, brother,male, white, age 23, single, born in Utah, father born in Nevada, mother born in Utah, pipe fitter at plumbing store, wage worker, not a veteran.
Line 13 - Peterson, Leon, lodger

5. Voter Registration: 1940, in Los Angeles, Los Angeles, California, United States.
McIntosh, Joseph A, 2027 E 130th st, farmer, D
McIntosh, Kenneth G, 2027 E 130th st, pipe machine operator, D

6. He appeared on the census in Apr 1940 in Compton, Los Angeles, California, United States.
Line 8 - **McIntosh, Kenneth, head, male, white, age 35, married, finished 8th grade, born in Utah, lived in Los Angeles, California in 1935, pipe machinist for oil well supply co, worked 52 weeks last year, earned $1310**
Line 9 - McIntosh, Grace, female, white, age 30, married, finished 7th grade, born in Illinois, lived in Los Angeles, California in 1935.
Line 10 - McIntosh, William, son, male, white, age 10, single, in grade 3, born in Missouri, lived in LA, CA in 1935.
Line 11 - McIntosh, Rose Mary, daughter, female, white, age 7, single, in grade 1, born in California, lived in LA, CA in 1935.
Line 12 - McIntosh, Beverly Jean, female, white, age 6, single, not in school, born in California, lived in LA, CA in 1935.

7. Draft Registration: World War II, 14 Feb 1942, Los Angeles, Los Angeles, California, United States. Description of Registrant: White; 5' 7"; 137 #; brown eyes, brown hair, ruddy complexion.

8. His obituary was published in the "The Daily Spectrum" on 19 Feb 1997 in Saint George, Washington, Utah, United

# Joseph Albert McIntosh and Annie Eliza Russell

States.
Hurricane, - **Kenneth Grant McIntosh**, 92, died February 17, 1997 at Dixie Regional Medical Center. Kenneth was born on July 29 1902 in St. John, Utah to Joseph Albert and Annie Elizabeth Russell McIntosh. He married Grace Chole Roberts in 1935 and their marriage was later solemnized in the Los Angeles, Temple. Grace preceded him in death in 1984.
Kenneth grew up east of Wasatch where he sheared sheep and was a cook on a chuck wagon and also worked in a sawmill. He was later employed and retired as a pipe fitter. He later moved to South Gate, California after serving an LDS Mission to Alexandria, Minnesota with his wife Grace. He and Grace moved to Hurricane, Utah 27 years ago.
Kenneth loved children and was known by the children of Hurricane as the "Candy Man". He always looked forward to seeing the children who also looked towards him as an example. Kenneth made a difference in many childrens lives including his son-in-law, Jack, whom he considered a son since the age of 9 years old. He was an unselfish man who was generous to anyone in need. Kenneth was a man with a big heart who never had a cruel word to say about anyone. He was an active member of the LDS Church holding various positions including High Priest and Stake Secretary in South Gate, California. Kenneth also faithfully served in the St. George LDS Temple for over 20 years. He is remembered by his family as being the most wonderful father. His life touched all of those who knew him and his loss will be felt by all.
Survivors include his two daughters, Rosemary (Edward) Brennon and Barbara Jean (Jack) Thompson both of Banning, California; one sister, Faye Gerrald of Logandale, Nevada; six grandchildren, 16 great-grandchildren and four great-great grandchildren. He is preceded in death by his six brothers and one sister.
Funeral services will be held Thursday, February 20, 1997; 10:00am, in the Hurricane LDS 5th Ward Chapel located at 274 South 100 West. Friends may call Wednesday, February 19, 1997 from 7-8 pm at the Metcalf Hurricane Valley Mortuary, 140 North Main, and Thursday February 20, 1997 from 9 to 10 am, at the church prior to services. Interment will be in the Hurrican City Cemetery under the direction of Metcalf Hurricane Valley Mortuary, 635-2211.

| 9 | M | **Rollo Henry McIntosh** [4,99] | |
|---|---|---|---|
| AKA | | Henry Rollo McIntosh, Joe McIntosh | |
| Born | | 29 Jan 1907 | Saint John, Tooele, Utah, United States[100] |
| Died | | 14 May 1951 | Beverly Hills, Los Angeles, California, United States[101,102,103] |
| Cause of Death | | Coronary Sclerosis (coronary heart disease) | |
| Buried | | 1951 | Inglewood, Los Angeles, California, United States[104] |
| Address | | Inglewood Park Cemetery, Inglewood, California, USA | |
| Notes | | No plot information. | |
| Bapt.(LDS) | | 25 Jun 1916 | |
| Endow.(LDS) | | 11 Oct 1963 | Los Angeles California Temple |
| SealP (LDS) | | 25 Jun 1924 | Salt Lake Temple |
| Spouse | | Ann Corinne Riley (1904-1982) | 24 Jul 1937 - Los Angeles, Los Angeles, California, United States |
| SealS (LDS) | | 9 Feb 2007 | Los Angeles California Temple |

**Events**

1. He appeared on the census on 19 Apr 1910 in Provo, Utah, Utah, United States.[105]
   Line 1 - McIntosh, J.A. head, male, white, age 41, married 22 years, born in Nevada, father born in Scotland -Scotch, mother born in Canada-Scotch, speaks english, teamster-freight, employee, out of work on Apr 15, 1910, out of work 8 weeks in 1909, can read and write, owns, house.
   Line 2 - McIntosh, Annie, wife, female, white, age 42, married 22 years, had 9 children, 8 living, born in Utah, father

# Joseph Albert McIntosh and Annie Eliza Russell

born in England-English, mother born in England-English, speaks english, can read and write.
Line 3 - McIntosh, Albert, son, male, white, age 20, single, born in Utah, father born in Nevada, mother born in Utah, speaks english, teamster, employee, out of work on Apr 15, 1910, out of work 4 weeks in 1909, can read and write.
Line 4 - McIntosh, Emily, daughter, female, white, age 18, single, born in Utah, father born in Nevada, mother born in Utah, speaks english, seamstress, can read and write, attended school since Sept 1, 1909.
Line 5 - McIntosh, Donald, son, male, white, age 16, single, born in Utah, father born in Nevada, mother born in Utah, speaks english, teamster, employee, out of work on Apr 15, 1910, out of work 2 weeks in 1909, can read and write, attended school since Sept 1, 1909.
Line 6 - McIntosh, Basil, son, male, white, age 14, single, born in Utah, father born in Nevada, mother born in Utah, speaks english, can read and write, attended school since Sept 1, 1909.
Line 7 - McIntosh, Marie, daughter, female, white, age 12, single, born in Utah, father born in Nevada, mother born in Utah, speaks english, can read and write, attended school since Sept 1, 1909.
Line 8 - McIntosh, Kimball, son, male, white, age 8, single, born in Utah, father born in Nevada, mother born in Utah, speaks english.
Line 9 - McIntosh, Kenneth, son, male, white, age 5, single, born in Utah, father born in Nevada, mother born in Utah, speaks english.
**Line 10 - McIntosh, Rollo, son, male, white, age 3, single, born in Utah, father born in Nevada, mother born in Utah, speaks english.**

2. He appeared on the LDS Church Census census in 1920.[68] Joseph Albert McIntosh, head, male, birthplace North America.
   Annie Russell McIntosh, wife, female, birthplace North America.
   Don Hyrum McIntosh, son, male,
   Daniel Kimball McIntosh, son, male,
   Kenneth Grant McIntosh, son, male,
   **Rollo Henry McIntosh, son, male,**
   Fay Maxine McIntosh, daughter, female, birthplace North America.
3. He worked as a foreman for a pipe fitting company.
4. He appeared on the census on 4 Apr 1930 in Los Angeles, Los Angeles, California, United States.
   Line 11 - McIntosh, Kenneth G., head, rents house for $30, does not own radio, male, white, age 25, single, born in Utah, father born in Nevada, mother born in Utah, checker at plumbing store, wage worker, not a veteran.
   **Line 12 - McIntosh, Rollo, brother,male, white, age 23, single, born in Utah, father born in Nevada, mother born in Utah, pipe fitter at plumbing store, wage worker, not a veteran.**
   Line 13 - Peterson, Leon, lodger
5. He appeared on the census on 16 Apr 1940 in San Antonio, Los Angeles, California, United States.
   Line 4 - **McIntosh, Rollo H., head, male, white, age 33, married, attended 3 years of high school, born in Utah, lived in South Gate, California in 1935, pipe fitter at fire sprinkler co, worked 52 weeks last year, earned $3300.**
   Line 5 - McIntosh, Corrina A., wife, female, white, age 35, married, attended 3 years of high school, born in Arkansas, lived in Shawnee, Oklahoma in 1935.
6. Draft Registration: World War II, 16 Oct 1940, Ventura, Ventura, California, United States. Rollo Henery McIntosh
   9825 McNerney St, South Gate, CAL
   Telephone: 8073, Age 34, Date of Birth Jan 29, 1907, Place of Birth St Johns, Utah, Country of Citizenship U.S.A.,
   Name of Person Who Will Always Know Your Address Mrs Anne McIntosh, wife, same address
   Employer's Name Viking Sprinkler Co, 2715 E 12th St, Los Angeles, Cal
   Description of Registrant: White, 5' 6", 155#, brown eyes, brown hair, dark complexion.

# Joseph Albert McIntosh and Annie Eliza Russell

| Children (cont.) | | | |
|---|---|---|---|
| 10 | F | **Faye Maxine McIntosh** [4,106] | |
| AKA | | Faye Jarrell, Fay McIntosh, Fay Maxine McIntosh | |
| Born | | 27 Mar 1911 | Provo, Utah, Utah, United States[107] |
| Died | | 6 Apr 2005 | Logandale, Clark, Nevada, United States[108,109] |
| Buried | | 14 Apr 2005 | Logandale, Clark, Nevada, United States[110] |
| Address | | Logandale Cemetery, 3201-339 N Lyman St, Logandale, Nevada, USA | |
| Bapt.(LDS) | | 21 Mar 1920 | |
| Conf.(LDS) | | 21 Mar 1920 | |
| Init.(LDS) | | 27 Feb 1971 | St. George Utah Temple |
| Endow.(LDS) | | 27 Feb 1971 | St. George Utah Temple |
| SealP (LDS) | | 25 Jun 1924 | Salt Lake Temple |
| Spouse | | Martin Clyde Jarrell (1915-2000) | 1 Jan 1937 - Yuma, Arizona, United States[111] |
| SealS (LDS) | | 27 Feb 1971 | St. George Utah Temple |

**Events**

1. She appeared on the LDS Church Census, Worldwide census in 1920.[68]
   Joseph Albert McIntosh, head, male, birthplace North America.
   Annie Russell McIntosh, wife, female, birthplace North America.
   Don Hyrum McIntosh, son, male,
   Daniel Kimball McIntosh, son, male,
   Kenneth Grant McIntosh, son, male,
   Rollo Henry McIntosh, son, male,
   **Fay Maxine McIntosh, daughter, female, birthplace North America.**
2. She appeared on the census on 2 Apr 1930 in Provo, Utah, Utah, United States.[112]
   Line 1 - McIntosh, Jos. A., head, owns house valued at $3000, not a farm, male, white, age 62, married at age 21, can read, write and speak english, born in Nevada, father born in Scotland, mother born in Scotland, laborer at ranch, wage worker, employed, not a veteran.
   Line 2 - McIntosh, Annie, wife, female, white, age 62, married at age 21, can read, write and speak english, born in Utah, father born in England, mother born in England.
   **Line 3 - McIntosh, Fay, daughter, female, white, age 19, single, in school, can read, write and speak english, born in Utah, father born in Nevada, mother born in Utah.**
3. She appeared on the census on 18 Apr 1940 in Compton, Los Angeles, California, United States.[113]
   Line 21 - owns house valued at $2500, not a farm, McIntosh, Joseph A., head, male, white, age 71, married, finished 4 years high school, born in Nevada, in 1935 lived in South Gate, Los Angeles, California, no occupation, has another source of income.
   Line 22 - McIntosh, Annie, wife, female, white, age 71, married, finished 4 years high school, born in Utah, in 1935 lived in South Gate, Los Angeles, California.
   **Line 23 - Garrell, Fay, daughter, female, white, age 28, married, finished 2 years college, born in Utah, in 1935 lived in South Gate, Los Angeles, California, saleslady at drug store.**
4. Memorial: After 6 Apr 2005.

# Joseph Albert McIntosh and Annie Eliza Russell

From Sandy, her daughter sandysing@comnett. nett
Dear McIntosh Family,I am sending this to let you know that mom, Faye McIntosh Jarrell, died Wednesday night, April 6, 2005 here at our home in Logandale. Our entire family surrounded her bedside with our Idaho family on the phone. Each child and grandchild and great grandchild had the opportunity to give her a hug and a kiss, tell her how much they loved her and anything else they wanted to do say. Afterwards Bruce offered a family prayer of tribute to her and expressed all our love as a family, then he told her that we were all okay and that she could go on according to the desires of her heart and the Lords approval. After the prayer as we stood talking about her and sharing wonderful memories in about 5 minutes her breathing slowed and she closed her eyes and took a last deep breath surrounded by her family. One of the little ones immediately said Grandma left…another said She waited for us to tell her goodbye. We were smiling through our tears and feeling the eternal link and love of Heavenly Father for her and for us. We spent the next while visiting and sharing with each other. As you all know Mom was the last of the original Joseph Albert McIntosh family, and I know her reunion with her brothers and sisters and her dear mother, Annnie Eliza, whom she had not seen in 65 years, was incredible. You may not know that she had an infant son, Thomas Russell, who lived 6 hours than died and was buried before she ever saw him. She will be seeing him for the first time, as well as her grandson Rich who passed away 20 years ago at age 15, Dad, and all the rest of the McIntosh and Jarrell Family. I know her joy is full. She was 94 years old on Easter Sunday, March 27. The funeral will be on Thursday, April 14, at 11Am in the Logandale Chapel and will be buried here in the Logandale cemetery next to Dad. I have many wonderful stories, a tape recording, and a lot of history about her life, which I will be glad to send after the funeral is over. I also will have a CD of the service which you can listen to if you would like. She often spoke fondly of the little gathering she was able attend a few years ago in the park and see once again some of her McIntosh family. Any who could come are most lovingly invited and we have plenty of available places to sleep that can be easily arranged. My love to you all. Sandy
Per FindaGrave: Faye is survived by her daughter, Sandra(Bruce)Cameron; three grandchildren and eleven great-grandchildren. Preceded in death by her Husband, Martin Clyde Jarrell; parents, Joseph Albert and Annie Eliza Russell McIntosh; one infant son, Thomas Russell Jarrell; one grandson, Rich Cameron; six brothers and three sisters.

# Source Citations


1. Brown, Beverly McIntosh and Marsha Lee McIntosh, *William McIntosh Diary, abridgement* (Self-published, Surprise, AZ. June 2002).

2. McIntosh Reunion Descendants, McIntosh - Descendants of John & Girsey (Grace) (Grizel) Rankin McIntosh (Attachment to Aug 17, 1958 Newsletter - copy in Collection of Bonnie S. Williams), Repository: Bonnie S. Williams, RR 1 Box 247, N Hwy 2, Wilburton, Oklahoma, USA.
Joseph Albert (son of William [McINTOSH] & Maria CALDWELL) md. Ann RUSSELL
Children:
 1. William Albert
 2. Emily Elizabeth
 3. Donald Hyrum
 4. Basil Hugh
 5. Annie Marie
 6. Alta Grace
 7. Daniel Kimball
 8. Kenneth Grant
 9. Henry Rollo
 10. Fay Maxine. Joseph Albert McINTOSH is a Grandson of John McINTOSH & Girsey RANKIN.
This single page attachment indicates that the parents of John McIntosh are William McIntosh & Isabell and is indicative of what our side of the family knew of our McIntosh cousins at that time in August 1958.

3. McIntosh, Donald H, *Joseph Albert McIntosh* (unpublished manuscript, 1961).

4. Family records of Joseph and Annie Russell McIntosh, In possession of Donald H. McIntosh 1515 North 3rd West Provo, Utah.

5. Utah, State Department of Health, Certificate of Death, death certificate state file no. 52180533; registrar's no. 423 (1952), William Albert McIntosh names his father as Joseph Elbert McIntosh.

6. California State Department of Health Services, Center for Health Statistics, "California. Death Index, 1940-1997," database, Joseph Albert McIntosh died 21 Jan 1950.

7. "Find A Grave," database (www.findagrave.com), Joseph Albert McIntosh, 28905722.

8. Brown, Beverly McIntosh and Marsha McIntosh, editors, *William McIntosh Diary 1857-1898, Abridgement* (Surprise, AZ: Self-published, June 2002).

9. Daughters of Utah Pioneers, *Our Pioneer Heritage* (Salt Lake City, UT: Infobases, Inc., 1996), 19: 422. Repository: Family History Library, 35 North West Temple Street, Salt Lake City, Utah 84150-3400, USA, Call Number: 979.2 H2.

10. Frank Esshorn, editor, *Pioneers and Prominent Men of Utah comprising Photographs-Genealogies-Biographies. Pioneers are those men and women who came to Utah by wagon, hand cart or afoot, between July 24, 1847 and December 30, 1868, before the railroad. Prominent Men are stake presidents, ward bishops, governors, members of the bench, etc., who came to Utah after the coming of the railroad. The early history of the Church of Jesus Christ of Latter-Day Saints. In One Volume, Illustrated* (Salt Lake City, Utah: Utah Pioneers Book Publishing Company, 1913), McIntosh, William: 331 and 1059. Repository: Family History Library, 35 North West Temple Street, Salt Lake City, Utah 84150-3400, USA, Call Number: 979.2 D3e.

11. Andrew Jenson, editor, *Latter-day Saint Biographical Encyclopedia: A Compilation of Biographical Sketches of Prominent Men and Women in The Church of Jesus Christ of Latter-day Saints*, 4 v.: ports. (Salt Lake City, Utah: Western Epics, 1971), William McIntosh: V 4, page 647. Repository: Family History Library, 35 North West Temple Street, Salt Lake City, Utah 84150-3400, USA, Call Number: 920.0792.

12. International Society of Daughters of Utah Pioneers, editor, *Pioneer Women of Faith and Fortitude*, Volume III (Salt Lake City, Utah: Publishers Press, 1998), Maria Caldwell McIntosh: page 1946. Repository: Family History Library, 35 North West Temple Street, Salt Lake City, Utah 84150-3400, USA, Call Number: 979 D36.

13. Brigham Young University-Idaho, "Western States Marriage Index," database (http://abish.byui.edu/specialCollections/westernStates/search.cfm), John Albert McIntosh and Annie E. Russell both of St. John married 6 Mar 1888.

14. 1870 U.S. census, Washington, Utah, population schedule, Panaca, p. 7, dwelling 54, family 48, McIntosh, Albert; digital images, *ancestry.com*; citing National Archives and Records Administration microfilm M593.

15. 1870 U.S. census, Lincoln, Nevada, population schedule, Meadow Valley, p. 186, dwelling 66-68, family 45, McIntosh, Albert; digital images, *ancestry.com*; citing National Archives and Records Administration microfilm M593.

16. 1880 U.S. census, Tooele, Utah Territory, population schedule, Clover, enumeration district (ED) 79, p. 6C, Mackintosh, Albert; digital images, *ancestry.com*; citing National Archives and Records Administration microfilm T9.

17. Brown, Beverly McIntosh and Marsha Lee McIntosh, *William McIntosh Diary, abridgement* (Self-published, Surprise, AZ. June 2002), p 71 October 20 [1891].

18. Brown, Beverly McIntosh and Marsha Lee McIntosh, *William McIntosh Diary, abridgement* (Self-published, Surprise, AZ. June 2002), p 72 October 14 [1891].


Produced by: Beverly McIntosh Brown, 15933 W Silver Breeze Dr, Surprise, AZ 85374, 623-584-0440, starfighteraz@gmail.com : 29 Jun 2021



Produced by Legacy

# Source Citations

19. Brown, Beverly McIntosh and Marsha Lee McIntosh,*William McIntosh Diary, abridgement* (Self-published, Surprise, AZ. June 2002), p 80 February 2 [1894].

20. Brown, Beverly McIntosh and Marsha Lee McIntosh,*William McIntosh Diary, abridgement* (Self-published, Surprise, AZ. June 2002), p 80 March 6, Monday [1894].

21. Brown, Beverly McIntosh and Marsha Lee McIntosh,*William McIntosh Diary, abridgement* (Self-published, Surprise, AZ. June 2002), p 80 March 10, Saturday [1894].

22. 1900 U.S. census, Tooele, Utah, population schedule, St. John, enumeration district (ED) 147, sheet 5B, p. 253, dwelling 94, family 94, McIntosh, Joseph A.; digital images,*ancestry.com*; citing National Archives and Records Administration microfilm T623.

23. 1910 U.S. census, Utah, Utah, population schedule, Provo, enumeration district (ED) 195, sheet 1A, p. 80, dwelling 116, family 120, McIntosh, J.A; digital images,*ancestry.com*; citing National Archives and Records Administration microfilm T624.

24. 1920 U.S. census, Utah, Utah, population schedule, Provo, enumeration district (ED) 210, sheet 7A, p. 112, dwelling 129, family 139, McIntosh, J.A; digital images,*ancestry.com*; citing National Archives and Records Administration microfilm T625.

25. 1930 U.S. census, Utah, Utah, population schedule, Provo, enumeration district (ED) 25-48, sheet 1A, p. 130, dwelling 1, family 1, McIntosh, Jos. A.; digital images (ancestry.com); citing National Archives and Records Administration microfilm T626.

26. 1940 U.S. census, Los Angeles, California, population schedule, Compton, enumeration district (ED) 19-103, sheet 16A, p. 1969, household 359, McIntosh, Joseph A.; digital images,*ancestry.com*; citing National Archives and Records Administration microfilm T627.

27. Utah, State Department of Health, Certificate of Death, death certificate state file no. 52180533; registrar's no. 423 (1952), William Albert McIntosh names his mother as Anna Elizabeth McIntosh.

28. *Family Bible Of William G Russell,* Repository: Bertha Russell, Saint John, Utah, USA.

29. *Ohio, Cleveland, City Directory, 1846.*

30. *Ohio, Cleveland, City Directory, 1848/9.*

31. Frank Esshorn, editor, *Pioneers and Prominent Men of Utah comprising Photographs-Genealogies-Biographies. Pioneers are those men and women who came to Utah by wagon, hand cart or afoot, between July 24, 1847 and December 30, 1868, before the railroad. Prominent Men are stake presidents, ward bishops, governors, members of the bench, etc., who came to Utah after the coming of the railroad. The early history of the Church of Jesus Christ of Latter-Day Saints. In One Volume, Illustrated* (Salt Lake City, Utah: Utah Pioneers Book Publishing Company, 1913), Russell, William Greenwood: 1145. Repository: Family History Library, 35 North West Temple Street, Salt Lake City, Utah 84150-3400, USA, Call Number: 979.2 D3e.

32. Utah, State Department of Health, Certificate of Death, death certificate state file no. (illegible); registrar's no. 4 (1946), Heber Curtis Russell names his father as William G. Russell born in England.

33. Daughters of Utah Pioneers, *History of Tooele County* (Salt Lake City, Utah: Publisher's Press, 1961), p.568 Photo p.568.

34. Utah, State Department of Health, Certificate of Death, death certificate state file no. (illegible); registrar's no. 4 (1946), Heber Curtis Russell names his mother as Elizabeth Vickery born in England.

35. 1870 U.S. census, Tooele, Utah, population schedule, St Johns, p. 1, dwelling 1, family 1, Russell, Annie E; digital images*ancestry.com*; citing National Archives and Records Administration microfilm M593.

36. 1880 U.S. census, Tooele, Utah Territory, population schedule, Rush Lake, enumeration district (ED) 77, p. 20, dwelling 92, family 92, Russell, Anne; digital images,*ancestry*; citing National Archives and Records Administration microfilm T9.

37. 1900 U.S. census, Tooele, Utah, population schedule, St. John, enumeration district (ED) 147, sheet 5B, p. 253, dwelling 94, family 94, McIntosh, Liza; digital images,*ancestry.com*; citing National Archives and Records Administration microfilm T623.

38. 1910 U.S. census, Utah, Utah, population schedule, Provo, enumeration district (ED) 195, sheet 1A, p. 80, dwelling 116, family 120, McIntosh, Annie; digital images,*ancestry.com*; citing National Archives and Records Administration microfilm T624.

39. 1920 U.S. census, Utah, Utah, population schedule, Provo, enumeration district (ED) 210, sheet 7A, p. 112, dwelling 129, family 139, McIntosh, A.E; digital images,*ancestry.com*; citing National Archives and Records Administration microfilm T625.

40. 1930 U.S. census, Utah, Utah, population schedule, Provo, enumeration district (ED) 25-48, sheet 1A, p. 130, dwelling 1, family 1, McIntosh, Annie; digital images (ancestry.com); citing National Archives and Records Administration microfilm T626.

41. *U.S., Newspapers.com Obituary Index, 1800s-current*; digital images, ancestry.com.

42. The Milford News, Milford, Beaver County, Utah, "Mother Local Man Killed Near Vegas (Annie Elisabeth McIntosh),"*U.S., Newspapers.com Obituary Index, 1800s-current*, 14 Jul 1938, p. page 1; digital images, ancestry.com.

# Source Citations


43. 1940 U.S. census, Los Angeles, California, population schedule; digital images,*ancestry.com*; citing National Archives and Records Administration microfilm T627.

44. McIntosh Reunion Descendants, McIntosh - Descendants of John & Girsey (Grace) (Grizel) Rankin McIntosh (Attachment to Aug 17, 1958 Newsletter - copy in Collection of Bonnie S. Williams), Repository: Bonnie S. Williams, RR 1 Box 247, N Hwy 2, Wilburton, Oklahoma, USA.
William Albert (son of Joseph Albert [McINTOSH] & Ann RUSSELL).
William Albert McINTOSH is a Great-Grandson of John McINTOSH & Girsey RANKIN
and a Grandson of William McINTOSH & Maria CALDWELL
no other information given.
Brother Donald Hyrum McINTOSH was active in the McIntosh Clan and genealogy at the time of this attachment.

45. Utah, State Department of Health, Certificate of Death, death certificate state file no. 52180533; registrar's no. 423 (1952), William Albert McIntosh.

46. Utah, State Department of Health, Certificate of Death, death certificate state file no. 52180533; registrar's no. 4231952 (1952), William Albert McIntosh names his wife as Grace Kirkman McIntosh.

47. Brigham Young University-Idaho, "Western States Marriage Index," database (http://abish.byui.edu/specialCollections/westernStates/search.cfm), William A. McIntosh and Grace G. Kirkman married 12 Oct 1916 in Juab County, Utah.

48. 1910 U.S. census, Utah, Utah, population schedule, Provo, enumeration district (ED) 195, sheet 1A, p. 80, dwelling 116, family 120, McIntosh, Albert; digital images,*ancestry.com*; citing National Archives and Records Administration microfilm T624.

49. *1920 U.S. Census Idaho, Bannock, Pocatello,* Repository: Heritage Quest.

50. 1930 U.S. census, Beaver, Utah, population schedule, Star, enumeration district (ED) 1-8, sheet 8B, dwelling 166, family 187, McIntosh, William A.; digital images (ancestry.com); citing National Archives and Records Administration microfilm T626.

51. McIntosh Reunion Descendants, McIntosh - Descendants of John & Girsey (Grace) (Grizel) Rankin McIntosh (Attachment to Aug 17, 1958 Newsletter - copy in Collection of Bonnie S. Williams), Repository: Bonnie S. Williams, RR 1 Box 247, N Hwy 2, Wilburton, Oklahoma, USA.
Emily Elizabeth (daughter of Joseph Albert [McINTOSH] & Ann RUSSELL).
Emily Elizabeth McINTOSH is a Great-Granddaughter of John McINTOSH & Girsey RANKIN
and a Granddaughter of William McINTOSH & Maria CALDWELL
no other information given
Brother, Donald Hyrum McINTOSH was active in the McIntosh Clan and genealogy at the time of this attachment.

52. "Utah, Select County Marriages, 1887-1937," database, William Roy Wymore married Emily E McIntosh on 29 Dec 1917 in Salt Lake, Utah.

53. "Western States Marriage Index, 1809-2011," database, William Roy Wymore married Emily E McIntosh on 29 Dec 1917 in Salt Lake, Utah.

54. 1910 U.S. census, Utah, Utah, population schedule, Provo, enumeration district (ED) 195, sheet 1A, p. 80, dwelling 116, family 120, McIntosh, Emily; digital images,*ancestry.com*; citing National Archives and Records Administration microfilm T624.

55. Church of Jesus Christ of Latter-day Saints, LDS Church Census, 1914-1960, Central States Mission, Amarillo Branch. Address: 205 Coroline St., Amarillo, Texas
Donald Hyrum McIntosh- Elder b. 1 Oct 1893, St. John, Tooele, Utah
Melba Cropper- female b. 19 Aug 1899, Hinckley, Millard, Utah
Meldon Joseph McIntosh- male b. 5 July 1925, Murray, Salt Lake, Utah
Marilyn Joy McIntosh- female b. 4 Mar 1928, Salt Lake, Salt Lake, Utah.

56. McIntosh Reunion Descendants, McIntosh - Descendants of John & Girsey (Grace) (Grizel) Rankin McIntosh (Attachment to Aug 17, 1958 Newsletter - copy in Collection of Bonnie S. Williams), Repository: Bonnie S. Williams, RR 1 Box 247, N Hwy 2, Wilburton, Oklahoma, USA.
Donald Hyrum (son of Joseph Albert [McINTOSH] & Ann RUSSELL). Donald Hyrum McINTOSH is a Great-Grandson of John McINTOSH & Girsey RANKIN and a Grandson of William McINTOSH & Maria CALDWELL
no other information given
Donald Hyrum McINTOSH was active in the McIntosh Clan and genealogy at the time of this attachment.

57. McIntosh, Donald H, *Autobiography of Donald Hyrum McIntosh* (unpublished manuscript, 1961).

58. Roberts, Barbara (editor), *McIntosh Clan 5th Annual Reunion Report* (Newsletter of 4 July 1960 in Collection of Bonnie S. Williams), Repository: Bonnie S. Williams, RR 1 Box 247, N Hwy 2, Wilburton, Oklahoma, USA. REUNION REPORT...
... It was unanimously decided to retain the same set of officers, with the addition of the office of Newsletter Editor and Reporter-at-large. The officers are now as follows:
President: Donald H. McIntosh
Vice Pres. &
Chariman of Genealogical Research: John McIntosh
Vice Pres.: Millie Tate
Vice Pres.: Alice Ward
Secretary: Lena Donaldson

# Source Citations

Assistant Sec.: Melba McIntosh
Assistant Genealogist: Fern Jacobs
Newsletter Editor: Barbara Roberts
Reporter-at-large: Margaret LaFollette [also Treasurer]
... The 5th Annual Reunion was held at Provo Park on 12 Jun 1960. Newsletter dated July 4, 1960.

59. Church of Jesus Christ of Latter-day Saints. Tooele Stake. St John Ward,*LDS Birth Certificate,* 21050, Page M. This Certifies that according to the Records of The Church of Jesus Christ of Laatter-day Saints -HYRUM D. McINTOSH-was born on the first day of October, Eighteen Hundred and ninety-three, at St. Johns, Tooele County, Utah
Father's name J. A. McIntosh
Mother's Maiden name Annie------
Recorded in Tooele Stake, St. John Ward Record of Members, 21050,page M.,
entered on 19 November 1983.
(signed) Joseph Fielding Smith, Historian of the Church and ex officio Custodian of its Records
A. Wm Lund, Assistant Historian of the Church.

60. Utah State Historical Society, "Utah, Cemetery Inventory, 1847-2000," database(https://www.ancestry.com/search/collections/utahburials/), Don Hyrum Mcintosh.

61. Utah, State Department of Health, Certificate of Death, death certificate (1976), Donald Hyrum McIntosh.

62. "U.S., Social Security Death Index, 1935-2014," database, Donald Hyrum McIntosh.

63. "Utah County, Utah Cemetery Index," database,*ancestry.com* , Don Hyrum Mcintosh.

64. Utah Division of State History, "Cemetery & Burial Database," database (https://heritage.utah.gov/history/cemeteries), Donald Hyrum McIntosh.

65. "Find A Grave," database (www.findagrave.com), Donald Hyrum McIntosh, 30812961.

66. "Utah, Select Marriages, 1887-1966," database, Melba Cropper and Donald H. Mcintosh married on 2 Aug 1924 in Utah County, Utah.

67. 1910 U.S. census, Utah, Utah, population schedule, Provo, enumeration district (ED) 195, sheet 1A, p. 80, dwelling 116, family 120, McIntosh, Donald; digital images,*ancestry.com*; citing National Archives and Records Administration microfilm T624.

68. Church of Jesus Christ of Latter-day Saints, LDS Church Census, 1914-1960.

69. "U.S., World War II Draft Registration Cards, 1942," database and images,*ancestry.com* , Donald Hyrum McIntosh.

70. *The Daily Herald*; digital images.

71. McIntosh Reunion Descendants, McIntosh - Descendants of John & Girsey (Grace) (Grizel) Rankin McIntosh (Attachment to Aug 17, 1958 Newsletter - copy in Collection of Bonnie S. Williams), Repository: Bonnie S. Williams, RR 1 Box 247, N Hwy 2, Wilburton, Oklahoma, USA.
Basil Hugh (son of Joseph Albert [McINTOSH] & Ann RUSSELL).
Basil Hugh McINTOSH is a Great-Grandson of John McINTOSH & Girsey RANKIN
and a Grandson of William McINTOSH & Maria CALDWELL
no other information given
Brother, Donald Hyrum McINTOSH was active in the McIntosh Clan and genealogy at the time of this attachment.

72. California State Department of Health Services, Center for Health Statistics, "California. Death Index, 1940-1997," database, Basil Hugh McIntosh.

73. "Find A Grave," database (www.findagrave.com), Basil Hugh McIntosh, 21982438.

74. 1910 U.S. census, Utah, Utah, population schedule, Provo, enumeration district (ED) 195, sheet 1A, p. 80, dwelling 116, family 120, McIntosh, Basil; digital images,*ancestry.com*; citing National Archives and Records Administration microfilm T624.

75. McIntosh Reunion Descendants, McIntosh - Descendants of John & Girsey (Grace) (Grizel) Rankin McIntosh (Attachment to Aug 17, 1958 Newsletter - copy in Collection of Bonnie S. Williams), Repository: Bonnie S. Williams, RR 1 Box 247, N Hwy 2, Wilburton, Oklahoma, USA.
Annie Marie (daughter of Joseph Albert [McINTOSH] & Ann RUSSELL).
Annie Marie McINTOSH is a Great-Granddaughter of John McINTOSH & Girsey RANKIN
and a Granddaughter of William McINTOSH & Maria CALDWELL
no other information given
Brother, Donald Hyrum McINTOSH was active in the McIntosh Clan and genealogy at the time of this attachment.

76. Idaho Department of Public Welfare, Bureau of Vital Statistics, death certificate 70110 (1930), Anna Marie Lee died on 16 Mar 1930; digital image, ancestry.com.

77. Utah Division of State History, "Cemetery & Burial Database," database (https://heritage.utah.gov/history/cemeteries), Annie Maria McIntosh Lee.

# Source Citations

78. "Find A Grave," database (www.findagrave.com), Anna M Lee, 28905702.

79. "Utah, Select County Marriages, 1887-1937," database, Marie Mcintosh and Ralph Lee.

80. Brigham Young University-Idaho, "Western States Marriage Index," database (http://abish.byui.edu/specialCollections/westernStates/search.cfm), Marie McIntosh and Ralph Lee.

81. 1910 U.S. census, Utah, Utah, population schedule, Provo, enumeration district (ED) 19 Apr 1910, sheet 1A, p. 80, dwelling 116, family 120, McIntosh, Marie; digital images, *ancestry.com*; citing National Archives and Records Administration microfilm T624.

82. McIntosh Reunion Descendants, McIntosh - Descendants of John & Girsey (Grace) (Grizel) Rankin McIntosh (Attachment to Aug 17, 1958 Newsletter - copy in Collection of Bonnie S. Williams), Repository: Bonnie S. Williams, RR 1 Box 247, N Hwy 2, Wilburton, Oklahoma, USA. Alta Grace (daughter of Joseph Albert [McINTOSH] & Ann RUSSELL). Alta Grace McINTOSH is a Great-Granddaughter of John McINTOSH & Girsey RANKIN
and a Granddaughter of William McINTOSH & Maria CALDWELL
no other information given
Brother, Donald Hyrum McINTOSH was active in the McIntosh Clan and genealogy at the time of this attachment.

83. "Find A Grave," database (www.findagrave.com), Alta Grace McIntosh.

84. "Find A Grave," database (www.findagrave.com), Alta Grace McIntosh, 28905724.

85. 1900 U.S. census, Tooele, Utah, population schedule, St. John, enumeration district (ED) 147, sheet 5B, p. 253, dwelling 94, family 94, McIntosh, Alta Grace; digital images, *ancestry.com*; citing National Archives and Records Administration microfilm T623.

86. 1900 U.S. census, Tooele, Utah, population schedule; digital images, *ancestry.com*; citing National Archives and Records Administration microfilm T623.

87. McIntosh Reunion Descendants, McIntosh - Descendants of John & Girsey (Grace) (Grizel) Rankin McIntosh (Attachment to Aug 17, 1958 Newsletter - copy in Collection of Bonnie S. Williams), Repository: Bonnie S. Williams, RR 1 Box 247, N Hwy 2, Wilburton, Oklahoma, USA.
Daniel Kimball (son of Joseph Albert [McINTOSH] & Ann RUSSELL).
Daniel Kimball McINTOSH is a Great-Grandson of John McINTOSH & Girsey RANKIN
and a Grandson of William McINTOSH & Maria CALDWELL
no other information given
Brother, Donald Hyrum McINTOSH was active in the McIntosh Clan and genealogy at the time of this attachment.

88. Church of Jesus Christ of Latter-day Saints - various Temples, *Temple originated records, 1970-1989* (Salt Lake City : Filmed by the Genealogical Society of Utah, 1971-1993), Batch T900120 - 1235257 Film.
Daniel Kimball MCINTOSH
Sex: M
Birth: 4 Oct 1901
Saint John, Tooele, Utah
Father: Joseph Albert MCINTOSH
Mother: Annie Eliza RUSSELL.

89. Social Security Death Index (Online publication - Provo, UT, USA: Ancestry.com Operations Inc, 2009.Original data), Kimball D McIntosh.

90. 1910 U.S. census, Utah, Utah, population schedule, Provo, enumeration district (ED) 195, sheet 1A, p. 80, dwelling 116, family 120, McIntosh, Kimball; digital images, *ancestry.com*; citing National Archives and Records Administration microfilm T624.

91. McIntosh Reunion Descendants, McIntosh - Descendants of John & Girsey (Grace) (Grizel) Rankin McIntosh (Attachment to Aug 17, 1958 Newsletter - copy in Collection of Bonnie S. Williams), Repository: Bonnie S. Williams, RR 1 Box 247, N Hwy 2, Wilburton, Oklahoma, USA.
Kenneth Grant (son of Joseph Albert [McINTOSH] & Ann RUSSELL).
William Albert McINTOSH is a Great-Grandson of John McINTOSH & Girsey RANKIN
and a Grandson of William McINTOSH & Maria CALDWELL
no other information given
Brother, Donald Hyrum McINTOSH was active in the McIntosh Clan and genealogy at the time of this attachment.

92. "Find A Grave," database (www.findagrave.com), Kenneth Grant Mcintosh.

93. "U.S., Social Security Death Index, 1935-2014," database, Kenneth G. McIntosh.

94. Utah Division of State History, "Cemetery & Burial Database," database (https://heritage.utah.gov/history/cemeteries), Kenneth McIntosh.

95. "Find A Grave," database (www.findagrave.com), Kenneth Grant McIntosh, 39414.

96. "Find A Grave," database (www.findagrave.com), Note: He was married to Grace Chloe Roberts - 23 Jun 1939.

97. California County Marriages, 1850-1952, marriage certificate ; digital image, familysearch.org, "Kenneth Grant McIntosh and Grace C McCall married on 23 Jun 1939".

# Source Citations

98. 1910 U.S. census, Utah, Utah, population schedule, Provo, enumeration district (ED) 195, sheet 1A, p. 80, dwelling 116, family 120, McIntosh, Kenneth; digital images,*ancestry.com*; citing National Archives and Records Administration microfilm T624.

99. McIntosh Reunion Descendants, McIntosh - Descendants of John & Girsey (Grace) (Grizel) Rankin McIntosh (Attachment to Aug 17, 1958 Newsletter - copy in Collection of Bonnie S. Williams), Repository: Bonnie S. Williams, RR 1 Box 247, N Hwy 2, Wilburton, Oklahoma, USA.
Henry Rollo (son of Joseph Albert [McINTOSH] & Ann RUSSELL).
Henry Rollo McINTOSH is a Great-Grandson of John McINTOSH & Girsey RANKIN
and a Grandson of William McINTOSH & Maria CALDWELL
no other information given
Brother, Donald Hyrum McINTOSH was active in the McIntosh Clan and genealogy at the time of this attachment.

100. Utah State Board of Health, Certificate of Birth 12-a (1907), Rollo Henry McIntosh; digital image, ancestry.com, "Birth Certificates, 1903-1911".

101. Social Security Death Index (Online publication - Provo, UT, USA: Ancestry.com Operations Inc, 2009.Original data), Rollo McIntosh.

102. California State Department of Health Services, Center for Health Statistics, "California. Death Index, 1940-1997," database, Henry Rollod McIntosh died 14 May 1951 in Beverly Hills, CA.

103. California, County Birth and Death Records, 1800-1994, death certificate no. 8102 (1951), Rollo Henry McIntosh; digital image, familysearch.org.

104. "Find A Grave," database (www.findagrave.com), Rollo Henry McIntosh, 216016638.

105. 1910 U.S. census, Utah, Utah, population schedule, Provo, enumeration district (ED) 195, sheet 1A, p. 80, dwelling 116, family 120, McIntosh, Rollo; digital images,*ancestry.com*; citing National Archives and Records Administration microfilm T624.

106. McIntosh Reunion Descendants, McIntosh - Descendants of John & Girsey (Grace) (Grizel) Rankin McIntosh (Attachment to Aug 17, 1958 Newsletter - copy in Collection of Bonnie S. Williams), Repository: Bonnie S. Williams, RR 1 Box 247, N Hwy 2, Wilburton, Oklahoma, USA.
Fay Maxine (daughter of Joseph Albert [McINTOSH] & Ann RUSSELL).
Fay Maxine McINTOSH is a Great-Granddaughter of John McINTOSH & Girsey RANKIN
and a Granddaughter of William McINTOSH & Maria CALDWELL
no other information given
Brother, Donald Hyrum McINTOSH was active in the McIntosh Clan and genealogy at the time of this attachment.

107. Utah State Department of Health, birth certificate File No. 309 (1911), Faye Maxine McIntosh.

108. "U.S., Social Security Death Index, 1935-2014," database, Faye M. Jarrell born 27 Mar 1911; died 6 Apr 2005.

109. "Nevada, Death Index, 1980-2012," database, Faye Maxine Jarrell.

110. "Find A Grave," database (www.findagrave.com), Faye Maxine McIntosh Jarrell, 10749763.

111. All Counties, Arizona, marriage certificate , Martin Clyde Jarrell married Faye McIntosh on 1 Jan 1937 in Yuma, Arizona-.

112. 1930 U.S. census, Utah, Utah, population schedule, Provo, enumeration district (ED) 25-48, sheet 1A, p. 130, dwelling 1, family 1, McIntosh, Fay; digital images (ancestry.com); citing National Archives and Records Administration microfilm T626.

113. 1940 U.S. census, Los Angeles, California, population schedule, Compton, enumeration district (ED) 19-103, sheet 16A, p. 1969, household 359, Garrell, Fay; digital images,*ancestry.com*; citing National Archives and Records Administration microfilm T627.

## Appendix C

# Stories of William McIntosh's parents, William's sister Agnes, and the eleven children of William and Maria Caldwell McIntosh

## John McIntosh and Girsel Rankin

John McIntosh was born on June 25, 1795 in Croy, Inverness, Scotland. We have been unable to find his official birth record. His birth date was found on a Temple Card that he had filled out himself. Girsel Rankin (known as Girsey) was born on September 17, 1794 in Old Monkland, Lanark, Scotland. Her birth record is shown at the end of this story. They married on June 15, 1817 in Rutherglen, Lanark, Scotland. They had two children in Scotland before they joined the Lanark Society Settlers and immigrated to Canada in 1821. They were 26 and 27 years old, respectively. Agnes was about 3 years old and William was about 2 years old.

They bought land in Dalhousie, Lanark, Ontario, Upper Canada. They built their own house out of trees they felled and helped their neighbors build theirs. They broke the rocky ground to plant crops. They helped build a church and a schoolhouse. They built a community.

They lived in Dalhousie, Lanark, Canada for 20 years, bore seven more children and raised them there.

By 1841, John had been baptized in the Church of Jesus Christ of Latter-day Saints and wanted to join them on their journey to Utah. He sold his land, packed up his family, and started out. They arrived in Monroe, Michigan a month later. They had walked along the shores of Lake Ontario and Lake Erie.

John and his family lived in Ohio and Michigan for about 12 years. By 1853, John was ready to move on. Girsey had just died on April 11, 1853 and was buried in Oregon, Ohio. His son James had died in 1844 in Monroe. His daughter Agnes had died in childbirth. His daughters, Isabel, Jennette and Girsey, all married and were staying in the Ohio area to raise their children. His last child David, also stayed in the area, and probably died in 1865. The last of his children, William and John, had gone on ahead in 1847 to join the Saints.

John travelled to Winter Quarters, Nebraska with the Caldwell family. The Caldwell's had been friends and neighbors in Canada. In fact, John's son William had married one of the Caldwell daughters, Maria, and his son John would marry another Caldwell daughter, Caroline, in Utah.

John and the Caldwell's arrived in Utah on September 17, 1853.

John settled in Session's Corner, later called Bountiful. He is mentioned several times in the Diary of his son William. He travelled occasionally to visit William and John and their families.

John himself died on March 5, 1875 in Bountiful. Here is his obituary:

*At Bountiful, Davis County, Utah, John McIntosh, aged about 82 years. Deceased was born in the Highlands of Scotland, when he immigrated to Canada in year 1824. In the later place he became a member of the Church of Jesus Christ of Latter Day Saints, being baptised in the year 1838 by John E. Page. Leaving there in 1851 he came to Salt Lake City, staying a year or two in Salt Lake City when he moved to Bountiful where he died. For twelve years preceding his death he had entire charge of the tabernacle at Bountiful, which place he ever kept warm and comfortable for the saints to worship in. He is thus known to many who respect him for his fidelity.*

None of the records we have researched tell us where John is buried. We can only hope he was buried in Bountiful near the tabernacle and the people he loved.

Here are the children of John and Girsey:

Agnes was born on January 28, 1818 in Glasgow, Lanark, Scotland. She married Abraham Isaac Vaughn, Jr. about 1846. They had two children. We believe she died because of giving birth to their last child in 1847. We do not know where she is buried, but probably in the La Salle Cemetery near Monroe, Michigan, since other family members were buried there.

William was born on September 16, 1819 in Barony, Lanark, Scotland. He married Maria Caldwell on September 27, 1841 in Bathurst, Lanark, Canada. They had eleven children. He died on May 4, 1899 in Mt. Pleasant, Utah. He and his wife are buried in the Mt. Pleasant City Cemetery.

John was born on November 14, 1821 in Dalhousie, Lanark, Upper Canada. He died on February 4, 1822, in the same location. He was born shortly after his parents had arrived in Canada.

A second John was born on August 17, 1824 in Dalhousie, Lanark, Upper Canada. It was common to give a child the same name as the one who just died. He married Caroline Caldwell on December 9, 1854 in St. John, Utah. They had three children. He died on December 6, 1859 in Clover due to pneumonia, at the age of 35. He is buried with his wife in the Clover Cemetery, Clover, Utah.

James was born about 1825 in Dalhousie, Lanark, Upper Canada. He died in August 1844, at the young age of nineteen. The family was living in Michigan. He was buried in the LaSalle Cemetery, near Monroe, Michigan.

Isabel was born about 1829 in Dalhousie, Lanark, Upper Canada. She married Jacob Sankas on December 12, 1856 in Lucas County, Ohio. They had one child. We do not have the death or burial records for her or her husband, but we know they were living in Toledo, Ohio during the 1860 U.S. Census.

Jennette was born on April 21, 1831 in Dalhousie, Lanark, Upper Canada. She married Charles Campbell about 1850 in Waterville, Ohio. They had two children. She then married Elijah Woodruff on December 31, 1866 in Waterville, Ohio. They had no children. Jennette and Elijah are found in the 1900 U.S. Census living in Toledo, Ohio. He is 97 and she is 70. We have no death records for either of them or burial locations.

Girsey was born on May 21, 1832 in Dalhousie, Lanark, Upper Canada. She married Henry Hinckley on April 3, 1852 in Toledo, Ohio. They had five children. She died on October 28, 1914 in Toledo. She and her husband are buried in the Woodlawn Cemetery in Toledo, Ohio.

David was born about 1834 in Dalhousie, Lanark, Upper Canada. We have been unable to find many records that ensure us which of the many David McIntosh's is ours. There is a David McIntosh in the 1860 U.S. Census living in Toledo, Ohio. He is married to Mary Landis and has one child. We next find a Civil War record that shows a David McIntosh, from Cleveland, Ohio, serving in the military from February 6, 1863 to June 27, 1865. He had a second child by then. According to the Civil War Pension Application filed by Mary, he died on April 17, 1865 in the Andersonville Prisoner of War Camp in Georgia. We think this one is the best match.

Here is the birth record of Girsel Ranken.

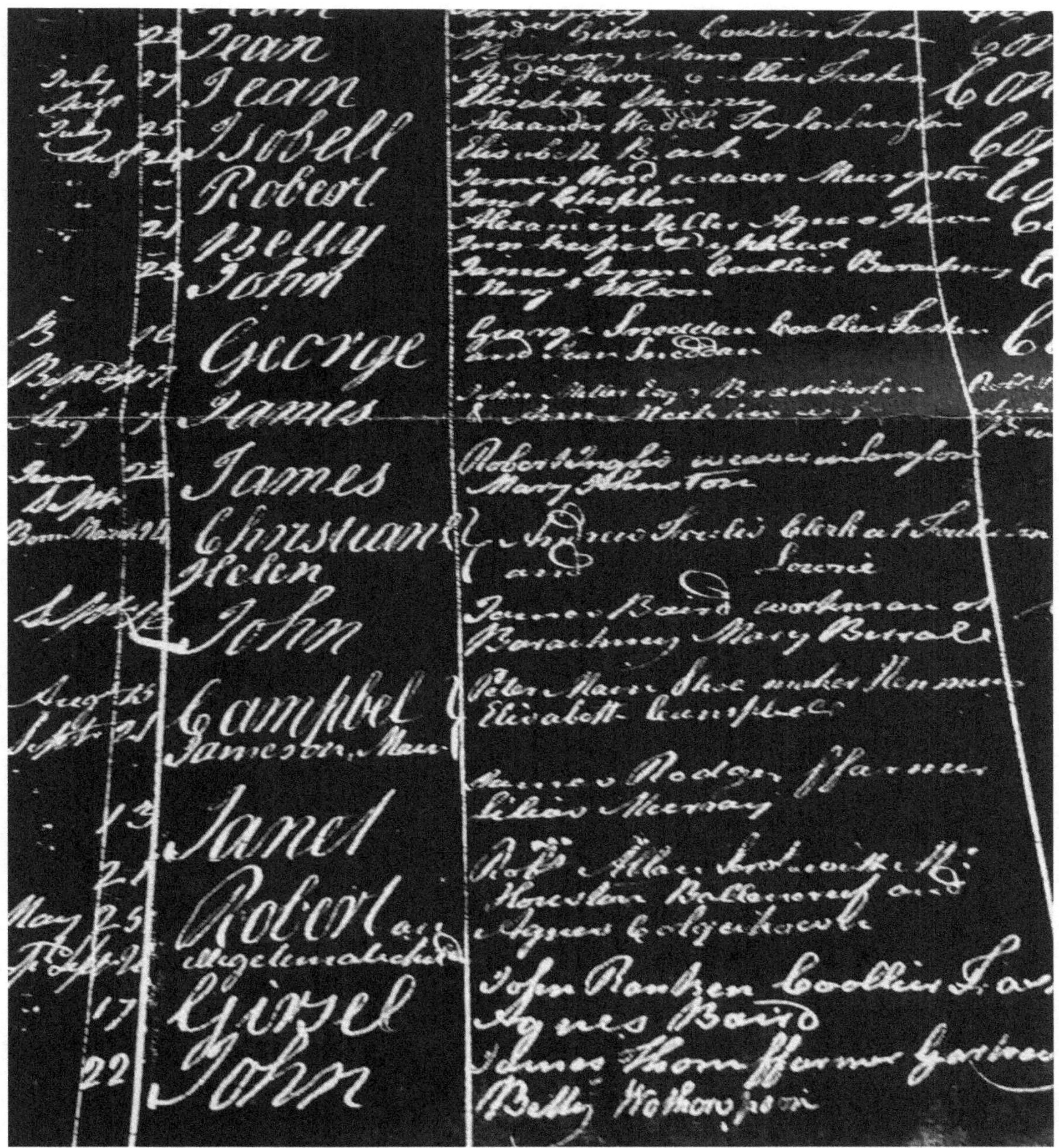

*Second to the last entry records the birth of Girsel Ranken. Source: Old Parochial Registers, Lanark, Scotland. Family History Library, Salt Lake City, Utah, Film 1,066,602. "Date: 1794 - Sept 17 – Name: Girsel – Father: John Ranken Occupation: Coollier (coal miner), Lasher (stevedore) – Mother: Agnes Baird.*

## Agnes McIntosh and Abraham Isaac Vaughn, Jr.

Agnes McIntosh was born on January 28, 1818 in Glasgow, Lanark, Scotland. She was the first child of John and Girsey Rankin McIntosh.

She emigrated from Scotland to Canada on May 11, 1821 with her parents and brother. Her brother, William, was born in 1819.

We do not know much about Agnes until she married Abraham Isaac Vaughn, Jr. in about 1846 in Michigan.

Abraham Vaughn, Jr. was an older brother of Mary Ann Vaughn Caldwell. According to immigration records, Mary Ann and her husband, David Caldwell, with five children, emigrated from Scotland to Canada, arriving on June 5, 1820, the year before the McIntoshes. We cannot find an immigration record for Abraham, so, since David and Mary Ann only had four children at the time, Abraham was probably included as the fifth child.

The Caldwell's and the McIntoshes bought land near each other around Lanark, Canada and became neighbors and friends.

The McIntoshes moved to Monroe, Michigan in 1841. The Caldwell's arrived in Monroe in 1845.

Abraham and Agnes met and married about1846 in Michigan, probably in or near Monroe.

They had their first child, Mary, in 1845 or 1846.

They had their second child, Isaac, in 1847.

In William's words, remembering back to 1847:

*At that time we lived about a half mile from Abraham Vaughan, my wife Maria's uncle who had married my sister Agnes. She had a child and was not able to be up yet. Maria went over to help her to do some work.*

William's Diary gives us vital information that we would not have had otherwise. This is how we know that Agnes had given birth and was possibly having a hard time recovering.

After that, there are no further records regarding Agnes, no record of her death and no record of her burial place. We assume that she died because of childbirth. And we assume she was buried in the LaSalle Cemetery, where other members of the family were buried. LaSalle Cemetery was an old Pioneer Cemetery for which no records remain.

What we do have is the 1850 U.S. Census of Monroe, Michigan on August 6, 1850. The two children, Mary and Isaac Vaughn, are living with their McIntosh grandparents, John and Girsey McIntosh.

In the 1860 U.S. Census, Isaac is living with his father's niece, Mary Caldwell Stuart, in Frenchtown, Michigan. There is no record of Mary.

There is no record of Isaac in the 1870 U.S. Census. He was the right age to join the military and serve during the Civil War. There were at least 27 Isaac Vaughns who served during the Civil War. Perhaps he was one of them. Perhaps he died in the war.

Meanwhile, in the 1860 U.S. Census, Abraham is a boarder with a family in a town near his niece and his son, Isaac. In the 1870 U.S. Census, he is living with that same niece in Frenchtown, Michigan. We cannot find him in any 1880 U.S. Census, so he probably died before then. We also have no record of his burial place, probably LaSalle Cemetery. Or he could have returned to Canada.

Here is a copy of the birth record of Agnes McIntosh.

*First entry records the birth of Agnes McIntosh. Source: Church of Scotland. Parish registers for Barony, 1672-1854 (Births, Baptisms, Marriages). Family History Library, Salt Lake City, Utah. Film 1041477: Date: January 1818, Father: McIntosh, John McIntosh, Occupation: dyer (probably dyed wool), Location: Bridgeton, Mother: Grace Rankin had their 1st child, born 28th January, baptized 8th February, named Agnes. John Montgomery and William McIntosh, wit.*

## William McIntosh

This is a copy of the birth record of William McIntosh in Barony, Lanark, Scotland on September 16, 1819.

*Record of the birth of William McIntosh*
*Public record from the National Archives of Scotland, Old Parish Records*
*The first entry reads: John McIntosh Grocer Bridgeton & Grizel Rankin had their 2nd child born 16th Sept named William. Wit. James Rankin James McIntosh. Top of the page: 1819.*

## John Ephraim McIntosh and Margaret Smith

John Ephraim McIntosh was born on June 13, 1842, just after his parents arrived in Toledo, Ohio. It had taken them one month to walk from Dalhousie, Lanark, Upper Canada to Toledo, Ohio, United States.

He lived in various places with his parents, as they made their way across the country to join the members of the Church of Jesus Christ of Latter-day Saints. The Saints were travelling to the Salt Lake valley in the Utah Territory.

John arrived in Utah with his parents on September 9, 1851. He was 9 years old. He lived with his parents as they moved to various places through-out Utah.

His father William was called on a LDS Church mission to establish a Mormon settlement, where the new pioneers could live, in Panaca, Utah [later Nevada] in 1867.

John was 28 years old. He did not travel with his family to Panaca. We cannot find him in any 1870 U.S. Census records.

In the 1880 U.S. Census, John McIntosh is living in Panaca, Nevada. He is married to Margaret McIntosh, nee Smith, age 31, born in Scotland. They have two children. John is 2 years old. Mary is 4 months old. We are unsure if this is "our" John McIntosh but this one is a close fit.

We know John died on February 2, 1889 in St. John, Tooele, Utah. Here is his obituary.

### Fatal accident at St. John.

### St. John, Tooele Co., Feb.8, 1889

A sad accident resulting in the almost instant death of Brother John E McIntosh occurred on the Johnson Pass, between Rush and Skull valleys about 1 mile below the divide at half past four on Saturday the 2nd. The deceased started from his parents house on the morning in question to his sheep camp in charge of a team laden with grain and provisions. He was accompanied by Mr. Henry Newman. Arriving on top of the divide and on going down the canyon the road being very difficult to travel and a considerable downgrade, the team started to run, throwing Brother McIntosh from the wagon. He fell between the two wheels. The hind wheels passing over his back, fracturing his ribs on both sides and slightly bruising the right side of his head. Mr. Newman stopped the team assisted the unfortunate man and laid him on some blankets and immediately afterward started down the canyon for help. He met Mr. S J Stookey coming up the canyon on horseback. On returning to the place of the accident they found him still alive but unable to speak and in about fifteen minutes from the time he received his injuries he breathed his last. His body was then conveyed to the home of his parents whom he had left only a few hours before in good health. The deceased leaves a widow and three children who reside at Eagle Rock, Idaho. There is also his aged parents brothers and sisters and a large circle of friends sadly mourn his loss. He was born in East Toledo, Michigan on June 13, 1842 and was a quiet inoffensive man and a devoted husband and father. An inquest on the body of the deceased was held at St. Johns precinct before Mr. John D. McIntosh J.P. the jurors found as their verdict that the said John E. McIntosh came to his death on Johnson Pass by being accidentally thrown under the wheels of his wagon which passed over his body causing almost instant death. The jurors were David H. Caldwell, David Charles and Nephi Draper. The funeral services were held on Wednesday last at St Johns. A. N. Ahlquist.

Note that it mentions his wife: *The deceased leaves a widow and three children who reside at Eagle Rock, Idaho* [present day Idaho Falls, Idaho]. We can only speculate about what this means.

I have searched Tooele County for the burial location of John Ephraim McIntosh with no success. We assume he was buried in the St. John City Cemetery. There are several small grave markers that are unreadable and overtaken by small bushes. Perhaps one of those marks his grave.

## Mary Ann McIntosh

Mary Ann was born on July 27, 1845 in Oregon, Ohio. She died on February 9, 1847 in Monroe, Michigan. She was just 18 months old.

Here is the story of Mary Ann's death in William's own words:

*At that time we lived about a half mile from Abraham Vaughan, my wife Maria's uncle who had married my sister Agnes. She had a child [Isaac Vaughan] and was not able to be up yet. Maria went over to help her to do some work. I was dragging up some wood with the oxen. And while I was after a drag of wood, Mary Ann's clothes caught fire. Before I could get to her, her clothes was all on fire. In this condition she came out to me. John had called to me that sissy's clothes was on fire and I came as fast as I could. She met me at the corner of the house. By this time the blaze was above her head. I put the fire out very quick. Water and snow being close by. After I had done this, her mother was not there, and I did not know what to do with her. I concluded I would take her to her mother. I had called several times but Maria she did not hear me. Consequently I started. Maria came out to meet me. Reader, you may judge how our feelings was in those circumstances. John Hall, the man I worked for at the moment, heard it and started his boy and a horse at the height of his speed for a doctor and soon had one there. We all did the best we could but all seemed of no use. She died in the eighth day of her illness. I was glad in one way to see her out of pain. This was in the 9th day of February 1847.*

William states, later, that she was buried in the LaSalle Cemetery near Monroe, Michigan.

## David Hirum McIntosh

In William's own words:

*On September the 5th, 1847, David Hirum was born. We lived there* [St. Louis, Missouri] *and enjoyed ourselves very well till David Hirum got sick. Whopping cough he got and was worse. We did all that we could until he died November the 16th. John, then our only child again, was very sick and came near dying. We began to think we was going to be bereaved of our children. John got well and we began to overcome our bereavement.*

We can assume that he was buried in the St. Louis area.

## William Henry McIntosh and Mary Elizabeth Keele

William in his own words:

*William Henry was born April the 18th, 1849* [St. Louis, Missouri]. *As soon as Maria was able to be up, we started* [continuing their journey]. *It was the 5th of May.*

During 1847, William and Maria had continued their journey to join the Saints in Winter Quarters, Nebraska. They stopped in the St. Louis, Missouri area in order for William to find work, so he could earn money to buy the supplies needed to continue their journey. They stayed about 5 years. With them, they had their son John, who was born in 1842 in Ohio. Their second child, Mary Ann, had died when her clothes caught fire in 1845 in Michigan. They lost their third child, David Hirum, in 1847 in St. Louis, when he died of whooping cough. Their fourth child, William Henry, was born in 1849, also in St. Louis, during the cholera epidemic. He survived, along with his brother, John, and his parents.

William Henry McIntosh traveled across the Mormon Trail when he was 2 years old, May 1 to September 9, 1851. He arrived in Salt Lake City, Utah Territory with his family.

They started out in Sessions Settlement in the North Kanyon Ward [later, Bountiful]; moved to West Jordon two years later; finally, to St. John, Utah in 1860, seven years later. William Henry [called Henry] was 11 years old.

William and his family were called on a LDS Church Mission in 1867 to settle a Mormon community in Panaca, Utah [later Nevada]. William Henry was about 17 years old when they got there.

He married Mary Elizabeth Keele on April 18, 1871 in Panaca. Her family were also among the early families who settled Panaca.

William's Mission was completed in 1871, when Panaca became part of Nevada. He and Maria moved to Panguitch, Utah with their five youngest children; the others having married and stayed in Panaca. Then, they moved back to St. John, Utah the next year, 1872.

Henry and Mary remained in Panaca for a few years. We do not have their complete story, but we can follow their moves by where their nine children were born.

Mary Elizabeth was born on February 2, 1872 in Panaca. She married James Ernest Cowdell on January 8, 1894 in Junction, Utah. They had five children. She died on January 22, 1962 in Los Angeles, California. Family records show that she and her husband are buried in Inglewood, California, but there are no records to confirm that.

William Henry, Jr was born on June 30, 1873 in St. John, Utah. He married Nora Morrill on April 18, 1894 in Manti, Utah. They had six children. He died on May 18, 1942 in Junction, Utah. He is buried with his wife in Junction Hill Cemetery, Utah.

Samuel John was born on March 26, 1874 in Panaca. He died on October 18, 1877, only 3 years old. He was buried either in Panaca or St. John, Utah. We do not know for sure.

Alice Maria was born on April 9, 1875 in St. John, Utah. She died on February 10, 1878, almost 3 years old. We do not know where she is buried, probably St. John, Utah.

Anna May was born on November 26, 1878 in Panaca. She married Daniel Lester Sprague on November 21, 1895 in Junction, Utah. They had six children. We do not know what happened to their marriage, but records show that she married Sidney Nephi Albert Black on July 2, 1918 in Richfield, Utah. They had no children. Again, records show that she married David J. Dunsire on February 27, 1928 in Sevier, Utah. They had no children. She died on November 22, 1956 in Ely, Nevada. We believe she is buried in California, but we do not have the exact location.

Abram was born on March 13, 1882 in Panaca. He married Charlotte Davis on August 3, 1904 in Junction, Utah. They had six children. He died on March 4, 1947 in Junction. He is buried with his wife in the Junction Hill Cemetery.

Olive was born on March 25, 1884 in Panaca. She married Joseph Sylvester Johnson on August 15, 1901 in Junction, Utah. They had one child. We do not know what happened to their marriage, but records show she married Louis William Lund on June 9, 1919 in Mt. Pleasant, Utah. She died on June 8, 1955 in Salt Lake City, Utah. She is buried at the Elysian Burial Gardens, Millcreek, Utah. Her husbands are buried elsewhere.

Elsie was born on March 3, 1887 in Junction, Utah. She married Joseph Jochein Ackerman on February 7, 1907 in Junction, Utah. They had eight children. She died on January 28, 1963 in Panguitch, Utah. She is buried with her husband in the Junction Hill Cemetery.

Raymond was born on July 30, 1899 in Junction, Utah. He married Telma Anderton on March 24, 1920 in Manti, Utah. They seven children. He died on February 3, 1954 in East Ely, Nevada. He is buried there with his wife.

Once Henry and Mary had moved to Junction (originally called City Creek), Utah, they bought a farm and remained there for the rest of their lives. Henry became a farmer and stock raiser. There was a large orchard on the farm and people came from surrounding towns to buy fruit for canning and apples for winter storage.

Henry was appointed Justice of the Peace from about 1887 to 1893 and performed many wedding ceremonies.

On April 28, 1901, at the age of 51, William Henry died. The cause is unknown since we are unable to find his death certificate. He is buried in the Junction Field Cemetery. It is located in a farmer's field east of the Junction Hill/Terrace Cemetery. It is open only on Memorial Day for visitors.

Four of their children remained at home after his death. The youngest child was only 2 years old.

Mary remarried, on July 15, 1909 in Manti, Utah, to James Empey. She brought her then ten-year old son to the new marriage; the other children having married and moved on.

James Empey had married her sister Harriet Keele in 1881 in St. George, Utah. Harriet died in 1906 in Panaca. So, when Mary married James, she raised her one and her sister's youngest children.

Mary divorced James Empey. We do not have the date. She took her young son, Raymond, and James took his children. Mary and her son moved to Henderson, Utah to live near her daughter, Elsie McIntosh Ackerman.

Mary rented out the farm in Junction when she moved. In Henderson, she went into the mercantile business and managed the only store in Henderson, Utah.

It was at Henderson where she had her fatal accident. She fell and broke her leg, just above the knee. Being 59 years old and unable to move, she probably died of pneumonia. We do not have her death certificate.

Mary Elizabeth Keele McIntosh Empey died February 26, 1916 in Henderson, Utah.

She is buried with her first husband, William Henry, in the Junction Field Cemetery.

## James Franklin McIntosh and Anne Mae Jordan

James Franklin McIntosh was called Frank. He was born January 8, 1852 in Bountiful, Utah, about 3 months after his family arrived in the Utah Territory.

Frank travelled with his family in 1869 to Panaca, Utah [later Nevada] when he was 17 years old.

He married Anne Mae Jordan on March 29, 1878 in St. George, Utah. He was 26 years old and she was 20.

Frank and Annie lived and worked in the Panaca area for several years, mainly farming and doing teamster work.

They were unable to have children of their own but were able to find a little girl who needed a home. Here is her story as told by her sister.

*This is a story of my life written June 1977 in Salt Lake City, Utah. My name is Dina Elizabeth Crow Burgess. I was born March 11th, 1881 to William Henry and Martha Ann Crow in Clover Valley, Nevada. My mother died when I was four years old. I was next to the youngest child. My mother was half Cherokee and half French Canadian. My father was Irish.*

*My father was left with six children to care for alone. Most of the people in those days were very poor and my Dad was one of the poorest. My baby sister Sharlet died soon after my mother left us. My father was very kind to us but I can imagine what a hard life he must have had trying to work and take care of us five kids. My mother gave little Sharlet to one of her best friends before she passed away, but she only lived a year so there were five of us left; two boys and three girls.* [They were living in Panaca, Nevada].

[In about 1886], *Mr. and Mrs. Frank McIntosh came to see if Dad would give them one of us girls. They didn't have any children so Dad let them have my sister just older than me. They were well off, so my sister had a good home. My dad took us four children, two boys and two girls; George and Joddie, Jannie and me and moved to Circleville, Utah but it wasn't any better for us, we were left alone most of the time.*

The little girl was Ica Minda Crow. She was born on November 7, 1879 in Panaca and was about 7 years old when she started living with Frank and Annie. They raised her as their own.

In about 1890, Frank, Annie, and Ica, moved to St. John, Utah, where Frank's father and mother, William and Maria, lived. Annie's parents, James Francis Jordan and Sarah Cannon also lived there.

Shortly after moving to St. John, the family decided to move to Mt. Pleasant, Utah.

William and Maria also moved there.

James Franklin McIntosh died of liver failure on May 2, 1896 in Mt. Pleasant, Utah. He was 44 years old. He is buried with his wife in the Mt. Pleasant Cemetery.

William wrote the following obituary for his son James Franklin:

*May 2, 1896. It has become my painful privilege to record the demise of J F McIntosh, my son. He died and was buried on Saturday May 2, Mount Pleasant, Utah. The son of William and Maria McIntosh of Mount Pleasant. We telegraphed for our people to come to the funeral but they could not get here in time for the funeral. We was obliged to bury him. He died from liver troubles. Ten days sick. He was born January 8, 1852. He was sick but a short time.*

Ica married Kimball Johansen in 1899 in the Manti Temple when she was 19 and he was 28. The two of them lived with Annie in Mt. Pleasant, Utah for about a year before they were able to support themselves. They lived and raised their five children in Mt. Pleasant.

Annie was living with them during the 1920 U.S. Census in Mt. Pleasant. The Census was taken in January and she died in September.

Anne Mae Jordan McIntosh died of a stroke on September 27, 1920 in Mt. Pleasant. She is buried next to her husband in the Mt. Pleasant Cemetery.

Ica and Kimball later moved to Millard County, Utah, southwest of Mt. Pleasant. They both died there but are buried in the Mt. Pleasant Cemetery.

Ica's obituary does not mention the fact that she was raised by Frank and Annie McIntosh.

## Melissa Jane McIntosh and Jacob Keele

Melissa Jane McIntosh was called Jane. She was born on June 27, 1854 in West Jordan, Utah. She lived in West Jordan with her family for about six years before they moved to St. John, Utah.

In 1867, she moved with her family to Panaca, Utah [later, Nevada]. She was 15 years old. She lived there with her parents until they moved to Panguitch, Utah in 1871. We are not sure if she returned to St. John, Utah with her parents, but we do know she returned to Panaca after she got married.

Melissa married Jacob Keele on October 10, 1872 in Salt Lake City, Utah. He was an older brother of Mary Keele, who had married William Henry in 1871.

The family of Jacob Keele and Mary Keele had also moved to Panaca to help settle the area.

We do not know much about their lives, but what we do know is based on where their children were born.

Maria Elizabeth was born on August 14, 1873 in Panaca. She married Frederick Walker Robinson on October 13, 1892 in Mesa County, Colorado. They had seven children. She died of the Spanish flu on December 7, 1918 in De Beque, Colorado. She is buried there with her husband.

Alice Melissa was born on October 16, 1874 in Panaca. She married Richard Burkitt on October 30, 1892 in Fruita, Colorado. They had four children. She died on January 29, 1920 in Fruita. She is buried there with her husband.

Alma Jacob was called Jacob or Jake. He was born on February 2, 1875 in Panaca. He married Dollie Garner on December 31, 1901 in Burlington, Wyoming. They had six children. He died on October 1, 1938 in Salmon, Idaho. He is buried there with his wife.

William Wallace was born in March 1880 in Panaca. He died in Huntington, Utah, when only four years old. We do not know where he is buried.

Annie Estella was born on August 2, 1883 in Huntington, Utah. She married Calvin Huston Kendall on December 25, 1899 in Fruita, Colorado. They had seven children. She died on April 26, 1965 in Fortuna, California. She is buried in Sunset Memorial Park in Eureka, California. We do not know where her husband is buried.

Lillian Jeanette was born on December 25, 1885 in Huntington, Utah. She married three times; to David Weir in 1903 and had one child; to David Armstrong in 1907 and had three children; Arvid Wiik in 1935 and had no children. She died on August 8, 1963 in Delta, Colorado. She is buried in the Mesa View Cemetery in Delta. Her husbands are buried elsewhere.

Abraham Deloss was born about 1887 in Fruita, Colorado. He is found in the 1910 U.S. Census in Meeteetse, Wyoming, at the age of twenty. He is found in no other U.S. Census records and we have no other information about him.

Jennie May was born and died in 1890 in Fruita, Colorado. We can assume she is buried in Fruita, but we have found no records.

Virgil Vaughn was born on July 27, 1893 in Fruita, Colorado. He married Claire Robbins on July 3, 1930 in Saint Anthony, Idaho. They had one child. He died on September 18, 1965 in Anaconda, Montana. He is buried with his wife in Humphrey, Idaho.

It always amazes us in the 21st century how often people moved around in the 19th century. But they moved for basically the same reason we do today, to find employment.

In 1895, William wrote about Melissa and Jacob living in Colorado:

*October 9, 1895. My wife is in very poor health. We are expecting Jacob Keele and family. His wife is our daughter Malisa Jane. They live in Colorado. They were coming on a visit to see their mother. She is sick. She feels a little better today.*

*October 14, 1895. We have had a letter from Jacob Keele's folks stating that they are disappointed about not getting their money and they cannot at this time come to see us.*

In 1900, for some reason, maybe looking for a better job, the family moved from Fruita, Colorado to Burlington, Wyoming. They lived there until 1902 when Melissa died. We cannot find her death certificate, so we do not know why she died at such a young age. She was 47. She died on March 9, 1902. She is buried in the Burlington Cemetery.

Jacob cannot be found in the 1910 U.S. Census, but in the 1920 U.S. Census, he is back in Fruita, Colorado. He died there on August 2, 1926 and is buried in the Orchard Mesa Cemetery/Municipal Cemetery in Fruita.

## Alice Maria McIntosh and Thomas Lorenzo Burridge

Alice Maria McIntosh was born on September 16, 1857 when the family lived in West Jordan, Utah. They moved to St. John, Utah in 1860; to Panaca, Utah [later, Nevada] in 1867; to Panguitch, Utah in 1870; and returned to St. John in 1872.

She was sixteen years old, living in St. John, when she met Thomas Lorenzo Burridge. His family had been like the McIntoshes as some of the early settlers of St. John.

Alice and Thomas married nine years later, on January 6, 1881 in Salt Lake City, Utah.

Thomas Lorenzo Burridge was born on December 2, 1853 in Valletta, on the island of Malta in the Mediterranean Sea. His parents, George Wilcox Burridge and Hannah Jane Shaw, were from Britain and his father was serving in the British Army, stationed at Malta, when Thomas was born. George had been in the Army for many years. Their first child was born in Greece; the second in England; the third while sailing on the Mediterranean Sea; then, Thomas in Malta. It was in Malta when George and Hannah joined the Church of Jesus Christ of Latter-day Saints. He began talking about his new religion amongst the other soldiers. The Army didn't like that so sent him back to England where he retired with his pension. The family then emigrated to the United States and joined the Milo Andrus Pioneer Company, arriving in Salt Lake City, Utah on October 24, 1855. They settled in St. John, Utah and had 3 more children.

Here are the children of Thomas and Alice.

George Thomas Burridge was born on June 19, 1882 in Iona, Idaho. He died of inflammation of the testicles resulting from a groin injury on July 18, 1911 in Provo, Utah. He was only 29 years old and had never married. He is buried in the Provo City Cemetery, Utah.

William McIntosh Burridge was born on October 4, 1883 in St. John, Utah. He died of a heart attack on November 29, 1905 in Mapleton, Utah. He had also died young, at the age of twenty-two. He never married. He is buried in the Provo City Cemetery, Utah.

Franklin Dennis Burridge was born on December 7, 1885 in St. John, Utah. He married Lurena Farrer on June 23, 1920 in Beaver, Utah. They had no children. He died on December 21, 1922, at the age of 37, in the Utah State Mental Hospital, Provo, Utah. According to his death certificate, he had *"acute mania for 14 days before his death, which was instantaneous."* He died of a cerebral hemorrhage, which can cause mania. He is buried with his wife in the Mountain View Cemetery in Beaver, Utah.

Alice Marie Burridge was born on January 1, 1888 in St. John, Utah. She died on May

12, 1896, at the age of 8. She is buried in the St. John Cemetery.

Jared Burridge was born on February 2, 1890 in St. John, Utah. He died on September 17, 1890, when only 7 months old. He is buried in the St. John Cemetery.

Theol Lorenzo Burridge was born on November 18, 1891 in St. John, Utah. He married Wanda Christison on October 15, 1919 in Salt Lake City, Utah. They had six children. He died on February 17, 1933, at the age of 41. He died of a manic type psychosis in the Veterans Hospital in Salt Lake City, Utah. He had served in the US Navy during World War I. Here are the comments the doctor wrote on the back of his death certificate: *"About last of Nov or first of December began to show some mental disturbance. While working on prospect in mountains on Feb. 4, 1933 he became greatly disturbed and jumped into a fire then ran away from camp during the very cold weather. This caused some freezing of toes and fingers. Burns, 3rd degree hands, feet, left leg, left arm, less extensive burns on neck and back".* He is buried with his wife in the Vine Bluff Cemetery in Nephi, Utah.

Thomas Lorenzo Burridge, himself, had been active in his community of St. John, and was appointed Justice of the Peace for a short time. He was also active in his church, the Church of Jesus Christ of Latter-day Saints. He was in the St. John Ward and was a ward teacher and assistant Sunday school superintendent.

He earned his living as a farmer and a sheep raiser.

Unfortunately, Thomas died on April 12, 1891 in St. John when he was only thirty-seven years old. We do not have his death certificate, so we do not know why he died so young. He was laid to rest in the St. John Cemetery.

Alice was left with a young family to raise. In a story told by her daughter-in-law, Wanda Burridge, Alice earned money by driving around Tooele County in her white top buggy selling milk, ice, cream, yeast, etc.

By 1900, Alice decided she wanted her children to have the best education possible, so she moved her family to Provo, Utah. Her two oldest sons George, and William, were already there attending Brigham Young University.

Alice Maria McIntosh Burridge died on October 31, 1914 in Provo at the age of 57. She had never remarried and did not live to see her grandchildren. Her death certificate states that she died of a duodenal ulcer. She is buried in the Provo City Cemetery.

## Abraham Edward McIntosh and Mary Louise Guhl

Abraham Edward McIntosh was called Abe. He was born on March 4, 1860 in Clover, Shambip County [later Tooele County], Utah. Clover was only a few miles from St. John, where the family later built another house.

When Abe was seven years old in 1869, the family was called on a mission by the Church of Jesus Christ of Latter-day Saints to form a community in Panaca, Utah [later Nevada] for the new Mormon families pouring into Utah.

The following information on this family came from the Diary kept by his father, William, and the stories he told his granddaughter, Fern McIntosh.

Fern wrote:

*These incidents were related to me by Abe McIntosh, my grandfather, as he remembered them.*

*The family went on a "Dixie Mission" to Panaca, Nevada. This was a mission in which you take your family and move to a particular vicinity to help settle. The Church authorities told William to go to Panaca so at this time my grandfather, Abe, was seven years old. He rode a horse 314 miles to his new home. Only the "best off" were called to settle a new place and this family was considered quite well-to-do for those times. Their wealth was not in gold and silver but in possessions such as cattle and sheep, etc.*

*With six teams of horses and 40 or 50 head of sheep, the father William, the mother Maria and eight children, with other families, started off. As they went along side of the Sevier River, a sheep fell in the water and nearly drowned because the river was so high. They had to lasso it and pull it to the shore. Again at a creek they had a queer experience. It happened at Chicken Creek south of Nephi, that one of the brothers threw a dog into the water to see how deep the water was and to watch him swim back to shore. They were having a great time watching him until some men from town came along and were going to shoot the dog because he was swimming in their drinking water.*

*They had a hard time getting to their destination. At Fillmore, they came upon hot and cold springs and had difficulty keeping the sheep out of them.*

*At Panaca, they lived in a dugout with merely an old quilt for a door. There was one large fireplace in the back of the room. The second year William and his boys built an eight roomed house. They had to pound the mud to make the adobes for the house and saw all the lumber by hand. William sawed the shingles for the whole roof by cutting the pine logs cross-wise.*

*Abe was 12 years old before he had any shoes of his own. In the winter he would borrow a pair from his older brothers to go out to do the chores. The next year they moved to a large ranch.*

*Grandpa, nearly 9, and his sister, a little past six, had to milk eight cows.*

*One day a strange man came past their ranch and decided he would like this prosperous looking place. So he decided to take it. As a result some of the boys had to ride 100 miles in a wagon to get a sheriff to help them quell this man's desires.*

*William and another man whom he thought he could trust, decided to start up a store. William put in $2000. All went well until one dark night, the "partner" ran away with everything but a basket of shoes.*

*When the states of Utah and Nevada were divided, Panaca was found to be on the Nevada side of the line, so William and family were released from their mission.*

*William tells in his diary of going to Panguitch to live for a while, but Maria was not well. She suffered eight years with throat trouble [Abe's story]. They moved back to Tooele and took out a homestead and after seven years received the "patent" on it. [Diary]. After suffering eight years, the inexperienced doctors in Tooele could find no cause for Maria's health problem so they started for Salt Lake City to find help. Near Magna, as William and Maria jogged along in their wagon, she had a hard coughing spell and coughed up a large piece of bone which had been lodged in her throat. It soon healed and she felt much better.*

*Abe married Mary Louise Guhl when he was 24 and she 22. She was born in Weber Canyon and had lived with her mother, sister, half-sister, and five half-brothers in Clover, near St John where the McIntoshes lived at the time. They met while going to school at St John's. [Mary's sister was Lena Guhl who later married William Abram McIntosh, Abe's cousin, and moved to Wyoming.] Mary tells of going to school and Mrs. Sworts, a sister to President Taylor, was her teacher.*

*Abe and Mary lived in St John for a while and Vance and William were born while they lived there. They decided to move to Mt Pleasant because it was supposed to be good sheep country. [Abe's story]. So with William helping them move, he drove the buggy with the children and Mary, and Abe drove the wagon filled with their furniture.*

*When they arrived in Mt Pleasant they lived in an adobe house in the west part of town but later built a nice brick home on the same lot. In 1892 [Diary] William and Maria moved to Mt Pleasant too. They had a nice frame house built for them on the West corner from Abe and Mary.*

*Maria had very poor health the last few years and finally at 73 years of age, died on July 27, 1897.*

*William was very witty and loved to tease. He lived with Abe and Mary and died May 5, 1899. Both William and Maria are buried in the Mt Pleasant City Cemetery.*

*Abe and Mary prospered in Mt Pleasant and had at one time a large ranch up towards the mountains north of Fairview and a big sheep herd and very choice ramboulette sheep. They built two lovely modern brick homes in town.*

*Abe's grandson Edwin remembered his Grandpa putting together food baskets throughout the year and delivering them to the widows who lived in town. He never told anyone, even his wife was surprised to learn of this during his funeral.*

Abe married Mary Louise Guhl on January 1, 1884 in St. John, Utah.

They became the parents of seven children.

Abraham Vance was born on April 26, 1885 in St. John, Utah. He married Florence Karna Monsen on October 15, 1913 in Salt Lake City, Utah. They had five children. Vance died on August 16, 1959 in Mt. Pleasant, Utah. He is buried with his wife in the Mt. Pleasant Cemetery.

William Edward was born on February 25, 1887 in St. John, Utah. He died on December 20, 1891 at the age of 4. He is buried in the Mt. Pleasant Cemetery.

Anna Estelle was born on December 24, 1889 in Mt. Pleasant, Utah. She married Joseph Schofield on November 2, 1912 in Salt Lake City, Utah. They had three children. Stelle died on January 13, 1973 in Los Angeles County, California. She is buried with her husband in the Rose Hills Memorial Park in Whittier, California.

Elvin Peter was born on January 28, 1892 in St. John, Utah. He married Muriel McArthur on November 27, 1923 in Provo, Utah. They had one child. Elvin died on March 18, 1958 in Los Angeles, California. He is buried with his wife in the Forest Lawn Memorial Park in Glendale, California.

Vernon Marenus was born on January 10, 1895 in Mt. Pleasant, Utah. After fighting in France in World War I, he returned home on April 1, 1919. He died three years later, on October 17, 1922. He was 27 years old. He never married. His death certificate states he died of diabetes, but his obituary gives more information.

> "Vernon McIntosh, 35 years of age, youngest son of Bishop and Mrs. A. E. McIntosh died suddenly this morning from diabetes. The young man was operated upon for the removal of his tonsils about a month ago and was seriously ill from severe hemorrhages at that time. After several blood transfusions had been resorted to, he began improving and was nearly well when he became suddenly ill and died after two day of illness".

He is buried in the Mt. Pleasant Cemetery. Vance also had a bleeding disorder thought to be hemophilia but now thought to be Von Willebrand disease. It is an inherited bleeding disorder and two grandchildren have been diagnosed with it.

Franklin Vaughn was also born on January 10, 1895, the twin of Vernon Marenus. Unfortunately, he died on February 7, 1895, not quite a month old. He is buried in the Mt. Pleasant Cemetery.

Grace Maria was born on September 6, 1903 in Mt. Pleasant, Utah. She married Robert Burns on November 14, 1923 in Provo, Utah. They had six children. She died on May 11, 1993 in Meadow Vista, California. She is buried with her husband in the Rose Hills Memorial Park in Whittier, California.

Fern ended her story with this:

*Abraham Edward always adhered to the faith of the Church of Jesus Christ of Latter-day Saints and since 1914 was bishop of the south ward of Mt. Pleasant. His political allegiance was given to the republican party and his personal popularity was indicated by the fact that on certain occasions he was the only republican elected to office on the local ticket. He continuously served as a member of the city council since 1894, or for a quarter of a century, save for two years when he filled a church mission to the eastern states, returning in 1897. As city councilman and as bishop he has endeared himself to the people of Mt. Pleasant because of his fairness and progressiveness and the wisdom which he has displayed, becoming recognized as one of the most valued and representative residents of Sanpete county.*

Mary died on August 21, 1936 in Mt. Pleasant, Utah at the age of 74. Her death certificate records that she died of chronic myocarditis [heart failure] and chronic arthritis. Her crippling arthritis is remembered by her grandchildren. She is buried in the Mt. Pleasant Cemetery.

Abe died on October 16, 1943 in Mt. Pleasant, Utah at the age of 83. His death certificate records that he died of chronic myocarditis [heart failure]. He is buried next to Mary in the Mt. Pleasant Cemetery.

## Lillian Elizabeth McIntosh and Heber Kimball McBride

Lillian Elizabeth McIntosh was born on January 11, 1863 in St. John, Utah. She lived with her family as they moved to Panaca, Utah [later Nevada]; then, Panguitch, Utah; and finally, when they returned to St. John, Utah.

Heber McBride was born on May 16, 1857 in Grantsville, Utah. His parents came to Utah two years before the McIntoshes and settled in Grantsville, a town near St. John.

Lillian married Heber Kimball McBride on October 9, 1882 in Salt Lake City, Utah in the Church of Jesus Christ of Latter-day Saints' Endowment House. The Endowment House was used temporarily, prior to the building of the LDS Temple. She was 19 years old and Heber was 25.

Lillian and Heber lived in Grantsville, Utah for a few years before moving permanently to Oakley, Idaho, as evidenced by the births of their eight children.

Following are the children of Lillian and Heber McBride:

Marie was born on August 1, 1883 in Grantsville, Utah. She married Arthur Marion Sanford on April 29, 1909 in Salt Lake City, Utah. They had six children. She died on February 17, 1967 in Boise, Idaho. She is buried with her husband in the Cloverdale Memorial Park in Boise, Idaho.

James William was born on August 1, 1885 in Oakley, Idaho. He married Julia Smith on April 9, 1909 in Salt Lake City, Utah. Julia died from an infection after giving birth to their last child in 1930. They had eight children. He remarried to Clarinda Beecher on July 11, 1942. They had no children. He died on December 1, 1960 in Tremonton, Utah. James and Julia, his first wife, are buried in the Oakley Cemetery.

Olive Marion was born on April 10, 1888 in Oakley, Idaho. She died on May 9, 1900. She was twelve years old. She is buried in the Oakley Cemetery.

Ephraim Heber was born on August 25, 1890 in Oakley, Idaho. He married Lydia Campbell on December 11, 1911 in Oakley. They had seven children. They divorced sometime after 1928. He then married Estella Bates on April 1, 1945 in Richmond, California. They had no children and also divorced. He then married Bessie Hansen on July 6, 1956 in Oakland, California. Ephraim died on November 16, 1965 in Oakland, California. He is buried in Evergreen Cemetery in Oakland, California. His wives are buried elsewhere.

Alice Lillian was born on November 15, 1892 in Oakley, Idaho. She married Moroni William Ward on November 12, 1914 in Salt Lake City, Utah. They had one child. Alice died on March 29, 1986 in Boise, Idaho. She is buried with her husband in the Salt Lake City Cemetery, Utah.

Edward Vaughn was born on May 9, 1895 in Oakley, Idaho. He died on March 20, 1905. He was nine years old. He is buried in the Oakley Cemetery.

Katherine Jane was born on February 2, 1898 in Oakley, Idaho. She married Leonard Campbell Livingston on June 7, 1916 in Salt Lake City, Utah. They had two children; then divorced. She then married James Squire on July 3, 1941 in Kansas City, Missouri. They had no children. She died on June 15, 1975 in Los Angeles County, California. She is buried in Rose Hills Memorial Park in Whittier, California next to James Squire, her second husband.

Dorcas Leah was born on January 25 ,1904 in Oakley, Idaho. She was called Leah. She married Karl Warren Collett on June 7, 1927 in Salt Lake City, Utah. They had two children. At some point after the 1940 U.S. Census, the family moved to Canada. Karl died on December 9, 1956, near Hope, British Columbia, Canada, in an airplane crash; his body was never recovered. Leah continued to live in Canada, in Calgary, until her death on May 18, 1987. She is buried in the Mountain View Memorial Gardens in Calgary, Alberta, Canada.

Heber Kimball McBride, himself, died on October 14, 1919 in Burley, Idaho at the age of sixty-two. He is buried in the Oakley Cemetery in Oakley, Idaho.

Lillian was alone for 24 years before she died on May 21, 1943. However, she was living with her daughter, Alice Ward, during the 1940 U. S. Census in Boise, Idaho. The Ward family then moved, with Lillian, to Tremonton, Utah where she died in 1943.

Lillian was buried with her husband in the Oakley Cemetery.

## Caroline Jeanette McIntosh and Joseph Clark Jordan

Caroline Jeanette McIntosh was born on November 1, 1865 in St. John, Utah. She moved with her family to Panaca, Utah, Panguitch, Utah, and finally back to St. John, all by the time she was seven years old.

Joseph Clark Jordan was born on April 2, 1863 in St. John, Utah. His family came to Utah three years after the McIntoshes and settled in St. John.

Caroline and Joseph married on January 5, 1887 in St. John, Utah. She was 21 years old and he was 23. They, then, moved to Mt. Pleasant, Utah.

They had three children, who were all born and died incredibly young, in Mt. Pleasant.

Fanny was born on September 13, 1887 in Mt. Pleasant. She died on March 19, 1889, not quite two years old. She is buried in the Mt. Pleasant Cemetery.

Then, they had twin girls. Marie Trinite and Anna Janette were born on August 23, 1889 in Mt. Pleasant. Marie died on November 15, 1889 and Anna died sometime after that. We do not know exactly when. They are both buried in the Mt. Pleasant Cemetery.

Caroline, herself, died on September 26, 1889, possibly because of birthing the twins.

Fanny possibly died from one of the epidemics/pandemics that were spreading throughout the United States and the World at that time, i.e., diphtheria in 1880, flu pandemic in 1889 and measles in 1890. There are many children in the Mt. Pleasant Cemetery who died during the same time frame.

Joseph remarried on October 23, 1895 in Manti, Utah to Lucina Madsen. They had seven children.

Joseph died on July 19, 1939 in Mt. Pleasant. Lucina died on May 29, 1944 in Mt. Pleasant.

Caroline, Joseph, their three babies, and Lucina, are all buried in the Mt. Pleasant Cemetery.

## Joseph Albert McIntosh and Annie Eliza Russell

Joseph Albert McIntosh, called Albert, was born in Panaca, Utah [later, Nevada] on March 8, 1869. He was just a baby when the family moved to Panguitch, Utah, and finally back to St. John, Utah, in 1872, where they had started.

Annie Eliza Russell was born on October 23, 1868 in St. John, Utah. Her parents had migrated to Utah the year after the McIntoshes and settled in St. John.

Albert and Annie got married on March 6, 1888 in St. John, Utah. He was 18 years old and she was 19.

The couple stayed in St. John for many years and had nine of their ten children there.

Albert became a sheep raiser.

Here are their children:

William Albert was born on November 28, 1889 in St. John, Utah. He married Grace Kirkman on October 12, 1916 in Salt Lake City, Utah. They had six children. He died on February 28, 1952. He is buried with his wife in the Wasatch Lawn Mortuary and Memorial Park in Millcreek, Utah.

Emily Elizabeth was born on September 14, 1891 in St. John, Utah. She married William Wymore in June 1918 in Provo, Utah. She was 26 years old and he was 27. They had no children because she died on December 11, 1918. She died because of the world-wide Spanish flu pandemic of 1917-1918. Here is the story behind her death. Emily's younger sister Marie married Ralph Lee in 1916. He went off to fight in World War I. He brought the flu back home with him. He and his wife, Marie, got extremely sick. Emily got time off from teaching school in Provo, Utah and went to Wyoming to take care of them. She was there three days when she got the flu and died. Ralph and Marie survived. Emily is buried in the St. John Cemetery, Utah. Her husband died on September 1948 in Los Angeles and is buried in Anaheim, California.

Donald Hyrum was born on October 1, 1893 in St. John, Utah. He married Melba Cropper on August 2, 1924 in Salt Lake City, Utah. They had nine children. He died on December 27, 1976 in Salt Lake City, Utah. He is buried with his wife in the Provo City Cemetery, Utah.

Basil Hugh was born on January 6, 1896 in St. John, Utah. He married Bernice Oates on June 14, 1919 in Tooele, Utah. They had 2 children. He died on August 28, 1956 in Inglewood, California. He is buried in the Forest Lawn Memorial Park in Glendale,

California. Bernice died on May 11, 1973 in San Bernardino, California. She is buried in the Wildomar Cemetery in Wildomar, California.

Anna Marie (called Marie) was born on March 4, 1898 in St. John, Utah. She married Ralph Lee on November 6, 1916 in Farmington, Utah. They had 4 children. Marie died on March 16, 1930 in Grace, Idaho. The cause of death was uremia from Bright's Disease and the flu. She was only thirty-two years old. She is buried in the St. John Cemetery. Her husband died on July 20, 1966 in Salt Lake City, Utah and is buried in the Salt Lake City Cemetery.

Alta Grace was born on April 27, 1900 in St. John, Utah. She died on May 11, 1900 in St. John. We do not know for sure, but we assume she is buried in the St. John Cemetery, since many of the family is buried there. There are many unmarked graves.

Kimball Daniel was born on October 4, 1901 in St. John, Utah. He married Pearl Dormet on August 15, 1947 in Reno, Nevada. They had one child. Kimball died on December 17, 1967 in Salt Lake City, Utah. He and his wife are both buried at the Wasatch Lawn Mortuary and Memorial Park in Millcreek, Utah.

Kenneth Grant was born on July 29, 1904 in St. John, Utah. He married Grace Roberts on June 23, 1939 in Compton, California. They had no children. Kenneth died on February 17, 1997 in Hurricane, Utah. He and his wife are both buried in the Hurricane City Cemetery.

Rollo Henry was born on January 29, 1907 in St. John, Utah. He married Ann Riley on July 24, 1937 in Los Angeles, California. They had one child. He died on May 14, 1951 in Beverly Hills, California. He is buried at the Inglewood Park Cemetery in Inglewood, California. We do not know where Ann is buried.

Faye Maxine was born on March 27, 1911 in Provo, Utah. She married Martin Jarrell on January 1, 1937 in Yuma, Arizona. They had three children. Faye died on April 6, 2005, at the age of 94, in Logandale, Nevada. She is buried with her husband in the Logandale City Cemetery.

In 1905, Albert and Annie move their family from St. John, Utah to Provo, Utah. It was Annie who insisted on the move, to allow better educational opportunities for their children.

Their last child, Faye, wrote the following about her parents:

*Dad was away from home much of the time attending to his contract hauling business so it was Mother who did most of the training of the children. She was patient and loving but not without some stern corrections when necessary.*

They lived in Provo, Utah for about 26 years - 1905 until 1931. They then retired to Compton, California, near Los Angeles.

Annie was killed in a car accident and Albert was severely injured, near Las Vegas, Nevada on July 10, 1940. They were on a road trip back to Utah to visit their sons.

The following is a description of her death, and is an excerpt from Annie's obituary:

*Funeral services for Annie Elizabeth McIntosh, 71, who was killed in a head-on motor car collision at Las Vegas, Nev., Sunday, will be conducted Friday at 1 pm at the St. John LDS ward chapel. Interment will be in St. John Cemetery. Mrs. McIntosh, with her husband, Joseph Albert McIntosh, and her son, Kimball H. McIntosh, was coming from her home in Los Angeles to Milford, Utah, to visit her sons, William Albert McIntosh of Milford and Donald H. McIntosh of East St. Louis, who was visiting in Utah. She was killed instantly when the automobile in which she was riding met head-on with another machine 62 miles west of Las Vegas. Mr. McIntosh lay critically injured in a Las Vegas hospital.*

Albert never fully recovered from the injuries he sustained in the car accident. He died on January 21, 1950 in Los Angeles, California, nearly ten years later. Both Annie and Albert are buried in the St. John City Cemetery, Utah.

# Appendix D

# History and Traditions of Clan Mackintosh

## Clan History

A clan is a kinship group among the Scottish people. Clans give a sense of shared identity among members. They generally identify with geographical areas originally controlled by their founders, sometimes with an ancestral castle and clan gatherings. Most clans have their own tartan patterns, usually dating from the 19th century, which members incorporate into kilts or other clothing.

It is a common misconception that every person who bears a clan's name has a blood tie of kinship with the clan chiefs. Many clansmen, although not related to the chief, took the chief's surname as their own to either show solidarity or to obtain basic protection. Most of the followers of the clan were tenants who supplied labor to the clan leaders. The tenant farmers took the chief's surname as their own in the 16th and 17th centuries when surnames came into common use.

Clan Mackintosh is a Scottish clan from Inverness in the northern Scottish Highlands. The chief of the clan is named The Mackintosh of Mackintosh. The Mackintosh of Mackintosh has traditionally also been the chief of Clan Chattan [pronounced Hattan]. It is a large confederation of twelve separate clans who grouped together for mutual defense.

Mackintosh is also spelled McIntosh, MacIntosh, Macintosh, MacKintosh, McKintoisch, McKintoch, McKintowse, Mhic an Tòisich, and other variations. The name *mc* means "son of". The name *toisich* means chief. So, McIntosh means "son of the chief". No matter the spelling, people named McIntosh are all part of the same strong and noble clan with a rich history.

The Scottish clan Mackintosh is traceable to the second son of Duncan MacDuff, the Earl of Fife, Shaw McDuff. Shaw McDuff took the name Mackintosh when he became the chief of the clan (son of the chief, Duncan). He was awarded lands in Inverness for his support of Malcom IV in the suppression of a rebellion in Morayshire in 1160. In 1163, he was made constable of Inverness Castle and was granted land in the Finhorn Valley. These lands became the heartland of the Mackintosh clan and the place where the chiefs would be buried.

The first Mackintosh clan castle was built on the island on Loch Moy [Lake Moy]. That castle has been rebuilt several times over the centuries, in different locations and in different styles. The clan home [always called Moy Hall] is now located on shore near the village of Moy, just south of Inverness.

Cruelties suffered under the English government after the failed Jacobite rising in 1745 forced many to leave their ancient homeland for the freedom of the North American colonies. These hardy settlers gave their strength and perseverance to the nations that would become the United States and Canada. Immigration and passenger lists have shown many early immigrants bearing the name MacKintosh, with all its various spellings.

## Clan Seat: Moy Hall, Scotland

Moy Hall, near the village of Moy and south of Inverness, has been the home of the Clan Mackintosh chiefs since the 14th century.

The original Moy Hall was built on the Isle of Moy on Loch Moy.

The second Moy Hall was built about the year 1700 on the north shore of Loch Moy. Its site is indicated by a stone a few yards from the approach road to the present building.

The third Moy Hall, built in 1803, was demolished after World War II having been overcome by dry rot.

The new and current Moy Hall is somewhat smaller but retains various features from the old place.

Mrs. McIntosh (mother of the current Chief, John, The Mackintosh of Mackintosh) lives in Moy Hall and welcomes all visitors to tour the small museum that contains Mackintosh memorabilia from the past centuries. It even has the bed in which Bonnie Prince Charlie (Charles Edward Stuart) slept when he was running from the English during the Jacobite rebellion.

Moy Hall is also the gathering place for the annual clan gathering.

*This is a map of Loch Moy, with its island, where the first Moy Hall was built.*

*Original Moy Hall on the island on Loch Moy*

*Current Moy Hall on the shore of Loch Moy*

*Loch Moy in summer*

The Mackintoshes Moy Hall near Inverness is not to be confused with Moy Castle. Moy Castle once belonged to Clan Maclaine. It is located on the Isle of Mull, near Argyll and Bute, on the western shore of Scotland. Moy Castle is a ruined castle built in the 14th century but abandoned in 1752. The ruins have been declared a National Monument. It has been used for scenes in several movies.

*Moy Castle on Isle of Mull, Scotland*

*Location of Isle of Mull on the western coast of Scotland*

## Coat of Arms of Clan MacKintosh

Coats of Arms were used for centuries to identify a particular family. They were created for the battlefield. Other knights could not tell who was inside a suit of armor, so they created symbols to attach to the armor. Thus, was born the coat of arms. The Crest is not to be confused with a Coat of Arms. The Crest is actually a portion of the coat of arms that is just below the helmet.

Touch not the cat bot a glove
MacKintosh

## Mackintosh Crest

The red lion at upper left on the shield signifies dauntless courage. Its red color indicates a warrior —brave, strong, generous, and just. The upper right includes a red hand which signifies sincerity, faith, and judgment; and a red heart which represents clarity and sincerity. The blue [shown here as black] ship at lower right shows a traveler to far places. The blue color depicts truth and loyalty. The lower left is blue with a gold boar's head to signify bravery—one who fights to the death. The gold color represents generosity and elevation of mind.

## Mackintosh Tartans

The wearing of the tartan kilt was banned after the fall of the last Catholic King of England and Scotland, James II. The Catholic Jacobite's [Scots] had lost their nearly 60-year-long rebellion against the Protestant English. This happened at the decisive Battle of Culloden in 1746. England instituted an act that made tartans and kilts illegal. Punishment was severe. Since the kilt had been widely used as a battle uniform, the garment acquired a new function – as a symbol of Scottish dissent. During the ban, it became fashionable for resistors to wear kilts in protest. So, the tartan faded from everyday use, but its significance as a symbol of Scottish identity increased. The ban was lifted in 1782 after any fear of a Scottish uprising had diminished. By that point, kilts and tartans were no longer staples of a Scottish wardrobe. But the tartan had turned into a potent symbol of Scottish individuality and patriotism and became the symbolic ceremonial dress that we know today.

*The Mackintosh modern tartan colors are red, navy blue and forest green.*
*Sample swatches were provided courtesy of Kinloch Anderson.*
https://www.kinlochanderson.com/tartan/macintosh

There are several other Mackintosh tartans that have been used over time. The one above is the one currently in use. The following tartans are only a few of the many plaids that are also part of the Mackintosh tartan group.

*Mackintosh Dress Tartan*

*Mackintosh Ancient Tartan*

*Mackintosh Hunting Tartan*

*Mackintosh Ancient Hunting Tartan*

*Mackintosh Modern Red*

*Mackintosh Muted Red Tartan*

## Mackintosh Crest on a Cap Badge on a Mackintosh Tartan

## Mackintosh Plant Badge

The plant badge, usually a sprig of a specific plant, is used to identify a member of a particular Scottish clan. It is usually worn on a bonnet behind the Scottish crest badge or attached at the shoulder of a lady's tartan sash.

*Red Whortleberry*

## Mackintosh Motto: *Touch Not the Cat Bot a Glove*

*Touch not the cat without a glove* is a warning to those who would be so imprudent as to engage in battle when the claw of the wildcat is ungloved. It is necessary to wear gloves if you are going to tangle with a member of the Clan because they are as fierce as wildcats.

Mottoes first began to be shown with coats of arms in the $14^{th}$ and $15^{th}$ centuries but were not in general use until the $17^{th}$ century. Thus, the oldest coats of arms generally do not include mottos.

## Mackintosh War Cry

*"Loch Moigh!"*(Meaning Lake Moy)

## Clan Chief

The current Clan Chief is John Lachlan Mackintosh of Mackintosh. He has been chief since his father died in 1995. He currently resides in Singapore, where he works as a history teacher at Nanyang Girls' High School. He returns to Scotland with his family every August for the Clan gathering and the Highland Games at Loch Moy.

## Official Book of Clan Mackintosh

*The History of the Clan Mackintosh and the Clan Chattan* by Margaret Mackintosh of Mackintosh. The Pentland Press Limited, Edinburgh, Scotland, 1997.

*Sources: The information presented above was gleaned from various websites on the internet. The Mackintosh Coat of Arms was purchased from ScotsConnection.com.*

**Map of the area around Moy, Scotland, including Loch Moy, Inverness and Culloden.**

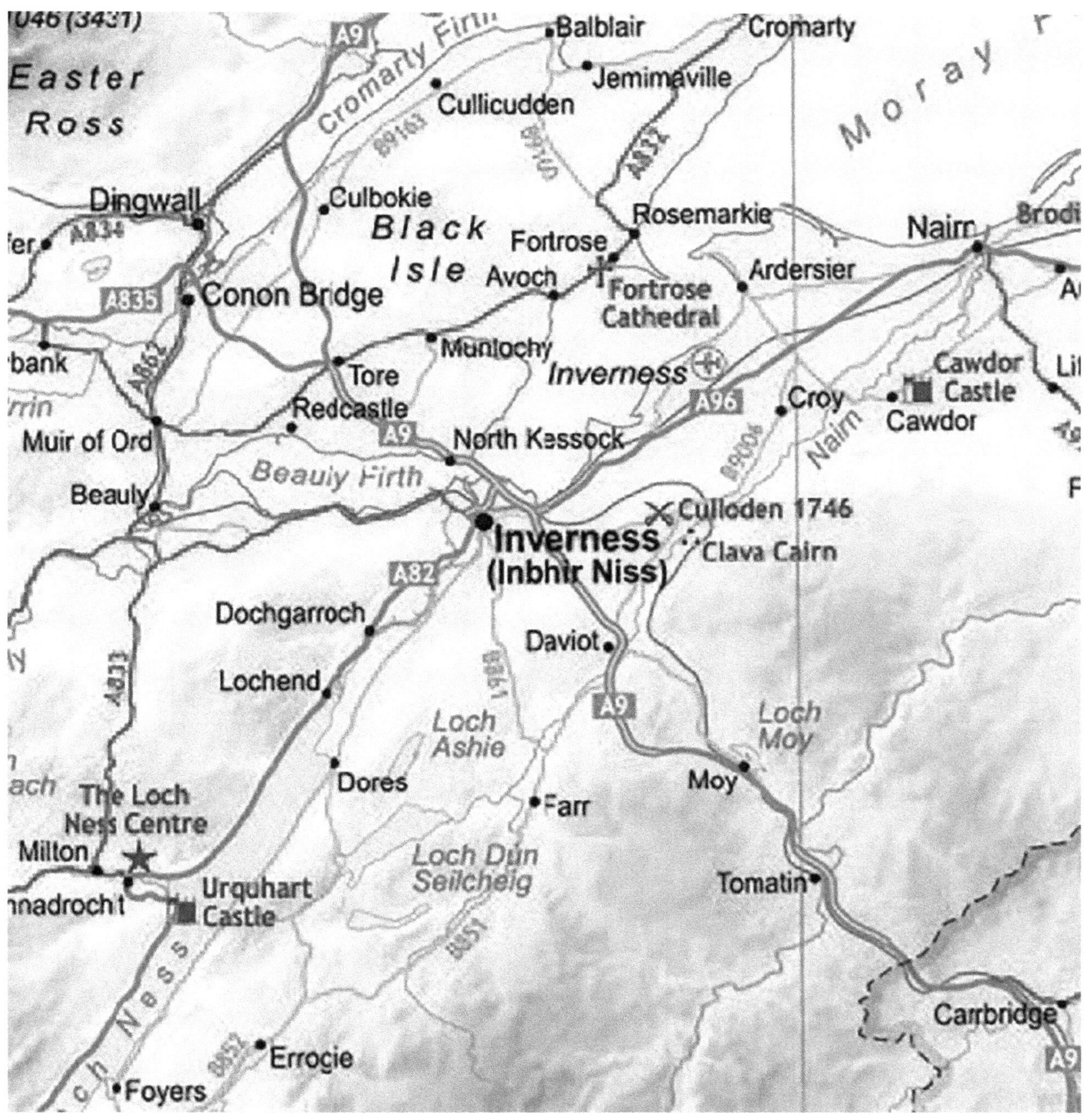

## Appendix E

# McIntosh Descendant Charts

# Descendants of John McIntosh

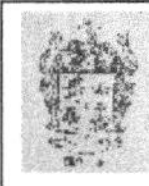

**John McIntosh Sr.**
b: 25 Jun 1795 in Croy, Inverness, Scotland, United Kingdom
d: 05 Mar 1875 in Bountiful, Davis, Utah Territory, United States

**Agnes McIntosh**
b: 28 Jan 1818 in Glasgow, Lanark, Scotland, United Kingdom
d: Cir 1847 in Monroe, Michigan, United States
Possibly died in childbirth

**Abraham Isaac Vaughn Jr.**
b: Cir 1783 in Lanark, , Scotland, United Kingdom
m: 1846 in Michigan, United States
d: Bef 1880

**William McIntosh**
b: 16 Sep 1819 in Barony, Lanarkshire, Scotland, United Kingdom
d: 04 May 1899 in Mount Pleasant, Sanpete, Utah, United States
bu: May 1899 in Mt. Pleasant, Sanpete, UT, USA
Le Grippe (Influenza)

**Maria Caldwell**
b: 17 Feb 1824 in Lanark, Lanark, Upper Canada, Canada
m: 27 Sep 1841 in Bathurst, Lanark, , Canada
d: 27 Jul 1897 in Mount Pleasant, Sanpete, Utah, United States
bu: 02 Aug 1897 in Mt. Pleasant, Sanpete, UT, USA
Epilepsy

**John McIntosh**
b: 14 Nov 1821 in Dalhousie, Lanark, Ontario, Canada
d: Cir 1822 in Dalhousie, Lanark, Ontario, Canada

**John McIntosh Jr.**
b: 17 Aug 1824 in Dalhousie, Lanark, Upper Canada, Canada
d: 06 Dec 1859 in Clover, Shambip, Utah Territory, United States
bu: 09 Dec 1859 in Clover, Shambip, Utah Territory, USA
Pneumonia

**Caroline Elizabeth Caldwell**
b: 03 Nov 1827 in Bathurst, Lanark, Ontario, Canada
m: 09 Dec 1854 in Saint John, Tooele, Utah Territory, United States
d: 10 Sep 1891 in Saint John, Tooele, Utah, United States
bu: 1891 in Rush Valley, Tooele, UT, USA
Typhoid Fever

**James McIntosh**
b: Cir 1825 in Dalhousie, Lanark, Ontario, Canada
d: Aug 1844 in Monroe, Michigan, United States
bu: 1844 in Monroe, Monroe, MI

**Girsel Rankin**
b: 17 Sep 1794 in Old Monkland, Lanark, Scotland, United Kingdom
m: 15 Jun 1817 in Rutherglen, Lanark, Scotland, United Kingdom
d: 11 Apr 1853 in Oregon, Lucas, Ohio, United States
bu: 1853 in Oregon, Lucas, OH, USA

**Mary McPherson**
b: 01 Mar 1797 in Galston, Ayrshire, Scotland, United Kingdom
m: 16 May 1860 in Bountiful, Davis, Utah, United States
d: 28 Feb 1879 in Fish Haven, Bear Lake, Idaho, United States
bu: 1879 in Fish Haven, Bear Lake, ID, USA

**Isabel McIntosh**
b: Cir 1829 in Dalhousie, Lanark, Ontario, Canada
d: Aft 1860

**Jacob Simkus**
b: Abt 1835 in Scotland, United Kingdom
m: 12 Dec 1856 in Lucas, Ohio, United States

**Charles Campbell**
b: 1829 in New York, New York, New York, United States
m: Abt 1850 in Waterville, Lucas, Ohio, United States
d: Aft 1858

**Jennette McIntosh**
b: 22 Apr 1830 in Dalhousie, Lanark, Ontario, Canada
d: 22 Aug 1908 in Toledo, Lucas, Ohio, United States
bu: 1908 in Oregon, Lucas, OH, USA

**Elijah Judd Woodruff**
b: 18 Sep 1802 in Watertown, Litchfield, Connecticut, United States
m: 31 Dec 1866 in Toledo, Lucas, Ohio, United States
d: 07 Jan 1904 in Toledo, Lucas, Ohio, United States
bu: 1904 in Oregon, Lucas, OH, USA
Chronic Interstitial Nephritis (kidney disease)

**Girsey McIntosh**
b: 21 May 1832 in Dalhousie, Lanark, Ontario, Canada
d: 28 Oct 1914 in Toledo, Lucas, Ohio, United States
bu: 31 Oct 1914 in Toledo, Lucas, OH, USA

**Henry Hinckley**
b: 04 Mar 1832 in New York, United States
m: 03 Apr 1852 in Toledo, Lucas, Ohio, United States
d: 23 Apr 1899 in Toledo, Lucas, Ohio, United States
bu: 1899 in Toledo, Lucas, OH, USA
Pneumonia

**David McIntosh**
b: Cal 1834 in Dalhousie, Lanark, Ontario, Canada
d: 17 Apr 1865 in Andersonville, , Georgia, United States
Probably died in the Civil War

**Mary Landis**
b: Cal 1833 in Pennsylvania, United States
m: Cal 1856

# Descendants of Agnes McIntosh

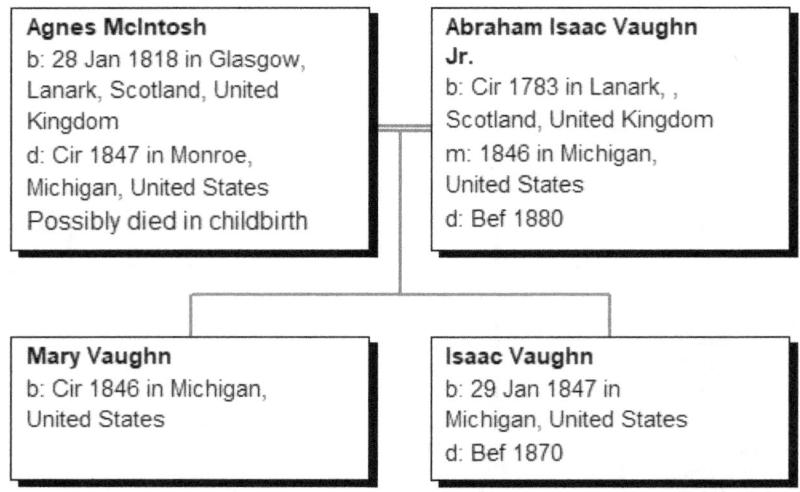
Agnes McIntosh
b: 28 Jan 1818 in Glasgow, Lanark, Scotland, United Kingdom
d: Cir 1847 in Monroe, Michigan, United States
Possibly died in childbirth
Abraham Isaac Vaughn Jr.
b: Cir 1783 in Lanark, , Scotland, United Kingdom
m: 1846 in Michigan, United States
d: Bef 1880
Mary Vaughn
b: Cir 1846 in Michigan, United States
Isaac Vaughn
b: 29 Jan 1847 in Michigan, United States
d: Bef 1870

# Descendants of William McIntosh

**William McIntosh**
b: 16 Sep 1819 in Barony, Lanarkshire, Scotland, United Kingdom
d: 04 May 1899 in Mount Pleasant, Sanpete, Utah, United States
bu: May 1899 in Mt. Pleasant, Sanpete, UT, USA
Le Grippe (Influenza)

**Maria Caldwell**
b: 17 Feb 1824 in Lanark, Lanark, Upper Canada, Canada
m: 27 Sep 1841 in Bathurst, Lanark, , Canada
d: 27 Jul 1897 in Mount Pleasant, Sanpete, Utah, United States
bu: 02 Aug 1897 in Mt. Pleasant, Sanpete, UT, USA
Epilepsy

## (continued)

**John Ephraim McIntosh**
b: 13 Jun 1842 in Toledo, Lucas, Ohio, United States
d: 02 Feb 1889 in Saint John, Tooele, Utah Territory, United States
bu: 1889 in Rush Valley, Tooele, UT, USA
Accidentally fell under wheels of his wagon on steep pass

**Margaret Smith**
b: Cal 1849 in Scotland, United Kingdom
m: Cir 1864 in Saint John, Tooele, Utah Territory, United States

**Mary Ann McIntosh**
b: 27 Jul 1845 in Oregon, Lucas, Ohio, United States
d: 09 Feb 1847 in Monroe, Monroe, Michigan, United States
bu: Abt 12 Feb 1847 in La Salle, Monroe, MI, USA
Died as a child from burns eight days after her clothing caught fire

**David Hirum McIntosh**
b: 05 Sep 1847 in Saint Louis, , Missouri, United States
d: 16 Nov 1847 in Saint Louis, , Missouri, United States
King's Cough - Whooping Cough

**William Henry McIntosh Sr.**
b: 18 Apr 1849 in Saint Louis, , Missouri, United States
d: 28 Apr 1901 in Junction, Piute, Utah, United States
bu: 1901 in Junction, Piute, UT, USA

**Mary Elizabeth Keele**
b: 29 May 1856 in Farmington, Davis, Utah Territory, United States
m: 18 Apr 1871 in Panaca, Lincoln, Nevada, United States
d: 26 Feb 1916 in Henderson, Garfield, Utah, United States
bu: 03 Mar 1916 in Junction, Piute, UT, USA
Probably pneumonia

**James Franklin McIntosh**
b: 08 Jan 1852 in Bountiful, Davis, Utah Territory, United States
d: 02 May 1896 in Mount Pleasant, Sanpete, Utah, United States
bu: 02 May 1896 in Mt. Pleasant, Sanpete, UT, USA
Liver failure

**Anne Mae Jordan**
b: 25 Oct 1857 in West Jordan, Great Salt Lake, Utah Territory, United States
m: 29 Mar 1878 in Saint George, Washington, Utah Territory, United States
d: 27 Sep 1920 in Mount Pleasant, Sanpete, Utah, United States
bu: 30 Sep 1920 in Mt. Pleasant, Sanpete, UT, USA
Cerebral Apoplexy (stroke)

## Descendants of William McIntosh (continued)

**William McIntosh**
b: 16 Sep 1819
in Barony, Lanarkshire, Scotland, United Kingdom
d: 04 May 1899
in Mount Pleasant, Sanpete, Utah, United States
bu: May 1899 in Mt. Pleasant, Sanpete, UT, USA
Le Grippe (Influenza)

**Maria Caldwell**
b: 17 Feb 1824
in Lanark, Lanark, Upper Canada, Canada
m: 27 Sep 1841
in Bathurst, Lanark, , Canada
d: 27 Jul 1897 in Mount Pleasant, Sanpete, Utah, United States
bu: 02 Aug 1897
in Mt. Pleasant, Sanpete, UT, USA
Epilepsy

**Melissa Jane McIntosh**
b: 27 Jun 1854
in West Jordan, Great Salt Lake, Utah Territory, United States
d: 09 Mar 1902
in Burlington, Big Horn, Wyoming, United States
bu: 12 Mar 1902
in Burlington, Big Horn, WY

**Jacob Keele**
b: 09 May 1847
in Council Bluffs, , Iowa, United States
m: 10 Oct 1872
in Salt Lake City, Great Salt Lake, Utah Territory, United States
d: 02 Aug 1926
in Grand Junction, Mesa, Colorado, United States
bu: 04 Aug 1926
in Grand Junction, Mesa, CO
Apoplexy; Stroke

**Alice Maria McIntosh**
b: 26 Sep 1857
in West Jordan, Great Salt Lake, Utah Territory, United States
d: 31 Oct 1914
in Provo, Utah, Utah, United States
bu: 03 Nov 1914
in Provo, Utah, UT, USA
Duodenal ulcer

**Thomas Lorenzo Burridge**
b: 02 Dec 1853
in Valletta, , , Malta
m: 06 Jan 1881
in Salt Lake City, Great Salt Lake, Utah Territory, United States
d: 12 Apr 1891
in Saint John, Tooele, Utah Territory, United States
bu: 14 Apr 1891
in Rush Valley, Tooele, UT, USA

**Abraham Edward McIntosh**
b: 04 Mar 1860
in Clover, Shambip, Utah Territory, United States
d: 16 Oct 1943
in Mount Pleasant, Sanpete, Utah, United States
bu: 20 Oct 1943
in Mt. Pleasant, Sanpete, UT, USA
Chronic Myocarditis

**Mary Louise Guhl**
b: 27 May 1862
in Weber Canyon, Weber, Utah Territory, United States
m: 01 Jan 1884
in Saint John, Tooele, Utah Territory, United States
d: 21 Aug 1936
in Mount Pleasant, Sanpete, Utah, United States
bu: 24 Aug 1936
in Mt. Pleasant, Sanpete, UT, USA
Chronic Myocarditis & Chronic arthritis

**Marie Leanora Monsen**
b: 13 May 1877
in Mount Pleasant, Sanpete, Utah, United States
m: 30 Jun 1937
in Manti, Sanpete, Utah, United States
d: 21 Apr 1954
in Castle Dale, Emery, Utah, United States
bu: 24 Apr 1954
in Mt. Pleasant, Sanpete, UT, USA
Chronic Myocarditis

# Descendants of William McIntosh (continued)

**Lillian Elizabeth McIntosh**
b: 11 Jan 1863
in Saint John, Tooele, Utah Territory, United States
d: 21 May 1943
in Tremonton, Box Elder, Utah, United States
bu: 23 May 1943
in Oakley, Cassia, ID, USA
Yellow Fever

**Heber Kimball McBride**
b: 16 May 1857
in Grantsville, Tooele, Utah Territory, United States
m: 09 Oct 1882
in Salt Lake City, Great Salt Lake, Utah Territory, United States
d: 14 Oct 1919
in Burley, Cassia, Idaho, United States
bu: 17 Oct 1919
in Oakley, Cassia, ID, USA
Nephritis (kidney infection)

**Caroline Jeanette McIntosh**
b: 01 Nov 1865
in Saint John, Tooele, Utah Territory, United States
d: 26 Sep 1889
in Mount Pleasant, Sanpete, Utah Territory, United States
bu: 1889 in Mt. Pleasant, Sanpete, Utah Territory, USA
Possibly from complications of childbirth

**Joseph Clark Jordan**
b: 02 Apr 1863
in Saint John, Tooele, Utah Territory, United States
m: 05 Jan 1887
in Saint John, Tooele, Utah, United States
d: 19 Jul 1939 in Mount Pleasant, Sanpete, Utah, United States
bu: 22 Jul 1939
in Mt. Pleasant, Sanpete, UT, USA
Carcinoma of stomach

**Joseph Albert McIntosh**
b: 08 Mar 1869
in Panaca, Washington, Utah Territory, United States
d: 21 Jan 1950
in Los Angeles, Los Angeles, California, United States
bu: 24 Jan 1950
in Rush Valley, Tooele, UT, USA
Conditions resulting from the car accident that killed his wife

**Annie Eliza Russell**
b: 23 Oct 1867
in Saint John, Tooele, Utah Territory, United States
m: 06 Mar 1888
in Saint John, Tooele, Utah Territory, United States
d: 10 Jul 1940 in Barstow, San Bernardino, California, United States
bu: 1940 in Rush Valley, Tooele, UT, USA
Killed in a car accident

# Descendants of John Ephraim McIntosh

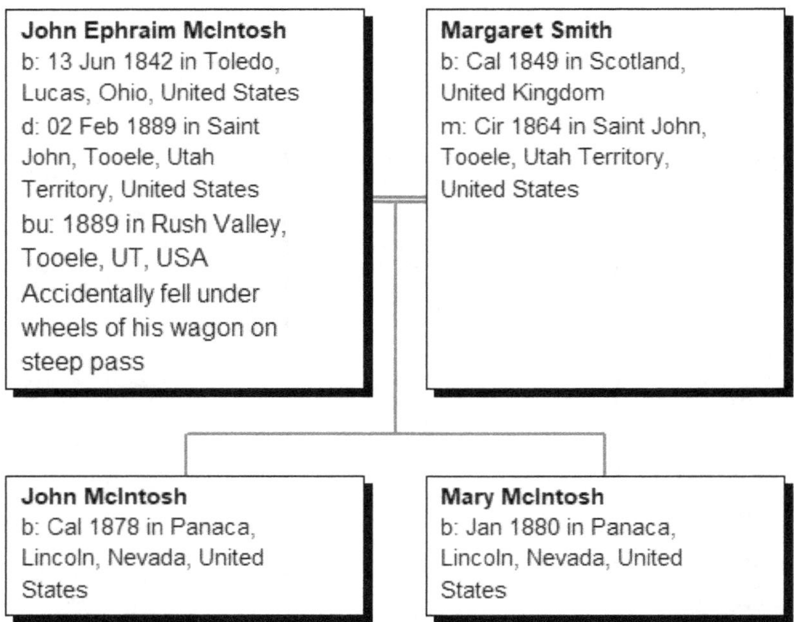
John Ephraim McIntosh
b: 13 Jun 1842 in Toledo, Lucas, Ohio, United States
d: 02 Feb 1889 in Saint John, Tooele, Utah Territory, United States
bu: 1889 in Rush Valley, Tooele, UT, USA
Accidentally fell under wheels of his wagon on steep pass
Margaret Smith
b: Cal 1849 in Scotland, United Kingdom
m: Cir 1864 in Saint John, Tooele, Utah Territory, United States
John McIntosh
b: Cal 1878 in Panaca, Lincoln, Nevada, United States
Mary McIntosh
b: Jan 1880 in Panaca, Lincoln, Nevada, United States

# Descendants of William Henry McIntosh

**William Henry McIntosh Sr.**
b: 18 Apr 1849
in Saint Louis, , Missouri, United States
d: 28 Apr 1901
in Junction, Piute, Utah, United States
bu: 1901 in Junction, Piute, UT, USA

**Mary Elizabeth Keele**
b: 29 May 1856
in Farmington, Davis, Utah Territory, United States
m: 18 Apr 1871
in Panaca, Lincoln, Nevada, United States
d: 26 Feb 1916
in Henderson, Garfield, Utah, United States
bu: 03 Mar 1916
in Junction, Piute, UT, USA
Probably pneumonia

## (continued)

**Mary Elizabeth McIntosh**
b: 02 Feb 1872
in Panaca, Lincoln, Nevada, United States
d: 22 Jan 1962
in Los Angeles, Los Angeles, California, United States
bu: 26 Jan 1962
in Inglewood, Los Angeles, CA

**James Ernest Cowdell**
b: 27 May 1868
in Salt Lake City, Salt Lake, Utah, United States
m: 08 Jan 1894
in Junction, Piute, Utah Territory, United States
d: 21 Jan 1947
in Los Angeles, Los Angeles, California, United States
bu: 1947 in Inglewood, Los Angeles, CA
Diabetes

**William Henry McIntosh Jr.**
b: 30 Jun 1873
in Saint John, Tooele, Utah Territory, United States
d: 18 May 1942
in Junction, Piute, Utah, United States
bu: 21 May 194
in Junction, Piute, UT, USA
Broncho-pneumonia

**Nora May Morri**
b: 16 Jul 1875 in Cedar City, Iron, Utah Territory, United States
m: 18 Apr 1894
in Manti, Sanpete, Utah Territory, United States
d: 19 Apr 1959
in Panguitch, Garfield, Utah, United States
bu: 22 Apr 1959
in Junction, Piute, UT, USA
Arteriorenal vascular disease, senility

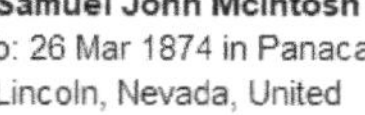

**Samuel John McIntosh**
b: 26 Mar 1874 in Panaca Lincoln, Nevada, United States
d: 18 Oct 1877

**Alice Maria McIntosh**
b: 09 Apr 1875 in Saint John, Tooele, Utah Territory, United States
d: 10 Feb 1878

**Anna Mae McIntosh**
b: 26 Nov 1878 in Panaca, Lincoln, Nevada, United States
d: 22 Nov 1956 in Ely, White Pine, Nevada, United States
bu: 1956 in Ely, White Pine, NV

**Daniel Lester Sprague**
b: 11 Jul 1874 in Grantsville, Tooele, Uta Territory, United States
m: 21 Nov 1895 in Junction, Piute, Utah Territory, United States
d: 03 Sep 1918 in Los Angeles, Los Angeles, California, United State

**Sidney Nephi Albert Black**
b: 22 Apr 1868 in U Territory, United St
m: 02 Jul 1918 in Richfield, Sevier, U United States
d: 29 May 1928
bu: Marysvale, Piu

**David J. Dunsire**
b: 06 Aug 1862 in Cowdenbeath, Fife, Scotland, United Kingdom
m: 27 Feb 1928 in Sevier, Sevier, Utah, United States
d: 02 Dec 1928 in Cedar City, Iron, Utah, United States
bu: 03 Dec 1928 in Cedar City, Iron, UT

# Descendants of William Henry McIntosh (continued)

**Abram McIntosh**
b: 13 Mar 1882
in Panaca, Lincoln, Nevada, United States
d: 04 Mar 1947
in Junction, Piute, Utah, United States
bu: 08 Mar 1947
in Junction, Piute, UT, USA
Cerebral hemorrhage due to hypertension

**Elizabeth Hanna Barnson**
b: 20 Aug 1884
in Manti, Sanpete, Utah Territory, United States
m: 29 Mar 1900
in Junction, Piute, Utah, United States
d: 04 Mar 1976
in Orem, Utah, Utah, United States
bu: 08 Mar 1976
in Ely, White Pine, NV

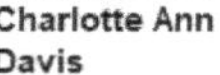

**Charlotte Ann Davis**
b: 06 Sep 1884
in Summit, Iron, Utah Territory, United States
m: 03 Aug 1904
in Junction, Piute, Utah, United States
d: 20 Mar 1939
in Junction, Piute, Utah, United States
bu: 22 Mar 1939
in Junction, Piute, UT, USA
Complications of diseases

**Olive McIntosh**
b: 25 Mar 1884
in Panaca, Lincoln, Nevada, United States
d: 08 Jun 1955
in Salt Lake City, Salt Lake, Utah, United States
bu: 11 Jun 1955
in Millcreek, Salt Lake, UT
Cerebral hemorrhage

**Joseph Sylvester Johnson**
b: 15 Sep 1881
in Junction, Piute, Utah Territory, United States
m: 15 Aug 1901
in Junction, Piute, Utah, United States
d: 14 Feb 1959
in Saint George, Washington, Utah, United States
bu: 16 Feb 1959
in Saint George, Washington, UT
Uremia

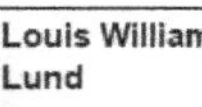

**Louis William Lund**
b: 01 Jul 1878 in Mount Pleasant, Sanpete, Utah Territory, United States
m: 09 Jun 1919
in Mount Pleasant, Sanpete, Utah, United States
d: 08 Jun 1962
in Salt Lake City, Salt Lake, Utah, United States
bu: 1962

## Descendants of William Henry McIntosh (continued)

**William Henry McIntosh Sr.**
b: 18 Apr 1849
in Saint Louis, , Missouri, United States
d: 28 Apr 1901
in Junction, Piute, Utah, United States
bu: 1901 in Junction, Piute, UT, USA

**Mary Elizabeth Keele**
b: 29 May 1856
in Farmington, Davis, Utah Territory, United States
m: 18 Apr 1871
in Panaca, Lincoln, Nevada, United States
d: 26 Feb 1916
in Henderson, Garfield, Utah, United States
bu: 03 Mar 1916
in Junction, Piute, UT, USA
Probably pneumonia

**Elsie McIntosh**
b: 03 Mar 1887
in Junction, Piute, Utah Territory, United States
d: 28 Jan 1963
in Panguitch, Garfield, Utah, United States
bu: 31 Jan 1963
in Junction, Piute, UT, USA
Heart Attack

**Joseph Jochein Ackerman**
b: 05 Dec 1885
in Loa, , Utah Territory, United States
m: 07 Feb 1907
in Junction, Piute, Utah, United States
d: 03 Jul 1979 in Panguitch, Garfield, Utah, United States
bu: 07 Jul 1979
in Junction, Piute, UT, USA

**Raymond U. McIntosh**
b: 30 Jul 1899 in Junction, Piute, Utah, United States
d: 03 Feb 1954 in East Ely, White Pine, Nevada, United States
bu: 06 Feb 1954 in Ely, White Pine, NV
Coronary artery disease

**Telma Clara Anderton**
b: 05 Jul 1905 in Monroe, Sevier, Utah, United States
m: 24 Mar 1920 in Sevier, Sevier, Utah, United States
d: 01 Mar 1976 in Ely, White Pine, Nevada, United States
bu: 04 Mar 1976 in Ely, White Pine, NV

# Descendants of James Franklin McIntosh

**James Franklin McIntosh**
b: 08 Jan 1852 in Bountiful, Davis, Utah Territory, United States
d: 02 May 1896 in Mount Pleasant, Sanpete, Utah, United States
bu: 02 May 1896 in Mt. Pleasant, Sanpete, UT, USA
Liver failure

**Anne Mae Jordan**
b: 25 Oct 1857 in West Jordan, Great Salt Lake, Utah Territory, United States
m: 29 Mar 1878 in Saint George, Washington, Utah Territory, United States
d: 27 Sep 1920 in Mount Pleasant, Sanpete, Utah, United States
bu: 30 Sep 1920 in Mt. Pleasant, Sanpete, UT, USA
Cerebral Apoplexy (stroke)

**Ica Minda Crow McIntosh**
b: 07 Nov 1879 in Panaca, , Nevada, United States
d: 03 Sep 1943 in Delta, Millard, Utah, United States
bu: 06 Sep 1943 in Mt. Pleasant, Sanpete, UT, USA
Cardio nephritis

**Kimball Johansen**
b: 24 Sep 1870 in Mount Pleasant, Sanpete, Utah, United States
m: 07 Jun 1899 in Manti, Sanpete, Utah, United States
d: 01 Feb 1953 in Salt Lake City, Salt Lake, Utah, United States
bu: 04 Feb 1953 in Mt. Pleasant, Sanpete, UT, USA
Natural causes

## Descendants of Melissa Jane McIntosh

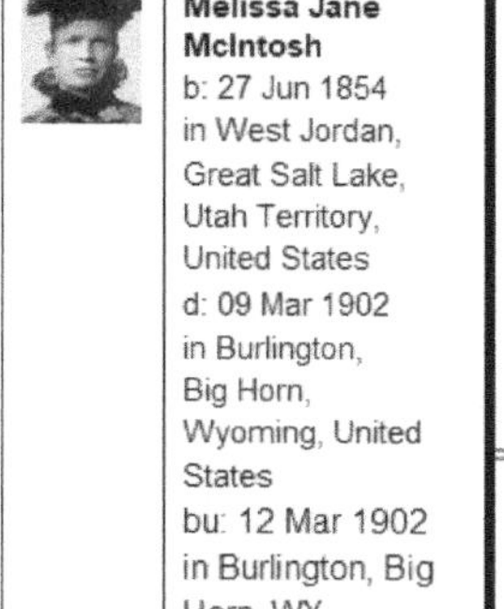

**Melissa Jane McIntosh**
b: 27 Jun 1854
in West Jordan, Great Salt Lake, Utah Territory, United States
d: 09 Mar 1902
in Burlington, Big Horn, Wyoming, United States
bu: 12 Mar 1902
in Burlington, Big Horn, WY

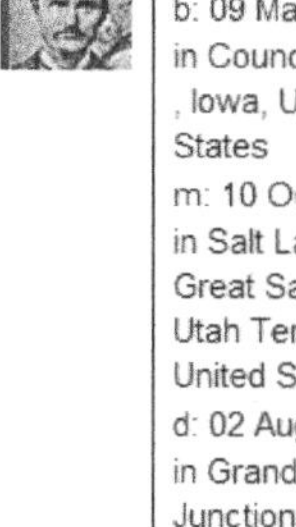

**Jacob Keele**
b: 09 May 1847
in Council Bluffs, , Iowa, United States
m: 10 Oct 1872
in Salt Lake City, Great Salt Lake, Utah Territory, United States
d: 02 Aug 1926
in Grand Junction, Mesa, Colorado, United States
bu: 04 Aug 1926
in Grand Junction, Mesa, CO
Apoplexy; Stroke

## (continued)

**Maria Elizabeth Keele**
b: 14 Aug 1873
in Panaca, Lincoln, Nevada, United States
d: 07 Dec 1918
in De Beque, Mesa, Colorado, United States
bu: Dec 1918 in De Beque, Mesa, CO
Spanish Flu

**Frederick Walker Robinson**
b: 27 Nov 1865
in Illinois, United States
m: 30 Oct 1892
in Mesa, Colorado, United States
d: 02 Oct 1920
in De Beque, Mesa, Colorado, United States
bu: 10 Oct 1920
in Mesa, CO, USA
Gastric Carcinoma

**Alma Jacob Keele**
b: 02 Feb 1875 in Panaca, Lincoln, Nevada, United States
d: 01 Oct 1938 in Salmon, Lemhi, Idaho, United States
bu: 03 Oct 1938 in Salmon, Lemhi, ID, USA
Heart Disease

**Dollie Coral Garner**
b: 09 Sep 1885 in Clifton, Franklin, Idaho, United States
m: 31 Dec 1901 in Burlington, Big Horn, Wyoming, United States
d: 10 Sep 1975 in Colfax, Whitman, Washington, United States
bu: Sep 1975 in Salmon, Lemhi, ID, USA

**Alice Melissa Keele**
b: 16 Oct 1875
in Panaca, Lincoln, Nevada, United States
d: 29 Jan 1920
in Fruita, Mesa, Colorado, United States
bu: 01 Feb 1920
in Fruita, Mesa, CO

**Richard Burkitt**
b: 08 Jul 1871 in Plainfield, Bremer, Iowa, United States
m: 30 Oct 1892 in Fruita, Mesa, Colorado, United States
d: 11 Nov 1939 in Delta, Delta, Colorado, United States
bu: Nov 1939 in Fruita, Mesa, CO

**William Wallace Keele**
b: Apr 1880 in Panaca, Lincoln, Nevada, United States
d: Abt 1884 in Huntington, Emery, Utah, United States

**Annie Estella Keele**
b: 02 Aug 1883 in Huntington, Emery, Utah Territory, United States
d: 26 Apr 1965 in Fortuna, Humboldt, California, United States
bu: 28 Apr 1965 in Eureka, Humboldt, CA, USA

**Calvin Huston Kendall Sr.**
b: 04 Mar 1875 in Springfield, Greene, Missouri, United States
m: 25 Dec 1899 in Fruita, Mesa, Colorado, United States
d: 03 Aug 1952 in Eureka, Humboldt, California, United States

# Descendants of Melissa Jane McIntosh (continued)

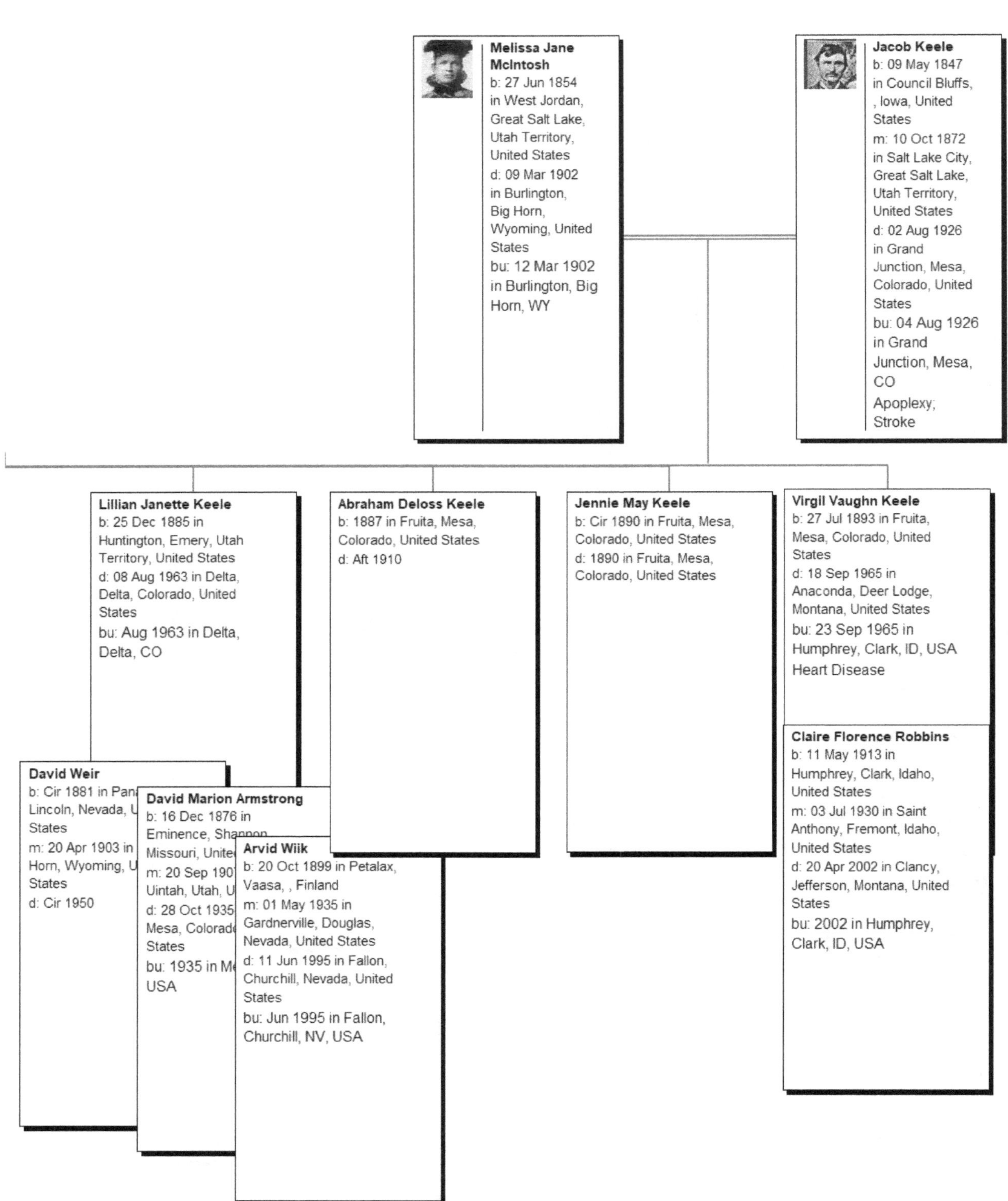
Melissa Jane McIntosh
b: 27 Jun 1854 in West Jordan, Great Salt Lake, Utah Territory, United States
d: 09 Mar 1902 in Burlington, Big Horn, Wyoming, United States
bu: 12 Mar 1902 in Burlington, Big Horn, WY
Jacob Keele
b: 09 May 1847 in Council Bluffs, , Iowa, United States
m: 10 Oct 1872 in Salt Lake City, Great Salt Lake, Utah Territory, United States
d: 02 Aug 1926 in Grand Junction, Mesa, Colorado, United States
bu: 04 Aug 1926 in Grand Junction, Mesa, CO
Apoplexy; Stroke
Lillian Janette Keele
b: 25 Dec 1885 in Huntington, Emery, Utah Territory, United States
d: 08 Aug 1963 in Delta, Delta, Colorado, United States
bu: Aug 1963 in Delta, Delta, CO
Abraham Deloss Keele
b: 1887 in Fruita, Mesa, Colorado, United States
d: Aft 1910
Jennie May Keele
b: Cir 1890 in Fruita, Mesa, Colorado, United States
d: 1890 in Fruita, Mesa, Colorado, United States
Virgil Vaughn Keele
b: 27 Jul 1893 in Fruita, Mesa, Colorado, United States
d: 18 Sep 1965 in Anaconda, Deer Lodge, Montana, United States
bu: 23 Sep 1965 in Humphrey, Clark, ID, USA
Heart Disease
Claire Florence Robbins
b: 11 May 1913 in Humphrey, Clark, Idaho, United States
m: 03 Jul 1930 in Saint Anthony, Fremont, Idaho, United States
d: 20 Apr 2002 in Clancy, Jefferson, Montana, United States
bu: 2002 in Humphrey, Clark, ID, USA
David Weir
b: Cir 1881 in Pan
Lincoln, Nevada, U
States
m: 20 Apr 1903 in
Horn, Wyoming, U
States
d: Cir 1950
David Marion Armstrong
b: 16 Dec 1876 in
Eminence, Shannon
Missouri, Unite
m: 20 Sep 190
Uintah, Utah, U
d: 28 Oct 1935
Mesa, Colorado
States
bu: 1935 in M
USA
Arvid Wiik
b: 20 Oct 1899 in Petalax, Vaasa, , Finland
m: 01 May 1935 in Gardnerville, Douglas, Nevada, United States
d: 11 Jun 1995 in Fallon, Churchill, Nevada, United States
bu: Jun 1995 in Fallon, Churchill, NV, USA

# Descendants of Alice Maria McIntosh

**Alice Maria McIntosh**
b: 26 Sep 1857 in West Jordan, Great Salt Lake, Utah Territory, United States
d: 31 Oct 1914 in Provo, Utah, Utah, United States
bu: 03 Nov 1914 in Provo, Utah, UT, USA
Duodenal ulcer

**Thomas Lorenzo Burridge**
b: 02 Dec 1853 in Valletta, , , Malta
m: 06 Jan 1881 in Salt Lake City, Great Salt Lake, Utah Territory, United States
d: 12 Apr 1891 in Saint John, Tooele, Utah Territory, United States
bu: 14 Apr 1891 in Rush Valley, Tooele, UT, USA

**George Thomas Burridg**
b: 19 Jun 1882 in Iona, Bonneville, Idaho, United States
d: 10 Jul 1911 in Provo, Utah, Utah, United States
bu: 12 Jul 1911 in Provo Utah, UT, USA
Orchitis (inflammation of the testicles) resulting from groin injury

**William McIntosh Bur**
b: 04 Oct 1883 in Saint John, Tooele, Utah Territory, United States
d: 29 Nov 1905 in Mapleton, Utah, Utah, United States
bu: 03 Dec 1905 in P Utah, UT, USA
Heart disease

**Franklin Dennis Burr**
b: 06 Dec 1885 in Sain John, Tooele, Utah Territory, United States
d: 20 Dec 1922 in Prov Utah, Utah, United Stat
bu: 1922 in Beaver, Beaver, UT, USA
Cerebral Hemorrhag

**Lurena Farrer**
b: 12 Jun 1893 in Beav Beaver, Utah, United States
m: 23 Jun 1920 in Bea Beaver, Utah, United States
d: 07 Aug 1974 in Ceda City, Iron, Utah, United States
bu: 10 Aug 1974 in Beaver, Beaver, UT, USA

**Alice Marie Burridge**
b: 01 Jan 1888 in Saint John, Tooele, Utah Territory, United States
d: 12 May 1896 in Saint John, Tooele, Utah, Unite States
bu: 1896 in Saint John, Tooele, UT, USA

**Jared Burridge**
b: 02 Feb 1890 in Saint John, Tooele, Utah Territory, United States
d: 17 Sep 1890 in Saint John, Tooele, Utah Territory, United States
bu: Sep 1890 in Saint John, Tooele, Utah Territory, USA

**Theol Lorenzo Burridge Sr.**
b: 18 Nov 1891 in Saint John, Tooele, Utah Territory, United States
d: 17 Feb 1933 in Salt Lake City, Salt Lake, Utah, United States
bu: 19 Feb 1933 in Nephi, Juab, UT
Burns, third degree

**Wanda Jane Christison**
b: 16 Sep 1893 in Nephi, Juab, Utah, United States
m: 15 Oct 1919 in Salt Lake City, Salt Lake, Utah, United States
d: 31 Dec 1986 in Tooele, Tooele, Utah, United States
bu: 03 Jan 1987 in Nephi, Juab, UT

# Descendants of Abraham Edward McIntosh

**Abraham Edward McIntosh**
b: 04 Mar 1860 in Clover, Shambip, Utah Territory, United States
d: 16 Oct 1943 in Mount Pleasant, Sanpete, Utah, United States
bu: 20 Oct 1943 in Mt. Pleasant, Sanpete, UT, USA
Chronic Myocarditis

**Mary Louise Guhl**
b: 27 May 1862 in Weber Canyon, Weber, Utah Territory, United States
m: 01 Jan 1884 in Saint John, Tooele, Utah Territory, United States
d: 21 Aug 1936 in Mount Pleasant, Sanpete, Utah, United States
bu: 24 Aug 1936 in Mt. Pleasant, Sanpete, UT, USA
Chronic Myocarditis & Chronic arthritis

**Abraham Vance McIntosh**
b: 26 Apr 1885 in Saint John, Tooele, Utah Territory, United States
d: 16 Aug 1959 in Mount Pleasant, Sanpete, Utah, United States
bu: 19 Aug 1959 in Mt. Pleasant, Sanpete, UT, USA
Chronic myocarditis

**Florence Karna Monsen**
b: 14 Sep 1887 in Mount Pleasant, Sanpete, Utah, United States
m: 15 Oct 1913 in Salt Lake City, Salt Lake, Utah, United States
d: 12 Jan 1966 in American Fork, Utah, Utah, United States
bu: 15 Jan 1966 in Mt. Pleasant, Sanpete, UT, USA
Natural Causes

**William Edward McIntosh**
b: 25 Feb 1887 in Saint John, Tooele, Utah Territory, United States
d: 20 Dec 1891 in Mount Pleasant, Sanpete, Utah Territory, United States
bu: Dec 1891 in Mt. Pleasant, Sanpete, Utah Territory, USA

**Anna Estelle McIntosh**
b: 24 Dec 1889 in Mount Pleasant, Sanpete, Utah Territory, United States
d: 13 Jan 1973 in Los Angeles, California, United States
bu: Jan 1973 in Whittier, Los Angeles, CA

**Joseph William Schofield**
b: 02 Oct 1887 in Spring City, Sanpete, Utah Territory, United States
m: 02 Nov 1912 in Salt Lake City, Salt Lake, Utah, United States
d: 16 Aug 1974 in Los Angeles, Los Angeles, California, United States
bu: 19 Aug 1974 in Whittier, Los Angeles, CA

**Elvin Peter McIntosh**
b: 28 Jun 1892 in Saint John, Tooele, Utah Territory, United States
d: 18 Mar 1958 in Los Angeles, Los Angeles, California, United States
bu: 21 Mar 1958 in Glendale, Los Angeles, CA
Bronchopneumonia

**Anna Muriel Vadis McArthur**
b: 26 Sep 1901 in Mount Pleasant, Sanpete, Utah, United States
m: 27 Nov 1923 in Provo, Utah, Utah, United States
d: 01 Aug 1965 in Los Angeles, Los Angeles, California, United States
bu: 1965 in Glendale, Los Angeles, CA
Heart attack

# Descendants of Abraham Edward McIntosh (continued)

**Marie Leanora Monsen**
b: 13 May 1877 in Mount Pleasant, Sanpete, Utah, United States
m: 30 Jun 1937 in Manti, Sanpete, Utah, United States
d: 21 Apr 1954 in Castle Dale, Emery, Utah, United States
bu: 24 Apr 1954 in Mt. Pleasant, Sanpete, UT, USA
Chronic Myocarditis

**Franklin Vaughn McIntosh**
b: 10 Jan 1895 in Mount Pleasant, Sanpete, Utah Territory, United States
d: 07 Feb 1895 in Mount Pleasant, Sanpete, Utah Territory, United States
bu: Feb 1895 in Mt. Pleasant, Sanpete, Utah Territory, USA

**Vernon Marenus McIntosh**
b: 10 Jan 1895 in Mount Pleasant, Sanpete, Utah Territory, United States
d: 17 Oct 1922 in Mount Pleasant, Sanpete, Utah, United States
bu: 20 Oct 1922 in Mt. Pleasant, Sanpete, UT, USA
Diabetes

**Grace Maria McIntosh**
b: 06 Sep 1903 in Mount Pleasant, Sanpete, Utah, United States
d: 11 May 1993 in Meadow Vista, Placer, California, United States
bu: 15 May 1993 in Whittier, Los Angeles, CA

**Robert Burns Sr.**
b: 20 Feb 1902 in Manti, Sanpete, Utah, United States
m: 14 Nov 1923 in Provo, Utah, Utah, United States
d: 04 Dec 1962 in Los Angeles, Los Angeles, California, United States
bu: 1962 in Whittier, Los Angeles, CA

# Descendants of Lillian Elizabeth McIntosh

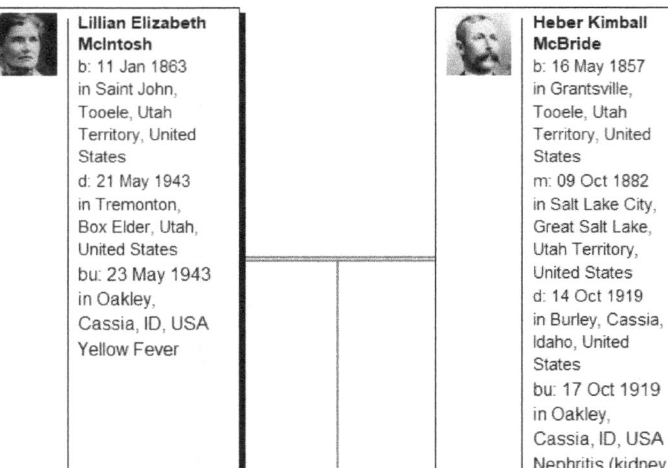

**Lillian Elizabeth McIntosh**
b: 11 Jan 1863
in Saint John, Tooele, Utah Territory, United States
d: 21 May 1943
in Tremonton, Box Elder, Utah, United States
bu: 23 May 1943
in Oakley, Cassia, ID, USA
Yellow Fever
**Heber Kimball McBride**
b: 16 May 1857
in Grantsville, Tooele, Utah Territory, United States
m: 09 Oct 1882
in Salt Lake City, Great Salt Lake, Utah Territory, United States
d: 14 Oct 1919
in Burley, Cassia, Idaho, United States
bu: 17 Oct 1919
in Oakley, Cassia, ID, USA
Nephritis (kidney infection)

**Marie McBride**
b: 01 Aug 1883
in Grantsville, Tooele, Utah Territory, United States
d: 17 Feb 1967
in Boise, Ada, Idaho, United States
bu: 1967 in Boise, Ada, ID, USA

**Arthur Marion Sanford**
b: 23 Mar 1884
in Basin, Cassia, Idaho Territory, United States
m: 29 Apr 1909
in Salt Lake City, Salt Lake, Utah, United States
d: 22 Nov 1971
in Boise, Ada, Idaho, United States
bu: 1971 in Boise, Ada, ID, USA

**James William McBride**
b: 01 Aug 1885
in Oakley, Cassia, Idaho Territory, United States
d: 01 Dec 1960
in Tremonton, Box Elder, Utah, United States
bu: 03 Dec 1960
in Oakley, Cassia, ID, USA

**Julia Maria Smith**
b: 04 Feb 1889
in Oakley, Cassia, Idaho, United States
m: 09 Apr 1909
in Salt Lake City
Salt Lake, Utah, United States
d: 10 Jul 1930 i
Rupert, Minidoka, Idaho, United States
bu: 13 Jul 193
in Oakley, Cassia, ID, US
Lymphatic Septicemia (infection after childbirth)

**Clotilda Desire Beecher**
b: 30 Nov 1882
in Elba, Cassia, Idaho, United States
m: 11 Jul 1942
in Preston, Franklin, Idaho, United States
d: 17 Nov 1960
in Tremonton, Box Elder, Utah, United States
bu: 1960 in Elba, Cassia, ID

**Olive Marian McBride**
b: 10 Apr 1888
in Oakley, Cassia, Idaho Territory, United States
d: 09 May 1900
in Oakley, Cassia, Idaho, United States
bu: May 1900 in Oakley, Cassia, ID, USA

## Descendants of Lillian Elizabeth McIntosh (continued)

**(continued)**

**Ephraim Heber McBride**
b: 25 Aug 1890 in Oakley, Cassia, Idaho, United States
d: 16 Nov 1965 in Oakland, Alameda, California, United States
bu: 19 Nov 1965 in Oakland, Alameda, CA, USA

**Lydia Campbell**
b: 12 Jul 1892 in Virgin, Washington, Utah Territory, United States
m: 11 Dec 1911 in Oakley, Cassia, Idaho, United States
d: 01 Sep 1970 in Grand Junction, Mesa, Colorado, United States
bu: 04 Sep 197 in Provo, Utah, UT, USA

**Estella Mae Bates**
b: 23 Oct 1889 in Marion, Cassia, Idaho, United States
m: 01 Apr 1945 in Richmond, Contra Co California, United Stat
d: 15 Nov 1955 in Mag Salt Lake, Utah, Unite States
bu: 21 Nov 1955 in B Ada, ID, USA
Myocardial infarction

**Bessie Henrietta Hansen**
b: 26 Nov 1895 in Chicago, Cook, Illinois, United States
m: 06 Jul 1956 in Oakland, Alameda, California, United States
d: 16 Sep 1973 in Alameda, Alameda, California, United States
bu: Oakland, Alameda, CA, USA

**Alice Lillian McBride**
b: 15 Nov 1892 in Oakley, Cassia, Idaho, United States
d: 29 Mar 1986 in Boise, Ada, Idaho, United States
bu: 01 Apr 1986 in Salt Lake City, Salt Lake, UT, USA

**Moroni William Ward**
b: 10 Apr 1890 in Elba, Cassia, Idaho Territory, United States
m: 12 Nov 1914 in Salt Lake City, Salt Lake, Utah, United States
d: 25 Jul 1967 in Salt Lake City, Salt Lake, Utah, United States
bu: 28 Jul 1967 in Salt Lake City, Salt Lake, UT, USA

# Descendants of Lillian Elizabeth McIntosh (continued)

**Edward Vaughn McBride**
b: 09 May 1895 in Oakley, Cassia, Idaho, United States
d: 20 Mar 1905 in Oakley, Cassia, Idaho, United States
bu: Mar 1905 in Oakley, Cassia, ID, USA

**Kathryn Jane McBride**
b: 02 Feb 1898 in Oakley, Cassia, Idaho, United States
d: 15 Jun 1975 in Baldwin Park, Los Angeles, California, United States
bu: Jun 1975 in Whittier, Los Angeles, CA

**Leonard Campbell Livingston**
b: 03 Apr 1895 in Moroni, Sanpete, Utah, United States
m: 07 Jun 1916 in Salt Lake City, Salt Lake, Utah, United States
d: 29 Mar 1937 in Dallas, Dallas, Texas, United States
bu: 01 Apr 1937 in Dallas, Dallas, TX
Neoplasm (cancer) of chest and lungs

**James Squire**
b: 18 Jul 1896 in Hancock, Houghton, Michigan, United States
m: 03 Jul 1941 in Kansas City, Jackson, Missouri, United States
d: 24 May 1963 in Los Angeles, Los Angeles, California, United States
bu: 28 May 1963 in Whittier, Los Angeles, CA

**Dorcas Leah McBride**
b: 25 Jan 1904 in Oakley, Cassia, Idaho, United States
d: 18 May 1987 in Calgary, , Alberta, Canada
bu: 1987 in Calgary, , AB, CAN

**Karl Warren Collett**
b: 29 Mar 1898 in Vernal, Uintah, Utah, United States
m: 07 Jun 1927 in Salt Lake City, Salt Lake, Utah, United States
d: 09 Dec 1956 in Hope, , British Columbia, Canada
Plane crash, body not recovered

# Descendants of Caroline Jeanette McIntosh

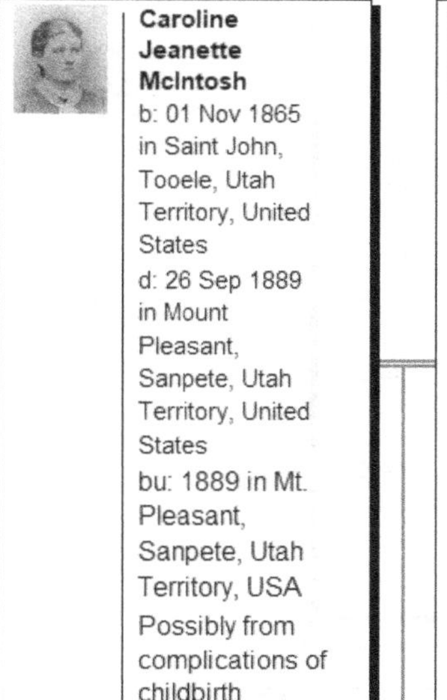

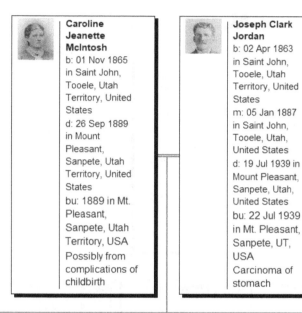

**Caroline Jeanette McIntosh**
b: 01 Nov 1865 in Saint John, Tooele, Utah Territory, United States
d: 26 Sep 1889 in Mount Pleasant, Sanpete, Utah Territory, United States
bu: 1889 in Mt. Pleasant, Sanpete, Utah Territory, USA
Possibly from complications of childbirth

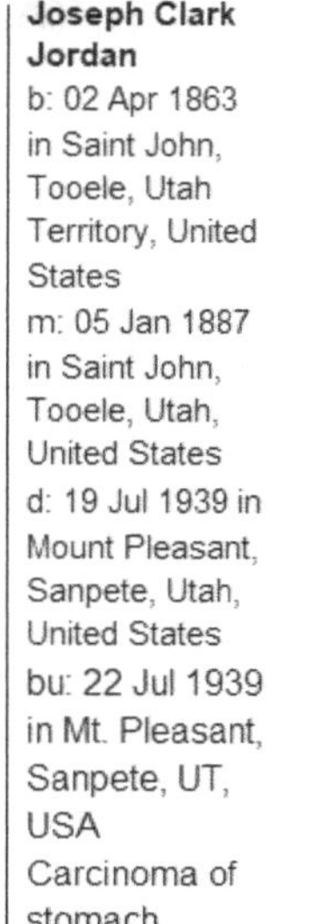

**Joseph Clark Jordan**
b: 02 Apr 1863 in Saint John, Tooele, Utah Territory, United States
m: 05 Jan 1887 in Saint John, Tooele, Utah, United States
d: 19 Jul 1939 in Mount Pleasant, Sanpete, Utah, United States
bu: 22 Jul 1939 in Mt. Pleasant, Sanpete, UT, USA
Carcinoma of stomach

**Fanny Jordan**
b: 13 Sep 1887 in Mount Pleasant, Sanpete, Utah Territory, United States
d: 19 Mar 1889 in Mount Pleasant, Sanpete, Utah Territory, United States
bu: Mar 1889 in Mt. Pleasant, Sanpete, Utah Territory, USA

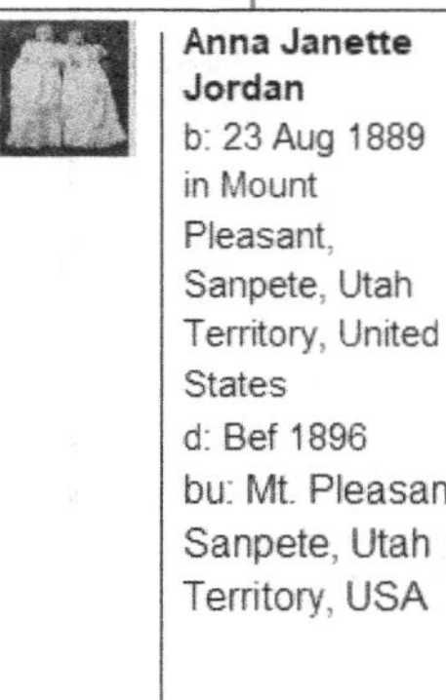

**Anna Janette Jordan**
b: 23 Aug 1889 in Mount Pleasant, Sanpete, Utah Territory, United States
d: Bef 1896
bu: Mt. Pleasant, Sanpete, Utah Territory, USA

**Marie Trinite Jordan**
b: 23 Aug 1889 in Mount Pleasant, Sanpete, Utah Territory, United States
d: 15 Nov 1889 in Mount Pleasant, Sanpete, Utah Territory, United States
bu: Nov 1889 in Mt. Pleasant, Sanpete, Utah Territory, USA

# Descendants of Joseph Albert McIntosh

**Joseph Albert McIntosh**
b: 08 Mar 1869 in Panaca, Washington, Utah Territory, United States
d: 21 Jan 1950 in Los Angeles, Los Angeles, California, United States
bu: 24 Jan 1950 in Rush Valley, Tooele, UT, USA
Conditions resulting from the car accident that killed his wife

**Annie Eliza Russell**
b: 23 Oct 1867 in Saint John, Tooele, Utah Territory, United States
m: 06 Mar 1888 in Saint John, Tooele, Utah Territory, United States
d: 10 Jul 1940 in Barstow, San Bernardino, California, United States
bu: 1940 in Rush Valley, Tooele, UT, USA
Killed in a car accident

**William Albert McIntosh**
b: 28 Nov 1889 in Saint John, Tooele, Utah Territory, United States
d: 28 Feb 1952 in Salt Lake City, Salt Lake, Utah, United States
bu: 03 Mar 1952 in Millcreek, Salt Lake, UT
Arteriosclerotic heart disease

**Grace Georgia Kirkman**
b: 14 Apr 1898 in Santaquin, Utah, Utah, United States
m: 12 Oct 1916 in Nephi, Juab, Utah, United States
d: 31 Oct 1972 in Salt Lake City, Salt Lake, Utah, United States
bu: 04 Nov 1972 in Millcreek, Salt Lake, UT

**Emily Elizabeth McIntosh**
b: 14 Sep 1891 in Saint John, Tooele, Utah Territory, United States
d: 11 Dec 1918 in Medicine Bow, Carbon, Wyoming, United States
bu: 18 Dec 1918 in Rush Valley, Tooele, UT, USA
Influenza

**William Roy Wymore**
b: 09 Jan 1891 in Liberty, Clay, Missouri, United States
m: 29 Dec 1917 in Salt Lake City, Salt Lake, Utah, United States
d: 11 Sep 1948 in Anaheim, Orange, California, United States
bu: 1948 in Anaheim, Orange, CA

**Donald Hyrum McIntosh**
b: 01 Oct 1893 in Saint John, Tooele, Utah Territory, United States
d: 27 Dec 1976 in Salt Lake City, Salt Lake, Utah, United States
bu: 30 Dec 1976 in Provo, Utah, UT, USA
Old age

**Melba C. Cropper**
b: 19 Aug 1899 in Hinckley, Millard, Utah, United States
m: 02 Aug 1924 in Salt Lake City, Salt Lake, Utah, United States
d: 26 Feb 1982 in Bennion, Salt Lake, Utah, United States
bu: 01 Mar 1982 in Provo, Utah, UT, USA

**Basil Hugh McIntosh**
b: 06 Jan 1896 in Saint John, Tooele, Utah, United States
d: 28 Aug 1956 in Inglewood, Los Angeles, California, United States
bu: 1956 in Glendale, Los Angeles, CA

**Bernice Christine Oates**
b: 14 Apr 1902 in Los Angeles, California, United States
m: 14 Jun 1919 in Tooele, Tooele, Utah, United States
d: 11 May 1973 in San Bernardino, California, United States
bu: 1973 in Wildomar, Riverside, CA

**Anna Marie McIntosh**
b: 04 Mar 1898 in Saint John, Tooele, Utah, United States
d: 16 Mar 1930 in Grace, Caribou, Idaho, United States
bu: 18 Mar 1930 in Rush Valley, Tooele, UT, USA
Uremia from Brights Disease

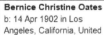

**Ralph Lee Sr.**
b: 29 Jan 1895 in Tooele, Tooele, Utah, United States
m: 06 Nov 1916 in Farmington, Davis, Utah, United States
d: 20 Jul 1966 in South Salt Lake, Salt Lake, Utah, United States
bu: 23 Jul 1966 in Salt Lake City, Salt Lake, UT, USA

# Descendants of Joseph Albert McIntosh (continued)

**Alta Grace McIntosh**
b: 27 Apr 1900 in Saint John, Tooele, Utah, United States
d: Aft 29 Jul 1900 in Saint John, Tooele, Utah, United States
bu: 1900 in Rush Valley, Tooele, UT, USA

**Kimball Daniel McIntosh**
b: 04 Oct 1901 in Saint John, Tooele, Utah, United States
d: 17 Dec 1967 in Salt Lake City, Salt Lake, Utah, United States
bu: 1967 in Millcreek, Salt Lake, UT
Heart Ailment

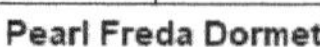

**Pearl Freda Dormet**
b: 28 Aug 1912 in McGill, White Pine, Nevada, United States
m: 15 Aug 1947 in Reno, Washoe, Nevada, United States
d: 15 Mar 2003 in Salt Lake City, Salt Lake, Utah, United States
bu: 20 Mar 2003 in Millcreek, Salt Lake, UT
Stroke

**Kenneth Grant McIntosh**
b: 29 Jul 1904 in Saint John, Tooele, Utah, United States
d: 17 Feb 1997 in Hurricane, Washington, Utah, United States
bu: 20 Feb 1997 in Hurricane, Washington, UT

**Grace Chloe Roberts**
b: 26 Nov 1909 in Jackson, Illinois, United States
m: 23 Jun 1939 in Compton, Los Angeles, California, United States
d: 19 Sep 1984 in Saint George, Washington, Utah, United States
bu: 22 Sep 1984 in Hurricane, Washington, UT

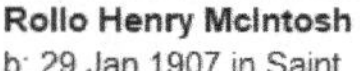

**Rollo Henry McIntosh**
b: 29 Jan 1907 in Saint John, Tooele, Utah, United States
d: 14 May 1951 in Beverly Hills, Los Angeles, California, United States
bu: 1951 in Inglewood, Los Angeles, CA
Coronary Sclerosis (coronary heart disease)

**Ann Corinne Riley**
b: 06 Aug 1904 in Arkansas, United States
m: 24 Jul 1937 in Los Angeles, Los Angeles, California, United States
d: 31 Oct 1982 in Los Angeles, Los Angeles, California, United States

**Faye Maxine McIntosh**
b: 27 Mar 1911 in Provo, Utah, Utah, United States
d: 06 Apr 2005 in Logandale, Clark, Nevada, United States
bu: 14 Apr 2005 in Logandale, Clark, NV

**Martin Clyde Jarrell**
b: 08 Dec 1915 in Vernal, Uintah, Utah, United States
m: 01 Jan 1937 in Yuma, Arizona, United States
d: 02 Mar 2000 in Saint George, Washington, Utah, United States
bu: 09 Mar 2000 in Logandale, Clark, NV

# Bibliography

## Books

Bennett, Carol, compiler. *The Lanark Society Settlers*. Renfrew, Ontario, Canada: Juniper Books, 1991.

Brown, Beverly McIntosh and Marsha McIntosh, editors. *William's Diary*. Surprise, AZ: Self-published, June 2002.

Carter, Kate B., editor. *Treasures of Pioneer History*. Salt Lake City, Utah: Daughters of Utah Pioneers, 1952-1957.

Church of Jesus Christ of Latter-day Saints, Grantsville Stake, Clover Ward, Genealogical Committee. *A History of Clover, Centennial Year, 1856-1956*. Tooele, Utah: Transcript-Bulletin, 1956.

Davenport, Dortha B. *Junction, Utah: Its History and Its People 1871-2004*. Self-Published: United States, 2005.

Esshorn, Frank, editor. *Pioneers and Prominent Men of Utah*. Salt Lake City, Utah: Utah Pioneers Book Publishing Company, 1913.

Hinton, Wayne K. *Utah: Unusual Beginning to Unique Present*. Northridge, California: Windsor Publications, Inc., 1988.

International Society, Daughters of Utah Pioneers. *Our Pioneer Heritage*. Salt Lake City, Utah: Infobases, Inc., 1996.

International Society, Daughters of Utah Pioneers, editor. *Pioneer Women of Faith and Fortitude*. Salt Lake City, Utah: Publishers Press, 1998.

Jensen, Andrew, editor. *Latter-day Saint Biographical Encyclopedia: A Compilation of Biographical Sketches of Prominent Men and Women in The Church of Jesus Christ of Latter-day Saints*. Salt Lake City, Utah: Western Epics, 1971.

Johnson, Paul. *A History of the American People*. New York, New York: Harper Collins Publishers, 1997.

Kimball, Stanley B. and Violet T. *Mormon Trail, Voyage of Discovery: The Story Behind the Scenery*. KC Publications, Inc., 1995.

Loveland, Carla Neves. *Sagebrush and Roses: A History of Otto and Burlington, Wyoming*. Lindon, Utah: Alexander's Digital Printing, 2003.

Mackintosh of Mackintosh, Margaret. *The History of the Clan Mackintosh and the Clan Chattan*. Edinburgh, Scotland: The Pentland Press Limited, 1997.

Miller, J.R. Ernest. *Scottish settlers to Bathurst Area for Bathurst District: includes Lanark, Leeds, Carleton, Frontenac, and Renfrew Settlers, Extracted from Dictionary of Scottish Settlers and Other Sources.* Kingston, Ontario, Canada: Ontario Genealogical Society, 1987.

Shaw, Ron W. *A Swarm of Bees: Lanark Society Settlers 1800-1900, A Journey from Scotland to Upper Canada and Utah.* Carleton Place, Ontario, Canada: Global Heritage Press, 2018.

Tooele County Chamber of Commerce and Tourism. *Tooele County: Visitors Guide and Business Directory.* Tooele, Utah: undated.

Walker, Dan & Robert W. Calder, editors. *The Marriage Registers of Upper Canada/ Canada West.* Ontario, Canada: NorSim Research and Publishing, Delhi, 1995.

Warrum, Noble, editor. *Utah Since Statehood, Volumes 1-4.* Chicago, IL, and Salt Lake City, UT: S.J. Clarke Publishing Co., 1919.

Wrigley, Russell F. *History of the United States Army.* New York, New York: Macmillan Publishing Co., Inc., 1967.

## Websites

Albert Sidney Johnston. http://eddy.media.utah.edu/medsol/UCME/j/JOHNSTON%2CALBERT.html

Alexander, Thomas G. *Military in Utah.* http://www.utahhistorytogo.org/military.html

Alexander, Thomas G. *Overland Migrations.* http://www.utahhistorytogo.org/overlandmi.html

Arrington, Leonard J. *Colonization of Utah.* http://www.utahhistorytogo.org/colonize.html

Brigham Young. http://eddy.media.utah.edu/medsol/UCME/UCMEFRAMES/y/YOUNG%2CBRIGHAM.html

Cemetery & Burial Database. Utah Division of State History. https://heritage.utah.gov/history/cemeteries

Cholera. http://vm.cfsan.fda.gov/~MOW/chap7.html

Death and Military Death Certificates, 1904-1961. Utah Department of Commerce, Bureau of the Census, database. ancestry.com

Dyer, William G. *Major Church Meetings.*

http://a-a-http://a-amormons.tripod.com/daily/activity/meetings/major_eom.htm

Embry, Jessie L. *The History of Polygamy.* http://www.utahhistorytogo.org/

historyofpolygamy.html

Fast Offerings. *Encyclopedia of Mormonism.* http://a-a-mormons.tripod.com/daily/activity/index.htm

Hansen, Larry. *Panaca's History.* http://pr.erau.edu/~hansena/hist.html

*History of the Office of Bishop.* http://a-a-Mormons.tripod.com/basic/organization/priesthood/aaronic/Bishop

Holzapfel, Richard. *The Civil War in Utah.* http://www.utahhistorytogo.org/utcivilwar.html

May, Dean L. *United Order Movement.* http://www.utahhistorytogo.org/united.html

*Mormon Pioneer Overland Travel, 1847-1868.* Church of Jesus Christ of Latter-day Saints, database. www.lds.org/churchhistory/library/pioneercompany

Morrisites. http://www.media.utah.edu/UHE/m/MORRISITES.html

Mount Pleasant. http://eddy.media.utah.edu/medsol/UCME/UCMEFRAMES/m/MOUNTPLEASANT.html

Mountain Meadows Massacre. http://www.britannica.com/seo/m/mountain-meadows-massacre/

Peterson, John A. *Black Hawk War.* http://www.utahhistorytogo.org/blackhawk.html

Poll, Richard D. *Utah War.* http://www.utahhistorytogo.org/utahwar.html

Scott, Patricia Lyn. *Bountiful.* http://www.utahhistorytogo.org/bntfl.html

Shirts, Morris A. *Mountain Meadows Massacre.* http://www.utahhistorytogo.org/mtmeadows.html

Thatcher, Linda. http://www.ce.ex.state.ut.us/history/stchron.htm

Tithing. http://a-a-mormons.tripod.com/daily/activity/tithing_eom.htm

Tooele County. http://eddy.media.utah.edu/medsol/UCME/t/TOOELECT.html

U. S. Federal Census Bureau, population schedules of various states. Digital images. ancestry.com/search/categories/usfedcen

*Utah History, A Brief Summary.* http://www.ce.ex.state.ut.us/history/uthist.htm

Utah Timeline. http://www.standard.net/~followme/timeline/utahtimeline.html

Western States Marriage Index, Brigham Young University-Idaho, database. http://abish.byui.edu/SpecialCollections/WesternStates/search.cfm

World War II Army Enlistment Records, 1938-1946, database. ancestry.com

# Index

## K



## L



## M

## N



## O



## P



## Q



## R

## S



## T



## U

## V



## W



## Y



## Z

CPSIA information can be obtained
at www.ICGtesting.com
Printed in the USA
LVHW060303180922
728635LV00007B/335

9 780578 334035